Uneven Zimbabwe

A Study of Finance, Development and Underdevelopment

Uneven Zimbabwe

A Study of Finance, Development and Underdevelopment

Patrick Bond

Africa World Press, Inc.

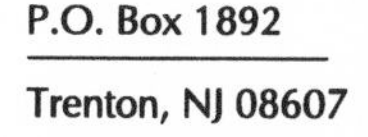

P.O. Box 1892
Trenton, NJ 08607

P.O. Box 48
Asmara, ERITREA

Africa World Press, Inc.

P.O. Box 1892
Trenton, NJ 08607

P.O. Box 48
Asmara, ERITREA

First Printing 1998

Cover and book design: Jonathan Gullery

Cover photo courtesy of the Ministry of Information, Harare, Zimbabwe

This book is set in ITC Galliard and Dolmen

Library of Congress Cataloging-in-Publication Data

Bond, Patrick.
Uneven Zimbabwe: a study of finance, development and underdevelopment / Patrick Bond.
p. cm.
Includes bibliographical references and index.
ISBN 0-86543-538-3 (cloth). -- ISBN 0-86543-539-1 (PBK. : alk. paper)
1. Finance--Zimbabwe--History. 2. Zimbabwe--Economic conditions--Regional disparities. I. Title.
HG187.5.Z55B66 1996
336.6891--dc20 96-35891
CIP

For Jan

CONTENTS

Part Two

Maps

Zimbabwe Economic Facts

Tables

Figures

PREFACE

> The private sector is ill-suited to allocate international credit. It provides either too little or too much. It does not have the information with which to form a balanced judgment. Moreover, it is not concerned with maintaining macroeconomic balance in the borrowing countries. Its goals are to maximize profit and minimize risk. This makes it move in a herd-like fashion in both directions. The excess always begins with overexpansion, and the correction is always associated with pain.
>
> —George Soros, *Financial Times*, 31 December 1997

> The credit system, which has its focal point in the allegedly national banks and the big money-lenders and usurers that surround them, is one enormous centralization and gives this class of parasites a fabulous power not only to decimate the industrial capitalists periodically but also to interfere in actual production in the most dangerous manner—and this crew know nothing of production and have nothing at all to do with it.
>
> —Karl Marx, *Capital, Volume III*, published posthumously, 1894

Precisely these sentiments have led me to ask why and how financiers aggravate the growing gaps between people, their economies, their geographies and the scales at which these are determined—and what sorts of political responses are effective and appropriate.

Such questions are of enormous importance to Zimbabwe at the end of the 1990s. To illustrate, in the waning weeks of 1997, as this book was being prepared for publication, the country's citizens suffered an economic nightmare punctuated by terrifying financial meltdowns. Surface-level symptoms included a spectacular crash of the currency (55% for the year as a whole, but 75% in a few hours on "Black Friday"—14

November—requiring a temporary central bank bail-out); dramatic increases in interest rates (6% within one month); a plummeting stock market (down 46% by the end of the year from peak August 1997 levels); renewed inflation, especially for food; and unprecedented fiscal stress.

Ironically, this particular calamity—reminiscent of the months following September 1991—unfolded at the tail end of a long-awaited economic revival (more than 8% GDP rise in 1996 and 3% in 1997). Yet that brief upturn on Zimbabwe's roller-coaster business cycle mainly reflected how extraordinarily far, on the one hand, the economy had plunged during the first Economic Structural Adjustment Programme (a 40% drop in the volume of manufacturing output from 1991-95, for instance), and, on the other hand, how mired Zimbabwe was in a long-term capitalist crisis dating to the mid-1970s. Not even the relatively high fixed capital investments of the late 1980s and early 1990s, following the stagnant, misnomered "socialist" era immediately after Independence, could undergird a financial superstructure that loomed speculatively—and parasitically, Marx would remind us—out of control. Thus the 1997 financial and currency turbulence set the stage for a long and potentially quite deep slump in the real economy.

Orthodox economic commentators were universally despondent. For them, the roots of Zimbabwe's late 1990s socio-economic crisis were to be found nearly entirely in the political sphere. Bucking strident advice and monetary arm-twisting from international financial institutions, President Mugabe had, after all, sustained his controversial October 1997 decisions to pay off a challenge from thousands of liberation war veterans—who received Z$50,000 each (plus a Z$2,000 per month pension)[1]—and at long last to begin implementing the 1993 Land Designation Act (1,500 mainly white-owned farms were identified for initial redistribution).[2]

At the same time, rancorous political background noise rose inexorably. There were vociferous demands from an indigenous business lobby still often shut out of white-controlled markets and financial institutions. Organized labor became increasingly militant, both in the public sector (where in mid-1996, 160,000 employees walked out and a general strike was contemplated) and around private sector wage struggles (in mid-1997, 100,000 workers were involved in strike action, even extending to poorly-organized agricultural plantations) (Saunders, 1997). Autonomous, shopfloor-based actions outran the ability of national union bureaucrats to control or direct the membership, and the corporatist strategy mistakenly pursued during the mid-1990s by the Zimbabwe Congress of Trade Unions (ZCTU) quickly became irrelevant.

More general popular alienation from government intensified during the late 1990s, as civil service corruption was repeatedly unveiled, as officials continued to rig tenders (e.g., construction of a new Harare airport), as shady and incongruous international investment partnerships (especially with Malaysian firms) were arranged, and as the political elites enjoyed conspicuous consumption (e.g., the extravagant presidential wedding) though not without the danger of socio-cultural delegitimization (e.g., of former president Canaan Banana, accused of serial sodomy and rape). Occasional but vicious police clampdowns did not, as of late 1997, deter growing public dissent. The opposition press continued to harangue government, the early 1980s Matabeleland atrocities were constructively publicized by human rights groups, and there were inklings of electoral challenges in the emergence of independent (mainly petty-bourgeois) candidates and in a widely-supported human-rights campaign to amend the country's constitution.

By year-end 1997, an anti-government stayaway and several large urban protests on "Red Tuesday," 9 December, were joined by more than a million people. A cross-class alliance of organized labor, the constrained petty bourgeoisie, sympathetic employers and various other activists had emerged around issues of accountability and abuse of public funds, fuelling a growing sentiment that after two decades in power, Mugabe and his ZANU party could potentially be voted down in the next (2000) general election. At the time this book was sent to the printers, it appeared that an uneasy blend of divergent ideologies might possibly coalesce to at least threaten such a feat—though it would unlikely be sufficiently influenced by ZCTU advocacy on behalf of its broader constituency of workers and the poor, and bedeviled by the apparent lock ZANU enjoyed on rural loyalties. Would such a coalition replay neighbouring Zambia's early 1990s conversion from stagnant authoritarian populism to democratization (at least in the initial stages) joined, as in Zambia (or for that matter post-apartheid South Africa), by even more rapid neoliberal economic decay?

There were two opposing ways of looking at the conjuncture. Mugabe's land "reform" and veteran payoff maneuvers surprised this author and many others who had watched ZANU drift steadily into market-oriented ways of running the government and the economy. Were these reflections of the leader's capriciousness and desire to divide-and-conquer his subjects by addressing the needs of discrete constituencies? Or did they, in contrast, represent the political last-kicks of an economic horse that could no longer perform even mundane functions? In short, did the political crisis set the stage for economic catastrophe, or was the sustained economic failure associated with the Economic Structural Adjustment Program and indeed nearly a quarter-century of falling living standards the proximate cause of the political crisis? (Or both?)

Political fluidity was certainly evident in the dramatic backlash against Mugabe's two very non-neoliberal turns, reflected in the international and local investor panic in November 1997, the December street protests, and the unprecedented rejection of tax increases (to pay for the war vets pensions) by delegates to a major ZANU conference and by parliamentarians in between. But perhaps of deeper significance here was the overall global economic trend during the mid- and late-1990s. From Mexico (1994) to Brazil (1995) to South Africa (1996) to Southeast Asia and even South Korea (1997), the semi-periphery of the world economy was subjected to formidable waves of currency speculation, raiding of foreign reserves, domestic credit crunches and stock market panic. This partly followed from the frenzied, footloose rush of international financial capital, but more fundamentally, from the awesome problem of systematic overinvestment, overproduction and overtrading in the productive sectors of the world economy.

Within this maelstrom, the Zimbabwe government's two emerging neoliberal strategies—"Zimprest" and "Vision 2020"—were taken less and seriously. The International Monetary Fund and World Bank erratically endorsed and then unendorsed the state's progress during the mid-1990s. By mid-1997, Zimbabwe debuted in the Swiss-based World Economic Forum's *Global Competitiveness Report* at third to last, out of 55 countries. True, the ineffectual, debt-ridden character of the state helped bring Zimbabwe's rating down. But this was at a time when, as shown in Part Three of this book, nearly all other neoliberal advice had been closely followed, and as even foreign investment (mainly mining, retailing and banking) had picked up from minuscule levels of the previous fifteen years.

As a result, a certain frustration must have emerged in Mugabe's inner circle regarding both state capitalism (1980s) and neoliberalism (1990s). One short-term gut reaction was a return to *dirigiste* methods, including the land grab and the takeover of foreign-currency denominated accounts (at a discount to the unwilling sellers)—thus doing great damage to government credibility on financial liberalization—as part of an initial, vain attempt to protect the value of the currency during the November 1997 tumble. But the medium term would see more dramatic reductions in the state budget, the introduction of Value Added Tax (largely to squeeze an extra 5% or so of the income of rural consumers who had avoided the general sales tax), as well as larger-scale privatizations.

If these aspects of Zimbabwe's political superstructure were related in any way to an underlying tendency to economic crisis, as was witnessed so frighteningly in the recurrent financial market upheavals, nevertheless, Mugabe's willingness to discard his mask of investor-friendliness does not necessarily warrant sympathy. Bank-bashing populism, at which Mugabe excels, is often a guise for conservative not progressive politics, based ultimately on slight adjustments to flows of resources for the sake of patronage, not economic transformation. The critique of global and local post-modern capitalism must go deeper, and thus has much to inherit from Marx's treatment of finance, development and underdevelopment, a theme to which the book returns repeatedly.

Indeed I think that once one gets a chance to study the laws of motion of capital, the more durable features of Marx's intellectual heritage are irresistible. Why make this case, though, given the enormous controversy surrounding this legacy, including over the theoretical treatment of money and finance?[3] I've decided, in fact, that remaining largely within the classical framework of *Capital*, many apparent internal contradictions can be resolved by considering that Marx applied his monetary and financial categories at different levels (and in different stages) of analysis. In *Capital*, Marx's sense of the displacement of economic contradictions into the sphere of finance, is illustrative:

> The credit system... accelerates the material development of the productive forces and the creation of the world market, which it is the historical task of the capitalist mode of production to bring to a certain level of development, as material foundations for the new form of production. At the same time, credit accelerates the violent outbreaks of this contradiction, crises, and with these the elements of dissolution of the old mode of production.

The Zimbabwe case confirms Marx's dialectical instincts here, it would seem (though the reader must be the judge of this). Yet as Engels explained in his preface to the tortured writings on finance in Volume Three of *Capital*, "We did not have a finished draft, or even an outline plan to be filled in, but simply the beginning of an elaboration which petered out more than once in a disordered jumble of notes, comments and extract material." This leaves political economists with a consensus that Marx's theoretical statements on finance are inadequate, and that, as Gary Dymski (1990, 42) put it in a helpful literature review, "a number of approaches are Marxian; the task of synthesis remains for contemporary scholars." What follows in this book, however, is no scholarly theoretical synthesis; instead, it is an attempt at taking two of the more powerful Marxian approaches to finance (those of the German socialists Hilferding and Grossmann) and considering them in the context of the unevenness of capitalist development.

I argue here that unevenness unveils itself (a) through various sectors of the economy; (b) over space; and (c) across scales. In having a stab at this, I have found very useful the interpretations of David Harvey and Simon Clarke, in which financial power is directly correlated to downturns in the accumulation process (specifically, to the periodic condition of "over-accumulation"). Drawing upon their insights, this book is one small empirical contribution to the task of a broader synthesis, I hope, in which the geographical features of finance are considered as interesting to theorists, researchers and critics as are the more common topics of "finance capital" power and speculative financial vulnerability. While also hoping to make a small contribution to the process of revitalizing latent left discourses in Zimbabwe and revisiting that country's rich, compelling political economy, I recognize all the same that intellectual conditions for propagating radical knowledge during the epoch of structural adjustment are not ideal, which only enhances my admiration for those many Zimbabwean democrats who resist as best they can under circumstances not of their own choosing.

I must go back quite a long way to begin to offer acknowledgements to those who helped in both intellectual and financial ways. Formal lecturers who introduced me to economic and social policy issues included David Weiman at Swarthmore College, Sydney Weintraub and Edward Herman at the University of Pennsylvania, and David Harvey, Vicente Navarro and Erica Schoenberger at Johns Hopkins University. I also learned a great deal about uneven development from Neil Smith and about finance from Paul Burkette and Doug Henwood. These post-Keynesian and Marxian perspectives only sunk in properly because of two years working in the United States Federal Reserve System (to counteract "redlining"—bank geographical discrimination against ghetto residents), where the pace of change was glacial. I left the Fed in 1985 and, in addition to studying at Hopkins, joined colleagues active on financial reform in progressive institutions in and around Washington DC during the late 1980s: the Institute for Policy Studies, Debt Crisis Network, Pacifica Radio News, some trade unions (in the mines, clothing/textile, and hotel sectors) and some visionary community reinvestment coalitions (especially in Washington, Baltimore, Philadelphia and New York), and the student anti-apartheid movement (and later, in 1995, the reformed Teamsters union and the International Liaison Office of President Jean-Bertrand Aristide of Haiti). The tenacity of these institutions' and movements' cadres, under conditions of struggle that—then and now—offer very little prospect for sustained success, still strikes me as remarkable.

During the early 1990s in Harare, the Street People's Organization and Zimbabwe Congress of Trade Unions, and in Johannesburg, Planact, the SA National Civic Organization and many of its township affiliates in Gauteng province, unions and the ANC/SACP Left all played a similar welcoming, and inspiring, role. Several critical Zimbabwean intellectuals—Tendai Biti, Rene Loewensen, John Makumbe, Dale Mckinley, Sam Matsangaise, Di Mitchell, Sam Moyo, my aunt Helga Patrikios, Ian Phimister, Brian Raftopoulos, Lloyd Sachikonye, David Sanders and Arnold Sibanda—and some brilliant expat doctoral students (Joss Alexander, David Moore and Richard Saunders) often shared their knowledge and enthusiasm. Tolerant editors at the *Financial Gazette*,[4] *Moto* and *Horizon* in Zimbabwe, the *Southern African Review of Books* in Germany, *African Agenda* in Accra and *Southern Africa Report* in Toronto, and several others since deceased—I still mourn the *Guardian* (NY) and the Jo'burg magazines *Work in Progress* and *Africa South and East*—taught me to write more fluidly about economics for popular audiences.

What I have often been most impressed by in most of these settings is that in inverse proportion to the way popular movements have begun to take seriously the challenge to human progress represented by high finance, there has been a qualitative worsening of bureaucratic supplication to—as the euphemism goes—"the markets": primarily, the buyers of government bonds, who ultimately wield veto power over economic policy. Recall Bill Clinton's response to a harshly neo-liberal economic briefing just prior to his taking office in early 1993 (as recounted by the journalist Bob Woodward in *The Agenda*): "You mean to tell me that my whole programme, and my re-election, hinge on the Federal Reserve and a bunch of fucking bond traders?" Nods all around the table. Uneven America the logical result.

We can be sure, from history and from a sense of the Zimbabwean people's renewed determination, that just as financial power has wreaked havoc on their lives, financial vulnerability will provide many opportunities over the coming period to resist neoliberal economics.

To all those colleagues, activists, political leaders, parents and siblings, tutors, distant authors of obscure materials, all of whom guided me along my haphazard journey ...far too many to list and thank individually... it is easy enough to dedicate this work in progress to you, in gratitude for bearing with me (mostly) thus far. In addition, six institutions provided material support and time so I could conduct the research in Harare and, in the Bvumba's placid if feudal surroundings, write it up: Johns Hopkins University's Department of Geography and Environmental Engineering, the US Social Science Research Council, the University of Zimbabwe Department of Political and Administrative Studies, Planact, the Hopkins

School of Public Health, the National Institute for Economic Policy in Johannesburg and the University of the Witwatersrand Graduate School of Public and Development Management. Standard disclaimers apply.

Finally, it is to my long-persevering family—especially wee Jan—that the greatest thanks and reciprocal support are due here, along with the (often waning) hope that our future will sooner rather than later witness a decline in the power of finance and a levelling of uneven development, so that we can all move on to more important things.

Patrick Bond
Johannesburg
December 1997

Notes

1. The amount (US$2,800 at the time) was transferred to the bank accounts of 50,000 combatants in late December 1997, following justified hand-wringing about how it was to be financed. There were approximately 60,000 combatants from the ZANU and ZAPU armies, of whom fewer than 36,000 were given demobilization pay of Z$2,420 in 1983. With high-profile exceptions, such as cabinet ministers and other high-ranking officials whose dubious disability claims plundered government's limited pre-1997 allocations, most veterans were needy povo. They were successful essentially because their 1997 demonstrations in Harare caused the ZANU government acute embarrassment. After the payout, however, intense popular resentment emerged given that a sales tax (and indeed initially an income tax and petrol tax increase) was imposed to partially cover the costs.
2. There would be only partial compensation, but again this raised the likelihood of fiscal convulsion. The damage to the commercial agricultural sector (and related industries) would be heightened by the fact—as conceded by the Agriculture Minister in a subsequent radio broadcast—that the recipients of the farms would be wealthy politicians not land-starved peasants. Patronage was the point, at a time other routes were closing. Government was once again apparently not serious about thorough-going redistribution, which would require vastly greater resources, support structures and administrative staff than were budgeted and planned, not to mention a shift in class power away from the emergent bureaucratic bourgeoisie. Nor was it likely that the ambitious designation exercise could be successfully brought to fruition even on its own terms; more feasible would be case-by-case compromises with only the most indebted designees agreeing to depart.
3. Not even *The New Yorker* (20/10/97) magazine's judgment that Marx is

"The Next Thinker" is likely to soon resurrect a reputation so unfairly earned in Zimbabwe and elsewhere.

4. A swift confession is in order regarding the reputation of the main press source upon which this book draws for contemporary empirical information, the *FinGaz*, a business journal with unusual social impact, printed on pink-dyed paper. Even prior to two badly-fumbled reports that led to a loss of nerve (and sharp political censureship) by owner Elias Rusike, here is a combatitive Robert Mugabe on his favorite press whipping-boy: "It was the usual pink lies. Don't take seriously what they publish in the pink lies." Replied the *FinGaz's* then-editor, Trevor Ncube (22/12/94), "The word 'pink' has several associations, one of which is: 'sympathetic to or influenced by communism; leftist or radical, especially half-heartedly.' In that context there can be little doubt who is really pink."

   Little doubt? Setting aside my own minor contributions to the *FinGaz*, Zimbabwe's political rulers always provide us a healthy measure of politico-ideological doubt, do they not?

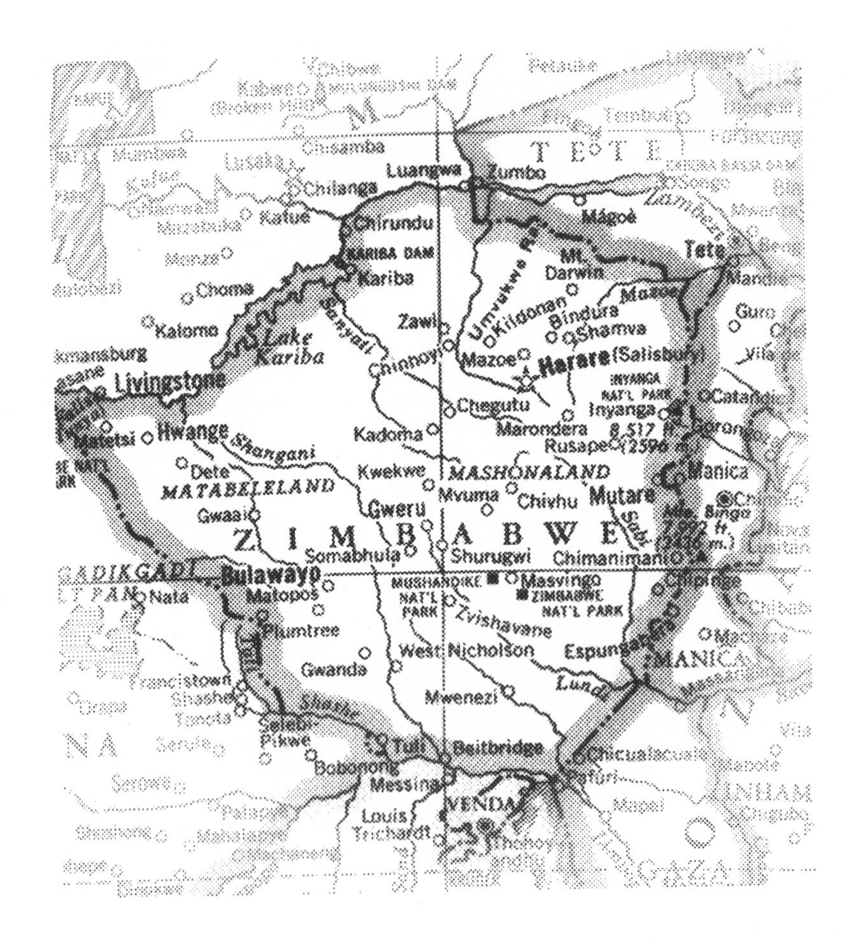
TETE
Chisamba
Lusaka
Luangwa
Zumbo
Chilanga
Kafue
Mazabuka
Chirundu
Mágoè
Zambezi
KARIBA DAM
Kariba
Mt.
Darwin
Tete
Choma
Kalomo
Lake
Kariba
Sanyati
Zawi
Kildonan
Bindura
Mazoe
Shamva
Guro
Chinhoyi
Mazoe
Harare (Salisbury)
Livingstone
INYANGA
NAT'L PARK
Inyanga
Chegutu
Marondera
Matetsi
Hwange
Shangani
Kadoma
Rusape
Dete
MATABELELAND
Kwekwe
MASHONALAND
Manica
Mvuma
Chivhu
Mutare
Gweru
Gwaai
ZIMBABWE
Somabhula
Shurugwi
Chimanimani
Bulawayo
Nata
Matopos
MUSHANDIKE
NAT'L
PARK
Masvingo
ZIMBABWE
NAT'L PARK
Chipinge
Plumtree
Zvishavane
Espungabera
West Nicholson
Gwanda
MANICA
Francistown
Lundi
Mwenezi
Tuli
Beitbridge
Chicualacuala
Bobonong
Messina
VENDA
Louis
Trichardt
GAZA

Zimbabwe

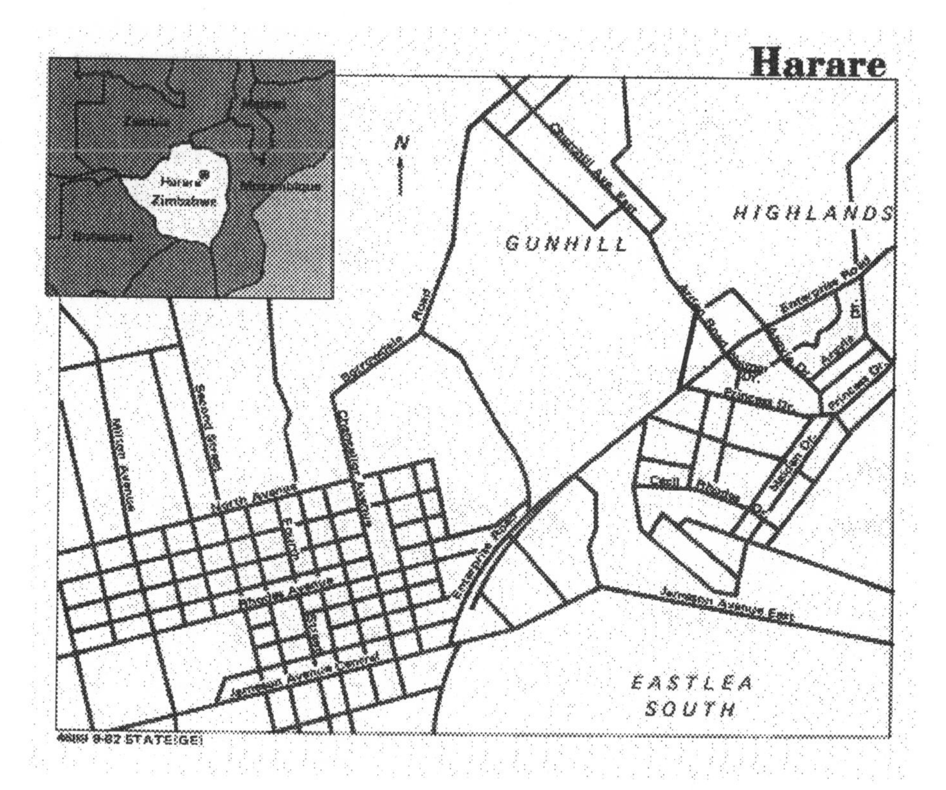

Harare
N
HIGHLANDS
GUNHILL
EASTLEA
SOUTH
Enterprise Road
North Avenue
Second Street
Milton Avenue
Rhodes Avenue
Jameson Avenue Central
Jameson Avenue East
Princess Dr.
Zimbabwe
Mozambique

Zimbabwe Economic Facts

Distribution of Gross Domestic Product and Employment (000) by Activity, 1991/96

Activity	1991 GDP	1996 GDP	1991 jobs	1996 jobs
Distribution, hotels, rest.	15%	18%	101	99
Agriculture	14%	18%	304	332
Manufacturing	24%	17%	205	185
Finance, insur., real estate	8%	9%	18	21
Transport,communications	5%	5%	56	51
Mining	4%	5%	51	59
Education	6%	4%	110	115
Public administration	5%	4%	95	74
Other	19%	20%	304	394
Total	100%	100%	1244	1240

Source: CSO *National Accounts*

Distribution of National Income (1996)
- Profits/GDP: 45.5/76.2
- Wages and salaries/GDP: 30.4/76.2
- Rent/GDP: 1.4/76.2

Gross Fixed Capital Formation/GDP (1996): 18.8/76.2
Gross National Savings/GDP (1996): 21.5/76.2
Exports/GDP (1996): 30.9/76.2
Visible Balance of Trade/GDP (1996): -3885/76200
Share of Electricity used by Major Consumers (1996)
- manufacturing, transport and construction: 40%
- domestic consumers: 18%
- mining: 17%
- agriculture: 10%
- others: 15%

Public debt/GDP (1996, 1991): 53.2/76.2 , 16.3/26.2
- Foreign debt/GDP: 21.8, 8.4
- Domestic debt/GDP: 31.4, 7.9

Distribution of Average Annual Household Consumption by Commodity

Sector	Rural	Urban	Total
Food	39%	22%	29%
Rent, fuel	16%	18%	17%
Transport	5%	11%	8%
Clothing	8%	8%	8%
Education	6%	8%	7%
Furniture	7%	7%	7%
Alcohol	6%	7%	6%
Other	13%	19%	18%
TOTAL	100%	100%	100%

Source: CSO *Income, Consumption and Expenditure Survey, 1990/91*

Distribution of Average Annual Income

Income Source	Rural	Urban	Total
Primary	80%	97%	93%
Agriculture	17%	0%	4%
Property	0%	2%	2%
Indiv. enterprise	3%	1%	1%
TOTAL	100%	100%	100%

Source: CSO *Income, Consumption and Expenditure Survey, 1990/91*

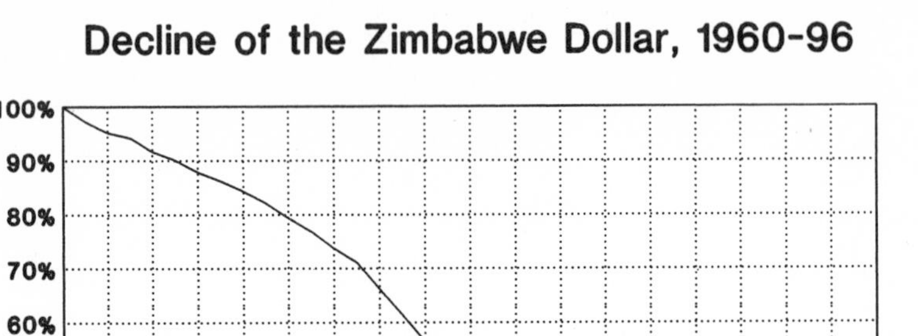
Decline of the Zimbabwe Dollar, 1960-96
100%
90%
80%
70%
60%
50%
40%
30%
20%
10%
0%
60 62 64 66 68 70 72 74 76 78 80 82 84 86 88 90 92 94 96
Year
Source: CSO Digest of Statistics
Consumer Price Index

Part One

Theories of Finance and Uneven Development

chapter one

Finance and Uneven Development

Introduction

Antonio Gramsci (1978:177–178) once explained the task of historical materialism: "In studying a structure, it is necessary to distinguish organic movements (relatively permanent) from movements which may be termed 'conjunctural' (and which appear as occasional, immediate, almost accidental)." For Gramsci, organic movements are of "far-reaching historical significance" and thus provide opportunity for "socio-historical criticism." Decades-long organic crises, for example, mean that "incurable structural contradictions have revealed themselves (reached maturity)." In contrast, conjunctural analysis is "of a minor, day to day character."

If we seek to understand movements of historical significance, as opposed to simply cataloguing those conjunctures which marked Zimbabwe's evolution as one of the most unequal countries in the world, it may be helpful to focus our attention on one set of organic, relatively permanent processes of uneven capitalist development. I have chosen to write primarily about the accentuation of uneven development *during times of heightened financial activity which accompany capitalist crises.* Of course, this is not a story reducible to a simple, monochromatic account, because each of our primary conceptual categories—crisis, rising finance, uneven development—is multifaceted and contradictory.

This first chapter is dedicated to exploring at a theoretical level the salient characteristics and contradictions of finance and uneven development. Further chapters tackle uneven development and the rise of finance in Zimbabwe in the same spirit. The goal is to build into the theory various layers of analysis that allow us to both draw new insights about complex socio economic realities and to enrich our understanding of how capital flows across space and through time in ways that, at surface level, often seem illogical, unstructured, and self-destructive.

After all, the world economy has suffered intense disfiguring due to financial bubbles and depressions the last few years, and Zimbabwe has not been immune. This we can glean from daily newspaper accounts of stock market crashes, unpredictable currency fluctuations, the ups and downs of speculative property markets, huge bankruptcies and unrepaid debts, unending financial innovations, or the ebb and flow of power—over so many facets of life—held by banks and institutional investors. Is there any discernable logic to all of this? Can the rise and fall of finance help explain the development and the underdevelopment of particular global regions, nation states, local economies, firms, households?

Very few theorists have been so ambitious as to try sketching a systematic relationship of finance to uneven development, and most who have done so worked from within the Marxist tradition of political economy, which is also broadly (though not exclusively) that within which the following pages lie. We begin by very briefly considering the traditional roles of money in capitalist production and circulation. But we try to promptly place these in the context of capitalist crisis, in which the accumulation of capital relies increasingly on financial, speculative activity. Speculative profits are often a good indication of ascendant finance and declining productive capital.

But—and this is ironic—financial power is far more vulnerable to system "breakdown" than many Marxists have foreseen, and it is worth taking a critical detour through some of the debates on "finance capital," particularly because the theorists Rudolf Hilferding and Henryk

Grossmann (and others) have made sweeping statements about financial power, control and crisis that bear close consideration. None of these are entirely satisfactory, however, due to their tendency to a singular monocentric logic. Instead, it is through far more subtle processes by which capitalist crises are *displaced*—essentially through time and through space—that I think we can draw out the prominence of finance. There is no singular logic, but on the basis of this theoretical exercise we can hypothesize that during such times of financial ascendance, ***uneven development is indeed most powerfully generated,*** across various sectors, spaces and scales.

The roles of finance in capitalism: Accommodation, control, speculation

What is it that we will focus our attention on, precisely? "Finance" is here considered to encompass *external sources of funding* beyond the normal revenue streams that generally consist of company profits, state tax receipts, the wages and salaries of households, and the revenues of other institutions. It thus includes myriad forms of debt, as well as corporate equity ("shares") issued on stock markets. *Financial capital* refers to the totality of financial institutions and instruments which advance money (and credit and other financial paper) for the purpose of gaining a return (interest, dividends, increases in value, etc.). But, like capital itself, financial capital is not a mere thing *per se*, but encompasses social processes as well. As Simon Clarke (1988:5) puts it, "The power of money is not the power of banks and financial institutions, although it is the latter who wield the power of money, it is the power of capital in its most abstract form." So it is to the basic relations between capital, money, and credit that we must first turn.

Why is finance integral to the dynamics of capitalism? In abstract terms, money plays well-known roles as medium of exchange and payment, measure of value, and store of wealth. But more to the point, Marx outlines ways in which credit—"interest-bearing money capital"—lubricates (or "accommodates") capitalist production and commerce. First, the smooth operation of markets depends on firms moving resources to where profits can be found, which has the effect of equalizing the rate of profit between firms. A well-functioning credit system is critical here, both because credit is an extremely fluid means of allocating capital to where it is most highly rewarded, and because new investments (which add to competition and hence profit equalization) normally occur through borrowing.

Second, credit allows more efficient forms of money (such as bills of exchange) to replace physical money handling. Hence, as Marx (1967:V.III, chap. 27, par. 6) put it, "credit accelerates the velocity of the metamorphosis of commodities, and with this the velocity of monetary circulation." In the process, the turnover time of capital is shortened and profits are realized more rapidly. In the *Grundrisse,* Marx (1973:359) goes so far as to argue that "the necessary tendency of capital is therefore circulation without circulation time, and this tendency is the fundamental determinant of credit and of capital's credit contrivances."

Third, credit also allows for greater centralization of capital, and this is a precondition for large firms to become publicly traded on the stock market and hence to raise further investment funds easily. Moreover, with credit the individual capitalist acquires "disposal over social capital, rather than his own, that gives him command over social labor. The actual capital that someone possesses, or is taken to possess by public opinion, now becomes simply the basis for a superstructure of credit" (Marx:1967, V.III,chap. 27, par.16).

But all of these *accommodating* characteristics of finance—providing lubrication to the payments system, speeding the velocity of capitalist production and centralization, and centralizing funds for investment or hiring large numbers of workers—are not the only ones to consider. With the "organic movement" of capital into more concentrated and centralized form, there also emerge *controlling* characteristics of finance. As conceptualized by Hilferding in his book *Finance Capital,* financial, industrial, and commercial capital supposedly merge under the guiding hand of the banks. Then there arise, as well, *speculative* characteristics of finance, which increase in importance as capitalist crises appear and intensify. It is here that investment funds are drawn into financial assets which become increasingly autonomous from the productive assets they are meant to represent (as securities, shares of stock, real estate titles, and the like).

The effect, in sum, is that as money and credit emerged from their most basic roles in the hoarding of wealth and early commerce to develop more fully as "financial capital" (money extended for the purpose of making more money), they also evolved from simply lubricating early capitalist relations to exhibiting controlling and speculative characteristics. But as we consider next, the ultimate determinant over which of these characteristics emerges and dominates at any given point in time and space, is the *capital accumulation process,* which gives meaning to the discrete acts of production and commerce which money and credit were ostensibly developed under capitalism to serve.

Capital accumulation, the tendency towards overaccumulation and the rise of finance

Let us again deliberate basic definitions. Capital accumulation refers to the generation of wealth in the form of "capital." It is capital because it is employed by capitalists not to produce with specific social uses in mind, but instead to produce *commodities* for the purpose of *exchange*, for profit, and hence for the self-expansion of capital. Such an emphasis by individual capitalists on continually expanding the "exchange-value" of output, with secondary concern for the social and physical limits of expansion (size of the market; environmental, political, and labor problems, etc.), gives rise to enormous contradictions. These are built into the very laws of motion of the system. It is worthwhile to cover these tendencies in some detail, and then assess how they are borne out through a review of historical evidence.

Perhaps the most serious of capitalist self-contradictions, most thoroughly embedded within the capital accumulation process, is the general tendency towards an increased capital-labor ratio in production—more machines in relation to workers—which is fuelled by the combination of technological change and intercapitalist competition, and made possible by the concentration and centralization of capital.[1] Individual capitalists cannot afford to fall behind the industry norm, technologically, without risking their price or quality competitiveness such that their products are not sold. This situation creates a continual drive in capitalist firms towards the introduction of state-of-the-art production processes, especially labor-saving machinery.

With intensified automation, the rate of profit tends to fall, and the reasons for this are worth reviewing. Profit correlates to "surplus value" which is actually generated only through the exploitation of labor in production. Why is labor only paid a certain proportion of the value produced, with a surplus going to capital? Since capitalists cannot "cheat in exchange"—buy other inputs, especially machines that make other machines, from each other at a cost less than their value—the increases in value that are the prerequisite for production and exchange of commodities must emanate from workers. This simply means, in class terms, that capitalists do not and cannot systematically exploit other capitalists but they can systematically exploit workers. Here arises the central contradiction: with automation, the labor input becomes an ever-smaller component of the total inputs into production. And as the labor content diminishes, so too do the opportunities for exploitation, for surplus value extraction and for profits.

This situation exacerbates what becomes a self-perpetuating vicious spiral. Intercapitalist competition intensifies within increasingly tight markets, as fewer workers can buy the results of their increased production. In turn this results in a still greater need for individual capitalists to cut costs. A given firm's excess profits are but only temporarily achieved through the productivity gains which automation typically provides, since every capitalist in a particular industry or branch of production is compelled to adopt state-of-the-art technologies just to maintain competitiveness. This leads to growth in productive capacity far beyond an expansion in what consumer markets can bear. (It is true that there are countervailing tendencies to this process, such as an increase in the turnover time of capital, automation, and work speed-up, as well as expansion of the credit system. But these rarely overwhelm the underlying dynamic for long.) The inexorable consequence, a continuously worsening problem under capitalism, is termed the *overaccumulation* of capital.

Overaccumulation refers, simply, to a situation in which excessive investment has occurred and hence goods cannot be brought to market profitably, leaving capital to pile up in sectoral bottlenecks or speculative outlets without being put back into new productive investment. Other symptoms include unused plant and equipment; huge gluts of unsold commodities; an unusually large number of unemployed workers; and, as discussed below, the inordinate rise of financial markets. When an economy reaches a decisive stage of overaccumulation, then it becomes difficult to bring together all these resources in a profitable way to meet social needs.

How does the system respond? There are many ways to move an overaccumulation crisis around through time and space, as discussed throughout this book. But the only real "solution" to overaccumulation—the only response to the crisis capable of reestablishing the conditions for a new round of accumulation—is widespread *devaluation*. Devaluation entails the scrapping of the economic deadwood, which takes forms as diverse as depressions, banking crashes, inflation, plant shutdowns, and, as Schumpeter called it, the sometimes "creative destruction" of physical and human capital (through the uncreative solution of war). The process of devaluation happens continuously, as outmoded machines and superfluous workers are made redundant, as waste (including state expenditure on armaments) becomes an acceptable form of mopping up overaccumulation, and as inflation eats away at buying power. This continual, incremental devaluation does not, however, mean capitalism has learned to equilibrate, thus avoiding more serious, system-threatening crises. Devaluation of a fully cathartic nature (of which the last Great Depression and World War are spectacular examples) is periodically required to destroy sufficient economic deadwood to permit a new process of accumulation to begin.

When overaccumulation becomes widespread, extreme forms of devaluation are invariably resisted (or deflected) by whatever local, regional, national, or international alliances exist or are formed in specific areas under pressure. Hence, overaccumulation has very important geographical and geopolitical implications in the uneven development of capitalism, as attempts are made to transfer the costs and burden of devaluation to different regions and nations or to push overaccumulated capital into the buildings (especially commercial real estate), infrastructure, and other features of the "built environment" as a last-ditch speculative venture. Moreover, the implications of overaccumulation for balance in different sectors of the economy—between branches of production (mining, agriculture, manufacturing, finance, etc.), between consumers and producers, and between capital goods (the means of production) and consumer goods (whether luxuries or necessities)—can become ominous. Indeed, because the rhythm of overaccumulation varies across the economy, severe imbalances between the different sectors and "departments" of production (sometimes termed "disproportionalities" or "disarticulations") emerge and introduce threatening bottlenecks in the production and realization of value, which further exacerbate the crisis. Such "uneven sectoral development" is discussed in more detail below.

These processes enhance the control and speculative functions of finance. The argument, simply, is that as overaccumulation begins to set in, as structural bottlenecks emerge, and as profit rates fall in the productive sectors of an economy, *capitalists begin to shift their investable funds out of reinvestment in plant, equipment, and labor power and instead seek refuge in financial assets.* To fulfil their new role as not only store of value but as investment outlet for overaccumulated capital, those financial assets must be increasingly capable of generating their own self-expansion, and also be protected (at least temporarily) against devaluation in the form of financial crashes and inflation. Such emerging needs mean that financiers, who are after all competing against other profit-seeking capitalists for resources, induce a shift in the function of finance away from merely accommodating the circulation of capital through production and increasingly towards both speculative and control functions. The speculative function attracts further flows of productive capital, and the control function expands to ensure the protection and the reproduction of financial markets. Where inflation may be a threat, the control functions of finance often result in high real interest rates and a reduction in the value of labor-power (and hence lower effective demand). Where bankruptcies threaten to spread as a result of overenthusiastic speculation, the control functions attempt to shift those costs elsewhere, in a manner examined in detail later.

Evidence of overaccumulation and rising finance

Can the first steps of the theory we have begun to outline above claim any empirical backing? In fact, historical evidence of financial ascendance during the accumulation cycle is impressive and can be reviewed briefly at this stage in the argument. For example, the existence of "Kondratieff"-style long-waves of capital accumulation is securely established, with global crises occurring roughly 1825–45, 1872–92, 1929–48, and 1973–present (Kondratieff 1979; Gordon 1980; Van Duijn 1983; Goldstein 1988). From either a Marxist or non-Marxist vantagepoint, though, a precise measurement of these cycles of accumulation is difficult. Variables such as estimates of price-series, profitability, and production are central to most studies whereas, ideally, measures such as capital intensity ("the organic composition of capital"), surplus value rates, the velocity of circulation of capital, the geographical expansion of capitalist relations, capacity utilization and inventory build-up would be preferable for Marxist analysis. (Some of these variables are investigated in later chapters.)[2]

Within the long-wave of accumulation, at a sub-global and sub-national scale, there are even more obvious "Kuznets cycles" of fifteen years to three decades in duration (Kuznets 1930), witnessed in particular by labor migration patterns and investment in buildings, infrastructure, and other facets of the built environment (Thomas 1972). David Harvey, in particular, has used empirical evidence of Kuznets cycles to reflect upon the Marxist theory of overaccumulation, followed by devaluation (Harvey 1989a:77).

Moving to the next step, we can verify the rise and fall of finance during the course of accumulation cycles, especially at the global level. During four particular periods—the late 1820s, 1870s, 1930s and 1980s—at least one third of all nation-states fell into effective default on their external debt following an unsustainable upswing of borrowing at a time of declining foreign-sourced productive-sector investment. With the exception of the 1980s (in which there was a significant lag), the onset of global debt crisis was the precursor for the onset of decades-long downswings in the Kondratieff cycles. Drawing on the world-systems perspective pioneered by Immanuel Wallerstein (1979), Christian Suter (1992) explains the "global debt cycle" by way of stages in the long-wave, beginning with technological innovation and utilizing international product-cycle theory.

At the upswing of a Kondratieff cycle, as basic technological innovations are introduced in a labor-intensive and unstandardized manner, both the demand for and supply of external financing are typically low, and in any case the residue of financial crisis in the previous long-cycle does not permit rapid expansion of credit or other financial assets into high-risk investments. As innovations gradually spread, however, peripheral geographical areas become more tightly integrated into the world economy, supported by international financial networks. As the power of innovation-led growth subsides, and as the consumer markets of the advanced capitalist countries become saturated, profit rates decline in the core. This pushes waves of financial capital into peripheral areas—where, instead of achieving balanced accumulation and growth, low returns on investment plus a variety of other political and economic constraints inexorably lead to sovereign default. In sum, at the global scale there is a three-stage process characterized by, as Suter (1992:41) puts it, "first, intense core capital exports and corresponding booms in credit raising activity of peripheries; second, the occurrence of debt service incapacity among peripheral countries; and third, the negotiation of debt settlement agreements between debtors and creditors."

Evidence for this theory is compelling at one level, the international scale. But to transcend the world-systems approach, a robust Marxist theory of accumulation must incorporate such evidence at other scales (national, regional, local, even household); more closely integrate the trends in the productive circuits of capital with the dynamics of finance; incorporate speculative and control features of finance as integral features of the debt crisis; and thus explain other forms of recent financial ascendance which have become common since the early 1980s—in the world and in Zimbabwe, as well as during other historical periods. These include high real interest rates (in relation to the historical record and in relation to the return on fixed capital investment); an explosion in share values and real estate prices; an increase in the outstanding debt of consumers, corporations, and governments, in relation to most measures of economic activity; and a qualitative increase in the political clout of financiers.

Although there is a good understanding of the overaccumulation problem and evidence of its recent manifestations (Clarke 1988:279-360; Harvey 1989:180-197; Mandel 1989:30-58; Armstrong, Glyn, and Harrison 1991:169-260), the rest of these issues have been addressed only fitfully, partially and imperfectly within Marxian political economy. To illustrate the controversies that remain, some of the methodological approaches that generated these, and the political implications of the analysis, we move next to the mistaken directions forged by explorers of what was termed "finance capital."

The rise of "finance capital"

As the twentieth century dawned (indeed from 1870 to 1920 or so, according to Paul Sweezy [1972:179]) it appeared to many observers that a new institutional form—"finance capital"—was achieving hegemony over the entire world economy. Testifying to this idea were the concentration and centralization of the major financial institutions; the organization of cartels of industrial capitalists, often by financiers; the exercise of financial control over corporate development more generally; and the powerful impetus of financiers in imperialism, manipulation of state policies, and the formation of ideologies. Indeed, many Marxists believed that banks and other financial institutions had actually pushed capitalism into a new and perhaps final stage, the era of monopoly, imperialist, "finance capitalism." The leading Marxist theorists of the first decades of the twentieth century—Hilferding, Kautsky, Bauer, Bukharin, Lenin and others—adopted this broad argument, although there was conflict about whether this final stage was one of strength or one of decay (Tickten 1986).

But the banks that were supposedly at the center of power in this new era of capitalism suffered tremendous bankruptcies, culminating in system-wide crashes that left the financial system in tatters from 1929 to 1933. Nonetheless, until then, the theory of "finance capital" had much to recommend it. Indeed, the notion of a financial power bloc that articulates with and controls industry has been resuscitated in several vigorous efforts since the early 1970s.

In 1910 Hilferding published *Finance Capital,* where he defined his subject as "the unification of capital. The previously distinct spheres of industrial capital, commercial capital and bank capital are henceforth under the control of high finance." In 1915, Bukharin used the phrase "the coalescence of industrial and bank capital." And in 1917, Lenin termed finance capital "the merging of industrial with bank capital." The terms used in the definitions are not substantially different (Brewer 1980:103-109; Howard and King 1989:chap. 5). Nor are they much different from modern-day conceptions of "finance capital" (Sweezy 1972:143; Aglietta 1979:253). These definitions each emphasize *institutional power bloc characteristics,* at the expense of drawing attention to the *vulnerability* implicit in financial relations.

Hilferding, for example, contends that the problem of rising overaccumulation in highly concentrated branches and sectors of production could be displaced (thanks to the coordination functions of "finance capital") into the more competitive, non-cartelized sectors of the economy. Thus the result of intensified uneven sectoral development during crisis is apparently, in Hilferding's (1981:298) formulation, *not* further destabilization of the economy, but rather its stabilization through deepening cartelization. "The difference in the rate of profit between cartelized and non-cartelized industries, which on average is greater the stronger the cartel and the more secure its monopoly, diminishes during times of prosperity and increases during a depression." The subsequent shake-out of the smaller producers permits the "finance capital" cartel to increase the level of industrial concentration and survive the broader downturn.

Indeed Hilferding goes so far as to argue that several factors "militating against a banking crisis" would combine with the increasing financial range of "finance capital" to ensure that conditions of crisis could be *ameliorated*. Those factors include, first, the ability of "finance capital" to manage and share risk effectively; second, the belief that a strong gold reserve and other state policies can shore up the creditworthiness of the system; third, a decline in the volume and importance of speculative activity (at the powerful urging of key institutions of "finance capital"); and fourth, the ability of production by joint-stock companies during a downturn to continue since such production need not realize an immediate return. Hilferding (1981:291) concludes that it is "sheer dogmatism to oppose the banks' penetration of industry... as a danger to the banks."

Hilferding (1981:180) even expressed faith that the centralization-and-concentration process would result in a giant bank at the center of the world economy. He predicts an "increasingly dense network of relations between the banks and industry... [which] would finally result in a single bank or a group of banks establishing control over the entire money capital. Such a 'central bank' would then exercise control over social production as a whole." (Bukharin [1972:73], too, predicted a "gigantic combined enterprise under the tutelage of the financial kings and the capitalist state, an enterprise which monopolises the national market.") Politically this is extremely important, for it provides a rationale for a route to socialism that entails the socialization of capitalist relations *via finance*. Hilferding (1981:368) at one point even asserted that "taking possession of six large Berlin banks would mean taking possession of the most important spheres of large scale industry, and would greatly facilitate the initial phases of socialist policy during the transition period, when capitalist accounting might still prove useful."

Hilferding was German Finance Minister later in his career (for a few weeks in 1923, and again in 1928-29) and was considered a "reformist" Marxist in the Bernstein/Kautsky tradition (Bottomore 1981:14). On this point his greatest subsequent rival, Grossmann (1992:198), offered scathing comment: "Hilferding needed this construction of a 'central bank' to ensure some painless, peaceful road to socialism, to his 'regulated' economy." Even as German Finance Minister (under difficult circumstances in the late 1920s)

Hilferding failed in any such mission—in no small part because of attacks against his party from the left which tragically equated social democratic politics (so-called "social fascism") with the actual fascism of Hitler.

Hitler, unlike Hilferding, had a strong command of the real power relations, and with the support of Albrecht Haushofer's Geopolitical School, stitched together a coalition of the German middle classes and disenchanted national capitalists aimed at creating an expanding geographical barrier ("Lebensraum") of economic autarchy against foreign financial power. As Kees van der Pijl (1984:14) explains, "The anti-Semitism of the Nazi movement portrayed the economic crisis as the result of 'German, creative' capital throttled by a rapacious international finance capital personified by the Jews ('schaffendes' versus 'raffendes Kapital')—an imagery that combined ancient prejudices with a distorted sense of Germany's actual subordination in the liberal world economy."[3] Distorted or not, in this instance the resistance to financial power was right-wing populism. But the real critic of "finance capital," Hilferding, was killed in Paris by the Nazis in 1941. Notwithstanding emerging problems with the "finance capital" concept (such as the collapse, not strengthening, of financial empires), Hilferding maintained his thesis even as late as 1931 (Sweezy, 1968:298).

The limits to "finance capital"

Where did Hilferding go wrong in miscalculating the power of "finance capital"? As a semantic construct, "finance capital" has, so far, been quarantined in quotation marks for a specific reason: to emphasize that its interpretation is a matter of protracted debate. As van der Pijl (1984:7) puts it, "the reality it conveys about the new empirical structure of capital does not obliterate the need for distinguishing the functional, 'original' fractions." But other criticisms have been levelled against Hilferding's profoundly institutional approach to finance. According to Suzanne de Brunhoff (1976:xiv), Hilferding makes a critical mistake that leads him to dissociate money and the credit system ("money as an instrument of hoarding" is ignored, she complains). "This dissociation has probably been one of the reasons for the overestimation of the role of finance capital."

Further objections emerge to the internal logic of Hilferding's "finance capital," as well as to its contemporary relevance. The first line of argument highlights the historical datedness of the concept, since banking capital was, during Hilferding's time, used nearly exclusively for financing the purchase of means of production (M-MP) and only rarely for purchasing labor power (M-L) (a function reserved for cash). Hilferding

(1981:70) observed a rising capital/labor ratio and concluded that "the growth of M-MP outpaces the growth of M-L, with the resulting more rapid increase in the use of credit compared with the use of cash." In the post-depression era, however, an enormous amount of finance was originally drawn from and allocated to M-L, in part through related processes such as pension and insurance funds, consumer credit, and government debt. Credit has now become a means of purchasing and reproducing labor power, in addition to its original role in arranging the purchase of means of production (as de Brunhoff [1978] has pointed out). Hence it would appear that Hilferding's reliance upon the rising organic composition of capital to explain the build-up of debt in the economy, and then to gauge the relative strength of the "finance capital" power bloc, is an insufficient (even if it remains a *necessary*) component of economic analysis.

It would appear too that without analysis of government and consumer debt, Hilferding's "finance capital" concept misses other insights about the influence of finance upon accumulation. One is the rise of labor's "social wage" as a result of access to credit, which is partly responsible for establishing a privileged consuming stratum of workers. Another is the ability of the credit system to maintain "effective demand" (buying power) in the economy, partly through government and consumer debt, thus avoiding crises of "underconsumption" but putting off until later the unavoidable need to repay the debt. Notwithstanding the subsequent hegemony of conservative policy, these credit-related functions remain vital components of economic management in advanced capitalist economies and they point to the need for more sensitivity to the meanderings of capital accumulation than that offered by a "finance capital" power bloc concept.

In addition, Hilferding's conclusion runs contrary even to much of his own prior analysis. First, the problem of uneven sectoral development between capital goods and consumer goods (disproportionalities between Departments One and Two, in the Marxist lexicon), upon which Hilferding based his crisis theory, tends to heighten as finance grows more important, notwithstanding the short-run amelioration provided by credit. Second, the same problems in the productive sector that lead to falling profit rates also force banks to look further afield, geographically and sectorally, in order to maintain lending and a healthy deposit base, and this brings added risk. Third, new forms of financial regulation which Hilferding suggests are responsible for stabilizing an inherently unsound banking system, are often incapable of dealing with a major financial crisis. Fourth, rather than declining in importance, speculation tends to increase dramatically prior to the climax of a crisis. Fifth, Hilferding's argument that joint-stock companies are relatively immune from downturns is contradicted by his analysis of how vital credit is to the smooth operation of stock exchanges. Sixth, given the tendencies already discussed (especially increasing risk, the breakdown of the state's protective role, and uncontrolled speculation), the combination of industry, commerce, and banking as "finance capital" increases temptations for insider lending and thus for greater than normal risk, leading to a greater chance of financial problems.

In sum, nearly all of Hilferding's previous analysis leads to the logical conclusion that, contrary to "finance capital" hegemony during a crisis, banks do indeed lose self-control—as well as control of outside entities and processes. Sweezy (1968:267) may have been correct in this respect when he commented, "Hilferding mistakes a transitional phase of capitalist development for a lasting trend." The "transitional phase" was one of recovery from the 1870s–1890s financial crises; these crises would emerge again in the early 1930s and again in the 1970s and 1980s, and would provide researchers—including Sweezy—a grain of salt in their considerations of the untrammelled power of "finance capital."

It was just prior to the 1930s crisis of "finance capital" that one of the most impressive critiques of Hilferding emerged, from the Frankfurt School economist Grossmann. Noting a remark by Hilferding in 1927—"I have always rejected any theory of economic breakdown. In my opinion, Marx himself proved the falsehood of all such theories" (*Liepziger Volkszeitung*, 27/5/27)—Grossmann (1992:52-53) replied, "No economic proof of the necessary breakdown of capitalism was ever attempted. And yet, as Bernstein realized in 1899, the question is one that is decisive to our whole understanding of Marxism.... Marx provides all the elements necessary for this proof." Specifically, as Grossmann (1992:200) concluded his 1929 book *The Law of Accumulation*, "The historical tendency of capital is not the creation of a central bank which dominates the whole economy through a general cartel, but industrial concentration and growing accumulation of capital leading to the final breakdown due to overaccumulation."

Space, time, and the displacement of overaccumulation

Notwithstanding the prescience of his pre-Depression argument, Grossmann's "final breakdown" has taken its time. In the wake of the polarizing Hilferding-Grossmann debate perhaps a theoretical modification is required which can account for the *displacement* of crisis, rather than its self-generating resolution or its degeneration into a full-fledged economic meltdown.

David Harvey (1982:285; 1985b:345) assists us by more clearly specifying "the contradiction between the financial system and its monetary basis," in part through introducing finance to geography. He unveils a set of countervailing tendencies to crisis which were hitherto unexplored within the Marxist tradition: "Absorption of capital (and labor) surpluses through temporal and geographic displacement played key roles in the history of crisis resolution." For Harvey, credit serves a temporal displacement function—a so-called "temporal fix" to overaccumulation—since finance not only speeds the turnover time of capital, as Marx observed, but also sends surplus capital into "the production of goods that have long term future uses in production or consumption." This helps to displace crisis in the short-term, but exacerbates the overaccumulation problem down the road.

There is also a "spatial fix" to overaccumulation: in serving a geographical displacement function (such as through foreign lending), finance can send "surplus money to another country to buy up surplus commodities." This amounts to a short-term solution to overaccumulation which comes back to haunt the lending country when, in order to pay off the debt, the borrower must cut imports from, and increase exports to, the lender. The same principle works at other geographical scales.

In sum, the tensions and contradictions in value production and realization can only be resolved, says Harvey (1982:xvi), "at the price of internalizing the contradictions within itself. Massive concentration of financial power, accompanied by the machinations of finance capital, can as easily destabilize as stabilize capitalism." Harvey (1982:283) thus highlights the constraints on the power of finance imposed by the full logic of the accumulation process, and "finance capital" is therefore seen, far more usefully, in terms of "the countervailing forces that simultaneously create and undermine the formation of coherent power blocs within the bourgeoisie."

With that, the primary Marxist conceptions of finance in the accumulation process have been reviewed, the most important abstract elements retrieved, the dangers of the "finance capital" concept disclosed, the rise of financial control and speculation explored, and spatial and temporal responses to crisis noted. But all of this has so far been accomplished with little or no discussion of ***uneven development***. We consider, first, the underlying dynamic of sectoral unevenness between and within the spheres of production, reproduction, and finance, followed, second, by uneven geographical development and third, by some considerations on the problem of scale in the relations between finance and uneven development.

The uneven development of sectors

The issue, simply, is whether the power of finance is asserted through an *intensification* of processes of uneven development, as opposed to *diminishing* (or levelling) such processes (in part through the imposition of universalizing standards). Georg Simmel (1971) seemed to support the latter view:

> To the extent that money, with its colourlessness and its indifferent quality can become a denominator of all values, it becomes the frightful leveller—it hollows out the core of things, their specific values and their uniqueness and incomparability in a way which is beyond repair. They all float with the same specific gravity in the constantly moving stream of money.

Although Marx also used phrases such as "great leveller and cynic" to describe money, the Marxist approach accepts this thesis only up to a point. Marx (1967:chap. 27, par. 15) commented on uneven development as a necessary process under capitalism:

> In the same relations in which wealth is produced, poverty is produced also; that in the same relations in which there is a development of the forces of production, there is also the development of a repressive force; that these relations produce bourgeois wealth, ie the wealth of the bourgeois class, only by continually annihilating the wealth of the individual members of this class and by producing an ever growing proletariat.

This "absolute general law of capitalist accumulation," as Marx termed it, offers a useful grounding for a theory of uneven development. For example, it provides the sort of insight into capitalism that will permit us to move beyond modernization theory's "dualistic" framework of development and underdevelopment as distinctly separate, unrelated systems. The pitfalls of modernization theory are taken up in later chapters. First, though, it is worthwhile to take the analysis of uneven development back to the point where finance emerges, in order to assess the processes through which unevenness intensifies or diminishes.

Whereas Neil Smith in his seminal study, *Uneven Development,* (1990), roots the equalization and differentiation of capital (the fundamental motions of uneven development) in the emergence of a division of labor, Ernest Mandel (1968:210) searched even further back, to "private production" among different producers within the same community. He insisted that "differences of aptitude between individuals, the differences of fertility between animals or soils, innumerable accidents of human life or the cycle of nature" were responsible for uneven development in production. As a result, societies faced a choice: either engage in mutual aid (usually feasible in a society based on cooperation) to ensure the subsistence of an entire community, or *save* and *lend money to those who need it* (eventually gaining some rate of interest). The latter route led to the historical development of money and credit, Mandel posited, which in turn paved the way for full-fledged commerce and, ultimately, for capitalist relations of production and distribution. In this abstract version of the capitalist development process, finance as an accommodating feature of early stages of economic growth had the effect of ameliorating uneven development, particularly in equalizing the rate of profit across firms and sectors.[4]

This could also, presumably, be the case in the sphere of *reproduction*, where the development of consumer and government credit markets offered finance the means to level certain reproductive relations. This phenomenon has been most important, of course, in advanced capitalist societies. When overaccumulation crisis is absent as a factor, then the inherent unevenness of the reproductive sphere—"disarticulated" development, as Alain de Janvry (1981) calls the differential production and consumption of durable goods along class lines—tends to be diminished by the role of credit in establishing what Michel Aglietta (1979:232) terms a "consumption norm." This sort of finance, Aglietta argues, also serves to level the unevenness of productive-reproductive processes because it "absorbs the divergence between the rhythm at which income is received and the rhythm at which it is spent, given the lumpiness of durable goods."

At the same time, the steady evolution of consumer savings and non-corporate contractual savings (pension and insurance funds), much of which is used to fund production, led finance "irrevocably into direct participation in determining the general strategy of accumulation." Spiralling government debt adds to this process, since, according to Aglietta, even the federal debt of the major capitalist power, the United States, "has no chance of being reduced or even stabilized in the near future." Astronomic growth in consumer credit—hire purchase, home mortgage bonds, car loans, credit for consumer durables, credit cards, etc.—after World War II reflected the mass consumption orientation of "Fordism" and the "intensive regime of accumulation."

What all of this implies is that under relatively good economic conditions—probably limited to the advanced capitalist countries—unevenness in the reproductive sphere can be ameliorated by finance, but the cost of this is growing indebtedness which in turn leaves the sphere of reproduction increasingly subject to the power of finance. In these theoretical arguments, in sum, the basis of finance-production-reproduction relations is one of amelioration; credit levels natural differences.

Finance has the opposite effect on uneven development under other conditions, however. It is only when we look beyond accommodating features of finance, and instead to the *control* and *speculative* functions, that we understand the roles of finance (as both cause and effect) in the uneven development of capitalism. To some degree, uneven sectoral development is most directly a function of imbalances in production between capital goods and consumer goods, and here the role of finance is by no means ameliorative. Such problems have "all kinds of manifestations in shifting investment flows from productive to speculative outlets," according to Aglietta (1979:359). For example, the increased turnover of short-term stocks of capital goods during the boom phase leads to ever-shorter terms for credit. More generally, Aglietta argues, "Uneven development creates artificial differences in the apparent financial results of firms, which are realized only on credit. These differences favour speculative gains on the financial market."

These rather different financial effects can be postulated at the level of abstract theory, but Aglietta also documents how uneven sectoral development reached crisis proportions in the 1920s, leading to financial chaos from 1929 to 1933 and the Great Depression. However, in considering the postwar era, Aglietta (1979:378) invoked the spirit of Hilferding, in suggesting that finance can stabilize itself. The devaluation of money (inflation) and deflation of debt (write-downs in selected sectors) together permit a "threshold of resistance" to crisis: "What is important to note here is that the entire structure of modern capitalism functions in such a way as to avoid this phase degenerating into financial panic." Indeed the general message from Aglietta's "Regulation School" of political economy is that the development of a "mode of regulation" to serve particular "regimes of accumulation" makes finance and uneven development a much less explosive combination.[5]

If, however, the intrinsic unevenness within and between finance, production and reproduction is not observable on the surface—thanks, temporarily, to successful strategies of regulation—that does not mean that overaccumulation crisis has been resolved, nor that we can dismiss theoretically-derived tendencies towards sectoral unevenness which ultimately manifest themselves in financial crisis. As argued above, the role for finance in accommodating production evolves into a much more contradictory function under conditions of overaccumulation crisis. It is here that finance *accentuates* other processes of uneven development in the productive circuit of capital.

Consider, especially, the phenomenon of speculation. According to Harvey (1982:326), financial speculation has the effect, at times, of restructuring productive capital, since it

> allows individualized and private experimentation with new products, new technologies (including organizational forms), new physical and social infrastructures, even whole new cultures, class configurations, and forms of class organization and struggle. It is this aspect to speculation that Marx ignores. The crash rationalizes and restructures production so as to eliminate extraneous elements—both old and new alike. It also disciplines all other aspects of social life to capitalist class requirements and hence typically sparks some kind of organized or unorganized response, not only on the part of labor (which goes without saying) but also from various affected factions within the bourgeoisie.

But then again there is the pure damage to the productive sector wrought by speculation, unmitigated by any meaningful role in restructuring production to support renewed accumulation. Indeed much of the displacement of capitalist crisis into speculative outlets, today and historically, is not merely unsustainable as the basis for regenerating productive development, it is also plainly self-destructive.

For capital, the challenge at this stage becomes undergirding unproductive financial assets with productive assets. This is most vividly expressed by Thomas Johnson, a leading US banker, in considering the potential implications of the Third World debt crisis during the 1980s: "There is a possibility of a nightmarish domino effect, as every creditor ransacks the globe attempting to locate his collateral" (Smith 1990:161). This is the point at which the dynamic of uneven development reaches the brink. Expressed here is the transition from finance as an accommodating agent in the development of the productive forces of capitalism, to finance as both a controlling power and a speculative vehicle gone awry.

The uneven development of space

It is by considering the process of spatial development during financial ascendance, that we can link analyses of unevenness more generally, between and within advanced capitalist settings and the Third World. Giovanni Arrighi and John Saul (1973b:145), for example, were well aware of

> *uneven development* thrown up by capitalist penetration in Africa. For the underdevelopment of Africa as a whole relative to the industrial centres of the West has been accompanied and mediated by uneven development as between regions, states, tribes, and races *within* Africa itself, and this fact adds important dimensions to the class struggle in Africa and to the character of the resistance of progressive African forces to contemporary imperialism.

While this phenomenon is often described as "articulations of modes of production" (Wolpe 1980), Smith (1990:156) explains it in more abstract theoretical terms: "The logic of uneven development is theoretically prior to the problematic of articulation of modes of production. The point is that today the 'articulation of modes of production' is a product of the developments and limits of capital, not vice versa. More concretely, it is the logic of uneven development which structures the context for this articulation." This insight leads us to again enquire of the role of finance in "the development and limits of capital" and the implications of this role for uneven spatial development.

Ironically, while spatial metaphors are often easy for visionary bankers like Thomas Johnson under conditions combining overaccumulation crisis and financial power, geographers have said very little about finance in economic development. This is a serious oversight, for, as Harvey (1989a:176) observes, "Money creates an enormous capacity to concentrate social power in space, for unlike other use values it can be accumulated at a particular place without restraint. And these immense concentrations of social power can be put to work to realise massive but localized transformations of nature, the construction of built environments, and the like."

But aside from Harvey and a very few others, there has been a near-complete theoretical neglect of the geographical aspects of finance and of the financial aspects of geography. This reflects, perhaps, theoretical satisfaction with the *accommodating* features of finance, in contrast to *speculative* or *control* features. The theoretical void is not limited to Marxist geography. In much of the mainstream geographical literature, finance is itself seen as a productive service enterprise with specific locational and employment features, and thus is incorporated into ordinary models of the space-economy. The location of financial institutions and the distribution of their physical lending and deposit-taking functions are considered effective barometers of economic vitality or of other productive sector activities less easily traced.

The obvious failure of such an approach, though, is that it assumes rather than questions the underlying rationality of the spatiality of finance. In the context of speculative financial markets and the rise of financial power, this assumption is immediately suspect. As the Zimbabwe case study demonstrates, the spatial structure of financial organization has all manner of contingent features that flow from institutional and historical accidents. As a result it is crucial to distinguish between the *necessary* and the *contingent institutional* features of a financial system in geographical terms. The financial penetration of space has, it seems, enormous implications for the nature of territorial divisions of production and reproduction, as well as for the operation of financial power across different scales.

How, then, can we get to the root of the relationship between finance and uneven spatial development? Smith (1990:150) situates the origins of uneven development in "the constant necessary movement from fixed to circulating capital and back to fixed. At an even more basic level, it is the geographical manifestation of the equally constant and necessary movement from use-value to exchange-value and back to use-value." The movement from exchange-value to use-value and back, after all, ***depends on money as a medium of exchange and store of value.*** (Later, credit amplifies these roles.) As a consequence, the dynamism of uneven development relates at least to some degree to the exercise of financial power. The abstract notion of money as a means of verifying trade and commerce takes on added meaning in practice, particularly when considered in relation to the actual development of capitalism. For example, during the epoch of imperialism, which Lenin described with such diligence, entire currency blocs battled each other for trading dominance. This sort of totalizing process was one through which finance seemed to level local dynamics of uneven development, in the course of imposing similar conditions drawing closer the various components of the global space economy into a universal law of value.

In moments such as these it may well appear that financial power overwhelms nations, regions, cities, and suburbs—or at least compels them to operate under a substantially similar global logic of credit-based expansion or contraction. Yet while finance levels certain local processes, this by no means implies the transcendence of uneven spatial development. To the contrary, there is growing evidence that under particular conditions—overaccumulation crisis, financial ascendance, and in turn financial crashes—the application of financial power exacerbates processes of uneven development.

This would appear to be the case particularly if frictional constraints to the movement of financial capital across space diminish over time. Such friction takes the form of technological-logistical, political-economic, or natural geographical barriers to the free flow of capital, commodities, or labor power. To the degree that these constraints are gradually removed, Harvey (1992) remarks, finance will "sharpen differences in the territorial division of labor because small advantages will be easier to capitalise upon." As overaccumulation sets in, as the power of money tends to increase, and as financial markets are consequently liberalized, there is then less scope for the ameliorative capacity of finance to level territorial differentials (as Mandel suggested was the historical basis for money). The reverse is also true, in that the existence of such friction—especially in impeding the geographical shift of funds to where they are most in need—

constrains the power of money. In other words, as finance exacerbates uneven development, geography simultaneously sharpens the contradictions within finance.

The depth of historical evidence for such phenomena varies depending on the contingencies of different national financial institutions and systems. Clarke (1988:110) has assessed historical processes in Britain which suggest the role of friction in financial crashes:

> In the initial phase of development of the credit system accumulation was frequently disrupted at an early stage by the failure of local banks. Although this was often put down to unsound banking practices, it was primarily a result of the geographical unevenness of accumulation which led to imbalances in the inter-regional flows of commodities and of capital, which resulted in an inflow of money into some regions and an outflow from others. Banks in some regions accumulated ample reserves of the money commodity, while banks elsewhere found themselves under increasing pressure.

In nineteenth-century South Africa, for example, Clarke's assessment would hold (Bond 1991a). But in colonial Zimbabwe, once established, the foreign-controlled banks avoided the worst excesses of financial collapse related to geographical funding flows (as shown in subsequent chapters).

Indeed the process seems to unfold in two directions, both extremely sensitive to issues of scale. On the one hand, geographically uneven development prevents locally-oriented banks from adapting to spatial changes in the productive circuits of capital. The solution to this problem, as discussed below, is to permit banks to "jump scale," such that highly-concentrated national banking systems have emerged to level such differentiation of scale.[6] On the other hand, though, the effect of overaccumulation on the rise and fall of financial power is most spectacular precisely because it is during these moments that geographical differentiation is most ambitiously generated. Space becomes a much more crucial "means of production" (Smith, 1990:85-87) when the circulation of capital in productive sectors is overshadowed by increasingly futile attempts to *realize* surplus value through commerce or financial speculation, regardless of where (and whether) it is being created.

It is at this point that speculation takes on crucial geographical characteristics. Ironically, Harvey (1982:398) appears excessively generous to "rampant speculation and unchecked appropriation" (particularly when it comes to their role in fostering uneven geographical development) when he argues that they "generate the chaotic ferment out of which new spatial configurations can grow." Harvey contends that "Waves of speculation in the creation of new spatial configurations are as vital to the survival of capitalism as other forms of speculation." The case would be firmer if opulent financial institution headquarters buildings (the premier outlet of speculative capital during peak periods) represented "the physical landscape necessary to future accumulation." But especially when land titles become the preferred form of financial capital, planting the seeds of future accumulation is often impossible. Indeed as Harvey (1982:349) acknowledges, "monopoly control guarantees that the problem of land speculation will acquire deep significance within the overall unstable dynamic of capitalism."

Speculation is both cause and effect in this respect. As Harvey (1982:397) continues, "The whole system of relations upon which the production of spatial configurations in the build environment is based, tends to facilitate and, on occasion, to exacerbate the insane bouts of speculation to which the credit system is any case prone." Examples of the insanity of financial speculation abound. "The postmodernist phenomenon seems irreducibly specific to the reckless overbuilding of commercial space that has taken place since 1974, continuing frenetically even through the trough of the severe 1981-82 recession," argues Mike Davis (1985:112). "This hypertrophic expansion of the financial service sector is not a new, higher stage of capitalism—even in America speculators cannot go on endlessly building postmodernist skyscrapers for other speculators to buy—but a morbid symptom of the financial overaccumulation prolonged by the weakness of the US labor movement and productive capital's fears of a general collapse."

Moreover, overaccumulation and financial speculation in the built environment together generate spatial bottlenecks, just as the productive sector suffers from uneven development and periodic bottlenecks in production and commerce. Harvey suggests that in generating "the chaotic ferment out of which new spatial configurations can grow," speculative tendencies in the built environment "are as vital to the survival of capitalism as other forms of speculation." However, "Too much speculation, to be sure, diverts capital away from real production and meets its fate of devaluation as a consequence." The trick, Harvey (1982, 398) posits, is to calculate "how much appropriation is appropriate. To that there is no clear answer and even if there were there is no guarantee that the forces at work under capitalism could ever achieve it."

Hence, at the local level, primarily through zoning decisions, the state attempts to work out the equilibrium of land as use-value and as exchange-value. That is sometimes helped, more often hindered though, by central bank decisions regarding credit supply, and by national housing and housing-finance programs which set out to achieve broad macroeconomic goals.

It will be useful to keep these divergent forces in mind when examining case studies of financial speculation in land.

We have traced the contradictory route of speculation through space and thus turn next to the control function of finance, where there are any number of spatial implications. Consider some examples of manipulative corporate decision-making of various types that have generated publicity in recent years: the provision of funds to corporations for overseas expansion ("loan-pushing"); the forced termination of the pension funds of overindebted companies (to speed loan repayments); wage takebacks imposed under similar circumstances; or the closing of factories deemed necessary by the financiers who pull industrialists' strings.

The urban, regional, and national—and, increasingly, global—implications of these control functions are legion. Indeed the reach of financial power extends beyond the corporation and into other arenas of production and reproduction where space is actively constructed. Various examples epitomize uneven geographical development. During the 1980s, financiers began to use "debt-for-nature swaps" to force overindebted nation-states to drop their sovereignty over tracts of land now slated for environmental conservation, having for years prior encouraged the degradation of such lands in order merely to record higher returns on Third World loans (Potter 1988).[7] The geographical impact of other forms of "structural adjustment" imposed by international financial power is vast, ranging from the desertification of the Sahel to the construction of cheap export platforms as in the Philippines or in the maquiladora region of Mexico (Broad 1988; George 1988). At a local scale, Harvey (1985a:88) argues that over time *urbanism* itself has "been transformed from an expression of the production needs of the industrialist to an expression of the controlled power of finance capital, backed by the power of the state, over the totality of the production process."

Across a variety of scales, uneven development is generally accentuated during those periods when financial institutions increase their range of movement, the velocity and intensity of their operations, and simultaneously, their power over debtors (whether companies, consumers, or governments). But specifying the control function of finance, within a multi-faceted relationship between financial power and uneven spatial development, is not uncontroversial.[8]

To illustrate, the legacy of the notion of "finance capital" can be seen in the work of the postmodern geographer Edward Soja. "Finance capital," in Soja's periodized account, was initially "relatively unimportant" in structuring urban space at the turn of the twentieth century (this was still the turf of productive capital). Later, with intensified concentration of capital and greater demands upon the built environment for "expanded reproduction," Soja (1989, 101) attributes to finance a primary role in the planning of cities.

At one level this is a compelling story, because it corresponds well to *descriptions* of urban development in advanced capitalist settings (Gordon 1978). But as the history of even a city like Harare, Zimbabwe demonstrates, there is no need to periodize in this manner to capture the *underlying dynamic* of financial circuits in uneven urban development. Finance-driven spatial changes (especially speculative land and investment booms) are typical outcomes of overaccumulation in the productive sectors. They do therefore supplant the circuit of industrial capital. And they occur according to a transhistorical rhythm that does not seem to respect as *determinate* the evolving role of the city in the reproduction of the capitalist system.

Still invoking periodization, Soja attributes to a post-Depression "coalition of capital and the state" factors such as the "intensified residential segregation, social fragmentation and the occupational segmentation of the working class." To the degree, however, that these factors do actually reflect an inner logic of urban capitalism (rather than being necessarily *functional* to the urban "consumption machine" as Soja seems to imply), this is surely not a logic constrained by the parameters of the institutional prerequisite that Soja identifies:the supposed planning power of "finance capital."[9]

In short, Soja demonstrates the sort of focus on institutional form, to the neglect of process, that must be avoided. The contemporary manifestations of this lesson are crucial, for, just as in the earlier period, financial power arises in ways that overwhelm built environment investment that came before it.[10] The dynamic here, however, is not primarily a new urban form which an omnipotent "finance capital" has appended to the existing socio-spatial landscape (though it may have that *appearance*), but in contrast a profoundly vulnerable reaction to a sustained crisis of overaccumulation which plays itself out increasingly in the financial circuit of capital.

As in the speculative booms of the nineteenth century or of the 1920s, the contemporary situation cannot continue in this state of displaced tension indefinitely. The search for surplus value realization in space becomes ever more fruitless, as the restructuring of the space economy becomes, concomitantly, more frenetically finance-driven. The power of finance over the course of uneven development is then at its most self-contradictory, and the spatial and socio-economic landscapes left in the wake of the inevitable collapse of financial power bear clearest witness to the fallibilities of the system.

Hence the need is clear to investigate the spatial dimensions of the non-accommodating roles of finance (speculation and the control function). To do so successfully requires us to decipher the underlying dynamics of financial relations and how they affect space and territory in very concrete ways. In a highly variegated Third World setting like Zimbabwe, such a study must immediately come to grips with the historical development of the spatial structure, especially patterns of industrial location, agricultural development, and residential housing segregation. The changing nature of these features of the space economy during the periodic rise and decline of finance will, presumably, reveal a great deal.

There is yet another concern, however: how to demonstrate the applicability of levers of financial power at different *scales*. Given the omnipresent dynamic of development and underdevelopment across scale, and the need to trace its well spring to the operation of the laws of motion of capitalism at scales appropriate for "socio-historical criticism" and informed political resistance, as Gramsci put it, these challenges will be central to the task ahead.

The uneven development of scale

The issue of scale, Smith (1990:134) insists, provides a "crucial window on the uneven development of capital, because it is difficult to comprehend the real meaning of 'dispersal,' 'decentralization,' 'spatial restructuring' and so forth, without a clear understanding of geographical scale." In this section, financial and monetary aspects of the integration of capitalist circuits at various scales are briefly considered, mainly with a view to establishing the theoretical basis for the power of international money in relation to economic processes determined at national and sub-national levels. But even power established and exercized at the highest scales is subject to challenge and to decay, depending on whether that power is geared to the accommodating, control, or speculative functions of finance at particular moments.

Smith, relying on ***production-bound*** understandings of scale derived from the division of labor, apparently considers the uneven power of finance at different scales a contingent (and relatively unimportant) feature of capitalist development. For Smith (1990:123), the key to uneven development is found in the changing basis of the centralization and dispersal of productive capital across international, national, and urban scales: "Certainly the spatial centralization of money capital can be considerably enhanced by the centralization of social capital as a whole, but in itself the spatial centralization of money capital is of little significance."

But is this really the case? Smith refers to the accommodating function of finance. But in the 1970s, for instance, as overaccumulation became generalized and financial power was ascendant, it was precisely the spatial centralization of money capital from petroleum consumers to the New York bank accounts of Arab rulers that represented the most proximate catalyst and facilitator for the flood of Petrodollars to the Third World (with all that that implied for the restructuring of the international division of labor and dependency relations of peripheral regions). After all, in contemporary times the main way in which spatially-centralized financial power is experienced is through the determination of national-level policies by the Washington, DC–based international financial institutions.

Smith's thesis is useful in advancing the theory of the geographical expansion of trade and investment beyond the limits of Lenin's *Imperialism* and other period works. But Smith possibly errs when addressing scale issues, especially at the national level, in concluding that point-of-production relations are definitive in a contemporary understanding of the nation-state.[11] In contrast, de Brunhoff (1978:61) draws the regulatory functions of both labor and money into the ambit of state policy:

> Public management of labor-power contributes to the reproduction of its value, which is something required by capital, but not guaranteed by capital itself. As for the reproduction of money as a general equivalent, this calls for state management of central bank money as the national currency lying "between" private bank money and international money. The circuit M-C-M', which represents the valorization of money capital, M, in circulation, cannot reproduce itself without these non-capitalist supports.

Indeed, while the nation-state ultimately acts to implement the workings of the law of value, such "political" functionality assumes vastly different forms under a system in which national accumulation is oriented to (domestic) production as opposed to (international) finance. Somewhere intermediate between national and international determinations, are super-regional currency blocs, such as those of the 1920s and 1930s, as well as what appear to be their 1990s revival in the form, initially, of hemispheric trade blocs. Just such variability—whether in the past (such as the 1930s-60s reign of import-substitution industrialization), or, as Samir Amin (1990) advocates, through the future "delinking" of the Third World from global circuits of trade, investment and finance—inspires the need for concrete investigations of the type that follows. Our beginning hypothesis is that while jumping scales to higher levels of determination occurs under conditions of ascendant financial power, the subsequent collapse of finance allows the issue of financial power to be broached, again, at lower levels.

It is important, therefore, to revisit de Brunhoff's (1978:40-43) typology of money according to three different scales: deposits in local banks, national currency, and international money. The dominant role of money during a particular stage of the accumulation process (whether accommodating, controlling, and/or speculative) and in different institutional settings, make a great deal of difference to the exercise of financial power at these various scales. At the lowest scale, the mobilization of deposits in local banks was central to early capitalist development. In contrast, in tightly-concentrated national banking systems characterized by high levels of financial power, local differentiation of scale can be washed away. Moreover, under certain institutional circumstances that tend to exist at the national scale, and during times when the tendency to overaccumulation is muted (such as the mid-1940s through the 1960s in most of the world), nation-state level policies emerge whereby control over financial power is quite feasible (a situation often described as "financial repression") (Burkett 1987). Indeed there are many historical examples of the repression of finance (and likewise financial power) by those states which are temporarily prejudiced by the dictates of national productive capital, or which are influenced, electorally, by populist sentiments.

From the standpoints of monetary policy and financial regulatory policy, the issue of scale returns again and again. All of the levers which concretize the uses and limits of financial power can, at times, be subsumed by the power of the nation-state (however that may be constituted at different stages)—and yet at other times, when applied by the IMF or World Bank from above (or from below, by financiers within the nation-state), they overwhelm state bureaucrats. Are these different power relations reflective of changing aspects of the necessary functions of money management in the reproduction of capitalism as an international system, or are they contingent? A sensitivity to scale is crucial to working out the modalities of financial power, as the geopolitics of international financial power demonstrate.

A starting hypothesis is that ***uneven hierarchies of scale are exacerbated during times of financial ascendance,*** at the same time unevenness in sectoral and spatial patterns of development is being generated. While the national scale of capitalist development usually occupies financial economists to the neglect of the sub-national, it is the international scale of financial power which, since the late 1970s, turns the heads and quickens the pulses of analysts and practitioners alike. Enormous evidence has accumulated over the past couple of decades to support the vivid claim of Hillel Tickten (1986, 37), that international financiers "have knowledge, global forms of action and speed on their side. Against them social democracy appears as clumsy peasants attached to one nation and with the horizon of village idiots." The power of international money over development strategies at the national scale is today reflected across the Third World, as well as in many advanced capitalist countries.

Sub-nationally, the ramifications of international financial power are increasingly evident. For smaller, home-bound manufacturing industries not well-located near air or shipping lanes to serve global markets, the fluctuating interest rates and national currency values dictated from Washington, DC, New York, London, Tokyo, Frankfurt and other sites of international financial control can be debilitating. The size of the national market, which was typically the key consideration in the expansion and contraction of production, has given way to trade liberalization enforced by the major financial institutions. Not just nation-states, but cities and regions are also increasingly caught up in the vortex of the international law of value, as more direct—often municipal-level—strategies of restructuring production and reproduction are brought into play, often at the behest of global financiers and aid agencies. In effect, the nation-state gives way to the city as a new unit of analysis, implementation and control, and as a means of enhancing the international competitiveness of production, via structural adjustment policies (Urban Institute 1990; World Bank 1991e).

There are plenty of other aspects of the determination of scale not by productive relations, but by financial power. Uneven development of the built environment at the urban scale, for example, intensifies principally because the land-rent structure becomes one in a set of portfolio options for financiers. "Rent," Harvey (1982:396) explains, "is assimilated as a form of interest identified specifically with locational attributes." Here Smith (1990:148) too is back on firmer ground (even if capitalism is not), in arguing that "To the extent that ground rent becomes an expression of the interest rate with the historical development of capital, the ground rent structure is tied to the determination of value in the system as a whole." Rent as an integrative lever—in this case, a means of universalizing capitalist space relations—is hence integrated into the broader capitalist economy by another lever of financial power: interest. The rate of interest in turn reflects a combination of factors, of which the most important are the demand for money and the concomitant balance of power relations between creditors and debtors of various sorts.

It is at this stage that Harvey (1982:396) asserts the "hegemonic role" of finance:

> The power of money capital is continuously exerted over all facets of production and realization at the same time as spatial allocations are

> brought within its orbit. The credit system affects land and property markets and the circulation of state debt. Pressure is thereby brought to bear on landowners, developers, buildings, the state and users. The formation of fictitious capital, furthermore, permits interest-bearing money capital to flow on a continuous basis in relation to the daily use of fixed, long-lived and immobile use values. The titles to such revenues can even circulate on the world market though the assets themselves are immobile.[12]

Harvey shows how the exercise of financial power includes the vision to monitor the markets in various types of financial capital—land, shares, debt instruments—so as to receive "elaborate signals for investment and disinvestment from one place to another... The effect is to reduce time and space to a common socially determined metric—the rate of interest, itself a representation of value in motion." Moreover, financial power imparts the capacity to avoid "one-shot devaluations" through their socialization of time and space, and the strength to occasionally absorb localized devaluations.

It appears now that, at its peak, financial power—specifically the interest rate, which becomes the main weapon in the battle between productive and financial circuits—has the capacity to level differences of scale altogether. As Dick Bryan (1995:41) insists, "the money form of capital most readily converts distinct and spatially diverse activities into a common unit of measurement" which in turn means that financial power can assert "the primacy of an internationally-determined rate of return on economic activity.... This calculation therefore operates as a limiting factor—dictating what class relations and what industrial organization are not sustainable, and specifying the criterion to which they must adapt." But contradictions are manifest, particularly in relating financial capital to surplus value extraction, and this means that, returning to Grossmann, the levelling process could as well represent a tendency to breakdown, not to renewed accumulation.

Conclusion: An investigation into finance and uneven development in Zimbabwe

Our theoretical overview has established the hypothesis that in the context of overaccumulation crisis, the rise of finance *intensifies the amplitude* of uneven geographical and sectoral development at crucial moments, accompanying a shift in the role of finance from accommodation towards speculation and control. And indeed, as shown throughout the book, this seems to occur at a variety of scales. Conversely, when finance experiences conclusive devaluation, this can be the signal for a revived accumulation process that is locally-determined, more proportional and tightly-articulated between sectors, and better-balanced geographically.

It remains next to begin to test these many concepts in Zimbabwe, prior to returning in the book's conclusion to review the relevance of theory to reality, and the implications for adjusting the theory and for testing it further through political struggle. Part Two begins in the next chapter with a rapid review of early economic trends in colonial Southern Rhodesia, from the speculative 1890s to the overaccumulation crisis of the late 1920s. Chapters Three and Four take the story into the next cycle of accumulation, from the 1930s through the early 1960s, describing how the financial system evolved (to the point of near-ruinous speculation) and how urban and rural unevenness was generated along the way. Chapter Five considers the inexorable process of accumulation and overaccumulation from the boom of the late 1960s and early 1970s to severe crisis during the late 1970s.

In the Third Part, the post-independence record of financial speculation and uneven development is examined. A discussion of the continuities between Rhodesian capitalism and Zimbabwean "socialism" and nationalism in Chapter Six sets the stage for detailed surveys of bureaucratic state support for financial capital and *comprador* class-formation in Chapter Seven, of speculation in shares and real estate in Chapter Eight, of housing and agricultural finance in Chapters Nine and Ten, and of precursors to (and introduction of) structural adjustment in Chapter(s) Eleven (and Twelve), respectively.

In Part Four, Chapter Thirteen brings together the experiences of a century of financial capitalism in Zimbabwe and assesses the theory we have just explored. It reiterates why the durable processes associated with capitalist crisis and the rise and fall of finance ensure that Zimbabwe will continue to experience terribly uneven development (when there is any development at all)—until the point at which resistance by a mass movement of poor and working people overwhelms the contradiction-ridden power of financial capital, and of capitalism itself.

Notes

1. There are other Marxist approaches to crisis theory which rely upon "underconsumption" and class-struggle "profit squeeze" explanations, but these are generally not utilised in the pages that follow and for simplification purposes can be omitted here.
2. The most rigorous Marxist analysis of such variables is Mandel (1980).

Other variables used to trace long-wave patterns include employment, social innovations, wealth inequality, social movements, political conflicts, and international wars.

3. As an aside, Deutsche Bank authorized a corporate biography in 1995 confirming its role in the economic persecution of Jews from quite early on during the Third Reich.
4. However, even if there was such a role for finance in societies which advanced rapidly from communal to capitalist relations, this abstract argument has little bearing on, for example, the imposition of credit in colonial Africa, a process we argue in subsequent chapters was characterised by intensifying polarisation most of the time.
5. An exception is Alain Lipietz (1985:109), but not without idiosyncracies we consider in the concluding chapter.
6. Although as Clarke (1988:110) points out with regard to the concentration of banking in 19th century Britain, "the increased integration of the financial system meant that when a crisis did strike it would reverberate through the whole system."
7. Consider too a well-publicised December 1991 memo by the World Bank's chief economist, Lawrence Summers: "I think the economic logic of dumping a load of toxic waste in the lowest wage country is impeccable and we should face up to that... Underpopulated countries in Africa are vastly under polluted" (cited in "Let Them Eat Pollution", *The Economist*, 8/2/92).
8. For example, David Harvey's urban analysis—which was, in the mid-1970s, concentrated on finance—came under attack, justifiably, from Soja (1989:100) and others, for its institutional view of "finance capital" which fostered both the idea of the "coalescence" of banking and industrial capital, and the idea that they are "permanently in conflict."

    > At times, he viewed finance capital as a separate fraction, a parasitic monopoly sector sucking up funds which would otherwise be available for housing and basic social services, and in direct conflict with industrial capital (from which it is able to extract part of the surplus in the form of rent and interest). At other times, Harvey treated finance capital almost in the Leninist sense as commingled with industrial capital in a monopoly imperialist union, cooperatively controlling the totality of the production process.

9. It is a logic, instead, that is rooted in the valorisation and devalorisation of space, in the manner described by Harvey, Smith, etc.
10. The 1980s consumption machine of the "urban spectacle" and real estate speculation dwarfed historical processes of accumulation in the urban built environment, as Davis (1991) shows in the case of Los Angeles.
11. Smith (1990:144) argues that the "historical stability" of the nation-state scale should be seen with respect to "political control over the working class. As economically obsolete as it is, the nation-state remains highly functional politically." Harvey's (1989b:194) position is more measured:

"The nation-state, though seriously weakened as an autonomous power, nevertheless retains important powers of labour disciplining as well as of intervention in financial flows and markets, while becoming itself much more vulnerable to fiscal crisis and the discipline of international money."

12. Paper representations of equities, other securities, real estate, etc., are termed "fictitious capital."

Part Two

Finance, Settler-Colonial Development and African Underdevelopment in Rhodesia

chapter two

Finance and Imperial Accumulation

Introduction

From 1890 through the 1930s, Southern Rhodesia's white settlers gradually took responsibility for ruling the colony from its founder, Cecil Rhodes' British South Africa Company. During these years, the colony experienced several dramatic shifts in political–economic character. Although driven by much larger forces, these shifts were perhaps best reflected in the fits and starts through which mines, farms, and industry suffered and prospered. All the while, the dynamic of change was resisted in various ways by African peasants and proletarians whose land and labor were expropriated in qualitatively greater degrees.

In short, uneven development emerged as a systematic though continually evolving characteristic of the local economy. All of this is well–known. What is less understood, however, is the systematic influence of financial flows, of the political power of finance, and subsequently of financial vulnerability upon capital accumulation.

In this chapter I seek to outline the most important confluences of finance and uneven development in the early imperial evolution of Southern Rhodesia's colonial–capitalist economy. There are several stages worth considering. The arrival of settler colonialism with the Pioneer Column of 1890, for example, depended upon mineral extraction. But the subjugation of mining to financial speculation during the 1890s forced the colony's rulers to introduce an agricultural bourgeoisie and to broaden the rest of the economy over the next three decades.

Notwithstanding the diversity of experiences over this stretch of early colonial history, the outcomes are comprehensible in theoretical, not merely contingent, terms. Of profound importance was the way in which control of space passed from merchants, miners, and farmers into the hands of foreign capital, landed speculators, and financiers. At the global scale, flows of finance ratified and often aggravated the various local processes.

Indeed this chapter first situates local political economy within the contradictions of global accumulation. In the process we are confronted with the regional (Southern African) geographical reach of financial power (1880s–90s). But the subsequent impact of financial crisis on the economy was unmistakable (1898–1910s). We move then to a period of more balanced capital accumulation (1910s–20s) which, however, culminated in a serious overaccumulation crisis (late 1920s). Finally we consider the evolving role of the banks and the currency system in the economy, before concluding with some theoretical observations about finance and imperial accumulation.

Primitive imperial accumulation

Rhodes, it is sometimes argued, had primarily geopolitical purposes in mind when, acting for the British government, he authorized the 1890 British South Africa Company (BSAC) invasion of what is now Zimbabwe: "If we get Mashonaland," he told associates, "we shall get the balance of Africa." The chartering of the BSAC was no historical accident occasioned merely by the notorious Rudd Concession which Rhodes obtained deceitfully from the Ndebele king Lobengula. It represented a structural switch from informal control of trade, to trade with rule. British imperialists assumed that competition for control of Africa would continue beyond the 1885 Berlin conference which partitioned Africa, and that only the chartering of private companies like the BSAC—"imperialism on the cheap"—would ensure geographical dominance over the interior of the continent in the face of hostile German, Portuguese, and Boer forces. Such a strategy was critical, they posited, to the protection of even the Nile Valley, which in turn represented the life-line to the prize of India (Loney 1975:31–32).

But there was, as well, an economic dynamic underway in Britain (and much of Europe)—beyond the never–ending search for gold—which undergirded Rhodes' conquests: chronic overaccumulation of capital, especially in the London financial markets, combined with social unrest. This dynamic fit, broadly speaking, the general thesis of financial control and capital–export advanced by, among others, Hobson, Hilferding and Lenin. Lenin (1986:75) illustrated ***Imperialism*** with the following quote of a remark Rhodes uttered in 1895:

> In order to save the 40,000,000 inhabitants of the United Kingdom from a bloody civil war, we colonial statesmen must acquire new lands to settle the surplus population, to provide new markets for the goods produced in the factories and mines. The Empire, as I have always said, is a bread and butter question. If you want to avoid civil war, you must become imperialists.

The settlement of Southern Rhodesia was undertaken with even more vigor than was the case in South Africa and other British colonies. All–encompassing racial domination was part and parcel of the widescale imposition of capital–labor relations upon what Arnold Sibanda (1985:16) argues was an indigenous "petty commodity mode of production" whose earlier contact with international capitalism was mainly mediated by Portuguese merchants.[1]

A telling incident involved Rhodes' top lieutenant in June 1893, and led directly to the first Ndebele massacres. When Lobengula harassed a Shona chief near Fort Victoria (now Masvingo), Starr Jameson argued for a forceful response: "The serious part is that every native has deserted from the mines and farms... There is no danger to whites but unless some shooting is done, I think it will be difficult to get labor even after they [Lobengula's men] have all gone" (Ranger 1985:93). Much shooting was indeed done by the BSAC's Maxim machine guns, as 1,000 Ndebele troops were killed in two major battles which led to Lobengula's defeat. The need for systematic labor control was clear to Jameson and the BSAC from the start, even if it took foreign financiers several more years to fully understand its importance.

Ironically, though, the BSAC overestimation of the region's gold reserves was, in the words of the country's first Marxist historiographer, Giovanni Arrighi (1973a: 336), "the most important single element determining the nature of economic and political development,"[2] for it involved enormous sunk costs by the company in infrastructure (especially a railroad) and land. Once the mistake was realised in 1894, Rhodes resorted to rampant looting, and ordered the conquered people of Matabeleland and Mashonaland to surrender as many as 200,000 cattle outright, to pay taxes (in the form of crops, cattle and goats), and to submit to forced labor. So extreme were these measures, and so overextended was the BSAC in the failed 1895 Jameson Raid on Johannesburg (conducted by the BSAC police), that Ndebele and Shona clans engaged in armed uprisings (respectively, "umvukela" and "zvimurenga") which dragged on for more than a year before finally being extinguished (Ranger 1967; Phimister 1988a).

Such circumstances created for the BSAC both a long-term commitment to full exploitation of the area and a desire, successfully fulfilled beginning with the "white agricultural policy" from 1908 to 1914, to recoup some return on its investments through the encouragement of white immigration and the development of a rural settler bourgeoisie. Recruitment offices were set up in London, Glasgow, and South Africa. It was only, however, in the 1920s that settler farming became commercially successful, having previously been undercut by African competition (Stoneman 1982:277; Leys 1959).

The financial basis for uneven regional development

The uneven direction and tempo of accumulation during this imperial era was profoundly influenced by the power of finance. The huge detour in the form of capitalist development orchestrated by the BSAC would not have transpired in quite this way were it not for the capacity of financiers—the London-oriented South African banks and stock exchange speculators—to segment the emerging geographical landscape of Southern Africa.

In what is now South Africa, for example, in the spirited battle over turf waged by British imperial capital against Afrikaner farmers and the Transvaal Republic in the 1880s and 1890s, bankers were on the front line, and won convincingly only with the takeover of President Kruger's National Bank during the Boer War (1899–1902). Lenders had infused small mining companies and farmers with excessive amounts of credit, which were then just as rapidly withdrawn during periodic overproduction crises, leading to waves of bankruptcies and an intense centralization of mining production and land holdings. Keegan (1986:44, 97) reports that in the Orange Free State (southwest of the Transvaal) "a chain of debt leading to the wholesalers was the basis of agrarian exchange relationships.... The grip of mortgage capital was an irksome burden, and farmers were deeply conscious of the greatly unequal exchange relations that their own dependence on the credit of others imposed."

Afrikaner nationalism was born from resistance to the power bloc comprising English–based financial and mining capital and the Cape government. This political and sometimes military struggle was an important impetus for Rhodes' northward thrust to Southern Rhodesia, which skirted the then Boer–controlled Transvaal. As was the case in earlier periods throughout the Cape, Natal, and the Afrikaner republics, it was the Cape Town–based Standard Chartered Bank—originally founded with London capital in 1860—that was most important in the geographical extension of financial power, earning it the moniker "gigantic devil–fish" by a resentful Broederbond, which in turn led Standard to drop "British" from its name in 1883 (Schumann 1938; Gilliomee 1989; Mabin 1989).

The close meshing of Standard with Rhodes' empire served the bank both because by 1900 it held deposits in Southern Rhodesia of £2.5 million against advances of just £250,000 (Standard attributed this imbalance to the difficulty of assessing underlying values of land and mines), and because it controlled nearly all local gold assaying and purchasing. Rhodes' close personal friendship with Standard's general manager, Lewis Michell, was one reason the bank opened its first branch in Salisbury just five months after the construction of a telegraph line in 1892. This offered the BSAC two crucial services: an acceptable currency supply to replace the BSAC's cheques (until then the chief medium of exchange); and local bank accounts which enabled money to be promptly transferred and thus "helped to put an end to the prevailing system of easy credit" (Standard Bank 1967:20). Indeed, according to one report (Irvine 1957), "A feature of the early days of banking in the Rhodesias was a drastic scarcity of ready cash. So bad was the position that an extensive and vicious credit system quickly grew, accelerated by the scarcity of goods and heavy transport costs."

The other influence wrought by financial power was the easy availability of foreign portfolio funding for local stock markets, which stemmed from a lengthy international economic depression, chronic excess financial liquidity (a symptom of general overaccumulation), and the global hegemony enjoyed by City of London financiers. Surplus capital was still concentrated in the London stock market in the early 1890s (Anderson, 1987), and flowed easily to the high-profile, well-tested initiatives of Rhodes.

This, Ian Phimister (1992:7) contends, was a period of increasing geopolitical turbulence across Africa emanating from "capitalism's uneven development during the last third of the nineteenth century, particularly the City of London's crucial role in mediating the development of a world economic system." As Britain faced industrial decline during the 1870s in both absolute and relative terms, manufacturers unable to compete in European markets joined ascendant London financial and commercial interests in promoting Free Trade philosophy (in contrast to the protectionism of other Europeans and the United States). Cain and Hopkins (1980:484–485) report that as London financial power increased, and as the prospects for domestic tariff protection waned, "industrial interests in Britain shifted, around 1880, into decisive support for the acquisition of new markets in Asia and Africa." Indeed it is here, and in a parallel crisis of French merchant capital in West Africa, that Phimister locates the well–spring of the "Scramble for Africa" which played such an important role in the region's subsequent development.

No matter how Africa was partitioned, the funding flows that fuelled Rhodes' adventures also reflected the last great speculative financial splurge of the 1870s–1890s global economic crisis. Some 35% of all nation–states had overborrowed during the 1870s and were in default by 1880. This figure dropped to 10% by 1890 thanks to British international financial coordination, and the 1890s were characterised by unprecedented numbers of debt settlements on defaulted foreign bonds. Nevertheless speculative surges continued during the decade, since the conditions for a new round of accumulation were not yet in place in most of the world. As a result, the percentage of nation–states in default rose again to 20% in the late 1890s (Suter 1992: 64,87,90).

It was in this global context that the City of London witnessed a "combination of sentiment, patriotism and opportunities for gain," as economic historian Sally Herbert Frankel (1938:20) put it. "Only against such a background can the almost incredible financial exploits of a Rhodes be understood, or the spasmodic, and at times exaggerated, bursts of capital investment which created the mineral industries of Africa be explained." The London capital investment in hundreds of mining and development company shares during this early period of speculation fundamentally altered the course of Southern Rhodesia's development.

Thus Charles van Onselen (1976:14) concludes that "the history of the mining industry between 1890 and 1903 is a story of the fluctuating fortunes of speculative capital." And drawing on accounts which note the appearance of an "enormous bladder unduly inflated and suddenly pricked," Phimister (1988a) surmises that anxious BSAC overseas investors' share price considerations were the basis for gross fraud, manipulation of the financial press, a smear campaign against Winston Churchill (whose mining experts were appropriately dubious about prospects), and, in part, the 1893 war against the Ndebele. Rhodes' DeBeers diamond company in South Africa assisted with bailout loans to the BSAC. Soon a Bulawayo stock market was established, became closely linked to Johannesburg, and itself promptly registered an astonishing £15 million worth of shares in 1894–1895.

Financial devaluation and geographical restructuring

The frantic pace could not be sustained, particularly in view of the speculative ebb and flow of capital and the concurrent geopolitical tensions emanating from South Africa. In 1898, comments Phimister (1988a:20–21),

> the flow of investment capital evaporated along with the value of Rhodesian mining and development company shares. This collapse of the speculative bubble forced the BSAC to try, much more seriously this time, to foster genuine mining activity. In short, the time had come to curb what critics had slated as "trading upon the unknown, this traffic in fairy tales, this capitalization of dreams." The new situation was to be one in which the large capitalist "should be encouraged, but only as a mining and industrial factor, not as a speculator pure and simple."

The Anglo–Boer War (1899–1902) dashed any further short–range speculative dreams, notwithstanding a major railroad investment program financed mainly by foreign bonds in the late 1890s. In 1903, in Arrighi's (1973a, 184) words, "The subordination of production to speculation ceased, and efforts were directed at reducing costs in order to enhance the profitability of those enterprises which had survived the crisis." According to the Standard Chartered Bank's Sir Lewis Michell, the share markets were "in no mood to absorb fresh issues of speculative capital" at that stage, mainly because the BSAC had not yet, after years of vigorous repression, secured a guaranteed cheap labor force for mining (Phimister 1988a:46). This state of affairs took some decades to remedy.

In retrospect, the role of finance had been decisive. Between 1891 and 1904, the London and Bulawayo stock listings of companies in the new territory accounted for the immense sum of £44.5 million, and cash investments were at least £10 million (Frankel 1938:150–157). The early rush of capital made an indelible impact, because, by rapidly broaching the limits of financial speculation, the BSAC was forced to make a more decisive commitment to African proletarianization. Arrighi (1973b:180–184) uses just this experience to refute the equilibrium labor market model of neo–classical economists, especially in explaining why African wages rose from 1893 to 1903 and were then stagnant until the 1940s: "The reason cannot be sought in the operation of market forces. The different behaviour of African wages before and after 1903 must instead be traced to the structural changes that occurred in the Rhodesian capitalist sector during the 1903–04 crisis."

Finance also forced the gradual geographical reorganization of the territory, as a result of efforts to gain a return on land titles which had failed in their previous role as speculative investment paper. Indeed, in a sea-change that lasted the next few decades, the emphasis of capital accumulation shifted from pure mining extraction to a combination of mining and agriculture. The BSAC transformed the territory's geography in order to make good the sunken rail and land investments, mainly through marketing cut-rate land to settlers (Ndlela 1980:27; Palmer 1977a, 1977b).

As a consequence, development or mining company shares were either wiped off the map to reflect their failure, or devalued and transformed into a longer-term commitment to undergird land titles with cash-crop production. This was not easy, because while the excessive flows of finance into Southern Rhodesia paved the way for this devaluation, the equally intemperate ebb tide of finance generally hindered the spatial expansion of capitalism into rural areas. Given the fortunes lost on land speculation, financiers like Standard Chartered Bank were so reluctant to pour medium-and long-term capital into agricultural credit that a Land Bank had to be established in 1912.

Uneven shifts in accumulation

In its first encounter with Southern Rhodesia, international financial power thus helped to establish a terribly uneven form of sectoral and spatial development. But the concentration of resources enjoyed by the BSAC subsequently made possible, at least temporarily, a more sustained process of capital accumulation. Establishing the sufficient conditions for broad-based accumulation—particularly an appropriate local class structure undergirded by cheap labor supplies and an imported agricultural bourgeoisie—was a responsibility the BSAC possessed through administrative rights over the region granted by the British government from 1890 to 1923.

The BSAC exercised substantial control over not only the gold and coal mines and railways, but also over citrus plantations, timber, some banking and insurance, and vast amounts of land. As the regional economy began picking up again, other major South African and British companies eventually followed, and became involved in asbestos, chrome, tobacco and land speculation. In 1909, for example, what is now Lonrho was founded as the London and Rhodesia Mining and Land Company.

It is important to note that, unlike in other African settings where foreign capital exploited and extracted resources and then moved on, the existence of a substantial agricultural bourgeoisie in Southern Rhodesia infused a decidedly "national" character. By 1902, three quarters of prime agricultural land was expropriated by whites. It was by no means virgin land. To one report that the territory's half-million Africans harvested over 600,000 acres of crops, Rhodes commented, "it shows what an important asset the native is" (Phimister 1975:258).

Yet the agricultural settler–bourgeoisie simultaneously discovered the need for an internal consumer market (whether settler or African) for the increasing farm produce. This was one reason for an early industrialization effort, which was unsuccessful because it conflicted with the short–run needs of the BSAC and foreign capital generally for sustained cheap labor supplies. "This represents the inconsistency inherent in the relations between international and national capitalism in pre–World War II Rhodesia," argues Arrighi (1973a:341). "The speculative interests [i.e., landholdings] of the former implied the expansion of the latter, but such an expansion might have threatened its more important productive interests." And still another source of conflict was the differential level of concentration in sectors controlled by (competitive) national capital and (relatively monopolistic) foreign capital. Such uneven sectoral development would haunt the colony well into the future.

One overriding concern shared by the emerging national bourgeoisie and foreign capital was expanding the supply of low–cost labor. To this end, the initial rise in African wages from 1893 to 1903 was "solved" by Native Commissioners' intensified coercion of Africans into labor markets, through various well–known methods. It was here that financial power was asserted at the microeconomic scale, since once mine workers were installed in compounds, a well–tested means of keeping them there was debt peonage to the mine store, even for such basic items as food and clothing. Van Onselen (1976:162,164–166) explains:

> Rhodesian mine owners and their commercial allies were quick to recognise and exploit this weakness: through extending credit to increasingly deprived black workers, they found the means to lengthen the labor cycle and enhance the process of proletarianisation. Peasants who had specifically left the rural areas with the purpose of earning cash found themselves trapped by the credit system in its various guises and were described as "demoralised." Workers from Nyasaland ensnared in the web of debt of the Rhodesian compounds spoke of their deep shame in going home without cash or goods for their kin. In some respects at least, the credit system as much as the

> compounds themselves were responsible for the passivity, frustration and despair of the workers.... As the cost of living rose and real wages declined, so the credit system spread throughout the compounds. So pervasive was the black workers' need for credit that their books of "work tickets" were printed with a special provision made for a space into which credit transactions were entered by the mine store. In many cases workers pledged their entire wages against the credit thus provided.[3]

As such financial controls were generalized as part of an overwhelmingly repressive compound system, African labor became relatively pliable and in good supply, and by 1922 wages were lower than in 1904. As a side effect of measures such as cattle–dipping and grazing fees, African peasant food production declined drastically. In sum, African labor markets went from discretionary to necessary as the BSAC expanded and a variety of other economic interests emerged. Arrighi (1973b:183–214) argues that the dichotomy of development and underdevelopment which permeated settler/African relations "was less an 'original state,' progressively reduced by market forces, than it was the outcome of the development of capitalism itself." Similarly, Frankel's (1938:14) exhaustive study of "investment and monocultures" led him to conclude that "there are limits to the extent to which it is possible to hasten returns to capital already invested. For the attempts to do so are likely to lead, directly or indirectly, to those systems of production which involve a large measure of direct or indirect compulsion."

The use of compulsion to draw out greater supplies of wage labor was unchecked either by the brief rise of militant white (racist) trade unions from around 1920, or the formal 1923 transfer of political power from the BSAC to a new Southern Rhodesian state representing 35,000 whites. "Self–governing status" was perceived to be in the interests of most whites, given the fact that a variety of groups registered periodic conflicts with BSAC rule: small miners, over royalty rights; white unions and labor, over wages; settler farmers, over their need to block African competition; the church, over social and political relations; and, within the BSAC, British and South African investors had different interests (the former received no dividends, while the latter desired a long–term, pro–settler policy) (Clarke 1980a).

As a result, the tentative import substitution program originally spurred by World War I continued well into the 1920s, as self–government matured. Manufacturing contributed an impressive 13% of Rhodesia's gross national product by 1926, mainly in the form of the railroad yard. Small firms engaged in subsidiary industries and production of rudimentary products for the local black consumer market (Wield, 1980).

But this strategy had its limits, as Africans—even those wage earners who attempted in 1927 to strike at the Shamva mines or, unsuccessfully, to organize a wing of the South African–based International Commercial Workers' Union, or who aimed for cooperation with white trade unionists in the late 1920s—remained mainly "appendages of the peasantry" with no prospects for petty bourgeoisification (except through collaboration), according to Arrighi (1973a: 349). The African labor force participation rate had increased from a stable 20% in the 1910s to 35% by 1926, a boon for settler agriculture. But it was not a boon for the peasantry, since it reflected their increasing deterioration as both subsistence and cash crop producers during the 1920s (with one–third less crop output over the period), which in turn contributed to insufficient buying power and ultimately the Great Depression itself.

By the late 1920s settler farming also began exhibiting classic capitalist crisis tendencies. As Murray (1970:67) recounts, "The local market was becoming too small to absorb local produce. What was true first of cattle and maize came in the course of the 1920s to apply to other commodities: more was being produced than could be consumed locally. The producers of each commodity in turn were faced with over–production and sought means of maintaining prices through an extension in the administration system for agriculture." Overaccumulation of agricultural capital led to the introduction not only of various state–capitalist functions, but of marketing cooperatives and consumer associations which, over time, came to play a powerful role in linking white farming elites to the political process.

At this stage, recently-settled white wage-earners and a nascent professional and commercial petty bourgeoisie moved into alliance with the settler farmers, the latter including many inexperienced immigrants who faced severe difficulties surviving hostile marketing conditions throughout the 1920s. While the Land Bank was a feasible state intervention, there was still neither the heart nor the muscle in the young Southern Rhodesian government to regulate seemingly omnipotent foreign capital (the failed effort in 1926 to control the BSAC–run railways was one key example). A deep economic crisis would bring matters to a head and lead to a change of government during the Great Depression.

Overaccumulation, overindebtedness and the Depression

After economic growth peaked in 1927, there appeared a very serious case of overaccumulation of capital in Southern Rhodesia's agro–mineral economy, reaching crisis point just before the climax of the global accumulation cycle in the late 1920s. In agriculture, and throughout the economy, growth was simply too rapid to sustain on the basis of available markets. National income had soared, in real terms, 20% in 1926 and another 13% in 1927, before stagnation set in (Barber 1961:104). As the Great Depression dawned, railway revenue was soon cut in half and mining lost even greater proportions of markets. And notwithstanding earlier marketing and cooperative schemes, overproduction remained a problem in agriculture. According to Murray (1970:78,81,83),

> When tobacco farmers had produced 23 million pounds of tobacco in 1928 and no market could be found for 10 million pounds of this, a large part of the farming industry was only saved by the Government contributing an estimated £500,000 (with an annual budget of £2.1 million)... By 1933 the economic circumstances of the Mashonaland maize and tobacco farmers had brought about major changes in the agricultural sector. The government had been forced to widen the scope of its activities by intervening to save tobacco farmers from bankruptcy and to prevent a similar fate overcoming the maize farmers... The slump in 1928 had driven out three–quarters of the tobacco growers, and in the ensuing five years the market had been able to absorb all that was produced, but in 1933 it was foreseen that another boom in tobacco growing was on the way, and as a result a further catastrophe was avoidable only through controls over production.

Extraordinary agricultural devaluation was partially mediated by the government and included further repression of the peasantry. Cattle exports declined from £340,000 in 1930 to £49,000 in 1931, land speculation collapsed, and there was a 30% cut–back in agricultural production nearly across the board. The Southern Rhodesian economy as a whole was facing devaluation of a third at that point. "The railway system, the merchanting and retailing organisation, the banks, could all handle a much greater volume of trade than they can get," commented one official report: "The country is in the position of a firm with heavy overhead expenses and an inadequate turn–over."[4] This, Frankel judged (1938:250–57), is "an analogy which can indeed be applied to most territories throughout Africa."

The analogy is even clearer if the firm is also externally overindebted, which was the case for countries throughout the world economy, and especially at the periphery, by the late 1920s and early 1930s. Then—as in the 1890s and the 1980s–90s—the tendency of overaccumulated finance to guide geographical and sectoral development became most intense, as much of Africa learned to its regret. For Southern Rhodesia, the situation was never as dire as it was elsewhere. Foreign debt to the public sector began accruing shortly after self–governing status was achieved. Considered a high risk in the mid 1920s, the new state issued £4 million in official bonds paying 5.0% interest on £4 million, in comparison to the 4.84% (on £64 million) that sub–Saharan Africa paid as a whole on outstanding foreign debt in 1925. By 1932, however, the Southern Rhodesian rate had diminished to 4.83% (on £5.7 million) as opposed to 4.85% (on £96 million) for Africa; and by 1935 Southern Rhodesia warranted an impressive 3.85% rate on stock issues of £8 million, the lowest on the continent and far below the average of 4.72% (for £99 million) and even South Africa's 3.91%.

On the one hand, the external debt of the continent rose 56% from 1925 to 1935, while Southern Rhodesia's had doubled. Yet on the other, Southern Rhodesia serviced the relatively low–interest bonds without excessive pain, thanks to the high gold price in relation to domestic currency after 1931. External debt as a percentage of export earnings remained under 10%. In contrast, in Kenya the debt servicing ratio soared from 12% in 1927 to 54% in 1934; in the Belgian Congo, the ratio exploded from 8% in 1927 to 45% in 1933. Nigeria and Tanganyika were similarly affected. Across the African continent, repayment problems were aggravated by a shattering 55% decline in the value of exports. Exports declined from £179 million in 1929 to £117 million in 1931, which was barely above the nominal 1913 value (Frankel 1938:173–193).

Southern Rhodesia's own exports rose to £6.6 million in 1929, then crashed by 50% two years later. A minor trade deficit in the late 1920s was thus replaced by a draconian enforced cut in imports (from £7 million in 1928 to £3.1 million in 1932). The devaluation was largely accomplished, and following the sterling area decision to go off the gold standard, Southern Rhodesian gold exports picked up. Total mineral exports increased from a low of £3.1 million in 1931 (the same as the nominal 1913 value) to £3.9 million the next year, and £6.5 million by 1935; gold accounted for some 80% of mining and 66% of total exports in 1933.[5] High profitability in the mining industry permitted imposition of a special tax in 1940, although, as Leys (1959, 103) notes, "after the war it was the government which had to be restrained (by the intervention of the International Monetary Fund) from subsidizing gold production for balance-of-payments purposes."

A parliamentary inquiry in 1945 found that gold was responsible for "a stabilising influence on the economy of Southern Rhodesia in times of world depression," from the standpoint both of fostering local employment and spending, and generating hard currency (Phimister 1988a:212). This was, in turn, a direct, if unintended consequence of a much deeper problem: at the global scale (and especially emanating from in the United

States), economic crisis was reflected in ever-tighter trade and financial circuits during the 1930s. Southern Rhodesia's government statistician (Shaul, 1946, 3,8) explained the (beneficial) impact of imperial economic disorder for his country's gold market:

> The economic policy of the United States in general sought to stimulate American exports, stimulate American shipping, prohibit imports from other countries, to grant loans accompanied by political and economic conditions, and in the depression to indulge in a panic measure of calling in of all loans irrespective of the repercussions on the currency and economic system of her debtors. As a result America became the trap for all the world's gold; her debtors could pay neither in goods nor services, and could not borrow from the creditor except on onerous conditions.

If 1930s-era international debt was manageable for Southern Rhodesia thanks largely to gold exports, much of the local debt—especially that owed by still-inexperienced white farmers—was not. The Land Bank's capital had grown from £300,000 at its founding to nearly £1 million in 1930. But asset growth accompanied unsustainable agricultural speculation. "My bankruptcy," said one farmer, "I attribute to the tobacco and land boom, and the easy way money and credit was obtainable. I consider the Government were at fault in encouraging farmers to go all out on tobacco—they should have insisted on farmers, before lending them big sums of money, to go in for mixed farming then if tobacco failed they would have something to fall back on" (Phimister 1988a:49,209).

It was a sympathetic enough plea, and a situation experienced by a large enough constituency, to compel government action. According to the Secretary of the Department of Agriculture and Lands, the 1935 Farmers' Debt Adjustment Act had "the specific object of relieving the burden of debt under which many efficient farmers, through no fault of their own, at present labor" (Phimister, 1988a, 175). Although the farmers won in the end, Murray (1970, 93) records the fierce debate over the issue of who would pay for the debt relief: "The Directors of the Land Bank pursued a policy which accorded with the wishes of the farmers' organisations and of the Minister of Agriculture in granting loans to help farmers to continue their farming. The Minister of Finance, backed by commercial interests, wished the Bank to administer the Act in a way that would enable mortgage holders and merchants to recover outstanding debts from farmers irrespective of whether or not this resulted in draining farmers."

The role of the banks

Over time, increasing popular hostility was aimed at the powerful Standard Chartered Bank, generating, during the 1930s crisis, the first national calls for a central bank as a solution to excessive "influence from South Africa" (though by now the banks were headquartered in London). This reflected, in part, a substantial imbalance in financial flows between Southern Rhodesia and England. Standard's role of providing money as a means of exchange rose to prominence again, briefly, in 1931, as Southern Rhodesia went off the gold standard (against Standard's counsel) while South Africa persevered until late 1932. "The intervening period had underlined the fact that Rhodesia could no longer be treated as an integral part of the South African administration of the Bank," reported Standard's official chronicles (1967:42,44).

In addition to Standard, the predecessor of Barclays Bank began operations in Southern Rhodesia in 1895. Between them, the two banks achieved such thorough penetration of white consumer banking that in 1938, the two banks in Gwelo (now Gweru) had 1,400 accounts at a time when the white adult population was 1,600. "Rhodesia had a reputation for being a country where credit was more general than cash in normal day to day business," Standard's biographer (1967, 53) noted, as "storekeepers would only allow credit to people who signed promissory notes payable at a bank and therefore people who otherwise would not have opened bank accounts were more or less forced to do so." With inadequate state regulation of money and finance, and significant changes in the nature of the Southern Rhodesian currency, the grounds for this reputation would increase even further in subsequent years.

Alongside providing currency and savings facilities, the banks played three roles which had longlasting implications for the colony's uneven geographical development. First, in the early 1910s Standard (and later Barclays) had established a wide branch network which provided bills of exchange—and thus stimulated much broader economic activity—for various small trading posts and mining centers. Following a dearth of new openings that lasted two decades, the branch networks were expanded to other mining towns during the 1930s. Second, the colony's 1933 purchase of BSAC mineral rights was supported by a £2 million overdraft from Standard, and was the first clear indication of what was to emerge as a symbiotic financing relationship with the local state.

Third, the banks assisted in the establishment of a monetary system, initially on the basis of their own notes—which typically accounted for a full 15% of banking system liabilities (although British coin was also accepted)—and then through supporting a new local currency in the late 1930s.[6] Unlike the banks, though, the new Southern Rhodesia Currency Board "exercised no control over any significant monetary variables, and had almost no power of discretionary action of any importance," according to Sowelem (1967: 24). The full transition from bank-issued money to the colonial British currency board system (which came into effect in 1940), reflected instead the declining capacity of Standard to administer currency and its unwillingness to grant loans locally, as well as the remobilized financial clout of the City of London within British imperialism more generally.[7] Southern Rhodesia was forced to maintain 100% foreign exchange cover for its local currency in London, using accounts at Standard and Barclays, which in practical terms meant that financial considerations now more directly shaped uneven development at the British colonial scale. According to Ann Seidman (1986:29),

> The colonial currency boards tied the colonial economy's money supply directly to the changes in the levels of the currency board's foreign assets, the pounds sterling or other foreign currencies which colonial company affiliates earned through exports. A fall in the colony's export earnings would cause an automatic decline in the stock of money available to the colony, with attendant depressing effects on the entire colonial economy: low foreign–exchange earnings led to a low demand, cutting back on imports or reducing local production, causing a negative multiplier effect throughout the country. An increase in foreign earnings, on the other hand, would lead to a direct increase in the money supply, causing an expansion of domestic demand. This stimulated increased imports, or, in a few cases, a positive multiplier effect stimulating an expansion of local production. In other words, the colonial currency boards spread the impact of the fluctuations in the value or volume of the colony's crude exports throughout its economy.

Thus there emerged a phenomenon of greater importance than the geographical spread of money through the banks, the financing of long-term state debt, or the banks' role in supplying money as a means of payment prior to the currency board. That was the capacity of the two banks to "accentuate" the "ups and downs of business," as a Bank of England envoy (Mynors, 1949) noted. A central bank and the application of moral suasion would be needed, he argued, to counteract the whims of "two well-established institutions with wide business knowledge and connections."

By the late 1930s the two local banks "were clearly conforming to the principles of British banking by providing only short-term capital and not long-term funds," the Central Statistical Office (CSO 1947:2,8,10) reported. "A world-wide trend for business to supply its own short-term capital by ploughing-back profits rather than by relying on bank advances appears to be in operation in the Colony," since banks "can always obtain Southern Rhodesian notes and coin which are legal tender in the Colony, from the Currency Board." The role of the currency board was limited to the most mundane aspects of central banking, "the ultimate source of supply of legal tender coin and notes." It soon became evident that the board's lack of control over banking credit would endanger the entire system, and that much more powerful forms of monetary regulation were required. The banks' power to exacerbate uneven development continued through World War II and, as the next chapter shows, even into a new era of financial deepening.

Conclusion: The dynamic of imperial accumulation

In case after case of uneven development, what this review of the contours of the early Southern Rhodesian economy suggests is that during particular periods, finance was at the switchpoint of the various circuits of local capital accumulation. How, then, do we understand this in more general terms? Was the relationship between finance and imperial accumulation accidental ("conjunctural") or structurally–determined ("organic")? David Harvey's (1982:410) argument on the capitalist characteristics of imperialism suggests a structural relation:

> Military conquest establishes state control. Surveyors establish private property in land (the laborer can then be excluded from the land by rent), transport and communications links are built, legal systems (conducive to exchange, of course) are established, and pre–capitalist populations proletarianised and disciplined (by force and repression, if necessary, but also through law, education, missionary activity, and the like). All of this costs vast sums of money. Beneath its surface ideological justifications, therefore, the politics of capitalist imperialism amount to a vast, long–run speculative investment which may or may not pay off. The debate over how much capitalists benefitted from imperialism is really a debate over whether this investment paid off or was effectively devalued. The destruction wrought on pre–capitalist populations and the high rate of exploitation achieved does not guarantee that colonial ventures were paying propositions. Nor does their failure prove that they were set in motion out of some benevolent attempt to bring enlightenment and development to "backward" regions in the rest of the world. They were simply caught up in the cap-

> italist dynamic of accumulation and devaluation. The investments were, in short, necessary but not sufficient conditions for the perpetuation of accumulation. The dynamic is not, however, without its pattern. The temporal and spatial horizons of capitalism are increasingly reduced to a manifestation of the rate of interest, itself a reflection of conditions of accumulation.

Harvey's argument is borne out by evidence from colonial Southern Rhodesia. Not only are the ebb and flow of accumulation and devaluation in evidence, there are clear signs of overaccumulation, uneven development and financial power which we will see again and again. Indeed, as the Southern Rhodesian economy matured during subsequent decades, geographical and sectoral flows of finance would play first accommodating, then determining, then rigorously delimited, roles in this process of uneven development.

Notes

1. Sibanda's argument departs from other researchers' theoretical notions of pre-capitalist social formation in Africa, including modes of production labelled, variously, communal, traditional, lineage, Asiatic, African, or undynamic caste system. Assuming that Sibanda is correct, within the broader theory of uneven development an "articulation of modes of production" perspective sensitive to different (sectoral and geographical) circuits of capital is, hence, at least partially appropriate for understanding these early superexploitative processes, especially in the development of mining and agriculture in Southern Rhodesia as well as labour migration processes involving the South African mines. However, this book is not aimed at resolving such controversies. For more information on pre-colonial economy in what is now Zimbabwe, see also Rennie (1973), Cobbing (1976), Mtetwa (1976), Beach (1977, 1994), Kosmin (1977), Bhila (1982), and Iliffe (1990).
2. The primacy of gold exploration (and its subsequent failure to realise returns for speculative London investors) in the development of capitalism in Southern Rhodesia is disputed by Sibanda, who places greater emphasis on the imposition of capital-labour relations (not an historical accident or miscalculation). It was not, he alleges, the failure of gold mining, but on the contrary its later success (in 1910) following the adoption of measures geared to disciplining labour, that indelibly stamped capitalist relations upon the territory and opened the door for settlers and for extensive penetration of foreign capital. Phimister's (1988a, Chapter One) subsequent interpretation—that labour discipline stemmed from the pressure imposed, in the final analysis, by international financial markets—may in fact reconcile the positions.

3. A comparable—but much more resistance-oriented—process was underway in South Africa, involving a struggle over the form which money ultimately took. Breckenridge (1992, 14) reports that gold was a form of wage payment that accounted for as much as 20% of the output, as migrants (especially from Mozambique) encountered the problem of paper money depreciation and contested currency exchange rates, not to mention the unfamiliarity of paper in rural home areas. Savings systems sprang up in the mines in part to "disrupt the binary exchange of labour between African migrants and white capitalists. Saving societies, like other forms of migrant organisation, were expressions of collective solidarity and mutual interest... Unlike other popular forms of worker association, the savings societies confronted the symbolic core of industrial and financial capitalism directly and sought to recast it on the collectivist terms of migrancy."
4. Professor Henry Clay's 1930 *Report on Industrial Relations in Southern Rhodesia,* C.S.R. 3-1930, cited in Frankel (1938, 243).
5. The attraction of gold was so strong as to work against processes of capitalist concentration: in 1936 the domestic gold mining industry was dominated by 10 producers responsible for 37% of output, while another 1700 produced the balance (in pre-depression years, the top ten averaged some 80% of output) (Frankel, 1938, 235).
6. The territory's first coins were Cape of Good Hope Colony coins, dating from an 1891 ordinance. Royal Proclamations in 1910 and 1911 allowed the use of British coins, and in 1922 commercial bank notes issued within the territory of Southern Rhodesia were made legal tender. With the gold standard of 1925, the 1922 Bank Notes Ordinance was repealed, but bank notes continued to circulate. In 1931 they were legalized again. A 1932 Coinage Act of Southern Rhodesia authorised the mining of Southern Rhodesian minerals to mint coins. The war-time nickel shortage was responsible for ending British coin convertibility in 1939. Bank notes were legal tender until 1940 (Central African Federation, 1959).
7. To use de Brunhoff's (1978, 43) framework, within the supposedly interdependent hierarchy, "international money" had thus displaced "private bank money." A truly autonomous "national money" didn't emerge in Southern Rhodesia until the 1950s.

chapter three

Growth, Crisis and Financial Regulation

Introduction

In the last chapter we considered the immense power of financial flows, largely emanating from London and South Africa, to shape the course of development during Southern Rhodesia's imperial era. In this and in the following chapter we take up issues of finance and uneven development between the early 1930s and early 1960s. With the Southern Rhodesian economy maturing during this period, we can now more directly assess some of the broad theoretical arguments of Chapter One, which have much to contribute to the story under consideration.

It should not be surprising that during this time of deepening capitalist relations and the emergence of a capitalist state, we find evidence of worsening uneven sectoral development, in particular imbalances between capital goods (machinery) and consumption goods (and, in the latter category, between production of luxury goods and basic goods), as well as between production, commerce, finance and landed (mining and agricultural) capitals. We begin, however, by observing how in the pre-war era sectoral unevenness was initially attacked and alleviated by a more interventionist government. The United Party (which had been elected to power as the populist Reform Party) sustained the emerging manufacturing bourgeoisie by making available new opportunities for industrial accumulation which would be controlled nationally and locally, rather than by the exigencies of international markets.

But sectoral unevenness inexorably returned in the early 1950s, as did the intrinsic tendency—fuelled by easy credit—to the overaccumulation of capital. Finance then rose in importance, its lubricating functions were accompanied by speculative impulses, and capital was increasingly centralized into financial groups closely associated with multinational corporations. Combined with outside factors such as the drop in copper prices and the uneasy African transition to neo-colonialism, a full-fledged crisis set in during the early 1960s in Southern Rhodesia, and financial investments crashed.

Throughout, the government of the day explored ways of responding to what were relatively new problems of rising finance. Here we trace uneven sectoral development as it was accentuated by overaccumulation and erratic credit flows, and combatted by somewhat ineffectual and *ad hoc* financial regulation—whereas the next chapter considers uneven spatial development and its political fallout. Throughout, there is also evidence of the uneven development of the scales at which economic processes are determined. By and large, Southern Rhodesia witnessed a transition from local and national determinations in the 1930s to global ones by the late 1950s—in production and agriculture, but with more variability in finance and mining.

By examining such facets of the 1930s–60s period, the role of financial power (both domestic and international) in the country's uneven development becomes clearer. This is a crucial exercise because overaccumulation and the rise and fall of financial power all ultimately had a profound effect upon the development of both black and white Rhodesian politics, and later, in the mid 1960s, upon Rhodesia's extraordinary ability to withstand international sanctions. That ability stemmed mainly from the advanced capacities of the state, which were codified in the 1950s—once hostility from a self-reliant, free-wheeling capitalist class had been overcome during the 1930s.

The state and financial capital

The Great Depression is considered to have lasted seven years in Southern Rhodesia, from 1931 to 1938 (Phimister 1988a). But to suppose this a period of wholesale, uninterrupted economic disaster (as indeed it was for farmers, many white workers and most Africans) runs the risk of overlooking vigorous political response to the crisis. For with the 1933 electoral victory of white urban and agrarian populists, this reaction ultimately was the basis for the early development of a capitalist nation-state and the restructuring of the economy in a manner conducive to somewhat more even, locally-controlled development. To talk of "even" development is not to suggest that the 1930s and 1940s witnessed racial reconciliation or even rural-urban equilibrium (precisely the opposite occurred) but is, rather, to think technically about how sectors in the economy moved towards a temporary equilibrium instead of continually growing more polarized in their functions. By way of proof that development of this nature is indeed feasible in Southern Rhodesia—on the periphery of global capitalism—it can be shown that the first extended upswing of a new cycle of capital accumulation lasted from 1932 through 1941. After the enormous devaluation of 1928-31 (including a massive 30% drop in net national income during 1931), real annual income growth picked up 16%, 20% and 21% in 1932, 1933, and 1934, respectively, followed by growth of 10%, 16% and 10% from 1935 to 1937, and then 6%, 3% and then 18% from 1938 to 1941 (Figure 3.1) (Barber 1961:103-104).

Initially, however, the recovery was so unevenly distributed that in the 1933 election the establishment-oriented Rhodesian Party was defeated by the Reform Party, led by the reputable surgeon Godfrey Huggins, who as a Rhodesian Party MP had represented his increasingly anxious white civil service constituency. Huggins also firmly endorsed segregation and a host of other forms of relief to beleaguered white farmers and workers. The election was, as Iden Wetherell (1975:61) observed, "fundamentally a populist protest designed to remind the State that its primary consideration lay not with the protection of profit, but with the promotion of institutional safeguards that would insure against a repetition of the recent experience." But although the Reform Party's initial, disgruntled programme was highly nationalistic, welfarist and racist, the more aggressively interventionist wing of the party was purged in 1934 (the Labor Party also gradually waned). Electoral calls for rescinding the BSAC's mineral rights, protectionism, nationalization, unemployment relief and white labor rights, a central bank for the colony, and the growth of government were all subsequently muted when conflict with powerful economic interests emerged. Huggins quickly deserted Reform and founded the United Party (subsequently, United Federal Party) in order to forge a new alliance with elements of the Rhodesian Party. For nearly three decades this remained Southern Rhodesia's ruling party, mostly under Huggins' reign (Gann and Gelfand, 1964). As the scale of the reversal became apparent, the bitter populist-segregationist (and former Reform leader) Neil Housman Wilson accused Huggins of restoring "the timid and fear and finance-riddled party that lost the battle of the mineral rights in 1933; gave the battle away rather than see it fought out to the possible detriment of the international financiers" (*New Rhodesia*, 26/10/34).

But a consensus remained across nearly all strata of whites that at least certain types of state intervention would be necessary to protect white workers from black competition, to ward off the worst effects of international Depression, to address debilitating supply bottlenecks, and ultimately (recalling the agricultural crises) to regulate the accumulation process itself. As even the first meeting of Southern Rhodesia's Associated Chambers of Industry (in 1944) conceded, "It is the considered opinion of this congress that when the industrial policy of the future is considered by the government, due weight should be given to the guarding against overproduction by existing or projected enterprises" (Murray 1970:182).

Even earlier, in the 1930s, a supportive state legal and political superstructure was being put into place: public works programs geared largely to solving white unemployment, parastatal industrial ventures to fill niches where the market failed, (white) state credit and trading networks, subsidies to white agriculture and to white workers of small and independent gold mines, anti-African labor laws (1934), and increased racial division and control of land (1930 and 1936). The state purchased from foreign capital the country's mineral rights in 1933 and its railroad in 1949, and set up major public investments in the Que Que (now Kwekwe) iron-and-steel and Gatooma (now Kadoma) cotton-spinning operations (Stoneman 1978).

The freedom to proceed along these lines was not merely established at the national scale. Locally, in the five main white population centers, commercial and industrial concerns projected their own sectional geographic power, reflecting the uneven development of scale. "To the extent that Commerce and Industry exerted any pressure on Central Government at all, it was mainly through the Municipalities," contends John Handford (1976:159-160). Nationally, in any case, Huggins' Finance Minister J.H. Smit "served Commerce so well that they had really no need of any organisation to lobby for their interests... Smit acted strongly in favour of free enterprise and restrictions on governmental spending—in face of opposition from farmers, smallworkers and employees." (He was later to resign from

Huggins' cabinet, however, over a slight leftward tilt during World War II.)

As capable and friendly as the United Party became to general business interests, the expansion of state intervention was, nevertheless, powerfully influenced by splits between (and within) national capital and international capital. "In general, the government found it easier to go along with what Industry wanted than with the aims of Commerce," Handford (1976, 161) suggests. Yet overall structural conditions ensured that, notwithstanding the impressive deepening of industry, the overall bias and orientation remained strongly towards mineral and agricultural export. "Partly this was due to the unequal strength of the contending parties," Phimister surmises (1988a:182); in any event, "London's financial clout was incomparably greater than any blow Salisbury might conceivably deliver."

Indeed, within the local capitalist class there was growing concern over the drain of financial surpluses to the two Southern Rhodesian banks' London headquarters. The banks "have consistently accumulated substantial excess reserves which have been held externally as balances with the head offices," Barber (1961:166-167) reports of the period spanning the 1930s–40s. "The lending policies of these organisations have been oriented towards short-term, liquid, and low-risk loans. Loans for fixed capital formation, the type of financial service most required in underdeveloped economies, have been precluded." Standard and Barclays held just 50% of their assets in local business loans (generally short-term advances for trade purposes) in 1936 (the first year such data were kept). Such local "earning assets" (which during the war also included government securities) declined to 41% of total assets in 1940 and a meagre 20% in 1945, while local deposits soared over the period from £8 million to £22 million (*P&F*, September 1957). As a result, the percentage of the banks' funds that accumulated in London rose from 49% in 1939 to 74% in 1945, accounting for £16.5 million. The banks did not invest locally, in part because war-time import and transportation restrictions affected opportunities for trade financing, but also because, according to the Central Statistical Office (CSO) (1947:9), "they were unable to find profitable outlets for their funds." Southern Rhodesia thus witnessed a war-time slump during which real income fell below 1941 levels until 1944 (Figure 3.2).

The banks' conservative outlook changed after the war, as loose Commonwealth-wide monetary policy, returning soldiers, new immigrants, and the lifting of import controls led to unprecedented consumer spending in Southern Rhodesia. The two banks' local assets (short- and medium-term loans, and investments in government securities) soared by 55% in 1946 and 71% in 1947. The Southern Rhodesian government was repaid a £2.5-million war-time loan from Britain and also floated a large sterling loan in London, so liquidity improved dramatically. Moreover, immigrants' remittances (mainly from Britain) rose sharply. Two immediate side effects of the surge in liquidity were rising inflationary pressures and highly uneven patterns of overindebtedness, both of which generated compelling demands for state intervention.

Early struggles over financial regulation

Heated debates catalysed by the feverish financial activity emerged over two issues: whether funds were being directed by financial institutions towards the most productive outlets, and whether the detrimental side effects of ascendant finance should be regulated by direct credit controls (which state bureaucrats and industrialists favored) or through interest rates (the preference of merchants). The position of many manufacturers was that finance remained the domain of foreigners who either sent hard-earned Southern Rhodesian money to London and Cape Town, or who encouraged excessive luxury-goods imports. Merchants, on the other hand, complained that attempts to deal with this problem through direct credit controls invariably hurt them the most.

As overindebtedness became a concern to Currency Board authorities in 1947 and as import bottlenecks were forming at the colonial Mozambican port of Beira and on the Rhodesian Railways, a new set of exchange and import controls were imposed, the effect of which was "to limit the supply of goods at a time when the supply of money is being steadily increased," the CSO (1948:3) acknowledged. This led to speculation in used cars and a black market in local land (at a time of temporary residential-only restrictions on development). At one point during the late 1940s, the threat of bank-fuelled generalized inflation was so great that the CSO (1947:15,19) recommended no future foreign borrowing by government, and limitations on immigration. Tough reserve requirements were mooted for the banks: "In view of the importance of the actions of the banking system and their effects upon the development of the Colony, control of the powers of the banking system to create credit is essential."

From a different but no less critical direction, renewed pleas by the Labor Party in Parliament in 1947 for a Southern Rhodesian central bank reflected the imbalance in credit allocation. It was a classic conflict between the loose money interests of productive capital (and workers) and the anti-inflationary bias of financial power. Productivist entreaties were consistently met by scorn from the extremely conservative administrator of the Currency Board, A.P. Grafftey-Smith (1954:1): "The idea seemed to prevail that a State Bank would control and compete with the commercial banks, and that a golden era of extended credit would succeed the Stone Age of the commercial banks."

However, more open-minded officials of the CSO (1948:3-4) began to firmly argue the case for formal state credit regulation, in large part due to the fact that the banks were fostering extremely uneven economic development:

> The commercial banks, by operating a sterling-exchange system, have caused wide fluctuations... When there is a direct inflow of external funds, bank advances to traders and merchants stimulate the import of consumer goods at the same time as the import of capital equipment. In other words, when funds flow in via the banking system the investment multiplier is much higher than if funds are raised and spent abroad on capital equipment as, in the former case, a much higher proportion of the total funds is directed towards consumption [which] has a much more immediate effect on the balance of payments. Conversely, in slumps, the balance of payments becomes adverse or, if favourable, it is because external capital is either flowing out or the net import is small. In these circumstances the banks enforce a multiple restriction of credit and incomes. The net effect of the banks' operations is to accentuate booms and slumps... Upon the above grounds it can be said that the present control of credits by the commercial banks does not always serve the best interests of these territories.

A Bank of England representative (Mynors 1949) commissioned to look into a new central bank agreed both that "the establishment of a central bank should not be long deferred" and that the two commercial banks were "accentuating" the business cycle. But he concluded that "the imposition of a 100% local assets ratio on the banks would in itself do nothing to influence the banks' local credit policy." That influence, he insisted, should arise through "moral suasion" and the personal (not legislated) capacities of the financial authorities (Sowelem 1967:33; Jucker-Fleetwood 1964:57-58).

But credit was still being allocated unevenly and on a short-term, low-risk basis, thus undermining industrial growth, many smaller manufacturers charged, blaming this condition on the fact that finance in Southern Rhodesia remained dominated by foreign concerns. As financial resources poured out of the colony—in 1949 the insurance industry received £1.4 million in premiums from Southern Rhodesia, but granted only £450,000 worth of claims[1]—Midlands business leaders recorded their anger at a Chamber of Commerce meeting: "As things were at present, the commercial banks virtually controlled credit at the insistence of either their head offices in Cape Town and London or the Government. They had all suffered from this and had asked themselves whether the general managements of the banks, 'with South African conditions in mind,' are the best judges of financial policy in Southern Rhodesia."[2] Standard's local office was now reporting to London directly (instead of to neighboring South Africa), as it had "become involved in public responsibilities which, from being only implicit became explicit sooner or later, entailing a redistribution of power and authority," according to the bank's biographer (Henry 1963:21).[3]

As the accumulation process gathered pace, credit continued to expand at a rapid rate, but in a manner deemed satisfactory by very few. By the late 1940s, total commercial bank assets had reached a level 60% as high as net national income. In the subsequent four years, the banks' domestic earning assets increased by £19 million while overseas balances diminished by £12 million (CSO 1947; CSO, *Monthly Digest of Statistics;* Barber 1961:103; Sowelem 1967:216). But in response to what indeed soon, inexorably, became a "golden era" of loose credit, Finance Minister Whitehead introduced rigid controls in 1952. In particular, he warned the banks to exercise special care "in those cases where [loan] applications result from the cessation or slowing down of financial assistance from the parent companies outside the colony," raising the spectre of multinational corporate swings in investment financing from foreign sources to local sources (this occurred at the end of the decade in substantial volumes) (Newlyn and Rowan, 1954, 174). There were other revealing provisions associated with the 1952 controls:

> The banks have been advised to give priority to credit facilities which will increase, or at least maintain, agricultural and mining output and also that of secondary industry. Also included in the priority class are credits which will directly benefit the export trade, and credits designed to facilitate the progressive and orderly liquidation of existing industrial stocks.... Credit will in no circumstances be made available for the carrying of supplies of non-essential imported goods, while requests by importers for finance after the placing of orders will be critically examined. (*Commerce,* April 1952)

Having chosen to support industrial capital against the merchant class in this round, Whitehead came in for withering criticism from (among others) the powerful head of the Salisbury Chamber of Commerce, A. Landau:

> Having deprived the Colony of the possibility of obtaining capital, the Finance Minister exhausted the bank by working up his own [government] overdraft to many millions of pounds, and then told the banks to clamp down on private credit. And this when credit was, and still is, most urgently needed and when any ordinary minister would have

> attempted to persuade the banks to ease up. Thus you see this strange man's plan unfolding. He wants a recession (*Commerce,* October 1952).

Merchants occasionally put forward constructive suggestions for financial regulation in response to the banks' uneven boom-bust credit cycles, such as the suggestion from the Midlands Chamber of Commerce that the Currency Board be replaced by an autonomous central bank which could regulate credit through interest rates rather than by direct controls on the volume of credit available. (Mindful of the economy's underlying dynamics, however, the chamber acknowledged that a central bank must "be prepared to check overtrading and undue speculation by an increase in its rate" [*Commerce,* September 1952].) Subsequently other London financiers arrived to advise the government on monetary policy, and a Bank of Rhodesia and Nyasaland (BRN) for the new Central African Federation was finally established in 1956 (Richards 1956).[4]

But the problems faced by emergent financial policy-makers intensified nevertheless. The condition of war-time economic stress attributable in part to the banks' tight credit and outflows of funds had now given way to a credit-driven crisis characterized by import bottlenecks, more general domestic overproduction, overaccumulation, and (as considered in the next chapter) even more pronounced uneven geographical development. Again, partly this reflected a variety of new financial institutions which emerged during the 1950s, calling again upon the state to intervene with new kinds of formal banking regulation. But underlying the threat of rising finance was the increasingly obvious productive sector overinvestment which followed a promising industrialization process.

Warnings of overaccumulation

Notwithstanding the limited circulation of funds through the banks during World War II, industrialization had gradually picked up, taking advantage of the severe strains in international trade. It was recognized from the early 1930s, as the world Depression deepened, that local accumulation based on import substitution industrialization was inevitable. This approach was cemented during the war, as the local food-processing industry expanded vigorously, accounting for a third of manufacturing output by the early 1950s. Another quarter of output was generated by the investment goods sectors, particularly construction materials. And low-quality consumables (for the black market) grew rapidly, especially clothing and textiles. Cheap textiles were also the leading manufactured export of Southern Rhodesia (Barber 1961:141; Thompson and Woodruff 1954:170). Indeed many small manufacturing enterprises initially aimed at the black market, which grew to encompass 28% of national income during the 1950s, of which about 90% derived from wage earnings (Sowelem 1967:18). On this basis manufacturing growth picked up spectacularly from 1944 to 1948, averaging 24.4% annually (Phimister 1988a:254).

Following the war, mining fell from 25% of GDP to 5%, in part due to the steady US dollar price of gold, but also because of constrained labor supplies and rising wages stemming from the rise of the Zambian Copperbelt, transportation bottlenecks, intense competition from South African mines, and the scarcity and high costs of mining capital equipment and supplies (Phimister 1988a:219-220). Foreign mining capital (especially the British South Africa Company, Anglo American Corporation, and De Beers) then diversified into other primary products and into manufacturing on the South African luxury goods model. In the process, corporate concentration intensified rapidly, with fewer than 10% of all firms soon responsible for more than two thirds of total output (Arrighi 1973a:353). Diversification by British and South African firms, much of it after World War II, was led by Anglo American Corporation into coal, iron, chrome, cement, steel, citrus and sugar plantations, and the country's newspapers (Innes 1984). Turner and Newall monopolized asbestos. Lonrho owned an oil pipeline, cattle and gold mines, and diversified further following Tiny Rowland's ascent to power in the 1950s.

Including the tobacco grown by white commercial farmers—which was sold to a single buyer—most of the country's primary products and (by 1960) most of the manufacturing output were effectively foreign-controlled. A third of Britain's largest firms set up subsidiaries and affiliates in Southern Rhodesia. Even in food processing and light consumer goods, domestic capital was quickly overrun by foreign investors, especially in the wake of the South African Customs Agreement and compliance with the General Agreement on Tariffs and Trade in the late 1940s. A 1949 trade agreement was to Southern Rhodesia's advantage as many South African goods continued to be subject to tariffs, and as a result of the fact that more expensive white labor was still employed in semi-skilled South African jobs (Thompson and Woodruff 1954:169). British-based foreign capital with South African connections flowed rapidly into Southern Rhodesia immediately after the Afrikaner nationalists' 1948 victory and, along with tens of thousands of skilled white immigrants, found hospitable conditions.

As Phimister (1988a:298) argues, the "wave of mergers and takeovers of local firms by international companies placed an important section of the domestic bourgeoisie in intimate alliance with foreign capital." As a result, liberal "Partnership" reforms were undertaken during the 1950s, but this occurred in the context of harsh repression of illegal strikes by black workers after World War II and extremely low wages. During the 1940-65 period, while manufacturing output increased by a factor of 34, the wage bill only increased by 26 times (Handover 1977:11).

In statistical terms, foreign direct investment rose from £13.5 million in 1947 to £50.7 million in 1951, and fixed capital formation was increased by an average of £50 million per year from 1946 to 1961 (Gann and Gelfand 1964:212; Clarke 1980a:15-38). Annual output in manufacturing rose from £5.1 million in 1938 to £105.1 million in 1957, doubling as a percentage of GDP. Real GDP growth averaged at least 10% annually for the period 1946-57 (Stoneman 1981:278). The reward, for foreign capital, was two thirds of all profits in 1960 (Arrighi 1973a:354-357).

But this was extremely uneven growth. In addition to widening technological differentiation between foreign and domestic capital at the point of production, consumer markets were extremely lopsided. Capital's turnover time, spatial horizons, and sectoral orientation had not, by the early 1950s, settled into a steadily reproducible pattern of any sort. Materials and financing bottlenecks were quick to emerge in the hot-house atmosphere, in sectors ranging across investment, production (especially construction), and consumption, leading to the dual threat of overindebtedness and overaccumulation. As Prime Minister Huggins remarked, "What is not generally realized is that the merchants of the Colony might be doing a very good business locally and at the same time importing so much that financially they are ruining the country, and the two things are not put together until you get currency difficulties and the difficulty of raising loans in any quantity to counterbalance the excessive spending of the country as a whole" (*Commerce,* July 1952).

Indeed, as early as 1952 *Commerce* magazine confirmed, "We are grossly overspent on consumer goods and to a somewhat lesser extent on capital development; there has been a steady decline in the flow of private capital into the Colony." (Such problems would look small in relation to those experienced later in the decade.) The top financial adviser to the government added, "The ratio of the loans and bills figure to deposits is around 65%. No one who considers these figures can possibly claim that the banks here are under-lent; they could hardly have gone further in making funds available to the country" (*Commerce,* April 1952, October 1952).

The conditions of emerging overaccumulation and uneven sectoral development in production and exchange were treated, in 1952, not only with credit restraints (in line with Britain's anti-inflation monetary policy), but also with ceilings on white immigration to 900 people (mainly Britons) per month and much tighter import quotas for goods produced outside the sterling area. Thus overaccumulation was initially ameliorated and devaluation was avoided at this stage.

Instead, new combinations of financial and geographical expansion were invoked to displace capital which began piling up in various outlets. At qualitatively greater scales than had ever been attempted before, both time and space were invoked, through the young financial markets, to switch capital from overaccumulated sectors of the economy into new fields of investment. These investments were on the one hand perceived as having longer-run possibilities for growth, but on the other, sometimes served merely as attractive speculative gambles. The geographical changes are considered in the next chapter. But the recourse found in displacing capital through time (the temporal fix), via credit, generated profound contradictions.

Financiers and friendly regulators

Once financial markets began to swell in the early 1950s, a friendly atmosphere within the financial elite prevailed. For relations between business and government, "The influence of clubs and a regular chat over a whisky-and-soda is all-pervasive in Rhodesia, and it has its merits," commented *Property and Finance* (September 1959). In the words of A.P. Grafftey-Smith, the head of the Southern Rhodesia Currency Board—and in 1956 the first Governor of the BRN—"It must be obvious that whole-hearted cooperation between the central banks and the commercial banks is essential" so as to avoid "friction where none should exist" (*Commerce,* October 1952).[5]

At that point the Federation deposits of Standard and Barclays amounted to 11% and 5% of their respective total international deposits. Although local advances increased, the two continued to record large balances in the London headquarters through the 1950s. In contrast, the other three subsequent arrivals—Netherlands Bank of South Africa (which opened in 1951), National and Grindlays Bank (1953), and the Ottoman Bank (1958)—consistently drew in deposits from overseas to finance operations in Southern Rhodesia and the Federation (Sowelem 1967:60-62), and by 1959 only 14% of total banking assets were held abroad, with nearly 50% of assets on the banks' books as loans at the time of the 1958 credit squeeze (Central African Federation Information Department, 1960; *P&F,* February 1960).

Profits in Federation banking and insurance rose 65% during the late 1950s, almost twice as much as other commercial profits (Pearson and

Taylor 1963:14). Across the Federation, the number of employees in the finance and insurance fields rose from 1,620 in 44 different companies in 1954, to 3,167 in 98 companies five years later. By the end of the decade, the five banks had opened 220 branches in 60 towns, but their lending remained geographically uneven, as discussed in the next chapter.

Rather than berate or forcibly compel the major banks to alter their lending behaviour or to drop their "Banking Agreement" (a services pricing cartel), the young BRN and Federation Finance Ministry followed a different path. A combination of new institutional innovations (such as acceptance and discount houses) and regulatory levers were meant to work in tandem to ease credit and balance of payments problems. For example, following 50% increases in advances during 1955, the Under-secretary of the Treasury, A.G. Irvine (1957) explained that the BRN "requested the commercial banks during the second quarter of 1956, to restrict credit, particularly for speculative purposes, for the acquisition or erection of fixed property, and for non-essential imports."

Facing such unpredictable conditions in the market for small-scale credit, the banks were satisfied that an emerging money market could provide new outlets for their liquid funds without representing excessive competition in deposit-gathering. A major boost to the money market was the commencement of regular government sales of Treasury Bills in 1957. Also new on the scene were a revived Rhodesian Stock Exchange[6] and a few "development corporations" providing medium- and long-term venture financing.[7]

But other innovations soon outran the authorities' control. Some emanated from multinational corporations, in particular the juggernaut mining finance expansion and diversification. With increasing levels of global trade and the success of similar institutions recently introduced to South Africa, prestigious international financiers joined the mining houses in establishing acceptance houses (also known as merchant banks) in Southern Rhodesia. Effectively controlled by the two major corporations, Anglo American and Roan Selection Trust, they offered bills of exchange on exports and imports, made private share placements on the stock market, and provided short-term sources of funds to hire purchase lenders.[8]

The growth of the money market also invited a wave of new discount companies to sell government securities and accept overnight deposits from commercial banks—and in the process to permit further centralization of the funds of major corporations and financial institutions.[9] The flavor of money market "finance capital" in the context of emerging overaccumulation is captured by an October 1959 *Property and Finance* editorial about "a determined struggle, behind the scenes, for the large amounts of uncommitted liquid funds now available in the Federation":

> The new house, British & Rhodesian Discount House Ltd, has been formed by the biggest individual customers of the pioneering concern, the Discount House of Rhodesia Ltd, which started business less than eight months ago. These customers are the Anglo American Corporation, the BSA Company, and the two main commercial banks in the Federation (Barclays and the Standard). They are strengthened by two large insurance companies, the Prudential and the South African Mutual, and have technical and financial backing from the London discount house, Smith St. Aubyn Ltd. Having formed themselves into the largest single finance group in the country, they are in an exceptionally strong position and, obviously, will now divert their "at call" funds to their own company for investment.

The response of the Discount Company of Rhodesia was to increase its capital by 200%, to £150,000, "the significance of the move being at least as much psychological as financial" (*P&F,* January 1960). In fact, however, the emergence of discount houses marked the last stage of the era's rise of finance.

Before this point, however, the financial markets created a speculative bubble in commercial credit. In 1958, *Property and Finance* (May, July) reported that "Both commerce and industry had been over-encouraged by the 'beckoning hand' of the banks, who had until recently extended over-generous credit facilities. There had also been a considerable growth of finance houses designed to discount hire purchase facilities, and nothing had been done to discourage new ones setting up in business in the federation." Hence the "incredible folly" of bankers who "were prepared to advance thousands of pounds on open account to companies with a paid-up capital of only £2 or £3. It was the public who paid for losses ultimately." In a quarter of the insolvency cases before the courts, prosecution was recommended.

Thus some additional state regulation was attempted. With Bank Acts in 1956 and 1959, supervisory controls were established and both reserve requirements and liquid asset requirements imposed.[10] But the controls were rather weak. According to one report on the 1959 legislation, "The draft Banking Bill circularised to major financial institutions has been severely criticised by the banks, and from under strong pressure from them, the Federal Treasury has produced an entirely new draft. This draft is now being considered by the institutions and is understood to be more acceptable to them" (*P&F,* June 1959), in part because the revised law increased barriers to entry of "mushroom concerns which might fail and do lasting damage to the financial system" (Sowelem 1967:279).

Thanks more to "voluntary" measures than active regulatory supervision, worrisome amounts of bank liquidity had declined to more reasonable levels by 1959, and the formal BRN ratios were thus used only once (in 1960) to control credit. Instead, testified the BRN's chief economist, "informal discussions held regularly with the commercial banks" were the basis for credit control (Grant-Suttie 1965:340). Thus financiers were rarely alienated by the various government financial interventions: imposition of credit controls in 1952, 1956 and 1958; dampening of interest rate fluctuations in the late 1950s and early 1960s; and application of tighter currency and exchange controls in 1961 and 1963. In sum, Southern Rhodesian and Federation financial bureaucrats experimented both with friendly suasion and with an *ad hoc* crisis management brand of regulation. State control over financial markets only gradually became comprehensive, and was never sufficiently firm to stave off the worst excesses of ascendant finance during bouts of overaccumulation. Nor did regulation alleviate what was perceived as a constant need for international financial investment.

The mixed blessings of international finance

Notwithstanding the fact that by 1960 annual local savings of approximately £60 million—representing a relatively substantial 21% of Southern Rhodesia's GDP—were sufficient to finance 70%-80% of new capital formation, access to foreign loans was considered increasingly essential by the government of Southern Rhodesia. During the 1950s, £72 million in official debt was issued on the London bond market as against £60 million on the local capital market. Total foreign and local public debt increased from £27 million in 1946 to £137 million in 1954, and two-thirds of the total domestic investment of nearly £300 million during those years was derived from international sources. In the late 1950s private corporations also became more active international borrowers, with an average of £23.5 million in net new annual foreign debt (Thompson and Woodruff 1954:171-81; Advisory Committee 1962:78-79).

Among the overseas funds were US$140 million in World Bank project loans during the 1950s and early 1960s (of which US$70 million fell into default in 1965). The Bank's largest single loan project ever through the mid-1950s was the US$80 million lent for the £114-million Kariba Dam (with a volume four times greater than the second biggest dam on earth). The dam brought enormous suffering to 56,000 people of the local Batonka tribe on the Zambezi River—who lost most aspects of their traditional riverside domestic economy—but it provided power to Northern Rhodesian copper mines owned by Anglo American Corporation and Roan Selection Trust. Cheryl Payer (1982:239) notes that "The needs of these two companies seem to have been the main impetus behind the entire project." The Bank also financed the expansion of Rhodesian Railways and the partial implementation of the intensely unpopular Land Husbandry Act, as well as certifying Southern Rhodesia fit for private sector sources of international credit.[11]

Yet while the initial boost to foreign reserves was appreciated, the subsequent repayment of these loans ultimately threatened the balance of payments. By the late 1950s, foreign financial flows turned against Southern Rhodesia in the form of interest, dividends, and profit repatriation. The impressive new foreign investments too quickly fostered an enormous net outflow of income from the Central African Federation (Southern Rhodesia, Northern Rhodesia and Nyasaland), averaging 8.4% of total GDP, but as high as 14% in 1956 (Pearson and Taylor 1963:15-21). By 1961, Southern Rhodesia's large debt to London bond holders, the World Bank, US Export-Import Bank and Colonial (Commonwealth) Development Corporation aggravated foreign reserve shortages so as to leave the BRN vulnerable to a controversial 1961 interest rate increase initiated by the London banks. As the vicious cycle continued, access to short-term international commercial bank loans became more important, yet a major barrier had already emerged in the mid and late 1950s: the borrower's reputation for racial problems and labor unrest (*P&F,* July 1955, June 1959, October 1959).

Ironically, the power of foreign financiers sometimes increased under such circumstances, and not merely through approval or amendment of particular loan projects. In 1960, when Chase Manhattan Bank agreed to grant a small loan in the wake of Salisbury's first major urban race riots, as Southern Rhodesia's international credit rating plummeted, Chase's visionary David Rockefeller also became involved with leading opposition politicians Jasper Savanhu, Stanlake Samkange, and Herbert Chitepo on the premise of providing "up-to-date business training for Africans" (*P&F,* August 1960). As documented in the next chapter, however, systematic attempts to gain favor with black nationalists through the financial system would ultimately run aground.

Rockefeller's geopolitical role in the region was heightened by other incidents, as well. South Africa's Sharpeville massacre in March 1960 prompted severe capital flight from that country, but it was stemmed by an emergency Chase Manhattan loan. Shortly afterwards, Rockefeller also had to assist the European bank Societe Generale in the Belgian Congo in fending off a takeover attempt waged against a local subsidiary (Union Miniere du Hart Katanga Company) by the British financial house

Tanganyika Concessions, managed from Salisbury. As *Property and Finance* (July 1960) reported, "The present financial struggle involving British, American, Belgian, Portuguese, Rhodesian and South African financiers, is the talk of the Johannesburg Stock Exchange and of the financial world."

Overaccumulation and its financial implications

Despite the interventions of foreign financiers, the Federation's uneven prosperity broke at the end of the 1950s. Fixed capital investment declined dramatically, leaving the regional economy mired in recession from 1961 (Figure 3.3). Although Northern Rhodesia's collapse due to falling copper prices was a catalyst for some of the subsequent problems in Southern Rhodesia,[12] endogenous factors cannot be discounted. Southern Rhodesia's industrial sectors (mining, manufacturing and electricity) produced enormous and consistent year-end inventories ("stocks") of £40 million from 1961 to 1966, generating a classic crisis of overaccumulation. Output slowed and new industrial capital spending declined far more than in the economy as a whole, to levels (£13.4 million in 1964) approximately one third the 1959 peak (Figure 3.4).

Manufacturing was hit particularly hard. The ratio of year-end manufacturing inventories to capital stock invested over the year—a ratio which indicates the degree to which overinvestment has already occurred—soared from 1.82 in 1958 to 5.2 in 1962, and 6.0 in 1965 (CSO, *Census of Production*). Southern Rhodesian manufacturing output had risen 88% between 1954 and 1961, while the domestic consumer market increased by only 70%. By 1962 leaders of the Association of Rhodesia and Nyasaland Industry complained bitterly of "considerable unutilized capacity" in manufacturing, and a government investigation found that "The problems inhibiting the further expansion of manufacturing are deeply rooted in the small dimensions of the domestic market" (Advisory Committee 1961:69,357). *Property and Finance* (January 1961) suggested that "mergers and rationalisation, particularly in the cement trade, would be an obvious remedy to overtrading," but in fact the crisis was one of overinvestment and overproduction, not merely overtrading. With more than a billion pounds sunk in gross capital formation in the Federation between 1954 to 1962, and with real gross national income up by just £113 million over the period, those investments had generated an extremely low output/capital ratio of 1:9 (Pearson and Taylor 1963:16-17).

The financial sector was a leading victim of the crisis. Whenever there is enforced deflationary devaluation of overaccumulated finance, it raises the age-old question of who is to blame, the speculative creditor or the errant debtor. The different views were expressed at the first meeting of the Association of Chambers of Commerce of Rhodesia and Nyasaland, in 1958: "The blame for the present position lay equally with merchants for overtrading, and with the commercial banks which had extended credit facilities on too big a scale when the price of copper was high... The credit system had got completely out of hand, and the present restrictions had not altogether overcome the situation, because a good many firms were subsidised by means of extended credit facilities from shippers or from firms with whom they had affiliations" (*P&F,* May 1958).

The results, during the long downturn of the early 1960s, included the collapse of finance-driven property speculation, a shake-out of the financial sector in which the number of building societies shrunk from eight to three and hire purchase contracted 25% (one major international lender, Lombard, quit the Federation for good), and a rise in company insolvencies from 68 in 1957 to 165 in 1962. There was such a sharp decline on the Rhodesian Stock Exchange that "for the stout-hearted these are possibly the cheapest shares available anywhere in the world," *Property and Finance* (January 1961) commented. In sum, according to the same source (August 1960), "It might be fair to ask whether the Federation's young money market has not become top-heavy in relation to the country's economy. The recession has disclosed serious over-trading in most sectors, and it could well be that lending by financial institutions, based on a 'boom' situation thought optimistically to be long-lived, has represented too much too soon. Overheads are enormous, and the banks' programmes, particularly in small towns, are probably uneconomic."

But while financial optimism may be an inevitable characteristic during periods of economic and geographic expansion, and while the decline of financial power inevitably follows a deeper-rooted crisis of overaccumulation (or merely "over-trading"), it is not sufficient to leave matters there. Financial regulation must be considered more closely to understand why the state took certain measures and not others to address the emerging problems.

The proliferation of red tape

Under conditions of financial overexpansion, a new round of credit restrictions had been imposed in January 1958, inspired in part "to prevent borrowing for speculative purposes, notably, property speculation," as well as by a serious balance of trade deficit during 1957, which in turn was traced to excessive luxury goods imports. These controls reduced the total level of commercial bank loans and advances outstanding in the Federation from £55 million in March 1958 to £44 million in mid 1959, with most of the (non-seasonal) drop coming from builders and contractors, wholesalers, retailers, and the motor trade. Loans for "personal and professional" use suffered an immediate reduction of 15%. Since personal income gained from rents and sales of property had increased from £2.8 million in 1954 to £5.3 million in 1958, this should have had some effect (*P&F,* February 1960; Grant-Suttie 1965:340). However, as a result of institutional investor interest in the construction of new financial headquarters, the momentum of property speculation carried on until 1961.

The credit squeeze of 1958 also converted a trade deficit of £14.5 million into a record surplus of £43.75 million the following year, as imports dropped by 15.5%. But as this happened, producer imports of raw materials and machinery declined substantially. "The country at large, it appears, found it easier to reduce purchases of capital goods for industry than of motor cars or toilet preparations," complained *Property and Finance* (May 1960) editorialists, reflecting upon the sectoral unevenness. "This trend raises the old problem of whether import controls would not, in the long run, have been more conducive to achieving the country's aims during the past years than was the credit squeeze."

While direct controls on luxury imports instead of the indirect cost burden on capital goods would probably have added balance to the trade accounts, they would not have rescued increasing numbers of middle-class white consumers who, credit squeeze or no, were already over their limits. There were 22,000 summonses for debts of less than £200 in Southern Rhodesia in 1959 (compared with 11,700 in 1956), 3,000 of which led to imprisonment (*P&F,* June 1960). The white population was about 220,000 strong, so this represented an enormous reliance by consumers on credit (black people had virtually no access to formal consumer credit). By 1960, white per-capita hire-purchase debt in Southern Rhodesia was twice that of Great Britain, amounting to a total of £10 million (*Sunday Mail,* 27/12/59; *P&F,* February 1960). However, following a series of credit restrictions on cars, televisions, radios, and other consumer goods, total hire purchase finance had fallen to £7.6 million by 1964 (Sowelem 1967:185). The hire-purchase credit squeeze was a substantial intervention by the state against the interests of its middle-class support base, one of several which fatally undermined the United Federal Party's support in the 1962 election.

This was not the only conflict arising from growing financial excesses and state regulation. Economic tensions generated by the displacement of overaccumulation into the sphere of finance were profound and had important political consequences. Struggles over access to resources and over commercial turf in turn began to reflect the traditional encounter between domestic and foreign capital. Certain controversies reflected a consciousness about Britain's own occasionally tenuous position at the head of the Sterling Area group—particularly given the country's Keynesian program and the post-war dollar debt—and hence its need to maintain high interest rates. Over time this seriously affected the circuit of Commonwealth financial capital and radically altered the velocity and direction of financial flows between Southern Rhodesia, South Africa, and Britain.

For example, increases in Bank of England interest rates in 1956 led the South African government to impose currency controls which in turn cut off a major source of Southern Rhodesian building society funds. Similarly, the 1958 credit squeeze was exacerbated by international conditions. More important, according to *Property and Finance*, was "the pull exerted by the abnormally high yield offered on treasury bills in London" initially in 1958. By 1960, "High interest rates and boom conditions in the United Kingdom combined with the political uncertainty in the Federation, are producing a seepage of money to Britain" (*P&F*, December 1956, March 1959, May 1959, July 1960). Thus Southern Rhodesia was ultimately forced to maintain high interest rates (Figure 3.5) in order to attract overseas investment capital.

Southern Rhodesia's nominal rates had been low (just 4.5% for overdrafts during the extremely liquid early 1950s) until mid 1956, when the commercial banks raised the overdraft rate to 6.5%. The BRN Bank Rate was established in 1957 at 4.5%, and increased in steps to 5.5% from 1960 to 1962 (thus driving the overdraft rate up to 7.5%). But with the recession deepening, it was again brought back to 4.5%. The BRN initially requested local banks not to change their rate structure in response to the wildly fluctuating Bank of England rate, but the banks refused at least once, in mid 1960, when, facing capital flight from the Federation, they took advice from their London headquarters and raised their rates by 0.5%, touching off a minor scandal (Sowelem 1967:288). *Property and Finance* (August 1960) interpreted this as the "Revolt of the Banks... It is common knowledge within inner financial circles that a difference of view developed between the [BRN's] 'British' executives and the 'South African' executives." The South Africans preferred the physical credit controls that had been used previously, while the British executives desired the power to regulate the cost of credit through the Bank Rate. The result was little action of any kind, leaving rates to follow international influences at crucial moments.

Already-tight exchange controls were toughened in 1961 to cover

Sterling Area transactions and to prevent any export of funds aside from profit remittances. In the process this gave local commercial banks the power of distribution of Southern Rhodesia's hard currency reserves. The main result of such controls was to increase local financial liquidity noticeably, yet the benefits were not typically passed on to the productive sectors, as government mopped up the funds through increased Treasury Bill issues. The BRN subsequently invested the surpluses not required by government. As *Property and Finance* (May 1961) commented, "Official intention, it seemed, was to throw on to the commercial banks the major responsibility for decision and discretion on what funds could, or could not, be sent out of the country."

Capital flight continued, thanks partly to the vast overinvestment of the late 1950s, partly to the stagnation of the early 1960s, and partly to the increase in what was termed "political instability." Banks aiming to meet domestic credit demand were forced to borrow larger amounts of short-term funds from their London headquarters, and in the course of doing so managed to persuade reluctant BRN authorities to raise interest rates to approximate the Bank of England's. This, it was said, "illustrates, once again, the financial authority London wields, for good or ill, on the Federal economy" (*P&F*, May 1961).

Even the tough 1963 exchange controls were imposed with the London headquarters of the banks firmly in mind, as Southern Rhodesia continued to seek foreign loans. "London financial confidence on such matters would depend on whether the balance-of-payments problem was seen to be handled properly, and this handling would depend on whether the Government had 'full and firm' possession, in advance of all the necessary powers of control, including, if necessary, control of luxury imports," Sir Edgar Whitehead (now in opposition) told Parliament (*P&F*, September 1963).

A London-instigated bank interest rate increase had recently led the *Herald* (18/8/60) to ask, rhetorically, "Has the time come to consider the formation of a purely Rhodesian commercial bank with all the control and management here in Rhodesia?" But such a bank was, in the end, unnecessary, as financial regulation finally tightened to the point of repression under the Rhodesian Front.

Conclusion: From capitalist crisis to financial repression

As shown in more detail in the next chapter, both the white and black nationalisms which played out the next act in Rhodesia's pre-independence political drama were doing so on an economic stage set in part by financiers' exercise of excessive power. As their sphere of operations increased and as their impact on the economy grew seemingly without limit, financial institutions came subject to more detailed governmental regulation in the late 1950s and early 1960s. This was not as effective as it could or should have been, but was generally deemed necessary because of the role of finance in uneven sectoral development, as credit promoted speculative and luxury consumption impulses and as the skewed economy faced a crisis of overaccumulation.

This is all familiar terrain, as developed in Chapter One. But while this chapter has helped to assess the broad, overarching theory of overaccumulation, finance, and uneven development, local details are extremely important and in some respects unique. For example, in both Southern Rhodesia and neighboring South Africa, the early basis for renewed post-Depression growth was gold, stemming from international financial crisis and growing geopolitical strife which sent cautious investors in search of a metallic store of value. Yet, as side effects of that great crisis, the two international banks continued to deny credit to Southern Rhodesia, and the British colonial Currency Board system unnecessarily transmitted and amplified global financial fluctuations to the local markets.

More generally, though, as in many semi-peripheral countries which then adopted an import substitution industrialization strategy, the accompanying global trade slowdown permitted the emergence of manufacturing industry on a substantial scale in Southern Rhodesia, all the while supported and extended by state intervention. Such intervention reached a qualitatively new phase with the advent of *ad hoc* and not always well-conceived financial regulation during the 1950s. Yet even as the role of the state evolved into larger tasks of macroeconomic management, the forces of internal and international funding flows were still capable of accentuating uneven development and overaccumulation in key sectors.

During this era, many other countries—especially semi-peripheral Commonwealth economies—also witnessed financial deepening (Crick 1965). There were similar state regulatory responses which, alongside monetary policy characterized by negative real interest rates, have subsequently been termed "financial repression" (Burkett 1987). Southern Rhodesia's uneven, unsustainable economic trajectory ensured that the rise of finance would be truncated more than in most Commonwealth settings. This helps explain why from an unsteady beginning, subsequent financial controls under the Rhodesian Front regime became perhaps the most rigid in the capitalist world. This in turn was possible because instead of serving effectively to displace overaccumulated capital, the 1950s rise of finance generated serious contradictions.

For example, accompanying the cooling of credit creation from 1958 was a decline in the social power of finance relative to that of other forces—in particular, white farmers and the now-threatened white working class, petty bourgeoisie, and many in the civil service. Since this economic transition was occurring simultaneously with the crucial "winds of change" in colonial Africa, it meant that finance gave way neither to industrial power (which remained in a state of serious overaccumulation from 1960 until six years later) nor to a neo-colonial black petty bourgeoisie (as happened elsewhere on the continent), but instead to a state capitalism based on the interests of national agrarian capital and those of the lower and middle strata of whites.

The state capitalist outcome was more profound precisely because of the prior excesses of finance. During the period of Unilateral Declaration of Independence, the interventionist Rhodesian state unhesitatingly applied the liberals' technical leverage over the financial system (both exchange and credit controls and, soon, investment directives). And the state could build into that white nationalist alliance a fanaticism and ingenuity surprisingly capable of withstanding efforts by any liberal local or international capitalists (especially financial) that threatened to undermine the project. As a result, there was very little subsequently that could be done to invoke meaningful financial sanctions against Rhodesia, or to encourage political change from within on the backs of liberal financiers. Finance was repressed in more ways than one.

But it would be a mistake to leave the subject of the economic crisis on essentially technical, regulatory matters. There was a much more substantive goal shared by liberal elements in the United Federal Party and their capitalist supporters (of both domestic and foreign origin): to achieve a longer-term solution to Southern Rhodesia's crisis of overaccumulation, uneven sectoral development, and growing political unrest. Yet financial interests so vital to the 1950s Partnership program were ultimately the victim of their own successes in establishing greater breadth and depth in the financial system, and subsequently in drawing funds away from productive circuits during the late 1950s and early 1960s. At that stage, as discussed next, uneven development had reached extreme proportions and the failure of financial Partnership initiatives were that much more disheartening. Intercapitalist rivalry took a decidedly political form, and nationalisms naturally prospered.

Notes

1. Noting this (in October 1952), *Commerce* magazine implied the rest was being hijacked by the insurers' foreign headquarters: "The desirability, from a national point of view, of an insurance company drawing its capital from and investing its profits in the country from which it derives its business has been felt for some time." The first insurance company with Salisbury headquarters was Rhodesian National Insurance Company in 1947, yet it too was established in association with a London firm of Lloyds brokers and underwriting agents.
2. *Commerce,* September 1952. Barber (1961:167) notes that until 1954, even "savings mobilised through the Post Office Savings Banks were also largely invested abroad."
3. These responsibilities included the securing of £24 million in credit in 1947 for one of the largest colonial public works projects ever, the nationalization and expansion of Rhodesian Railways.
4. This set the stage for subsequent conflicts between advisors from England and from the South African Reserve Bank. The central bank that emerged from various debates over autonomy, ownership and powers was a different animal than most that had preceded it. The new central bank was prohibited from financing government deficits (as Central European reserve banks did) and its capital was held by the Federation government instead of the commercial banks (the latter was the case in South Africa). But aside from acting as banker to the Federation, the Bank of Rhodesia and Nyasaland had the limited objective of the "regulation of the monetary system of the Federation." This was the responsibility of nine directors, of whom seven were drawn from business sectors, whereas other central banks established following the war (e.g., India, Ceylon, New Zealand, Australia and Malaysia) depended on direction from either the Finance Minister or Parliament. One important consequence was the Federation governments' lack of dependence on the central bank for financing assistance.
5. Upon becoming BRN governor, one reflection of Grafftey-Smith's attitude was, as expressed to the Radcliffe Committee on the Working of the Monetary System, "a desire 'not to alienate the commercial banks' by raising reserve requirements and thus reducing the profitability of their operations" (Sowelem 1967:277.) The key personality in sustaining that attitude over time was the former Federal Cashier, who was named Governor of the Rhodesian Reserve Bank in 1965 and who, according to Handford (1976:43), played "a major part in organising the Rhodesian economy after UDI."
6. Following the debacle of the 1890s, a stock exchange was not established

again until 1946. But by the late 1950s, nearly 100 companies were listed (including the mining houses and several financial institutions), and annual share issues averaged £1.5 million (Sowelem 1967:166-67).

7. There were no state loans available to industry prior to the Second World War, and although an Industrial Loans Board was set up, briefly, after the war, it was not until 1958 that the government established an Industrial Development Fund. In 1960 the Federation established an Industrial Development Corporation, supported by the Reserve Bank and the Commonwealth Development Finance Corporation. In addition, Barclays Overseas Development Corporation invested more than £11 million in the Federation during the 1950s, in 82 ventures where loans ranged from six to twelve years, and occasionally an equity stake was involved. Former shareholders of the British firm Cable and Wireless also made long-term investments (though some could be described as property speculation), and Rhodesian Anglo American Corporation and Rhodesian Selection Trust also had development finance subsidiaries (Barber 1961:151,167).
8. A stellar list of international financial institutions participated in the founding of Rhodesian Selection Trust's Merchant Bank of Central Africa: N.M. Rothschild and Philip Hill, Higginson of London, backed by Rothschild Freres (Paris); Banque Lambert (Brussels); Dillon Read & Co. (New York), and the Tanganyika Concessions and Messina Transvaal Development. Meanwhile, Anglo American founded Union Acceptances (South Africa's first accepting house, which subsequently expanded north), and then joined with Lazard Brothers of London to promote Rhodesian Acceptances, Ltd (RAL). The new institutions had no problem in raising local funds, since the mid-1950s was a period of high liquidity for both the copper mining companies and the growing commercial banking sector, and the fact that the BRN now existed in the Federation meant that there was a "lender of last resort" in the event of major liquidity problems. Whereas the Southern Rhodesian money market was modeled on London's, its introduction was due to "the success of similar institutions established, after the Second World War in South Africa," according to Sowelem (1967:81-87). Similar efforts three decades earlier had failed to establish money markets in South Africa, Australia and New Zealand, but these countries—as well as Canada, Ghana and Nigeria—all gained a variety of new financial intermediaries during the 1950s (Grant-Suttie 1965).
9. In 1959, Gillett Brothers of London founded the Discount Company of Rhodesia—the first such international venture approved by City of London authorities—with support from the local banks. Competition soon appeared from the British and Rhodesian Discount House Limited, and again with the arrival of Colonial Banking and Trust Company, which

was supported by the US entrepreneur S.A. Schlesinger (who also helped found a local finance company, Scottish Rhodesian Finance, Ltd) (*P&F*, September 1956, January 1958, May 1958).

10. Initially, for commercial banks, 8% of demand deposits and 3% of time deposits were to be held with the BRN, although the demand deposit requirement was relaxed to 6% in 1960 as recession set in. Furthermore, 25% of all bank assets, and 20% of other financial institutions' assets, had to be in liquid form, although only from mid-1962.
11. A public relations officer of the Bank conducted a two-week visit in 1956: "The two note-books full of notes which he had made on the trip would be used both internally by the Bank, and as a source of information for use by Swiss, USA and other financial interests" (*P&F*, May 1956).
12. As a result of the 1957-58 copper price collapse, total profits earned in the Federation, led by the multinational copper companies, had dropped from £109 million in 1956 to £57 million in 1958. But Federation export revenue was buoyed by rapidly rising tobacco sales, and net GDP was much less affected—a decline from £356 million to £332 million over the same period—due to Southern Rhodesia's stronger industrial base (Central African Federation Information Department 1960:397). Moreover, the copper price drop was short-term, and the major producers rapidly reduced output to stabilise the price during the early 1960s (Pearson and Taylor 1963:10).

chapter four

Finance and Uneven Development in City and Countryside

Introduction

We observed in the last chapter that when pushed to the wall during the 1930s, Southern Rhodesia's ruling establishment—in government, industry, mining, farming and commerce—could partially alleviate uneven sectoral development even under conditions where financial sources were not particularly cooperative. But as the colony became reimmersed in circuits of international trade, investment, and finance after World War II, it became much harder to continue along this route. The economy's development became sectorally more uneven.

And while the rise of domestic finance may have displaced overaccumulation temporarily, it ultimately made the economic problems more difficult to resolve for the medium and long runs. Financial reforms and regulations which were identified in the 1930s and 1940s—but imposed only weakly during the 1950s and early 1960s—proved impotent against more durable processes of capital accumulation.

In this chapter we continue along this line of analysis, moving now from the impact of the changing financial system upon sectoral development, to relationships between finance and uneven geographical and indeed political development. This chapter, like the last, draws out evidence of finance and uneven development during the period from the Depression through the early 1960s. Here the three-decade-long "Kuznets cycle" can be measured by investment in property and by the ebb and flow of ill-considered credit schemes for black urban and rural residents. And here too prospects for resolving Southern Rhodesia's socio-political crisis, seemingly so promising during the economic expansion of the 1950s, were shattered as overaccumulation crisis and financial devaluation heightened social tensions.

Many of those tensions reflected struggles over space. Several geographical outlets (spatial fixes) for overaccumulated capital became more pronounced and drew finance into new areas: a qualitative increase in commercial property investments in the center of Salisbury, a tentative home-ownership policy for black residents of townships and loans for black farmers, and resource conflicts between the different regions of Southern Rhodesia and the Central African Federation. Through the lens of finance, each source of uneven development will be examined in turn, followed by a glance at related political processes.

Uneven property development

In Salisbury, Southern Rhodesia's major urban hub, a deluge of commercial office buildings arose impervious to the overcrowded, degraded housing which most of Salisbury's residents suffered in. Entering the Central Business District (CBD), we encounter characteristics which led observers to easily remark, "Salisbury is essentially a modern city, and the CBD resembles that of many smaller American or South African cities, with multi-storeyed office blocks and modern architectural styles" (Heath 1990:33). The story behind this contradiction-laden urban form reflects many of the ways in which finance exacerbates uneven geographical development.

Dating from its emergence as the young colony's administrative center at the turn of the century, Salisbury claimed a long track record of uneven investment patterns. "Large areas in the neighborhood of Salisbury lay dormant in the hands of speculators," according to A.J. Christopher. Some 40% of the CBD was controlled by just five companies, which purchased whole blocks in some cases and alternative stands in others, Christopher (1977:16,18) indicates, "so as to control any development that might take place." Such concentrated control of land was attacked but not defeated by a municipal anti-speculation ordinance in 1914. Under conditions of tight land management and financial liquidity, Salisbury remained mired in the 1930s Depression, and by 1937 the annual value of building plans was still just £70,000, having dropped from a peak of £290,000 in 1931.

Subsequently, with immigrant artisans arriving and new factories opening, construction activity picked up dramatically. By the end of World War II, Salisbury claimed a white population of 17,000, and its geographical expansion eastward and northward catered well to the residential needs of the skilled immigrant male workers, with model urban planning designs copied from the United States (Wilson 1980). There was strong financial support for the 1950s surge in suburban housing from building societies, which increased in number from two to twelve between 1948 and 1951 and were rewarded by soaring assets—from £7.8 million in 1954 to £51.5 million in 1960—and average deposits of £82 per head by 1956, compared with £37 in British societies (Pearson and Taylor 1963:14; *P&F* March 1957).

In addition, infrastructural investment also contributed to uneven property development. Roads, public works, water systems, railways, electricity, iron and steel, and a national airline were all considered essential for the rapid expansion Southern Rhodesian policy-makers projected. Some of these projects relied on foreign funding because of the scope of capacity required to break into new spaces and sectors of the economy. The infrastructural loans were a relatively easy way to acquire foreign exchange, but at the expense of falling into a foreign debt trap as discussed in the last chapter.

As for the CBD, property investment was slower to take off, due to late 1940s restrictions on non-residential building, material shortages, and surveying delays. Moreover, it was initially hard to know precisely where to invest, since the city center was experiencing the geographical flexibility which is characteristic of immature property markets. From its 1890s origins in the Kopje district slightly southwest of the town center, according to Smout (1971:35), the Salisbury shopping district had migrated "more than a kilometer and has resulted in a rather extensive and varied business area with an overall low density of buildings." But beginning in the early

1950s there arose a virtual forest of major skyscrapers, and in particular a discernable financial district along the north side of the CBD (Bond 1992a).

Imposing new £200,000-£500,000 modernist structures soon towered over the colonial architecture—by twenty stories in one case—and lured further opulent commercial property investments by banks (Standard, Barclays, and a spate of new market entrants), building societies (Beverley, Founders), finance houses (Syfrets) and insurance companies (SA National Life and Mutual, Southern Life, African Life, Pearl, Northern). And there were also several luxury buildings constructed for the newly centralized regional headquarters of the Central African Federation's major multinational corporations (Anglo American, Lonrho, Roan Selection Trust). Indeed, international property speculators—Cable and Wireless, London bankers M. Samuel & Co., and Kenneth de Courcy's Overseas Land Purchasing Trust—also continued to acquire Salisbury stands for development as late as 1959. The valuation of Salisbury as a whole peaked at £117.6 million in 1960, comprising land worth £52.1 million and improvements worth £65.4 million. Five years earlier, the land was valued at £40 million and improvements were just £37.5 million (*P&F*, April 1960).

But built as it was on a collapsing industrial base, the property bubble was destined to burst. The speculators quickly experienced declining demand and excess supplies of office space, shrinking rental revenues, higher financing charges as interest rates rose, and a few major defaults on mortgages (in de Courcy's case, to a South African pension fund) (*P&F*, May 1959, August 1960, December 1961). Indeed, as early as 1957, serious concern was being expressed about the new buildings' foundations:

> The biggest single item of investment over the last few years of rapid development in Salisbury has been the purchase of central city property and the building of multi-storey shops and office blocks. With so much outside capital, as well as internal investment capital, being sunk in this type of property, many people are asking whether the provision of new offices is not being overdone. (*P&F*, September 1957)

Such concerns proved valid, as we see below. But, in their early manifestations—as wild fluctuations in building society funds during the late 1950s—they did not shut off the supply of property investment funds but instead spurred financiers to explore certain other geographical routes to displace the excess liquidity. These were ultimately nowhere near as significant in magnitude as even one office block, but during the peak property speculation years nevertheless finance also found its way into black urban "locations" (townships) and even into rural credit programs.

Uneven township housing development

As in formal apartheid towns, black people were forced by law to reside in underdeveloped conditions to the south and west of the city of Salisbury, consistent with the direction of ill winds blowing through the industrial sites which lay between the black townships and the CBD. Even before attempts were launched to create a black middle class as a negotiating partner for Kenya-style neo-colonialism (the "Partnership" program of the 1950s), there was concern about the conditions of the urban workforce by far-sighted politicians like Prime Minister Garfield Todd (1953-58), based on their connections to fast-growing manufacturing industries which had recently suffered intense labor unrest (railroads in 1945 and a general strike in 1948).

"The problem here," Arrighi (1973a:361) observes, "was the stabilization of the proletariat, because the high rate of turnover associated with migratory labor retarded specialization within the manufacturing sector." Of high priority among several Partnership initiatives aimed at overcoming the urban impermanence of the working class was to encourage financiers to tear down traditional barriers to black housing or small business credit. As Davies and Dewar remark (1989:48), "What was being achieved was the cooptation of a black property owning class which would favor stability and oppose resistance to the existing social order."

The financial circuit was required in the townships for another reason (Bond 1993a). Industrial development had, by the late 1940s, reached the point at which companies could no longer expect to house workers on their own premises. Some 75,000 black people lived in Salisbury at this stage, of whom only 28,000 were housed in municipal housing, while another 17,000 were domestic servants living with their employers (Mafico 1987:7). Once prevented from urbanization by pass laws, many more women and children (40% of the total population by the late 1950s) had now joined men in the townships, and the government oriented new housing development towards female and married accommodation.

Nevertheless, with a huge backlog developing and official rents still the same for single and married accommodation, the hated hostel system also persisted and families were forced to become lodgers in other households, which fostered petty intraclass and gender divisions within the proletariat. Urbanized women were increasingly controlled by male relatives, their sexual lives stringently regulated. Although there is evidence that patriarchy was also initially bolstered by specific state policies (Schmidt 1991), Barnes (1992a:588) argues that "restricting the mobility of women had become an unworkable policy by the mid 1930s" and a new framework consistent with the requirements of capital accumulation was needed (Barnes 1992b).

Thus a more explicit urban-based reproduction of labor began to gain the support of state policy-makers. This was reflected in the fact that the spatial organization of the township was now guided less by traditional apartheid administrative control and health-related concerns and more by addressing family, transport, and industrial location problems. Rational spatial planning, the embedding of bourgeois social norms, and workplace-control methods were being perfected in many capitalist settings during the 1950s. Southern Rhodesia was not immune, as the spatial question began to mesh with industrialists' evolving approach to black social and residential conduct.

The best hope was to match consumer demand with labor supply, which would have encouraged the local construction industry to provide an appropriately-priced housing product. Early on it seemed that sufficient buying power might emerge among black workers (who, all told, earned £20 million in the money economy in 1953) so that at least a privileged few might gain access to a nuclear family home through the market. The industrialists' congress unanimously adopted a resolution to this effect: "Congress recognises that there are today Africans who have reached a degree of education and culture far beyond the mass of their fellows and strongly urges that suitable land be made available within urban areas so that housing and recreational facilities can be provided by private enterprise commensurate with the degree of advancement of this section of the population" (*Commerce*, September 1953).

There were interesting prospects here for black housing to serve as a new route for capital accumulation. But meager progress was made on this front, partly as a result (policy-makers hypothesized) of a lack of formal housing finance available to blacks prior to 1958. At £515 for a commercially-constructed four-room detached house in 1960 (including separate meters for water and electricity), "The total is quite beyond the normal capacity of an African to pay," noted *Property and Finance* (March 1960). Under such conditions, an emerging consensus in the late 1950s was that black urban buying power could be augmented only through credit.

The building societies played a crucial ideological role in the subsequent campaign to make homeowners out of black urban dwellers. As political agitation by black militants reached new heights, a leading South African financier, Gordon Collins of UBS, emphasized to an international conference the role of building societies "in the development of the African and in the struggle against Communist influence" (*P&F*, November 1962). Or as Clive Wright, leader of the Building Societies Association of Southern Rhodesia, put it: "A brief glance at the history books will show that wherever these institutions have been allowed to develop, social revolution has been gradual and has not taken a violent form. In fact, it is these countries which today form the major bulwark against the spread of communism. Home ownership is the priceless heritage and practical aim of most English-speaking peoples. Compare this with the teeming millions of the earth's population who can never hope to achieve this object" (*P&F*, March 1956).

For white immigrants, the building societies had extended certain European working-class traditions which did indeed transfer well to Southern Rhodesia during the post-war era of economic expansion. Generous 90% government loan guarantees played a major role in the extension of property ownership, covering by 1962 more than 6,000 building society loans worth £23 million (Advisory Committee 1962:389).

There was every expectation that simply extending this tradition into the black townships would solve the growing housing crisis. Through legislation arising from the 1958 Plewman Commission on Urban African Affairs, societies were empowered to offer, for the first time, mortgage bonds to blacks on residential or commercial properties carrying 99-year leasehold tenure. According to the Minister of Local Government and Housing, the target market for the new borrowing privileges would be "the middle-lower income group and the upper-income group" in townships outside Salisbury and Bulawayo: "We have also encouraged banks to open branches there, and building societies have already commenced business" (*P&F*, April 1958).

Although credit restrictions intervened in 1958, within a few months after their withdrawal cheaper money arrived, leading to higher expectations in financial circles that black housing finance would pick up where the white residential market was fading. As *Property and Finance* (August 1959) remarked, "There is a great deal of surplus cash in the country... The building societies are anxious to stimulate as much as possible a building trade now very much in the doldrums; and in this stimulation, they have the sympathy of the Government. They are not unduly worried over the general fall in demand for bonds for European housing: as announced in the Southern Rhodesian Parliament, African home-ownership schemes will offer an outlet for their surplus funds, and demand from Asian and Colored people is growing steadily."

Another spur to the societies was the fact that the Salisbury City Council, which administered township accounts with Federal monies, failed to receive an £800,000 Federal housing commitment in early 1960. The Council quickly lobbied for home-ownership and private construction. The proposal to permit full black homeownership (not just the 99-year leases) coincided with increasingly hospitable money market conditions.

With a general slump in demand for credit stemming from industrial overinvestment and the waning of the property boom in both CBD and white suburbs, building societies and institutional investors were indeed excessively liquid again, if only temporarily. As late as 1960, according to one account, the societies "warmly welcomed the opportunity to invest embarrassingly-large surplus funds in Government-sponsored schemes for black housing, which came indeed as a blessing at a time when normal 'European' demand for mortgages had fallen off steeply" (*P&F*, March 1961). Such conditions may have generated optimism in Partnership policy-makers, who hoped that enlightened financiers could reduce the uneven urban development of Southern Rhodesia's racial capitalism. But as in the CBD, there were insurmountable contradictions, which will be explored shortly.

Uneven rural development

"We do not want native peasants," Garfield Todd once told Parliament. "We want the bulk of them working in the mines and farms and in the European areas and we could absorb them and their families." According to Arrighi (1973a:362), underlying Todd's program was the need "to substitute an African agrarian bourgeoisie and proletariat for the peasantry." To this end the Native Land Husbandry Act of 1951 aimed to transform communal-owned land under the guidance of tribal chiefs into monetized land owned by more productive black farmers, partly in the name of conservation and as concern grew over the vast overcrowding of peasant lands (Roder 1964; Ranger 1985; Alexander 1993; Phimister 1986, 1993). Following a slow start to implementation in 1954, a £2 million World Bank loan in 1960 made possible expanded implementation of the Act, if only partially and temporarily.

Loan programs for small commercial farmers—invariably men—were viewed as crucial to the commodification of the countryside. As the government's Advisory Committee on Economic Resources (1962:54) recommended, "At the risk of being criticized for seemingly over-playing the theme of credit, we must once again state how much importance we place upon the provision of adequate, soundly administered credit for the stimulation of both the petty and the somewhat more expansive activities of the rural producer."

But all of this would be attempted in the context of intensifying rural crisis which was a consequence not only of informal expropriation of land, cattle, and labor during the initial decades of colonial settlement, but of a variety of formal laws and regulations in subsequent years. In particular, the Land Apportionment Act of 1930 stipulated that most Africans would live and farm in generally arid "Reserves" or "Tribal Trust Lands" (now known as "Communal Areas"). People already forced into the Reserves in earlier cycles of dispossession experienced another round of cattle destocking in the 1930s and 1940s on a massive scale, as authorities purportedly concerned about soil erosion then resold many of the stock to white farmers. Overcrowded villages and eroding fields were swelled by many further victims of displacement as white commercial tobacco growers brought more land into cultivation (Palmer 1977a:1977b).

Official price controls, marketing systems and the naturally polarising tendencies of agricultural markets also intensified uneven rural development. "African producers' and consumers' interests may differ considerably from those of their European counterparts," the Advisory Committee (1962:276-279) pointed out diplomatically. "Europeans are primarily interested in the highest quality and Africans in the lower quality produce and the needs of these two different markets may clash." Instances of price "manipulation," for instance, were not "to the advantage of either the most needy or the greatest number of producers and consumers" and entailed an "often unjustified subsidization of a small body of producers at the expense of the general body of consumers and taxpayers."

In addition, overproduction—or what the Advisory Committee (1962:187-189) termed "under-consumption of the higher value produce"—continually threatened the local agricultural markets, especially in maize, potatoes, vegetables, pigs, milk, munga, sorghum and rupoko. In response, white farmers took advantage of subsidies, credit, and marketing support to diversify, especially into tobacco. This is reflected in the steady rise of white farmers' gross output from £23.4 million in 1954 to £41.5 million in 1961, whereas over the same period the value of all black farmers' production for their own consumption increased from £10.4 million to £14.7 million, but for the market from just £3.7 million to £4 million (Pearson and Taylor, 1963, 20).

Much of the structural unevenness was rooted in land inequality. Having allocated and restricted the purchase of the better two-thirds of Southern Rhodesia's land to whites alone (of which there were 7,000 commercial farmers by the late 1950s), the Land Apportionment Act provided a small number of black farmers (6,500 by the late 1950s) with protection from white competition on another 7% of the land, termed "African Purchase Areas" (now "small-scale commercial farming" areas) (Weinrich 1975). Here modern accumulation—production for the market and individualized ownership—ultimately evolved so as to co-exist with a traditional mode which entailed shared wealth, cooperation among farmers in crop production, polygamy, and large families, all legitimized by religious ideology.

The hybrid system encouraged men to use "selected aspects of traditional entrepreneurship in order to accumulate without becoming subject to any redistribution of their accumulated capital," according to Angela Cheater (1984:xv). As a result, Purchase Area farmers began to view themselves as having much closer interests to white commercial farmers than to black peasants. This class differentiation process affected struggles over credit during the 1950s, leaving many aspirant Purchase Area farmers dissatisfied with what was being offered by the government and private sector sources.

From the 1950s, credit was seen as a means by which leading Purchase Area farmers could be drawn into selective market processes, since their land could be put up as collateral. As early as the 1930s, credit-linked irrigation programs in the Reserves were established, relying upon repayments through deductions from produce sales. In 1947 the Chief Native Commissioner persuaded Parliament to pass legislation enabling Purchase Area farmers to formally borrow from the state Land and Agriculture Bank. This suited the Purchase Area farmers, as it heightened the latter's distinction from the African peasantry in the Reserves.

But loans to black farmers would always be far smaller (at roughly £50 each) than those received by the 80% of white farmers who borrowed from the Land Bank, and this was a source of continual complaint at African Farmers' Union (AFU) congresses. Government officials had to be careful not to provoke white resistance to the new Land Bank loans, since "Credit for capitalization of farming was a critical issue to settler racism, in ways that registration of title and marketing were not," as Cheater (1984:167) records. Bringing such loans into racial parity would have "created competition with whites for essentially limited resources, and embittered those whites who lost out in the competition. It would also have been interpreted, among the white electorate, as a public commitment to black advancement."

By the 1950s, however, as Southern Rhodesia's financial markets burgeoned, the rural credit system began to open slightly (Yudelman 1964:158). The Native (later African) Development Fund, a new state agency funded (until 1979) through a 10% tax on all goods marketed by black farmers, began to improve Reserve and Purchase Area infrastructure, although in a manner so non-transparent and so duplicative of envisaged government expenditure that the Advisory Committee called for its abolition in 1962. The Development Fund granted credit to groups of small farmers who belonged to government-registered African Cooperative Societies, which administered the loans.

However, as happened in other cases where finance was introduced in a non-organic manner, its modalities would initially exacerbate—not dampen—unevenness between white commercial and black Purchase Area farmers. Through their organization, the AFU, Purchase Area farmers struggled for many years to enjoy similar institutional support as had been won by the white Rhodesian National Farmers' Union in the 1920s and 1930s. The AFU opposed certain Development Fund policies, such as lending only through the cooperatives (which again differentiated Purchase Areas from the white farms). And a 1959 AFU conference resolution insisted that Purchase Area farmers would no longer pay the 10% tax, since white farmers did not pay such a levy in exchange for their credit. When this was rejected by government, loan repayment levels declined significantly (Cheater 1984:167; Whitsun Foundation 1980:35).

Nevertheless, in the wake of enabling legislation passed in 1956, the registered cooperatives deemed capable of on-lending mushroomed from just two (representing 187 farmers), to 52 in 1962 (representing 4,500 farmers) (roughly 1% of the total small farmer population). With cooperatives proliferating, in part through US government credit support, the Development Fund loan program also expanded, from £5,000 in 1958/59 to £40,000 in 1961/62. This was still a minuscule amount, but in 1964, following Advisory Committee recommendations, an Agricultural Loan Fund (ALF) was established, and within two years a further £600,000 in funds were available not only for cooperatives, but also for individual farmers vetted by their District Commissioner.

In addition, private sector sources of funds began to materialise. Lay-by credit was extended to small farmers by larger numbers of suppliers and manufacturers. Cooperatives borrowed £75,000 from suppliers in 1962, mainly for maize and groundnut inputs. And the African Loan and Development Company (ALDC) was founded in 1961 by 26 companies, including mining houses, fertilizer companies, and banks, and initially collected loan repayments from a small elite of Purchase Areas farmers easily. The ALDC's capital was £250,000, with working funds drawn from the banks and guaranteed by the government (Sowelem 1967:193). Unhappily for black farmers, the private sector fund charged higher interest rates than were available to white farm borrowers (and higher than those charged by the Development Fund and ALF). For example, the 1970s government rate for white farmers was 6.5%, while the ALDC's not-for-profit successor (whose administrative costs were roughly 15% of each loan) charged 10% to black farmers, and as high as 15% for short-term credit for cattle purchases (Whitsun Foundation 1980:40,44).

Ultimately, though, even sharply differential rates would not be sufficient to make up for what became a rash of defaults which, as we see below, threatened not only the viability of the main private loan fund but also the legitimacy of the Rhodesian Front government's bureaucratic personnel and hence its small farmer co-option strategy.

Uneven regional development

Policy-makers tackling urban and rural underdevelopment through credit during the 1950s expansion also turned their attention to achieving better-balanced economic expansion within Southern Rhodesia as well as with neighboring countries. But there quickly emerged substantial controversy over which regions would receive infrastructural, commercial and industrial investments. And as uneven regional development became a more obvious phenomenon during the 1950s, financiers were again criticized for magnifying already-divergent patterns of investment between Salisbury and smaller towns. At a 1955 national congress, business leaders from outlying areas arguing (unsuccessfully) for a decentralization policy even insisted that "An Industrial Bank is needed to help new industries in small towns" (*Commerce*, September 1955).

Such concerns corresponded to international trends. "Muted during the Great Depression and in the immediate post-war period, the regional question took on new importance in the 1950s," according to Soja (1989:167-168), though in most countries, "Awareness of the countervailing spatial strategies of capital was minimal." Yet in Southern Rhodesia those in the regional hinterlands expressed awareness and a general dissatisfaction with the geographical distribution of credit. According to *Property and Finance* (March 1960), "There was often 'loose talk' that building societies took money from the smaller centers for investment in Salisbury."[1]

Under such competitive and hotly-contested internal conditions, one obvious way for authorities to sustain accumulation and encourage foreign investment in the Southern Rhodesian economy was a geographical reorganization far more profound than introspective regional decentralization: the merger of Northern Rhodesia (Zambia), Nyasaland (Malawi) and Southern Rhodesia during the decade 1953-63 in a "Federation of Rhodesia and Nyasaland." Aside from the visionary official propaganda (Phillips 1960), many Southern Rhodesian whites approved of the Central African Federation in order to delay the transition of the two northern colonies—with their fewer white settlers and relatively more powerful nationalist movements—to majority rule (Keatley 1963). Remarked Peter Joyce (1974:77) in his biography of a then-emerging opposition politician (Ian Smith), "Northern Rhodesia and Nyasaland could, in effect, serve as firebreaks. Godfrey Huggins, father of the Federation, very probably took Ian Smith aside and explained all this." (Smith subsequently dropped his resistance to Federation, which had been based on fear of an increased British role in the region.) Likewise a generation of black nationalists aggressively opposed Federation.

But another powerful impetus behind the Federation's establishment was Huggins' desire to expand the protected manufacturing market for his supporters' commercial gain (as for Smith, notes Joyce [1974:76], "the economic possibilities of the federal arrangement would naturally have appealed to him"). According to Murray (1970:193), "The goal of a closer association between Southern Rhodesia and the colonies to the north was shared by the Federated Chambers of Commerce and the United Party government, and it was this which, despite periodic crises, attached the Federated Chamber to the government." As Gann and Gelfand (1964:227) report, "The wealthier strata, businessmen with their eyes turned towards northern markets, the bulk of the press, the mining companies and financial concerns backed Federation in the same way as they once advocated Southern Rhodesia's joining South Africa," notwithstanding the costs to the mining companies, which bore the brunt of Federation financing through stiff taxes on the copper mines.

No matter what class alliances ultimately supported Federation, ultimately there was a deeper economic drive behind the extension of capital northwards, Phimister (1988a:298) explains: "With no capital goods sector to speak of, and largely restricted to food processing and the manufacture of light consumer goods, Southern Rhodesian industry's capacity for autonomous development was severely compromised... If the market could not be readily deepened, however, it could at least be widened." And indeed Southern Rhodesia's manufacturers increased their output by 90% from 1954 through 1961, partly on the basis of the economies of scale and new markets that Federation permitted.

Conversely, however, Federation strengthened Salisbury and Bulawayo manufacturers at the expense of Northern Rhodesia and Nyasaland, whose "rates of growth of manufacturing industry have been less than they would have been had there been no Federation," according to Pearson and Taylor (1963:16-19). There were few improvements in trade from Northern Rhodesia and Nyasaland southwards (Stoneman 1982:279). Moreover, Southern Rhodesia benefitted immensely from the transfer of headquarters (and hence profit repatriation) of numerous firms that extracted resources from Northern Rhodesia and Nyasaland. To underscore Salisbury's new importance, the primary multinational corporations active in the Federation transferred their registration from London to Salisbury in search of lower tax rates.

This was matched in the public sector by a concentration of major Federation infrastructural projects in Southern Rhodesia, paid for ultimately through appropriation of taxes on Northern Rhodesian mines. The location in Salisbury of Federation functions as diverse as armed services and the new BRN exacerbated the surplus drain. Workers from the northern territories also migrated at a much faster rate—and many permanently—to Southern Rhodesia's mines, farms, and factories, importing whatever meagre resources they had accumulated.

Moreover, Pearson and Taylor (1963:9) point out that the Federation's expanded property and infrastructure investments accentuated uneven development not only because they were overwhelmingly geared to the interests of big mining and financial capital, but also because of their temporal characteristics:

> An inordinately high proportion has been invested in those assets whose income-producing potential is either intrinsically low, such as office buildings, or into types of investment whose income-producing potential cannot be realized until a very long time has elapsed. An example of this latter type is the Kariba hydro-electric scheme. It is open to question whether, in an underdeveloped country like the Federation, attention should be concentrated on those types of investment which can be expected to yield fairly quick returns, or upon those types of investment which are unlikely to prove to be real economic assets until some very considerable time in the future.

In sum, nearly all facets of regional geographical change increased the biases in favor of centralization against decentralization. Uneven Central African development therefore intensified at the same time that the spatial solution which federation had seemed to represent was reaching its limits. Southern Rhodesia's industrial economy was essentially extended—widened, as Phimister put it—in the process, rather than deepening into one more balanced between various sectors (which would have to wait until sanctions compelled a revival and transformation of fixed investment).

Thus as the 1950s financial innovations also ran out of steam, neither the temporal nor geographical expansion of investment served as a basis for renewed or better-balanced capital accumulation, as reflected in the ultimate failure of those investments to achieve lasting returns through the reorganized cities and countryside, and through development ventures at regional and even Central African scales.

The collapse of property

It was inevitable that overextended financial assets and the geographically-diverse investments which they represented would crash in the early 1960s. As overaccumulation worsened from 1957 onwards, the withdrawal of foreign accounts and the consequent crisis in liquidity served as catalysts for quite severe financial devaluation, as noted in Chapter Three.

Several building societies and hire purchase firms closed their doors forever, in part because many of the 56,000 whites who fled Southern Rhodesia in 1961-64 (representing a 10% net white emigration) simply walked away from their homes and debts. And as manufacturing growth petered out, the property slowdown of 1958-59 turned into a severe slump. The number of mortgage bonds granted in Southern Rhodesia (virtually all in commercial and white residential areas) dropped from a peak of 7,654 in 1957 to 6,846 in 1959 and then plummeted to 3,048 in 1961 (Central Statistical Office, *Bulletin of Statistics*). The value of new housing construction across Southern Rhodesia fell from £16 million in 1956 to £1.3 million in 1962. From 1958 to 1964, the annual value of new commercial buildings planned fell from £12 million to £2 million. Whereas from 1955 to 1960, 26 suburban shopping centers were established in Salisbury (about half the cumulative total to that point), in the subsequent five years just two more were built (Smout, 1977:73). The total value of new building plans passed by municipalities and peri-urban areas fell from a peak of £22 million in 1957 to just £8 million in 1961 (Advisory Committee 1962:357).

Retrospectively, considered *Property and Finance* (April 1962), "The property boom was due chiefly to transfers of big blocks of land for [white] township development and subsequent heavy sales of plots, and to speculation in city center property." The slowing of new immigration from 1957 and the uneven ebb and flows of mortgage bond availability affected the first factor, while CBD buildings coming on line found the oversupply problem treacherous. Noting critically that during the latter 1950s more than half of all Federation fixed capital formation was in "building and works," the government's Advisory Committee (1962:15) remarked,

> We can only conclude that substantial capital outlays have been on forward-looking or grandiose projects, which either only promise a return in the distant future or yield, at best, a low return because of the wasteful character of the investment... In a hectic investment boom, when incomes are growing rapidly, it is inevitable that scarce capital resources should frequently be misdirected, or that surplus capacity should emerge because of the failure of the economy to grow at some

> anticipated rate. This is undoubtedly the situation in Southern Rhodesia, which today possesses an agglomeration of buildings, merchanting, retailing, banking, power and other productive facilities constructed to meet the demands of a substantially larger volume of activity.

The larger volume of economic activity might conceivably have emerged, had Southern Rhodesia's social structure evolved according to the Partnership plans of the 1950s liberals, including not only new urban and rural property relations, but a limited black franchise, education of a black elite, and improved labor relations (Holderness 1985). However, the real agenda of the United Federal Party and of large-scale capital in Southern Rhodesia was revealed in a famous pronouncement by Central African Federation Prime Minister Huggins: "Partnership between black and white is the partnership between horse and rider."

With Southern Rhodesia Prime Minister Todd's 1958 ouster by his party's more conservative wing, even Partnership languished. The United Federal Party's failure to convert significant portions of small farmers and proletarians into an aspirant black middle class was evident in the rural areas—where Todd had dreamed naively of transforming each peasant into a commercial producer—and also in the townships, where the grand visions of homeownership faded quickly. As just one reflection of the mixed signals, the Salisbury central business district was cleansed of black businesses throughout the post-war period (West 1993).

But underlying Partnership's political failure of nerve, which is discussed in more detail below, were deep-rooted economic contradictions. Some reflect the essential requirement that overaccumulated capital fall victim to devaluation prior to the resumption of a new round of vigorous capital accumulation. In Southern Rhodesia's case, this lasted more than seven years, as growth only resumed in earnest in 1966. Other economic contradictions, Arrighi (1973a:364) argues, stemmed from powerful "centrifugal reactions" that inter-racial competition provoked amongst reactionary whites.

Still other economic contradictions which surfaced in the early 1960s are emblematic of the dangers of debt as a device for alleviating uneven development. To illustrate, it is worth considering in detail the outcome of both township housing reforms and the rural credit programs, for each not only contributed to the broader socio-economic crisis of the early 1960s, but also materialized again in the 1980s.

The false hope of township housing bonds

Notwithstanding the early availability of township housing finance and the enthusiasm with which the Plewman Commission and others suggested it be deployed, Partnership failed in the sphere of urban housing due to a combination of volatile liquidity and limited buying power. From government, there was a diminishing commitment to addressing these forms of market failure, and as economic growth slowed, state subsidies were reduced. Direct expenditure on housing by the Southern Rhodesian government fell from a peak of £1.8 million in 1956/57 to just £375,000 in each of the following two years. Even local government found itself facing shortfalls of external finance during these crucial years, as loans raised by municipalities shrunk from £5 million in 1956/57 to £3 million the next year, with even lower amounts registered during the early 1960s (Advisory Committee 1962:84).

The barrier of insufficient buying power bedevils capitalist housing markets across the world. One related problem in Southern Rhodesia was that building societies themselves contributed to the relatively high cost of urban housing—due in large part to racial bars protecting whites in the powerful building trades—by refusing to grant bonds on houses constructed by black workers (*P&F*, April 1961). (The number of registered black carpenters had risen from 456 in 1945 to 937 in 1955, before falling back to fewer than 900 in the subsequent decade; the number of registered black builders and painters also leveled off after rapid increases between 1945 and 1955; only brickmakers continued to tap an expanding market through the early 1960s [West 1990:266].) The head of the Salisbury Master Builders' Association persuaded government to shut down a site-and-service program under which blacks could build their own shack-houses for £60 each: "I told the Minister that he dared not go ahead with the scheme, otherwise it would cost him his post and also create such slums in this country that we would never overcome the thing he had built" (*P&F*, August 1962).

Regardless of such interventions, the market for housing was surprisingly small. In 1960, of approximately 200,000 black residents of Salisbury (and 141,000 in Bulawayo), the Plewman Commission reforms would affect a tiny class of blacks: "a virtually 'European' suburb will be established for those who, like people of all races, wish to get away from the hoi-polloi," *Property and Finance* (November 1960) announced. "Africans will also be able to obtain freehold title to land, a provision of great psychological importance."

In reality, Southern Rhodesia's urban workers were so severely underpaid that the normal operations of business societies just could not apply.

A government survey conducted in 1963 and 1964 found that the tiny classes of black "professional, technical and related workers" (3% of the population) and "administrative, executive and managerial workers" (0.4%) earned £25 per month, while clerical workers (6%) received £21. This proved an insufficient basis for a substantive homeowning population, given that average monthly household expenditures amounted to £18.9 as against average monthly income of £19.4. Household overcrowding was the rule, and rural-urban migratory patterns continued to exert a heavy influence, so that disposable income quickly disappeared. Indeed, the "hoi-polloi" were distributed everywhere, and average household incomes in the different Salisbury townships were remarkably consistent, varying by not more than 8% from the "elite" Mufakose to the older ghetto of Highfield (CSO, 1965:7-11).

As a result of the effective demand constraints, Brian Raftopoulos (1995:87) observes, "The inability of the Southern Rhodesia economy to stabilise broadly the reproduction of labor in the cities provided a general environment of instability for the urban population." Doing business in an urban space—the townships—where politics were getting hotter while buying power remained cool, was not what the comfortable Salisbury financiers had in mind. The recession, rising unemployment and dreadful living conditions formed an economic terrain which easily cultivated discontent, such as the "Zhii Riots" sparked in July 1960 by the arrest of three nationalist leaders (Bhebe 1989:77). In reaction, and characteristic of the ruling United Federal Party's degeneration, all political meetings were banned for three months, following which a Vagrancy Act was passed to prohibit the presence in towns of unemployed blacks (hundreds of people were arrested and deported in its first few days of implementation). In the wake of an earlier (1957) banning of the African National Congress, its successors the National Democratic Party and the Zimbabwe African People's Union (ZAPU) were sufficiently threatening as to attract bans in 1961 and 1962. Then, in the wake of the Rhodesian Front's introduction of school fees in 1963, urban protest exploded. By August 1964, the People's Caretaker Council of ZAPU and the more militant, breakaway Zimbabwe African National Union (founded in 1963) were finally banned permanently and their leaders—Nkomo, Sithole, Mugabe and many others—jailed for many years by Southern Rhodesia's new premier, Ian Smith.

Given the lack of business opportunities in the stagnant Southern Rhodesian economy, one result of intensified political dissent was another dramatic surge of capital flight, which hit the building societies' foreign deposit accounts very hard. "As in many businesses, [societies'] policies have been based largely on boom conditions and on a 'sky's the limit' psychology which encouraged overextension of activity and put no premium on efficiency or shrewd operation," commented *Property and Finance* in March 1961. As financial devaluation intensified, the societies' attempts to draw blacks into their circuit of capital waned, and, notwithstanding the financiers' generally liberal instincts, this contributed to the sense of resignation about broader prospects for a modernising, neo-colonial solution to Southern Rhodesia's political crisis.

The mismatch beyond growing needs, raised expectations and generally shrinking government resources allocated to fulfilling them during the last years of the Partnership era precluded a state solution. Ironically, during the period financial capital was most liquid and urbanization was most geared to the expansion of industry—and hence the period that greatest resources existed for housing provision—the opportunity for developing a partnership between state and capital capable of incorporating as junior partners urban blacks otherwise susceptible to radical nationalist agitation, was lost. This failure was also obvious in another area, small farmer credit.

Defaults on small farm debt

By the early 1960s, new contradictions in the rural Partnership strategy emerged. The imposition of individual titles on communally-grazed land in accordance with the Native Land Husbandry Act was creating further rural differentiation, and meeting stiff resistance from peasants residing in the roughly 40% of Reserves where by 1961 the Act had been at least partially implemented (Duggan 1980; Ranger 1985; Alexander 1993; Phimister 1993). And with the rise of tobacco as Southern Rhodesia's major export, the interests of white farmers shifted away from internal markets, which further undercut attempts at cross-racial class alliance by AFU leaders like Aaron Jacha (who also, in 1934, had founded the African National Congress). The broader economic crisis of the early 1960s was also felt in rural areas. The total number of cattle held by Reserve farmers actually declined between the years 1954 and 1966, from 1.9 million to 1.7 million, while white-owned cattle increased from 1.2 million to 1.7 million. And there were poor rainy seasons during 1963-65, just as small farm credit programs began attracting increased government funding support.

Moreover, without radical improvements in the basic production and marketing conditions faced by black farmers, the infusion of credit would neither raise the competitive standing of black farmers in relation to whites, nor achieve sustainability (in the form of regular repayments) on its own terms. Before long, increasing numbers of defaults—particularly by rural traders—began to affect the books of the formerly-profitable ALDC (*P&F*, September 1964, October 1964). Tail between legs, over a two year period the ALDC requested and finally received a £166,000 bail-out from Oxfam, but on the condition it transform into a non-profit trust (Whitsun Foundation 1980:39).

By 1964, £500,000 in unpaid loans were outstanding from various programs, and nearly 10,000 individual peasants were in arrears to the government African Loan Fund (Ndlela, 1981, 145). "Cooperative officers spent an increasing proportion of their time as debt collectors to the detriment of their other cooperative functions," the Whitsun Foundation (1980:36,29), a strong proponent of small farm credit, observed wistfully:

> A number of organizations had offered facilities without adequate supervision or knowledge of peasant farming conditions and experienced severe losses, resulting in either their closure or the withdrawal of their credit schemes... Loans would appear to have been issued fairly liberally and without adequate recovery plans... The poor level of repayments almost brought the demise of the cooperative movement as it became heavily indebted to the Agricultural Loan Fund. With the problems facing the Fund and the Cooperative Movement, Government decided that both should be transferred to the Ministry of Internal Affairs.

This administrative home reflected the political/control functions of credit (Internal Affairs had many policing functions), although agricultural lending was subsequently centralized when the Agricultural Finance Corporation was founded to replace the Land Bank in 1971. By then the failure of rural finance had generated, even amongst technicist bureaucrats, a "growing realization in many quarters that the assumption of credit by individual Reserve farmers is a non-essential prerequisite for agricultural advancement," as Ndlela (1981:135) put it. But this realization faded away at independence, as Chapter Ten shows, when credit was utilized again to tackle agricultural underdevelopment, in a manner again geared to market processes. However, in spite of rather more legitimate government-sourced finance, the result was an even higher, not lower, rate of small farmer default.

The rise and fall of indigenous finance

Blacks were not merely on the receiving end of credit. The failure of formal financial institutions to penetrate the urban and rural markets compelled another strategy: promotion of indigenous savings and credit systems, especially through a "friendly society" movement which came to the notice of the capitalist press in the late 1950s, and which by the early 1960s was "accounting for an increasing amount of African savings" (*P&F*, April 1961).

Such savings were not insignificant, for by 1930 over 2,000 African men and 117 women had opened savings accounts through the Post Office Savings Bank (Barnes 1992b:22) and by 1954 black savers accounted for nearly half the accounts. The post office was popular, recounts Barber (1961:165), because "The commercial banks have not always welcomed accounts by Africans. The earlier reluctance of the commercial banks to accept African accounts is now, however, breaking down." By 1963, the banks registered 15% of their fixed and savings deposits from blacks. (Other long-standing forms of grassroots savings, such as burial societies and stokvels, are discussed in Chapter Ten.)

But on the credit side, the market remained highly uneven; in spite of holding £3.6 million in deposits with the banks, blacks received less than £100,000 in advances (Sowelem 1967:57). In contrast, their access to trading credit had been impressive and, according to Michael West (1990:290), "the primary reason for the huge expansion in the number of African general dealers in the postwar years was the ease with which wholesalers now gave credit to budding African traders." There was an "astounding" amount of credit circulating, complained the Chief Native Commissioner, and "It can well be imagined that the number of civil claims against Native storekeepers is on the increase."

But even the well-established petty bourgeoisie became increasingly thwarted in the search for credit (Wild 1997:53). Although in 1956 the Southern Rhodesian African Chamber of Commerce claimed 150 paid-up members—shopkeepers, eating-house owners, pedlars, carpenters, shoe makers, traders, and transport operators—there was ultimately very little financing available to get major projects off the ground (white control of business credit was airtight).

Thus the friendly societies were meant to fill a market vacuum, beginning with small household loans (such as funeral expenses) and moving on, perhaps, to bigger financial projects, as the young Afrikaner financial elite were in the process of proving in South Africa (O'Meara 1983). One black politician claimed of his Central African Mutual Association, "The Association has demonstrated beyond all doubt that the African can discharge financial responsibilities without constant European supervision" (*P&F*, December 1960). Thanks to the fact it was chaired briefly by the country's leading nationalist, Joshua Nkomo, Central African Mutual was able to quickly raise £50,000 in deposits. But after three years of operations it had lost more than 60% of the funds, which were purportedly aimed at providing credit for funeral expenses and other small loans. "Administration" costs accounted for £11,000 in the society's first year of operation, 1958-59. By 1962, Nkomo denied any connection with the Association (*P&F*, May 1962, July 1962; Wild 1997:242).

Nkomo had also been chair of the Bulawayo-based Bantu Cooperative Society in the late 1950s. The BCS was founded in 1938, but according to West (1990 :285), "Perhaps in part because of a lack of sound business practice on the part of its managers" (who were "advised" by two whites), had "not lived up to its envisaged role as a major vehicle of African capital accumulation."

Leading white liberal businesspeople were drawn into the black self-financing schemes, to their ultimate discomfit. Former Prime Minister Todd and B.S. Higgs (a high-profile white businessperson) were embarrassed by the 1964 failure of a black retail group managed by Higgs—the United Consumer's Cooperative Society—which lasted just four months. It was chaired by Leopold Takawira and included on its board notables such as Rev. Ndabaningi Sithole, J.T. Malulke and the wife of the prominent doctor Samuel Parirenyatwa (*P&F*, June 1963, March 1964). Earlier, in 1960, the managing director of Provident Assurance had helped establish the First African Friendly Society, which occupied what were considered "luxurious" offices in a converted warehouse in Sinoia Street. The society's trustees included Nathan Shamuyarira (then Editor-in Chief of African Newspapers Ltd, later Zimbabwe's Foreign Minister), the prominent medical doctor E.M. Pswarayi, and the well-known journalist Stanlake Samkange. As *Property and Finance* (July 1962) reported, "These offices were closed without warning in March 1961, and numbers of Africans wishing to transact business were somewhat disconcerted to find the doors locked."

Such failures led to highly-restrictive, paternalistic regulation of friendly societies in 1962: "In view of the average African's ignorance of financial affairs, and of his probable gullibility when faced with highly-colored 'salesmanship,' mismanagement, misappropriation and misrepresentation are the three risks which the Bill seeks primarily to control" (*P&F*, October 1962). In several high-profile court cases, black financiers were convicted of fraud and mismanagement.

Unfazed, leaders like Nkomo, Herbert Chitepo and Kenneth Kaunda (of Northern Rhodesia) looked to even greater financial challenges in the Federation in 1961, but framed them in a careful political light. A Conservative member of Britain's Parliament, John Foster, lauded "the Bank of Africa Project, to which great importance is attached by African leaders, who regard its establishment as a useful counter to possible nationalist demands for the expropriation of European assets when the Africans attain political power... African realization of the importance of a sound banking system, would influence British investors who fear expropriation." Foster warned that "if British bankers refused to finance the project, black political leaders would look elsewhere." Notwithstanding such faraway rational calculation, local reports by *Property and Finance* (December 1961) undercut the viability of an indigenous black financial venture: "The City of London has cold-shouldered the Bank of Africa, thus showing itself impervious to extravagant aspirations or veiled blackmail." Subsequent efforts to get black financial institutions off the ground under Rhodesian Front rule failed (Chimombe 1983:78). As discussed in Chapter Seven, bias on the part of white-controlled financial institutions met by indigenous banking myth-making and mishaps, continued well into the post-independence era.

Finance and uneven political development

In the last chapter we observed evidence of economic imbalances, overaccumulation crisis, and the rise of finance. We have so far reviewed several related economic processes in this chapter, including the excessive speculative binge of property speculation, the failure of formal and indigenous finance to take root and prosper in underdeveloped urban and rural areas during the post-war era, and the economic limits of the Central African Federation. While all of these developments were accentuated by financial market malfunctions, there were certainly crucial social and political factors working against Partnership, including higher levels of white opposition, black rural resistance, urbanization, and labor market inflexibility than planners had anticipated (Cliffe 1981:18).

There are interesting political implications of the failed 1950s reforms, in relation, first, to the capabilities and limits of local financiers under these changing conditions; second, to the nature of the black nationalist movement that began to emerge as a potent force in many areas of Southern Rhodesia; and third, to white reaction, observed through intercapitalist competition over policy objectives, interclass alliances opposed to black advancement, and the Rhodesian Front's disregard for geopolitical processes established at superpower level.

First, financiers faced a qualitatively new level of political pressure, and in a period of declining profitability and devaluation of assets, they reacted without a coherent plan. For example, the fact that by the early 1960s the hoped-for geographical solution in Central Africa was petering out left Southern Rhodesian financiers fretting over the emerging constitutional transformation. Of enormous concern was the impact of the break-up of Federation on the size and vitality of their currency base, for which they now enjoyed increased foreign exchange responsibilities.[2]

More frightening still, the South African alternative, which financiers had always considered an option, now appeared unviable in the wake of the Sharpeville massacre, as a leading Salisbury banker emphasized: "I cannot stress too heavily we in Rhodesia do not even appear to align ourselves with the Republic. London is still the premier financial market, and we are much more dependent on London—and, thus, on the rest of the world—than we ever have been on South Africa" (*P&F*, July 1961). Subsequent developments changed financial power relations with London quite convincingly, of course, reflecting how brittle the international alliances had become. There were limits to even Chase Manhattan's support.

But even more urgent for the financiers were the barriers to overcoming uneven urban and rural development which Southern Rhodesian capitalism itself constructed in the course of the accumulation cycle. For these contributed to increasingly polarized racial politics and a sense that the black petty bourgeoisie would never get a fair deal from local banks. For example, the distinct lack of investment in housing in black townships (and the manner in which such investment was envisaged) demonstrated by its absence the ultimate limits of financiers to structure social life in their image, for what were then generally sound short-term economic reasons. Black urban entrepreneurs suffered a similar fate.

And like small overindebted farmers everywhere, many Purchase Area and Reserve borrowers were left poorer by the loss of their collateral, to the point, as the Whitsun Foundation (1980:25) noted, that "Subsequently government extension staff were withdrawn because their service image was becoming tarnished by having to dun loan defaulters." Although the most prosperous 30% of Reserve farmers managed to increase their relative incomes during the 1954-61 period (when the Native Land Husbandry Act was partially implemented) these "Reserve entrepreneurs" also joined the landless in contributing to militant rural nationalism (Phimister 1991:17). But as the United Federal Party panicked over the Act's failed implementation, the political punishment conferred upon peasants was the installation of chiefs, headmen, and community development councils as replacements for the Native Commissioners and technicist Partnership administrators (Alexander 1993).

In sum, the circumstances under which capitalist reproduction failed in underdeveloped black areas—in part because finance failed to alleviate uneven development and indeed intensified it in many respects—only fuelled a variety of fires set by nationalist activists and intellectuals (including a crew of failed indigenous bankers). It was, hence, the uniformity of the unhappy experiences with capitalism that joined the petty bourgeoisie of the liberation movement to aspirant black capitalists, West argues (1990:307): "Were black capitalists a part of the evolved African middle class in 1965 or had they, by this time, come to constitute a separate class? The answer is that there was only one African middle class, of which the capitalist stratum was an integral part."

This raises the second issue, the nature of black resistance that emerged in the early 1960s. From around 1957—the point at which militant youth revived the Southern Rhodesian African National Congress—the political alliance between black peasants, Purchase Area farmers (many of whom were political leaders in their own right), workers, and the petty bourgeoisie prospered under the banner of African nationalism. Setting aside regional and ethnic divisions (which were overcome in the past, and in later years, during important moments of struggle), it was primarily strategic and tactical differences and uneven leadership which prevented unity within the liberation movement at that stage. The militancy of ZANU won the day, as the constitutional route advocated by Nkomo's ZAPU in the early 1960s consistently proved a fruitless *cul de sac* (Shamuyarira 1965; Bhebe 1989).

Yet it was mainly due to the frustrated character of the movement's limited middle class component, Arrighi concludes (1973a:365-367) that Zimbabwean nationalism was not "suitable for a solution of the 'neo-colonialist' type. Hence large-scale capitalism (and the British government) were in a weak position vis-a-vis the white workers and petty bourgeoisie, who are thus enabled to consolidate their power position in the political as well as economic sphere." As state repression intensified alongside economic crisis in the early 1960s, nationalist organizations turned to armed struggle, which completely "deprived the British government and the reformist groups (manufacturing and foreign capital) of an alternative to the settler's rule."[3]

Third, if the United Federal Party and its backers among large-scale industrial and financial capitalists desired a black urban middle class and rural bourgeoisie, it was as a means of limiting and controlling social unrest and as a (consumer market) basis for further industrialization. Opposed, however, were mining and agricultural capitalists (because of the implications for wage levels and competition, respectively), as well as white wage earners and petty bourgeois elements. In the latter camp, an especially important group in the give and take over state policy direction was the

Public Service Association of civil servants, which retained effective control over "native affairs." This coalition of white reaction was able to sabotage various United Federal Party reforms through legislative compromises and bureaucratic manoeuvres during the 1950s. According to Murray (1970:359), "The [opposition] Dominion Party and [its successor] Rhodesia Front, besides giving voice to European dismay at the challenge posed by Africans, also expressed the widespread hostility of Europeans to the established administrative system and to the dominant groups in the political system of each sector."[4]

Despite efforts of the enlightened sectors of the capitalist class, matters had deteriorated too far, leading the United Federal Party to class disintegration and in December 1962 to its first defeat in nearly three decades. According to Murray (1970:367), "The election result in 1962 involved not a subtle shift within the limits of an established system but the overturning of it; and on what remained of it a new one was being built up." One way the Rhodesian Front upset existing political norms and practices was through the disregard shown for international forces mandating neo-colonial reform. As Federation Prime Minister Welensky (1964:364) interpreted the geopolitics of the day, his British counterpart "was concentrating on two principal objectives: a relaxation of tension between the Soviet Union and the West, and Britain's entry into the European Common Market. If, in order to achieve one or both of these, British influence and responsibility in Africa had to be liquidated, so be it... This 'realistic approach,' as Mr. Macmillan's colleagues and supporters called it, was explained to me with considerable emphasis."

In colonies such as Northern Rhodesia and Nyasaland where settlers were extremely weak, Britain's realistic, neo-colonial architects had their way. The Central African Federation was dissolved at the end of 1963 and Zambia and Malawi were granted independence in 1964. But in Southern Rhodesia, in the years between a reform-oriented 1961 constitutional referendum and the Rhodesian Front's November 1965 vote for international isolation through the Unilateral Declaration of Independence (UDI), hopes for local reform faded away entirely.

The class structure of Rhodesia was by this time such that an extremist reaction to the British decolonization and neo-colonization policy (and to black unrest) was feasible, logical, and supported by a broad coalition of white Rhodesians. UDI, according to Arrighi (1973a:367), "was directed as much against large-scale capitalism as against the Africans. The populist undertones of the UDI campaign were very noticeable." Those undertones harked back to the 1933 Reform Party victory, Wetherell insists (1975:76) since Smith's intention was "undoubtedly to conserve a system of safeguards that the radicals of the 1930s fought so hard to establish... The inheritors of the pre-war populist or 'left-wing' legacy [were] now self-defined as 'right-wing'."

Conclusion: The limits to space, time, and financial capital

We have explored in this chapter various ways in which uneven development in city and countryside prior to UDI was directly affected by the contradictory roles of finance. There was, for example, the 1950s evolution of finance from an accommodating to a more speculative mode, as epitomized by the rash of opulent skyscrapers which played host as either headquarters or investment outlets for banks, building societies, insurance companies, and other financial institutions.

In addition, controlling characteristics of ascendant finance also emerged, even if in a somewhat erratic form. For example, the last chapter reviewed the power of international bankers to dictate interest rate policies at the stage when local overaccumulation became acute. Yet at a different scale, the gradual increase in national financial regulation was an example of the Southern Rhodesian government's realization, after consistent prodding from productive capitalists, that local credit flows would have to be better controlled in the national interest. In contrast, rather ironically, was the government's lack of microeconomic financial power over small farmers in the Purchase Areas, whose growing indebtedness and increasing default rate contributed to the crisis of state legitimacy.

If there is anything to be drawn from these diverse examples, it is that theoretical propositions concerning financial power ("finance capital") cannot rest—as did so many from Hilferding's (and even Grossmann's and Sweezy's) work—on singular, discrete trends (such as the centralization of capital, overaccumulation and the increase in speculation, or the rise of oligopoly through industrial concentration). Instead, the various factors we have been observing, such as scale, space, and sectoral unevenness in the context of rising finance and overaccumulation, must be integrated into a holistic argument. By now, five working propositions have emerged which in future chapters can be explored forward and backward over time and across space.

First, we have seen in the last two chapters an accumulation cycle with a duration of roughly thirty years evolve from rapid growth through to the onset of crisis. The endpoint of this cycle was generalized overaccumulation in the early 1960s. Second, during this process finance emerged as more of a speculative force, and as one incorporating ever greater control functions.

Third, we have also seen that uneven sectoral development worsened over the period, and that more, not fewer imbalances emerged between imports and exports and between incoming financial flows and remittances (balance of trade and payments); between production and consumption and in consumption between luxury and basic goods; and between the broader socio-economic interests of manufacturers and merchants as opposed to primary (minerals and agricultural) producers.

Fourth, we have seen uneven geographic development grow worse, over time, in cities, countryside, and regions. In the CBD there was overbuilding fuelled by easy liquidity and the proliferation of financial institution headquarters. In townships, the growing class of manufacturers required an increase in housing for their employees but were unable after a certain point to assure this on their own. But the building societies' efforts to bring working-class blacks and even a petty bourgeoisie into the financial system failed, for reasons of limited buying power and receding liquidity. So too did tentative government attempts to expand credit into Purchase Areas and Reserves.

And fifth, we have seen the unevenness of scale at which productive development was determined evolve from local (municipal-scale) circuits of capital in the field of manufacturing, to national-level initiatives which supported industry and agriculture, to international market fluctuations which ultimately had a disruptive effect on local accumulation in areas ranging from copper prices to geopolitics. But while this holds broadly true for productive capital, finance exhibited a somewhat different trajectory. During the 1930s and 1940s financial power had international roots—in the British colonial currency boards and London banks—but, while these presented serious irritations to Southern Rhodesian capitalists, they did not prevent the renewal of an accumulation cycle, and in any case financial control and the reaction it provoked (government regulation) moved decisively to the national scale during the 1950s before being buffeted again by international forces (such as the Bank of England interest rate).

Each of these five propositions concerning overaccumulation crisis, rising finance, and uneven sectoral, spatial, and scale development may warrant the conceptual weight Gramsci conferred on his "organic movements": permanent tendencies which exhibit incurable structural contradictions. In addition, we have considered the displacement of overaccumulated capital through time and across space in order to understand how these deep-rooted tendencies mesh together. In particular, we explored why spatial strategies which aimed to mop up excess financial liquidity or to widen capital's reach, whether into townships, rural areas, or new regions, were ultimately untenable. The same conclusion held in the previous chapter regarding temporal extensions through the rise of finance.

An additional insight into the interrelatedness of our concepts emerges as Pearson and Taylor (1963:9,7) describe how spatial (infrastructural expansion) and temporal (delayed returns on investment) fixes can exacerbate uneven social development:

> There are general economic reasons for assuming that people with low incomes—and this applies to the majority of the Federation's inhabitants—have almost immediate preferences; in other words, they will attach less importance to benefits which will accrue in the distant future. If this is true, there are considerable grounds for doubting whether much of the actual disposition of public investment resources which has taken place in the Federation over the last ten years reflects the time preferences of the majority of the consuming and producing population... It would seem that some imbalance between [infrastructural investment] and the pressing desirability of an immediate increase in incomes and the production of consumer goods has occurred.

Finally, this brings us to the pressing matter of uneven political development, witnessed by Partnership's dual failure to gradually mould a cooperative black petty bourgeoisie and to win the white electorate to a reformist point of view. With the intransigence of racism, the rigidity of the dominant class structure under conditions of emerging overaccumulation crisis, the contradiction-ridden rise of finance, continuing uneven sectoral development, and the skewed nature of the various geographical strategies, all routes forward to neo-colonialism were subsequently found barricaded.

Worsening uneven development exacerbated nationalist tendencies in opposite directions, leading black freedom fighters to a Marxist-Leninist-Maoist-inspired guerilla war, and whites to proto-fascism. The situation had built up inexorably from the 1950s in a manner "strikingly similar to what happened south of the Limpopo roughly a decade earlier" in Arrighi's words (1973a:364).[5] As in late 1940s South Africa, the nature of the economic crisis Rhodesia faced in the late 1950s meant that there was greater scope for a temporarily renewed internal accumulation cycle, beginning with UDI in 1965, based in large part on increasing import substitution, financial controls, and racial polarization. As the next chapter demonstrates, this stands in stark contrast to the external and internal interests of finance which included economic liberalization and political reform (the power of which was demonstrated in early 1990s South Africa) (Bond 1994a;1994b). But what makes the 1950s expansion of state monetary responsibility most interesting is the subsequent ability of the Rhodesian

Front to hijack the bureaucratic controls (and the bureaucrats themselves). With them, and with the help of enforced autarchy from the international economy, the rebel government temporarily and partially compelled capital to balance more evenly across different sectors of the economy, as shown next.

Notes

1. It was not, however, until 1976 that a full-fledged regional decentralisation policy was adopted (Heath, 1990), although as early as April 1952 *Commerce* was reporting, myopically, on "Decentralization as the Answer to the Problems of our Big Cities."
2. The head of the largest discount company pleaded, in vain, "I must point out that the company, and indeed, the continued growth of a virile money market in Central Africa, are dependent on a monetary system embracing the three territories of the Federation" (*P&F,* May 1961).
3. Under such circumstances, according to Astrow (1983, 13), "British imperialism had no fundamental disagreements with this [Rhodesian Front] strategy" and "maintained its interests in the country through the settlers" (see also Verrier, 1986 and Mandaza, 1986a). The main supporting argument for this interpretation is that British sanctions against Rhodesia were the minimal possible response when armed intervention was widely called for. It is an interesting—if controversial—interpretation, in part because it offers an explanation for the power of the Rhodesian Front that does not rely on either Arrighi's concern with contradictions of Partnership by which whites feared black competition, or my own sense of the failure of Partnership reforms in the context of economic crisis.
4. Hence the Dominion Party was viewed as a potentially populist space by well-known former Labour Party leaders and even those like the idealistic Ahrn Palley, who was, according to Murray (1970, 361), "a recent immigrant who brought with him the tradition of left-wing politics in the South African Cape. He was pre-eminently a critic of government by an established ruling group who saw in the existence of this circle and the antagonism to it in European society the opportunity for a non-racial, class-based political movement."
5. It was the weakness of English-speaking finance in South Africa in the 1940s which contributed to an analogous set of objective conditions: disunity within the capitalist class, in that instance over World War II; traditions of discrimination against Afrikaners and, in response, the "Economic Movement's" harnessing of anti-bank populism to build, for the first time, a nationalist economic power-base; followed by the "swart gevaar" (black

panic) over African urbanisation and proletarianisation. The apartheid electoral outcome was thus possible in 1948. Yet in turn those underlying objective conditions encouraged the development of a new class of enlightened ("verligte") Afrikaner financiers (in state ministries and the Reserve Bank, and in financial conglomerates like Sanlam, Rembrandt and Volkskas, and related institutions). By the 1960s, they had imposed on the Nationalist Party sufficient respect for economic rationality and the rule of private property such that the Nats would begin to jettison their traditional electoral base and, significantly, even terminate support for the Rhodesian Front regime (Bond, 1991a, Chapter One).

chapter five

The Rise and Fall of The UDI Economy

Introduction

The 1965–79 Unilateral Declaration of Independence is sometimes described as providing a "hothouse" atmosphere for accumulation, due to extraordinary rates of growth until 1974 as well as to the various barriers to free financial flows erected by the state. These barriers imposed a condition of semi-autarchy on the financial circuit of capital and allowed for an initial amelioration of uneven sectoral and geographical development, but ultimately exacerbated capitalist boom-bust tendencies.

In the wake of a half-decade of economic stagnation (1960–65), UDI featured a shift in the Rhodesian economy's general sectoral orientation of accumulation, its geographical orientation, and the financial intermediation it required. Finance was at the heart of the shift, but this time in a dominated, not dominant way. With financial capital repressed, it was the resurgence of manufacturing—responsible by that stage for one quarter of GDP—that powered the 1966–74 boom in which annual GDP growth averaged 9.5%.

This in turn demonstrates how even on the semi-periphery of world capitalism, a relatively autarchic economy can grow extremely rapidly, and an increasingly empowered state can direct investment in a manner conducive to corporate profitability. It is important, however, to understand some of the preconditions for this centrally-directed economic dynamism: the powerful yet flexible state economic policy apparatus, the cohesion and class solidarity of industrialists, existing manufacturing production overcapacity, and the availability of cheap, repressed labor.

Capitalist crisis emerged, nevertheless, and decimated most spheres of manufacturing in the late 1970s. It is difficult to abstract locally-generated economic factors from issues such as political conflict, civil war and global economic recession (the conventional explanations for the crisis). But the organic roots of overaccumulation crisis can be traced to untenable new fixed capital investments in various manufacturing subsectors, which in the context of limited buying power resulted in year-end stockpiles and inventories at record levels.

The crisis was met with various kinds of capitalist and state responses. From the mid 1970s, Rhodesia experienced an ambiguous process of uneven development, in part reflecting weaknesses in state policies aimed at levelling growth across space and at stimulating financial sector activity. Ultimately, both spatial and temporal attempts to deal with overaccumulation and uneven development in the late 1970s—in particular, regional decentralization initiatives and loosely-guarded credit markets during a period of monetary conservatism—were an ineffectual combination, leading to yet another major political transition.

Financial repression and buying power

Control over the Rhodesian financial system was vital for the first, high-growth period of UDI (1966–74), both because reigns on finance encouraged capital accumulation to proceed in a direction that was temporarily sustainable in the local hothouse, and because the state effectively prevented geographical capital flight (Seidman 1986:64–67). "The directors of the national economy were already using their main weapon," recounted Rhodesian Front economist John Handford (1976:16): "bottling up capital by severe exchange control restrictions."

In the same vein, Roger Riddell's extensive study of the country's manufacturing sector boom concluded that (contrary to accepted wisdom), "the major import-substitutions thrust occurred prior to UDI, with the major source of manufacturing growth in the UDI period being domestic demand expansion." According to Riddell (1990:341,344), increased buying power within Rhodesia was responsible for a vast amount (61%) of the manufacturing growth which occurred during the years 1964–78, as compared with import substitution industrialization (30%) and export-based growth (9%).[1] Subsequently, excessive new capital investment in the mid 1970s adversely affected accumulation, as discussed later. But it is important, first, to stress the sources of buying power, because in view of the hostility the Rhodesian Front initially faced from financiers who had earlier influenced monetary management so profoundly, the new regime's management of key financial markets was by no means predetermined.

The basis for a shift of monetary and financial regulatory responsibilities from the London-based banks to the state had been established during the 1950s, as discussed in Chapter Three. Extraordinary levels of state intervention in the financial system ultimately proved crucial in deflecting the financial brouhaha that surrounded the declaration of UDI itself, in late 1965.[2]

Ever-tighter exchange controls brought the entirety of Rhodesia's international financial dealings under government purview. The Reserve Bank assumed responsibility for overall coordination of exchange control in 1965. Also that year, exchange controls on dealing in external shares began the process of reflating the economy. And industrialists, still suspicious of the Rhodesian Front and still suffering from overinvestment and stagnation, won surprisingly generous import tariffs and export incentives.

Partly as a result of the local restrictions, Southern Rhodesian economic vulnerability to a potentially punitive British government and City of London was qualitatively reduced in the period leading to UDI. Rhodesian external government bonds suffered devaluation (by some 23%, compared with Zambia's 20%) at the hands of City traders in the months prior to UDI as racial politics deteriorated. Yet a growing sense of self-confidence was felt by the Rhodesian Front—and in particular by Ian Smith, who in 1964 became Prime Minister after a spell as Finance Minister—after whites provided a unified show of support in the May 1965 elections. In November, when UDI was declared and the financial doors slammed shut, the Rhodesians responded by defaulting on R$82.6 million in foreign debts. Handford (1976:18, 50) gloated about how successful the countervailing efforts had been:

> When the full story of the "whisking away" of considerably more than half of the fixed and liquid Rhodesian reserves in London is eventually told, it will read like a James Bond thriller. Weary officials of the Reserve Bank and of the Treasury regard the secret removal, only a matter of hours before the Independence Proclamation, as the auspicious

> start of Rhodesia's counter-attack against the British sanctions.... Probably the biggest British miscalculation of all was on the extent of the funds which would be available once money was bottled up inside Rhodesia through the operation of the closed economy.

Whereas Britain's Prime Minister Harold Wilson claimed that "the cumulative effects of the economic and financial sanctions will bring the rebellion to an end within a matter of weeks rather than months," in reality, according to Elaine Windrich (1978:69–70), Whitehall had acted too slowly, waiting three weeks after the UDI declaration to impose the sanctions: "Criticism of the Government's delay ranged from the *Financial Times,* which pointed out that during the interval preceding the controls the Reserve Bank of Rhodesia had been buying up all the gold it could, to the *New Statesman,* which said that if the financial controls had been imposed with the UDI they might have toppled the Smith regime."

South African banks offered support in the evasion of sanctions and in lubricating anonymous trade (Clarke 1980a:104), while London *Sunday Times* investigations also established that from 1972, imports of steel-making equipment were being financed by Swiss and Austrian banks.[3] Thus perhaps the only significant domestic effect of what was termed the "financial squeeze" was a temporary decline in bank credit outstanding, which was addressed by an immediate Reserve Bank infusion of £13 million a month after UDI. This was accomplished by lowering reserve balances from 6% to 3% for commercial bank demand deposits, which freed funds for lending. By 1966, notes Handford (1976:48), "The money market seemed flooded with funds which, for one reason or another, holders wanted to keep fairly liquid."

Short- and medium-term cooperation between the regime and the major financial institutions was an integral component of UDI's initial economic successes. "British-controlled banks in Rhodesia, presumably not wishing business to foreign banks, reportedly put their foreign currencies in South Africa before UDI, and it appeared that this helped them to extend credit against blocked accounts," reports Handford (1976:18). In the words of top Barclays bank officials (Crossley and Blandford, 1975:251–252), "UDI had in effect been anticipated and made no change in the administration of the bank's affairs save that London could no longer approve nor reject proposals put forward by Salisbury... (By 1971) the best possible use had been made of six difficult years." Simultaneously, Seidman (1986:65) contends, "The foreign banks became more closely interlinked, not only with each other but also with other financial institutions, on account of their collaboration in the face of United Nations sanctions to mobilise locally generated investable surpluses, primarily to finance the transnational corporate affiliates' expanding activities in the modern sector."

Exchange controls trapped not only local financial resources and the profits of multinational corporations, but also existing bank deposits of non-residents, which by the late 1970s accounted for a third of the stock of surplus funds that banks had available for loans. According to Duncan Clarke (1980b:325), the system of financial autarchy was convincingly in place by the late 1960s:

> The controls worked, especially when combined with buoyant growth conditions in the economy associated to high net white immigration (and rising mortgage demand), rapid industrial development through diversification (and demand for hire purchase and leasing facilities), and expanded primary sector output (with demands for short- and medium-term financing). All these developments widened the base of the institutions, led to diversification within them, increased intra-sectoral linkages and flows, and strengthened the financial sector's structure.

A good example of the impact of blocked liquidity was the development of the white housing sector, the main beneficiary of property finance in the late 1960s (Figure 5.1). The imposition of financial sanctions, "if anything, boosted the business of the building society movement," argued the chair of the country's largest society, leading the *Herald* (27/9/67) to report, "It appears that a rapid build-up of funds available for housing combined with a popular conviction of political certainty, has taken the cork out of the bottle."

At the time, residential building costs in Salisbury were only a quarter of those in Lusaka and 40% lower than in South Africa, and this encouraged a further development of the Salisbury suburban sprawl and flow of finance into land improvements (*Sunday Mail*, 1/10/67). But commercial property also benefitted from financial repression, according to estate agent John Parkin: "The recent surge in development can be attributed to various factors which are not altogether necessarily indicative of political confidence. It is certain that some building, essentially large developments, has been prompted by a need to find acceptable investment for surplus funds rather than because of any great expectations" (*Herald*, 18/6/70).

Finance was an especially strong driving force behind the real estate boom in its later years. In 1974, some 11,670 mortgage bonds (including second mortgages) were issued against just 8,611 property sales in Rhodesia as a whole—as compared, in 1971, with just over 9,000 mortgages issued against the 10,690 property sales. And while the total number of *urban* property sales peaked at 9,200 in 1972 (a year the societies granted 5,200 bonds) two years later the societies granted 6,734 bonds against just 7,735 sales (Central Statistical Office, *Statistical Yearbook*

1987:132,223,224). Although these bonds included a greater number of second mortgages (typically lower in value than the first mortgages), the overall value of the average bond issued during the early 1970s was higher than the average property sales price, which is indicative of a very ready flow of surplus funds into property. But the subsequent crash of the property market once building societies withdrew funds in 1975 was even more extreme, as we shall see below.

The cohesion of the capitalist class

The manner in which the industrial base of the economy closed ranks to support UDI is worth some comment. Rhodesian Front politicians and government bureaucrats intensified state intervention to sustain capital accumulation on a wider scale and to organise the disparate parts of an economy under siege. From late 1965, the state focused unprecedented resources on controlling external account balances, encouraging immigration of skilled white males, ensuring labor market stability, cementing land inequality, expanding police and military control, and subsidising all manner of white business ventures. This entailed waiving overseas firms' production rights, licensing arrangements, and trade marks, as well as other constraints against technology transfer. UDI state spending also included new investments in transport (especially rail and airlines), energy, posts and telecommunications, and purchasing and marketing authorities (Kadhani 1986:104-105; see also Sutcliffe 1971 and Makgetla 1980). And there was other aid given to the Rhodesian economy from neighbouring states, namely sanctions-busting, transport arrangements, loans and other assistance from South Africa and Portuguese-ruled Mozambique.

Earlier, organised business lobbies ACCOR and ARNI had officially and energetically opposed UDI, and in 1965 had published reports on the "potentially disastrous" effect of an independence declaration. It was widely assumed that a crippling set of economic penalties would be the minimum response from Britain. At the outset, South Africa's *Rand Daily Mail* reported that "there is confusion in all sections of the business field" in Rhodesia (Metrowich 1969:43). Initially, in 1966, the fear of sanctions appeared well-founded, as manufacturing gross output declined 6.5% (in nominal terms) and, more disturbingly, manufacturing volume declined 9.3%.

The head of Dunlop's local subsidiary later explained, "Having taken a deep breath and having assessed the direction in which the economy should go, by the end of 1966 Rhodesian businessmen were exhibiting a remarkable degree of optimism, ingenuity and determination that the economy must not be destroyed by the new conditions produced by world sanctions" (Handover 1977:12). Merchants and financiers who had earlier backed an anti-UDI compromise, organised the import control system nearly overnight. Handford (1976:6,7) describes how "Rhodesian industrialists jumped in quickly, made arrangements with overseas organizations, set up things in back alleys—one thousand new industries in a few years." Sanctions-busting became a national pastime, with "a network centred on obscure offices in back streets of cities in Europe—as fast as one London press-man uncovered a hide-out, another would be set up."

There were only rare desertions by business leaders. In late 1968, the heads of Rhodesian Iron and Steel Corporation (E.S. Newson) and Standard Bank (E. Campbell) issued critiques of UDI and called for a settlement and fresh infusion of foreign funding. Prime Minister Ian Smith's reaction, according to Windrich (1978:149), was quick and dirty: "This was the first real opposition the Smith regime had encountered since their decision to go ahead with the illegal declaration of independence, in spite of the dire economic forecasts announced at that time. In response, Mr. Smith launched a fierce attack on the 'old gang,' in league with the Argus Press, for trying to prepare the country for a sell-out." The sell-out allegation became yet more concrete in December 1969, when the main financial journalist of Argus' *Rhodesia Herald* (R. Nicholson) was convicted of spying on behalf of the Central Intelligence Agency, and was bailed out of prison by the United States government (Joyce 1974:315).

More important than business leaders' willingness to participate in the illegal UDI was the unprecedented manner in which capital was accumulated. Overcapacity had been the rule across industry prior to UDI, with capacity utilization down to below 60% in 1962 (Ramsey 1974; Davies: 1982). What was particularly important about how that capacity was taken up during UDI was the extraordinary flexibility shown both by capitalists (who organized an extension of product lines largely on the basis of existing plant and equipment prior to 1970) and by black workers (who adapted to the initial skills shortage caused by early 1960s white emigration and to the new production demands).

Rhodesia suddenly produced its own breakfast cereals, cube sugar, high quality furniture, lollipop sticks, canned asparagus, bird seed, fifteen varieties of hair shampoo, ten different hand cleaners, five lipsticks, seven varieties of swimming pool paints, and ten varieties of pet foods. These corresponded to a vast expansion in local industrial production units (i.e., with ten or more workers) from 665 at UDI to 1,036 five years later, as the number of different products increased from 1,059 in 1967 to 3,837 in 1970 (Wield 1980:107, 127; Nyathi-Mdluli 1980:84). By 1971 it was said that the homes of even high-income whites could be entirely furnished with Rhodesian-made goods (Handford 1976:141). The backward and forward linkages of luxury goods production were tightly coordinated, aided by very high levels of corporate concentration within most sectors of the national economy.[4]

Even so, fixed capital investment remained relatively meager in manufacturing until 1973, and the capital intensity of industrial production remained inordinately low until the mid 1970s investment deluge. One calculation of the incremental capital-output ratio for manufacturing for 1971–74 was 1.76, as against comparable figures in developing countries of between 2.5 to 3.5 (World Bank 1983a:23). Moreover, thanks to import protection, Rhodesian manufacturers showed a learned capacity to produce on relatively "short runs" and thus, according to Handford (1976:145), local manufacturers had "the opportunity of taking immediate advantage of changes in market demands, in a way that is not possible with the great industrialised countries."

Extensive (capital-widening) rather than intensive (capital-deepening) investment was initially the rule not only in manufacturing but also in agriculture. White commercial farmers attributed 41% of their growth in output for 1965–74 to land expansion, which also involved increasing the number of black employees by 70,000 during that period. Notwithstanding the hardships inflicted by extremist Rhodesian Front land policies, peasant farmers also managed to increase their land under cultivation by 26% during the first few years of UDI, as output increased by 32%—hence four-fifths of growth was a result of land expansion (Mumbengegwi 1986:208). Uneven sectoral development between capital goods and consumer goods was, partly as a result, kept effectively in check for a full decade, even if unevenness in luxury versus basic needs consumption was increasing.

Also during this time, the balance of power in the industrial class struggle swung heavily towards capital, and a lowly 8% of gross industrial revenues were spent on black workers' wages in 1969. Even in the mid 1970s, with a liberation war underway, Handford (1976:145) could brag, "At present, possibly the biggest advantage enjoyed by Rhodesia in regard to the more developed nations is its absence of labor troubles." There were, interprets Lloyd Sachikonye (1986:251), no fewer than 68 trade union leaders in detention in 1973:

> It is scarcely surprising that in the 1960s and 1970s a dark cloud hovered over trade unionism in Zimbabwe. A decimation of the leadership of unions through its incarceration in detention or exile, the onerous labor laws, in addition to the dubious role of international labor institutions such as the Brussels-based International

Confederation of Free Trade Unions—all had a generally weakening impact on the unions.

In sum, not only did finance stimulate buying power, but at least three other accommodating features also help account for the success of UDI in broadening and deepening the economy: state-directed investments, the prior overcapacity in manufacturing, and an extremely repressed labor force. Sanctions and planned investment ensured that the law of value did not fully operate according to international norms. Capital expenditure did not become excessive until the mid 1970s, and overproduction tendencies were initially muted.

Initial explanations for the mid 1970s crisis

But an economy-wide downturn ultimately set in following the first UDI decade of growth. The manufacturing sector witnessed immense increases in accumulated stocks and inventories, and an extraordinary decline in capacity utilization. By all accounts, the resulting drought of industrial investment has remained the single major constraint on the economy's growth through the late 1970s, 1980s, and early 1990s. And efforts to displace the economic problems through space and through time also came to naught, as demonstrated below.

The late 1970s crisis was of Great Depression-scale. From 1974 to 1978, manufacturing production declined 27%, capacity utilization fell by 38%, and there was a net loss of 50,000 urban private sector jobs (from a peak of just over one million in the entire national economy), mainly in manufacturing and construction (World Bank 1989c:9).

How to explain this awesome slump? Economists have loosely interpreted Rhodesia's problems by recourse to a wide variety of factors exogenous to an internal logic of market failure. Riddell (1990:352–353), for example, cites:

- major political disruption and uncertainty (especially war);
- a series of poor agricultural seasons;
- the international rise in oil prices; and
- the increasing foreign-exchange dependence of manufacturing growth and decreasing role of manufactured exports in the economy.

But these are unsatisfactory, for several reasons. Sanctions, for example, cannot be held wholly responsible for long-term deterioration in income terms of trade, since they mainly affected export volumes (not export values or imports). In any case, by 1968 their effect was "negligible, causing a fall in export volumes of only about 5%," according to Rob Davies (1982:297–299). "Sanctions are likely to have had a once-and-for-all effect on the terms of trade, causing an initial but not a continuous deterioration." And international influences were muffled, as a brief global downturn in 1971 had no visible effect on the Rhodesian economy (GDP growth increased from 2.2% in 1970 to 8.8% in 1971 and 8.5% in 1972).

Even foreign exchange dependence of manufacturing production could not have been the crucial factor, since in 1975, when net capital investment in manufacturing reached a peak of R$125 million, manufacturing import allocations were a third lower than in 1974, when net capital investment was R$102 million. There were even greater capital investments in normally import-intense major projects (mining, electricity, and water supply) in 1976 and 1977, despite steadily diminishing foreign import allocations (Central Statistical Office, *Census of Production 1979/80,* 21; RAL *Executive Guide to the Economy,* December 1983).

Indeed most manufacturing subsectors had reached unprecedented levels of import self-sufficiency by the late 1970s, well after the crisis had set in. Exports as a percentage of imports in the manufacturing sector had risen from 15% in 1952 to 40% at UDI to more than 70% just prior to independence. Even in the metals and metal products sub-sector, the self-sufficiency ratio reached 70% by 1979. Foodstuffs, beverages and tobacco, textiles, clothing and footwear, and wood and furniture all recorded export levels far greater than import levels.

As for the war, this was the main reason for increased government spending—to more than 40% of GDP by 1979 (there was also extensive investment by the parastatal electricity supply authority, which recorded huge capital spending in 1975–78). While in aggregate economic terms the war may have been counter-cyclical during this period, nevertheless the skills shortages, social tensions, and physical destruction that accompanied it probably overpowered any economic stimulation. However, Davies (1982:300) argues that "Because of the substitution of black for white workers that has taken place, I would argue that the effects of the war on output have not been great, and that one has therefore to look elsewhere for the primary reasons for the recession."

Davies and Colin Stoneman (1981:95–96) instead take recourse in "underconsumption" as an explanation: "it is generally accepted that the discrimination against the rural population and the low level of black wages must have restricted the size of the internal market." Industrialists themselves viewed the problem primarily in these terms at particular junctures, with 57% of those polled by the University of Zimbabwe in 1981 (a year in which large real consumption increases actually occurred) citing insufficient domestic buying power as a factor constraining industrial expansion. It is true, too, that during 1974–78, as the recession hit black workers especially hard, larger purchases such as furniture (blacks made up 51% of the domestic market) and even clothing and footwear (68% of the market) suffered reductions of 28% and 12%, respectively (Wield 1980:128,107).

On the other hand, however, total consumption expenditure by private residents actually increased in real terms in 1974–76. The single most substantial annual decline in total consumption during the crisis was then 12% (in 1977), a smaller drop than that experienced elsewhere in the economy (for example, in manufacturing capacity utilization) (CSO, *National Income and Expenditure Report*). And while black wages were extremely low, the share of gross operating profits relative to wages was actually lowest (36%) in 1977 and 1978, the two years of deepest recession. Moreover, from 1978 to 1980, profits took a high and increasing share of national income, yet this was the period in which recovery began (Kadhani 1986:106). Moreover, while manufacturing and agricultural investment were devastated by the downturn, private consumption expenditure in the (mainly white) luxury-goods market was not nearly so badly affected, which in turn suggests that underconsumption was not obviously the driving force behind the crisis.

Stoneman (1981:281) quickly advanced beyond simple underconsumption theory by noting the disarticulation of production and consumption, in Rhodesia's notoriously skewed racial context:

> The market became more distorted in the direction of luxury consumption, a tendency reinforced by sanctions against imports. A number of manufacturing industries (in particular in food processing and clothing) had developed to supply black needs both domestically and in the Federation, and their attention was redirected to the white market... Much of the new industry has therefore been at the expense of far more urgently needed rural investment and is furthermore geared to supplying luxury products on a very small scale, rather than the basic requirements of the population as a whole.

This kind of uneven sectoral development closely matches other more general arguments about failed import substitution industrialization models in the Third World (de Janvry 1982).[5] Nevertheless, the blame for Rhodesia's crisis cannot be laid primarily at the door of low-income blacks' failure to gain access to "basic need" commodities relative to their consumption of these in prior years. Throughout the 1970s, the major food processing industries reflected the residual strength of consumption in both white high-income and black low-income markets. Beer suffered virtually no underconsumption crisis, and along with cigarettes, represented the largest single item (15%) of personal consumption expenditure. Similarly, meat processing and dairy products experienced significant build-up of inventories mainly during the few years occasioned by factors in the fields, but both subsectors continued growing in real terms during the four worst years of economic slump.

Finally, underspending in key counter-cyclical sectors (like construction) is not a convincing reason for the crisis because, if such were the case, post-independence state fiscal expansion and increased building activity would have led to a more sustainable growth path than was ultimately experienced. In sum, with factors such as investment, capacity utilization and production falling far faster and further than consumption, it is on the supply side, not the demand (underconsumption) side, that we might better focus our attention.

Overaccumulation crisis

While by no means denying the reality of (unquantifiable) exogenous problems, a classical Marxist approach attempts to unveil structural constraints to growth that continued well beyond the 1970s era of war, drought, high oil prices, and lack of foreign exchange. To follow this approach we can employ official data covering manufacturing output, investment, year-end inventories ("stocks"), and capacity utilization for evidence of overinvestment, overproduction and overaccumulation in the UDI economy.

Some aggregate data and a few graphs illustrate the intensity of the overaccumulation problem. Taking 1970 as a base year, in real terms, new investment rose by a factor of more than three by 1975, manufacturing output rose to levels 60% higher, and capacity utilization and profits rose significantly (Figure 5.2). During the process, plant and equipment grew enormously as the manufacturing process deepened substantially. In contrast to earlier small-scale, extensive investments, the mid 1970s investments were extremely capital-intensive (Figure 5.3).

Then, following the 1975 peak, ratios of inventories to output and especially of inventories to new investment soared, as the problem rapidly became full-blown (Figure 5.4). (This is as clear evidence of overaccumulation as may have existed at this point anywhere; yet it was by and large ignored by Rhodesia's period economists.[6]) Net profit rates as a percentage of gross national income rose to more than 20% in the early 1970s, but declined rapidly thereafter, to 12% in 1977 (Wield 1980:118).

Can the origins of overaccumulation be specifically pinpointed to a specific Department and sector of the economy? In Rhodesia, the rhythm of overaccumulation in various manufacturing subsectors relative to the growing overaccumulation crisis in the economy as a whole can be crudely measured as a ratio of year-end stocks to gross output, an "overaccumulation ratio" which for the manufacturing sector as a whole increased from 21% in 1970–73 to 28% in 1976, before falling to 24% at decade's end. It was an extremely high level at this stage, far higher than any comparable figure over the two-decade period for which data were recorded. This ratio suggests how the rhythm of overaccumulation affects various departments, sectors, and subsectors of the Rhodesian economy. (Table 5.1 provides overaccumulation ratios for 22 major manufacturing subsectors.)

Beginning with the sectors responsible for the greatest volume of manufacturing output—base metals, metal products, textiles, grain milling, dairy, fertilizers, and meat processing—it is clear that the worst overaccumulation (with ratios double the average in the late 1970s), was experienced in base metals (mainly steel). Moreover, the dramatic increase in steel overaccumulation from 1974 is timed exactly with the onset of general manufacturing stagnation. Metal products showed overaccumulation tendencies no worse than those of the economy at large, while textiles hit record levels of overaccumulation in 1975, 1976, and 1978, approximately 50% higher than the economy's average. Each of these sectors was producing some R$250 million in output by the end of the 1970s.

The next four major subsectoral sources of output, ranging from R$120 million to R$140 million by decade's end, were grain milling, dairy, fertilizers, and meat processing. These agriculture-driven sectors were profoundly affected by weather conditions, but their periodic introduction of new machinery also had some effect on the tendency to overaccumulation of stocks relative to output, as previous figures have demonstrated. Most importantly, however, because the capacity to hold such stocks is extremely limited, the overaccumulation ratios of these four subsectors in relation to those of the rest of the manufacturing sector were extremely low. Just as noticeable, was the tendency to increase stocks in the early 1970s rather than the mid and late 1970s.

Further unpredictable patterns of overaccumulation can be observed in the next most important sectors, namely clothing and transport (ranging from R$100 million to R$120 million by 1980), which both witnessed extremely high ratios in the early 1970s (in the vicinity of double the national average), followed by average ratios in the mid 1970s and an increase at decade's end. Other subsectors which drove the overaccumulation process in the mid 1970s (i.e., with a significantly higher ratio than the average from 1974–78) were tobacco and knitted products.

In sum, there is a relatively uneven sectoral pattern evident, with areas of potential export such as metals and textiles having vast overcapacity problems in the mid 1970s. It is difficult to pin this down to disproportionalities between departments of production. Instead, the importance of this data is in its reflection of the geographical limits to growth, a subject touched on shortly.

To put the mid 1970s problem into perspective, consider the period 1957–60, a time when the limits to spatial expansion in the Central African Federation were also drawing near. Those years experienced much higher real levels of net capital formation than any subsequent years save 1973–75. "The rather high industrial investments of the 1950s include plant which is by all accounts still in use in a number of branches and rather old," noted Wield (1980:111). The circumstances of the late 1960s—when relatively small volumes of industrial capital were invested in rather wide sectoral extensions—provided little scope for a full-fledged manufacturing transformation towards intensive export-orientation (as was happening in East Asia). (Rhodesian manufacturing investment was subsequently extremely intensive, but never achieved the economies of scale required for export-competitiveness.) The economy was cemented into a disarticulation of production and consumption that portended inevitable crisis at some stage, notwithstanding the impressive flexibility many producers showed within that framework.

Thus the nature—and depth—of the 1970s crisis of the Rhodesian economy was already predetermined, in a sense, by the ruling class failure to come to grips with the challenge of constructing a trajectory of sustainable accumulation during the early 1960s. In spite of the state's valiant efforts to balance investment in the appropriate sectors, UDI-era manufacturers placed exorbitant emphasis on luxury goods production for the domestic white market, rather than expanding into extensive low-cost basic consumer goods which might have helped generate increased buying power in the process and which would have had greater export potential into independent Africa. Not only did the political-economic climate overencourage producers of certain capital goods, it ultimately widened the socio-economic and political divisions between whites and blacks within Rhodesia. Soon, the depth of the economic crisis proved a greater threat to the business establishment than the prospect of government by nominally "Marxist-Leninist" forces, with whom business leaders increasingly sought reconciliation.[7]

This survey of overaccumulation in Rhodesia during the 1970s highlighted the relationship between investment and build-up of year-end stocks that was at the root of the economic slump. But overaccumulated capital may have been displaced, temporarily, or at least more effectively managed, were it not for other exogenous factors that drained the regenerative capacity of the productive sectors. To some degree, crisis displacement was subsequently attempted through both spatial and temporal processes, as described next. Both ultimately proved infeasible, and in order to deepen our insights into the depth and direction of Rhodesia's economic demise, it is worthwhile to examine why space and time did not displace capitalist crisis more potently, in contrast to experiences in other places—or even in Zimbabwe during the more recent period.

Geographical limits to crisis displacement

We have observed evidence of overaccumulation in Rhodesia in the form of a massive increase in unutilized plant, equipment, and stocks as well as unemployed workers. Capital had piled up in a variety of sectoral bottlenecks with fewer and fewer opportunities for reinvestment in the productive process. Devaluation of overaccumulated capital appeared inevitable, but as always would be resisted. Thus we turn to countervailing state-led strategies—in particular, expansion of public works projects and decentralization of industrial activity away from the main business centers (Salisbury and Bulawayo)—which were deployed, rather weakly, as a response to these problems.

In fact, in much of the world during the mid 1970s, geographical responses to overaccumulation were emerging at qualitatively greater scales. These often entailed dangerously high levels of government debt as the basis for expanding public infrastructure, often in outlying areas (beyond the major urban centers). In part this strategy reflected the inability of the market to lead new geographical investment, at a time when a global property market collapse sent clear signals that new construction offered an unattractive outlet for overaccumulated capital.

This was also true in Rhodesia's case, where the property market collapse was all the more devastating because the previous round of activity was due, in such large measure, to the excessive availability of housing finance. Building society loan policies heralded the collapse of real estate in 1975 (a year in which real gross fixed capital formation was near the 1974 record and in which real gross domestic product, gross national income, and private consumption expenditure all continued to rise). The societies' mortgage originations dropped 53% in nominal terms from 1974 (R$77 million) to 1975 (R$36 million). Whereas it appears that the societies had earlier pushed the real estate boom, their exit accentuated its collapse. Taking together all real estate investments, building societies controlled more than 40% of the bond market during the decade (except 1975–76, when commercial banks played a larger role by default).

The disintegration of the property market is illustrated by the decline in the total nominal value of total commercial, industrial, and residential sales in Salisbury (which has always represented more than half of the country's total real estate market) from R$87.4 million in 1974 to R$40.6 million in 1977. The number of construction industry employees had risen from 45,000 in 1970 to more than 63,000 in 1974, but dropped back to fewer than 40,000 in 1979. Investors recognised the problem of overbuilding, and in any case real estate was considered too long-term an investment in such politically uncertain circumstances. Even staid pension and provident funds rapidly disinvested their property loans and building society shares at a rate of more than 10% per year during the late 1970s, and insurance companies pulled back even faster.

With the market's failure to explore geographical outlets for liquid capital, the state initially undertook to shift funds into gross fixed capital formation of various sorts. Central government and public enterprises increased their share of total capital formation from 37% in 1974 to 43% in 1976 largely on the strength of military infrastructure, black township housing, posts and railways and water/electricity supply investments. However, the ratio steadily declined as government expenditure was subsequently redirected towards recurrent war costs. (The brutal nature of counterinsurgency imposed other constraints to geographical expansion and in the process further accentuated rural underdevelopment.)

As even state investments failed to mop up overaccumulated capital, another geographical strategy presented itself as a socio-economic option. In many parts of the world during the 1970s the locational pattern of cities within regions was being placed on the agenda more urgently than ever before. Officials in underdeveloped territories kicked off new rounds of interurban and interregional competition between themselves through promotion of decentralised investment, including the establishment of capital cities in their hinterlands.[8] Often decentralization policies were inspired by efforts by central governments of any and all persuasions to establish "growth poles" in underdeveloped regions within their boundaries.

Decentralization of investment was the subject of long-running debates in Rhodesia. As economic crisis and war intensified in the late 1970s, the urban/rural divide was more striking than ever. Planners traced regional underdevelopment to the suboptimal location and the lack of maturity of secondary economic centers. Basing their analytical framework on a theory of an urban-rural "dual economy," they generally advocated the extension of urban market-related institutions and systems (such as credit) into geographical areas not fully penetrated by the market.

The implications of this framework for Rhodesia's emerging regional policy are important. "Urbanization is well developed at the upper levels but poorly developed at all other levels," according to a seminal 1978 study by Robin Heath (1990:179, 181). "If the growth of medium-sized cities can be encouraged by implementing a vigorous policy of decentralization, they may become true 'growth points,' each serving separate regions, attracting migrants from surrounding rural areas, and contributing significantly to the national economy and overall national development." This sort of logic emerged from an idealised notion that the spatial extension of capital would improve the lot of the rural peasant. It was a particularly easy recommendation to make at a time when urban markets were relatively saturated with investment, as was the case in the mid and late 1970s.

Thus, in 1974, the state launched an initial attempt to address the question of regional and rural underdevelopment through a White Paper, but this "failed to offer specific incentives or disincentives, or to promote particular growth points in the Tribal Trust Lands (TTLs), expressing instead merely a desire for decentralization anywhere outside Salisbury," according to Dennis Davies (1981:76), who labelled it "a pre-majority rule concept concerned only with the developed parts of the national space economy." Subsequently, a 1976 Regional Town and Country Planning Act delineated six planning regions, which were hopelessly biased towards administrative not functional boundaries.

By 1978 a revised policy was issued. According to Heath, "Official thinking appears to be that if 'growth points' can be created in the TTLs, regional disparity will be lessened and the economic development of the problem areas will be boosted."[9] Economic functionality was behind this approach ("consultation" with community residents was given lip service and ignored in practice). But the intellectual reliance upon both orthodox planning models (such as Christaller central place theory) and the dual economy thesis, which saw the trees but not the forest, ensured that the root causes of uneven regional development would be ignored.

In fact, moderate as it was in reconstituting spatial relations, the regional development scheme was adopted in modified form by the Zimbabwean government after independence. Its lack of real potential to "solve" uneven development (particularly rural underdevelopment), though, is probably a function of the *overdevelopment* of urban centers. The cities were shaped by factors such as the substantial flow of capital into white suburban-sprawl development and to a lesser extent into Salisbury CBD property. And intensive investment processes had, by the mid 1970s, cemented into the Rhodesian economy such powerful overaccumulation tendencies in the key cities and towns that there appeared no feasible short-term geographical outlet for those funds. Outside of the half-dozen main manufacturing centers, nowhere else in Rhodesia could begin to offer the requirisite infrastructure, amenities, or reserves of skilled labor, given that the basic disarticulated structure of the economy was not seriously challenged by the planners.

On balance, therefore, geographical strategies—whether through public investment programs or through decentralized private investment—proved a relatively ineffectual factor in crisis resolution at the time it was most desperately needed, during the late 1970s: this is one reason for the great depth of the downturn that Rhodesia experienced. The contrast with other times and places is evident enough. For example, during the 1950s Southern Rhodesian industrialists and farmers could depend (for at least a few years) upon expanding Federation and international markets in order to overcome the tendency to overaccumulation. Likewise, in South Africa during the 1970s there was a powerful, multi-faceted geographical approach to the displacement of overaccumulation, one implemented by capital as well as government. In contrast, such spatial routes were barricaded in late 1970s Rhodesia.

What was most wrong, it appears, is that massive and ultimately extravagant *intensive* manufacturing and mining investments characterised the mid-1970s. These consequently made it difficult for state and capital to accomplish a smooth and sustainable switch of funds into more spatially and sectorally *extensive* productive circuits. Moreover, the ability of the state to increase infrastructural investments (water and electricity) or black housing in counter-cyclical fashion during the late 1970s was constrained by mounting budget deficits and by war. The war itself may have provided some stimulation to the besieged economy, yet to the degree that it amplified uneven sectoral development by drawing resources into military production, this further curtailed buying power in the consumer market, as witnessed by ever-higher levels of taxation and the interruption of rural trade in many areas. Furthermore, there were diminishing prospects for further import-substitutions given the small absolute size of local markets.

As a result, uneven geographical development was also accentuated during the late 1970s crisis. By the mid 1970s intensification of production processes in industrial districts, in mines, and on commercial farms centralised investment and led to even more inequality in urban, rural, and regional development. The towns were overwhelmed by flows of war refugees, at the same time employment levels in the urban manufacturing sector suffered enormously, and there were also deep (white) emigration-related cuts in domestic services employment (black maids and gardeners). Commercial farms were in the midst of their purge of farmworkers, which affected (between 1974 and 1983) some 100,000 employees and their families.

The Rhodesian Front regime is largely to blame for the way the brunt of the crisis was borne by those in society who were already worst off. Yet the preceding litany of geographical unevenness and human degradation is not the full story. Many of the other factors determining the economy's spatial limits—world recessionary barriers to exports, the intensive (not spatially extensive) nature of the mid-1970s investment wave, the limited buying power for housing commodification in black townships, overproduction (and subsequent land underutilization) on commercial and communal farms—can be traced not merely to state oppression and neglect, but quite directly to the very laws of motion of Rhodesian capitalism.

Neither is this meant to excuse the Rhodesian Front regime for failing to creatively invest surpluses that had built up in the economy. However, it is to argue that the geographical barriers to growth were substantial and that, in a sense, capital imposed some of these upon itself. The proof of the argument lies in the endurance of the distorted geographic logic of capitalism following independence.

In sum, given the contingencies of the UDI period, all these diverse geographical factors ultimately limited rather than enhanced the capacity of capitalists and policy-makers alike to cope with the economic crisis by systematically displacing it across space. Perhaps even more troublesome, in contrast to the deepening of financial markets during the previous (late 1950s) period of overaccumulation crisis, a new set of constraints emerged in the 1970s which prevented a temporal solution through recourse to finance.

Temporal limits to crisis displacement

Across the world the 1970s and 1980s were littered with attempts to expand financial markets in a manner which effectively (if only temporarily) displaced overaccumulated capital through time, and in the process provided the illusion that economic stagnation was being postponed indefinitely (Magdoff and Sweezy 1987).

Indeed, by paying attention specifically to developments in the Rhodesian financial system, a great deal more about UDI-era economic processes and state policies in general can be understood. For one, the financial system played a short-lived role in capturing some flows of funds directed away from the circuit of productive capital by manufacturing firms. However, notwithstanding a tightened monetary policy in the late 1970s, the low rate of return on financial assets—and especially the lack of likely speculative outlets—limited the attraction of the financial circuit to increasingly liquid investors. In any case, long-term financial investments were to be avoided in view of the generalised search for greater liquidity that was underway as an uncertain political transition approached.

In 1974-75, as manufacturing fixed capital investments peaked, there were noticeable shifts in funding flows between productive and financial circuits. As overaccumulation became apparent, Rhodesia's four commercial banks were the immediate beneficiaries. When they offered a new three-year time deposit, their fixed and savings deposits soared to extraordinary levels—R$313 million in 1975 (a 92% increase over 1974)—partly on the basis of R$15 million in new funds drawn from firms in manufacturing, mining, and agriculture (Figure 5.5). Indeed, from 1973–77, the share of GDP contributed by finance and insurance rose impressively from 3.9% to 6.6%. Bank profits were consistently strong, and in relation to total gross operating profits jumped from 1% in 1965 to nearly 5% in 1977 (although they receded when industrial capital subsequently began to recover).

Later, the banks' tendency towards a relative "delinking" from industry under such conditions was subsequently confirmed by a rapid decrease in loans to manufacturing and mining concomitant with a slight increase in loans to finance and insurance companies between 1976 and 1979. Financial sector borrowers were the only ones to increase their debts to commercial banks in real terms in the late 1970s, as even public sector borrowing declined, which suggests the depth of the overinvestment crisis.[10]

On the other hand, even bank accounts were not without a risk component for depositors, since potential nationalization of the country's banks was beginning to be taken seriously by 1978, with Rhobank publicly lobbying against it (Clarke 1980a:106). Bank nationalization was the one sustained radical proposal made during subsequent UNCTAD discussions (Stoneman and Cliffe 1989:42).

Overall, though, there was an absolute lack of viable speculative investment prospects. Aside from bank deposits, which provided listless returns, other outlets for holders of liquid funds looked even gloomier as the downturn deepened and as foreboding political change grew closer. The real estate market had crashed decisively and the Rhodesian Stock Exchange offered little relief, as it only began a mild recovery in 1978, with turnover well below the level reached in 1980. Insurance company investments in property, stocks, and shares were anemic in 1978 and 1979.

Soon another important funding shift occurred within the financial system. Liquidity rose significantly as the transition to majority rule approached. In 1975, financial liquidity levels were generally close to the regulatory minimum required for building societies and finance houses, but over time they increased considerably in all financial institutions (banks, for example, at one point in 1979 held R$120 million more in liquid assets than required). In 1977, investors moved tens of millions of dollars from the commercial banks to a "flexi-deposit" scheme of the building societies which featured easier liquidity. Then investors switched time deposits worth tens of millions of dollars into yet more liquid savings and checking accounts (demand deposits) in commercial banks, with the outflow peaking in March 1980, a month before the election. Similarly, the "cash-on-hand" of pension and provident funds rose from R$25 million in 1978 to R$48 million in 1980.

In sum, the expansion of the financial sector in the last years of the Rhodesian economy was not sustainable under conditions where liquid funds could simply not be invested in well-established speculative markets such as shares and property. Partly because of the anticipated political turmoil, partly because with regulated interest rates and innumerable restrictions the returns on financial assets were low, and partly because the emergence of overaccumulation in the productive sectors was relatively recent, the Rhodesian financial circuit lacked the prospects for growth and power evident in many other parts of the world. A decade later, things would be very different, partly as a result of state policies adopted soon thereafter, which for the most part were sustained into the 1980s.

State financial policy and politics

There are several areas of financial policy to consider. First, the devaluation of the Rhodesian dollar in the mid 1970s represented an about-face on a twenty-five year old practice. Second, a relatively conservative monetary policy continued to exist simultaneously with an active counter-cyclical fiscal policy. Finally, in broader debates about the impact of the transition to majority rule, financial capital played a nearly invisible role.

In 1975 the Rhodesian dollar was devalued by 10% against the South African rand and 8% against major currencies. In late 1977, Rhodesia announced another 3% devaluation against the rand and 6% against the major currencies. And again in April 1978, there was a devaluation, this time 5% against the rand and 8% against the major currencies. Exchange controls—especially multinational corporate profit repatriation—were toughened marginally in 1976, reflecting an emerging foreign exchange crisis as Rhodesia's net foreign assets declined.

Simultaneously, in real terms monetary growth slowed in 1975 and 1977, and monetary velocity slowed even in years (1976, 1978, 1979) that the money supply increased, thanks to what Xavier Kadhani (1986:106) calls "radically restrictionist policies of the classical IMF short-run stabilization variety." As Reginald Green (1985:61) suggests, "Over 1974–79 Rhodesia (as it then was) ran an IMF type stabilization programme—for different reasons and also without using Fund resources." Yet the bank rate was consistent at 4.5% and treasury bills were offered at a low 3.5%, so this was not a case of a restrictive interest rate-based monetary policy. Instead the Reserve Bank's "compensatory monetary policy" allowed the money supply to expand gradually. Only in May 1979 were liquid asset requirement ratios of the banking sector increased by 10%. As statistics cited earlier suggest, liquidity in financial markets remained high. The "IMF short-run stabilization" effect was apparently achieved through higher taxes (including a huge 12% surcharge imposed in 1977) and wage restraint, which together were key vehicles for slowing consumer spending.

But while the brakes were on for monetary expansion, the accelerator was pushed down hard on state spending. The government budget deficit reached an alarming 15% of GDP in 1979, nearly entirely funded by domestic sources.[11] But the use made of the capital markets by investment authorities was probably not optimal. Fiscal policy could have played a stronger counter-cyclical role if even more borrowing had replaced the tax increases and also if longer-term infrastructural investments had taken the place of huge recurrent war costs. And while the Finance Ministry and Reserve Bank adopted an excessive degree of monetary conservatism in the late 1970s—pleasing to equally-conservative bankers concerned about rising inflation and the potential for currency degradation—the corresponding deflationary impact on the economy did little to pave the way for a smoother political settlement.

And indeed there exists little concrete evidence of a positive role played by financial institutions in the political transition. What little information there is does not contradict the general thrust of these conservative trends. Local financiers tried, for example, to attract foreign investors and donors to Rhodesia. This would have more than a psychological impact—it would also tie the future state to the dictates of foreign creditors (including the parents of the Rhodesian bank branches) (Windrich 1978:49).

However, notwithstanding promises of billions of dollars in development finance by British and US negotiators in the event of a political settlement, relatively tight financial sanctions prevented international financiers from playing anything beyond a very minor role in the Rhodesian economy (in contrast to South Africa's a few years' later) (Bond 1991a). Nor was there any discernable role in the Lancaster House settlement (aside from financial aid to the combined ZANU–ZAPU Patriotic Front from the Bank of Credit and Commerce International).

There was, of course, the ubiquitous World Bank, still concerned about pre–UDI era projects and outstanding loans, as well as the transition process. Back in 1966, a top Bank official had served as an "obscure" back-channel between Prime Minister Wilson and Ian Smith (Joyce 1974:327) and, over time, the Bank's involvement became more direct. As Robert Mugabe (1979:i) put it,

> In the wake of the escalating war and the flight of so many European settlers, an African petit-bourgeoisie is being formed very rapidly as Africans move into white farms, suburban homes and even jobs. In 1974, with the help of the World Bank, local European businessmen launched a fund and a Foundation, called the Whitsun Foundation, to provide capital to the new black petit-bourgeoisie to buy property and to initiate a variety of economic studies. The national development plan proposed by the Foundation is a blueprint for neocolonialism that militates against the freedom of the future independent State of Zimbabwe to embark upon programs for socialist transformation.

These words proved prophetic. Both the Bank and the Whitsun Foundation strongly promoted credit expansion as a rational—and still profoundly market-oriented—approach to post-independence "development." However, in contrast to such far-sighted liberal initiatives, local financial institutions played only a muted role in the political transition, in spite of their economic power.

While Rhobank, for example, called for "a planned transition to majority rule" in late 1978, it argued that "expanded credit and loan facilities to indigenous entrepreneurs should not itself be a criterion but should occur as a process of upliftment of these individuals through improved basic technical know-how and information" (Clarke 1980a:106). Other banks appeared far less psychologically prepared for the transition, for as Neva Seidman Makgetla (1983:IX,10) points out, Standard banned the use of African languages (even for relaxation) during working hours in 1978, and both Standard and Barclays officially opposed equal pay for women employees who were said to be of "less value" than men in the same jobs.

In sum, the attempt to find a temporal means of displacing overaccumulation through expansion of the financial sector—both in terms of assets and in terms of political power—was not effective. Ultimately, for a variety of contingent reasons, the rise of finance was truncated and politically irrelevant.

Conclusion: Financial repression and political transition

This chapter has explored aspects of the rise and fall of Rhodesia's UDI economy. We noted, in particular, that overaccumulation crisis was characterised by unevenness of investment, output and consumption between the luxury and basic consumer goods industries and certain of the capital goods industries. In part this sectoral unevenness can be attributed to particularly malevolent reactions by state and capital to economic crisis and guerrilla war, which made for increasing disparities of income and power between races and between classes. What is most important is that industrial overinvestment in the mid 1970s is mainly what underlies the subsequent prolonged period of underinvestment.

This is not an uncontroversial finding, because during the late 1970s even self-described Marxist researchers adopted a variety of non-structural interpretations of the most pressing issues: the impact of sanctions, the scope for post-independence redistribution, economic power relations, engagement with the international system, the forthcoming "transition to socialism" (see the survey by Burdette and Davies 1987). There was, unfortunately, very little effort to root these issues in the dynamics of sectoral accumulation, space, and time. Instead both the 1970s crisis and the stagnation which enveloped Zimbabwe for much of the next decade was either attributed to exogenous, once-off factors, or too closely derived from the international crisis, or at best seen merely in terms of "underconsumption" (only one half of the equation). Deeper problems in sustaining accumulation, following the deluge of mid 1970s capital investments, were passed over without comment, and their longer-term ramifications—such as tendencies towards increased financial liquidity, corporate indebtedness and speculation, all of which exploded in the late 1980s—were largely ignored.

In contrast, this chapter identified overaccumulation as the underlying economic dynamic of the 1970s, and showed how displacement of overaccumulated capital across space and through time was half-hearted and infeasible. As previous chapters suggested, the role of space in crisis displacement appears initially as a palliative, a geographical solution to overaccumulation tendencies, a means of removing excessively liquid capital from one place to another in search of higher returns. But geographical extension can also magnify underlying problems, especially if the strategy amounts merely to the reproduction of existing relations in new spaces. New spaces for accumulation were hard to find in 1970s Rhodesia, and so, internally, uneven spatial development was accentuated, especially between town and countryside.

Time was just as ambiguous a factor in both crisis formation and late 1970s attempts at its resolution. This was partly because of the immobilising effect of the huge fixed capital investments of 1973–76, and, later, because of limited prospects for political stability that the Rhodesian Front could offer investors. But perhaps the most important barrier to expanding time horizons was the relative lack of power of financial elites even in the late 1970s.

Credit usually offers the most efficient means of displacing crisis through time. Domestic credit expansion might have helped, but was not possible. Finance was ascendant in the late 1970s at exactly the stage of accumulation that credit demand collapsed, broader monetary discipline was applied, and political uncertainty peaked. Moreover, Rhodesia (unlike so many semi-peripheral economies) had no real access to foreign loans, which were the vehicle for so much international crisis displacement during the 1970s. In any event, the main basis for foreign loans to a Rhodesian economy already suffering severe overaccumulation would have been in expanding the economy's spatial horizons through development projects (transport, communications, energy, water, and the like), as was occurring throughout the Third World at the time. This route, we have suggested, was strewn with difficulties in Rhodesia. Thus in spite of its enhanced profitability, finance continued to exhibit characteristics of repression, not expansion and strength.

At the end of the day, only a political transition would (temporarily) remove the geographical and temporal constraints to crisis displacement. From the time of Britain's Pearce Commission—which in 1972 found overwhelming opposition to any settlement that left intact the racial pillars of Rhodesian colonialism—Handford (1976:29) discerned a "dramatic mood change" among whites: "From now on the general feeling was that something always seemed to be going wrong." There ultimately emerged a powerful psychological sense, from 1977 or so, of the difficulty of displacing the economic crisis to a future time through long-term public works infrastructural investment (especially when that investment came under increasing military attack). Notwithstanding the barrage of official propaganda about the unpopularity of the Patriotic Front amongst the masses, smart investors turned decidedly liquid during the late 1970s, fearing the eventual outcome, a government led by Mugabe and the nominally-socialist ZANU.

What then, of finance during the UDI era? The political significance of financial repression becomes fairly clear at this point. There was, during the late 1970s, a belated and incomplete rise in financial power, and the social role of financiers was nothing like it had been two decades earlier (or a decade later). There was, simultaneously, a belated effort to set the stage for a transition of formal state power to black nationalists that would retain the basic features of the Rhodesian capitalist system, but in deracialised form. Ideally, this would have been substantially assisted by infusions of credit into black townships, rural areas, and small black-owned businesses.

To this end, the most substantial credit-oriented rational capitalist programme—that of the Whitsun Foundation—revealed the influence of the World Bank and its ideas. Yet this was not a period in which international-scale geopolitical considerations or the power of international financial institutions were anywhere near as dominant over Zimbabwean nationalists as they would later be. And Rhodesian financiers had not yet discovered any truly effective means of providing sustainable, large-scale levels of credit to black borrowers (with the exception of those from the middle classes beginning to desegregate the northern suburbs). This was due, as usual, to insufficient levels of black consumer buying power. But it was also due to restrictive monetary policy and tight controls on finance (including, until a very late stage, laws regulating black land ownership). Ultimately, the scope for a finance-driven economic reform strategy was, ultimately, uneven and basically unsuccessful.

The termination of colonial-capitalist Rhodesia, at Lancaster House, was therefore less influenced by the emerging (but very low-key) financial elite, and more by residual military calculations. But before long, the sustained nature of the economic crisis of neo-colonial capitalism eventually paved the way for the hegemony of finance over crucial aspects of Zimbabwe's uneven development, as subsequent chapters demonstrate.

Nevertheless, what is striking about the partial rise of financial markets during this period is that, notwithstanding a set of political and policy-related contingencies that limited the operation of geographical and temporal strategies through finance, the underlying tendency was indeed operative: *overaccumulated capital flowed out of fixed manufacturing capital investment and into the financial markets.*

It was only in the mid and late 1980s that this tendency was given free reign, and that the long-term crisis of stagnation experienced by Zimbabwean capitalists, whose roots we have traced to their vast overinvestment in fixed capital during the mid 1970s, ultimately led to a full transformation in the nature of the Zimbabwean economy. But this was not a transition to a socialist Zimbabwe, as the liberation movement promised, but ultimately to a decontrolled, deregulated, peripheralised capitalism subservient to extremely powerful international and local financial markets.

Notes

1. Manufacturing subsectors which grew especially quickly through domestic market expansion were transport equipment (whose growth was entirely due to domestic demand), beverages and tobacco processing (93% due to domestic demand), construction materials (88%), chemical and pharmaceutical products (77%), and foodstuffs (75%). In contrast, import substitutions were made to good effect mainly in textiles (responsible for 56% of the subsector's growth), metals (37%) and paper products (37%), while exports during UDI were nearly insignificant, making an impression only in textiles (responsible for 14% of growth) and metals (13%).
2. For summaries of various institutional aspects of the financial system in the first years of UDI see Grant-Suttie 1965; Beak 1967; Sowelem 1967; Askes 1971; Cole 1973a, 1973b, 1973c, 1974; Clarke 1980a, 1980b; Chimombe 1983; Makgetla 1983; and Seidman 1986.
3. This rare publicised case of financial sanctions-busting is instructive. The US$63 million deal doubled Rhodesia's iron and steel production capacity, and involved a US$29 million loan, split between the Austrian equipment vendor (Voest), the Union Bank of Switzerland, European-American Bank and the Austrian bank Girozentrale (which expressed nervousness at the implications of the deal for UN Secretary-General Kurt Waldheim, an Austrian). A clause was even inserted to ensure immediate repayment of the loan in the event of "political risk." Rhodesian offices of Standard, Rhodesian Acceptances Limited, Barclays, Merchant Bank of Central Africa, National and Grindlays, and Neficrho Acceptances put up a guarantee, and other local financing came from SA Mutual insurance, Central African Building Society and Founders Building Society. A South African "dummy" corporation was established by the Rhodesians as the borrower, and a shell financier was set up in Zug, Switzerland "to satisfy Swiss authorities." With so many actors involved, the loan was sure to be exposed. Within eighteen months a British banker living in Rhodesia slipped information to the *Sunday Times* (14/4/74), and subsequently fled to Malawi. There, however, he was arrested, extradited to Salisbury and briefly jailed in 1974 (United Nations 1975).
4. Bennell (1991:5) found that in 1970 Rhodesia's four firm concentration ratio in most manufacturing subsectors was extremely high, and he observed "the growing dominance of large enterprises" during the subsequent fifteen years.
5. According to Nixson (1982:50), "ISI does not in general result in greater self-reliance or self-sufficiency. ISI has been heavily dependent on foreign capital, technology and expertise, it has been based on the consumption patterns, tastes, marketing techniques, and so on, of the developed capitalist economies and the changes in the import structure and the failure to alleviate the balance-of-payments constraint have exacerbated the dependence of the IS economy on the external sector."
6. There was a single Zimbabwean researcher who put a finger on the theo-

retical basis for the crisis of manufacturing overaccumulation—if only partially and momentarily—and it is worth recording this. Angela Cheater (1986:143-149) examined "Zimtex" (a pseudonym for a major textile firm in the Midlands), and discovered a clear "crisis of overproduction" in the early 1980s. However, Cheater's subsequent analysis reveals a naive expectation that the "The orthodox marxist view [of] crises of capitalism, such as the one which Zimtex faced," would lead to a resolution in the interests of the working-class through intervention by what in reality was a state-capitalist (not "Marxist-Leninist") post-independence government.

7. The Centre for African Studies (1979:42) printed a series of statements of local business leaders, who, from mid 1976, finally established that "white minority rule is an anachronism."
8. Rhodesia may have been tempted to follow the highly visible model of South Africa. In large part through mid 1970s foreign borrowings, Pretoria financed wide-ranging parastatal expansion, emphasising improvements in transport and communications, and the extension of electricity grids and water supply. The Vorster regime was also in the midst of an ultimately futile effort to prop up its Bantustans with regional decentralisation initiatives. By the early 1980s this had degenerated to giving billions of rands in incentives to Afrikaner, Taiwanese and Israeli industrialists in order to attract them to "deconcentration points" (Tomlinson and Addleson 1987; Bond 1992b).
9. Some of the new growth centres would serve barren, arid areas (Sanyati in Mashonaland West, and Tshotsholo and Nkai in Matabeleland North); others would centralise livestock (Maphisa, Mataga, Ngundu and Rutenga in Matabeleland South); others still would support mining and forestry (Chisumbanje, Pungwe and Hauna in the eastern highlands); and others would serve densely-populated regions (Mharadzano, Gutu, Nyka, Jerera). Basic services to be offered included town planning, infrastructure development, building and housing construction, and business promotion.
10. Under the prevailing conditions, however, it would be wrong to treat these symptoms of a rising financial circuit of capital—in particular the large 1975 bank deposits by industrialists—as "speculative." The rate of return on financial assets was often guaranteed (especially in time deposits) and was generally negative in real terms. Indeed negative real interest rates were common across the developing world prior to the 1980s-90s era of positive real rates. (For a defense of the policy in relation to productive sector growth, see Burkett and Dutt 1991.)
11. Aside from the illegal US$29 million loan for RISCO in the early 1970s and a US$15 million loan floated in the Eurodollar market in 1978, there were no other placements to speak of. Although a public sector loan of R$195 million was arranged from South Africa to cover deficits in 1978 and 1979, total foreign liabilities declined by 40% during the 1970s.

Table 5.1 Manufacturing Overaccumulation, 1970s
Year-end stocks/Gross output
and sector ratio in relation to manufacturing average

Sector (inflation adjusted to $1980)

(1975 output)	ratio	1970	1971	1972	1973	1974	1975	1976	1977	1978	1979
manufacturing average		.206	.210	.214	.213	.229	.255	.279	.271	.257	.237
	ratio	**100**	**100**	**100**	**100**	**100**	**100**	**100**	**100**	**100**	**100**
1. base metals		.228	.301	.318	.283	.276	.384	.396	.588	.548	.515
(R$238m)	**ratio**	**110**	**143**	**149**	**133**	**121**	**151**	**142**	**217**	**213**	**217**
2. metal products		.236	.213	.199	.229	.255	.270	.260	.272	.249	.244
(R$212m)	**ratio**	**115**	**101**	**93**	**107**	**111**	**106**	**93**	**100**	**97**	**103**
3. electrical machinery		.258	.242	.243	.248	.273	.249	.316	.347	.307	.249
(R$60m)	**ratio**	**125**	**115**	**114**	**117**	**119**	**98**	**113**	**128**	**119**	**105**
4. rubber		.198	.175	.176	.272	.268	.219	.238	.260	.273	.251
(R$37m)	**ratio**	**96**	**83**	**82**	**128**	**117**	**86**	**86**	**96**	**106**	**106**
5. transport		.289	.280	.417	.336	.325	.299	.319	.316	.321	.316
(R$80m)	**ratio**	**115**	**180**	**169**	**176**	**168**	**206**	**258**	**116**	**88**	**91**
6. bricks/clay		.105	.113	.109	.136	.163	.199	.272	.329	.213	.197
(R$11m)	**ratio**	**51**	**54**	**51**	**64**	**71**	**78**	**97**	**121**	**83**	**83**
7. construction mat.		.205	.224	.192	.165	.188	.202	.241	.284	.335	.341
(R$63m)	**ratio**	**100**	**107**	**90**	**77**	**82**	**79**	**86**	**105**	**130**	**144**
8. fertilizers		.226	.165	.188	.150	.193	.245	.198	.161	.173	.202
(R$107m)	**ratio**	**110**	**79**	**88**	**70**	**84**	**96**	**71**	**59**	**67**	**85**
9. meat products		.071	.064	.119	.072	.064	.071	.106	.172	.127	.080
(R$128)	**ratio**	**35**	**31**	**56**	**34**	**28**	**28**	**38**	**63**	**49**	**34**
10. grains		.087	.103	.113	.129	.162	.129	.129	.105	.102	.103
(R$96m)	**ratio**	**42**	**49**	**53**	**61**	**71**	**51**	**46**	**39**	**40**	**43**
11. tobacco products		.296	.256	258	.236	.441	.354	.338	.400	.360	.249
(R$43m)	**ratio**	**144**	**122**	**121**	**111**	**193**	**139**	**121**	**148**	**140**	**105**
12. dairy products		.133	.157	.200	.215	.182	.227	.201	.227	.219	.216
(R$119m)	**ratio**	**65**	**75**	**93**	**101**	**80**	**89**	**72**	**84**	**85**	**91**
13. beer/wine		.114	.085	.095	.105	.136	.166	.221	.189	.162	.149
(R$74m)	**ratio**	**55**	**41**	**44**	**50**	**60**	**65**	**79**	**70**	**63**	**63**
14. textiles		.254	.186	.220	.287	.243	.372	.416	.330	.394	.325
(R$176)	**ratio**	**123**	**88**	**103**	**135**	**106**	**146**	**149**	**122**	**154**	**137**
15. knitted products		.380	.401	.403	.347	.407	.466	.455	.479	.440	.409
(R$26m)	**ratio**	**185**	**191**	**189**	**163**	**177**	**183**	**163**	**177**	**171**	**173**
16. clothing		.334	.436	.322	.312	.318	.294	.290	.281	.291	.289
(R$102)	**ratio**	**162**	**208**	**150**	**147**	**139**	**115**	**104**	**104**	**113**	**122**
17. footwear		.280	.242	.257	.281	.271	.213	.248	.257	.228	.259
(R$36m)	**ratio**	**136**	**115**	**120**	**132**	**119**	**84**	**89**	**95**	**89**	**109**
18. furniture		.237	.251	.219	.213	.267	.231	.224	.255	.262	.259
(R$31m)	**ratio**	**115**	**124**	**102**	**100**	**117**	**91**	**80**	**94**	**102**	**109**
19. wood products		.194	.207	.221	.189	.236	.250	.234	.204	.169	.146
(R$26m)	**ratio**	**94**	**98**	**103**	**89**	**103**	**98**	**84**	**75**	**66**	**62**
20. paper products		.224	.222	.195	.198	.221	.241	.240	.277	.233	.219
(R$62m)	**ratio**	**109**	**106**	**91**	**93**	**97**	**94**	**86**	**102**	**91**	**93**
21. printing		.152	.138	.162	.172	.171	.205	.210	.196	.176	.191
(R$54m)	**ratio**	**74**	**66**	**76**	**81**	**75**	**81**	**75**	**72**	**69**	**83**
22. pharmaceuticals		.255	.267	.240	.232	.318	.339	.305	.303	.297	.271
(R$63m)	**ratio**	**124**	**127**	**112**	**109**	**139**	**133**	**109**	**112**	**115**	**143**

Part Three

Finance and Uneven Development in Zimbabwe

chapter six

Post-Independence "Socialism," Nationalism, and Capitalist Stagnation

Introduction

In the last chapter, the 1960s boom and 1970s economic crisis were explained in large part using classical Marxist insights about the push and pull factors which direct flows of capital into different sectors over space and time. Under the prevailing conditions, very little scope existed for tightly-controlled financial markets to operate freely, to send liquid capital into more auspicious investments, or to exercise control over the direction of the country's political evolution during the transition from Rhodesia to Zimbabwe. But following independence in April 1980, the relative power and importance of financial flows in the economy changed dramatically. In view of the fact that subsequent chapters are devoted to speculation, debt and financial control issues, this chapter downplays the financial aspects of uneven development so as to turn attention to the underlying conditions of stagnation in the productive sectors of the economy.

The perseverance of economic stagnation is, by nearly all accounts, the single most important constraint Zimbabwe experienced in its political and social life since independence. (As structural adjustment policies did their damage in the early 1990s, there was a perceptible shift from nagging concerns amongst even the business elite over stagnation to outright panic regarding the growing prospect of full-fledged deindustrialization.) The legacy of stagnation is very often blamed in popular discourse on ZANU's 1980s "socialist" orientation, which requires a bit of debunking. In reality many of the policies adopted by the new government in the field of economic development represented continuity from the worst of Rhodesian state capitalism, rather than change. Ironically, perhaps, it was as a result of the failure of such policies that the opportunity arose for the power of finance to make itself felt. Throughout the 1980s, the existing economic structure—classic monopoly capitalism, with key sectors still controlled by whites and foreign companies—and many supportive state policies were sustained, and these were important in setting parameters on how development would proceed. In particular, they made it difficult to generate new options for accumulation. Instead, it would take a decade of capitalist stagnation before radically free-market policies were deemed necessary.

Post-independence stagnation and crisis can be easily illustrated by surface-level statistics.[1] Following the boom of 1979–81, only in 1985 and 1987–90 was there real per capita GDP growth. The years 1982–84 and 1986–87 witnessed negative per capita GDP growth (in 1984 and 1987, of -4%) and 1992 showed an enormous per capita GDP loss of 11% followed by a paltry, uneven recovery. The most conspicuous symptom of stagnation is the incessant decline in the percentage of the population formally employed, which peaked in 1960 at 19%, declined but peaked again in 1975 at 17%, and steadily dropped to around 11% in the early 1990s. By then the unemployment rate had reached 50%, as 200,000 young people were discharged from schools each year but looked forward to job creation of 20,000 in a good year. The result was often described as a "time-bomb," and a consensus thus eventually emerged among the country's elites, under heavy pressure from international financial institutions, that the only possible means of defusing it was economic liberalization in the form of a draconian "Economic Structural Adjustment Program" which was applied from 1990.

This chapter explains the persistence of stagnation and uneven development in the context of surface claims of a transition to socialism. The intention is not to offer a comprehensive survey of social and spatial developments since Zimbabwe's independence but to provide, instead, a series of snapshots of different aspects of the Zimbabwean experience. These help us to locate processes of class formation, financial speculation, uneven urban and rural development and international financial control in subsequent chapters.

Repression, class formation, and socialist rhetoric

One of the first chores any commentator on Zimbabwe faces is separating socialist rhetoric from raw capitalist reality. During the 1970s both ZANU and ZAPU adopted what were termed "scientific socialist" principles, although these were distinguished for their pragmatism. The ZAPU Revolutionary Council (1977:4), for example, once insisted that "profit is the mainstay of all exchange, bargains or trade and is not *per se* a contradiction to socialism." Marxists with more integrity were to be found in the Zimbabwe People's Army and March 11 Movement (which were both suppressed), but, according to David Moore (1992), their "challenge did not extend significantly beyond the intelligentsia on the road to power, and thus did not gain hegemony within the popular classes."

While the class character and ideological legacy of the Zimbabwean liberation struggle are still bitterly contested,[2] one theme stands out: in contrast to more romantic notions of the possibility for radical transformation of the living conditions of peasants and workers under a friendly nationalist government,[3] the connection between those directing the struggle and the constituencies meant to benefit was ultimately tenuous. Ian Phimister (1988b:8) concludes that "The alliance of rural class forces underpinning the guerilla struggle which eventually overthrew Ian Smith's Rhodesian regime was united in opposition to colonialism but little else. There was no shared vision of the future beyond the recovery of land lost to the whites."

It is in this sense that there was no durable basis amongst existing social forces for the liberation movement's socialist ideology. And it should not be surprising, therefore, that from colonial days through the post-independence period of Zimbabwean "socialism," capitalist relations persisted without substantial threat of upheaval. Three years prior to independence, an exceptionally accurate prediction was made by R. Murapa (1977:28):

> The present alliance is not dictated by ideological homogeneity, rather, it is one of convenience between a politically ambitious petty-bourgeois leadership, a dependent and desperate proletariat and a brutally exploited and basically uninitiated peasantry. The hope to neutralise the real capitalist forces of exploitation remains distant. After national liberation, the petty-bourgeois leadership can abandon its alliance with the workers and peasants and emerge as the new ruling class by gaining certain concessions from both foreign and local capital and, in fact, forming a new alliance with these forces which they will need to stay in power. Of course, lip service commitment, *a la* Kenya, to the masses, will be made.

Indeed Zimbabwe perseveres long after independence as a semi-peripheral neo-colony—witness its profound reliance on exports of primary commodities, extreme differentiations in domestic income and wealth (which remained among the most skewed in the world), and Zimbabwe's wholesale adoption of the economic and social policies of international financiers. However, this reality was somewhat veiled during the 1980s by the combination of radical-populist rhetoric from government (and especially government-controlled media) and the steady hand of a strong and visible national capitalist class (especially in manufacturing and agriculture). The notion that a socialist experiment was underway in the years after independence, all evidence to the contrary notwithstanding, served both groups well.

To illustrate, the white capitalist class firmly overlapped with Zimbabwe's vocal but small liberal elite, who generally looked down upon the liberation forces with scorn. This was a long-standing characteristic, as thinly-veiled racist overtones often distinguished liberal attacks on the socialist project in Africa. In her biography, renowned writer Doris Lessing recounted, from early adulthood (during World War II), membership in a tiny, lily-white Southern Rhodesian Communist Party which soon disintegrated, apparently because of the group's total failure to tap into the kind of organic radicalism of black workers that generated a general strike in 1948. Bitter, Lessing (1994:279) had inexplicably concluded that "Communism was too abstract and inhuman an idea to satisfy Africans—and in fact, when later there were Communist or Marxist regimes, they did not last long." Lessing (1994:367) considered post-independence Zimbabwe a "Communist government, too extreme for the natural temper and style of the black people."

To local white elites and their allies in international financial institutions responsible for development aid, blacks' alleged temper and style were, it seemed, better geared to the inculcation of petty-bourgeois norms and values, through a variety of well-known methods (Chapters Four and Nine describe the key example of housing finance). Under such pressures, the post-independence class-forming process soon degenerated into a situation in which not only would any residual socialist consciousness wither but full-blown ***compradorism*** ultimately prospered. As Arnold Sibanda (1988:62) explains,

> The reconciliation with whites, together with some fundamental aspects of their colonial rule and patterns of ownership of the means of production, constitutes nothing beyond an institutionalization of class alliances as a condition for an orderly transfer of power from a settler-colonial state to nationalist militants without disruption of the reproduction of capitalism. Thus the [Lancaster House] constitution was a concrete manifestation of the triumph of the condensed class-strivings of monopoly allied with settler capital over the national democratic bloc, a triumph which successfully prevented the materialization of a full national democratic revolution. The new state thus emerged with features of a classical neo-colonial formation with the corresponding class structures.

How, then, to explain the decade-long maintenance of official socialist discourse in Zimbabwe under such conditions? A brief review of the challenges to ZANU hegemony suggests that the country's nationalist leadership spent the 1980s maintaining left-wing discourse apparently in order to repress protest mainly from the Left.[4] Workers, for example, engaged in 150 formal and wildcat strikes against private firms immediately before and after independence (accounting for 72% more lost days than Zimbabwe's much larger, more proletarianized neighbor South Africa experienced in 1980). Brian Woods (1988:286) considers the circumstances in which newly-elected Prime Minister Robert Mugabe found himself in May 1980:

> The Prime Minister's crucial meeting with Harry Oppenheimer, head of southern Africa's largest transnational corporation, the Anglo American Corporation, coincided with the start of two large and relatively prolonged strikes at the company's major coal mine in the north-west and its sugar estates in the south of the country. It was at those two strikes that the police, and in the case of the Wankie Colliery, the army, were sent to protect installations and those who returned to work, as well as to arrest thirteen miners under the provisions of the Industrial Conciliation Act [of 1934].

Also in 1980, Mugabe declared one strike of bakery workers "nothing short of criminal," while his Labor Minister Kumbirai Kangai sent in police to end a strike at a transport firm and declared: "I will crack my whip if they do not go back to work."[5] A second wave of strikes, beginning in early 1989 and lasting through mid 1990, was met with police violence (for example, against teachers in downtown Harare), and also featured the detention without charges of Zimbabwe Congress of Trade Unions leader Morgan Tsvangirai under the 1965 Rhodesian State of Emergency, still in force at that stage. Subsequent strikes were generated largely from the public sector, in health, the postal service, airlines and railways. Aside from the occasional minor success, most were dealt with in authoritarian manner and ended with the workers defeated and despondent.

To illustrate the importance of ideological concerns, Tsvangirai's 1989 detention was specifically motivated by his mild support for a courageous verbal attack on the government by University of Zimbabwe students, who remained a consistent thorn in the government's (left) side during the late 1980s and early 1990s. The students were periodically harassed, locked up in the course of demonstrations, and faced university closure on several occasions. A draconian law was introduced to control the students by effectively making the university a parastatal institution, and ZANU functionaries used left-wing rhetoric to paint the students as "counter-revolutionaries."[6] Official political repression of a more dangerous sort was experienced by opposition parties ZAPU (coinciding with an estimated 5,000 murders of innocent Ndebele civilians by government forces during the 1981–86 Matabeleland conflicts) and the Zimbabwe Unity Movement (which opposed ZANU from the right but which gained the support of many urban dissenters) (Lawyers Committee for Human Rights 1986; Mandaza and Sachikonye 1991).

In addition, landless urbanites faced an unsympathetic government in the early 1980s when on two occasions, different groups of 30,000 people were forcibly removed from the Harare "high-density suburbs" (i.e., black townships) of Chitungwiza and Epworth. High-profile displacement on a somewhat lesser scale occurred in the early 1990s when the Queen of England visited Mbare (formerly "Harari," the closest high-density suburb to the city centre) and was protected—through forced removals—from the unsightly spectacle of squatters. Later, when opposition politician Ndabiningi Sithole attempted to initiate a shack settlement on his Churu Farm, the authorities clamped down rapidly and remorselessly, "clearly motivated by political interests," as the Catholic Commission for Justice and Peace put it (*FG* 19/5/94). More generally though, evictions were carried out under the pretence that, in the words of Harare's Director of Community Services, "squatting is not an acknowledged form of shelter in Zimbabwe" (Taylor 1985:27).[7]

Women, too, both experienced sustained structural discrimination and received severe treatment at the hands of the authorities throughout the post-independence period, as witnessed, for example, by instances in 1982, 1983, 1986, and 1990 in which hundreds of single urban women were ignominiously rounded up at night for alleged prostitution (Barnes and Win, 1992, 126). The Zimbabwean constitution prohibited discrimination in theory, but exempted gender discrimination based on adoption, marriage, divorce, burial devolution of property on death, or other matters of personal law (Kazembe 1986; Batezat, Mwalo and Truscott 1988). By the early 1990s, Mugabe himself forcefully defended women's oppression on national television, and also displayed hints of anti-Semitism. And in 1995–96, fierce bigotry against gay men and lesbians, bordering on paranoia, became a presidential sport worthy of international condemnation.

Putting down challenges from social forces with potential left-wing tendencies was the only conceivable function of ZANU's protracted socialist rhetoric. That rhetoric was maintained religiously for the first decade of independence, notwithstanding the fact that petty-bourgeois party leaders repeatedly violated even their own leadership code prohibiting excessive personal capital accumulation.[8] As Lloyd Sachikonye (1995b:180) argues, "The assumption of the petty-bourgeois leaders of the liberation movement was that socialist cadres and party members were largely moulded through ideological education... The elements of choice and voluntarism underlay this rationale for the adoption of socialism from amongst a menu of ideologies."

The evolving words and actions of leading ZANU politician and liberation war hero Maurice Nyagumbo are telling, beginning in 1983: "I do not fear that some monster called the black elite will jeopardise the revolution, because we are educating people on socialism and this is being accepted so that no single class of people will or can make people follow them. We do not believe in the elite, they must identify with the rest of the people" (1983:7). But by 1986, Nyagumbo was sufficiently worried to call for "an emergency congress (to) tell the people that we are unable to fulfil one of our important resolutions... mainly that of scientific socialism, because the leaders acquired property... appear to have adopted capitalism, become property owners and appear to be deceiving our people" (*Herald* 21/7/86). In 1989, Nyagumbo, then the third-ranking government official, committed suicide as a result of his involvement in the Willowvale car distribution scandal.

By the late 1980s, the ruling party's decaying bona *fides* became the subject of some debate amongst Zimbabwean intellectuals who queried the status of the ZANU's "socialist project." Some were misled by the rhetoric—late in the day the country's premier geographer, Lovemore Zinyama (1989:234), forcefully argued that "Zimbabwe is slowly heading towards state socialism" on the basis of red herrings such as the one-party state issue. But just as much as other sectors of society, radical intellectuals, too, had to be brought aboard the national project. Ex-President Canaan Banana (1987:vii) noted that while "socialism based on Marxist and Leninist principles" has made "remarkable advances" in Zimbabwe, it was "regrettable" that "there does not seem to have been a corresponding development in the intellectual sphere that would enable rational conceptualization and evaluation of the content, mode, and pace of our national development strategies."

This was, notwithstanding the fallacious preface, fair criticism. Whether caused by romanticism, or perhaps occasionally by subtle and overt pressures applied by government, the intelligentsia's "failure of analytical nerve" permitted such optimistic arguments as—in this case in the (otherwise extremely critical) work of Colin Stoneman (1988b:4)—"a process, full of contradictions, gains and reverses, is under way that could eventually lead to a socialist society in line with government pronouncements." Likewise, positing that "Zimbabwe, like Rhodesia before it, is somewhere in between socialist and capitalist parameters," the (self-described) postmodernist Christine Sylvester (1991:183,187) hence found "few sharp conclusions to draw or clear lessons to reiterate." A less timid group of indigenous intellectuals led by Ibbo Mandaza and associated with the magazine *Southern African Political and Economic Monthly* was on the one hand anxious to avoid the alleged "revolutionary mythology" of Northern Hemisphere Africanists (namely, John Saul). But on the other hand Mandaza (1986a, 1986b) generally stood ready to place the blame upon "international finance capital"—which, remarked Sibanda (1990:2), "approximates an 'apologia' for the ruling petty bourgeoisie"—while effectively neglecting the deeper structural process of capital accumulation.[9]

There were others yet, such as Paul Teedon and David Drakakis-Smith (1986:310,323), who contended that Zimbabwe's failure to break with settler-capitalism reflected (the otherwise socialist) ZANU's inability to withstand "the pressures and blandishments of international capitalism" which was in part due to an anti-urbanism inherent in the "general Maoist tendencies within African socialism." In the urban areas, Neil Dewar (1987:47) recounts an idealized version of ZANU party organization, pointing to the means by which geographic hierarchy was established by "a party inspired by a Marxist-Leninist conception of socialism... into party Cells, Branches and Districts. This served both to politicise and mobilize the people while at the same time ensuring that members of the District executive who also became city councillors would be sensitive to, and able to respond to, problems experienced at 'grassroots' level."[10] That ZANU was in reality neither pro-peasant "Maoist" nor urban-oriented "Marxist-Leninist" will become evident in later chapters.

More practical than intellectual observers of Zimbabwean "socialism," perhaps, even if ultimately as misleading, was Mugabe himself, who in an interview not long after independence spoke of delays in socialist mobilization "until we have managed to establish an adequate infrastructure and a basis of human skills, and until we have proceeded to educate our people on our principles so that by persuasion they can see the goals as we see them" (*Herald* 10/6/81). Until then, ZANU would reign over a state monopoly capitalist economy inherited from Rhodesia, and would do so, ostensibly as a Marxist-Leninist party, because state ownership could be legitimized (in the minds of official pundits) as a stepping stone to socialist relations of production. As Mugabe explained, "Some people argue that ownership by the state amounts to state capitalism. That may very well be; it depends entirely on how state ownership translates itself... The state, acting as custodian of the people and the society, will ensure that capitalism diminishes and that the area of socialism is augmented" (*Moto* #6 1984).[11]

In this spirit, the most charitable statement of Zimbabwe's 1980s doctrine—in the words of the Government of Zimbabwe *Transitional National Development Plan* (1982:i)—was that ZANU "recognises the existing phenomenon of capitalism as an historical reality, which, because it cannot be avoided, has to be purposefully harnessed, regulated and transformed as a partner in the overall national endeavour to achieve set national Plan goals. Accordingly, whilst the main thrust of the Plan is socialist... ample room has been reserved for performance by private enterprise." Even if completely implausible as a description of the Plan itself, this was a coherent ideological call for ever-elusive capitalist development in some "national interest," and coincided with other rhetorical statements usually—as in the following example by leading state ideologue Cain Mathema (1988:9,10)—aimed at establishing popular-front politics:

> Our local capitalists, regardless of race and nationality (Shona, Ndebele, Khalanga, Tonga, English, etc.) have to be mobilized against neo-colonialism, they have to be allowed to operate in those areas of the economy which at any particular time are found to be operated best by the local capitalist class... Also, our capitalists have to be educated to see that as long as the multinationals remain in control of the commanding heights of our economy, they (our bourgeoisie) will always play a peripheral role. It is in their interests therefore to work hand in

> hand with the government because their role will be clearly defined and their interests better protected.

Rhetoric of this sort suggests that multinational corporations would not get red carpet treatment in Zimbabwe during the 1980s (although individual tycoons such as Tiny Rowland of Lonrho, Tony O'Reilly of US-based Heinz, and British mining tycoon Algy Cluff were fast friends of the socialist rulers, and the influence of Oppenheimer, the continent's greatest magnate, was remarked upon earlier). But in reality, ZANU's corporatist approach presented no great threat to capitalist interests, even those headquartered in London and Johannesburg.[12] On the contrary, foreign investors were periodically wooed with much more frank admissions about the state of socialism in Zimbabwe, in this case by Finance Minister Bernard Chidzero speaking at a 1982 investment conference in New York:

> Does the government of Zimbabwe have something up its sleeves? We are socialists, are we encouraging you to come so that tomorrow we can grab you? If that's what you think, I can assure you that we have nothing up our sleeves, we are simple pragmatists... Let us not fight the battle on ideological grounds. Life is more serious than to be controlled by ideologies. Life is very down-to-earth, let us just look at the realities of life. And I believe that good businessmen enter into riskier areas than areas where *we talk about ideologies without doing much about it* [emphasis added].

The cowering presentation by the normally urbane Chidzero was immediately followed by the more calculated view of the US State Department's Chester Crocker:

> The US believes that Zimbabwe can become a showcase of economic growth and political moderation in southern Africa, a region of substantial strategic importance to us. That belief rests on facts, not illusions... As part of the Reagan administration's worldwide policy of support for economic development, we have embarked upon several new approaches in our assistance programs. We believe these will strengthen the role of indigenous private sectors and facilitate US private investment to stimulate developing economies.

Providing the icing on the cake, the head of the Confederation of Zimbabwe Industries (CZI) quite prophetically

> concurred with the view expressed by Dr. Chidzero that it is time to put away "isms" and that over time, more emphasis is likely to be placed on private enterprise development than on the public sector... What is needed in Zimbabwe is export-led growth, and over time, the spectrum of opinion between far right and far left will converge, caus-

> ing "isms" to disappear. (African-American Institute/American Bar Association 1982:4–12)

The result was an operating environment termed "business friendly" by a United States Agency for International Development (US AID) industrial consultant (Oakeshott 1987:xv). At the time of independence Stoneman (1982:290) had warned, presciently, that

> Piecemeal or pragmatic state action (seeking accommodations, guidelines, joint ventures, minority holdings, some nationalization with generous compensation and management contracts, and so forth), that is, the type of policy often erroneously described as "socialist" or "African socialist," will in the face of such an economic power bloc be no more successful in reducing inequality, tackling rural poverty, establishing economic independence or producing rapid economic growth than in many other African states.

In contrast to the socialist promises, ZANU's corporatism allowed large local companies to ultimately exercise considerable influence over state regulatory policies. A former president of the CZI, David Long, exhorted other executives:

> Our role is to change the overall picture, to look at the overall environment and seek to change that for the good of our members through bringing constructive pressure to bear on government in bringing about policy changes and creating an environment conducive to free enterprise and the efficient operation within that environment. And this we have done most successfully during the past decade. Government makes the rules. We hope, at most, to play on the same team and to have some opportunity to influence policy decisions. Compare this to the situation in which we were in 1980, across the table, daggers drawn. (*Industrialist,* July 1991)[13]

But regardless of radical rhetoric—and it remained fiery and occasionally anti-imperialist even into the 1990s—not long after independence ZANU effectively jettisoned any socialist baggage it may have carried from the liberation struggle. US AID (1982:15) soon expressed satisfaction that "The Government of Zimbabwe has adopted a generally pragmatic, free-market approach... and this approach has the full support of the US AID." The view from inside a large US bank in 1982 was also one of reassurance:

> The management of the more sophisticated large companies, i.e., TA Holdings, Lonrho, and Anglo American, seem to be impressed by and satisfied with Mugabe's management and the increased level of understanding in government of commercial considerations... I feel it is a political pattern that Mugabe give radical, anti-business speeches before

> government makes major pro-business decisions or announcements. (cited in Hanlon 1988:35)

A decade after Lancaster House, a ZANU leftist, Lazarus Nzareybani, Member of Parliament from Mutare, agreed:

> The socialist agenda has been adjourned indefinitely. You don't talk about socialism in a party that is led by people who own large tracts of land and employ a lot of cheap labor. When the freedom fighters were fighting in the bush they were fighting not to disturb the system but to dismantle it. And what are we seeing now? Leaders are busy implementing those things which we were fighting against. (*Sunday Mail*, 10/12/89)

Such commentary merely illustrates the persistent surface-level search for explanations of what were actually much deeper-rooted commitments to the existing economic order. For as the 1980s witnessed a dramatic backpeddling from the socialist vision, ZANU's main goals were reduced to Africanizing the colonial state and forcing some limited inroads into white capitalist old-boy networks. Sibanda (1988:275) concludes, correctly it seems, "We cannot therefore justifiably measure the actions of the present Zimbabwean state on the basis of a scientific socialist yardstick, for the socialist project was not seriously on the agenda and *could not have been*, without the working class either being organized, or represented, or acting as a combatant class on the stage" (emphasis original).

In this context, the incongruous persistence of left-wing official rhetoric has done great damage to more organic left prospects—as in Prague, where socialism "is a really awful word, for ordinary people it has been destroyed completely" (according to a leading young activist who inspired Wainwright's [1994] *Arguments for a New Left*). Actually, when as late as September 1991 ZANU reaffirmed its commitment to Marxism-Leninism, Senior Minister of Political Affairs Didymus Mutasa responded in an interesting (apparently Trotskyist?) way to the general global collapse of the "communist" movement: "The political system in eastern Europe could be best described as state capitalism and therefore not different from that in Western Europe, except that there it is carried out by individuals" (*FG*, 19/9/91).

Ironically, it was at precisely this point that the failures of Zimbabwe's Economic Structural Adjustment Program (ESAP)—which was supported by the party in no uncertain terms—made it virtually impossible to sustain the idea of socialism.[14] This was aptly remarked upon by Nkosana Moyo (1991:4), managing director of Standard Chartered Bank: "What is rather forlorn about the continuing ZANU debate on socialism is that it is basically a sinister manoeuvre of deliberately flogging a dead horse to hoodwink and confuse the nation in order to win sympathy among the weak minded." And as for ESAP, "How can it succeed when it is being spearheaded by political sharks who, devoid of business values, are using political clout accumulated over the last eleven years to invade the private sector under the assumption that business is politics and politics is business?"

Monopoly capitalist reality

Indeed business was a matter of politics, in important ways. The role of the "political sharks" among Zimbabwean financiers and bureaucrats is reviewed in more detail in the next chapter. More generally, state officials maintained the responsibility to taking over failing firms on the one hand, and on the other were easily intimidated by monopoly capital. Writing in the late 1980s, Stoneman (1988c:48) could still argue,

> Zimbabwe is a market economy, in which firms' decisions are based on calculations of profitability. It is not, however, a *free*-market economy, and if the workforce does not question managerial prerogative, then government does. In investing, in importing inputs, in exporting output, in paying or firing workers, in expatriating profits, firms are under tight governmental control. In exchange, they benefit from a high degree of protection, and in many cases, of monopoly on the local market; the workforce is also effectively constrained from striking, and state provision of social services, including education, healthcare and housing, relieves firms of the costs of ensuring a healthy and reasonably contented workforce.

There were certainly bureaucratic controls and often excessively-tight regulation (mainly inherited from Rhodesia, rarely initiated from scratch by ZANU). Yet the state did not attempt, either through bureaucratic fiat or its extensive industrial holdings, to interfere in the corporate profit calculus or otherwise fundamentally alter the logic of capital accumulation.

Government ownership of capitalist means of production occurred mainly through the Industrial Development Corporation, and amounted, by the end of the 1980s, to a 4.6% stake in Zimbabwe's manufacturing sector. The main post-independence acquisitions were in metals and metal products, and in pulp and paper and agri-industrial subsectors. Large post-independence government ownership shares of in excess of 40% were registered in the pharmaceutical (CAPS Holdings) and food processing (Olivine Holdings) subsectors. Other majority-ownership acquisitions included Zimbank and Wankie Colliery, and a majority holding was maintained in the Zimbabwe Iron and Steel Corporation.[15] What this often led to in practice, Sibanda (1990:8) points out, was "a 'shadow' management implementing real decisions which are taken in the metropolis, the proportion of shares held by the host state notwithstanding. This shadow petty-bourgeois partner is at a disadvantage since the imperialist partners have more knowledge available to them concerning the productive operation of the enterprise."

The young government also faced monopoly control of markets. With no regulations prohibiting monopolies, trusts or cartels, some 80% of Zimbabwe's 6,000 manufactured products were made under monopoly or oligopoly conditions (Deloitte & Touche, 1990:4). Half the local output of Zimbabwean industries was produced by a single firm in each sector (and another 20% by two firms and 10% more by three). Hence, reported Ndlela (1984:73), "New applicants found it difficult to gain entry to the system in an effective way." Chapter Seven shows Ndlela's complaint was particularly true in terms of entrepreneurs' access to the banking system.

Recall, too, that foreign ownership of the productive sectors—especially mining, but also manufacturing and agriculture—was central to ZANU's anti-imperialist rhetoric during the 1970s. Yet it is important not to overplay the surface form of capital (its "foreign"-ness) to the neglect of underlying dynamics of capital accumulation. The 1980s, after all, witnessed substantial foreign disinvestment (caused in part by inhospitable profit remittance regulations in the context of overaccumulated domestic markets).[16] Even the World Bank (1989d:2, 63) commented, somewhat sheepishly, that "high expectations on new inflows would be inappropriate, even with a highly favourable (foreign investment) regime."

Still, residual foreign ownership was not an insignificant phenomenon. In 1989, of 667 firms surveyed by Zimbabwe Institute for Development Studies researchers, 56% were still at least half owned by foreigners (accounting for 38% of manufacturing assets), and 21% of the firms were 100% foreign-owned. Major clothing firms were entirely foreign-owned, while the ownership of the furniture and foodstuffs subsectors was approximately half foreign. Foreign ownership of manufacturing as a whole was dominated by Britain (54%), followed by South Africa (18%), the Netherlands (10%), and the United States (7%). The major firms in which multinational corporations held at least 51% equity included (in order of size of capitalization) Dunlop Zimbabwe, Delta Corporation, Triangle, David Whitehead Textiles, Lever Brothers, B.A.T. Zimbabwe, Zimbabwe Bata Shoe Company, Eastern Highlands Tea Estates, Lemco Zimbabwe, Metal Box Central Africa, and Plate Glass Industries. These eleven companies represented 30% of the total capitalization of the 667 major manufacturing companies in Zimbabwe at that point (Maya and Tongoona 1989).[17] Though disinvestment was announced regularly, multinational corporate control of Zimbabwean manufacturing was still so widespread in the early 1990s that 40% of a Z$900 million African Development Bank loan package "lay idle" because foreign-owned companies were initially ineligible (*FG*, 22/7/93).

The importance of attracting new foreign investment was even greater as a ruse used by domestic capitalists to express their own desires for a more friendly economic environment. First Merchant Bank chief economist John Robertson illustrates the relevance of even semantic symbolism: "When a foreign investor hears the word comrade, he leaves immediately. I do not believe that black Africans know how emotive the word is" (*FG*, 1/7/93). Yet the treatment of foreign investors was far more hospitable than ZANU's rhetoric might suggest to the uninitiated. According to Ticharwa Masimba (1994:4), mining magnate Algy Cluff invested Z$17 million in Zimbabwe and then proceeded to raise Z$55 million on the Zimbabwe Stock Exchange in 1990 and another Z$25 million in 1992:

> This money from the Zimbabwean public accounts for 80% of total injection and yet represents less than 20% of the ownership of the company. That is foreign investment for you. The company declared dividends of Z$98 million from 1990 on a thin dividend cover of 2,82% of the dividend, representing Z$80 million which has all been shipped back to Mr Cluff. In addition, the country has been forced to provide gold loans to the company of Z$150 million. If the government can do so much for one white man, it can surely afford to do the same for a black man who will inject the dividends back into the economy. It is sad—the matter is regarded as sensitive—precisely, because this is the way investors continue to drain the economy. The investment has been paid over and over again. What development did the country get from Mr Cluff? He has hardly put in any infrastructure.

Nevertheless, ZANU's political alliances ensured that multinational corporations were never seriously threatened. As an example, in 1992, then-Commerce Minister Kangai praised Lonrho's Rowland for demonstrating that "Multinationals have and can become our economic ambassadors and promote, not just their own products but everyone else and all other goods produced here" (*FG*, 9/1/92).[18] At the end of the day, government's political perspective offered few substantive ideological obstacles to direct investment, although the payoff was minimal: the early 1990s witnessed no new takers aside from South African firms buying new subsidiaries (notably, banks such as Standard buying out Grindlays, and Nedbank taking a major stake in Merchant Bank of Central Africa)—and that thanks mainly to the rapidly-devaluing Zimbabwe dollar—and notoriously-fickle international mutual fund investments in the Zimbabwe Stock Exchange. Later, Zimbabwe attracted South African retail, tourism, and mineral-extraction capital, and Malaysian investors bought into land development and (existing) energy projects.

The underlying reason for the lack of new investment—multinational or local—can be traced to deeper tendencies of stagnation in the productive sectors of the economy. And these in turn meant that a decisive break with Rhodesian-era structural racism in business and banking would be extremely difficult.

The nationalist response to corporate racism

One reality of monopoly capitalism in Zimbabwe felt painfully by workers, junior managers and entrepreneurs is crucial to record: its racial bias. This was not absolute, as the case of powerful black financial elites makes clear (Chapter Seven). Nevertheless, as Brian Raftopoulos (1993:7–8) argues,

> It is not surprising that racial inequality has continued to be a problem in Zimbabwe. Put simply: the economic structures that produced and sustained a white elite are, in their essentials, still prevalent. It is equally unsurprising that opposition to this continued inequality should be coming not only from a state unable to meet the increasing demands of the majority of its citizens, but from fractions of the black petty-bourgeoisie unable to make their fortunes on a sustained basis. Having occupied the structures of political office, the board rooms of the private sector remain an area rarely dominated by anything approaching a black "national bourgeoisie."

The ceiling on the black petty bourgeoisie was, ironically, a function of continuing state programs which in key sectors favored white settler capital, according to Tom Ostergaard (1991:24): "Moreover, while doing this, the Mugabe government has neglected—if not directly opposed—the development of a class of indigenous, black industrialists." The reason for this paradox is that "the governing groups reckoned that the well-being of the national economy and their personal livelihood depended on the continued success of the inherited industrial machinery." Such sentiment was certainly dominant until, in the early 1990s, racial tensions again became more serious, as broader economic changes increased the desperation of an aspirant black business elite.

Throughout, a large proportion of white Zimbabwean businesspeople remained unabashedly racist, fomented anti-government cynicism (and charges of reverse racism), fostered a siege mentality ("We are first class passengers on the Titanic" was the favored metaphor of a leading white professional), and fortified old boy networks wherever possible. As the CZI's own (white) affirmative action consultant reported in 1989, "One of the primary factors affecting the pace and nature of black advancement in industry is the racial attitude of white management. There is still white management at all levels that believes blacks are incompetent and cannot do the job" (cited, Raftopoulos 1993:10).

As in the early 1960s, post-independence nationalism was readily fuelled by the difficulties blacks faced breaking into—much less breaking up—the institutions of monopoly capital. The executive management of major firms remained more than 60% white through the 1980s (the CZI consultant conceded), and in effective control of the private sector's commanding heights. One study of 38 small-scale metal-working industries (most of which were founded after independence) showed that "34 (89%) were owned by Whites, four by Asians and 'Coloreds,' and two by Blacks" (Raftopoulos 1991:14). A *Herald* editorial (23/3/91) concluded: "It is worrying that almost eleven years after independence and the banning of racial discrimination in Zimbabwe, there is still such a strong perceived need for an association grouping indigenous [black] businessmen... The largely hidden problem is the old boy networks."

One answer was affirmative action, the essence of which was captured rather candidly by writer Nevanji Madanhire (1994:28):

> There is trepidation within the white community and over-excitement among black entrepreneurs. The former sees affirmative action as a threat and as racism in reverse, while the latter view the policy as offering new business opportunities. Now it emerges the policy was wrongly put across. As it is it will benefit only an upwardly mobile middle class and generates the view that those it helped would never have made it on their own. The policy is open to abuse and only a vocal and well-connected elite will benefit.

Another strategy for conclusively breaking the white networks was to establish a competing *black* old-boy bloc. But to this end, the highly-touted Indigenous Business Development Centre (IBDC) developed serious problems nearly immediately after its founding in 1991. Founding member Leonard Nyamutsamba soon alleged that the IBDC was "run by a clique" without a constitution or treasurer. Leading IBDC members were blacklisted by government for illegally reselling vehicles they received through a special IBDC allocation, while other members publicly alleged that the organization's leadership and government practiced favoritism in the allocations (*FG*, 19/9/91; *Weekend Gazette*, 13/12/91).

The split widened, leading to the formation of the Affirmative Action Group (AAG) in mid 1994 by the young entrepreneur Phillip Chiyanga, reportedly supported by disgruntled ex-leaders of the IBDC who had been voted out of office (Chiyanga spent Z$100,000 of his own funds on the AAG). Politicians like Didymus Mutasa took sides, and there was acrimony regarding the alleged purchase by IBDC secretary general Enock Kamushinda of Z$130 million worth of buildings in the Avenues and Kopje areas of Harare in late 1994. By 1995 Norwegian funders had withdrawn Z$14 million in IBDC funding as leadership squabbles continued. Chemist Siziba eventually defeated Ben Mucheche's faction, after intervention by Vice President Joshua Nkomo (*FG*, 18/8/94, 8/12/94, 12/1/95, 2/2/95, 15/12/95). In addition, a National Reconstruction and Development Board was initiated by intellectual leader Ibbo Mandaza to link black empowerment advocacy groups.

Ultimately, though, even without such distractions, the operations of black business organizations and nascent black-owned banks and companies were still mainly limited to the *circulation* of capital. The opening had come, in the immediate wake of independence, from black merchants' capacity to mop up the marginally increased effective demand (e.g., as a result of the expansion of hire purchase lenders), especially through geographical expansion. And what with an expansion of government regional decentralization initiatives, there were further opportunities for black petty-bourgeois accumulation in trade and commerce, since white-owned monopoly capital was far less interested in exploring new geographical outlets in the poorer rural areas.

But with most of the economy mired in stagnation during the 1980s, such meager countervailing strategies could not break open significant niches within which black entrepreneurs could begin to accumulate. It was in part due to the CZI members' monopoly power and privileged access to resources, in part to the flood of imports in the early 1990s, and, as we shall see, in part to relentless overaccumulation tendencies, that the *productive* (especially manufacturing) circuit of the Zimbabwean economy remained essentially locked shut to potential black capitalists.

Stagnation in the productive economy

Until ESAP, the response by state and capital to the 1980s stagnation, as in the late 1970s, could be characterized as "muddling through." The main socio-economic principle seemed to be maintaining the existing economic structure intact so as to renew (and extend slightly downwards into the mass of potential black consumers) the trajectory of growth that was interrupted during the 1970s. As a US AID (1980:10) report naively put it at Independence, "The country's unemployment problems date from the 1974 downturn in the economy." According to this line of thinking, revival of growth would solve an unemployment crisis that stemmed, simply, from the 1974–78 economic collapse (not from decades of colonial-capitalist uneven development). Here it is worth returning to Sibanda's (1985:12) critique of the prevailing "dualist" policy wisdom: "Unemployment is thus seen as *the* problem and not a consequence of or manifestation of a deeper and *real* problem."

Stagnation in the key sector of the economy—manufacturing—essentially represented a continuation of crisis tendencies which had surfaced in the mid 1970s (Figure 6.1). Profits in all the productive sectors (manufacturing, mining and agriculture) were anemic during most of the 1980s. Although agriculture experienced a healthy upturn when there were rainy seasons, most corporate profit rates were stagnant (manufacturing) or falling (mining, and all other private sector firms). If we factor out the "unincorporated enterprises" (basically the several thousand commercial family farms), the decline in corporate profits as a percentage of GDP is startling (Figure 6.2). Improvements were witnessed in the years just prior to the implementation of ESAP, but (as shown below) these were not sustainable since they did not entail a resolution to the condition of overaccumulation.

Other aspects of the economy reflect the overall deterioration. Exports rose an average of 3.5% annually during the 1980s in local currency terms, but this was largely as a result of an erratic but significant devaluation of the Zimbabwe dollar and, given chronic balance-of-payments problems was barely noticed. As the private sector languished, government expenditure became increasingly responsible for Gross Domestic Product formation, though this occurred less in terms of traditional (and costly) civil engineering projects (which would have kept capital formation at respectable levels) and more in terms of recurrent expenditure, including straight income transfers.

The government deficit thus typically exceeded 10% of expenditures, as much as three-fifths of which paid for interest due on past debt. Government debt repayment to foreign creditors rose from 4% of export earnings in 1980 to an excruciating peak of 35% in 1987, before falling off to around 20% at the time a fresh round of ESAP borrowing began in 1990. Inflation averaged 15% during the 1980s, with nominal interest rates at 12%, yet the savings rate averaged a respectable 20% of income. Chapter Eight shows how, in this context, dramatic speculative investment patterns emerged in the mid-1980s, while Chapters Nine and Ten demonstrate the uneven impact of debt on urban and rural development.

Underlying the generalized stagnation, by all accounts, was a lack of fixed investment. The World Bank (1991a,v.I:5) attributed stagnation to "low levels of investment in the productive sectors of the economy. Investment has probably not been adequate to maintain the capital stock, let alone increase it and raise productivity." What the Bank would probably not concede is that this stemmed from the overinvestment of the mid 1970s and the skewed nature of effective demand in the economy. The Bank (1989d:44) noted that total new investment by corporations listed on the Zimbabwe Stock Exchange amounted to US$466 million in 1980–82, and just US$355 from 1983–87 (in 1980 prices).

As noted earlier, it was particularly difficult to attract multinational corporate investment. The African-American Institute and American Bar Association sponsored a conference on "Investment in Zimbabwe" in New York City in early 1982, but of the many major corporations present at the conference[19] only HJ Heinz Company made a high-profile new investment (in Olivine Holdings along with the government).[20] In the wake of a global shift from direct foreign investment by multinationals in the 1950s and 1960s, to portfolio investment (loans and other credits) by banks in the 1970s, to a reverse net flow of funds from South to North in the 1980s, it was naive to think Zimbabwe could buck the trends. The reasons for lack of new multinational direct investment are varied. According to an unusually honest assessment by the World Bank (1989d:iv,44),

> Some observers emphasise low returns to multinational parent companies, the extensive government restrictions over decisions over most aspects of production and investment, and the high degree of political and economic uncertainty surrounding any new investment. Others point to high profits, a comfortably protected economic environment and the dearth of new investment inflows from parent companies, despite a stream of remittances. Both views have some truth in them... Perceived from the viewpoint of foreign-controlled companies, there is also an important element of strategic behavior; thus their reluctance to invest may be seen as a strategic tactic intended to elicit more favorable terms and to establish a set of ground rules which would be more akin to their long-term interest.

And indeed, of industrialists active in Zimbabwe during the 1980s, the multinational corporations performed much worse in terms of reinvestment in plant and equipment than even the local industrialists (who are widely known to favor personal luxury consumption over and above a long-term commitment to Zimbabwean capitalism). The World Bank found that in the first three years after Independence, investment by foreign companies totalled US$338 million (in 1980 dollars), while the following five years (1983-87) witnessed a mere US$191 million in new investments by foreign firms.

It would, however, have been unreasonable to expect foreign firms to invest in a stagnant economy when local producers were putting their surpluses elsewhere. Fixed capital expenditure across the manufacturing sector—still the motor of the economy, representing more than a quarter of GDP—was low because it had been so high a decade earlier, and because at the end of sanctions a minor burst of investment activity also took place which soon left markets saturated again.

The early post-Independence moment of investment is worth brief consideration, for it confirms the most unstable trends in the productive circuit of capital. The upturn in manufacturing had actually begun about a year prior to the transfer of power, in mid 1979 (most accounts merely acknowledge 1980-81). Some subsectors of manufacturing—furniture and fixtures, for example—increased their net capital expenditure by nearly 500% from 1978 to 1979 and then doubled it again over the next two years. But this led to enormous increases in stocks, which exceeded the annual investments by a factor of at least four from 1981 to 1984. Net capital expenditure in clothing also picked up by a factor of ten from 1977-78 to 1980-81, and this generated a doubling of inventory. The pattern was the same for footwear. In all of these cases during the early 1980s, consumer capacity was too quickly saturated and export markets difficult to penetrate. Economist Rob Davies (1983:7) reported "a large amount of excess capacity in Zimbabwe's industry at present. An increasing number of firms are going on to short-time etc., leaving plant and labor idle. In one sense therefore there is a lack of demand rather than excess demand in the economy."

The overaccumulation problem was by no means evenly felt. Some light consumer good industries (especially food processing) continued to experience a steady expansion. Heavy investments continued in beer, wine and spirits, printing and publishing, meat processing, milling, dairy products, soft drinks, and bakery products. But given persistent income inequality and the previously better-balanced nature of Zimbabwe's industrial base, the swelling of smallish food subsectors made little impact on macroeconomic growth. Capital goods appeared terminally weak.

Overall, the most important reflection of manufacturing investment inactivity was the existing low level of capacity utilization experienced virtually across industry. While bottlenecks and shortages appeared periodically, and while the first two years of independence certainly witnessed large imports of foreign machinery to replace old equipment (although much of it was on tied-aid terms such as that of US AID's Commodity Import Program), overall there remained an excess of capital already invested in the manufacturing production process to realise a rate of return competitive with other investments. By the time the CZI began quarterly surveys in late 1984, capacity utilization rates were down to 75%, and they fell to as low as 62% in 1987.

CZI members' capacity utilization rates rose following the 1987 downturn, in part because such extremely small amounts of money had been invested in equipment, plant and machinery throughout the Zimbabwe economy during 1985–88. With low levels of existing utilization in the mid 1980s, the perceived need for new capital investment had diminished even further, and remained very low (from 1985–88, according to official statistics, the rate of increase in gross fixed capital formation as a percentage of GDP averaged just 13%, one of the lowest on record, and well below fixed capital replacement rates). In real annual terms (measured in 1980 Z$), such investments amounted to only two thirds (around Z$200 million) of the amount invested in 1974 (R$325 million). In the manufacturing sector in particular, the entire investment in new plant and equipment amounted to just Z$60 million in 1986, and total fixed capital formation in manufacturing was just Z$116 million—as compared to total fixed capital formation in manufacturing of R$180 million in 1975 (also 1980 Z$). Moreover, other outmoded plant and machinery had been taken off-stream at this stage.

The late 1980s finally witnessed a genuine recovery in the economy—due in some degree to good agricultural seasons—following an extremely bad period (1982–87) in which gross national income either declined or rose by less than 1.5% in five out of six years.[21] There was, particularly, an expansion of real manufacturing output—5.9% in 1989, 6.1% in 1990—in excess of growth of the economy as a whole (4.6% and 2.2%, respectively). Although manufacturing grew by just 2.7% in 1991 (against GDP growth of 4.3%), capital investment was by now picking up sharply. Capacity utilization and new investments had little choice but to show improvement at this point. There was a substantial increase in manufacturers' real fixed investment in 1989. In 1990 total real gross capital formation reached levels achieved in 1980–82, and in 1993 and 1995, manufacturing investment approached GDP ratios of 1974-75 (figure 13.1)

But many companies leading the investment mini-boom—for example, the Z$1.5 billion sunk into textiles and Z$230 million into paper and packaging during 1990–93 were nearly all by the largest firms—regretted doing so, according to Sachikonye (1995a:118), since it "resulted in huge financial exposures as interest rates soared above 40% in 1992 and early 1993." Not only was investment financially burdensome for many large enterprises (industry leaders Cone Textiles and Hunyani packaging essentially went bankrupt), but government had then to be lobbied hard for the reimposition of protective tariffs against imported clothing, textiles, and paper.

Moreover, few jobs accompanied the new investments. Even in commercial agriculture, which according to the World Bank (1995b, v.II:119) witnessed a real increase in fixed investment of 450% from 1985–91, the number of permanent commercial farmworkers rose from just 145,000 to 155,000 during that period. The Bank (1995b,v.I:6) argued that the excessively capital-intensive nature of the late 1980s investments was due to several factors:

> foreign exchange was overvalued and depreciation expected, subsidized foreign exchange cover was provided, real interest rates were negative, foreign companies were forced either to reinvest or deposit blocked and surplus funds in accounts at 5% interest, corporate taxes were high (50%) and investors were allowed to immediately write-off 100% of investment cost from taxable income... The manufacturing sector uses capital very inefficiently and has a very high incremental capital to output ratio... Over the last few years, the capital productivity has been declining and labor productivity increasing, leaving overall productivity very low.

Thus, despite becoming vastly more productive during the late 1980s, labor's share of total output crashed from a high of nearly 20% in 1982 to 14% a decade later. As a corollary, in relation to the earlier period of stagnation, manufacturing profitability was extremely impressive during the late 1980s (gross profit margins of 21% of sales, compared to 15% from 1980–85), with firm earnings "much higher than the rate observed in developed countries" (World Bank, 1995b,v.II:121, 123).

Yet the economy's contradictions could not be suppressed for long. What with adding these new capital-intensive investments to a chronically overaccumulated economy, it would only be a matter of another few months (late 1991) before manufacturing again found itself the victim of massive overcapacity, plummeting investor confidence and the need for enormous downsizing. Exports were by this stage considered the only route open for manufacturing growth. But as shown in more detail in Chapter Twelve, rigorous marketing research had not been undertaken by exuberant boosters of liberalization in the Finance Ministry and CZI, and in fact there was no reason to think that past failures would be reversed (*Africa South*, January 1991, May 1991, February 1992).

One result of "export-led growth" was a shift from healthy trade surpluses during the 1980s to mild trade deficits in 1989–90, which in turn exploded to untenable levels (more than 10% of GDP) beginning in early 1991. Another was, by 1993, the reappearance of enormous underutilized capacity in manufacturing. Indeed, reported the Bank (1995b,v.II: 129–30), using existing equipment and modes of operation, firms could at that point still increase their output by an astonishing 80% before hitting technical barriers: "These numbers are dramatic as they do not incorporate stretching of capacity through extra shifts. However, it is not clear whether the firms in Zimbabwe will be capable of expanding, as it requires exporting and maintaining their shares in the domestic market in the face of increasing import competition."

The continuation of a condition of overaccumulation, even in the midst of a deeper devaluation process, is revisited in Chapter Twelve; but suffice it to say the main subject of devaluation during the early 1990s was variable capital, i.e. the real wage. Yet in a world characterized by increasingly cheap labor, that would not be a substantial enough advantage to wrest Zimbabwe from its chronic problems of economic stagnation.

The alleged "forex constraint"

Finally, a perennial excuse for the economic stagnation of the 1980s was the alleged constraint to fixed investment that foreign exchange "forex" shortages represented. Indeed, this shortcoming became the rallying cry for industrialists throughout the decade, allowing them to also account for the decline in production quality, consistency, and output. Later, the need to earn forex became the primary rationale for switching emphasis from an internally-oriented manufacturing sector to one which would sink or swim based on international competitiveness.

Though the "forex constraint" requires debunking, it was not an entirely misleading hypothesis. There were, in the capital goods subsector, increasingly serious foreign import shortages, and some 30% of raw materials for manufacturing still had to be imported (although this ranged from just 2.5% in foodstuffs to more than 90% for some types of electrical machinery and transport equipment).[23] Transport was first hit by a deficiency in foreign exchange, and a crisis in rail haulage capacity along with shortages of diesel and petrol reverberated throughout the economy (especially the agricultural markets) within a year of independence. Foreign currency allocations to manufacturers had been at near-record (real) levels in early 1981, but were then quickly halved in 1982 and 1983 largely as a result of the 1982 devaluation of the dollar and subsequent increases in import prices. In 1982 the CZI conducted a survey of manufacturers and concluded that "of the Z$942 million capital investment envisaged for the sector under the three year *Transitional National Development Plan*, some 73% would consist of direct imports" (Girdlestone 1983:8). The foreign currency crisis emerged in heavy industries, but created further bottlenecks which would be felt later.

As international prices for primary products failed to improve and manufacturing exports appeared stymied in the mid-1980s, a renewed urgency began to take hold. "The most important single factor influencing manufacturing sector performance since 1980 has been the extent of availability of foreign exchange to import material inputs required to sustain production levels," according to Chidzero's Ministry of Finance (Government of Zimbabwe 1986:133). And indeed the import content of investment in the existing stock of plant and machinery was about three times as high (in relative terms) as the import content of consumption expenditure such that under the prevailing circumstances, according to Davies (1986:4), "raising the investment ratio would reduce consumption by more than it would raise capacity growth and would thus reduce GDP."

Yet there is contrasting evidence to suggest that foreign exchange was *not* in fact the *most* crucial barrier to manufacturing fixed capital investment. For example, the Whitsun Foundation (1983:124) reported in 1983 that a high proportion of foreign exchange was "used for raw materials and spare parts, rather than for new capital equipment." And fixed capital expenditure did improve in the late 1980s, when hard currency remained in short supply. Dan Ndlela (1984:73) argues that even where foreign exchange was used for capital expenditures, "there was no attempt to streamline allocations in such a way that priority branches of production could receive more in order to produce goods that would be key in the expansion of other sectors of the economy."

Moreover, Zimbabwe's economic elite had regular access to foreign exchange for certain types of conspicuous luxury product consumption (which, if profits were to be had from higher levels of reinvestment, could have been redirected). Foreign currency was also squandered on capital flight, in unknown but probably significant amounts. What there was available could certainly have been allocated more rationally. In the wake of a 1990 banking scandal involving foreign exchange, a Member of Parliament, J.C. Kufandada (*Hansard*, 15/8/90:1472), implored to his colleagues,

> Now the question that has often begged the answer, which answer has

> not been forthcoming, is do we indeed have a genuine foreign currency problem in Zimbabwe or is it not a question of allocation?... I wonder how long it will take us to wake up and plug up all these loopholes to make sure that whatever monies we have will be legitimately used for the development of this country and not for those well-placed manipulatory thieves that would like to get this money out of the country for their own designs elsewhere.

Even Chidzero, when facing bitter complaints from industrialists that there was only 30% as much foreign exchange in the mid-1980s as in 1972, responded bluntly: "Statistics can be made to lie. During the UDI period, there was inventiveness and drive. Where is that drive today? The problem as I see it is one of identification. The industrialists are not identifying with the nation" (*Herald*, 4/7/86).

This particular argument can be sustained only at a subjective level, yet the interests of a supposed "national capitalist class," as represented originally by the CZI (prior to the ascendance of a pro-ESAP faction), should be taken into consideration.[24] Through most of the 1980s, the majority of domestic manufacturers were definitely not oriented to international markets (in terms of which they would have required cutting-edge imported capital goods and advanced technology), but on the contrary to protection from international competition (Riddell 1983). In the early 1990s, the move to export-led growth justified industrialists' access to vast amounts of foreign exchange through the Open General Import License system.

Yet it is difficult to conclude that the renewed availability of hard currency on its own was responsible for increased fixed investment beyond late-1980s levels, given that much of the early 1990s borrowing was used instead as a means of stockpiling raw materials and speculating. And as interest rates soared to 8-10% in real terms in 1991, and remained at this level over subsequent years, it also became clear that many domestic private sector borrowers of foreign capital were simply seeking lower interest rates for investments they would have made anyway.

In turn, the Zimbabwe Reserve Bank had guaranteed the lower cost of foreign debt by insulating such borrowers from the cost of repaying hard currency loans with their rapidly-declining local currency, through "forward cover" protection. Zimbabwe taxpayers paid not only these direct costs (amounting to Z$2 billion in 1991 alone [World Bank 1995b, v.II:21]), but also indirectly, in the form of a huge foreign debt whose servicing was certain to become extremely onerous again in the late 1990s.

In point of fact, a valid argument may be that it was not the *lack* of foreign exchange during the 1980s, but rather the *surplus* of foreign exchange in the wrong hands and wrong sectors of the economy that most adversely affected the manufacturers. This is the argument of Ndlela (1984:72), who identifies in Zimbabwe what he terms a

> "Dutch disease" because of the observed impact of the North Sea gas production on the Dutch economy. The strong export revenues from gas caused an appreciation of the Dutch guilder against other currencies which then exposed local industries to more intense foreign competition, causing unemployment. Large foreign aid inflows can be a special case of the "Dutch disease." Such large foreign aid inflows have in fact had similar effects on Egypt, as those generated by export revenues from cocoa on Ghana's economy, copper on Zambia and petroleum revenues on oil producing countries.
>
> In the Zimbabwean case, the large inflows of foreign aid were likely to raise the price of inputs demanded by a certain sector (what we may call the booming sector) and initially increase the wages and salaries in this sector. In Zimbabwe, the booming sector was invariably the public sector at the beginning but it later on spread to other sectors. The other sectors that were likely to benefit directly from the boom were the services, utilities and transportation sectors... Thus the sector that stands to lose in this spending and resource movement effect is the manufacturing sector and in particular the still fragile heavy-industrial base of the economy, the capital goods sector.

Conclusion: Beyond stagnation?

In this chapter, an attempt has been made to paint the transition from Rhodesia to Zimbabwe in colors of continuity rather than change. Perhaps this has been best articulated by Cornelius Hoffman, a white (Afrikaner) commercial farmer who explained to *New York Times* journalist Joseph Lelyveld (1985:368–369) that he now "had a workers' committee, linked to the [ZANU] party organization, that had to give its approval before he could apply to the authorities to discharge an employee for cause. But the system worked smoothly and to his advantage... [Hoffman], far from grumbling about Marxist interference, as other whites were then doing, showed every sign of deriving a sportsman's satisfaction from his ability to play by the new rules."

The "new" rules may have been flexible enough, but the economy wasn't. As in the mid and late 1970s, the problem of overaccumulation stood as the key constraint to both absolute growth and to a more balanced form of development during the 1980s. Neither ZANU's ersatz socialist vision nor increasingly militant nationalist rhetoric confronted this reality effectively. It was, in the early 1990s, left to ESAP and its sponsors—international financiers and their local allies—to somewhat more conclusively break with certain of the traditions and institutions that were considered by orthodox economists to be most responsible for Zimbabwe's persistent stagnation. Yet, as documented in Chapter Twelve, this process occurred in a manner that led to depression, not revival. It also dramatically heightened unevenness and inequality.

Actually, ESAP was not as qualitative a break with the past as often claimed, for it was foreshadowed, we shall see in the next five chapters, by rising financial power and an increasing commitment to market-oriented social and economic policy. That the adoption of a market-oriented, "modernization theory" approach to development did nothing to cure stagnation was rarely considered.

Was there an inward-oriented, basic-needs alternative? The basic argument for moving along an export-oriented road was well-summarized by the CZI (1986:17–19):

> Zimbabwe has passed the "shallow" stage of simply replacing formerly imported consumer goods. It is standing on the threshold of a deeper phase, in which equipment, intermediate goods, machine tools and processes are being designed, modified and manufactured for use in the manufacturing sector itself and other sectors such as agriculture, mining, energy and telecommunications... Within Zimbabwe's manufacturing sector there is a very elaborate and diverse system of linkages. At the level of its 33 subsectors, it is estimated that about 70% of all possible linkages within manufacturing are taking place.

But the CZI's analysis accepts as a premise the structure of the economy—especially the skewed structure of effective demand—and in doing so begs three questions: first, what of the 30% more "possible linkages" within manufacturing; second, what of the disproportionalities between capital goods and consumer goods that could conceivably be addressed with certain forms of state intervention; and third, what of the discrepancies between luxury and basic-needs consumer goods?

The last point in particular bears closer attention, since the potential for further "inward industrialization" along this path was substantial. For example, as shown in Chapter Nine, housing is a commodity that can be produced with very minor import costs in Zimbabwe. Had there been a more equal distribution of income and strategic targeting of government subsidies after Independence, housing could easily have been the basis for a successful Keynesian "kick-start" and antidote to stagnation. And thorough-going land reform (as well as proactive intervention in financial markets and industrial organization) had been a key element of some East Asian industrializing countries' strategy for developing an internal class base for consumption of basic manufactured goods, and was occasionally suggested as the basis for inward-oriented capital accumulation (Robinson 1988).

Such approaches would not have solved the deep-rooted industrial overaccumulation crisis, but would probably have delayed and dampened the crisis by combining the best tendencies of manufacturing growth in the early UDI period (the broadening of production, the closer articulation with local markets, the localization of decision-making, and the control of financial markets that would make all the above feasible) with the post-Independence "Growth with Equity" rhetoric of meeting democratically-determined basic needs. But to understand why such a strategy would not be pursued in Zimbabwe, no matter its manifold advantages, requires consideration of how financial power-brokers and processes operated within and outside the state (Chapter Seven), in speculative markets such as the Zimbabwe Stock Exchange and real estate (Chapter Eight), and in both urban areas (Chapter Nine) and rural settings (Chapter Ten). Only then can the devastation caused by international financial control of much policy-making in Zimbabwe (Chapter Eleven)—and specifically the imposition of ESAP (Chapter Twelve)—be understood from the perspective that there were indeed paths to less uneven development, even if these were never really terribly well-mapped, much less explored.

Notes

1. All statistics not otherwise cited are from Central Statistical Office, *National Income and Expenditure Report* and the CSO *Quarterly Digest of Statistics* and—even when somewhat dated—reflect the latest and most accurate figures available.
2. For critiques of the "petty bourgeois" class character of the Zimbabwean liberation struggle see Yates (1980), Astrow (1983), and Sylvester (1990), and for an assessment of some of the more repressive aspects of the guerrilla strategy, see Kriger (1988).
3. See Martin and Johnson (1981), Lan (1985) and Ranger (1985).
4. Sender and Smith (1986:133) conclude their analysis of African capitalist development with the contention that "It is not a coincidence that working-class activity has been muffled by many post-Independence African governments in name of 'unity' or 'African socialism,' since it is precisely from organised labour that such regimes have most to fear."
5. Kangai, later the Minister of Industry and Commerce responsible for early

implementation of the Economic Structural Adjustment Programme, and then Agriculture Minister during the 1990s land redistribution scandal, was also noted for plagiarising, word-for-word, paternalistic speeches of a former Rhodesian Front Labour Minister (Woods 1988:290-291).

6. The ZANU Youth League, for example, issued a statement following one incident which accused the students of being "lawless reactionary elements... misguided by enemies of our revolution" (*Herald*, 10/10/89). Shortly afterwards even Education Minister Fay Chung (one of the more serious of left intellectuals within ZANU) labelled the protesting students "neo-Nazis" (*Africa South*, January 1990). For a full analysis of the initial round of conflict, see Ncube (1989:324-328). Major outbreaks of violence and rioting occurred at the university in following years, grounded in generally progressive student critiques of various government policies.
7. In the same spirit, Ron Davies and Dewar (1989:56) inexplicably found in Harare a "strictly applied policy of severe containment of informal and squatter housing development (appropriate to socialist thought)" (*sic*).
8. The scandal involving Willowvale assembly plant car allocations was only the tip of the iceberg, but did have the effect of leading to five ministerial resignations in 1989.
9. John Saxby (1989:79) offers this perceptive critique: "There is little here by way of a materialist analysis (in terms of the social base of the nationalist movement, for example) to explain why an emergent petty-bourgeois class has secured power. Nor... does the reader have a sense of the possible trajectories of social and political change." Four exceptions to the rule within the SAPES circle were Sam Moyo, Brian Raftopoulos, Lloyd Sachikonye and Arnold Sibanda. See also Saul's (1993) eloquent rebuttal to Mandaza's charges.
10. What, then, was the reason for the failure of urban socialism in Zimbabwe? Davies and Dewar (1989:43,52,55) argue that "The productive capacity of the national economy is limited. Furthermore the state is constrained by the capitalist economy in the degree to which it may determine the redistribution of surplus value." They also point to "a change of [state] actors, but not of fundamental structure," to "ongoing development momentum in existing new self-help, ultra-low cost home ownership schemes" as well as to recalcitrant colonial city officials and U.S. Agency for International Development guidelines. But the actual accumulation process (including the role of the state), as discussed in this and following chapters, is absent from their account. Like Teedon and Drakakis-Smith, Dewar (1987:24-26) also cites, as constraints to socialism, the prioritisation of rural over urban development, overambitious black expectations, the "difficulty in breaking the patterns of people historically engaged in survivalist strategies," and the risk to Zimbabwe's economic infrastructure.
11. But as Sachikonye (1995b:182) points out (and as is elaborated in the next chapter), "The proliferation of state development corporations should not be viewed as an altruistic strategy of the newly-installed state bourgeoisie to limit or pre-empt the expansion of the private sector. It can

be interpreted as a conscious attempt by the state-based bourgeoisie to carve a niche for itself for its own accumulation requirements."

12. One exception may have been DeBeers, which following conflicts with the Minerals Marketing Corporation of Zimbabwe—DeBeers insisted on imposing its Central Selling Organisation diamond cartel arrangement—was encouraged to leave. However in 1993 Mines Minister Eddison Zvobgo invited DeBeers back (*FG*, 28/10/93).
13. As examples of corporate influence, the CZI claimed successes in lobbying for removal of parastatal subsidies (and eventual privatisation); reduction in the size of the civil service; upgrading of the Zimbabwe Investment Centre; a variety of government assistance in export markets; and reductions in taxes (*The Industrialist*, October 1991).
14. "It is important to note that socialist countries have also had structural adjustment," rationalised the irrepressible Chung (*Sunday Mail*, 16/12/90):

    > Structural adjustment can therefore be utilised to strengthen socialism. It can also be utilised to strengthen capitalism. It very much depends on whether the belt-tightening is for the benefit of the people; for the benefit of capitalists who will use the accumulated wealth to develop the country; or for the benefit of capitalists who aim to expatriate the wealth without developing the country. All three possibilities are there today.

15. ZISCO is emblematic of failed state enterprise, as it suffered marketing problems, rising transport costs and bottlenecks, unfavourable export prices, a flight of skilled labour, and a shortage of foreign exchange for key inputs. As a result, government subsidies increased from Z$20 million in 1982-83 to Z$100 million two years later (Government of Zimbabwe 1986:138). ZISCO's early 1990s crisis was based largely on three factors: massive overcapacity (amounting to 50% of production); suicidal attempts to engage in what ZISCO's managing director termed "cut throat price competition" on the declining international markets (which the government demanded, for the sake of earning foreign currency); and debt financing which ate up 8% of gross sales revenue in 1990. The result was a loss of Z$675 million in the year ending in mid 1991, which in turn sparked renewed calls for ZISCO's privatisation. By 1994 ZISCO had been shut down after losses continued to mount, as even efforts to refurbish through Chinese suppliers came to naught.
16. For a list and case study analysis of disinvestment—though thoroughly misleading conclusions—see Zinyama (1989).
17. However, a study released simultaneously by the CZI's chief economist defined foreign ownership as 50% or more of equity, and found that only 141 out of 550 large manufacturing companies (26%) were foreign-owned. This compared with 48% surveyed in 1987 and 52% in 1985. Humphrey (1989, 4) explains that "since early 1987 there have been a

number of localisations of large previously foreign owned companies." In 1991, the CZI updated the survey, and found that the foreign ownership figure had declined to 23%. Of 105 foreign-owned firms (out of 516 surveyed), 58 had annual turnover in excess of Z$12.8 million, which accounted for 33% of the 174 total firms in this latter category (*The Industrialist*, November 1991). There is no obvious reconciliation of the ZIDS and CZI findings.

18. For an analysis of Lonrho that spells out in more detail personal relations between Rowland and Zimbabwe government leaders, see Hall (1989). Lonrho spokesperson Paul Spicer explained the dynamics openly: "Our relations with governments are very good. Our investments are very substantial, and if I have to put it like that, we get preferential treatment. If you've got muscle you can talk to the government and come to an understanding. Small people can't do that" (*South*, October 1988).
19. These included Leon Tempelsman and Son, Johnson and Johnson International, Ford Motor, Caltex, Xerox, Westinghouse, Ingersoll-Rand Company, Mobil, NCR Corporation, General Motors, Goodyear, Union Carbide Southern Africa, and PepsiCo.
20. Of note is the fact that O'Reilly is "pleased with our Zimbabwe investment in every respect," and that Zimbabwe profits and remittability compare favourably with other Heinz operations worldwide (Lowe-Morna, 1989, 34).
21. As a reflection of the (inflation-adjusted, Z$1980) effective demand shrinkage over this period, private final consumption expenditure, which had reached Z$382 per capita in 1983, sunk to Z$226 in 1987, a decline of 41%.
22. In 1995, the World Bank (1995b, v.II:118-121) reported a remarkable rise in gross fixed capital formation, allegedly beginning in 1985 and proceeding at "a real rate of 20% per annum. The increase in investment has been quite broad based with all sectors experiencing a significant increase; most of the investment has been in plant, machinery and vehicles and not so much in buildings." In particular, private sector fixed investment apparently rose from a low of 9.4% of GDP in 1983 to a high of 20.6% in 1991, according to the Bank. But the new finding—a deluge of (non-building) investment during the stagnant pre-ESAP period—is counterintuitive. It contradicts both the Bank's (e.g., 1989, 1992) own earlier reports on manufacturing cited above—a 1992 Bank study openly argued that the lack of fixed capital investment was the "principal cause of Zimbabwe's modest economic growth" (*FG*, 29/1/93)—and data from the CSO's Census of Industrial Production, which recorded an enormous real decline (not increase, as the Bank claims) in real investment during 1992. The Bank's response (1995b, v.II:120) was that the CSO numbers "seriously underestimate" the investment "surge," but it offers no explanation of how or why. This issue is revisited in Chapters Eight and Twelve.
23. Other subsectors where the import content was less than 5% in the early 1980s included cement (5%), machinery for mines (3%), plumbing and

irrigation equipment (5%), cables (2%), and tissue paper (2%). Subsectors which had extremely high levels of import content included pesticides and insecticides (90%), aluminum extrusion for the building industry (90%), moulding for plastics (100%), televisions and radios (80-100%), trailer axles (98%), rubber products (95%), ball pens (90%), and carpets (98%) (Government of Zimbabwe 1986:139-41).

24. There is reason to doubt the value of an ascription like "national capital" in view of the fact that over time, foreign ownership of the Zimbabwean manufacturing sector declined, whereas the orientation of the CZI moved progressively towards international markets. The difference is observed, for example, in the approaches of two different CZI chief economists, namely Roger Riddell's unbridled hostility to the World Bank in the mid 1980s, as compared to Mike Humphrey's early 1990s fawning over ESAP. For an analysis of the evolution from a liberal-pluralist perspective, see Skalnes 1993.

chapter seven

Financiers and Bureaucrats

Introduction

This chapter explores the exercise of power over the Zimbabwean economy by financiers and financial bureaucrats. On the surface it is easy to pose of the financial system a question that emerged from the previous chapter, namely, why did underdevelopment of a section of the population persist in a sector of the economy overseen by a new breed of ostensibly radical bureaucrats? After all, more than any other sector, finance was permeated with tight regulation, state ownership, and high overall visibility amenable to ZANU's populist rhetoric.

But the 1980s bureaucrats were not the same breed as the technocrats of the mid-1960s, steeped in monetary and financial interventionism, who with Ian Smith had so effectively bottled up capital to serve the new national project, UDI. Instead the Finance Ministry was led initially by the hot-headed populist Enos Nkala. Bank nationalization had been mooted even by UNCTAD's major economic study, and the 1981 "Growth with Equity" framework included a commitment to greater state intervention. Mugabe asserted, at one point, "We reject a policy which accepts money from the peasant farmers, the small traders, and the cooperatives so it can be re-directed to the big corporations" (*Herald*, 14/4/84). Yet, ultimately, that is precisely what happened within the banking system, and with the active participation of the government.

Unlike the economy as a whole, finance was a high-growth sector, particularly during the late 1980s when speculative tendencies were rampant. Most branches of the financial system benefitted from extremely rapid asset growth. In the first decade of Independence national income tripled in nominal terms (inflation ran at approximately 15% annually), but was far outpaced by the assets of financial institutions: commercial bank assets increased by a factor of 6; merchant banks' by 5.5; and finance houses' by 7. The profits of financial institutions, in relation to other companies, were very healthy throughout. Unprecedented escalation was witnessed in stock market share values and real estate prices and was mainly concentrated over an even shorter period (1984-91). The Zimbabwean stock market was the world's fastest-growing during 1987-90 (and again in 1993-94).

To comprehend all of this requires analysis not only of the economic "structure" and its contradictions, but also of "agency"—which I take to include extreme institutional (and perhaps personal) biases within the system, as well as the failure of state bureaucrats to correct these biases in spite of having formidable powers at their fingertips. This requires a study of how, concretely, bias operated and of the scope for action of leading state personnel. What freedom and power, in other words, did the Finance Ministry, Reserve Bank, and other national-level agents possess? What personal interests and ideological influences intervened to prevent them from using that power to change the system in line with official pronouncements?

We cannot conclusively answer these questions, of course, without considering the constraints imposed on local actors by international financial power (the subject of Chapters Eleven and Twelve). Nevertheless, before returning in later chapters to a structural analysis that seeks explanations of the role of finance in speculation and uneven geographical development, a review must be undertaken of some central issues of financial sector agency—i.e., discrimination in lending and employment, corruption, and the rise of a black financial petty bourgeoisie over whom the figure of Finance Minister Bernard Chidzero towered.

Bias in the financial system

During the immediate post-Independence period, financial institutions managed to carry on business as usual, expanding their depositor base while maintaining tight control over the direction of flows of funds in the economy. State intervention was aimed in part at buying a small piece of the banking system for the emergent black financial elite, rather than at transforming it for the country's majority. Various researchers have compiled adequate institutional descriptions of the numerous public and private sector financial institutions in Zimbabwe, and these need not be repeated here (Chimombe 1983; Clarke 1980b; Makgetla 1983; Seidman 1986; Whitsun Foundation 1983). Instead, we consider how credit distribution was affected by Zimbabwean financiers' institutional biases.

In early 1981 the government bought Johannesburg-based Nedbank's 62% share of Rhobank (for "a very fair price") and renamed it Zimbank (Makgetla 1983:IX, 20). Six months later it bought 47% of a new local subsidiary of the Bank of Credit and Commerce International (BCCI). (BCCI went bankrupt in 1991, and its Zimbabwe subsidiary apparently suffered such severe financial problems that the government was able to purchase the remaining 53% of the shares for less than Z$1 million—and then changed the bank's name to Commercial Bank of Zimbabwe.) Thanks to official patronage (including, we shall see, turning a blind eye to fraud), Zimbank and BCCI vastly increased their share of commercial and merchant bank deposits during the 1980s. The government also gained a leading stake in Fidelity Life Assurance of Zimbabwe in 1988, following the sale of shares by Legal and General Society of London through the state-owned Zimbabwe Reinsurance Group.

In addition, the 51% government-owned Zimbabwe Development Bank was initiated in 1983 to make loans to medium- and large-scale businesses. The Industrial Development Corporation, once responsible for the initiation of major industrial expansion (in the days of Rhodesian state capitalism), was given continued support by the new government. At the low end of the market, a Credit Guarantee Corporation half-heartedly supported, in a manner, small businesses by offering collateral to their commercial bank lenders.[1] In addition, a Small Enterprise Development Corporation (SEDCO) was founded and immediately given good access to international loans and financial expertise (although, as noted below, the attached conditionality may have been more harmful than the assistance).

But in achieving ZANU's economic objectives—especially, broadening ownership of the means of production to black entrepreneurs—these myriad state interventions failed miserably. SEDCO's ineptitude was reflected in, among other statistics, an administrative costs/total assets ratio of 39% in the mid-1980s, and by 1990 a low loan/job cost of Z$14,500 (on the basis of Z$36 million in loans to more than 1,000 borrowers) (World Bank 1986b:9; *FG*, 10/8/91). In the rural areas, the Agricultural Finance Corporation also proved broadly ineffectual for both peasants and small commercial farmers, who defaulted on their debts at record rates, as Chapter Ten shows.

Attempting to support an emergent petty bourgeoisie through making credit available or through financial sector employment was not the only basis for government intervention, of course. Just as important, though even less successful, was the concerted effort of bureaucrats and financiers to expand the actual boundaries of the money economy. But if, as the *Herald* (29/7/84) reported, "IMF experts believe that the base of taxpayers should be widened to create awareness of the cash economy and monetary constraints," they soon had to come to grips with limited buying power. Typical was the following sad refrain from *Financial Gazette* editorialists: "A great deal was said in the previous budget of the need to add the informal sector to the tax base by the end of the 1993/94 fiscal year. Nothing much has been done about it despite the tight financial problems faced by government" (*FG*, 28/6/95). As former World Bank official and Finance Ministry chief economist Norman Reynolds concluded after extensive attempts to enhance rural savings and credit, "The fact is that in Zimbabwe cash hardly circulates outside of the cities" (1988:73).

Raising access to formal credit for urban residents through building societies (see Chapter Nine) and for small farmers through the Agricultural Finance Corporation (Chapter Ten) remained a priority of government economic development strategy. However, to qualitatively expand the money economy—both geographically and socially, across the class (and ethnic, gender, and generational) spectrum of Zimbabwe—would necessarily entail more than just the introduction of new financial mechanisms, incentives, and institutions. There were apparently still severe racial biases (especially lending and employment discrimination) in Zimbabwean finance, and these were never effectively addressed.

Lending and hiring bias

Bank discrimination against small entrepreneurs has been recorded across Africa (Iliffe 1983:68) and, in a country like Zimbabwe where financial acumen was relatively high, its persistence long into the Independence era was easy to identify and rebuke.[2] Black access to business finance was a long-standing problem. Even as free enterprise-oriented reforms escalated in the late 1970s, the credit barrier proved nearly insurmountable. Over a four-year period through early 1983, bank credit to black entrepreneurs amounted to a meager 414 loans for Z$2.25 million (most for the retail trade) (Chimombe 1983: 109). There was not much improvement during the 1980s, as Professor Tony Hawkins noted in the *Financial Times* (21/8/89):

> While the money markets are awash with funds and the banks underlent, investment levels are inadequate to the task of maintaining the capital stock intact, let alone generating the 200,000 new jobs needed each year. The banks deny that they are turning away potentially viable black entrepreneurs simply because they lack collateral, the most frequent complaint levelled by black businessmen... [Yet] ***official figures show that only 3% of bank lending goes to black Zimbabweans.*** (emphasis added)

The Reserve Bank ultimately ordered the commercial banks to increase their black borrower ratio from 3% to just 5%, or face punitive reserve requirements (Zimbabwe has a 99% black population so this should not have been extremely difficult). Responses ranged from the defensive rebuttal that "banking returns do not reveal the full extent of actual lending to blacks" (Girdlestone 1990), to the acknowledgement that, as the chief executive of Standard Chartered put it, "Banks have been criticized, not entirely unjustly, for perhaps being overly cautious in their lending policies. This caution has to a large degree arisen through a lack of understanding of the exact nature of the requirements of the borrower operating outside what has become known as the formal sector" (*Herald*, 1/11/90).

Government officials such as John Nkomo often tried to explain bank discrimination in terms of foreign control: "I am well aware that most banks in Zimbabwe have their roots and still maintain links with parent head offices in the industrialized countries of the west and their work-methods and perspectives derive from there. In other words, in assessing and determining courses of action and prospects for expansion, their judgement is largely influenced from outside" (Zimbabwe Department of Information 1988). But even government-owned Zimbank, one Member of Parliament (J.C. Kufandada) alleged in 1990, "has a very good reputation of being anti-black. The statistic speaks for itself. It is clear and I think we now begin to understand why there is a certain species of Zimbabweans that is given priority when it comes to loans in our own bank" (*Hansard*, 15/8/90, 1472).

According to commentator Matthew Chandavengerwa (1994:4), small entrepreneurs viewed banks as a whole as "arrogant, obstructive and insensitive." Specific complaints were that "too often banks raise invoices late, impose interest charges without notice and usually in retrospect and keep their operations under constant conditions of fear and uncertainty by threatening to call in their loans at any time." The role of the banks' solicitous black spokesperson (Barclays' Isaac Takawira), the increase in black bank managers, and the opening of small business bureaus were all viewed by Chandavengerwa as tokenism: "simply an attempt to keep indigenous enterprises at bay."

At one point, even the *Financial Gazette* (28/10/93) was moved to editorialize,

> It is increasingly becoming difficult to do business when one is black in Zimbabwe. Financial institutions, most of which are white-dominated, have used their economic power effectively. They have pulled the plugs on corporations headed by blacks and imposed onerous conditions to keep the financial tap flowing to the same executives. The effect of this has been to thoroughly humiliate black executives, most of whom have been caught by the current harsh financing environment. On the other hand handsome rescue packages amounting to spoon-feeding have been put in place to whites in similar positions. White mismanagement and general financial problems have been tolerated and encouraged through an unlimited and unconditional availability of loan funding. The banks and the white community will vehemently deny that there is racism. But this is a futile exercise. If they deny its existence then they clearly do not understand the predicament of their black countrymen.[3]

Nor did non-bank financial institutions accomplish much in opening their doors to black businesses. Fifteen years after Independence, the chair of the National Reconstruction and Development Board, Elton Mangoma (a chartered accountant and former group financial director of the Hunyani paper/packaging conglomerate), complained, "Blacks are being marginalized on the [Zimbabwe Stock] Exchange, and are being told they are not good enough. The few companies that have a majority of black members are so heavily discounted on the stock exchange, reinforcing the same sentiment that blacks are incapable as big business managers" (*FG*, 2/2/95). In any case, black board members were rare. Ticharwa Masimba (1994:4) points out that of 62 companies registered on the Zimbabwe Stock Exchange (ZSE) in late 1994, the boards of just five were majority-black (Delta, Mhangura Copper Mines, Wankie Colliery, Zimbabwe Financial Holdings, and Zimbabwe Newspapers). About a quarter of the ZSE-listed companies had no black board members and the remainder had just one or two. Cluff Resources—which Masimba accused of draining so many millions from Zimbabwe—had only one black out of a dozen board members.

As discussed in more detail in Chapter Ten, gender discrimination was also a standard operating practice of Zimbabwe's financial institutions, partly because of slow legal changes which made it difficult for women to gain housing and land title rights. The World Bank (1991b:18) noted that "An adequate legal framework for lending to women still has not been created." Banks seemed to ignore the fact that women made up the bulk of the 5,500 savings clubs established in Zimbabwe between 1970 and 1985, and thus had something of a collateral and regular payment record to fall back on (Nowak 1989:71).

Seen from below, discrimination was a devastating experience. As Rasmussen (1992:226) concluded in an exhaustive study of small-scale enterprises in two outlying towns (Murewa and Gutu), 39% of respondents used their local banks for savings (an equivalent number use the Post Office Savings Bank), yet "Most small enterprises state that capital access is a problem, and, evidently, the enterprises would not mind obtaining a heavily subsidised loan without presenting any collateral security."

But in Zimbabwe, the government was unsuccessful in assisting banks to meet such needs. Even state-owned banks (such as Zimbank and BCCI) and "indigenous financial institutions" proved either as biased as the expatriate banks in their lending, or too small to be effective. For example, the Zimbabwe government inherited a Development Finance Company, founded with R$3 million in 1979 to make loans to black small-scale enterprises, but which "dissipated its resources during the regime immediately preceding Independence by making politically-motivated loans, many of which had to be written off," according to the World Bank. This initiative was formally shut down in 1984 (World Bank 1986b:5).

The post-Independence state, which was able (for a full decade) to bolster an emergent middle class through civil service employment and welfare spending functions, was ultimately unable to carry off a sustainable credit-based expansion of the commercial petty bourgeoisie (which instead resorted to mark-ups on retail pricing that, by 1994, were so high as to invite direct competition from wholesalers and even manufacturers) (*FG*, 19/5/94). SEDCO was provided a Z$1 million capital base in 1983, and about 90% of the first batch of SEDCO loans were to merchants, with a small percentage to emergent industrialists. Half were in urban areas, and cooperatives received a quarter of the initial loans. Loan terms were generally two years and the average interest rate was 14.3%. However, World Bank conditionality subsequently raised this to 18% for urban projects and 16% for rural areas.

Indeed Bank conditionality on SEDCO was extensive. The need for SEDCO credit was greatest in rural areas, and according to the Bank

(1986b:18-27), "Government has indicated that it would like SEDCO to assist, on a selective basis, cooperatives and Small Scale Enterprises in rural growth points with limited infrastructure. Government and SEDCO, however, are keenly aware of the potential risks of such lending to SEDCO's financial integrity and its cost to Government." The Bank therefore insisted on controlling this process through a different fund and, in the negotiations over a US$10 million loan to SEDCO in 1986 noted that "Bank supervision missions would also closely monitor SEDCO's performance."

The Bank decided that the root of the rural loan problem was that "Rural businesses cannot offer title deeds as collateral for bank loans because land in the communal areas is not privately owned," and mandated that title deeds in Growth Centers be made available. Moreover, SEDCO was told it must "not modify its policy statement without prior consultation with the Bank." SEDCO was promised Z$500 million in government funds over a five-year period in the mid-1990s, but in 1993/94 it received only Z$40 million.

Notwithstanding continuing financial support from government, Rasmussen (1992:226) reported, "The knowledge of SEDCO as a possible supporting institution is not impressive in the district centers. Only half of the potentially eligible small enterprises know what SEDCO is." The Credit Guarantee Company was even more obscure and ineffectual. Loan insurance functions, supported by the Reserve Bank, reached a level of only 150 loans per year because, as the World Bank concluded, "Despite the increasing demand from the emerging short-term as well as medium-term credits, the banks remain reluctant to significantly expand their lending levels."[4]

Other private sector small business development funds of an earlier generation—Anglo American Development Corporation and the Industrial Promotion Corporation of Rhodesia and Nyasaland, and a Zurich-based development finance agency, EDESA—had been introduced by international capital in part for politically-motivated reasons, and were just as ineffective at getting credit to the black petty bourgeoisie. A subsequent World Council of Churches small business credit fund administered through the Zimbabwe National Chamber of Commerce (ZNCC) demanded loan repayments in hard currency, which carrying an offshore interest rate of 9% in 1994 translated into 30% in local terms, according to the ZNCC, compared with the 5% then being charged by the Reserve Bank for an IBDC loan fund (*FG*, 5/5/94).

Under such circumstances it is easy to see why credit remained an emotional issue. When the Indigenous Business Development Center was established in 1990, a key priority was to gain better access to small business loans, and the IBDC rapidly collected a membership of 4,000, doubled it to 8,300 by early 1994, and made itself a highly visible lobby group

(Raftopoulos 1991:16; *FG*, 13/1/94). In 1992, the World Council of Churches Development Fund advanced a Z$30.6 million loan (and Barclays advanced Z$40,000) (*FG*, 20/6/92). But controversy arose over a government budget allocation of Z$100 million to the IBDC in 1992. In the words of the then secretary-general of the IBDC, Strive Masiyiwa, "There are certain non-indigenous people who are frantically lobbying to be part of this money. But we will fight tooth and nail to ensure that they won't get any cent from that money since it is us who solely went to the government begging for that money as far back as February."

Masiyiwa was given assurances by Chidzero that "government would ensure that the funds would be exclusive to indigenous businessmen" (*FG*, 27/8/92). Yet Chandavengerwa (1994:4) insists that instead, the banks—given responsibility for managing the Z$100 million—partially redirected the monies into paying off the outstanding loans of members of the IBDC. This "created a great deal of anguish," for even after the loans had been paid off, "some banks were not prepared to extend working capital facilities." Chemist Sibiza (then IBDC president) agreed that "the Z$100 million credit facility made available through the commercial banks never benefitted IBDC members" (*FG*, 13/1/94).

Finally, in January 1994, the IBDC was appeased when Z$400 million was reserved by the Reserve Bank for black small-scale business credit, to be administered through the Credit Guaranty Company (CGC). Offering loans at 5% interest, the CGC quickly took in more than 6,000 applications worth Z$165 million and granted 4,583 loans worth Z$142 million. Ordinarily, the CGC processed 800 loan applications per year, up from just over 100 during the 1980s (*FG*, 12/1/94).

Masiyiwa was also a vigorous campaigner when commercial banks were an issue. In mid-1992, he publicly accused Standard Chartered Bank of being "the most conservative bank when it came to dealing with indigenous people," arguing that a century "was a very long time for the bank to start considering localising part of its external shareholding." Masiyiwa demanded that Standard Chartered Bank appoint a black chief executive: "Certainly this would be a good time for some serious management changes. Do we have to wait another one hundred years before they make a commitment to black advancement?" (*FG*, 13/9/92).[5]

Due to the objective conditions imposed by overaccumulation, it was possible for there to coexist excessive flows of funds into financial markets, a limited market of local borrowers, and a lack of prospects for international expansion—alongside well-structured, time-honored discrimination which appeared pervasive in the business norms and practices of Zimbabwe's banks and bankers (both expatriate and indigenous). Even the few exceptions suggest the levels to which entrepreneurs had to sink to gain access to capital. In the late 1980s, for example, Isaac Takawira of Barclays and Willie Ford and Fanuel Muhwati of Merchant Bank of Central Africa (MBCA) together bought a South African-owned company (Flexible Packaging) for which they were financed by MBCA, leading one Member of Parliament to comment, "It would appear to me that there had been what is termed overseas as some form of insider trading." Employees of Flexible were expecting to buy 25% of the company as it became the first black-owned listing on the stock market. But according to MP Byron Hove, "The employees felt cheated, and felt that the big sharks, as it were, grabbed the cake from their very lips" (*Moto,* May 1992).

A few new financial institutions emerged out of the black petty bourgeoisie's frustration.[6] Yet aside from the single area of short-term insurance,[7] penetrating the well-established and tightening financial markets appeared next to impossible, as big capital simply continued to ignore black entrepreneurs. With the state unable or unwilling to force banks to change their lending policy, by 1990 the situation was so desperate that the CZI stepped in. Purporting to support the development of a petty-bourgeois manufacturing class (i.e., its potential competition), the CZI chief economist (Mike Humphrey) firmly advocated less government intervention in credit markets rather than more:

> Interest rates should be decontrolled, the rigid controls on the areas of operations of the various types of institutions should be loosened, and financial institutions should be allowed to offer venture capital in the form of equity. It is only under these changed conditions that the financial institutions will obtain the resources needed, and the incentive, to consider financing more of the financially riskier new enterprises. (CZI 1990:3)

Some of the CZI misconceptions should be countered at once. The incentive to invest in certain black businesses did in fact exist, as witnessed by the extension of some limited forms of credit by a few financial institutions (particularly the merchant-oriented finance houses), but did not extend as far as funding new manufacturing enterprises. Chinyoka (1988:103) explains,

> Despite the fact that some of the finance houses are subsidiaries of commercial banks, they tend to have a more liberal attitude with respect to assisting small enterprises. This might be due to the inherent nature of lease financing that it is self-secured. While they have yet to make an impact in the manufacturing sector, they have been assisting significantly in the service sector—that is commercial trucks, passenger vehicles, etc.

Yet when considering the cost of credit, Chinyoka continues, "small-scale entrepreneurs are often crippled by the high rates of interest charged by finance houses." Mupandiki (1985:143) notes that even the relatively mild (in retrospect) early 1980s increase in commercial interest rates (from 4.5% to 9.5%) "contributed to shifting income from the poor to the financial institutions—most of which are foreign-owned. While the large foreign-owned companies can afford to pay higher interest rates, their increased cost had squeezed many smaller would-be African entrepreneurs out of business."

Thus the sorts of interventions the CZI proposed—especially higher rates—would not result in the predicted redistribution of finance, but would instead limit the commercial petty bourgeoisie at an earlier point in their business trajectory. Indeed the arrival of positive real interest rates in the early 1990s was accompanied by a credit crunch of unprecedented proportions. As the deputy minister for industry and commerce, Simon Moyo, observed in 1994, "Small and medium-scale enterprises are plagued by an assortment of viability problems including lack of access to finance due to under-capitalization and limited development of institutions for the provision of financial and technical support for this sector" (*FG*, 19/5/94).

Racial discrimination in the banking system is a real phenomenon, though probably no more so than in other parts of the white-controlled economy. Barclays, Zimbank, and Standard all eventually opened small business loan departments to serve emergent black firms, but such incremental institutional change would not make much difference. Part of the problem, it was alleged, was the race and class composition of high-ranking bank officials.

Although employment in the finance, insurance, and real estate sector grew dramatically during the 1980s, outpacing everything else in the economy save public health and education, institutional power was maintained at the top of a very steep, white-dominated hierarchy (a few blacks managed to climb to higher rungs, but these were mainly government financial sector ladders, which tended to move personnel from state finance into industry, not into private finance). As the number of financial sector employees rose by 35%, the per capita salary of those employees in relation to the national economy declined noticeably during the early 1980s. The result was a potential for severe conflict not only between banks and their clients, but within banks as well.

In 1985, the press began picking up some of the allegations. According to the chair of the Zimbabwe Society of Bank Officials, Richard Mawoyo, "Discontent among black bank workers is the result of promotion expectations built up over the past five years" (*Herald*, 11/10/85).

Allegations of bias led Barclays officials to announce that "all branches of Barclays Bank will have to submit to their head office names of all candidates considered for promotion along with those of the candidates they are recommending" (*Herald*, 30/10/85). Two years later, Standard Chartered employees embarked on a formal work stoppage, based on claims "that management was practicing racial discrimination in employment and other conditions of service... Employees also alleged that black advancement had been resisted with the result that there were no blacks in decision-making positions at all despite the fact that the vast majority of the workers in the bank were black." The allegations led to an extensive investigation by the Labor Ministry, and a finding that

> many of the employment practices pursued by the bank though neutral on their face, tended to perpetuate past discrimination while others tended to discriminate in practice. These practices include: exclusion of blacks from key decision-making organs and sensitive posts such as in the advancements department; absence of any open recruitment or promotion policy which tended to favor the insiders, friends and relatives, a haphazard grading structure which resulted in large disparities in salaries, benefits and other conditions of service between whites and blacks; appointing white pensioners and giving high salaries to security positions which could have been filled by younger qualified persons including blacks; the existence of an unhealthy and almost hostile relationship between some members of the management team and the Workers' Committee. (Department of Information 1987)

With tensions throughout the financial services industry still not resolved by the end of 1987, Chidzero told a meeting of bankers, "I would like to reiterate my call made about two years ago about black advancement in our financial sector... Although there has been some positive response by some institutions, others still have to work harder to ensure that their management structures reflect the new order in the country" (Department of Information 1987). But controversies continued raging at Standard Chartered and other banks over discrimination.

In addition, Anglo American Corporation's Bard Discount House faced resignations by five senior black managers in late 1994, when a white managing director was granted a Z$475,000 profit-sharing bonus while many blacks received nothing. Anglo Zimbabwe chair Roy Lander defended the profit sharing and attributed problems to "a lack of communication within the organization" (*FG*, 15/12/94). The Discount Company of Zimbabwe also lost two top black managers. As the *Financial Gazette* (5/1/95) reported, "most of the black workers in discount houses and stockbroking firms are crying foul over alleged racial inequalities in terms of promotions and remunerations."

Suffice it to say, the perception of discrimination continued even after the elite (e.g., Leonard Tsumba of Zimbank) attained senior bank management positions. Protests, work stoppages, and full-fledged strike action at Zimbabwe's financial institutions were common throughout the 1990s.

Corruption

If discrimination persisted, so too another form of economic activity prospered beyond the boundary of rational market exchange relations: corruption. According to Sachikonye (1995b:183), clientelism led to "widespread nepotism in recruitment and promotion practices, embezzlement of funds and corruption." This was not the sole preserve of a new government bureaucratic elite intent on personal capital accumulation, although this ubiquitous phenomenon must not be discounted. Corruption also found its way into the banks, which as a matter of ordinary business practice not only maintained price-fixing retail cartels, but regularly inflated interest charges on overdrawn accounts (*FG*, 2/6/94).

Briefly consider two of the more spectacular cases of banking system fraud—involving BCCI during the 1980s and Zimbank in 1990—which between them suggest several telling features of Zimbabwean finance. According to a United States Senate Foreign Relations Committee report, *The BCCI Affair*, a briefcase containing £500,000 was delivered by a BCCI official to a London hotel during the course of Lancaster House negotiations in 1979. As another bank official, Akbar Bilgrami, confirmed to Senate staff, "We paid Mugabe and [Joshua] Nkomo." Then in 1981, BCCI Chief Executive Officer Agha Hasan Abedi, his personal assistant Nazir Chinoy, and BCCI officer Aluddin Sheikh went, in Chinoy's words, "to the opening of a joint venture with Zimbabwe. I think to get permission for establishing a bank in Zimbabwe that money was paid to President Mugabe and to Nkomo." Chinoy claimed that Sheikh

> went off on his own to see Nkomo who was the chief opposition at the time, and then he went off to see President Mugabe, and when they talked they wanted me out of the room... Mr Sheikh carried a bag with him. At the time I had a suspicion that you don't get permission as a foreign bank so easily without a payment. Without favors, it wouldn't be so easy to get a bank that fast, especially given the opposition of the British banks who were already established there.

BCCI failed in July 1991 when its global pyramid-scheme of deposit-taking, drug money laundering, and rampant bribery of international officials imploded, and the national railways of both Zimbabwe and Zambia reportedly lost Z$330 million in deposits. Member of Parliament Edson Ncube alleged that this stemmed from political appointments to the parastatal railroad: "Because of these political appointments, at one stage our bank account for the National Railroad of Zimbabwe was transferred from this one bank to BCCI. What has happened to these funds has not been fruitful" (*Weekend Gazette*, 13/12/91). Zimbabwe was also a prolific borrower from BCCI. In March 1991 the government owed the bank US$17 million, according to the Senate report, all of which had to be repaid, even if Zimbabweans' deposits had vanished.[8]

In a second case, Zimbank—the main state-owned bank—was the subject of a national scandal involving top politicians. A Member of Parliament, A.T. Mangwende, alleged "gross irregularities involving substantial amounts in foreign exchange, import licenses and other related malpractices" at Zimbank and a white-owned shell company (Lorac Pvt Ltd). Although the facts of the case were never conclusively established, the charge illustrates the power of Zimbabwe's financial institutions, both materially (in their foreign currency-handling responsibilities) and psychologically (in their relations with small black businesspeople). According to Mangwende,

> The unsuspecting emergent businessman goes to a bank with his import license to organize funding for whatever transaction he will have obtained the license for. In the bank, this particular bank, there are senior banking officials who would then direct the unsuspecting emergent businessman to this particular company to be funded. Instead of the bank doing it, the officials in the bank choose to direct the poor emergent businessman to this financial shark. What happens, of course, is that as soon as the businessman gets there and is introduced by some officials in Zimbank, he surrenders his license because he wants to get funds.

In other words, the Zimbank officials refused to process the application, instead directing the clients to their colleagues in Lorac (one Zimbank official was actually employed by Lorac inbetween stints at the bank).

> What then happens, Mr. Speaker, is that after some time, the emergent businessman is advized that in fact, his goods have arrived and had been sold at a much less prices than otherwize and therefore he has a shortfall. The next thing when the man starts to complain, summons are quickly issued. I have a list of over 40 emergent businessmen who are in that predicament as a result of this financial chicanery. (*Hansard*, 15/8/90:1460-1461)

But the chicanery came to light because Lorac itself ran into repayment problems and owed Zimbank Z$8 million on an unsecured bank overdraft by the time the scandal broke. There were also alleged political contacts with Lorac involving one of the country's two vice-presidents and as many as seven cabinet ministers, who reportedly had received certain favors.[9]

But perhaps more tellingly, the incident revealed several features of the institutional bias of Zimbabwean finance. Most obvious was the direct collaboration of white and black financiers (even in a state-owned bank) with a corrupt form of merchant capital (Lorac), a combination which served to make short work of Zimbabwe's fabled exchange and import control system. But also clear in this incident was the role of the black entrepreneur, who willingly—and illegally—turned over import licenses to unauthorized dealers. The so-called "briefcase businessman" phenomenon was, by the late 1980s, an oft-criticized but well-trod path to petty accumulation, given the great potential in the sphere of finance for precisely these sorts of invitations to corruption.[10] Lastly, there was the suspiciously passive role of key government civil servants and politicians. As J.C. Kufandada complained in Parliament,

> I do not understand why the Senior Minister [Chidzero] did not institute enquiries when press reports surfaced and in particular when the former Minister of Trade and Commerce who himself reported to the Senior Minister of Finance, expressed concern at the racket. I wonder why such senior banking officers that we have entrusted with our national patrimony should be given such protection. (*Hansard* 15/8/90:1468)

While Zimbank's relationships with clients were spotlighted in this particular instance, an underlying aspect of the entire operation of the banking system was, in a sense, unveiled. That friendly relations between regulators and regulated turn quickly to corruption under conditions of overaccumulation crisis is nothing new. In the late 1980s such conditions gave way to corruption scandals involving high finance in Japan, Greece, Jordan, and even the United States, in each case toppling heads of government (or in the US case, the first-and third-ranking Democratic Party officials in Congress).

The depths of visible financial corruption never plunged so far in Zimbabwe. But Bulawayo lawyer David Coltart testified in 1991: "From the evidence before me as a lawyer I believe that corruption within government and Zimbabwean society is rife and that the Willowvale scandal pales into insignificance compared to the level of corruption now" (*FG*, 19/9/91). Brian Raftopoulos (1991:12) describes the Sandura

Commission investigation into Willowvale as

> an epic tragedy: an heroic liberation struggle, the transfer of power, the making of individual reputations within the broader framework of social transformation; and then the antithesis, of the corrupting influence of power, the untidy, grubby manipulations of accumulation, the trial, exposure and, in one case, suicide. To many analysts, this process represented the almost ineluctable logic of the propensity of the political elite to accumulate at any cost; the ubiquitous neo-colonial denouement of the predictable petty-bourgeois project.

Aside from complaints by white outsiders and dissident left intellectuals, the degeneracy of the petty-bourgeois bureaucrat was confirmed by the man in charge of the civil service, Eddison Zvobgo, who acknowledged in 1992 that there was "a high incidence" of corruption in a government "wrought with bribery, patronage, embezzlement and extortion" (*FG*, 25/6/92). Bribery was uncovered in ministries responsible for environment, tourism, and construction and public works (*FG*, 24/3/94). Of note in this regard is that many of the most important of the emergent financial elite began their ascent from the public sector, especially, as Arnold Sibanda (1990:8-9) comments, from parastatal managerial positions:

> The reactionary petty bourgeoisie fills these management posts either with an incompetent element that is ideologically bankrupt in terms of the philosophy of socialist transformation, or that is anti-socialist pure and simple, and sees its appointment as an opportunity to establish links with foreign capital for purposes of carving a base for its own primitive accumulation. Corrupt appointments on the basis of "class friends," "ethnic comrades," or "regional home boys" take precedence over radical ideological inclination, competence and qualification for the job and recognition that the task is a struggle which is part of the general class struggle against imperialism.[11]

The most important aspect of this in relation to the early growth of the black petty bourgeoisie as a class was probably the "briefcase businessman" phenomenon, as noted above, but there emerged black financial elites who had a much more respectable orientation. On the one hand, bank personnel largely consist of "black people not in meaningful positions," as MP T. Mudariki put it. One ironic result, already noted, is that black access to credit is typically suffocated by white "old boy" networks, notwithstanding the fact that today most mid-level bank employees (including the bulk of branch loan officers) are black.

On the other hand, however, the apparent discriminatory nature of banking—affecting primarily the black commercial petty bourgeoisie—was not able to detain a few key individuals who springboarded ahead of the classical black petty bourgeoisie as compradors with domestic and international finance. In doing so, their protestations to the contrary notwithstanding, they effectively ratified the continuation of black petty-bourgeois subordination to financial capital. It is important, hence, to go beyond chronic charges of race discrimination and strong hints of financial intemperance, in order to search out the particular class orientation of changes that took place in Zimbabwe's financial system after Independence. Again, the point of such a study is to identify where personal agency, working through state institutions, has a material effect on the exercise of financial power.

Emergent financial elites

A poignant cry rang out in Parliament in 1990:

> Our party has called for the democratization of the banking sector several times but nothing so far has been done, ten years after Independence. Is this what our heroic combatants fought for? It appears that there are people who are not willing or who benefit from the non-democratization of the banking sector. Maybe they are benefitting from the crumbs that fall off the table, who knows? If you go into any of these banks you will find that a lot of black people are not in meaningful positions (T. Mudariki, *Hansard,* 30/8/90, 2081).

This was, a decade after Independence, an increasingly plaintive complaint. Even President Robert Mugabe (1989:358) openly expanded on the theme in his surprisingly frank contribution to Canaan Banana's nationalist text *Turmoil and Tenacity:* "There exists among the membership of the new ZANU(PF) a minority, but very powerful bourgeois group which champions the cause of international finance and national private capital, whose interests thus stand opposed to the development and growth of a socialist and egalitarian society in Zimbabwe." Yet, as Theresa Chimombe (1983:17) pointed out, it was under Mugabe's patronage that this group had initially emerged: "The state is increasingly participating in the banks and this signifies the development of state monopoly capitalism. It is significant to note that after Independence, government appointed some board members of banks to serve as directors of some companies."

Political commentator Jonathan Moyo (1992:4) expressed growing frustration about the demise of accountability, not (as Mugabe griped) because of the new elites' hostility to the cause of socialism within ZANU, but simply on grounds of national interest:

> In most cases, the World Bank and the IMF prefer to infiltrate the minds of bureaucrats in ministries of finance, trade, industry and commerce and in parastatals such as reserve banks as well as private financial institutions such as merchant banks and other influential business concerns. This is what happened in Zimbabwe between 1987 and 1990 when the World Bank started inviting Zimbabwean bureaucrats in the Ministry of Finance and the Reserve Bank to Washington, DC and elsewhere, to indoctrinate them with ESAP under the guise of "training" and "seminars." Others were treated to lavish dinners and parties locally to give the feeling of being "important." This is how some critical personnel in the national bureaucracy were baptized into ESAP... The result is that the politicians have lost control of policy formulation in the economy. That is why every ZANU central committee these days is a classroom for Dr. Chidzero to lecture dumbfounded politicians on ESAP. All this is happening because, while politicians have been reduced to bystanders, economic policy in this country since 1990 has been driven by the World Bank and the IMF, with the assistance of Zimbabwean bureaucrats whose hearts and minds were won years before the implementation of ESAP.

The challenge here is not to pose a "great person theory of history" to explain Zimbabwe's biased financial system in terms, mainly, of the "minority, but very powerful bourgeois group" (which we shall term the "emergent financial elite") which benefitted from bankers' breadcrumbs and thus left the pre-Independence system intact. Instead, it is to place people of the ilk of Finance Minister Bernard Chidzero, a man rarely understood or analyzed, yet of profound importance for Zimbabwe's post-Independence development, in their appropriate class and political setting.

Chidzero may have felt lonely, for he once commiserated, "There is a dearth, even near complete absence, of skilled personnel with a requisite grasp of policy instruments" (*Horizon*, September 1991). (If so, the logical question arises, why would Zimbabwe embark on dramatic changes in economic policy in the early 1990s?) In an otherwise unreasonably favorable report on ESAP's implementation, the government conceded to the World Bank (1995a:48) that, indeed, there was "limited institutional capacity" in its ranks and that "weak capacity in line ministries and implementing agencies led to an overstretching of resources devoted to policy analysis and formulation in a period when far-reaching policy reforms needed to be designed."

Moreover, there were few with political credentials sufficient to make ESAP stick. "We fail to identify individuals with the political courage to successfully defend and hold back any strong and persistent opposition to the reform program," lamented the *Financial Gazette* (5/9/91) at the precise point at which interest rates were doubled and financial liberalization conclusively began: "We stand to be corrected, but the only individuals who have shown commitment to the program and hence are capable of raising a finger in support of it are, the Ministry of Industry and Commerce, Mr. Kumbirayi Kangai,[12] Dr. Tichaendepi Masaya,[13] the Minister of State for Finance, Economic Planning and Development and the Senior Minister, Dr. Bernard Chidzero."

Another logical candidate would have been Reserve Bank governor Kombo Moyana. Yet by the time he left his position in mid-1993, his popularity with financiers had evaporated. Under Moyana, the Reserve Bank had the distinction, according to the *Financial Gazette* (17/6/93), of being "the most secretive, most feared and least-understood institution in this country... Perhaps the lack of transparency at the bank is attributable to the fact that it now effectively has two masters, the government and the IMF." Moreover, Moyana "cultivated a culture of fear and intimidation in the financial sector... The Reserve Bank wants to treat the administration of monetary policy like guerrilla warfare. It takes immense pleasure in springing surprises on the unsuspecting public."

From corporate Zimbabwe, a few emergent, highly-respected financial elites stood in support of ESAP upon its introduction, including Ariston Chambati, Morrison Sifelani, Isaac Takawira, and Leonard Tsumba. Chambati is worth close attention, for he was head of the conglomerate TA Holdings for a decade and in 1995 was named successor to Chidzero as Finance Minister (Chambati unexpectedly passed away within a few months). Previously he had worked for the US Consulate in Salisbury during the early 1960s, then studied in New York and at Oxford, returned to University of Rhodesia where he was a senior lecturer in political science during the 1970s, served the liberation movement at the Geneva, Malta, and Lancaster House conferences, was elected to parliament in 1980, and was immediately made ambassador to Germany. Later he was named to the Business Advisory Council of the World Bank's International Finance Corporation, as well as to the advisory board of Coca-Cola Africa.

Yet in business, Chambati's actual record did not warrant the glowing reputation he enjoyed as the ideal financial bureaucrat to replace Chidzero. According to Ibbo Mandaza (1995:4), Chambati had started masterfully at TA Holdings, that corporate "*laager* for the 'old Rhodies' during the 1980s," because "He used his political contacts in government to confront his enemies in TA Holdings and in the private sector as a whole, thereby creating a functional link between sectors of corporate Zimbabwe and the state into which he was slowly gravitating." But over the last few years of

Chambati's reign, TA's results were most embarrassing. More so than other listed companies, the company's share price had plummeted dramatically beginning in September 1991 (from 410c to 55c two years later). The key problem was debt management, for TA's 1993 interest bill of Z$73.8 million was 128% higher than in 1992, which in turn had been 132% higher than in 1991 (interest payments varied between 23% and nearly 50% of operating profit).

Not only was the huge conglomerate over its head financially (even by 1994 the debt load was still Z$350 million). Chambati's vaunted Botswana hotel investments were also losing money, and TA was ultimately forced to dispose of its recently-acquired bicycle plant, a clothing firm, and a motor transport company. "TA Holdings' situation would come in handy as a case study for MBA students at the University of Zimbabwe," the *Financial Gazette* (25/2/93) stock market commentator remarked sarcastically:

> Two years ago, at a time when its cashflow was already encountering rough seas, two acquisitions were taken on, Bernstein's Clothing and Johnston Transport. Now, in the half-year statement for the period to the end of November, shareholders are told that both are losing money. It was clear at the time that there were not enough financial resources to justify the takeovers... Just what the reason was for buying the clothing factory was unknown. There seems to have been some vague notion that clothing was the business flavour of the month because of tales about all the export profits being made... There also seemed to be little relevance between clothing and the other group businesses, but then this is true of the whole group. TA of course is well known for its disastrous investment decisions. The Macey's saga left one with the feeling that management barely knew what the stores did, while there was no real attempt to check on stockholding... Selling the tobacco floor has got to rank among the most memorable business blunders since Independence. Remember that tobacco was the group's foundation. Transport has never been one of the greatest successes... Despite such an erratic divisional performance TA saw fit to buy yet another transport company, doing so with borrowed money.

Chambati followed up with an ill-timed Z$100 million rights issue in 1994 that was only 55% subscribed. Underwriters, including Merchant Bank of Central Africa (chaired by Chambati), had to buy the balance. Baring's Securities reported in their October 1994 *Zimbabwe Stock Market Review* that it was only because of "the protective nature of Zimbabwean banks that TA Holdings survived in its existing form." It was clear to Barings that TA's executives "had never operated in a competitive environment and were eager to issue more scrip to cover past mistakes... In most other markets, the company would have been forced into liquidation" (*FG*, 20/10/94).

Nor could Chambati's trendy commitment to "vigorous implementation of and adherence to the philosophy of Total Quality Management" turn his company around, and by early 1995 he had to acknowledge that "We in TA have come in for a great deal of criticism in the past two years." He blamed the high cost of debt for his difficulties. Yet in spite of having being burned not only by interest rate liberalization but also by exaggerated expectations of rewards to TA from export markets and foreign investments, Chambati continued to support ESAP (*FG*, 5/1/95, 23/3/95).

Moreover, his short reign as Finance Minister enhanced Zimbabwe's uneven development, according to a *Read On* (November-December 1995) magazine commentary:

> Chambati's [1995] budget showed no mercy at all for the ordinary worker. Instead, his budget was more cruel than the ones Bernard [Chidzero] used to present... [for it] favors the industrialists and business people who are already rich. For example, duty on spares and computers was reduced. Duty on beer was also reduced. Beer prices are likely to go down as a result. Tough luck, children cannot feed on beer. As a result of the removal of subsidies and the increase in sales tax, mealie meal prices have gone up. A 50kg bag of ordinary roller meal, for example, used to cost Z$112. It now costs Z$143.

Enjoying nearly as high a profile as Chambati, Morrison Sifelani had been a key Lonrho representative, once the head of the CZI, and under ESAP the director of the public-private export agency Zimtrade.[14] He also chaired the insurance company Fidelity Life, which was partially owned by government. Working with Sifelani at Fidelity was Forbes Magadu, an assistant general manager responsible for marketing—when not busy chairing Chitungwiza Town Council and the ZUPCO bus company.

Another ESAP-booster was Takawira of Barclays: "Contrary to popular opinion, ESAP is good for the country and its people—and it is working. Positive results are emerging in our sector, like the introduction of foreign currency accounts for individuals" (*FG*, 5/8/93). (No doubt ESAP worked for the banking fraternity and those who had access to forex, but as "for the country and its people," Chapter Twelve provides contrary evidence.) Takawira's background included courses in corporate finance at the Manchester Business School, in financial policy at the IMF, and in international capital markets in Sweden. In 1986-87 he served on the Council of African Advisors to the World Bank.

A more important candidate—also, perhaps, "lacking the requisite grasp of policy instruments," but clearly well-positioned in this small group of emergent financial elites—was Leonard Tsumba. Tsumba was an assistant vice president at Citibank during the 1970s and served as a consultant to the UNCTAD study *Zimbabwe: Towards a New Order.* Returning to Zimbabwe to become general manager of the Reserve Bank in 1981, he was elevated to the position of deputy governor in 1986. Tsumba later became chief executive of the majority government-owned Zimbank, where he raised his voice to demand liberalization of financial markets, access to world futures markets, and the freedom to develop new financial products and services (*FG,* 27/7/91).

During the period Tsumba led Zimbank, his staff showed no great propensity to work in partnership with blacks in industry and commerce. The allegations of the bank's racism were noted above. Just as disturbing, Tsumba himself allegedly fired a middle manager who protested internal corruption prior to the public revelations concerning the Lorac scandal. Member of Parliament Mudariki attacked Tsumba in mid-1990: "What does that person do when he is appointed to that top position? He snubs the President, he snubs the party, he snubs the heroic people of Zimbabwe and he creates new criminal friends who subsequently baptise him in the River Jordan of corruption" (*Hansard,* 30/8/90, 2081).

Nevertheless, Tsumba was made governor of the Reserve Bank when Moyana's term ended in August 1993. Inheriting the highest real interest rates in the country's history and an economy suffering a deep crisis of effective demand, Tsumba kept the rates up at around 10% after inflation, earning flattering reviews from other financiers. After a year of such extreme policies, Barings Securities reminded Tsumba of his "mandate to maintain real interest rates and implement several reforms" and, based on his ability to sustain the most severe monetarism in Zimbabwe's history thus far, named him "one of the best central bankers in sub-Saharan Africa" (*FG,* 20/10/94). Yet Tsumba also came under attack when he backtracked on liberalising foreign investment policy in early 1994, leading the usually pro-Reserve Bank commentator Eric Bloch to comment, "This shows that the government makes announcements first and then thinks about them afterwards. It is time the government ensured that it put its brain in gear before putting its mouth in motion" (*FG,* 21/1/94).

Like Chidzero, Tsumba was not impressed with the colleagues he found around him, and once even blamed rising levels of foreign debt on his government's negotiating teams: "It is largely true that civil servants involved in loan negotiations have had little or no formal training in this crucial aspect of debt management" (*FG,* 21/4/94).

Yet another financial bureaucrat of note was Xavier Kadhani, who earned his degrees from York and Sussex and was in all likelihood the only Zimbabwean economist ever to cite French Marxist Suzanne de Brunhoff in a published work (see Chapter Five). Kadhani then taught economics at the University of Zimbabwe before joining the Ministry of Finance as an economist. Then, as a fellow of the Economic Development Institute of the World Bank and the Institute of Directors, he was made managing director of the Zimbabwe Development Bank and, from there became managing director of a huge state-owned firm concerned largely with paper and packaging, Hunyani Holdings Ltd. By 1992, Kadhani had built himself a Borrowdale mansion valued at Z$15 million, but he ran Hunyani into debt so far in excess of company assets that his merchant bank creditors began preparing emergency rescue plans.

Like Hunyani, Kadhani himself faced personal financial ruin, for he borrowed in order to finance the personal purchase of 4.6 million shares of the company's stock when it was priced at 160 cents per share. When the price fell to 35 cents in May 1992, Kadhani left Hunyani. Chidzero had mooted Kadhani for the post of senior secretary to the Finance Ministry, but withdrew the nomination in 1993 as the scandal mounted. Facing personal bankruptcy, Kadhani's house was auctioned at a sheriff's sale (the mortgagor, CABS, was the only bidder, at Z$1.3 million, but was requested by the Sheriff of the High Court to raise the bid because it was "a bit on the low side"). Kadhani was also forced to sell his restaurant in the elite Chisipite suburb, hence aborting an exemplary accumulation of capital for a former university teacher and civil servant (*FG*, 14/5/92, 21/5/92; 5/8/93; 8/12/94; 19/1/95). In retrospect, the route Kadhani followed may have seemed attractive but in fact proved dangerous: from left-wing academic, to acceptance within the community of international finance, to ineffectual local development banking, to crisis-ridden corporate management and personal luxury consumption brought to a grinding halt by excessive indebtedness.[15]

Ultimately the largest black financier was Joshua Nkomo, and not merely because of his political office and connections to Lonrho, BCCI and other high-flying (and sometimes nose-diving) corporations. Nkomo also chaired the Development Trust of Zimbabwe (DTZ), an enormous investment and holding company founded in June 1989 by Mugabe with trustees drawn from the highest ranks of ZANU. The DTZ promptly bought the country's biggest ranch (Nuanetsi) for just Z$15 million, which was said to be less than the value of its 26,000 cattle alone (the number of cattle had dwindled, by 1994, to 5,000, leading to a major police investigation). Often in conjunction with international investors, Nkomo began to embark upon projects in the Zambezi Valley (a tourist resort, tire factory, and timber project which was subsequently canceled), growth point development in outlying towns, horticulture, coffee farming in the Bvumba, and the like (*Horizon,* January 1992).

In one 1994 deal featuring a no-competition bid, the DTZ and a Bulgarian construction firm won a Z$240 million toll bridge contract at the Beitbridge border with South Africa, to be owned and operated by the joint venture, which also received a government guarantee so as to raise financing, inexplicably, in the form of a Standard Chartered Bank pound sterling loan. Residents of the Beitbridge area who were dependent upon nearby Messina, South Africa, for trading, medical, and other services, were likely to be most detrimentally affected by the privatization of the Limpopo River crossing and imposition of a US$6 motor vehicle crossing fee (*FG,* 26/5/94); SA's Transport Minister, Mac Maharaj, was also incensed that a non-toll alternative was not offered. But the DTZ also drew criticism for its ravenous and insensitive acquisition of land and monopoly control of development in several other locales, including Bulawayo and Beitbridge, and actually lost Bulawayo land options when vociferous local public opposition emerged (*FG,* 22/4/93, 23/6/94).

The DTZ paralleled ZANU's Zimbabwe Development Corporation, whose early 1990s estimated annual turnover of Z$350 million was drawn from stakes in National Blankets Ltd (in partnership with Lonrho, and with US$6.5 million in credit from the World Bank's private sector investment arm), the Treger Group, Zidco Motors, Woolworths, and Catercraft (*Horizon,* April 1992; *FG,* 18/8/94, 9/15/94). Other ZANU ministers and functionaries accumulated wealth through land meant for redistribution to peasants, as well as through state-supported commercial and industrial enterprises, practicing what student leader Arthur Mutambara (1991, 139) termed "monopolistic politics of domination, corruption and petty-bourgeois accumulation." There were other leading entrepreneurs—including Mucheche of the IBDC and Chiyangwa of the AAG—who contributed financially to ZANU, which, as Iden Wetherell remarked, "clearly locates indigenous business advocates within the ruling party's patronage network" (*FG,* 9/15/94).

Nevertheless, in a Zimbabwe increasingly oriented to Western bourgeois cultural norms, there remains a degree of social respect accorded to the black financial elite. Madanhire (1995:4) argues incongruously that in contrast to other emergent businesspeople from both pre- and post-Independence eras,[16] black financiers had become Zimbabwe's "true entrepreneurs" by the early 1990s by virtue of having "worked for years in large conglomerates and in banks" and having succeeded "without the help of underhand deals or political connections. Most of them made their money on the money market, therefore their origins in the world of business are traceable. They took advantage of the liberalization of the financial sector." Leaders of Kingdom Security (Nigel Chanakira), National Discount House (Never Mhlanga), Intermarket Discount House (Nick Vingirai), National Merchant Bank (Julius Makoni), and Allied Capital Markets (Bigson Mpabanga) should, Madanhire suggests, "be brought to the fore to take a leadership role in addressing the imbalances in the Zimbabwean economy."

The experiences of Finance Minister Chidzero should be instructive, for, progressive social-democratic rhetoric to the contrary notwithstanding, his policies clearly led to a dramatic heightening of such imbalances.

Bernard Chidzero

Chidzero was not only Senior Minister for Finance, Economic Development and Planning until he formally stepped down due to ill health in 1995, but was also recognized as a global political figure when he was voted runner-up in the race for the Secretary-Generalship of the United Nations in 1991 (his influence waned once illness overtook him in 1993). A comprehensive profile is warranted in view of the near-complete lack of critical material about Chidzero to date.[17] Such omission is puzzling. While it is important not to bend the stick too far the other way by focusing excessive attention on a single personality, it is, nevertheless, the lack of attention to the roles of key individuals, of ideology, and of systems of public administration, that most discredits structural analysis. Such attention is repaid many times over in this instance, for Chidzero's personal political background is of relevance to his role in shaping Zimbabwe's economy. Hence we must consider how he was outwardly, over time, a liberal, nationalist, socialist, social democrat, and ultimately full-blown neo-liberal.

Chidzero, after all, arose from the all-pervasive racial oppression of mid-twentieth century Rhodesia to become arguably the most influential black banker in history, and this reflects not merely a substantially mutating international social and economic environment. More importantly, as the wave of ascendant finance subtly altered class relations within the international economic system, we must consider why Chidzero was so well-placed within the Zimbabwe power structure to take advantage of the emergent order.

On the one hand, Chidzero adapted well to the milieu of high finance, but on the other hand, he was also tightly constrained by international forces, no more so than at the height of his own domestic influence when a politically unpopular structural adjustment program was implemented in the early 1990s. Indeed, throughout the post-Independence era, the Finance Minister played a schizophrenic game, generally arguing for rational market processes within a state-party nexus that was for many years geared to personal and clientelist accumulation while parroting "Marxism-Leninism." It will be clear in Chapters Eleven and Twelve that the international constraints were ultimately determinant.

But if the question is whether there was "space" available in the national political economy for a different economic program, the answer is relatively straightforward: there was. As noted in the previous chapter, a far more transformatory economic program could have been embarked upon, centered on expansion of basic needs-related industries. In contrast, Chidzero's chosen trajectory exacerbated the underlying processes of ascendant financial power and vulnerability. Indeed the broad mandate of international finance was adopted as official policy largely because of the promotional role played by Finance Minister Chidzero.

His mother was Shona, his Malawian father a farmworker then a shop assistant, though able, finally in the 1950s, to set up his own storehouse.[18] After Bernard, six more children were reared. During Chidzero's childhood, especially in the late 1940s, popular opposition largely emanated from working class struggles in mines and industry (Sibanda 1989). Young Chidzero was fortunate, both because he was befriended by an early nationalist leader, Abraham Chirimuta, and because he managed to attain a slightly delayed but nonetheless illustrious education. Following a stint at a primary school in the Seke reserve, Chidzero gained a place at the well-known Kutama Marist mission in Mashonaland West, served as the drummer in a band led by fellow-student Mugabe, and was there converted to Roman Catholicism. He studied through standard six at Kutama and in 1945, at the age of 18, transferred to Marianhill College in Natal, where he matriculated first class four years later, renowned in black education as the premier debater in South Africa.

In 1950-52 Chidzero earned his undergraduate degree in psychology (with distinction) from Pius XII University College, now the National University of Lesotho. A Canadian family provided initial assistance for his post-graduate education, first at Ottawa University (MA cum laude in political science) and then McGill, which conferred on the hard-working student a doctorate in political science in 1958. His thesis on *The Influence of International Trusteeship on Tanganyika* was published by Oxford University Press in 1961, Chidzero having spent two intervening years at Nuffield College, Oxford. Post-doctoral research at Oxford focused on politics, economics, and labor relations in the Central African Federation. But Chidzero's first book, in 1957, was a lighthearted Shona novel which, as one of just fifty novels in the vernacular, was used widely in schools.

Nzvengamutsvairo ("Broom-Dodger") offers substantial insights into Chidzero's early thinking, for its main theme illuminates the author's own political calculations. The book is centered on the lives of three friends, Matigimu, Tikane, and Samere, who reside in the Seke communal lands during the 1950s. Matigimu is an easily-influenced young peasant possessing little experience with white society, while Tikane, his mentor, has worked in the capital, Salisbury. Tikane has had brutal experiences with oppression at the hands of white bosses and advocates anti-colonial struggle while enjoying working-class vices like petty gambling. Samere, a Standard Six student who speaks fluent English, is the novel's protagonist, and urges:

> It is our country together. For us to fight with them with sticks, axes, spears and knives only, drunkards can say that... What surprised me, fellows, is that what you eat, what you put on, what gives you happiness, are all things of the white man... Whites are our blessers. It is true that they wrong us many times. Many of them think we are baboons with tails... We must show them that even though we are in darkness we are people who love the white, even if we are people of a black skin we are the sons of one father, we are children with soft hearts and kindness. (Chidzero 1957:56-57)[19]

While Tikane and Matigimu are initially determined to fight oppression, their mistaken ways are shown in the course of fruitless attempts to win girlfriends (Samere, in contrast, has no problem finding a mate). The desired girls are "broom-dodgers," in that they neither want to work for the white man nor go to school; instead they need men to support them. This presents a problem for the two, until Samere quits school to work for a farmer as a "baasboy" and soon influences his boss to hire the others. At that point Tikane and Matigimu acquire their girlfriends, and the story ends with the three couples gazing romantically at the moon on Christmas evening. Samere's political viewpoint is thus vindicated; he occupies a position between the black farm laborers and the boss; his salary is much higher; his smoothness and education place him in a position of being able to make decisions on behalf of the farmer. *Nzvengamutsvairo* is a telling piece of fiction, and it is little wonder the book was used by the colonial government as part of the general barrage of propaganda aimed at demobilizing nationalist inclinations.[20]

Two years after its publication, in 1959, the Ford Foundation helped Chidzero return to Salisbury. He was even offered a teaching job at the young University of Rhodesia and Nyasaland. But a year earlier Chidzero had married a white French-Canadian, and as a result of such forbidden racial mixing the job offer was withdrawn. Chidzero lost little time in reconnecting with the nationalists. He joined the new National Democratic Party in 1960,[21] arguing (in the *African Daily News,* 8/8/59) that the black middle class must "realize that it has a vital role to play in the destiny of the Africans—it is the spearhead and the tool of the masses, and must never lose sight of the fact." Along with nationalist figures like Nkomo, Takawira, Silundika, and Dumbutshena, he succeeded in convincing the British government to retain power over Southern Rhodesia as constitutional evolution was underway in the early 1960s (Bhebe, 1989). But Chidzero soon left the struggle, taking up employment with the United Nations in Addis Ababa in 1960 as Economic Affairs Officer. From 1963 to 1968 he served in Kenya as the UN Technical Assistance Board representative and then as UN Development Program resident representative.

Chidzero's formative years, hence, saw him emerge quickly and convincingly from an environment of racial repression and ambitious petty-bourgeois circumstances. Shaped by the rigors of Catholic missionary education, an education in political science, and contacts at two of the world's elite universities, he ultimately secured an esteemed post within the upper levels of the rapidly-growing international civil service. The coterie of international financial and development bureaucrats Chidzero joined in the 1960s would soon begin to shape the Third World in fundamental ways, replacing other spent forces such as colonialism, superpower interventions, and sundry superpower client dictators.

He achieved the directorship of the Commodities Division of the UN Conference on Trade and Development (UNCTAD) in 1968 and then in 1976 the position of UNCTAD Deputy Secretary-General. Also that year Chidzero was economic advisor to both the liberation movement and Bishop Muzorewa's ANC team at the ill-fated Geneva conference,[22] and subsequently, through UNCTAD, chaired the group that produced the voluminous study *Economic and Social Survey of Zimbabwe: Towards a New Order.*[23] The UNCTAD study was published in 1980, just as the war of liberation was won, in the context of intense "Marxist-Leninist" triumphalism and, specifically, a variety of radical restructuring initiatives mooted by ZANU's *Zimbabwe News.* In contrast, according to Stoneman and Cliffe (1989:42), *Towards a New Order* "was very cautious, analysing existing inequities and arguing for their reduction, but almost entirely in a spirit of reform rather than structural transformation." Chidzero's own research work during his last years of exile dealt mainly with education and labor skills, and did not have even as much bite as the UNCTAD study (Chidzero 1979; Chidzero and Moyana 1979).

Back home at last in independent Zimbabwe, Chidzero was promptly named Minister of Economic Planning and Development, to which was added the Finance portfolio in 1982, and in 1988 he was made a Senior Minister. For a time, Chidzero was effectively the fourth leading official in government, after Mugabe, Nkomo, and vice-president Simon Muzenda. Moreover, Chidzero also continued to play an extraordinary role in the international development industry.[24] Among global elites, he was often considered the voice of reason in the Zimbabwe government, a view codified by political scientists Ronald Libby (1987) and Jeffrey Herbst (1990) in their differentiation between ZANU's "technocrats" and "populists." In Chapters Eleven and Twelve, the international implications of Chidzero's technocratic approach are spelled out.[25]

But what of Chidzero's domestic politics? As Trevor Ncube (1995:4) put it, "He was seen as a political outsider. He lacked the political authority to rally his cabinet colleagues around his 'vision thing.' He was without the political clout that would whip dissident civil servants into line." His role as a Zimbabwean politician was not easy, Herbst (1990:128) argues, because "he did not fight in the war and, therefore, had little standing on ideological issues." In reality, Chidzero's problem was not ideological flexibility. What is just as interesting is that as a function of playing both sides of a complex, fluid ideological game, Chidzero failed to sustain a solid national-capitalist support base within Zimbabwe.[26] This is worth some detailed consideration. Even while the *comprador* class, in Mugabe's words, "champions the cause" of national private capital, Chidzero was outwardly ambiguous towards many white businesspeople, and it is revealing to understand why.

Chidzero was particularly disturbed by slave-like conditions experienced by commercial farmworkers, and told the Commercial Farmers Union—which represents most of the white farmers—how "horrified he was to revisit a farm he had seen in his childhood only to find that absolutely nothing had been done to improve conditions" (*Herald*, 2/8/85, 24/7/88). It is thus ironic that the commercial farmers, on the other hand, respected Chidzero as if he were one of their own. "I reckon he's a good bloke," said top agricultural estate agent Pip Hutchinson. "He's a clever boy. For the rest of them they don't think" (interview, January 1991). This mainly reflected the farm fraternity's confidence that Chidzero's Finance Ministry recognized the importance of tobacco and other export cash crops to the country's balance of trade. So although Chidzero might occasionally have used the white farmers as whipping-boys (as most of Zimbabwe's nationalist politicians are wont to do), and even to their faces, he would at other times reward their self-interested loyalty by welcoming them into "the spirit of oneness and national unity growing somewhat imperceptibly, but steadily in this country" (*Herald*, 31/5/83).

Aside from the white farmers, major industrialists also occasionally drew Chidzero's wrath, especially when they crossed him in public over legitimate concerns such as delays in long-anticipated ministry policies or plain old government corruption. Chidzero even criticized the lack of patriotism of white industrialists generally (*Herald*, 28/4/87). Indeed his analysis of Zimbabwe's debilitating investment crisis was pointed: "It is rather unfortunate that within the private sector, there exists a tendency to interpret general government policy in ways that engender uncertainty and therefore, inhibit investment expansion" (*Herald*, 10/8/83). In other words, for Chidzero it was the non-patriotic *psychology* of the ruling economic elites, not the fact that the economy was in a long-term overaccumulation crisis or that the stock market and real estate provided Zimbabwe's investors with much higher rates of return, that was at the core of the problem.

Surprisingly, perhaps, the bulk of Chidzero's public enmity was reserved for local bankers. He berated them, at various points, for having lily-white senior management, for their failure to support black businesses, and for their hesitancy to penetrate rural areas (*Herald*, 25/1/86, 10/12/87, 5/17/90; Maliyami 1990b). "The present situation where little credit is going towards rural area development is even more disturbing, even scandalous, when one considers that more than 80% of our population live in the rural areas and especially the communal areas, and that with the success of our agricultural policies, increased savings are now coming from communal farmers," he told the Institute of Bankers, threateningly, in 1990. "We have one economy to expand and develop without being shackled by considerations of race or color. I could say more but let this suffice" (*FG*, 3/7/90). Chidzero even called on national television for an investigation of bank discrimination (but never carried through with it) (*Herald*, 12/6/89). Yet at the same time, the institutional independence, policy-making clout, and ownership relations that bankers came to expect in doing business with the government remained intact. Most importantly, with respect to the Reserve Bank, Chidzero insisted to parliament that "we must maintain its probity and keep it free of political interference" (*Herald*, 21/10/83).

This sort of approach allowed Chidzero to situate himself in the middle on thorny problems and to fit in well with the hegemonic ideology, even when it differed radically from his own.[27] As a result, to conclude this brief biography, we must carefully consider the *ideology* that motivated Chidzero and that permitted him latitude in applying and even defending repressive economic policies in the midst of "Marxist-Leninist" political party rhetoric,[28] for it is complex and contradictory. Indeed, it would be a mistake to look back on Chidzero as a mere puppet of the World Bank and IMF, or as simply functional and reactive to the requirements of international capital. Chidzero explained his approach in 1982: "We are aiming at a society with more socialized forms of production and distribution. At the same time we wish to encourage individual enterprise. Let us have a dialectical [*sic*] process—and we will see who wins in the end" (*Herald*, 18/2/82). Capitalism writ large was, in both Chidzero's oration and his official economic policy statements, an abstract and essentially flexible historically phenomenon. Zimbabwe had to live with capitalism, yet capitalism could be, nevertheless, simultaneously and unproblematically "transformed." This reflects Chidzero's uneasy relationship with "Marxism-Leninism."

However, the legacy of Rhodesian capitalism was so appalling for the majority of Zimbabweans that appropriation of the term socialism seemed to (at least initially) come easy for Chidzero:

> We are anxious that the economy should continue to grow, and grow more rapidly. We are a socialist government, but we are a socialist government which stands very firmly on *terra firma*, solid ground. Our motto, if we have any in the economic field, will be "growth with equity"—in other words it is not just equity, not just distribution, not just sharing of a diminishing cake, it has to be sharing based upon a growing or a constantly enlargening cake (cited, Goldring, 1980).

Hence Chidzero spent the 1980s nurturing an unlikely yet truly organic Zimbabwean marriage of "simple pragmatism" (i.e., bowing to economic laws imposed by settler and international capital) and idealist "socialism" (the latter reflecting the memory—and continual need to refer to such memory—of a time when ZANU really did stand for the aspirations of the masses and against Rhodesian capitalism and imperialism), the offspring of which might be termed populist developmentalism. Such populist ideology can often be progressive: if "self-reliant" development is taken seriously; if use-values for poor and working people are actually produced with labor-intensive, ecologically-sensitive technology; and if the organizational empowerment of dominated classes and social forces is achieved. However, in Zimbabwe's case it is a fundamentally right-wing ideology of artificial nationalist unity, used to smash political enemies (ZAPU prior to 1988, and subsequently other opposition parties), workers, the homeless and students.

An example of the contradictions engendered in the marriage of pragmatism with socialist rhetoric that proved important during the 1980s was multinational corporate investment. On the one hand, Chidzero (under the influence of the traditional ZANU critique of imperialism) would claim that Zimbabwe didn't need an investment code because of constitutional guarantees and "undoubted good intentions and policies about security of investment and property" (*Herald*, 25/8/83). Moreover, "If the African history is anything to go by, the record has been disappointing with regard to the flow of investment capital even to those countries which have adopted legally-binding national investment codes or signed bilateral investment agreements" (*Herald*, 13/6/85).

On the other, Chidzero's late 1980s statements bubbled with pride at signing one investment code after the other (e.g., MIGA, OPIC and other bilateral agreements). Sibanda (1988:270) traces much of the contradictory rhetoric to a particular class project: "In seeking to pose the issue of a stronger economic base for itself, the ruling petty bourgeoisie has made public its dissatisfaction with domination by foreign and settler capital in the field of the economy. It has been constrained by the constitutional provisions not to attack settler capital domination."

And so even Chidzero turned occasionally to outright attacks on his own ultimate benefactor, international capital (*Herald*, 29/5/84, 20/9/84, 14/6/85, 3/8/85, 7/9/85). Again, Sibanda (1988:271) explains:

> In a move that surprised most Zimbabweans, at the height of the 1985 election campaign, Chidzero complained that "far too much of our economy is still in foreign hands"... I argue that in order to understand the petty-bourgeois bloc's articulation of this anti-imperialist discourse, one must understand the fundamental relationship between the instances of the social formation... Expressed more concretely, the petty bourgeoisie cannot say: "We detest domination by imperialism in our political field," while keeping a complete silence over the glaring fact of domination in the economic field. Furthermore, where "socialism" is proclaimed without seeming to produce any meaningful and sustained improvements in the lives of the would-be beneficiaries, a scapegoat must be found. In our context, once the litany of the "world recession" and the "drought" became exhausted, the focus seemed to turn to a guarded anti-imperialism in the economic field.

This flexibility is consistent with the objective conditions Chidzero himself experienced as a product of a dual background—locally, of a stunted petty bourgeoisie (1927-early 1960s) and internationally, of an ascendant new-class of technocrats based in multilateral financing and development agencies (1960s through 1970s).

Locally, consider Chidzero as politician. In a country in which political speeches are considered mandatory print for the slavish official media, the *Herald* made just two references during the entire decade of the 1980s to Chidzero's role as parliamentary representative for central Harare. On one occasion, he delivered pre-election speeches to local police and to citizens gathered in a central shopping center in June 1985. To the latter, reported the *Herald*, "He appealed to Harare voters to vote for ZANU(PF) to show that 'Harare is a one-party state.'" Chidzero went on to slam dissidents "being sent by leaders of minority parties who want to rule this country"—a very serious charge that referred to rival ZAPU leaders. ZAPU had by that time, however, made clear its opposition to the so-called "super-ZAPU" dissident movement in Matabeleland, which just a couple of years earlier had provoked ZANU massacres of thousands of innocent Ndebele people. Chidzero's indelicate use of this as an electioneering scare tactic fed the general flame of ZANU intolerance which soon developed into an inferno of harassment, detentions and bannings, and hastened the *de facto* formation of a one-party state, a situation which, ironically, Chidzero won praise from liberal and international quarters in mid-1990 for firmly opposing.

On other occasions, though, Chidzero appeared uninterested in improving his local profile. Addressing the ever sensitive issue of wage-setting in 1987, for example, his growing power allowed him to overrule his colleagues with ease. As one commentator put it, "Significantly, the decision to freeze wages, despite the fact that an informal agreement to raise wages by 10% had already been made, was announced by Minister Chidzero, without EMCOZ, the ZNFU, or (apparently) Minister Shava being informed in advance" (cited, Herbst 1990:214). Chidzero was sometimes viewed as operating without much regard for procedure, and amongst business leaders his haughty attitude was well known. He was once confronted by ZANU party leaders at a Gweru meeting, following a two-and-a-half hour defense of his controversial structural adjustment policies:

> In an emotionally charged voice, Gweru businessman Enias Mabodza, speaking in Shona, set the ball rolling. He started by saying he was convinced Ministers Chidzero and Kumbirai Kangai lied to party members when they issued policy statements on government's incentives on the encouragement of new investments, especially by indigenous businessmen...
>
> Speaker upon speaker fired hard words at Chidzero and other chefs for neglecting the blacks despite a majority rule government. Some of the

> delegates even went to the extent of telling Chidzero that because of the failures of policy makers, they, the party leadership, had no explanations to give to the povo who now say Ian Smith was better than the ZANU government. In reply, a visibly angry Chidzero said first he wanted it known that he was not a mere politician who issued empty statements "to beg for your votes. I am a professional. Where I was before I came here after Independence, I was being paid five times what I am getting now, so don't take me for granted" (*Moto,* May-June 1992).

Chidzero's ideology, in sum, was laden with convenience, eclecticism and contradiction. It was invoked with arrogance at times, even against some of the most important local forces (e.g., financial and farming capital, organized labor and even the black petty bourgeoisie on occasion). But notwithstanding the high degree of respect he gained in international financial circles, his ideological flexibility was not sufficient to gain the Secretary-Generalship of the UN (he came in a close second to Boutros Boutros-Ghali of Egypt in the October 1991 vote).[29] Ultimately, even if it was based on some of the more contingent, irrational aspects of Zimbabwean politics, Chidzero's ideology served the structural interests of finance—international and domestic—much more than it empowered ordinary Zimbabweans.

Conclusion: Finance and class formation

ZANU ideologues' visions of an anti-imperialist alliance of peasants, workers, the black petty bourgeoisie, and even a national patriotic bourgeoisie, never materialized. The potential glue of the mythical coalition was a petty bourgeoisie which theoretically could have demanded state support for a new trajectory of socially-oriented accumulation based on regionally-decentralized, labor-intensive production of low-cost basic goods. This might have been part of a broader program of progressive transformation, which would have blended vastly increased state subsidies with funds from overaccumulated financial markets, aimed at a revolutionary upheaval of the wide variety of barriers to progress (through more opportunities for petty-bourgeois accumulation, peasant access to land, mass housing construction, gainful employment in public works projects, etc.). If power relations had been different, if the Patriotic Front had conclusively won the war, if the cadres had been better developed, if working-class organizations had put self-emancipation firmly on the agenda, and if freedom to carry out transformation existed with respect to international finance and regional geopolitics, the role of the black petty bourgeoisie might have had an entirely different tenor.

But Zimbabwe's petty bourgeoisie met racism and "old boy" networks in the corridors of finance on the one hand, and on the other hand monopoly-controlled productive circuits of the stagnant economy which offered few opportunities for accumulation. In this context, a select group within the petty bourgeoisie saw an obvious means of prospering through state-related clientelism and even corruption. The most lucrative terrain soon appeared to be within the financial circuit of capital. Although some indigenous financial enterprizes and entrepreneurs foundered, the bulk of evidence of Zimbabwe's emergent financial elite suggests that this small clique became extremely powerful, in part through the symbols and imagery of nationalism, but in a manner which led, ultimately, to only minor changes in the *status quo*. Indeed the climb up the financial-comprador career ladder depended precisely upon the intensification of that *status quo*.

The accomplishments of the emergent financial elite put to shame the experience of the early 1960s, when the failure of the friendly societies resulted in the loss of many individuals' life savings. But the harm to Zimbabwe by the contemporary group of financiers is far deeper and longer-lasting. Viewing similar developments elsewhere in the Third World, Clive Thomas (1989:335) held out no hope that a strategy of industrial development and commercial reform would ever appeal to the likes of the emergent financial elites:

> The emerging capitalists in the periphery are, *as a social class*, underdeveloped in comparison to their counterpart in the center. In spite of the emergence of some "vibrant" business elites and the increasing sophistication of some state classes, I believe that at this stage peripheral capitalists are incapable of seeing their class project in terms of the need for historic reforms. To most of these ruling groups, reform is anathema. Also, the capitalist classes in the periphery generally rely on the exploitation of economic rents through strategic control of assets instead of pushing a constant revolution in productive techniques.

This fits Zimbabwe's emergent financial elites. Indeed it is as if Franz Fanon had Zimbabwe in mind when he proclaimed, long ago,

> In its beginnings, the national bourgeoisie of the colonial country identifies itself with the decadence of the bourgeoisie of the West. We need not think that it is jumping ahead; it is in fact beginning at the end. It is already senile before it has come to know the petulance, the fearlessness, or the will to succeed of youth. (cited, Loney 1975:16)

Beginning at the end, for those like Chidzero at the Finance Ministry or Tsumba in Zimbank and the Reserve Bank, was not merely a matter of *com-*

pradorism. It also reflected the ineffectual nature of institutional forms of state regulation (including ownership in Zimbank and BCCI). It reflected, as well, the persistence of bank biases which caused so many black Zimbabweans to suffer in the post-Independence period. More worrying still, all of these appear to be inextricably linked phenomena. As a result, the class project of the emergent financial elites was consistent with both continued broad-based racial discrimination against the petty bourgeoisie and ineffectual state interventions. What will be addressed in next three chapters is the impact of this warped institutional framework on the processes of speculative financial expansion and uneven urban and rural geographical development.

Notes

1. The Credit Guarantee Company emerged from a small business credit insurance firm, Finance Trust for Emergent Businessmen, founded in 1978 and owned 60% by the Rhodesian government and 40% by the four major banks.
2. This section considers the credit problems of small black businesses, but they were not alone. Accusations of lending discrimination and steering against prospective black homebuyers were also common, and a "Fair Lending Law" was even deemed necessary by some in government (although never formally mooted) (*Herald*, 14/7/81, 13/4/82). Not long after independence, the Deputy Minister of Local Government and Town Planning accused banks, building societies and insurance companies of discrimination "in various forms" in the past, and threatened to strike any institution off the register if it showed racial prejudice in granting loans (*Herald*, 14/7/82). Rebuttals by the building societies included arguments that high density suburbs were not yet surveyed and title deeds not registered, and that it was unprofitable, due to administrative costs, to grant loans of less than Z$6,000 (*Herald*, 8/11/82). But discrimination complaints continued through the mid 1980s (*Chronicle*, 28/12/84, 30/1/85), and a decade later, confronting a market study which showed building societies rejected applications "far more often than the high income group even after allowing for differences in borrower-income and size," the managing director of the black-controlled Zimbabwe Building Society, Francis Nhema, conceded, "We all can and we all must do a great deal more" (*FG*, 2/3/94).
3. Strong charges, but after incessant repetition their impact tended to fade. After a while, it became difficult to shame even liberals on this score. *Financial Gazette* columnist Di Mitchell (writing under the name Mwana Wevhu) refuted the charges of bank racism: "The issue of how to grow rich ('capital formation' [*sic*] in the jargon of Marxists, now happily adopt-

ed by capitalists) has been further confused by false information about the source of such capital. Some people, it seems, were seriously considering interference in correct banking procedures" (*FG* 26/1/95). Revealingly, Mitchell also (selectively) recalled her experience in white Rhodesia: "This columnist, long ago, worked—for a very short year—in a Bulawayo bank. Then, such instant success, such adroit corner cutting as 'affirmative action' was unheard of" (*FG*, 18/8/94).

4. According to Chinyoka's (1988, 102) report on the Credit Guarantee Company,

   "Commercial bank conservativeness as well as the black entrepreneurs' lack of a track record and adequate collateral, have resulted in a modest level of operations for the credit guarantee scheme. Less than Z$1 million is advanced on an annual basis and despite the increasing demand from the emerging black entrepreneurs for short-term as well as medium-term credits, the banks remain reluctant to significantly expand their lending levels. Commercial banks including the Credit Guarantee Company have no programmes to develop entrepreneurship just as they devote no time and resources to upgrade management and other skills of small-scale enterprises. This is despite their preoccupation with the strict pre-requisites of a good track record and good management skills to their would-be clients."

5. Standard Chartered subsequently began accounting for "Loans and overdrafts to small business and personal sector borrowers" and claimed that as of July 1992, Z$180 million had been extended, more than any other lender (*FG*, 27/8/92). At the same time, the IBDC also demanded that government permit it to purchase a majority stake in the Commercial Bank of Zimbabwe (formerly BCCI) following the government's purchase of 53% of the bank's shares for less than Z$1 million in 1991 (*FG*, 2/7/92).

6. A Z$100 million Venture Capital Company was launched by the Zimbabwe National Chamber of Commerce in early 1991, funded by the Reserve Bank, the World Bank's International Finance Corporation (IFC), the Commonwealth Development Corporation (CDC) and local commercial financiers, but was not expected to break any of the structural barriers to the success of the black manufacturing petty bourgeoisie. A second fund, Continental Capital, was started by a syndicate of institutional investors in early 1992, with projected share capital of Z$60 million and loan capital of Z$60 million. The Zimbabwe Building Society was founded in late 1991 by a consortium of insurance companies and what were described as "unnamed businessmen and 'big guns' in ZANU(PF)." The National Merchant Bank of Zimbabwe was founded in early 1993, with Ariston Chambati chairing and financial support from the IFC. Julius Makoni of the IFC was the first chief executive, and was assisted by the founder of a Ghanaian merchant bank (William Nyemba) partly owned by the IFC, CDC and a US bank. The first black-owned commercial bank, Prime Bank—the joint venture of an MP from Bikita West, Great Makaya, whose grain mill had in 1993 been the subject of a demonstration by

Nykia Growth Point communal maize farmers for paying out millions of dollars in dishonoured cheques, and an Austrian partner—lost investor confidence even before opening its doors in 1995 (*FG*, 5/12/91, 26/3/92, 25/2/93, 9/6/94, 2/9/95).

7. In 1989, firms like Nicoz, Shield and Lion were not major contenders, but by 1994 reports surfaced that "significant market penetration achieved by predominantly black-owned and state-controlled short-term insurance firms is sending shock waves through the industry." The response of white-controlled firms was apparently to end one pricing agreement and replace it with "a sweetheart non-aggression agreement" which acted as "a cartel" to ensure that the insurance market was split into black and white sectors (*FG*, 24/2/94).
8. Later, Bashir Shaik, the former managing director of BCCI's Zimbabwe subsidiary (as late as mid 1993, following its conversion into Commercial Bank of Zimbabwe), was tried for drug money laundering and sentenced to several years in jail in the US. The charge stemmed from his relationship with Manuel Noriega when Shaik worked for BCCI in Panama (*FG*, 28/10/93).
9. According to a Member of Parliament quoted in the *Financial Gazette* (17/9/92), the Lorac owner "built a house for one vice-president... in his home province. He also built a house for minister 'X' in Midlands."
10. The phenomenon actually began just prior to independence, as the Rhodesian Front government attempted to build up black petty bourgeois allies through forex allocations. (Even earlier, there were repeated prosecutions for foreign exchange control violation by whites, including 100 at a single point in 1974 [*Chronicle*, 1/4/74].) Entrepreneurs made repeated post-independence claims that the foreign exchange system was biased against blacks, and therefore required extensive affirmative action: "Foreign exchange allocations at the moment are granted mainly to the people who received these during the sanctions period. It's always the old boys who get the money. No matter how good an idea a black businessmen brings up, he will always find the door closed." A government official responded that of 184 new recipients of foreign exchange in the first four months of independence, 158 were black (*Herald*, 30/9/80). Nevertheless, the press reported that among others, "Leonard Nyamutsamba (a prominent businessman) alleged those benefiting [from foreign exchange scams] were blacks being used as frontmen by whites and white-controlled companies which had no desire to export to black Africa, and sought markets in South Africa and Europe" (*Herald*, 4/10/80). Such controversies continued through the 1980s.
11. Raftopoulos (1991, 14) argues, however, that the "brain drain"

    > ultimately slowed because those employees entered the racist employment structures of capital, and have often been neutralised and absorbed. Secondly, those public servants who were poached by the private sector because of their assumed knowledge of the government machinery and government contacts, often lost credibility with the

State itself. In addition, White employers began to develop their own linkages and lobby groups within the State, and have developed a decreasing need for such ex-State official intermediaries.

12. There was at least one other at that point. Under Kangai at Commerce was Mudzi Nziramasanga—formerly a US-based professor of neo-classical economics—who in 1991 was "imposed" on Zimbabwe by the World Bank and by the US Agency for International Development, replacing a more progressive official (Stoneman, 1991). Cliffe (1991, 28) notes that Nziramasanga earned a salary "more than four times that of other Permanent Secretaries—payable, in US dollars, in an overseas account, by US AID!"
13. A few years later, however, the paper's opinion of Masaya was revised: "more of a technocrat and would not withstand the political pressure that goes with the post" of Finance Minister (*FG*, 14/7/94). Masaya later chaired the Trust Merchant Bank, which was started with National Railways of Zimbabwe pension money.
14. The fragility of the emergent financial elites under conditions of an emerging financial crisis is witnessed in the threatened collapse of Zimtrade in mid 1992, as the government provided only Z$3 million out of Z$4 million pledged to the public-private promotional body. In addition to Sifelani (whose Lonrho support base was threatened by the 75% crash of Lonrho's share values in late 1991-mid 1992), another prominent Zimtrade official was former CZI chief economist Mike Humphrey, perhaps the Zimbabwean most responsible for promoting ESAP, and least capable at the time of acknowledging the risks to CZI member companies which eventually doomed many of them (*Africa South*, May 1990).
15. Kadhani brought others down with him, notably ZANU liberation war veteran Crispen Mandizvidza, who faced bankruptcy when what was once a majority shareholding in Hunyani (and was later a stake of 28%, valued at $21 million in 1991) evaporated to a value of $2 million in 1993. This forced 11 of his 15 companies into judicial management, and Mandizvidza claimed that in instructing him to retain the 28% share at a time the Industrial Development Corporation and Mass Media Trust were buying 60% of Hunyani, government was responsible for "manipulation of his investment" (*FG*, 24/3/94).
16. Madanhire's (1995, 4) list of the "five generations" of the black petty bourgeoisie is interesting. First came the tiny businesses dating to the 1950s, especially in the transport and hospitality sectors, with family empires emerging in the Machipasa, Mwaera, Zemura, Mpofu, Mverechena, Matambanadzo, Mundondo, Madondo, Mpepu, and Mucheche clans. "What is most admirable about them is that they worked for their wealth over decades. The amount of risk they were prepared to take, some investing their lifetime savings in areas where they could never dream of getting title deeds or other forms of security, is unimaginable."

    Next came a generation of politically-connected businesspeople who, upon independence, followed the first rather too closely. According to Madanhire, "There were more bus fleets and in a way it can be argued this new breed of transport operators destroyed the first generation and, come to think of it, themselves, for most of them packed up within ten years of being established." Leading lights included Chris Chigumba (an MP), and Sampson Paweni (caught for fraud during the transport of drought food relief).

A third, more sophisticated generation of younger entrepreneurs included Phillip Chiyangwa, Peter Pamire, Leo Mugabe, Enoch Kamushinda, and Moses Mlauzi. Access to guerrilla demobilisation money plus smuggling of ivory and emeralds in the early years gave way, Madanhire notes, to larger-scale scams involving Ericsson cellular telephones, pay-TV and an airport construction contract. A fourth generation, emblematised by the former Labour Minister and ZANU leader Frederick Shava, includes politicians whose access to cars, buses, grain and other speculative commodities assured them a process for capital accumulation. The fifth generation is based on finance.

17. There are, for example, no post-1960 citations of Chidzero in *Turmoil and Tenacity* (notwithstanding Mugabe's hint). And in the three major leftist studies—Mandaza's *Zimbabwe: Political Economy of Transition 1980-86;* Stoneman's 1988 collection *Zimbabwe's Prospects;* and the 1989 Stoneman/Cliffe book *Zimbabwe*—Chidzero is barely mentioned. Moreover, he gets cursory, superficial treatment in Herbst's *State Politics in Zimbabwe,* and perhaps most surprisingly, no reference (aside from supplying a single statistic) in Weiss' *Zimbabwe: The New Elite.* Critical journalistic profiles of Chidzero are also non-existent.
18. Biographical notes from *Zimbabwe News,* November 1988; Mitchell (1980); and Chidzero's modest 1990 *Curriculum Vitae.*
19. Translation by T. Biti.
20. In 1992, *Nzvengamutsvairo* became required material for A-Level Shona examinations.
21. According to Shamuyarira (1960, 10), this was a coup for the nationalists in that along with Herbert Chitepo and Rev. Ndabaningi Sithole, the presence of the new "eggheads" would "be tremendously reassuring to those Europeans and Indians who fear for their future and their property."
22. According to Mitchell (1980), the conference ended before his services could be utilised by either side.
23. Among the contributors were noted Marxist intellectuals such as Duncan Clarke, Lawrence Harris, Tonderai Makoni, Ibbo Mandaza, Dan Ndlela, Martyn Ngwenya, David Sanders, and Colin Stoneman.
24. Chidzero served on the boards of the Dag Hammarskjold Foundation from 1972 and the North-South Roundtable from 1980, and accepted any number of other appointments during the 1980s, including membership on:
    - the UN-sponsored World Commission on Environment and Development, chaired by the Norwegian prime minister Gro Harlem;
    - The Commonwealth Consultative Group on International Economic Issues, also known as the Commonwealth Group of Eight;
    - the Independent Group on Financial Flows, chaired by Helmut Schmidt

and oriented to increasing loans to the Third World;
• the Rome-based Society for International Development, an international meeting of which he hosted in 1988 and whose Zimbabwe chapter he chaired since 1982;
• the board of the United Nations University's World Institute for Development Economics and Research;
• the editorial board of the prestigious *Journal of Modern African Studies;*
• the advisory group of the UN Committee for Development Planning; and, most importantly,
• the Development Committee of the International Monetary Fund (IMF) and World Bank, which he chaired during the second half of the 1980s.

In 1985 Chidzero led a major South-South conference in Harare, sponsored by Aga Khan's Third World Foundation, which Chidzero served as board member since 1979. The Third World Foundation was a prime vehicle for BCCI influence-peddling, according to the US Senate Foreign Relations Committee (1992) report: "BCCI would make a form of payments to high ranking officials through one of its Foundations, which would create an annual 'prize,' and bestow it upon a person either whom BCCI wished to influence, or whose receipt the prize would provide BCCI needed legitimacy." The Third World Foundation's US$100,000 annual prize was given to leading figures from whom BCCI was attempting to gain favors. The 1988 prize, won by Brundtland, was presented by Mugabe.

In 1987, Chidzero was briefly drawn back to UNCTAD, as chair of the seventh session of that UN division. And Chidzero chaired both the ineffectual eastern and southern African "Preferential Trade Area" (PTA) Trade and Development Bank in the mid 1980s and the Board of Governors of the African Development Bank and African Development Fund from 1986. His c.v. grew longer and longer, and by 1986 *Euromoney* magazine had named him a "Banker of the Year," and in 1991, the runner-up "Finance Minister of the Year."

25. Technocratically, Chidzero's skill as a manager of a key bureaucracy was also subject to debate. For example, for at least three years beginning in 1990, Chidzero failed to appoint a board to run the holding company of the Zimbabwe Development Bank (which falls under the Finance Ministry), leading to lack of oversight and to two executives eventually being fired for fraud (*FG*, 5/8/93). And he also appointed the discredited Xavier Kadhani to be his senior secretary at the Finance Ministry in 1993, although this was withdrawn (*FG*, 28/10/93).
26. As one reflection, Raftopoulos (1991:14) recounts "a meeting between the President, senior economic ministers and an emerging businessmen's association, the Senior Minister of Finance, Economic Planning and Development responded to the continuous criticisms of emerging businessmen by stating that 'We were not trying to create a petty bourgeoisie in this country!'"
27. Moore (1991) argues that—contrary to Sylvester's (1990) interpretations

of "simultaneous revolutions"—"Zimbabwe's recent political history was indeed constituted by a single, albeit contradictory, successful revolution: that of the rise of a new group of intellectuals to power and the construction of their own form of hegemony within the strictures of the international and domestic socio-economic status-quo."

28. To the relief of a great many Zimbabweans of all ideological stripes, Mugabe in 1991 finally opened to question whether the official philosophy of state and ruling party should remain "Marxist-Leninist" (*FG*, 22/3/91).

29. Chidzero explained his defeat to *Southern Africa Political and Economic Monthly* (Dec/Jan 1991/1992):

    > I would be naive to think that everybody was applying objective criteria. There must have been a lot of arm-twisting in the end, horse-trading; not to mention pressure which must have made some of our colleagues change their minds... I believe that in the post-Cold War era, the industrialised countries would like to control the United Nations in a more subtle manner than through the veto in the Security Council.

    This was one of the few occasions in which a well-placed government official publicly revealed perceptions of outside pressure and international geopolitical interests.

chapter eight

The Fortunes of Speculators

Introduction

The average Zimbabwe Stock Exchange (ZSE) share bought at the beginning of September 1991 crashed in value by an extraordinary 65% within the next nine months. Prime real estate bought a couple of months earlier crashed by 45%. The losses are far greater when roaring inflation, which reached nearly 50% in 1992, is taken into account. Many billions of Zimbabwe dollars—paper investments, but nevertheless representing the life savings of many hundreds of thousands of people—essentially went up in flames. Why? Who won and who lost? And what do the fortunes of speculators have to tell us about uneven development in Zimbabwe?

Speculation—particularly in stock market shares—is an intrinsic feature of capitalism, according to Rudolf Hilferding (1981:134): "The specific activity of the stock exchange is really *speculation*. At first sight, speculation looks like any other purchase and sale. What is purchased, however, is not commodities but titles to interest." In that sense, plenty of real estate also qualifies as purely speculative, since it is not necessarily the price of the commodity—the rental income—that determines the return on investment, but instead the appreciation of the property itself.

Since speculation is therefore not necessarily linked to real production, the gamble tends to be a zero-sum game. For Hilferding (1981:138) this appeared as a moral and distributional challenge, for

> The great public which simply follows the lead of the big speculators, and continues in the same course after the latter have already pulled out with the gains they have made—these naive people who believe the moment has now come for them to share in the fruits of prosperity—are the ones who have to bear the losses, and to pay the balances arising with every turn in the business cycle or in the mood of the stock exchange, which are pocketed by the speculators as the reward for their "productive activity."

Raising distributional questions (for instance, concerning the exposure of worker pension funds to share price volatility) is one of several ways to understand the dynamics of speculation. But in addition, speculation is just as interesting a phenomenon for what it reveals about the course of uneven sectoral and spatial development, particularly during periods of overaccumulation crisis when financial turbulence becomes particularly vivid and potentially devastating. Indeed Henryk Grossmann's (1992:200) theory of *The Law of Accumulation and Breakdown of the Capitalist System* pivots around the role of speculation in drawing funds from productive to financial circuits: "When the overaccumulated capital of a certain industry finds no such scope for expanding into other industries defined by a lower degree of accumulation, funds are channelled into the New York money market, where they play a crucial role." Likewise, the impact of speculation upon geographical development is intimately related to the state of the property market: how is the market organized and who is driving it, what is their access to finance, does the real estate host real productive activity that can be sustained over time, and so forth.

The important issue is, how, concretely, did *delinking* occur between claims to interest (stock market shares, as well as real estate) and real production in the Zimbabwe economy, notoriously protected as it was for so long against both international economic processes and market determinations of interest rates? The implications of this delinking were most evident in the period of the most decisive *relinking* between Zimbabwe and the world economy in mid and late 1991, as tariff barriers crashed, import restrictions crumbled, and interest rates soared on the explicit instruction of the World Bank. Thus a seven-year burst of speculation—unprecedented since the great Bulawayo stock market boom and bust more than nine decades earlier—came to a fitful end.[1]

There was no predetermined path for capital to flow within Zimbabwe, as we observed from the lack of attractive speculative outlets during the late 1970s. The process must be examined, instead, with an eye to decisions taken by the major institutional investors, which in Zimbabwe commanded sufficient financial power to kick-start dormant markets by virtue of the institutions' need to displace centralized, overaccumulated capital. This chapter considers the two main channels for the emergence of speculative fevers in Zimbabwe, the reasons for their subsequent ebbing in 1991, and the basis for an erratic recovery under conditions of structural adjustment. The ZSE and commercial real estate are targets of this chapter's inquiry, but other kinds of speculation—foreign currency, luxury consumer durables, stockpiled goods and materials—were also rampant until 1991 in spite of receiving official condemnation.

The regulation of speculation is also of great interest, given the small and generally clubby atmosphere of the Harare financial markets. Indeed, there was ample warning of the dangers of letting the small crew of financiers pursue their own ends. As Chidzero's Finance Ministry observed as early as 1984, "An increase in non-productive, speculative activity is [occurring simultaneous with] income transfers from the poorer to the well-to-do classes."[2] That warning signified a vigilance and official consciousness of what was to become, arguably, the single most important organic economic sensation in Zimbabwe during the subsequent eight years. Speculation ultimately captured billions of dollars which would have otherwise either escaped the country had there been no exchange controls, or alternatively which could have been rechannelled into productive investment had government transformed the nature of the economy as promised at Independence in 1980. Instead, the process of capital accumulation followed its own short-term profit-oriented logic, and the result was a steady and untenable shift of funds into unproductive financial and property markets.

Notwithstanding Chidzero's 1984 warning and periodic Reserve Bank interest rate interventions, the stock market and commercial real estate actually received a *de facto* government blessing (for example, through access to foreign exchange for luxury office construction, and a blind regulatory eye to share scandals). Related perhaps was the fact that, until the bursting of the speculative bubble, shares and property were also the prime indicators of skyrocketing wealth within Zimbabwe's ruling class (including some of the emergent financial elite considered in the previous chapter) in the midst of both increasing immiserization of the citizenry and stagnation of the productive economy. The stock market drew in more funding and lost far more, ultimately, but speculation in real estate more fundamentally affected uneven geographical development (in a manner not dissimilar to that of the late 1950s, as shown in Chapter Four). As discussed in the next two chapters, there were also massive, inappropriate financial flows into other spaces and sectors (especially urban housing and rural agriculture) that could not contain them. However, it is to the stock market that we turn first.

The Zimbabwe Stock Exchange

In relative terms, we might consider stock market speculation to exist if a simple principle holds: increases in values of company shares vastly outstrip increases in the company's fixed capital stock and other assets which the shares are meant to represent (i.e., assets which provide, in the near future, reasonable anticipations of increased profitability).

Recall from Chapter Two that the country's first stock market, in mid-1890s Bulawayo, generated wild speculative surges in gold mining claims and land titles, but ended in financial chaos. Yet the market attracted foreign capital in amounts great enough to fund infrastructural development and ensure the arrival of Cecil Rhodes' agrarian settler bourgeoisie. As the local economy became more balanced in the course of world depression and war, a need again arose to raise capital, not for speculative mining ventures, but for nascent manufacturing concerns. The Rhodesian Stock Exchange was founded in Bulawayo in 1946, and opened a Salisbury office in 1951.

A flurry of new financial institutions during the 1950s offered intense financing competition in the context of what proved to be a short-lived boom. A serious case of financial overaccumulation emerged, especially in retail banking, as discussed in Chapter Three. In the early 1960s, as a full-fledged economic crisis set in, the new Rhodesian Front government's control of the financial system tightened considerably (see Chapters Three and Five). The Unilateral Declaration of Independence in 1965 entailed further financial repression by the state. Notwithstanding GDP growth rates among the world's highest during 1966-74, new production was initially based mainly on existing unutilized capacity and generated little need for new capital issues. The unprecedented 1973-75 deluge of fixed capital investment was generally financed through retained earnings, and the stock market's performance was uneventful until just prior to Independence. A brief but temporary rise in share values in the late 1970s, in the context of the devastating 1974-78 economic collapse, testified to the increasing volume of floating speculative capital unsure of what political change would bring.

At Independence in 1980, the ZSE was not well-known to the nationalists, and was thus neglected in the "transition to socialism" discourse. Whereas the prospect of nationalising the foreign-owned banks was raised (even by Chidzero's colleagues in the UN Conference on Trade and Development), the stock market was let off the hook. As Leonard Tsumba (1980:399), ZANU's Citibank-based financial advisor (later to become managing director of Zimbank and then governor of the Reserve Bank) put it in the UNCTAD study *Zimbabwe: Towards a New Order,* "At Bulawayo [*sic*], the local stock exchange has become highly specialized—and if some capitalist type development strategy should be retained during the transition period, or whatever—the exchange could prove invaluable as a mobilizer of both savings and capital."

Reflecting the official bafflement with the stock market, at one point in 1981 the generally conservative Chidzero slandered the ZSE and then later apologized and withdrew his remark: "I once referred to the Stock Exchange as the harlot of the economy because I believe in shock tactics and shock therapy" (*Herald,* 30/11/81, 29/4/82).

In fact there was good reason for Chidzero's suspicion. The dramatic decline in the ZSE industrial and mining indices between Independence and late 1981 reflected, in the words of its president, Bill Burdett-Coutts, the supposed confirmation of the speculators' worst fears: "It does appear possible that the government is now following a more radically socialist policy than appeared likely 12 months ago, examples being the almost hostile attitude it adopts in numerous statements to any extension of foreign control of companies and also to multinational companies" (*Herald,* 11/10/81). More to the point, however, Burdett-Coutts later conceded that the real reasons for the 1981 decline were Chidzero's doubling of interest rates that year, which served to attract capital into competing financial assets, and the worldwide recession, which led to declining mineral markets (*Herald,* 3/5/82).

Whatever the reasons, material or ideological, the sinking state of the productive economy continued to spark a withdrawal of funds from the ZSE by the large investors. Whereas about 70% of ZSE activity at Independence was due to institutional investors, that figure had slipped to 10% by 1982 (*Herald,* 21/10/82). With falling share prices, companies searched elsewhere—mainly at the banks—for infusions of capital, rather than float new stock issues. Commercial banks were not ideal sources of funds, what with interest rates doubling from Independence to late 1981. Immediately after Independence, in the midst of the brief economic boom, the banks initially were extremely cautious about funding new fixed capital in production.[3] By late 1981, however, corporate debt ratios for some leading local firms had risen to what were considered uncomfortable heights (*Herald*, 15/10/81).[4] By early 1983, Zimbank's chief economist (Girdlestone 1983:8) disclosed "the deteriorating cash flow positions experienced by many manufacturers," the result of a Z$60 million increase in net borrowing over a thirty-month period.

Then the mini-investment wave tailed off and the demand for external financing waned. A World Bank (1989d:17) study of the 50 companies listed on the ZSE during the 1980s showed that whereas the companies' internal funds (retained earnings and depreciation) accounted for 41% of financing sources in 1981, in 1984 and 1985 they were well above double that ratio.[5] Notwithstanding a general rise of debt in the economy and the fact that effective costs of debt averaged negative 1.2% per year through the 1980s, corporate borrowing (other than trade credits) actually declined.[6] As the Bank (1989d:17) reported, "Firm interviews confirm that external finance is little used for fixed investment and predominantly for the companies' operating requirements, including funds for working capital to pay for stocks and work in progress, financing trade debtors and for holding cash and other liquid assets." Even these tasks, however, were minimal.

Underlying the lack of corporate credit demand was the chronic condition of excess capacity, illustrated by high inventories—reaching a level of 23% of total corporate assets in 1983—in relation to the inventory holdings of companies in other countries which by late 1983 were in a new upswing of the business cycle (Japan, 14%; US, 15%; Korea 18%). Also in Zimbabwean companies' financing favor were low effective corporate taxes (28% for 1980-87) and relatively high profit rates (22.6% after-tax return on local shareholders' equity, and 16% for foreign shareholders' equity).[7] Thus Zimbabwe's companies initially had little need for liquid assets (which amounted to 2.5% of total assets in 1983, in comparison with 13% in Japan).

In considering corporate debt, however, it is important to distinguish between long- and short-term debt. Asl Demirguc-Kunt and Vojislav Maksimovic (1995, Appendix) show that during the entire period 1980-91, Zimbabwe's ratio of private sector debt to GDP was the lowest among 30 countries surveyed, at 14%, far behind South Africa (72%) and debt-reliant Switzerland (301%). But although long-term corporate debt was extremely low, ZSE companies' short-term debt—averaging 62% of total share equity book value during the 1980s—was higher than that of listed companies in Brazil (42%), Mexico (44%), South Africa (52%), and even Canada (54%). This contributed to speculative impulses and short-termism, even if it did not necessarily harm profits, given that during the 1980s low (sometimes negative) real interest rates prevailed.

In many other parts of the world chronic overaccumulation in the productive circuits led to intensified overindebtedness, as falling corporate profits during the course of the stagnation encouraged borrowing for the purpose, largely, of purchasing other companies (Pollin 1986; Bond 1990:155). Zimbabwe was different during most of the 1980s, for a few reasons worth reviewing.

First, as noted, with practically no new fixed investment planned, there was little demand for credit for that purpose. Second, there was little need or incentive to maintain high levels of corporate liquidity since the financial system was powerfully equipped to handle simple monetary circulation functions and since the Zimbabwe dollar was undergoing a steady decline. Third, it was still relatively unprofitable in the early 1980s—due to negative real interest rates and the weak property and share markets—to purchase the limited range of liquid financial assets that were available in Zimbabwe. Fourth, the fact that most of the main private sector financial institutions were well-established, foreign-based, and seemingly secure in their "corset of controls" (as Chidzero termed the government regulatory framework), meant there was little opportunity (in terms of market openings) for Zimbabwean corporations to become financial engineers as was happening elsewhere in the world.

Under these conditions, the ZSE faced both dwindling institutional investor interest and a declining market for raising corporate financing through share issues. The effect was devastating. By the end of 1983, ZSE market capitalization had plummeted to Z$52.5 million for industrial shares and Z$32.3 million for mining, as compared to Z$911 million and Z$249 million in 1980. One fifth of the listed companies paid no dividend and, according to Burdett-Coutts, "a number of companies are dependent on their banks for survival." But he added, optimistically, "Recently there have been indications of a more pragmatic approach being adopted by the government and for a readiness to understand the problems facing industry. I trust this trend will continue and be expanded" (*Herald*, 29/12/83). And, indeed, within two and a half years Burdett-Coutts could report, "despite the rhetoric, the policies followed by our government have been mainly pragmatic" (*Herald*,20/6/86). In the meantime, however, the market had bottomed out in 1984 when ZSE dealings in external shares were prohibited by government decree during the foreign exchange crunch. Although, according to press reports, "financial spokesmen do not believe that the ZSE's demise can be long delayed" (*Herald*, 19/4/84), a recovery did soon commence.

The speculative rise of the ZSE

Four years into the new regime, Zimbabwe's capitalist class grew far more comfortable in the knowledge that commercial property rights were sacrosanct and that increasing corporate influence on economic policy-making would pay off. The industrial index picked up slowly at first, from a low of 150 in mid 1984, to 550 by late 1987, to reach 2,732 by September 1991 (Figure 8.1).[8] Mining shares also saw an eighteen-fold increase over the 1984-90 period, from 28 on the index to nearly 500 in mid 1990.

This behavior was incomprehensible to some observers. The World Bank (1989d:31) argued in May 1989 that the ZSE was "undervalued," but, on the contrary, Standard Bank's *Economic Review* reported in September that year, "Major institutional investors already consider even quality shares highly overpriced on current dividend yields." Within six months, business consultants Deloitte and Touche (1990:14) advised clients as follows: "The shortage of scrip and the high liquidity levels in the economy have contributed to the share price inflation. There has also been a marked reduction in the number of individual investors—while an increased proportion of issued equity has found its way into the portfolios of long term institutional holders."

In money terms, the ZSE capitalization of approximately 50 listed companies rose to Z$1.4 billion by 1987, and soared to a peak of Z$9.5 billion in September 1991. (By comparison, the total savings in the country's financial institutions in September 1991 was Z$9.7 billion.) While the average major bourse across the globe was losing 20% in price terms during the course of 1990, the ZSE industrial index soared by 160% (second only to Venezuela) and continued rising nine months into 1991.

Bard Discount House economist Nigel Chanakira (1990:4) explained the speculative euphoria: "Investors appear to have grown indifferent to fundamental factors and information, in a stampede to acquire shares way beyond historical levels." The delinking of Zimbabwean finance from the real sector is perhaps best observed in the stagnation in the underlying net asset value reported by ZSE companies: 311 cents per share in mid 1988; 295c at year-end 1988; 322c at year-end 1989; and 359c at year-end 1990. Yet the period experienced a 400% increase in industrial share prices. With the lowest share-price/net-asset-value ratio during the period at 0.77, and the highest 1.93, this represented a phenomenal 150% delinking in just 30 months. Thus in spite of a solid rise in corporate profits in the late 1980s, the average ZSE price/earnings ratio climbed uncontrollably, from 4.64 in early 1988 to 10.81 three years later, unprecedented by Zimbabwe standards.

The most important ZSE shares at this stage included the big conglomerates (TA Holdings, Delta, Apex, Hunyani); food and agriculture (National Foods, Hippo Valley); and (in the late 1980s) blue-chip mining houses (Rio Tinto, Bindura Nickel, Wankie Colliery). The most active shares vary according to fashion and global commodity prices. The primary share-owners are Old Mutual, Anglo American's "Security Nominees," Barclays, Art Corporation, Southern Life, Colonial Mutual, Fidelity Life Assurance, Standard Bank, the railway and mining industry pension funds, and various state investment bodies. The 1990 merger of three insurance firms—Colonial Mutual, Norwich Union, and Prudential Assurance—increased concentration of share control immensely.

The ZSE's hothouse atmosphere was exacerbated by scrip shortage. There were only five new share listings and only Z$98 million in rights issues during the 1980s (until mid-1989), again reflecting the stagnation in industrial investment. And until 1991, retiring outstanding debt was not an incentive for corporations to issue new stock, given the low levels of long-term debt and the negative interest rates. (At last, in 1990 and 1991, a huge surge of listings were enticed by the high prices offered in the super-speculative ZSE. Also in 1991, corporate borrowings increased markedly and interest rates rose dramatically.)

Nevertheless, the ZSE bubble kept from bursting until September 1991 largely because the market was controlled by a few major players. What with the lack of scrip, share turnover was remarkably low (total ZSE turnover in 1989 was just Z$75 million, and in 1990 Z$125 million) in comparison with the vast increases in share values, revealing the highly concentrated and interlinked nature of the institutional investor community. Some trusted leaders in the investment field even fuelled the speculative flames, including the chairperson of the Zimbabwe Association of Pension Funds, Labani Hove: "Equities could prove to be very profitable during the days of boom and despite the risk involved pension funds should consider putting some of their surplus funds in equities" (*FG*, 23/5/91). Within four months, Hove would regret this advice.

Soon, the ZSE provided the same temptations as were corrupting stockbrokers everywhere. "The pool of big investors in Zimbabwe is small, and they do know each other, often socially," remarked the *Herald* (19/3/92) following one scandal. "The ZSE could easily be manipulated in a few key counters by someone with a few million dollars in cash, simply because the share turnover and the actual size of the economy are not that large." Two well-known stockbrokers were fired from the top brokerage firm Sagit in June 1990 for insider-trading, which involved using Z$600,000 of Sagit's bank clients' money to purchase shares in a firm just before its public listing.[9]

The *Financial Gazette* (22/6/90) condemned "A situation where brokers, of all the people, buy huge blocks of shares and hold on to them while speculating, completely distorts the market mechanism. It is not surprising that some counters continue to bid upwards on the Zimbabwe Stock Exchange, even if there are no tangible indicators that the companies' fortunes are due for better times." (Even in 1995, there were still just eight brokerage houses on the ZSE, four of which were owned by blacks.)

Other hints of share manipulation occasionally surfaced. For example, when a gold mining company (Cluff) was listed in October 1990, Old Mutual in particular pulled out of subscriptions that were expected to be in the range of Z$10 million. "It is difficult to explain why people suddenly developed cold feet but we have a suspicion that some circles within the market deliberately killed the issue by spreading malicious market gossip," the *Financial Gazette* (13/10/90) commented. "The fact that Cluff is coming in as an outsider has not gone down very well with some mining companies which have held sway for a long time."

The most debilitating scandal (involving the black owners of Flexible Packaging) occurred in late 1991, and cost state Post and Telecommunications (PTC) workers a large part of their pension fund. When Flexible was bought in 1989, eyebrows were raised, since the buyers (Willie Ford and Fanuel Muhwati of Merchant Bank of Central Africa) had earlier been approached—in their capacity as MBCA officials—by the sellers. Ultimately, MBCA financed Ford, Muhwati, and Isaac Takawira (a top Barclays Bank official), but in late 1991 Flexible aimed to raise more money. Realising that they had missed the ZSE peak, the company's owners wined and dined Labani Hove, who was also the PTC Pension Fund's principal officer. Hove then dumped more than Z$15 million of pensioners' money into the company. Flexible's early 1992 ZSE debut as the first black-owned firm to appear on the ZSE was thus an enormous success, in a period in which share values were sinking rapidly. Flexible's bankers were effectively bailed out by the PTC workers. Realizing his mistake, Hove began unloading shares, which was one contributing reason for the Flexible stock's dramatic drop following its listing (*Moto,* May 1992). By mid 1992, ordinary Flexible shares in the PTC Pension portfolio which were purchased at a cost of Z$15.4 million were valued at Z$6.1 million. This was, unfortunately, at a time when the existing valuation of the PTC's assets (dating from mid 1990) showed a shortfall of Z$16.9 million, and reflected the fact that workers were beginning to pay the cost of speculation (Bond 1993b:35). And it was downhill from there, for in 1993-94, Flexible was losing Z$14.3 million a year, followed up in 1994-95 with a loss of Z$8.8 million.

The vast overvaluation of shares during the most intense period of speculation provided the underlying conditions for insider-trading and other forms of manipulation. It also raised the prospect of what a "correction" might bring. Nigel Chanakira (1990:4) had raised this as a possibility:

- Is a stock market crash similar to that which occurred on several major international markets in 1987 possible in Zimbabwe and if so when?

- Is the value of shares traded on the ZSE likely to dry up because institutional investors have adopted a "buy and hold" strategy in an economy with limited financial alternatives and investment outlets for their funds?

- Are the world-renowned stories of insider-trading, tax frauds and general financial misdemeanors likely to capture our newspaper headlines?

While hedging his bets, Chanakira implied affirmative answers to his questions. The rates of return from share speculating, he argued, were "approaching those occurring in sophisticated capital markets such as Japan... It is rather disturbing to note that in a period where some policies and conditions could change dramatically, investors on the stock market have thrown caution to the wind."[10]

Commercial property

The stock market took the bulk of liquid institutional investor funding in the late 1980s, but at the same time commercial property—especially in Harare's Central Business District (CBD)—also witnessed vast increases unrelated to any underlying prospects for value creation in the economy, much less in the specific properties themselves. It is in this sense that the commercial real estate market can be considered "speculative." As Chanakira (1990:4) put it, "One must sympathize with the institutional fund managers who receive thousands of dollars per month for pensions and insurance policies, as well as investment income, all which must be in an economy which has seen little growth of investment opportunities and innovation in financial assets."

This was not the first time such conditions existed. As noted in Chapter Four, the late 1950s was a period of dramatic property speculation. A crash followed in the early 1960s, and although some commercial real estate was developed during the economic boom of 1966-74, much faster growth occurred in industrial and white residential property. In 1974, that too came to a stunning halt as a result of generalized overinvestment and a series of exogenous shocks (especially guerrilla war and declining terms of trade). At Independence, prime Harare CBD office space cost about half of that in Johannesburg's Carlton Centre (*Herald*, 10/1/80).[11] According to a Whitsun Foundation (1983:57) report on insurance company investments, "In non-residential properties the combined effects of economic downturn, excess capacity and an absence of projects have proved damaging." But there was political pressure to combat high rents in the CBD, which led to a rent freeze on commercial and industrial properties in November 1982, withdrawn a year later and replaced with a Rent Board.[12]

It was not until early 1982 that a potential upturn was signified by vague institutional investor interest in the CBD. At that point, the stabilization and centralization of financial capital began to pay off, as two of the largest players—Old Mutual and the National Railways of Zimbabwe Contributory Pension Fund—agreed on a property investment worth Z$5 million. According to Old Mutual property manager David Frost, "The market value of our rent producing properties in our present portfolio is about Z$30 million and that is not enough in a portfolio of our size. We have a further Z$26 million of property development in the pipeline" (*Herald*, 11/3/82). From 11 buildings in 1981, Old Mutual built up a portfolio of 105 properties by 1992.

But most institutional investors remained wary of real estate throughout the early 1980s. The long-term nature of such investments, added to fresh political uncertainty (e.g., the Matabeleland conflicts), kept money in much more liquid form. And the government's increase in prescribed asset requirements (from 55% to 60%) in late 1983 temporarily mopped up a small amount of institutional investors' available speculative capital.[13] As late as mid 1984, there were reports that "Demand for large space office accommodation remains poor with an excess supply currently remaining available" (RAL *Executive Guide to the Economy*, September 1984). When in early 1984 the Rent Board replaced the rent freeze, this was a clear signal that commercial property might again become a profitable investment. As in the case of the near-bankrupt Zimbabwe Stock Exchange, this was the point that the market hit rock bottom and then turned.

The rise of property speculation

The key impetus appears to have come from commercial banks, which sank an unprecedented Z$70 million into 550 Harare mortgage bonds (mainly commercial) during six months from May 1984 (Figure 8.2).[14] The banks' share of what was then a Z$335 million market in new mortgages thus rose from Z$70 million to Z$150 million during 1984, while building societies' share of new mortgages declined from Z$110 million to Z$90 million (the other Z$95 million in mortgages were held by other investors). It was not long before the banks' decision paid off. As the RAL *Executive Guide to the Economy* reported in June 1985: "Demand for central business district investments is becoming increasingly buoyant with the majority of funds and institutions not presently able to satisfy demand for prime commercial properties. A bullish attitude is being adopted by fund managers and prices have tended to harden for the best located quality properties."

The phenomenon was not limited to the CBD (notwithstanding continuing stagnation elsewhere in the economy). Industrial sites were also gaining institutional investors' attention: "Sale of properties to an investment institution and the granting of a long lease by the institution back to the previous owner is becoming a popular investment concept. A number of businesses have survived the recession because sale and leaseback agreements have provided them with the cash they needed in difficult times." Thus difficult times for manufacturers corresponded to windfalls for financiers. Reminiscent of the late 1950s, government took various countervailing actions. In mid-1986, the Reserve Bank clamped down on speculative property acquisition, temporarily prohibiting any financial institution (including the institutional investors) from lending to individuals or corporations for property designed for non-owner occupation. But this was only a slight hindrance to further investment in commercial real estate.

During 1986, as the supply of available CBD office space dropped from 5,000 square meters to 1,100, the commercial banks again found means of increasing their advances to developers. The value of their new mortgage bonds doubled from Z$125 million to Z$250 million in 1986 alone, with the expectation that another 35,000 square meters of new office space would come on line by late 1987. Even so, in 1988 estate agents described Harare's commercial and industrial property market as "full," with shortages expected to continue into the foreseeable future. Industrial land was in such short supply in Harare by 1989 that new development in Msasa, Willowvale, and Graniteside (a new industrial suburb which commanded Z$10 per square meter) was restricted by the municipality to owner-occupiers, which prevented the popular lease-back development of stands by insurance companies and pension funds.

However, the real action continued to occur in Harare's CBD. (Bulawayo's speculative boom was delayed through most of the 1980s—

until the signing of the ZANU-ZAPU Unity Accord in late 1987[15]—while after a brief mid 1980s upturn related to the opening of the Beira Corridor, building in Mutare declined and picked up only in 1990).[16] From 1987 to 1994, some 185,000 square meters of new office space would be added to the Harare CBD, an amount equal to the existing office space built over the previous thirty years. More than 100,000 square meters were scheduled to come on line in 1992, 1993, and 1994 alone. In 1992 this amounted to Z$500 million worth of CBD property investments, much of it "airconditioned, Grade A space incorporating state-of-the-art technology, high speed lifts and car parking," according to a Knight Frank & Rutley executive (*FG*, 19/10/90).

The cost of office rent was now becoming exorbitant. Prime Harare space fetched Z$30 per square meter in 1991—up from Z$3 in 1980 and Z$15 in 1987 (rentals on the Charter Road in the Kopje area soon fetched as much as Z$50 per square meter, still not as high as the Z$100 per square meter paid for a prime First Avenue retail site). From 1975 to 1990, the official valuations of office buildings in Harare increased by between 317% and 721%, with land prices rising by between 455% and 1,488% over the period (*FG*, 16/7/92).

The value of all property sales in Zimbabwe reached Z$636 million in 1989, 25% higher than the year before, partly on the basis of a 65% increase in the value of mortgages granted; financiers had become so confident about the value of property that they invested Z$1.4 billion in 17,600 bonds (including second mortgages for improvements). In 1990, the value of property sales was up to Z$860 million, and 21,000 mortgages were registered worth Z$2.1 billion. The pace was maintained into the first half of 1991, with Z$1.374 billion in (10,700) mortgage bonds registered.

The residential property market was by no means immune from speculation (see Chapter Nine). Moffit Saunders (1990:1), a leading developer and head of the National Property Association, was so frustrated by the lack of new space for middle- and upper-class housing that he prepared his association for a full-fledged attack on non-resident owners of vacant land:

> While there is a raging crisis with respect to the acute shortage of residential accommodation at all levels, particularly middle and low income brackets, 8,545 surveyed and serviced residential stands mostly in the low-density suburbs are lying idle in the hands of "land speculators." Most of these residential stands have been idle for more than two years and the owners, some of whom are out of the country, seemingly have neither the intention to develop nor the inclination to sell these properties.

The geography of speculation

On the ground, the flows of funds into real estate became highly visible by the early 1990s. Multinational property capital stepped up its activity, as UK-based Knight Frank & Rutley controlled a pool of Z$100 million in mainly pension fund investment capital, pioneered a property unit house which promptly won a ZSE listing and purchased several CBD and shopping centre properties. The demand for Harare CBD offices seemed to be unquenchable. On the seedy west side of the CBD, space in the Zimre Centre (Zimbabwe Reinsurance Corporation's headquarters) was fully rented soon after its completion in early 1989 (RAL *QGE,* March 1989). In mid-1991 Zimre and another parastatal, the Urban Development Corporation, announced a Z$200 million redevelopment of land just to the north of the CBD for restaurants, shops, supermarkets, and high-quality office space.

On the east end of the CBD, the Z$120 million Southampton Life Centre (on the site of the Meikles carpark, at African Independence Square) was financed mainly by Southampton Assurance (which held just Z$410 million in total assets) (*Herald*, 28/2/91). The building's ground-level shops would host "high class specialist traders" (*FG*, 28/9/90). Next door, the Meikles Hotel began a Z$120 million refurbishing which included a postmodern rooftop architectural touch (as tens of millions of dollars more were pumped into refurbishing other hotels in Victoria Falls and the Eastern Highlands) (*Herald*, 11/7/91). On Samora Machel Avenue, the octagonal silo-shaped Z$130 million Reserve Bank building, Zimbabwe's tallest at 23 stories, would soon tower over the financial district at First Street and Samora Machel Avenue, its ground-level frieze ironically depicting scenes of production in fields, factories, and mines.[17] Nearby, Lonrho's local headquarters, untouched since its construction in the 1950s, received a Z$200,000 facelift. As the executive director put it, "Our building, because of its central location, is one of the most valuable in Harare, and we feel it is part of our responsibility to ensure that the building maintains the look of the area" (*FG*, 11/5/90).

One report noted that "Most of the developments are from institutional investors who, in the light of the current financial stranglehold on building societies, are the only players with the funds to invest in property" (*FG*, 12/12/91). Of these, Old Mutual—whose assets increased from Z$3 billion to Z$4 billion in the twelve months to June 1991—was still the major player in property speculation, with Z$300 million worth of building underway in 1991. According to a senior Old Mutual property manager, "We like to keep a low profile, except about Chitungwiza [a high-density suburb shopping mall], which is good propaganda" (interview with M.P. Musto, Old Mutual Properties, January 1991). The company invested Z$90 million in two "prestigious" commercial CBD properties (on Samora Machel and Union Avenues) in 1991-92 (*FG*, 28/9/90). The biggest CBD project yet, however, was destined for the east side of the CBD, a Z$300 million shopping-office complex behind the Meikles Hotel (near the Southampton project). With 26,000 meters of office space in two seven-storey buildings connected by a series of bridges, "Eastgate" would be the "First serious attempt to provide quality office accommodation at affordable rentals," according to Old Mutual's Frost. "The flexible office layouts will permit both large and small tenancies in self-contained premises" (*FG*, 9/1/92).

But the west side of the CBD was even more densely populated with construction activity, catalysed by the successful Zimre development. There, the Mining Industry Pension Fund's monumental new headquarters would face architectural competition from the Agricultural Finance Corporation headquarters, from the Posts and Telecommunications headquarters, from the luxurious new Zimbabwe Development Bank in the potentially-gentrifying Kopje district just west of the CBD, and from a postmodern Construction Industry Pension Fund development (*FG*, 31/8/90, 14/9/90). On the south side, the Metro Peach Group and MacLellan's Prestige Homes were preparing for a development on Robert Mugabe Road, while Ximex redeveloped an old Macy's Hypermarket on Jason Moyo Avenue. Zimre also purchased properties for redevelopment, including one on Chinhoyi Street in the Kopje and the Tattersalls building on Jason Moyo Avenue, together valued at Z$150 million. In the centre of the CBD, the sixty-four year old Dominion Building at First Street and Union Avenue was demolished in late 1991 (and attempts to retain the facade proved futile) (*FG*, 23/5/91), as the National Railways of Zimbabwe Pension Fund prepared a Z$53 million building to replace it (*FG*, 18/7/91).[18] Fidelity Life was another major institutional investor, holding in its portfolio office-shopping complexes costing Z$68 million in Harare and Z$50 million in Bulawayo. Fidelity also drew profits from office and shopping developments in Mutare, Gwanda, Gokwe, Beitbridge and even Plumtree (*FG*, 12/12/91).

How far would the CBD's speculative bubble expand? Putting the touches on the new Construction House in early 1990, a London-based Knight Frank Rutley executive wondered aloud about the impact of a bust on the stability of the financial system:

> In some ways the market here can be compared to Tokyo, where property is quite impossible to buy. However, the proposed redevelopment

> of Tokyo Bay may release enormous amounts of property which the authorities, and banks in particular, are extremely worried about because these sales may cause values to drop. The same could be said about properties here if large amounts were available. I wonder if statistics are available to show what levels of institutional bank lending exist, against property in comparisons with total lending, and also what effect a 20% fallback in values would do this lending. (*FG*, 18/5/90)

But while Tokyo tottered, Harare maintained momentum well into 1991. The advantage was a closed economy which continued to trap profits and the willingness of institutional investors to continue pumping funds into property. "The investment of pension funds in the area of fixed properties is one which is of utmost importance in times of inflation. Fixed properties appreciate in value and hence are a hedge against inflation," argued Labani Hove, the chair of Zimbabwe Association of Pension Funds (and later of the scandal-ridden PTC). "But to successfully invest in fixed properties, pension funds require foreign exchange in sufficient doses" (*FG*, 23/5/91). These doses were made available as 75% of developer applications for components like lifts and air-conditioning units received allocations. Indeed according to Geoff Brakspear of Frank Knight Rutley, from 1988, it was "easy" to acquire foreign exchange for special glass and tiles, air conditioning systems, lifts, and other components.[19]

Geographical barriers to CBD office expansion were probably more important than foreign exchange availability. Following suggestions about rezoning the Avenues (already *de facto* commercial zones, as many private businesses were run from homes), the City Council ordered developers to go south—"to the railway"—instead (*FG*, 17/8/90). The developers responded initially by going much further, stepping up their *suburban* activity. The ubiquitous Old Mutual opened the Z$68 million "Mutual Gardens," its new headquarters at Emerald Hills eight kilometers from town. One of the biggest buildings in Zimbabwe, it would boast spacious gardens, shops, sport facilities, and middle-class housing in the immediate vicinity (*FG*, 24/5/90). The northeastern suburbs of Newlands and Borrowdale were also prime suburbs for speculators (such as MacLellan Homes and Sam Levy), though not without pitfalls.[20] A Z$60 million office and shopping complex was to be built in the western suburb of Belvedere (*FG*, 24/10/91). Yet "the most significant retail project" in Zimbabwe in 1989 was the Chitungwiza town centre developed by Old Mutual. The company's property manager, Frost (1989:7)—then also president of the National Property Association—explained that the Chitungwiza centre was approved by the Town Council, "who have opted for a planned centre by a single developer with a full range of national retailers, with plenty of competition to keep prices down, yet without over-trading. This can only be achieved by having a planned retail mix, hence the necessity to have a single developer." It was a prescient statement of the anarchy of speculative overbuilding that would soon prove disastrous.

Speculation and gentrification

To the west of Harare's railway, the developers began to fuel what became a speculative inferno in the old Kopje district. The unfortunate recent history of the Kopje—namely, its systematic devaluation—suggests the reasons that development travelled in this direction. According to news reports in the mid-1960s, "owing to the difficulty in letting offices in the western area of the city, the City Council ... allowed a business block in Cameron Street to be converted completely to residential rooms" (*P&F*, January 1964, June 1964). This would mark an important watershed, as the area's decline was reflected in its transition to a lower land use. By the early 1970s, Smout (1971:39, 49) characterized even the busy central hub of the Kopje by its

> wide variety of low quality retail establishments of which representatives of the motor trade are most frequent. Unfortunately many of the buildings in the southern Kopje are poorly maintained and the general aspect is that of a run-down, rapidly ageing, twilight zone... Many structures are in need of a new coat of paint and where outer walls are plastered repairs are urgently needed. Further, as the area is socially and financially inferior to the rest of central Salisbury it receives minimal attention from those engaged in providing Municipal services.

The systematic devaluation of the area continued beyond Independence, and in the mid 1980s the Kopje was described as "dying slowly, as little or no care is being taken to maintain the blocks of flats, cottages and houses" (*Herald*, 9/11/84). The problem, surmised an Estate Agents Council spokesperson, was that "Kopje rents are too low... Most of the buildings have broken windows, peeling paint or cracked walls. Some of the roofs are held down by large stones and bricks so that they are not blown off by the wind" (*Herald*, 10/11/84). Several estate agents simply refused to manage properties in the area. Many flats became brothels or shebeens (informal bars).

According to Brakspear, the owner-occupied (not institutional-owned) nature of the Kopje slowed its redevelopment. Moreover, another barrier to successful redevelopment was excessive passive speculation.[21] Absentee landlords were "scattered all over the world," their full-bulk buildings underutilized (*FG*, 17/8/90). Indeed the majority of older properties in both the Kopje and the CBD were held by non-residents.[22] As Old Mutual's Frost (1989:8) informed the National Property Association, "The result is that large areas of our city centres have become sterile. A number of major development schemes have foundered because of the difficulty in persuading non-resident owners to sell their old properties, many of which are little more than single storey slums."

Notwithstanding such problems, a "rent gap"—between the devalued real estate and the potential for commercial property development[23]—emerged which was finally attacked, though carefully, by foresighted developers, on the basis that small office space was becoming impossible to acquire in the CBD. Indeed, following an initial rezoning in 1989 and extensive consultations in 1990 and 1991 with Harare City Council about a new plan for the area, the National Property Association announced that it "took issue with the retention of a residential precinct in an area intended for vibrant commercial and office activities. The present 'run-down' look which is a feature of the area is likely to continue and is incompatible with upmarket intentions for the area" (*FG*, 11/5/90). As with gentrification everywhere, the existing residents would have to go, having successfully completed their role in the devaluation process. According to one single mother, "Even though we have seen other surrounding flats being destroyed our landlord has not yet given us notice. We understand that our flat is going to be turned into an office for the building society. I am looking for alternative accommodation in the high-density suburbs."[24]

The first major inroad into the Kopje came not from private developers backed by institutional investors, but instead from state-owned finance in the form of a new Z$3.4-million headquarters for the Zimbabwe Development Bank (ZDB). ZDB managing director Rindai Jaravaza "hoped that other developers can emulate the bank's lead in providing above average standard of office accommodation and thereby help to uplift the scenic beauty of the area" (*FG*, 7/9/90). In 1991 Harare's director of works confirmed, "Our main objective is to give the area a face-lift and commercialize it" (*FG*, 8/1/91).

When speculation in the Kopje finally took off, it was unprecedented. In one transaction Brakspear bought a property in 1990 for Z$460,000 and sold it three months later for Z$2 million (interview, January 1991). Indeed Z$2 million was a typical price for a stand (plot) in the Kopje by 1991, and this amounted to a higher price per square meter than that found in the CBD. In the heart of the Kopje area, the famous old Queens Hotel and its musical venue was targeted to become an office block. The Cotton Marketing Board planned in Rotten Row, at the west side of the Kopje, at a cost of Z$18 million. Fidelity Life Assurance would take a site nearby (the third largest in the Kopje) for its Z$80-million headquarters, next to the ZDB, not far from the Z$32-million Caltex building (*FG*, 24/3/94). On the very western end sat the postmodern ZANU house, nicknamed Chibuku for its similarity to the cardboard carton used for indigenous beer.

The fall of commercial property

The demise of speculation had to arrive at some point, and the spectre of the Economic Structural Adjustment Program—with its promises of increased access to foreign goods and, in a few years, of free access to foreign financial markets—certainly made Zimbabwe's financial elite think twice about domestic speculation. In addition, there were warnings from other countries that real estate price inflation might not last in Zimbabwe.[25]

The main catalyst for the fall of commercial property was the interest rate increase that occurred first in February 1991 and then again in September. These had their greatest immediate impact on the residential market.[26] By August of 1991, the *Financial Gazette* (1/8/91) reported, "Sellers are now experiencing delays in finalising property sales because of the buyers' difficulties in raising mortgage finance." Ironically, in June and July 1991, a record-breaking Z$700 million in mortgages were registered, of which Z$240 million came from the commercial banks, yet these were mainly commercial and industrial mortgages. In July building societies began to sharply curtail their lending, dropping from an average of Z$60 million per month in early 1991 to Z$35 million in mid-year (CSO, *Digest of Statistics*). Thus residential real estate, which had taken longer to develop as a speculative commodity, broke badly, losing some 20% of price levels in the last six months of 1991 (*Herald*, 12/12/90).

Second, on the commercial and industrial side of the market, the high mark-up construction firms enjoyed had reached self-destructive levels: with building costs in March 1984 at Z$980 per square meter, and with rents at Z$12 per square meter, the initial yield to the developer was 11%; but according to Frost (1991, 3), "an entirely comparable building under construction to finish in March 1993 costs Z$7,086 per square meter for construction, but can only get Z$44 rent and yield of only 6%."[27] Frost attacked "the cozy pricing policies of Zimbabwe contractors [who] thereby achieve markups and margins they have not experienced in their wildest dreams" and he warned them, "You can not assume that financial institutions will continue to invest in new property development."[28] (The problem may also have reflected inflation in building materials, which continued to soar. The overall building materials price index was up 38% from September 1990 to September 1991, more than double the consumer price index.)

Developer Moffit Saunders commented in mid-1992 that "the once unthought-of spectre of industrial buildings lying empty is fast becoming a reality in Harare" (*FG*, 13/8/92). According to Mitchell Real Estate,

> with the exception of a few pension funds and insurance organizations, most concerns had stopped buying industrial and commercial space. For the past three or so months, large institutions were buying up industrial and commercial space from developers who needed the funds to meet production expenses... However, pension funds were now channelling their funds into short-term investments on the money market where they received returns of over 35%. (*FG*, 13/8/92)

Given the ongoing collapse of the ZSE, there were still a few institutional investors with excess funds available for property in 1992.[29] But the extreme variability in financial flows—sometimes exorbitant (whereby Frost's Old Mutual fuelled the construction overpricing so enthusiastically, even into 1992) and sometimes repressed (as they were for building societies)—was also to blame. Indeed it was Frost (1991:3) who first publicly predicted the vast overextension of commercial property speculation, in July 1991: "It is now clear that the property industry is facing a surplus office accommodation in Harare for the first time since Independence. This surplus is reliably calculated to be 3.3% in 1992 rising to 6.3% in 1994." A symbolic event was Lonrho's May 1991 decision to withdraw from construction of a major new hotel between 3rd and 4th Streets and Samora Machel and Union Avenues.

Some developers (like MacLellan) were teetering on the edge in late 1991. Property prices fell by a quarter during the first half of 1992, according to the *Financial Gazette* (6/8/92): "Estate agents said all classes of property had experienced reductions in prices, with some agents saying the property market was 'virtually dead' or 'non-existent.'" Impressive Harare property registrations in 1992 were based on "old contracts signed a year or two ago." From 1992 to 1993, plans approved fell from Z$916 million to Z$51 million in nominal terms. The commercial property market hit bottom in mid-1993, and with inflation running at more than 40% the best improvements in prices subsequently were just 5-10% (*EIU*, March 1994).

Even in the mid-1990s, as several suburban office parks were planned (*FG*, 2/9/95)—as well as luxury office-shopping developments like Eastgate and a Z$1 billion Borrowdale complex (with luxury housing, hotel, medical centre, golf course and offices)—the future for commercial property in

Harare looked grim. Revenue from office rentals continued to decline in real terms (*FG*, 21/7/94) and, when 38,000 square meters suddenly became available, the *Financial Gazette* (10/3/94) headlined, "Property developers near panic over unoccupied office space." At that stage, new office buildings including Finsure House, Corner House, Fidelity Towers, Southampton Life Centre, National Social Security Administration House, Unity Court, Beverley Court, Eastgate, and the Zimbabwe Electricity Supply Authority building all had vacancies.

As Rory O'Donoghue, managing director of Richard Ellis Real Estate, put it in September 1994, "An awful lot of office buildings have been built which have come on stream over a short period and several more will come onto the market over the next 18 months, and it is fair to say that a number of these buildings were not market-driven but merely followed from the speculative burst of buying land prior to 1990." O'Donoghue worried that ESAP had "changed the perceptions of some of the users who would have gladly taken up offices had they been available a couple of years ago." And, he concluded, the oversupply problem would have been worse, but "virtually every building was running behind schedule" (*FG*, 15/9/94). Moreover, there was the issue of alternative investments, for as Moffit Saunders put it in late 1994, "With short-term interest rates about 30% and 10-year bonds at 20%, there was little incentive for the institutions to move out of the money market back into property" (*FG*, 15/12/94).

A sorry but revealing example of the commercial property crisis could be found in Chitungwiza in September 1995, where the much-heralded Old Mutual shopping centre development had fallen into "a depressed state," due in part to Old Mutual's withdrawal of a subsidy to the Zimbabwe United Passenger Company to transport workers from Harare to the Chitungwiza Town Centre. With the bus service cancelled, and with the satellite city's major employer, Cone Textiles, having laid off 6,000 workers, many of the Centre's smaller retail outlets were forced to shut down and its major tenants (OK Bazaars and TM Supermarkets) found that "Things have never been this bad" (*FG*, 21/9/95).

Given the problem of generalized overproduction of office and shopping space, by late 1995 the major prospects for new construction were largely state-related. The National Social Security Administration announced commercial office/retail developments worth Z$120 million in Bulawayo and Z$70 million in Mutare. The Post Office planned a Z$50-million office in Gweru, SEDCO began work on a Z$20-million headquarters in Harare, while the Zimbabwe Reinsurance Corporation announced several multimillion dollar projects across the country. In the most grandiose state-backed project, the Industrial Development

Corporation began the first (Z$500 million) phase of what it claimed would be a Z$14-billion, 20-square-kilometer industrial park to the east of Harare, supported by a Malaysian partner (the Sungeiway Group). The park would, the IDC proclaimed, be "earmarked for corporations and entrepreneurs seeking areas of cheap but literate labor and global competitiveness of new industrial sitings" (as an export-processing zone it would allegedly generate 30,000 jobs and exports of Z$1 billion per year in sectors such as high-tech electronics and motor components). Meanwhile, the private sector remained stagnant, with the exception of the cash-flush Mining Industry Pension Fund, which after a year-long suspension of all property development would in 1996 embark upon projects in Harare valued at Z$100 million, none of which, however, were for commercial office or retail space (*FG*, 28/9/95, 19/10/95, 9/11/95, 21/12/95).

More generally, the variety of structural problems surfacing in the commercial property market appeared, at least for the time being, insurmountable. Overaccumulation of speculative real estate threatened to synthesize with other negative factors such as the envisaged purchase of some of Zimbabwe's best companies by eager South Africans as business relations were normalized and investment restrictions in both countries fully removed. At that point, it would not be unlikely for Harare to increasingly appear to Johannesburg as Lusaka did to Salisbury during the late 1950s, a shell of its former self, with administrative and financial control functions (in sectors such as banking, tourism, and the retail trade) stripped and transferred south.

The ZSE shakeout

The interest rate increases of 1991 caused the ZSE crash in two ways. Funds were quickly shifted away from the ZSE into bonds or other interest-bearing assets. And an abundance of now unrepayable corporate debt, beginning with a wave of borrowing in September 1990 (and cooled only slightly by the February 1991 rate hike), also suggested that financial markets had become far too loose.

The market peak, 3 September 1991, came two days prior to a phenomenal rise in short-term interest rates (from 20% up to 40% following a World Bank ultimatum) which suggests a rather detailed level of insider information. Share trading on the ZSE peaked in September and October (Z$95 million total volume) as investors fled shares for the money markets. In the two months immediately preceding (Z$27 million) and following (Z$16 million), ZSE trading value was much lower. As the *Financial*

Gazette (12/12/91) observed: "Individuals have been active [in selling ZSE shares], and perhaps so have the banks, having to call in former loans against share portfolio values now barely covering them." While some smarter individuals, banks, and companies liquidated early, ordinary pensioners were tied in to the ZSE through their life-savings.

Within three months, the industrial index was at November 1990 levels, having dropped 30% from the September 1991 peak. By March 1992, it was down by 60% and by February 1993 by 70%. Even as the index began to plummet, a dozen companies issued shares in order to "reduce or extinguish high interest-bearing debt as an immediate requirement," as the *Financial Gazette*'s (12/12/91) anonymous ZSE columnist put it. "At one time there were moanings about shortage of script. Now we have a situation where there are more than double the number of issued shares on the market than a year ago and nobody seems to want them." In 1992, total trading on the ZSE was worth just 3% of the ZSE total value, compared with 50% in New York and Tokyo.

The proximate cause of the ZSE crash was the interest rate hike, and the fact that international finance was now calling the monetary policy shots did not escape the attention of domestic financiers. According to the *Financial Gazette* writer,

> Added to [the interest rate increase] was the World Bank's insistence that the Zimbabwe dollar was still over-valued and that the country should act accordingly. The Reserve Bank duly obliged with a quick succession of lower exchange rate fixes. These might have stabilized at the lower levels, but doubt remains whether we have seen the last of interest rate adjustments. The institutions became so attracted by the unprecedented rates then obtainable in the money market that they justifiably saw fit to unload large parcels of high-value, low-yielding shares accumulated over the years at peanut prices.

It is true that some of the investment volatility can be traced to exchange-rate movements, which at the zenith of speculation in imported commodities led to a disastrous series of delayed export orders and rushed imports (in order to take profits from declines in the Zimbabwe dollar). Under the new Open General Import License system, there was also widespread hoarding of "unnecessarily large stocks of certain finished products and raw materials as some importers have speculated on demand prospects and on currency exchange rate changes," according to FMB (*QGE,* September 1991). One direct result was that financial markets were "in disarray." The effects spread beyond the financial markets: "This practice has already had unfortunate consequences as it has not only tied up scarce foreign exchange, it has also slowed the extension of the OGIL list to other products and helped to generate an over-supply of the products that could result in wastage or price-cutting and losses to the traders." Moreover, as the economic misery of average Zimbabweans increased visibly, shortages emerged in basic goods while luxury products (at unprecedented prices) abounded in shop windows.

But even without such import speculation, the conditions for the demise of financial-speculative capital was inevitable, given excessive levels of profiteering, overbuilding in the CBD, and the overindebtedness of some key companies. "Company liquidations have become the order of the day as heavily borrowed companies fail to meet the increased interest rates and send workers onto the streets to swell the ranks of the unemployed," the *Financial Gazette* (23/7/92) reported. Zimbabwe Banking Corporation economists added, "Institutional investors are increasingly being called upon to bail out the Zimbabwe economy... Over the past six months, the number of businesses that have come forward to sell their factories and premises, and immediately enter into long-term leases with the institutional investors buying their property has increased" (*FG*, 4/6/92).

Corporate debt, once relatively trivial, had become a millstone for many companies. Hunyani required an official Z$37-million bail-out due to overindebtedness in early 1993 (although simultaneously, the company's compensation payments to directors rose from Z$75,000 to Z$1.9 million) (*FG*, 1/4/93). Art Corporation's 1993 interest bill of Z$72 million was more than two and a half times the conglomerate's profits, leading to a Z$280-million debt restructuring by local banks and the European Investment Bank (*FG*, 3/3/94, 10/6/94). Accounting gimmicks proliferated. Zimpapers' pension fund was used to fund an Z$8-million bank overdraft (*FG*, 3/6/93). Art Corporation admitted that it understated the debt of its plastics division in 1995 (*FG*, 19/10/95). And the ZSE's biggest company, Delta (at that point more than a third government-owned), excluded short-term loans from current liabilities (which were renamed as "interest free liabilities") in mid-1993 and instead placed them at the end of shareholders funds. As the *Financial Gazette* (22/6/93) remarked, "Cynics and skeptics would immediately say the reason for this change is that short-term borrowings would make the balance sheet look extremely vulnerable if classed as current liabilities. So vulnerable that liabilities would outmatch assets by 1.4 to one."

The radical change in the market was reflected in the rise in dividend yields on industrial shares (just 3.36% at peak in September 1991, and a year later 11%) and earnings yields (11% in mid-1991, and 30% a year later). Price-earnings ratios were 11.3 at peak and had fallen to just 3.3 a year later. The World Bank's International Finance Corporation (1992:46) called the ZSE "the worst performer among world equity markets" in 1992 in part, interestingly, because "The success of the Structural Adjustment Programme was in doubt after the first year."

The crises of domestic debt and speculation worked hand in hand, as the *Financial Gazette* (12/12/91) observed: "Individuals have been active [in selling ZSE shares], and perhaps so have the banks, having to call in former loans against share portfolio values now barely covering them." While some smarter individuals, banks, and companies liquidated early, ordinary pensioners and insurance policy-holders were tied in to the ZSE through the institutional investors which controlled their life-savings.

The implications of speculation for workers

Who lost in all of this shakeout, then? Among the "great public" who—as Hilferding had it—followed the speculators innocently to the slaughter, were workers (Bond 1993b). Members of pension funds contributed Z$800 million in net new savings in 1992 and many also depended upon fund payouts to survive the wave of early 1990s retrenchments. Pensions were a relatively common means of working-class saving, given Zimbabwe's inheritance of so many British working-class institutions. In the late 1980s, of a total non-agricultural working population of 818,000, some 658,000 workers were members of funds.

But in the wake of the 1991-93 ZSE collapse—which coincided with the industrial depression—many workers learned to their dismay that for a variety of reasons payouts would now be delayed and that benefit levels were falling precipitously. In spite of inflation reaching more than 48% in late 1992, the Registrar of Pension and Provident Funds mandated maximum increases in pension fund payouts of only 30% (a huge drop in even the most fortunate pensioners' standards of living).

Behind the payment shortfall was the speculative nature of the major pension fund managers' investment portfolios. Herd investment mentality characterized the major firms—Old Mutual, Southern Life, Colonial Mutual, and Fidelity Life—as well as self-administered funds such as Anglo American Corporation and the railway and mining industry funds. At year-end 1992, Zimbabwe's pension funds controlled Z$7.62 billion in assets. Of these, property (mainly commercial) accounted for Z$1.2 billion, while Z$745 million was held in ZSE shares, debentures, unit trusts, and building societies—assets which were falling spectacularly in value.

Assets invested in the collapsing property market were particularly galling to workers, since some of it was speculative high-cost residential property (housing in high-density areas was *terra incognita* to the pension fund managers). The Mining Industry Pension Fund (MIPF), for example, ventured into residential property in mid 1983 with the Z$2.3-million "Wansford" development in a fashionable section of the Avenues in Central Harare, a project which "could become one of the most exclusive addresses in central Harare," according to one report. It is worth examining this particular fund, since its 45,269 mineworker members saw little in the way of socially-productive returns on the 5% of earnings they contributed each month. In addition to Wansford, the MIPF invested in other high-priced residential properties, including a Z$5.8-million development in another exclusive section of the Avenues. To its credit, the MIPF recognized the social incongruity of diminishing supplies of low- and middle-income housing occurring simultaneous with increasingly speculative housing investments. In 1989 MIPF chief executive Sam Nkomo argued, "We could use our investment more profitably by developing in the commercial sector, but we feel we have a social responsibility to society." Nevertheless, that "social responsibility" was still geared to higher-income housing, with rentals on MIPF properties in the Avenues fetching more than Z$1,000 per one bedroom unit per month (*FG*, 20/10/94).

All told, MIPF's residential properties accounted for Z$8.6 million at historic cost, which enjoyed mid 1992 property valuations of Z$31.3 million. The total MIPF property portfolio had a historic cost of Z$100.2 million, with mid-1992 valuation of Z$185.7. Even considering that the mid-1992 valuations were excessive in view of the emerging oversupply of commercial property, the residential component enjoyed a higher increase in value, notwithstanding the fact that most of the residential buildings were purchased later than the commercial property.

A large residential property developed by the Construction Industry Pension Fund was also designed for an upmarket segment (the project cost before escalations was Z$29 million). But when it ran into major problems in 1991, the fund had to record a Z$8.2-million contingent liability. The entire asset value of the Construction Industry Fund was just Z$72.8 million in late 1991, with fixed property accounting for 36%. This sort of fluctuation is important, because construction industry employees are possibly the most transient and vulnerable of any economic sector, with nearly 30,000 new members joining the pension fund in 1991 along with 12,700 withdrawals (total membership was 76,000).

In an even more incongruous situation was the National Railways of Zimbabwe Pension Fund (which owns commercial property including Ambassador House and Karigamombe Centre in Harare, as well as National

Railways of Zimbabwe headquarters and the hotly-contested Ascot Flats in Bulawayo). The fund attempted to sell to the Harare City Council the railway employees' high-density suburb of Rugare just southwest of the city, but according to press reports, "The offer was initially rejected because of the poor state of the roads and stormwater drainage in the suburb."

In sum, the shakeout had a profound class bias that Hilferding would easily recognize. "Workers are being stabbed in the back by a capital-hungry private sector which has blown millions on stock market gambling and high-flying real estate speculation," *Horizon* magazine (November 1992) commented. "Meanwhile, as workers' money goes into putting up flashy post-modern office blocks in downtown Harare that most workers only enter as sweepers and cleaners, at least 80,000 are queuing for low-cost housing in the capital." And Morgan Tsvangirai (1992:4-5), secretary general of the Zimbabwe Congress of Trade Unions (ZCTU), confronted the Zimbabwe Association of Pension Funds during the midst of the collapse:

> It is workers' money that is being used to fuel this speculative roller coaster, that at the end of the day benefits the speculators, but does not put finances into productive investment and jobs. This is an untenable situation for us—who then walk the streets unemployed.... Like the rise of luxury high rise blocks in a city where the people cannot afford food and transport, rising financial speculation on a withering industrial base does not bode well for sustainable development.

The rebuttal by Association chair Sam Nkomo was so obdurate—"Once money is in the hands of the fund it is no longer the workers' money. The trust laws rule supreme" (*FG*, 13/8/92)—that the ZCTU intensified its efforts to reform the existing pension funds, to redirect their assets into housing, and to promote the National Social Security scheme as an alternative (*Horizon*, November 1992; Bond 1993b).

The precise effect of the ZSE crash on pension funds remained difficult to calculate due to historic-cost accounting policies and the re-purchase of lower-priced shares in the wake of the crash. The MIPF is an example, because by mid-1992 shares (including government stocks listed on the ZSE) purchased by the MIPF at a cost of Z$212 million had devalued 31% in nominal terms to Z$146 million. A year earlier, when an actuarial valuation was carried out, the MIPF investments had appeared extremely healthy, and a surplus of Z$82 million was discovered. According to the MIPF, "In the light of this valuation it was decided to declare a 15% bonus" to members.

Similarly, the Construction Industry Pension Fund commissioned an actuarial valuation in late 1990, discovered a Z$5.6-million surplus, and declared a 10% bonus. A year later, however, ZSE equities valued at Z$5.9 million in the pension fund had dropped 39% to Z$3.6 million (with far further to go still in 1992). The Zimbabwe Electricity Supply Authority Staff Pension Fund also made large ZSE acquisitions during the dramatic share price rise, and by mid 1991 recorded 11.33% of its aggregate asset value in ZSE shares (the highest of any pension fund). The Z$5.7-million ZSE historic-cost exposure (recorded as Z$7.5 million middle market value) was untimely, in view of the fund's 1988 actuarial valuation shortfall of Z$9.3 million and a decision taken in 1991 to merge with the E.S.C. Weekly-Paid Staff Pension Fund (which itself carried a Z$8.8 million shortfall). By 1993, authorities began investigating the alleged "misuse of millions of dollars in funds" (*FG*, 22/4/93).

It was at the time of these shortfalls, in 1992-93, that retrenchments increased dramatically and hence that pension funds came under intense payout strain, leading to numerous incidents of non-payment and conflict over control of the funds (Bond, 1993b). The National Railways of Zimbabwe, for instance, refused to pay its pension fund—already crippled by the BCCI collapse—Z$40 million (though workers put the figure owed at Z$196 million), and in 1993 even failed to make its monthly fund contribution (*FG*, 13/5/93). Nevertheless, with a revival of the ZSE in 1993, unrepentant pension fund managers began reinvesting in both commercial property and shares, inviting the prospect of further losses and a repeat of the 1992-93 liquidity problems further down the road.

The ZSE comeback

The ZSE finally began a recovery after hitting an exceptionally low trough in February 1993, when the industrial index plunged to 850. Because the depth of collapse had been so great, the subsequent rise—fueled by a new breed of foreign institutional investors and supported by local speculators and more pension fund cash—was equally impressive. New fortunes were made essentially because of uneven global stock market speculation which spilled into Zimbabwe through foreign mutual funds. Indeed, an estimated US$50 billion flowed from North to South via Third World stock markets during the late 1980s and early 1990s, until the 1995 Mexican crash cooled speculative fevers in the emerging markets. The reforming, formerly "Marxist-Leninist" Zimbabwe was advertised internationally as a favored African child of the World Bank, and was hence sure to get at least a small piece of the action. And although many ZSE-listed companies continued to withhold dividends during the 1991-93 depression, their share prices began rising rapidly when prohibitions against foreign dealing on the ZSE were lifted in June 1993.

Within a few weeks, the 1993-94 budget featured a capital gains tax reduction from 20% to 10% and a reduction on the dividend tax. This was the result, according to the *Financial Gazette* stock market commentator, of "several representations by securities firms that excessive tax on securities had cost the country several millions of dollars in lost portfolio investment and direct foreign investment." In reality, foreign investors were now storming into the ZSE, joining funds flowing from the local money market where rates had fallen. But as the tax cuts were announced, ordinarily gung-ho *Financial Gazette* editorialists cautioned, "Little attempt has been made to see what are the targets of the foreign money and no one is questioning whether the interest rate fall is a blip on a graph that might be rising inexorably" (*FG*, 5/8/93).

But the foreigners seemed to be hooked. From mid-1993 through early 1994, based initially on the erratic inflow of several tens of millions of dollars of investment from Switzerland, the UK, and a major New York investment bank, the ZSE soared. Local speculators who emerged to take advantage of the upsurge included between 50 and 100 extremely wealthy individuals, according to a Sagit stockbroker (*Horizon*, September 1993). Many were tobacco farmers who had access to large seasonal cash infusions in mid-1993 (notwithstanding the recent collapse of tobacco prices) and who benefitted from capital gains tax cuts and falling interest rates (leading to transfers from the money market to the ZSE). Pension and insurance funds then moved back in once the new bull market gathered speed.

A renewed surge of foreign mutual fund investment occurred in early 1994, rippling out from the Johannesburg Stock Exchange (in anticipation of successful elections scheduled for April, South Africa had attracted massive new inflows). But *Financial Gazette* commentator Ticharwa Masimba (1994, 4) was right to complain, "The ZSE has been crowing about the Z$500 million net inflow through the capital market. What is not said is, this money is temporary and can be shipped back to investor countries at the drop of a hat. It has not flown into the companies but has gone into the hands of shareholders, who are mainly white. With this windfall, the whites have the capacity to increase their ownership of the economy." In the *Financial Times* (7/12/94), Tony Hawkins soon termed the ZSE "the white man's casino."

Indeed, the prospects for another crash remained high, given the continuing shakeout of Zimbabwe's productive sector, volatility in international trade, and the extreme vulnerability that accompanied global financial liberalization. South Africa's boom was shortlived, as the rand suddenly devalued. Bitter foreign fund managers withdrew, many taking huge dollar-denominated losses of 5%-10% (for a few weeks' worth of investment). Zimbabwe also devalued its currency dramatically at this stage, leading to a sudden drop in the ZSE index from 3,800 to less than 3,000. A resurgence in foreign funds brought the index back up again to 3,800 very quickly, but like a yo-yo it then dropped again by 25% in March 1994.

Meanwhile, most listed Zimbabwean companies had not yet come to grips with the new situation, and were recording declining real turnover and profits for 1993. "There is therefore again little justification in the published results for the rapid stock market index rise that has been occurring, and which must therefore be put down to speculative factors following the opening of the stock market to foreign investors," surmised the *Economist Intelligence Unit* in June 1994. High inflation levels had also eroded the value of the ZSE to levels far lower than the September 1991 peak.

Moreover, there were unfortunate spinoffs of the capital inflows elsewhere across the economy. Foreign currency accounts and foreign investment in the ZSE were the primary cause of a 40% increase in money supply growth during the first half of 1994, which in turn—"to neutralize these inflows," in the words of Reserve Bank governor Tsumba—led to increases both in overnight interest rates (from 28.5% to 30.5%) and in the reserve ratio for banks (from 13.5% to 17%) (*FG*, 11/8/94).

A substantial (if rather gradual) decline occurred in share prices over the following months, as hedge funds disinvested from the ZSE in the wake of a downturn in the global bond market (though at least one pundit also cast blame on "the hate campaign which is presently being waged against multinationals and local minority groups on racial and political grounds") (*FG*, 14/7/94, 20/10/94). By the time of the 1995 Mexican peso crisis and stock market crash, there were few foreign investors left in the ZSE. The Zimbabwe dollar was being prepared for another devaluation, so fund managers took the hint and liquidated half of their investments, leaving a net of just US$67 million (still substantial in local dollar terms, however). As the *Financial Gazette* (31/1/95) noted, "Mexico and Zimbabwe are similar in that both nations have massive budget deficits and their currencies, prior to the downward correction in the former country, are perceived to be artificially supported. This correlation has left our market vulnerable to flights of equity and there has been very little foreign buying since the beginning of the year."

Indeed, it was no longer the institutional investors who now managed speculative capital. The scale at which finance determined uneven development in Zimbabwe had clearly moved from national to international. A Soros Fund Management executive explained how global speculators had come to view emerging markets by the mid-1990s:

> What is being made clear by the Mexican problem is that in traded securities, you are going to have to be very careful about where these flows are going and where the herd is. When everyone is wild to get into a place, it is often better to just stay away... What a lot of people have missed are the implications of the global flow of equity funds—and the new alignment, where the maniacs, like ourselves, are driving the flow of funds around the world. (*African Agenda*, April 1995)

Thus, as Zimbabwe's currency controls evaporated, financial globalization would—as in the late 1890s and late 1920s—prove enormously threatening, in contrast to the 1987 and 1989 stock market crashes which caused not a flutter in Harare.

But more generally, foreign finance merely amplified the ZSE's casino-like atmosphere. In August 1993, when the industrial index had climbed back to just 1,350, the overvaluation of shares had already reached 20% (according to the Sagit broker), which in turn prompted—as the *Financial Gazette* (13/8/93) ZSE columnist observed—"signs of manic depression. Overwhelming and instant euphoria takes over when some slight piece of good news comes along, blotting out the previous total despair." It was emblematic, the same source complained in early 1995, that an uptick in the money market attracted vast funds out of the ZSE and in the process "accentuated the short-termism of most Zimbabwean investors. This partly explains the relative failure of new and rights issues in 1994. Out of 12 such issues, nine are trading below offer price" (*FG*, 19/1/95). By May 1995, the real interest rate (the Negotiable Certificate of Deposit rate minus inflation) had hit a peak of 13%, leaving the ZSE comparatively unattractive.

And reflecting not only the temporal feature of finance but also its spatial flexibility was that in early 1995 the ZSE issued its first share offer denominated in US dollars (to finance Falcon Investments' foreign mining operations). Then (after a 17% decline in ZSE share prices due to the attractive money market interest rates and the ongoing drought)[30] by September 1995 (as real interest rates very briefly dropped to 1%) the ZSE again hit record levels. But as the *Financial Gazette* (19/10/95) warned, "Of course the surge in the index bears no relation to the pulse of the national economy. Speculators searching for short-term profit rather than long-term investors have been active in pushing up the index." And they pushed it above the 4000 mark by year-end 1995 and then to 12,000 in August 1997, far higher than underlying values merited.

In sum, the increasing ease with which investors could switch funding from one portfolio to another, from local to international currency investments, and from long- to short-term paper, apparently meant that not even the immediate memory of the ZSE's awesome 1991-93 crash had taught Zimbabwean stock market players the lessons of speculation.

Conclusion: The meaning of speculation

Throughout the first decade of Independence, Harare's bankers, investors, and estate agents generally overlooked the machinations of the rest of the speculative financial world and for good reason, namely, their protected status thanks to exchange controls. But they could not remain innocent forever. The spectacular rise and tumultuous fall of international property markets—and of players such as Ivan Boesky, Michael Milken, Alan Bond, Donald Trump, and Robert Maxwell—finally, and too late to do any good, began to raise a few Harare eyebrows. What, however, are the lessons *from* Zimbabwe?

There are several aspects of the analysis that correspond to earlier theoretical arguments concerning speculation. These include the delinking of an exploding financial system from a crisis-ridden productive base; the weakness of a post-liberation state in relation to an ascendant financial fraction of capital; the emergence of a state-based bureaucratic petty bourgeoisie unwilling to take substantial steps to identify and to control the more parasitical elements of the economy; the dynamics of financial collapse that necessarily follow an orgy of speculation; and the fact that without a successful restructuring of the productive circuits of capital, speculative embers can remain hot enough to reignite, especially when foreign funds catalyse a resurgence of local investor confidence.

Boasting such a volatile, mixed record, how can we judge the two main speculative financial markets in Zimbabwe in the post-Independence period? First, real estate must be seen in terms of not only the crash of rent and property values in highly speculative markets in the CBD and low-density suburbs, but also in the context of uneven urban development (extraordinary urban land, housing, housing finance, and building material backlogs and shortages), which is the subject of the next chapter.

Second, the ZSE must be judged a profound failure over most of the Independence period, even on its terms. This was conceded by even its natural allies and enthusiasts: the World Bank, International Finance Corporation and associated intellectuals. A 1995 World Bank conference on "Stock Markets, Corporate Finance, and Economic Growth" ranked the ZSE miserably in most categories. A few findings are illustrative.

Eric Chang and Peter Montiel (1995) concluded that during the period 1975-92, Zimbabwe's market liquidity (0.35% per month share turnover) was lower than all emerging and developed stock markets (for which the average was 8.79%) except Nigeria (0.05%). Chang and Montiel also conducted measurements of "mispricing"—deviation from international trends—and noted that the ZSE was the most consistently distorted of all emerging stock markets: "The Zimbabwe stock market shows generally high levels of adjusted mispricing."[31]

Charges of low liquidity and distorted pricing would not surprise ZSE observers. But in a variety of other categories considered by Asl Demirguc-Kunt and Ross Levine (1995), the ZSE also ranked poorly. Zimbabwe scored in the lower half of developed and emerging stock markets with respect to market concentration as the top ten firms comprised 44% of the entire market's capitalization (compared to 14% in the US, 24% in Great Britain, and 51% in Nigeria). Zimbabwe's high degree of volatility over the 1986-93 period also ranked the ZSE among the least stable of all stock markets.[32] In the aggregate indicators of market capitalization, turnover, concentration and mispricing, the ZSE ranked below the markets in all countries except Nigeria, Venezuela, and Colombia. And in most categories, Zimbabwe did not exhibit marked change (either improvement or slippage) during the period 1986-93.

Third, and most importantly, the fundamental reason for the overall poor ranking was, perhaps, the comparative degree to which the Zimbabwean economy suffered productive sector overaccumulation, exacerbated by volatile capital flows into the country's immature financial circuits. As we have seen, this entailed a long and circuitous process, beginning with the crisis of industrial overcapacity (1974), taking on new forms as a result of political transition (1980), and ultimately reaching a speculative climax (1991) that presaged one of the country's worst-ever depressions. The process depended upon key actors overcoming their political qualms about Zimbabwe's government and "making the market," whether in shares or property (or other markets, such as art and imported machinery, which also served speculative purposes during the 1980s).

Grossmann (1992:196-197), too, posits speculation not as a mechanical switch from productive to financial circuits upon the first appearance of overaccumulation, but as an unpredictable process that sometimes takes many years to come to fruition: "The worst orgies of speculation are possible in a period when, with the transition from individual forms of property to its social form in share-capital, enormous fortunes accumulated over several decades are thrown on to the market and sacrificed on the exchange." In the sense that these fortunes were less the product of individual capital accumulation, and were increasingly located in pension funds, this sacrifice was all the more "social":

> Under these conditions, speculation is badly debilitated, not through the "conscious intervention" of banks which supposedly centralize command over the economy into their own hands [here, a reference to Hilferding's thesis], but because there is not enough "material" for the exchange to "digest." At an already advanced level of concentration of share-capital, speculation on the stock-exchange is bound to lose its impetus as its middle-class base of small rentiers, workers, civil servants, and so on, dries up. Yet this only compels the idle money-capital to rush into other outlets, into export of capital, as the only investments promising greater returns. This alone is one reason why world market struggles for investment outlets become increasingly sharper.

Grossmann was prophetic in suggesting the "rush" of capital into other outlets. Following the 1991-93 crash, the ZSE's subsequent roller-coaster performance was largely a function of the "increasingly sharp" searches for investment outlets by New York and London fund managers, joined by local capitalists. But for loose domestic capital that had not been devalued during the crash of share and property speculation, the era of ESAP also opened up many opportunities to engage in "world market struggles." Prior to considering some of these in Chapters Eleven and Twelve, however, more of the ground-level implications of footloose financial capital are examined in the next two chapters, first in the cities, then in the countryside.

Notes

1. The subsequent upturn in share values, from mid 1993 to early 1994 and from 1995 through mid-1997, was fragile and based to a large extent upon international speculators, but does deserve some comment; the upturn in real estate is little more than could have been expected.
2. Press Statement 203/84/RM, 29/3/84. It was not an easy time for Chidzero, who faced a foreign exchange shortage on top of an enormous drought- and South African destabilisation-related budget deficit. He used this new development to rationalise the imposition of harsh foreign exchange control measures both against multinational corporate profit remittances and against Zimbabweans dealing in overseas stock markets. However, such policies were anathema to the International Monetary Fund, which immediately severed a US$375 million line of credit to Zimbabwe.
3. Outstanding loans to the manufacturing sector reached their lowest level in three years in mid 1980 (Z$67 million) notwithstanding an infusion into banks of record levels of checking accounts by manufacturers (Z$45 million at that point). The mining and distribution sectors also witnessed

declines in bank lending immediately after independence, notwithstanding enormous increases in demand deposits.

4. Some of the most indebted companies included major firms like TA Holdings (63% debt/capital ratio), the Art Corporation (49%) and Natfoods (46%).
5. The data cited in this and the following paragraphs are drawn from the Bank report unless otherwise noted.
6. In 1987 the debt/capital ratio for local corporations was 33% and for foreign corporations 17%. This permitted a decrease in the interest expenditure of corporations from 31% of total operating income in 1983 to 15% in 1987, with an average of 19% from 1980-87.
7. It was noted in the previous chapter that corporate profits declined during the 1980s, picking up again from 1987-91. Nevertheless, over the entire 1980-91 period, ZSE firms' profitability (pre-tax income as a percent of total assets) was fourth highest among major national economies, at 13% (after Turkey at 24%, South Africa at 21%, and India at 13%). Measured by dividend yield, ZSE firms also ranked in the top five internationally. Finally, ZSE firms enjoyed an extremely high "tax shield" (measured as pre-tax earnings minus the ratio of corporate taxes paid to corporate tax rate, deflated by total assets, and excluding debt). At 3.3%, Zimbabwe firms' tax shield was below only those of South Africa (6.6%) and Pakistan (5.5%) (Demirguc-Kunt and Maksimovic 1995, Appendix).
8. Data in the following paragraphs are drawn from Bard Discount House, *Zimbabwe Money and Capital Market Review; Dataworld Shareworld Crosstables;* Reserve Bank of Zimbabwe *Quarterly Economic and Statistical Review;* and Sagit Stockbrokers, *Statistical Information on Companies Listed on the ZSE.*
9. Sagit felt compelled to advertise the fact that "The majority of shares in Sagit Stockbrokers Pvt Limited were owned by companies controlled by Mr. Jeremy Cochrane and Mr. Amos Nota. In June 1990 they were asked to resign from the Stock Exchange and as directors of the company and the shares have been lodged with Reserve Bank of Zimbabwe in trust" (*FG,* 15/6/90, 19/9/91).
10. Chanakira's analysis is compelling, but comes up short on theory: "It becomes increasingly evident that our stock market is inefficient and defies text book theory of rational investors, all of which, one may conclude, is due to scrip shortage, excess liquidity and influential market psychology." The problems in the productive sector of the Zimbabwean economy are nowhere mentioned.
11. Zimbabwe's prices ranged from Z$1.61 to Z$3.76 per square meter, compared to Z$7.53 in South Africa.
12. The Board dealing with commercial and industrial land had 78 meetings from 1984 through 1990, where they considered 92 cases, 97% of which involved white businessmen. Of 3,000 commercial lease negotiations that take place annually, only 14 go to the board. Rent Board members are nominated by government and business groups (Frost 1989:5).

13. Insurance companies funded just Z$9 million in new mortgages in 1983, compared with Z$16 million the year before. With respect to prescribed assets, the requirements were apparently not enforced, and in the mid 1980s life offices held only 45% (not the required 60%) of their assets in the form of government stock.
14. Unpublished data from the Deeds Office, Harare. Unless otherwise cited, all other quotes and data in this section are drawn from official sources (CSO, *Digest of Statistics)* and from property reports in RAL EGE (June 1985, September 1986, March 1987); RAL *QGE* (December 1988, June 1989, September 1989, March 1990); and FMB *QGE* (June 1990, September 1990).
15. In June 1989 RAL *QGE* reported rental rates of Z$14 per square meter in the Bulawayo CBD, compared with $6 to $8 in mid 1987: "This rapid increase in rentals has come as a shock to some Bulawayo businessmen."
16. Fidelity Life Assurance developed a multimillion dollar mixed commercial complex, while Prudential Assurance refurbished a major building.
17. The building, with its 46,000 square meters floor space, was designed to reflect the luxury of ascendant finance. The eighteen tower blocks are air-conditioned and serviced by thirteen lifts and escalators, as well as by thirteen staircases. In addition to a two-storey international trading room with state-of-the-art communications equipment, there will be four high-level managerial floors, with "high standard internal finishes." The concrete framed building is clad externally with glass valances and polished local granite. An initial outlay of Z$3 million was required simply to reroute communications signals which would otherwise be blocked by the tower (*FG*, 28/9/90, 9/5/91).
18. Indeed many historical buildings with important architectural value were lost to redevelopment, including the Grand Hotel, Meikles Hotel, the Land Bank Building and Jameson House.
19. Interview, January 1991. It was only in mid 1992 that some luxury office developers finally ran out of foreign currency when the Open General Import License system omitted lifts. Suppliers of lifts and airconditioners in the AFC's Hurudza House headquarters were still owed foreign currency by the developer. An MIPF office development in Bulawayo was also delayed because Z$300,000 in foreign currency was not available (*FG*, 30/7/92).
20. Levy bragged about using his influence to have city officials overlook zoning prohibitions for his addition to the Borrowdale shopping centre, leading to widespread condemnation by ratepayers and the daily press.
21. Within a year, the need to reclaim the land had intensified, and a policy was adopted by the Association:

    Even in Central Business District properties which are ripe for redevelopment, the problem of absentee landlords who in many cases now resident outside Zimbabwe was uncovered. In many cases, these property owners own more than one property... The National Property Association feels that it is in the public interest that the City of Harare should develop a policy which will induce these speculators to release land at market value for development... Such policies exist in developed countries and are designed to serve the public interest against the selfish interests of speculators (*Newsletter of the National Property Association*, 13/12/90).

22. After an initial selling spree in 1984 forced by new exchange control regulations prohibiting remittance of rentals, it gradually became clear that the benefits of selling, whereby the proceeds went into a blocked account or a 4% external bond, were diminishing to the point where some investors simply held on to the property (Frost 1989:7). (Contributing to the problem were capital gains tax, a 20% remittance tax and the depreciating value of the dollar.)
23. Neil Smith (1979, 1982) invented the concept, applying it mainly to residential gentrification in the United States, but the applicability to Harare should be clear.
24. Fortunate Chikafu was an employed mother of two, and a resident of Manlyn Court in the Kopje. By late 1991, Beverley Building Society bought Chikafu's block and prepared to demolish it (*FG*, 8/1/91, 5/12/91).
25. After surveying the international collapse of property in 1990, from Japan to Australia to Britain to the United States, Saunders (1990:5) of the National Property Association queried to his members,

    Is there a lesson for Zimbabwe where this year's wild rush to convert cash into tangible assets, whether it be property or shares, has pushed prices up to the level at which yields are not commensurate with the cost of borrowing money? Is our economy so watertight and cut off from outside influences that we can avoid a turn in the market which could have a disastrous effect on highly geared owners of property whether it be houses or offices?

    Saunders' message at the following year's meeting hit even closer to home: "Over the past couple of years we have seen the property recession reaching worldwide proportions yet leaving Zimbabwe unaffected. The recession continues and has started to affect our buoyant neighbour, Botswana, where house rents and prices have stabilised and industry peaked out" (*FG*, 12/12/91).
26. "With the increases in mortgage rates announced on September 5, several proposals that were of a speculative nature have been shelved for the time being" (*FG*, 17/10/91).
27. The construction industry's rebuttal came quickly: "Mr. Frost should take off his jacket and leave his nice air-conditioned office and try getting a building put up in this country. I would like to see his expression working with 15-year old vehicles that break down every day, pathetic work forces and materials that just never seem to arrive" (*FG*, 1/8/91).
28. Frost (1991:3) was speaking at the contractors' 1991 annual general meeting: "You have all had a good run... and I doubt whether there has been a more profitable period in the history of the building industry in

Zimbabwe... Apart from the perception that we are no longer getting value for money, new investment opportunities in private and public stock issues following economic reforms will compete for funds that would otherwise be earmarked for property development." CIFOZ is notorious for maintaining the old boy patronage system, which attracted hostility from the World Bank in 1991 and led to some minor affirmative action steps. CIFOZ represents just 25% of all registered in the country, and fewer than fifteen companies handled 90% of all construction work (which in total in 1990 accounted for Z$930 million, or 6.5% of GDP). The *Financial Gazette* (9/5/91) reported CIFOZ members' "victimisation of black contractors, abuse of human rights and dignity, unfair trade practices against black contractors and obstruction of access to materials and machinery."

29. As one example of an institutional investor which still had funds for property, the National Railways of Zimbabwe Pension Fund spent Z$44 million in mid 1992 on two CBD buildings (the mid 1980s Globe House and mid 1950s Electra House) and a warehouse (2 Rezende St), all purchased from Aberfoyle Holdings. And in another example, even as late as mid 1992 Old Mutual was attempting to construct a Z$20 million shopping and factory complex in an area of Graniteside which one report called "the most valuable retail and industrial site in the industrial areas of Harare." And other buildings approved by the Harare City Council in the first seven months of 1992 amounted to Z$87.4 million, of which Z$68 million were commercial offices (*FG*, 27/8/92).
30. We may note here that persistent drought did play a substantial role in lowering what Keynes would have termed the ZSE investors' "animal spirits"; the *Financial Gazette* (19/10/95) reflected, with unintended but revealing racial bias, the nature of its dominant audience: "Right now, the crucial factor for the stock market must be the rainy season. It remains to be seen whether umbrellas or sun tan lotion will be required."
31. There were three prolonged periods of mispricing when the ZSE's average adjusted pricing was at least 80% higher than the international norm: most of 1980, part of 1986, and from the crash of October 1987 through most of 1988. Surprisingly, high levels of mispricing remained in late 1992, when ZSE price ratios were still, Chang and Montiel found, 40% higher than the international norm.
32. Of secondary importance, the ZSE also ranked second least accessible (after Nigeria) with respect to publication of share data, and the most restricted during the 1986-93 period for capital investment and repatriation. Zimbabwe's quality of accounting standards was considered merely "adequate" (a blow, given the profusion of Big Eight firms and the rigorous British heritage), as were investor protection and market regulation.

chapter nine

Housing Finance and Uneven Urban Development

Introduction

After unemployment, the desperate need for housing ranks among the worst of Zimbabwe's post-Independence social problems. The scope of the backlog reached an officially estimated cost of Z$30 billion by the early 1990s. According to one study, only 41% of Zimbabwe's houses were constructed from modern building materials, with the rest based on thatch, pole-and-dagga, and other flimsy materials. Of 2.3 million total housing units, piped water was available inside just 324,000, with water available outside another 536,000, while electricity was connected to only 450,000 homes (*FG*, 5/1/95). Another study, by the Civic Groups Housing Project (a loose coalition of unions, the development industry, non-governmental organizations, and community-based organizations), found that fully 40% of urban residents were lodgers with other households, resulting in a rise in the number of Zimbabwean households requiring decent homes from 965,000 in 1985 to 2,212,000 in 2000 (Civic Groups Housing Project 1995:5; ***Sunday***

Gazette, 10/12/95).

As a result, Zimbabwe's cities were fast degrading, in the words of government planner Andrew Mlalazi, into a "vast spread of squatter settlements and backyard houses in low cost housing areas, ill-supplied, if at all, with basic amenities. Accompanying this are rapid environmental deterioration and declining standards in health and sanitation." And because of "non-revenue generating incentives" being offered to investors to come to all urban areas outside Harare,[1] there was emerging the danger of a "country-wide collapse in levels of infrastructure... The only effective demand which may remain in these cities and towns is the demand for housing by people who can ill-afford the houses they queue for" (*FG*, 16/6/94).

The housing crisis reflects Zimbabwe's extreme, and worsening, uneven urban development. Any observer will immediately comment on the roomy atmosphere of Harare and the obvious surplus of vacant land. Boasting more than a dozen (mainly unutilized) golf courses within the city limits and vast suburban lots for wealthy homeowners, Harare must set a per capita record for luxury consumption of land, certainly in the Third World.

The ebb and flow of housing finance has been central to this socioeconomic and geographical problem. The city's low-density suburbs received, ultimately, excessive flows of speculative capital while, in contrast, high-density suburbs could never attract sufficient housing finance to create a sustainable urban fabric. Related to this were extraordinary shifts in residential property values during the mid-1980s (up) and early 1990s (back down).

The failure of government, the private financial sector (mainly building societies) and international institutions (in particular the World Bank and US Agency for International Development) to establish a suitable housing finance system was one of the most vivid reflections of how little things really changed with Independence, notwithstanding this promise by then-Housing Minister Eddison Zvobgo (1981, ix): "The first democratically elected government of the Republic of Zimbabwe has vowed to assure for all its people shelter, food and clothing... Nobody, we say, should be allowed to be so poor as to starve, live in the open field or go naked."

The failure of Zvobgo and his successors to achieve social welfare goals in the field of housing can be laid largely at the door of orthodox, market-oriented financing principles upon which far too great a reliance was placed by government bureaucrats and their international aid agency advisors. These are characterized by a diminution of state subsidies, an emphasis on full cost-recovery, and the single-minded promotion and deregulation of private sector institutions. Following from such principles were three government policy approaches which closely paralleled the advice of international aid agencies:

- government subsidies to assist prospective home owners/tenants were minimized;
- building societies were the primary means by which people acquired finance for housing; and
- real estate speculation was not effectively prevented (other than through minor reforms to interest rate policy).

There were certainly other explanations of the housing crisis, advanced by analysts who favor market-oriented solutions. Early in this chapter we assess, in particular, the claim that there was an *insufficient* market in high-density areas, due to the "dual" nature of the housing system. Other justifications for Zimbabwe's lack of progress include excessively rapid urbanization, limited availability of land for housing development, bureaucratic barriers, inappropriate building standards, and foreign exchange shortages which hampered building materials supply.[2] Regardless, however, of the merits of these arguments, it will be clear that because government refused to adopt a creative subsidy policy, failed to channel private monies in an efficient manner towards housing, and permitted chaotic financial market activity, underlying processes of uneven development were invariably exacerbated by finance.

Manipulated policy

Uneven urban development was understood by key policy-makers, particularly in the international agencies, not as a logical outcome of the capitalist nature of Zimbabwe's cities, but instead as a simpler, discrete problem related to the country's supposedly dualistic housing system. The financing of low-density suburban housing inhabited by whites was, since the late 1940s (when building societies proliferated), the sole preserve of single-family mortgages. (As noted in Chapter Four, a minor effort was launched by the Partnership-minded government in the late 1950s to provide bonds to a tiny middle-class black population, but this petered out.) In contrast, public housing in the high-density suburbs was financed by the beer accounts of local authorities and by central government housing funds (which gained indirect bond-financing support from building societies, insurance companies, and finance houses in the late 1970s).

The view of the international agencies was that Harare's dualistic residential system revealed distinctly different and unrelated patterns of housing finance (World Bank 1983b;1985; and National Council of Savings Institutions 1985). Hence, the broad solution arrived at by US AID and the World Bank for reversing the colonial legacy was *to provide the same sorts of market-oriented institutions and practices to the high-density areas as were available in the low-density areas.* In the main, this strategy relied upon expansion of the scope of homeownership and upon increasing the delivery of housing finance through the private sector.

This was not the only distortion of reality required to justify market-oriented policy interventions. The World Bank (1983b:2) downplayed serious urban problems already reaching crisis stage by the early 1980s: "Zimbabwe's cities and towns have coped successfully with the demands that have been placed on them. Housing shortages exist for lower income households, but these have for the most part been reflected in overcrowding rather than squatting or illegal subdivision..." Just weeks after the Bank made this statement, the Zimbabwe central government cut housing funds by 65% and reallocated housing spending from urban to rural areas. Within a few months, the government raided the Harare suburb of Epworth late at night, burned and bulldozed thousands of shacks, and forcibly removed 50,000 people (Patel 1984).

Such mistakes in analysis, which are biased either to sustain the *status quo* or to support the adoption of market-oriented policy, cannot be dismissed lightly, for the international agencies were extremely influential. As Ann Schlyter (1990:206) points out, "dependency on international funding makes it difficult, if not impossible, to follow an independent housing policy."[3] The agencies' generic approach to policy was not only misguided, but even on its own terms was insufficiently nuanced to contend with Zimbabwe's peculiarities. According to Chris Mafico (1991:147),

> Public low-income housing policy gives the impression of having been formed in a "vacuum" without adequate knowledge of the target population... Public sector urban low-income housing policy is the product of a "top-down" approach where the important decisions on housing are taken by the planners and policy makers. Consequently, the housing policy is far from being a well oiled and coordinated response to the low income housing problem.

In spite of such flaws, the market-oriented approach won overwhelming favor in Zimbabwe, much as it won the initial political struggle over the course of rural development (the "willing-seller, willing-buyer" Lancaster House compromise). But it was soon clear that housing policy was emerging without proper regard to other local and national economic dynamics (ranging from interest rate fluctuations to real estate speculation). As Carole Rakodi (1993:5) put it, "no thought seems to have been given either to the likely outcome of introducing a private market in property into the high-density areas in a situation of housing shortage or to the possible widening of tenure-related inequalities amongst the low-income population."

Other policy options, such as public housing or subsidized cooperative housing, were not seriously considered (notwithstanding the fact that Harare city council continued to control tens of thousands of housing units which were constructed during the Rhodesian era; cooperatives were only given support beginning in 1993). Instead, hard-sell tactics by the two international agencies succeeded in part due to the general lack of experience and perspective within the Ministry of Local Government and Housing, as witnessed in the May 1980 "Five Year Plan: Low-Cost Housing Construction Program 1980/85." Consisting of just six pages of text and three tables, the initial government plan nevertheless included specific provisions for housing construction at a rate sufficient to meet the existing backlog as well as new household formation (167,000 units) within five years; relatively high minimum standards (four walls, at least two rooms, a supply of fresh water, sewage services, standard roads, and an "electric fuel supply"); and sufficient durability that the house would last 40-50 years.

Significantly, nowhere in the ministry's plan was full cost recovery stressed ("Housing must be of a cost which the different income groups can afford to occupy" and "Each house must be capable of being sold to the occupant"). And more explicitly, the option of "aided self-help" was "not anticipated... to have a significant impact on the development program within the five year period." (These provisions became important later, in US AID's willful misinterpretation of the early policy.)

To fulfill its objectives, the ministry projected spending Z$738 million over the five years, and anticipated some (unspecified) degree of cost recovery from recipients. But for prospective buyers in the Z$800-1,100 per annum income category (the lowest considered to have formal employment), the cost of an "ultra low-cost" house was Z$1,920—whereas the maximum feasible amount of capital borrowed at 8% interest for 25 years (based on a 22.5% monthly repayment/income ratio) was just Z$580-1,360. Clearly, substantial government subsidies would be needed for this low-income group (70% for the lowest-income buyer), as well as for those in income categories below Z$2,300 per annum. It was in this initial confrontation with market realities that the manipulation of government policy began.

US AID's (1980, 13) first major housing report, in September 1980, noted somewhat disingenuously—by explicitly ignoring the contribution made by local and national government in late 1970s Rhodesia (Figure 9.1)—that

> In Zimbabwe, there have been no subsidies for urban low-income housing. The new policy calls for housing to be constructed at a cost that low-income people can afford. It also calls for housing to be sold with total cost recovery on an instalment rent/purchase basis which leads to freehold tenure. At the same time, much of the existing rental housing stock is now being offered for sale to the tenants. These policies offer a foundation upon which an AID shelter program can be developed.

Thus, in US AID's interpretation of Zimbabwe's housing plan, the market was established as the bench-mark by which production, financing, and distribution would be carried out, in spite of the fact that only the top 4% of the black population had access to formal market financing at the time. In harmony with US AID, the Whitsun Foundation (1981:31)—the Rhodesian-era policy think-tank which enjoyed close links to the World Bank—rationalized the market in the following terms:

> Some countries take the view that, since housing is a "social good," the provision and pricing cannot be left to market forces. For rich countries it may be possible to adopt policies which prescribe projects that are delivered at prices below cost. But in developing countries already overcommitted to the provision of food, defence, health and education, a more market-oriented approach to housing is necessary.

And in its *Urban Sector Review*, the World Bank (1983b:57) considered the question and came to similar conclusions:

> The longstanding, financially sound practice of full cost recovery for housing and urban infrastructure may be endangered under the political pressure to provide subsidized housing; if such a course evolves, it could threaten the program's viability and ability to expand. Therefore, a housing policy which preserves the tradition of cost recovery must be designed quickly.

Under such influence, housing delivery according to the market was quickly adopted as official policy. The 1984 "Long Term Plan for the Construction and Housing Sectors of the Zimbabwe Economy: 1985-2000" committed that government would "minimise subsidies" for housing, which, according to US AID's primary housing finance consultants (Manson and Katsura 1985:2), "represents a correct and constructive step in the necessary direction."

But Rakodi (1993:23) points out the obvious shortcomings of the agencies' manipulation of policy in this direction: "insufficiently thorough analysis of the likely effects of adopted policies; an inadequate understanding of markets; and a failure to respond to the needs of the urban poor majority while placing too much emphasis on the interests of middle and upper income groups." As the *Daily Gazette* (20/1/93) aptly editorialized, "Surprisingly a capitalist rather than socialist policy has been applied to housing... If the government and local authorities really want to ensure every family has decent housing, they must accept that not every family can afford to acquire this at its own expense." Nowhere was this point more obvious than in the excessive reliance which government and the aid agencies placed on building societies as the sole financiers of housing, even in the high-density suburbs.

Faith in the building societies

"The most serious financial problem now confronting urban Zimbabwe is the funding of low-cost housing and its supporting infrastructure," the World Bank (1985:56) pronounced in 1985. The Bank posed this "financial problem" in such a manner that it could be solved by simply expanding the existing market system: "The institutional infrastructure exists to do this, in the form of well-developed building societies, but it will be necessary to direct this focus to the low-income end of the market and to reverse current government policies that hamper their operations." By following such a strategy, the Bank (1985:3-5) claimed, it would indeed be possible to flood the high-density suburbs with building society funds. "It is, therefore, not overly ambitious to aim at getting up to scale in the short term so that *house creation equals housing needs in all urban areas.* This will, however, require policies that encourage private sector savings institutions to enter the low-income housing field" (emphasis added).

To assess this logic requires not only moving forward in time to the early 1990s, when the Bank's outlandish promise of meeting all housing needs through the market was broken by the market itself, exacerbated by Bank interest rate directives. It requires, in addition, going backward in time, to the years just before and after Independence, to understand what grounds there might be for the Bank's optimistic argument. What experience would have evoked such faith in the building societies?

Ironically, it was apparently not the experience of success, but of the societies' *failure* (in their normal business) that appeared to most impress the Bank (1985:81) (in this assessment originally made in a 1983 version of the Bank's Urban Sector report):

> A case could also be made for involving the building societies in low-cost housing simply to preserve their dynamism during the period of

> a depressed upper-income housing market. At present, there is no sign that the slump is abating and it may well last for years. It is not clear that building societies could survive, as mortgage lending institutions, without entering the low-income housing field in one way or another.

Why building societies might not have survived is revealing. Just prior to Independence, as a legacy of the tight financial controls during the Rhodesian Unilateral Declaration of Independence, Zimbabwe's building societies had initially offered "among the lowest interest rates in the world," according to an industry spokesperson (*Herald*, 3/4/80). Yet the societies were also among the most conservative, partly because, as the Whitsun Foundation (1979:67-79) reported,

> the net flow of funds to the societies can be irregular. A substantial decrease in this inflow at a time when a society was close to the statutory minimum [liquidity requirement] would necessarily involve a sharp cut-back in, or the cessation of, mortgage lending with a disruptive effect on the housing market to the disadvantage of both the society and the public. The societies greatly prefer a relatively stable monthly lending program which enables them to be selective in their investments, even if this restraint does involve high liquidity ratios and, thus, a lower income.

The stability of lending to white middle-class homebuyers was suddenly a practice of the past, not only because of white flight from Rhodesia, but because profound economic forces began to affect the building societies. When the manufacturing investment boom of the mid-1970s was followed by a rapid and extremely deep contraction (leaving surplus capacity throughout the productive economy), financial mechanisms emerged to funnel new flows of surplus capital into other, non-productive circuits. The dual conditions of relative financial liquidity and lack of investment demand elsewhere in manufacturing made it possible for the Rhodesian Front regime to raise capital in order to provide unprecedented numbers of houses to low-income blacks during the waning years of white rule.

Although building societies were unlikely vehicles, given their roots in Rhodesia's middle-class housing market, they became increasingly important in mobilising funds for low-cost housing. In 1977 Beverley Building Society provided a total of Z$10 million in new housing loans, 20% of which was for public housing construction in the black townships in the form of "block loans." According to the Whitsun Foundation (1981:67-79), "in 1979 and 1980 there was a dramatic rise in provision of block loans. Building societies explain this by their very high liquidity ratio, caused by an almost non-existent demand for new loans just prior to Independence."

However, it was not merely diminished demand for funds by white homebuyers, but their increased supply, that made the societies as liquid as they were. Beverley's chairperson explained (in his 1979 *Annual Report*), "It has been a policy of the Board in recent years to maintain a high liquidity ratio in view of the uncertain political climate." Indeed, this also affected the type of loans now being considered: "As private enterprise, we believe that the African housing problem has, for too long, been borne by Government and Local Government alone." But notwithstanding good intentions by Beverley and other societies, the Whitsun Foundation (1981:24, 32) reported soon after Independence that "building societies have stopped making block loans to government [for high-density suburb housing] and virtually stopped new loans to individuals."

The reasons for this can be traced to macroeconomic flows of funds, and to the lack of effective demand for housing purchase (housing rental prices, on the other hand, were still moderate, as reflected in a reasonable ratio of housing costs to income). For example, higher interest rates proved a substantial deterrent to housing turnover. From a base at Independence of 7.25% for houses costing less than Z$12,000, the rate rose in March 1981 to 8.75% and in September 1981 to 12.5%.

But in the high-density suburbs, the loss of public housing stock meant that the supply of rental property would decline, ultimately pushing costs up dramatically. The first reflection of the market-oriented policy approach to low-cost housing was the rapid privatization of the state-owned housing stock. Within fifteen months of Independence, 16,000 out of 19,000 Harare public housing tenants had confirmed their desire to buy their properties. Yet the move to homeownership by tenants was not one of free choice, for if not purchased within six months of the offer, rent increases of 30% were imposed (World Bank 1985:69; City of Harare 1985:5; Teedon and Drakakis-Smith 1986:321). Rakodi (1993:5) evaluated the privatization: "As the existing housing enters the private market, values are increasing in response to the excess of demand over supply. The prospects of low-income tenants becoming owner-occupiers are, therefore, receding even further, leading to greater differentiation in housing terms and diverging opportunities for asset accumulation for this and future generations." And indeed, as noted above, Harare was forced to retain large amounts of its public housing stock.

What is most important here is that, whereas earlier financing mechanisms were ultimately segregated by race and geography, an official mandate (and popular political pressure) existed in the post-Independence period for a much more uniform system incorporating building society activities in both the high- and low-density suburbs. But the result of enticing building societies into high-density suburbs, contrary to World Bank and US AID promises, was an *intensifying* crisis in urban housing. This followed directly from the fact that "government and the local authorities have rapidly passed their traditional responsibilities in the high-density areas to the private sector, mainly building societies," as cautioned Matika (1987:1), a CABS official.

Hence the urban poor and the working class saw the ratio of their housing costs to income soar in the early 1980s, as housing loan interest rates increased by 72% and as urbanization rates, demand for housing, rents, and service charges also rose rapidly. Bearing witness to the squeeze, the Whitsun Foundation (1981:41) at one point asserted (on the basis of surveys) that "Chitungwiza respondents are willing to pay up to 35% of their income in repayments" for housing loans (the global norm is in the range of 20%-25%).

Yet even by sacrificing other basic consumption, the reality was that at Independence, only 4% of the population could afford a housing bond; the next 16% could afford standard low cost housing; the next 8% could afford "core housing" (a living room, bedroom, rudimentary kitchen and bathroom); the next 35% could afford "transitional housing" (an ultra low-cost unit with living room, bedroom and toilet); the next 8% could afford site and service facilities; while the bottom 28% could not afford any of these. Even by 1985 only 16% of the population had a sufficient monthly income (Z$260) to afford the average Z$71 per month rent for a four room core house in a high-density area. Two-thirds of Zimbabweans could not afford any shelter better than a serviced site, while 16% could not even afford to pay for that (Rakodi and Mutizwa-Mangiza 1989:29).

As might have been expected, building societies were not terribly interested in reaching into the lower 96% of the market once their excess liquidity evaporated. The number of bonds issued by building societies was halved following changes in interest rate regulations in February 1981 (*Herald*, 22/3/81). As a spokesperson for the real estate industry confirmed, "many prospective buyers of houses have been put off by increased interest rates, higher down payments and larger pay-back installments" (*Herald*, 22/10/81). The situation did not improve, and within a year an editorialist complained,

> A combination of last year's bank rate increases and this year's wage restraints, continues to keep home ownership out of the reach of many Zimbabweans... It was suggested by building society bosses that home-owners would need to push for higher salaries to absorb their increased

repayments... What does 1982 have in store for "Mr Average" home-owner or prospective buyer?... If you're in the market, you have repayment problems. If you're out of it, you still have to get into it before you can get anything out of it. You can't win. (*Herald*, 16/2/82)

Even landowners came under pressure from the tightened financial environment, as a rent freeze on residential property in 1981 had the unintended consequence of dramatically increasing arrears by landlords who were squeezed between the freeze and rising mortgage rates. Building societies lobbied government to remove private houses (not flats) from the rent restrictions, but were initially unsuccessful (*Herald*, 8/12/82). (In high-density areas, rent control on tenants was ignored.)

Properties costing under Z$13,000 were "few and far between," and there was little in the way of new construction anywhere in Zimbabwe (*Herald*, 16/2/82). As a building society official grumbled in early 1982, "Housing is taking a back seat and it has been given a very low priority" (*Sunday Mail*, 7/3/82). The largest building society, CABS, admitted it had run out of the meager funds that it allocated to the high-density suburbs (*Herald*, 27/5/82). According to one report, "The major difficulty facing agents in selling properties was the lack of mortgage finance from the building societies" (*Herald*, 22/7/82). The combination of dramatically higher nominal interest rates, the wage freeze, the rent freeze, and intensified pent-up demand for housing contributed to an epidemic of tenant evictions (particularly for flats that were being turned into share block schemes). Responding to the pressure, in 1982 the Reserve Bank shifted funding flows again, back to the building societies, resulting in a few more loans (*Sunday Mail*, 12/9/82).

On the one hand, there is no question that certain government interventions—such as the unfavorable interest rate structure for deposits and increased reserve requirements—were hostile to the building societies. But, on the other hand, more significant forms of direct government intervention supported the societies. According to US AID consultants from the National Council of Savings Institutions (1985:48), the government's primary accomplishment was to expand the Housing Guarantee Fund: "Since many building society residential loans today have a government guarantee, this has helped assure the flow of building society assets to the housing market, something that would not have occurred since Independence due to the softness of the market in the higher income brackets, the traditional building society market."

Nonetheless, the absolute lack of new housing construction meant that rising demand from low and moderate income households was not satisfied. Although the cost of many properties in high-density areas had risen to

Z$20,000 or higher, the continued gap between low purchase prices and high construction costs also hampered the supply side. In terms of financing, liquidity remained tight during 1983, with societies recording three-month waiting lists (CABS rejected 1,800 of 6,000 bond applications, while Beverley simply ceased taking new mortgage applications) (*Herald*, 10/8/83). By September 1983, building societies were forcing house-sellers to reinvest the sales proceeds with the societies for four years ("rolled-over takeover bonds"). The societies—which, according to a spokesperson, were "going through difficult times, and can't help people sell their homes unless they reinvest their money"—also suffered the loss of pension and insurance company withdrawals subsequent to increased prescribed asset requirements (*Herald*, 15/9/83). Moreover, the Post Office Savings Bank now offered top tax bracket savers a 23% return on savings, as opposed to 11.25% from building societies, while finance houses were offering 18%.

Government intervened once again, this time in the societies' favor. In March 1984, Reserve Bank restrictions were imposed on foreign remittances (including prohibitions on external rent payments), which had the effect of dramatically increasing property availability at the top end of what was a stagnant market, as a large proportion of non-residents with property sold in order to purchase external bonds. However, given the continued lack of mortgage funds, many properties were sold only on a cash basis. This had the dual effect of lowering prices substantially but simultaneously keeping lower and middle income buyers (in need of financing) out of the market. Such conditions were ideal for speculators (*Herald*, 6/10/84, 10/11/84).

Conditions were changing on the demand side as well, as witnessed by the fact that by 1983 the first wave of thousands of new post-Independence civil servants had accumulated sufficient funds for much more substantial inroads into the low-density suburbs, since they had served the two years required to acquire a 100% government bond guarantee.[4] Hence although the total number of bonds issued during 1983 rose by 49%, the average value of bonds granted declined by 15%, indicating the bulk of activity in the market was in the middle-income residential range. This was, as a result, a critical element of ZANU's implicit strategy of new class-formation within the civil service. Further declines in average bond values were subsequently recorded as sales of sectional title in formerly foreign-owned flats increased. Companies were also increasingly willing to finance their employees' homes, and the number of mortgages they issued more than doubled during 1983.

In sum, in the years just before and after Independence, building society finance went through ebbs and flows, but generally left working- and middle-class potential buyers frustrated. Although, as noted in Chapter Seven, racial discrimination was one way in which the lack of building society funding was interpreted—and may indeed have been an important feature of the housing market—other government interventions also played a role. However, notwithstanding the failure of the market-oriented approach to date, the most important subsequent development was the attempt by international aid agencies in the mid-and late 1980s to use municipal government as a base from which to address the growing housing crisis, still via financial flows through the building societies.

Aid agencies, local authorities and building societies

As low-income housing construction stagnated in high-density areas where building societies lacked a ready market, the World Bank, US AID, and other international agencies began to turn increasingly to city government (formerly a major housing developer)[5] in search of partners. The agencies and government officials renewed ties with the building societies and, in the process, revitalized the market-oriented approach to housing. The ultimate effect, however, was to add new dimensions to the crisis (including real estate speculation).

Perhaps the most important point that this alliance glossed over—and which returned to haunt the building societies when high interest rates were imposed by the World Bank in 1991—was the unnecessary use of foreign financing for locally-produced basic needs commodities such as housing. Even the Bank (1983b:46) had earlier commented on the fact that the total import cost of low-income housing was just 7.6%, consisting of only glass, putty, some imported copper and plastic used in electrical installations, and some imported paint pigments. Moreover, other inputs such as steel and cement benefitted from vast excess local capacity at Independence (40% and 20% respectively).

Under these conditions there were, apparently, some astute Zimbabwe government officials who opposed foreign-denominated loans for locally sourced housing materials and labor; indeed, in the Bank's own assessment of its 1980s housing program, there emerges the concession that the government's "interest in seeking alternatives to hard Bank money is understandable" (World Bank 1994:13). Yet from the standpoint of the international agencies, hard currency lending was non-negotiable, whether it was needed or not. As US AID (1980:31) forthrightly commented in its US$50 million 1980 housing loan proposal, "Because over 95% of the inputs for housing investment are produced locally, the proposed loan will make an important short-term foreign exchange contribution... External debt is a very small part of central government debt. The estimated debt servicing ratio for 1981-83 is about 10%."

However, US AID miscalculated, for by 1983 the debt service ratio was in fact 16%, whereas foreign exchange allocations undertaken on the backs of debt contracted by low-income housing consumers (among others) had little or no relation to meeting their basic needs. At this point, US AID was switching from grant to loan support consistent with Reaganomics budgetary pressure, and its 30-year housing loan was not terribly generous in any case, for it required a full repayment guarantee from the Zimbabwe government regardless of the success of the project; an interest rate "consistent with rates of interest generally available for similar types of loans made in the long-term US capital markets"; and an annual fee (in US$) of 1/2% of the outstanding amount of the loan plus a fixed amount of 1% of the loan.

Most importantly, perhaps, foreign loans for housing (or other basic developmental goods) were unnecessary because Zimbabwe's own financial system was, from around 1984, experiencing unparalleled liquidity. Nevertheless, in spite of the declining value of the Zimbabwe dollar (which increased the effective interest rate on the foreign loans) and in spite of abundant domestic public finance available to local authorities, expensive foreign loans were signed to pay for what in reality was by this time less a housing program than a low-cost, "site-and-service" scheme.[6]

With the encouragement of the Bank, US AID, and other foreign development agencies, four Zimbabwe cities (Harare, Bulawayo, Mutare, and Masvingo) began expanding "aided self-help" projects, which partially included financing for housing and construction. But "self-help" is a misnomer, according to the housing director of the City of Harare (1985:12), because "Relatively few actually carry out the building work themselves as they have neither the time nor the skills to do so. Instead they hire small informal building contractors to do the work." Mafico (1991:75) describes the system as "not for the faint-hearted. It demands considerable sacrifice and input from the allottees. Consequently it is still too expensive an option for many low-income earners. The loans are insufficient to finance a full four-roomed house and allottees have to contribute their own resources."[7]

Beginning in 1984 US AID's US$50 million loan scheme was brought into implementation phase (the details had been agreed upon with government officials in 1982, and the project was formally completed in mid-1987). Three quarters of the loan (US$38 million) went to the western Harare high-density suburb of Kuwadzana, where more than 7,000 aided self-help participants paid a 5% deposit (typically Z$30) for 330-square-meter plots, and were required to complete four rooms and ablutions within eighteen months.[8] A 25-year loan of Z$2,500 was allocated to each participant, with the provision that it be used to build at least the concrete slab floor, one room, and ablutions. The program's eligibility required that housing payments (for stand and loan) not exceed 27.5% of income (up from the 22.5% in the original housing policy). The result, as observed at the surface level, was a relatively impressive initial increase in entrepreneurial activity and housing delivery, as Kuwadzana reportedly hosted some 2,000 independent builders.

A critique of Kuwadzana, however, would point out that women heads of households were continually in danger of being cheated by builders and that since almost all recipients of housing worked during the day there was very little self-help involved. As Schlyter (1987:214) put it, "The building period was difficult, not just for the poorest strata and women-headed households. Enormous sacrifices were made in order to raise the money needed in addition to the loan." The recipients were not truly of low-income status; as Schlyter notes, "It would be more honest to call Kuwadzana a middle-income housing project in which the low-income population comes in as lodgers."

Indeed, the cost of building and servicing a house in 1985 was at least Z$9,000 (Butcher 1986:9), leaving the government loan far short of the minimum resources required to provide decent shelter. Such schemes became particularly vulnerable to raiding by higher-income groups and absentee landlordism, a problem that was to become widespread over the years. Moreover, there were no land-purchase or -ownership cooperatives at Kuwudzana to assist the poor, since people previously had no contact with their future neighbors and were not allowed to live on the site during construction. Moreover, Kuwadzana's excessive distance (11 km) from the employment and shopping offered by the city meant that very little in the way of township planning appeared to change from Rhodesian days. In addition, according to Colleen Butcher (1986:10), there was "very little flexibility to individual households with respect of the location and sizes of dwelling units available."

While generally lauding the project as "quite successful," US AID's own Kuwudzana evaluation report (Abt Associates Inc 1988:ii) revealed two systemic problems: growing arrears on payments by recipients, and violations of US AID's cost-recovery policy (due to the existence of hidden subsidies). The arrears problem reflected the fact that

> Over one-third of the beneficiaries report having problems making

> payments and nearly 80% indicate that they now have less money to spend on items other than housing... Given that beneficiaries have exhausted most of their currently available funds; that few have completed four rooms; and that a large gap apparently exists between beneficiary and official estimates of costs, it is clear that arrears will continue to be a major problem. (Abt Associates Inc 1988:53)[9]

Arrears were high notwithstanding subsidies which included "land acquisition at below cost or no cost, failure to consider off-site infrastructure in service charges, failure to account for administrative costs, or subsidized interest rates." The initial sales price for Kuwudzana sites, developed by government, was particularly generous at Z$0.30 per square meter, or Z$90 for a 300 square meter stand. When "a substantial number" of repossessed Kuwudzana stands were sold in 1986, the US AID evaluators estimated that the stand value was in fact several thousand dollars (in the cases of similar US AID schemes in the smaller towns of Marondera, Chinhoyi, and Kadoma, the estimated cost of land and site servicing was upwards of Z$8,000). In view of the urban land shortage, this represented an enormous subsidy, one that ran against the grain of US AID's philosophy: "Private sector developers, without benefit of this type of subsidy, cannot replicate the project with the same assumptions about target groups and affordability" (Abt Associates Inc 1988:53).

US AID's evaluators noted that this was one area where "A government's housing policy can be influenced by a continuing dialogue based on evident achievements in project implementation" (Abt Associates Inc 1988:56). Ironically, US AID was thus encouraged to attack any inclusion of subsidies in housing policy, on the basis of a housing project which succeeded (to the degree it did, merely in terms of production of housing units) largely because of those very subsidies.

With such significant problems and contradictions embedded in the project, what, indeed, was the point? According to Abt Associates (1988:57),

> Overall, the project is viewed as a success from the perspective of US AID interactions with the Government of Zimbabwe. Both the policy dialogue and the achievements in project implementation have influenced the evolution of housing policy in Zimbabwe... As the main bottleneck in the housing delivery system came to be identified as a scarcity of serviced land and as public sector housing finance became smaller relative to the demand for loans, the government modified its strategy. It would now lend public funds to local authorities for the servicing of land while calling for the totally private financing of the houses themselves.

Hence even though the evolving housing policy must be considered a failure both in terms of meeting people's needs and even on its own terms (measured merely by problems such as middle-class raiding, the high arrearage—addressed through cutoffs of vital services—and the inaccurate costing of the project to the end-user), it was "quite successful" because it forced government into a deeper commitment to market-oriented housing policy. In Kuwudzana, cost recovery was even promoted for the primary schools and clinics which as a result "threatened to delay construction." Meanwhile, concluded Schlyter (1990:215) "no lessons were drawn from the observation that low-income earners and women had limited access to the project."

The World Bank, on the other hand, paid greater lip-service to the need to target low-income recipients, yet Bank staff developed high-density suburb pilot projects which utilized similar cost recovery principles for what also amounted to site-and-service schemes. Through the US$36.4 million "Urban I" loan, Harare, Bulawayo, Mutare, and Masvingo received financing for infrastructure (water, electricity, roads) on 21,000 plots, loans to build houses on 11,350 of those, and some improvements in public transport. But because of increasing land prices—an issue the Bank generally did not view as appropriate for government intervention—the bulk of the Bank's housing initiatives were geared to peripheral locations which exacerbated the existing apartheid-style colonial planning framework.[10]

As a model, the Bank was particularly impressed by a self-help site and service scheme at Glenview, a distant southeasterly suburb of Harare, which was begun in 1978 and entailed the provision of minimal services to 8,000 plots. The Bank (1985:77) judged Glenview as "very successful," but with the reservation that the municipality financed too much of it, namely the full cost of infrastructure (a Z$1,000 loan was provided residents for building the house). In contrast, in subsequent Bank schemes involving the City of Harare (1985:15; 1986:2), full cost recovery principles were applied.

Eligibility in these schemes, which began in 1985, was originally limited to those "salaried workers in the formal sector" (hence disqualifying the majority of low-income Zimbabweans) with monthly incomes of less than Z$400 per month, and with 70% of the funding allocated to those earning less than Z$200 per month (a year later this impossible target was adjusted by Harare officials to a target group between Z$190 and Z$400 per month).[11] Construction deadlines of 18 months were also imposed, following a dispute between the Bank and government officials regarding minimum housing standards.[12] The next task was to attract private sector housing finance.

But a glaring contradiction soon emerged. Private finance would be available only if borrowers could repay their loans. But with the Bank projecting an internal rate of return on the project of 12%, the monthly payment on each Z$25,000 four-room housing unit would have to be Z$400 (World Bank 1994:23). In other words, a family earning the maximum allowed (Z$400) was expected to shell out its entire monthly income (or, in the case of the majority for whom a Z$200 monthly income was anticipated, twice its monthly income). To afford the monthly payments, at least three families renting rooms from the recipient would have to squeeze in, in order to bring the housing payment ratio down from 100% to something more reasonable (such as 25%).

In its project assessment, the Bank (1994:8) begins to acknowledge that affordability may have been a problem: "This finding is common among site and service schemes in the Africa region: these programs rarely meet the homeownership needs of the bottom quintile of the income distribution. However, the poorest fifth of the urban population were the major beneficiaries of the rental opportunities created under the project which permitted partial subletting of owner-occupied dwellings." Yet such rental opportunities are also a recipe for overcrowding, lack of privacy, poor health and sanitary conditions, and excessive strain on housing and community infrastructure—all problems noted to have increased markedly in Zimbabwe's cities since Independence (but unmentioned in the Bank assessment).[13]

Without thinking through the unintended consequences, Bank staff prepared the first sites of its new housing project, once again in a high-density suburb (Glen Norah) on the apartheid-style far southwestern periphery of Harare. Age discrimination may have been a factor in the early going, since many people on the City of Harare's housing waiting list had been there for decades, were over 55 years of age, and hence would not meet building society specifications. Beverley was the only society participating at the early stages, and although it was expected to approve 112 applications per month, after four months not a single one had been approved. The City of Harare's (1985:4-5) disappointed housing director called for "a more radical approach which would speed up loan application approvals." Building societies responded that local authorities' own failure to produce sufficient serviced plots was the main constraint (Beresford 1990:A37). But the building societies found themselves increasingly at the center of attention.

New building society incentives

Both the World Bank and US AID regularly insisted that Zimbabwe housing policy take on an entirely market-oriented character, and in 1986 US AID co-hosted a conference on "Housing and Urban Development, Public and Private Partnership" to promote its policy perspective. As Schlyter (1987) reported, however, Zimbabwe government representatives in attendance "seemed less convinced about such propositions," and also made clear that the market was unable to deal with gender discrimination in access to housing finance (a point that was censored from the printed version of the government's "National Report" tabled at the conference). Similarly, the Bank (1994:13) also remarked that government officials involved in Urban I "expressed concern about the ideological thrust of World Bank training efforts."

In reality, the private sector—in particular the building societies—would require huge government interventions to achieve higher levels of housing production. What in effect were subsidies (via foregone tax revenue) ultimately came in the form of the tax-free "Paid-Up Permanent Shares" (PUPS) which government allowed the building societies to offer depositors from late 1986 in order to compete with the Post Office Savings Bank.[14] But by then, the societies were unable to provide loans to borrowers earning less than Z$250 per month (due to rising construction costs). The societies' front-end charges also proved excessive for many home purchasers with paltry savings. And the lenders' stipulation that a formal transfer of property title precede disbursal of the funds caused further bureaucratic delays. As the housing director of the City of Harare (1987:14) concluded,

> These problems are magnified when beneficiaries are mostly full-time workers from the lower-income group, who lack the time or the sophistication to find their way through the complex Municipal Building Society and conveyancing procedures. Even after the mortgages are eventually registered, beneficiaries have difficulty in constructing their houses because the largest building society insists that mortgage draw-downs can only be made after progress in construction. It is apparent that building societies have overestimated their capacity to handle high-density housing on a large scale.

The societies' interests were in increasing their PUPS deposits, only about half of which were used to fund houses in high-density areas. As the CABS Housing Projects Manager (Beresford 1992:1) put it, "The building societies appreciated that they could not remain on the fence or [they would] gain the reputation of being borrowers from the poor and lenders to the rich. For the sake of their own survival they had to get in on the low-cost housing act." Unfortunately, as a result of the societies' involvement in high-density suburbs, the situation actually deteriorated for the low-income target group, because their housing came under pressure from higher-income raiding (purchases of low-cost houses by desperate middle-class families). The City of Harare's (1987:15) Housing Director complained, "The average mortgage loan of Z$6,384 [during 1986-87] is now clearly insufficient to enable a beneficiary to pay for his stand and erect a four-roomed house within eighteen months. If the objective is to have as many houses built in the shortest time then a more flexible approach to the present income ceiling is required."

Similar schemes supported by US AID and the United Nations Development Program were attempted in the mid-1980s in Kwekwe and Gutu, again using Beverley Building Society. But as Rakodi and Mutizwa-Mangiza (1989:35) conclude, "The housing finance component of the project had a number of teething problems, as mechanisms were devised to satisfy the building society's administrative and collateral requirements." The World Bank also used Z$9.6 million from the Commonwealth Development Corporation to sweeten the pot for further involvement by the reluctant building societies.

From the building societies' point of view, this was still a difficult way to make money. In the end, a variety of building society minimum standards and operating procedures changed under the various forms of economic and social pressure. Computerization made more cost-effective the administration of smaller loans. The societies overlooked requirements that ceilings and special floors be included in finished houses, and that the fully finished house must be entirely financed (instead, only part—for example two out of six rooms—could be considered eligible for bonding). Borrower income was adjusted to take into account the possibility of a low income home owner having a Z$20/month tenant. Even Cuban-style "building brigades" initially qualified as contractors on a bonded house (which made the local building societies far more flexible than US AID staff, who rejected this option for ideological reasons) (Teedon and Drakakis-Smith 1986:320).[15] And the building societies eventually went so far as to grant loans for "paper" houses made from corrugated waxed void formers with a conventional concrete floor foundation (*FG*, 14/9/90).

But there continued to be persistent problems in lubricating financial flows from aid agency to government to building society to homeowner and back again. According to Matika (1987:2) of CABS, "the collection of repayments in the instance of self-help constructions is proving to be of great concern. This is mainly a result of the fact that the methods of construction chosen by the prospective buyer are slow." The chief executive of CABS added, "The self-help house has taken the beneficiaries on average two years to construct, prices have risen considerably during this time, and interest charges have added to the repayment burden" (*FG*, 12/12/91).

The PUPS scheme did, proponents argue, open up a new funnel for money into townships, albeit through a subsidy that empowered building societies not borrowers. The 21,000 loans that were ultimately granted in high-density areas over the period 1987-91 averaged Z$10,700, and supported not only new site-and-service developments, but also, to a limited extent, the growth of a market for existing houses in high-density suburbs. But Beresford (1992:2) later conceded that "in practice, we make very few loans of under Z$10,000" and summed up the role of the societies as follows:

> Local authorities have been relieved of their former cost recovery functions and this has been taken over by the building societies. House construction by the public sector has dropped dramatically and very few rented units are being built. A genuine real estate market has developed in the low cost housing field which is governed by market forces. What lessons have we had to learn during this process? Firstly, the low income client has not proved to be a credit risk. Housing is a scarce commodity and the demand is so high that most borrowers will make extraordinary sacrifices to maintain payments. High resale values ensure that clients can sell at a profit if they have to. In the very few instances where repossessions have become necessary, we have had no difficulty in recovering arrears due from auction sales.

Notable here is the degree to which the societies' very limited success, in relation to the vastness of the problem at hand, depends on factors such as scarcity of housing, rising prices, and an effective foreclosure method. These factors were not likely to be sustainable forever, though, in the face of a sudden drop in financial liquidity that paralyzed the building societies. In sum, while there were gradual improvements in housing supply to selected middle-class strata through the innovations in housing finance, these fell far short of meeting needs, for they consistently failed to confront the market as a barrier to housing delivery.

As a result, the 1990 portfolio of Founders, as an example, included Z$53 million invested in nearly 1,700 outstanding housing bonds, but only Z$3.5 million (6.6%) of this amount was located in high-density suburbs (*FG*, 6/4/90). The building society industry average was just 14% (*Horizon*, February 1992). The societies were simply not, in Beresford's (1990a:40) words, "the appropriate agencies for reaching the very poor or those living on land with no security of tenure. By the same token, they could not directly assist those in need of subsidized shelter or individuals in squatter upgrading schemes":

> The point I am trying to make is that, while Building Societies can make a major contribution to the national low-income housing programs, they cannot be all things to all men. They are creatures of their environment and susceptible to many influences outside their own control: changes in interest rates, national liquidity levels and political stability are examples of such influences.

All these factors suggest a need to reexamine the international agencies' strategy of making building societies the sole providers of housing finance, attempting to prevent central government housing subsidies going to housing recipients, and permitting local authorities to provide only serviced sites instead of housing. In addition, one other factor—uncontrolled real estate speculation—must also be taken into account to understand the full role of finance in exacerbating uneven urban development.

Real estate speculation

By the mid-1980s, housing prices were no longer too low to encourage new construction, but on the contrary were rising so quickly that they shut even greater numbers of poor and working-class people out of the market. In 1985 alone, medium-priced houses in Harare's low-density suburbs doubled in nominal terms. In the even wealthier northern suburbs, price increases began in 1985 (38%), and spectacular hikes of 50% in 1986, and 1987 were recorded. Total price increases for low-density suburbs across the country amounted to 26% in 1985, 53% in 1986 and 28% in 1987. Individual owners were now accumulating sufficient funds within Zimbabwe (thanks to exchange controls) so as to drive the residential market at as fast a pace as the booming commercial office market (RAL *EGE*, March 1986, December 1987; *Northern News*, August 1989).

By 1987, there was a brief respite in demand for residential property in central Harare. As another rental price freeze (as part of a general price freeze) was imposed in mid-1987, owners of blocks of flats began offering their properties for sale at (overinflated) prices equivalent to the buildings' aggregate sectional title prices. According to RAL merchant bank (*EGE*, December 1987), "At these prices the yield from rental is far too low to attract long-term investors," who subsequently shifted funds back into the commercial property market.

But the high-density suburbs were the victims of even worse distortions. In the southern high-density area of Epworth, Butcher (1986:11) reports that "Unsuspecting rural migrants and families desperate for any accommodation have often fallen prey to illegal land speculators and conmen." According to a resident of the largest high-density suburb,

> the fact of the matter remains that Chitungwiza's housing shortage is not only desperate, but has also reached a point where it has become pathetic, especially when one takes into account the fact that on average up to 30 people live in a single housing unit. It's even sadder when one considers that the majority of Chitungwiza residents are the so-called lodgers who occupy dwellings of varying sizes at rent-to-die rates... In fact, the exorbitant rents the majority of people in Chitungwiza are paying, the anguish, and the frustration that has become so evident means that the time bomb... cannot be far off from exploding. (*Sunday Mail*, 17/3/91)

Chitungwiza was not alone in facing such shortages. Less than 19,000 units were built annually on average during the late 1980s, just 11% of the minimum necessary rate of housing construction to meet Zimbabwe's national goals by the year 2000. With such shortages, and under such speculative conditions, prices soared (until 1991) even at lower and middle ranges. The average advertized price in high-density areas of Harare (surveyed through *The Herald*) rose from Z$30,068 in 1989 to Z$61,133 in 1990 to Z$100,000 in 1991, with areas such as Highfield, Warren Park, and Kambuzuma recording average sales prices of more than Z$115,000 in 1991. The average price per room rose in roughly proportional amounts (Rakodi 1992:33). At that point the (highly-skewed) median urban income was Z$700 per month, but a quarter of urban households earned less than Z$270 per month (Butcher 1992:2).

The massive housing price rise was dependent upon the financing supplied by building societies. The societies generally failed to consider what would happen in the event the prices being paid for land and housing were not matched by their intrinsic values. The price determined the bond level, and building societies failed to vary the size of deposits to try to cool the speculative fires. Indeed, according to a *Herald* (17/12/90) editorial, a new "trick" emerged in the late 1980s involving

> people with modest amounts of capital who wanted to enter the game. These people used the smallish sums they had as deposits, borrowing vast sums to accumulate property holdings. They did nothing to develop or improve these holdings, simply keeping them for a worthwhile capital gain. Meanwhile, the certainty of high rents meant they could service the loans and get an income. It was simply the chance to make a fortune without risk.

But the motor behind the supposedly risk-free property speculation was not merely the actions of clever individuals. A structural feature that soon appeared unmanageable was excessive liquidity within the building societies. From a low of Z$67 million in new mortgage bonds registered in 1982, the three societies granted Z$114 million in 1986; Z$217 million in 1988; Z$746 million in 1990; and Z$395 million in the first half of 1991 (at which point interest rates began to rise, causing a drain of the societies' deposits and a reduction in new bonds registered in second half of 1991 to Z$224 million) (Figure 9.2). This excess liquidity had a profound impact on prices. Notwithstanding the fact that lower-cost houses were being marketed and financed in the late 1980s, the value of the average bond granted (including commercial and industrial property bonds) soared. With prices of land and property rising to unprecedented heights, the ratio of the average bond value to the average sales price continued its steady post-Independence climb.

In mid-1990, the Reserve Bank's response was, once again, to increase interest rates and minimum deposits on mortgages for non-owner occupiers, but (as usual) this merely slowed, but did not deter, the underlying dynamic of speculation.[16] Indeed the failure to regulate or self-regulate the overheated supply of finance in the real estate market (for example, by adding checks and balances such as investment referees, a chartered institute of arbitrators and complaints officers) was subsequently condemned by the managing director of Intermarket Discount House: "The 'speculative bubble' of 1989-90 resulted in careless property lending on the part of some banks and building societies at low interest rates" (*Daily Gazette*, 3/3/93).

Careless property lending followed naturally from high liquidity. "Building societies complain of excess funds in their coffers," reported the *Financial Gazette* (3/8/90). In early 1991, the Reserve Bank tried again with higher interest rates aimed at arresting the "roaring" inflation rate:

> The interest changes have also been designed to specifically discourage speculative residential and commercial property developments, which might create short-term jobs in the economy but which do not contribute to the overall economy in any lasting way. Dr. Moyana particularly criticized the luxury home developments aimed at the super-rich, which he said were draining the economy of the bricks and cement needed to build factories and create jobs. (*Herald*, 14/2/91)

The speculative property boom proved profitable to some, but debilitating to the majority without capital. When Harare houses and buildings were revalued in January 1990, the average value was fifteen times higher than in 1975, and many homeowners feared the implications for their rates and taxes (*FG*, 30/7/92). In its editorial "Curse of Land Speculation," the *Herald* (17/12/90) warned,

> While those owning homes might be impressed by the present market values there is little they can do to benefit from these unless they want to join the speculative paper chase; they after all still need somewhere to live and if they want to upgrade their home they will find the gap between the market values of existing and proposed homes prohibitive. Even if they want to will the home to children, death duties will be far higher thanks to speculators.

By the early 1990s, unmet housing needs had climbed to Z$950 million annually (which matched the entire output of the construction industry), as against supply of Z$196 million worth (14,000 homes) (*FG*, 13/6/91). Out of 60,000 families on Harare's housing waiting list in early 1990, only 10,000 were middle-income (*FG*, 17/8/90) and the country's leading popular magazine headlined in 1991, "Mr Average can't afford a house in Harare" (*Parade*, April 1991).

Intensified international financial pressure

In the late 1980s and early 1990s it was clear that earlier policies were failing and that property speculation now threatened even the housing prospects of the middle-class. Paradoxically, this provided the international aid agencies an even greater opportunity to intervene. As expressed by a US AID official in 1991, the agenda of the agencies was clear:

> An objective of the program is to have the private sector provide all financing for low-cost housing. Broader-based investment in building societies will occur through the creation of several new mechanisms to raise long-term housing finance. The result is that the societies' low-cost mortgage portfolio will expand and government's long-term portfolio will correspondingly diminish. (*FG*, 24/10/91)

But now government appeared desperate, faced with rising land prices, inappropriate zoning, bureaucratic delays, difficult conditions in the construction industry, and excessively liquid financial markets yet insufficient means of funnelling credit towards middle- and working-class Zimbabweans. Since dramatic changes in either budget allocations or policy direction were not feasible during this era of structural adjustment, government's only recourse appeared to be continued adherence to market-oriented principles, but now increasingly under the rubric of "public-private partnerships" (Government of Zimbabwe 1986).

In the *Second Five Year National Development Plan*, the government blamed the rapid growth of housing waiting lists upon "limited resources to fund housing schemes." The National Housing Fund—which provided loans at 11% (i.e., below market) rates to local authorities—was cut back, as total public spending on National Housing and on Housing Construction declined dramatically in real terms after 1987-88. The private sector was asked to pick up more of the burden.

This was not the first time such partnerships were suggested, for the *First Five Year National Development Plan* had introduced numerous incentives for housing, including the 9% paid up permanent shares for building societies, tax rebates for employee housing, and possibilities for joint ventures with local authorities. But as the *Second Plan* (1986:53) noted, "although a few housing schemes were launched as private sector initiatives, the bulk of the private sector did not show interest to invest in low-cost housing."[17]

The problem of housing sufficient workers in proximity to the city, which had motivated so many urban capitalists of an earlier generation (Chapter Four), was less pressing during a period of structural unemployment and workforce downsizing. But even if employers were slow to react, Zimbabwe's building societies had long demanded the right to purchase land for development themselves. After several years of lobbying, according to the general manager of Founders, "Government is supporting us on this one and is in the process of drawing up the relevant legislation. Building societies can then go into joint ventures with private developers and municipal authorities to develop housing." In the same spirit, the National Property Association recommended, "For residential property, encouragement of larger scale financing in conjunction with developers of medium cost housing developments," along with the "release of larger tracts of presently undeveloped land by the municipality" (*FG*, 29/6/90).[18]

Such private sector-led efforts remained small in relation to the size of the crisis. Recognising this, the World Bank and US AID poured unprecedented resources into incentives for vast expansions of building society loans. In May 1989, the Bank hinged 40% of its "Urban II" development strategy on the three building societies. As planned, the exercise would ultimately cost an estimated US$580 million, of which US$248.3 million would go towards housing finance. The Bank would contribute US$80 million in loans to the project, joined by a host of other international aid agencies including those of the US, Britain, Sweden, and the Commonwealth. In addition, the Zimbabwe government would advance US$234 million, and building societies US$242 million (earned through the tax-free accounts), the latter two in local currency.

Ignoring the subsidy to the building societies, the project would purportedly be on a full cost recovery basis:

> The proposed project would reduce the need for central government resource transfers to local governments by replacing public with private sector sourced housing finance and by improving local authority financial management, as well as by investing in social and economic infrastructure targeted on poverty alleviation and equality. This is evident in the nearly 70% of total project costs allocated for the development and financing of housing and housing-related infrastructure, which, it is estimated, will benefit approximately 500,000 people under the project (about 65% of all new urban residents during the project period) of whom 50% will be at or below the urban poverty threshold. In addition, 70% of the housing supplied under the sector program would be affordable to households at or below the 30th percentile of the income distribution of urban residents. Access to housing opportunities and related mortgage financing for female-headed households is assured under similar procedures to those utilized successfully under Urban I. (World Bank 1989c:3)[19]

A parallel contribution by US AID in 1991 included tough conditionality on a loan aimed at boosting the private sector construction industry's access to foreign exchange. US AID insisted that a highly-touted secondary market for securitized housing bonds had to be established with "limited government involvement."[20] Moreover, the government would have to permit building societies to issue Negotiable Certificates of Deposit (NCD) at market rates to raise funds for housing finance. Changes would also be made in land use and zoning procedures, and minimum shelter quality standards would be lowered.

To consider just one example of US AID's stubborn misguidedness, the 30-60-90 day NCDs were expected to fund 25-year-long bonds, an extreme version of the liability mismatch which hapless US savings and loan institutions themselves had experienced a decade earlier when they borrowed short (during a period of rising interest rates) and lent over the long term. The chairperson of the Association of Building Societies concluded that this approach "will not enable building societies to fulfil their complete function of long-term mortgage financing" (*Business Herald*, 14/1/93).

Had the design not been based on purely market-oriented principles, the secondary market could have been a source of more appropriate financing, particularly by tapping pension funds for investments and blending them with government subsidies to bring the interest rate down to a reasonable level (Bond 1993b). But without direct government intervention, there was little chance of this happening naturally. As the chairperson of the Labor Relations Board, Ignatius Chigwendere, remarked caustically,

> The assumption at the moment, until proved wrong, is that the biggest contributors to these pension funds, by their sheer numbers, are the black employees. Little is known of the extent at which these are represented at the highest level of the pension funds. One gets the impression that most of these funds are manned by mainly retired whites and ex-civil servants... In all this, the Registrar of Pension Funds has been most conspicuous by his silence, and very little seems to have been initiated in terms of changes that will make this institution more consistent with the ten years of Independence. In parliament, not a single voice has been raised in enquiring whether or not there may be changes needed to open up this institution to play its full part in extending its development capacity to the high-density areas.

In contrast, US AID would never challenge the sources of power that lay behind the extremely uneven flow and control of institutional funds, and US AID interventions would, as a result, be effective only at the margins at best. Like some of the building societies' institutional reforms, US AID funds did, naturally, have some minor impact in expanding the housing finance pool to a slightly larger clientele. But the broader crisis of housing and housing finance was continually exacerbated by precisely those market-oriented dynamics that US AID and the World Bank encourage.

Thus by the early 1990s, notwithstanding the disappointing results of the existing municipal housing program and the earlier dismal failures to extend housing finance to the lower 50% of the population, government agreed to place an increasing responsibility on local authorities to fund housing infrastructure on a cost-recovery basis. In 1992, as budgets were tightened due to the Economic Structural Adjustment Program, local authorities judged it necessary to tap building society funds for even infrastructure provision. Although such suggestions would never have been considered during the period when local government was run on behalf of whites, a Town Clerks' Forum recommended that the societies provide access to funds for water supply expansion as part of what the *Financial Gazette* referred to "the entire development of local authority areas under ESAP."

Local authorities' own regulations—such as rent control[21]—"were in conflict with ESAP" and would also have to be scrapped. Moreover, "in line with the ESAP principle of full cost recovery, the Ministry of Transport should deregulate itself and pay in full to the local authorities the cost of maintaining state roads which pass through local authority areas" (*FG*, 3/9/92). As for providing municipal land for housing, Harare's Director of Housing and Community Services explained that he would now "focus on applicants with the capability of developing the stands... buttressed by council's resolution of May 1992 which put more emphasis on applicants with proven hard cash or with financial assistance from their employers" (*FG*, 6/1/94).

The thrust of the evolving strategy had become clear: the privatization of much of the Zimbabwean urban form would occur via local government, and with the cost recovery discipline of private sector intermediaries such as building societies.[22] As Harare's town clerk put it,

> The main problem in the question of servicing of stands is that all of them are serviced through loans from the World Bank and other financial institutions. Those monies have to be repaid with high interest. It is, therefore, not possible for the city council to allocate serviced stands at reduced cost. It has to be at full cost. (*Daily Gazette*, 17/5/93)

The effect of all this was that while the housing crisis intensified, central government (and the Bank) became increasingly capable of avoiding any visible responsibility. The problems of urban management were localized, privatized, dislocated as a competitive process between cities, and yet simultaneously bureaucratized in a new (municipal) form, such that government could offer no effective solution even if the political will had existed (in contrast to the land issue, where pronouncements of imminent widespread redistribution accompanied the intensification of the rural crisis).

The immediate danger of transferring the housing subsidy responsibility of central government to the municipal level was apparent during the severe financial crisis experienced by various municipalities in the early 1990s. Some towns, including Chitungwiza, were effectively disqualified from borrowing from the Bank's loan fund because accounts were not in order; this, in turn, partly stemmed from the unprecedented wave of ESAP-related retrenchments of Chitungwiza's ratepayers, and subsequently their growing arrears on municipal payments (in Bulawayo, there were reports of 25,000 residents of high-density suburb in arrears, mostly attributable to ESAP, and in Harare, arrears rates in high- and medium-density suburbs rose to 35%) (Ziana wire report, 16/7/92; *FG*, 25/11/93). As a result, in 1993 the Urban Councils Association of Zimbabwe requested central government to extend repayment of loans to forty years, which "would make houses affordable to the low-income group" (*Daily Gazette*, 22/5/93).

Reflecting one of the economy's most intense contradictions, the Bank had simultaneously insisted that at a macroeconomic level, Zimbabwe seek positive real interest rates (whereas government budget deficits remained at 10% of GDP and required increased POSB funding at the expense of the building societies). Following the February 1991 interest rate increase, which favored the POSB and other financial institutions, the societies sharply restricted mortgage lending, and one society simply refused to take new applications. Thus by late 1991 a Z$200-million backlog in applications to building societies had developed.

The chairperson of the Association of Building Societies did not fail to make the connection: "The [monetary policy] measures are having the effect of substantially reducing the availability of funds for home ownership at a time when the building societies were to play a major part in the provision of finance for low-income housing under the second World Bank urban development project" (*FG*, 20/6/91). In the nine months following the September 1991 rate changes, building societies lost Z$360 million in deposits. The backlog of applications reached Z$1 billion by August 1992, as compared to a little over Z$2 billion in total mortgage assets on the societies' books (*FG*, 6/8/92). Even in late 1993, most building societies had not begun granting new loans except on a tied-basis (by which companies deposited funds specifically for their employees' housing bonds); as a result Beverley's mortgage loan approvals fell from Z$95 million in 1991-92 to Z$28 million in 1992-93, enough for fewer than 600 new loans (*Daily Gazette*, 20/10/93).

Conclusion: The collapse of the residential property market

The combination of extremely tight liquidity and the peaking of the property market's speculative bubble ultimately led to a dramatic self-correction, namely a rapid decline in residential property prices that began in mid-1991. It was at this point that a number of factors converged, conclusively throwing real estate into doubt as a speculative investment. At a meeting of the Auctioneers, Estate Agents and Valuer's Institute shortly after the February 1991 monetary policy took effect, the regional chairperson predicted that higher interest rates "might control or even depreciate property values" (*FG*, 30/5/91). But it was not merely monetary policy. "The market is beset with problems," said a spokesperson for Borrows estate agents in mid-1991, citing the

> rampant inflation spiral, causing an increased demand for land and property as a protectionary measure; and out of control inflation resulting in building and general costs outstripping wage and salary increases thereby reducing prospective buyers' and lessees' purchasing power.

> The recent imposition of high interest rates on non-owner occupied mortgages which curtails building for investment and reduces rental accommodation, and the lack of available lending funds by the building societies have made the market inactive. (*FG*, 11/7/91)

From "inactive," the residential property market slumped some 20% in the last six months of 1991. Building societies went from surplus liquidity in 1990 to a deficit that mounted to Z$200 million in backlogged applications by late 1991. In the first six months of 1992, residential property suffered another 25% drop in values (*FG*, 6/8/92). By mid-1993 "there was generally very little activity on the property market," according to Bulawayo estate agents, witnessed by diminished real estate prices and a 30% drop in sales (*Daily Gazette*, 2/6/93).

At this stage Zimbabwe was introduced to the phenomenon of "negative equity," whereby a borrower owes more for his/her house than the house could be sold for on the open market. This was a particularly difficult case of negative equity, for it involved a combination of rapidly-falling housing prices and rapidly-rising interest rates. The extreme degree of negative equity in Zimbabwe again reflects the danger of too much reliance on a market-oriented housing finance system, as building societies made no efforts to cool the overheated speculative property market, and then stood exposed—along with their unfortunate borrowers—when the market collapsed.

The World Bank (1994:12), meanwhile, appeared indifferent to all of this, and actually went so far as to term its Urban I project (still underway during the building society liquidity crisis) "an excellent example" of privatized housing finance. The pressure of two inordinate increases in the interest rate (mandated by the Bank's macroeconomic department) during 1991 and the building societies' failure to grant home loans to new prospective borrowers for two subsequent years were barely mentioned in the project evaluation, and were attributed merely to "the cyclical vagaries of Zimbabwe's financial sector" (World Bank 1994:13).

After nearly a year of unprecedented building society illiquidity, Finance Minister Chidzero reacted to the problem in his 1992 budget address by proposing that a 20% withholding tax on interest be applied to building societies, as opposed to a 30% tax on banks. But Greville Burmester of the Association of Building Societies responded, "Everybody in the movement is extremely confused over the senior minister's statement as it does not address the problem at hand... Every month that government waits precipitates the problem and does not help at all" (*FG*, 6/8/92). On another occasion, Burmester alleged that government "feared that if it sufficiently accommodated the building societies in the way of allowing their interest rates to go up considerably, it would defeat its monetary control objectives and set it on a collision course with the International Monetary Fund which is overseeing Zimbabwe's fiscal and monetary policy reforms" (*FG*, 11/6/92).

Yet subversion of monetary control was one result of US AID's next major housing finance intervention, aimed at providing 8,000 low- and middle-income families with housing finance each year, thanks to "immediate liquidity to the private building societies to enable them to maintain low income mortgage lending during the high inflation period accompanying economic structural adjustment, while the policy changes help the financial system develop mechanisms to attract new capital" (US AID, Undated, Annex 1:2). Once again, the enormous (US$75 million) boost in liquidity came with regrettable foreign currency exposure, for the Housing Guarantee Loan took the form of 30-year paper placed by Lazard Freres in the New York market at 7.91% (this was a considerable interest rate premium notwithstanding the US government's backing, especially considering Zimbabwean currency devaluation and the already-multiplying foreign debt) (*FG*, 21/7/94). As for the loan's policy conditionality, USAID regional and urban development officer Michael Enders announced that the desired framework would be based on

> private, tradeable and enforceable rights to property... Governments must rationalise and eventually eliminate subsidies, and, rather than relying on subsidies to increase access to housing, other methods such as regularising insecure tenure, improving access to market-rate housing finance or removing regulatory barriers to the production of affordable housing should be attempted. If subsidies are necessary, they should be well-targeted, measurable, transparent, transitional and avoid creating market distortions. One time capital grants or housing allowances are preferable to continuing subsidies which create an increasingly large burden on the public budget. (*FG*, 24/6/93)

And yet, as was the case throughout the 1980s, the contradictions intrinsic to this orthodox strategy proved overwhelming. For US AID to acknowledge the practical urgency of channelling its funds into actual houses (not merely amenable policy statements), it would have to completely ignore its own counsel.

Thus US AID administrators did, ultimately, reject both "market-rate housing finance" and "one-time capital grants" in favor of blending Z$237.5 million of US AID-originated government funds (interest-free) with Z$237.5 million in commercial funds (ostensibly at 18.5%), to reach a (still excessively high) rate of 14.5%. Together, in a Z$475 million pool, US AID predicted the program would ultimately fund 43,200 new low income bonds—but at an average loan of just Z$11,000 per site, leaving next to nothing for building materials and labor. The implications for affordability were not hopeful, however, particularly when the price of an average high-density suburb house had risen to Z$100,000 by the time the program began (the minimum cost of constructing a very basic unit was on the order of Z$40,000). By the time the program was finally initiated in April 1994, inflation and devaluation had increased US AID's on-lending to Z$600 million in local currency terms, with the average loan increasing to Z$25,000 and the income ceiling to Z$1,000 per month, still far below both construction costs and affordability levels.

The housing finance market clearly needed additional support, and whereas under more hospitable conditions (such as before ESAP, when liquidity was high) the World Bank's millions could have been a palliative and the US AID secondary market proposal might have generated an added boost, the housing market in fact deteriorated markedly. US AID's promises of expanded building society lending failed to materialise for several years, and by 1993 Minister of Public Construction and National Housing Enos Chikowore "recognized the inability of the building societies to provide adequate mortgages for either house purchase or construction" (*Daily Gazette*, 22/5/93). There were substantial declines in bonds granted by the building societies—Z$184 million in the first half of 1992, and as low as Z$16 million in the month of August 1992—as CABS reported "a noticeable increase in the number of mortgagors falling in arrears on loan repayments," from 3.8% in early 1991 to 5.4% in early 1992 (foreclosures were up from 0.7% to 1.2%) (*Herald*, 2/4/92).

This was at a time of financial crisis not only for the poor (because of higher prices) and workers (due to real wage declines and retrenchments). The largely white-collar civil service was also in the process of being downsized by 25% from 1991-95, thus throwing into question the earlier ZANU strategy of building a supportive class base from within the bureaucracy. As trade union leader Morgan Tsvangirai noted in 1992, "The middle-classes are now vulnerable. Interest rates are unbearable and building societies will have to increase repossessions" (*Africa South*, February 1992). The foreclosure pace increased, and by mid-1993 Minister Chikowore (himself the victim of foreclosure, along with former Labor Minister Frederick Shava) had convened a committee comprising three ministries "tasked with ensuring that the repossession of stands by building societies due to failure to pay mortgage rates was immediately reversed" (*Daily Gazette*, 21/4/93, 22/5/93; *Sunday Gazette*, 4/7/93; *FG*, 10/6/93). When market failure was met with this sort of heavy interventionist hand, the futility of the market-oriented policy should have been evident.

Finally, when liquidity began to improve, such experiences kept the societies out of the housing market and into other (typically money market) investments. In 1993-94, for example, the four building societies (CABS, Beverley, Founders, and Zimbabwe Building Society) increased their assets by 34% (to Z$4.4 billion), but mortgage bonds grew by only 3% (to Z$2.2 billion), due to what the president of the Association of Building Societies of Zimbabwe, Richard Parke, called "problems of affordability." Promised bond rate reductions by the societies did not materialise, and moreover, in July 1994, the 3% government subsidy to high density borrowers was withdrawn (*FG*, 8/12/94). Hence the residential market remained in the doldrums. By 1995, a spokesperson for Mitchell Real Estate confirmed, "very few properties appreciated in value" in the high-density suburbs (which he partly blamed upon "the sudden increase in the number of housing cooperatives" that presumably sidetracked demand and won, through collective struggle, an increased supply of municipal land for housing).[23]

As a result of the market-oriented approach, there was very little scope for, on the one hand, increasing the supply of affordable low-cost housing and, on the other, preventing either land speculation or downward raiding. Moreover, as new programs were implemented which depended even further upon private sector financing, such financing effectively dried up, throwing into question all other aspects of housing policy. Housing finance, in sum, was one of Zimbabwe's most powerful generators of uneven urban development. Simultaneously, as we see next, farm credit had parallel effects in rural areas.

Notes

1. In Gweru, the city council offered incentives including free land, a five-year rates holiday, and reduced water tariffs, while Mutare business leaders complained that similar investment incentives were taking too long to establish. As for those municipalities which had not yet entered the interurban race to the bottom, Zimbabwe National Chamber of Commerce vice president Shadreck Beta warned, "The competition among cities for investors must not be taken lightly" (*FG*, 28/9/95, 21/12/95). This mirrored the urban neo-liberal "urban entrepreneurialism" being practiced by cities nearly universally during the 1990s. As articulated by a senior advisor to the United Nations Conference on Human Settlements, Shlomo Angel (1995, 4), the challenge of global urban management would encompass "creating a level playing field for competition among cities, particularly across national borders; on understanding how cities get ahead in this competition; on global capital transfers, the new

economic order and the weakening of the nation-state..." for after all, "The city is not a community, but a conglomerate of firms, institutions, organisations and individuals with contractual agreements among them."

2. Each justification can be briefly considered. Urbanization was indeed rapid, insofar as rural areas and outlying regions were not given sufficient developmental support, in the form, for example, of radical land reform or generous decentralisation subsidies. But in any event, such support cuts against the grain of neo-liberal policy, which has no durable answer to stemming excessive (and crisis-driven) rural-urban migration.
Land shortages have long been cited as a major facet of the housing crisis. Yet there is certainly the physical land available to solve the housing problem, were it not being warehoused mainly by private owners. Not including Chitungwiza, Harare's residential property market in the mid 1980s included 25,000 low density houses and 25,000 medium density homes on 20,000 hectares, and another 60,000 homes in high density areas (World Bank 1983b:47). (The total land within the city limits of Harare amounts to 54,000 hectares, of which, at independence, about 8,000 were undeveloped.) While high density areas are very dense indeed (some 300 square meter plots had as many as 30 people in residence), density in the middle- and upper-class areas of the city is, according to one press report, "extremely low... a situation not found in any capital city anywhere in the world" (there were 24.8 persons per hectare in the low-density suburbs of Harare, in comparison to 1,600 persons per hectare in Kenya's Mathare Valley). Indeed, in 1990 it was determined that "in-fill" housing in low-density areas could nearly double the city's housing stock—ie, by as much as 100,000 units (at even the very generous scale of 400 square meters per plot)—and thus easily accommodate more than half a million new residents (*FG*, 13/7/90, 9/5/91). But breaking up the plots of the old and new bourgeoisie was not a realistic proposition. Again, the market was the barrier, not the solution. Moreover, none of the normal state interventions that are feasible in most countries—whether land taxes or expropriation with compensation—were taken to remove underdeveloped land from the control of speculators and non-resident investors.
Bureaucrats and excessively high housing standards were indeed a barrier, although these were addressed through ESAP, with no evident improvement in housing construction. Finally, the foreign exchange constraint was not in evidence when it came to acquisition of building materials required for luxury office construction.

3. There were also nascent efforts to extend beyond the market, with vehicles such as housing cooperatives and building brigades. But until the early 1990s the cooperatives applied generally to the purchase of land and construction of housing, with no serious effort made to explore more collective approaches to home ownership (such as community land trusts, housing associations or limited equity housing cooperatives). And building brigades soon proved more expensive than self-help housing (Schlyter 1985).

4. The guarantee protected the building society's first 30% of the loan, as opposed to the standard 20% guarantee offered by government to non-civil servants on the basis of a 10% deposit.
5. Local government provision of houses was most impressive just prior to independence. Subsequently, construction in Harare's high density areas fell dramatically, from a total of 5,581 new houses and stands made available for allocation by the City of Harare (1985:6) during fiscal year 1979-80, to 2,201 in 1980-81, 3,416 in 1981-82, and just 200 in 1982-83. Although with the help of the international agencies the rate picked up again (and remained above 1,500 annually in eight of the next nine years), by 1992 the allocation of stands or houses was back to just 200 (*FG*, 6/1/94).
6. For critiques of self-help housing, see Burgess 1978, 1985.
7. Mafico also criticizes the cost-reduction principle of omitting ablution facilities. The government rationale was that locating toilet facilities at one end of the plot reduced the options for plot use, which Mafico concludes is "hardly a plausible argument" since allottees already have extremely limited options.
8. Only a quarter of the participants ultimately managed to do so, hence the argument that Zimbabwe's low-cost housing construction standards were excessively high.
9. Ironically, Michael Stone (1993:6,7) notes that fully one-third of US residents also suffer "shelter poverty," due to the fact that an unrealistically high percentage of their income is applied to housing. US AID officials often remark that they are most satisfied when they succeed in recreating US-type institutions and processes in countries they work in.

   In a similar scheme at Chinhoyi, cumulative arrears reached five times the monthly revenue potential. In Marondera, inhuman tactics were employed, according to US AID consultants (Abt Associates Inc 1988:47,48,52): "Failure by beneficiaries to pay after notice of being in arrears is then followed by some incentives, such as turning off the household's water supply. This appears to be effective since the ratio of monthly arrears to monthly revenue potential fell from .43 to .07 between June and September 1987."
10. For example, the Bank had no objection to allowing Chitungwiza to remain a separate, self-sustaining municipality in spite of the fact that its employment and consumer tax base were structurally depleted by its dormitory status (Harare employers and retailers paid taxes to the Harare Council on earnings taken from Chitungwiza residents). This did not escape the attention of Chitungwiza residents, for as one complained, "The donor community, e.g. the World Bank, which has funded many housing schemes in other towns and cities, seems to be shunning Chitungwiza like a leper" (*Sunday Mail*, 17/3/91.) By mid 1993, the Chitungwiza housing backlog was rising dramatically and the number of people living on each stand had increased to 13.2, but the World Bank disqualified Chitungwiza from its most recent housing loan scheme due to

poor bookkeeping by the town council (*Daily Gazette*, 9/7/93).

11. This change in income targeting may not have come to the attention of Bank personnel, who noted that in each of the four cities comprising the Zimbabwe housing programme, fewer than 10% of recipients fell below the Z$200 income target. Incredibly, over the course of the entire project (which was originated in November 1981), while the Zimbabwe dollar was severely eroded by inflation, the income eligibility did not change. Allegedly, the Z$400 income ceiling was largely adhered to, for the Bank insists—stretching plausibility—that only in Masvingo did more than 20% of the recipients earn more (World Bank 1994:8).
12. Government initially wanted to insist on the construction of a full four-room house prior to occupation, which would have limited the aided self-help component; the Bank largely won this dispute. The Bank (1994:11) also found fault with government's failure to abide by loan covenants, "particularly with regard to the employment of consultants (few were used) and to the enforcement of the income guidelines for property ownership." Yet those conditions—force-feeding US$7.5 million worth of overpriced foreign consultants who parachute in for a few days, and recipient income guidelines that the Bank also confessed made little sense (especially reserving 70% of the sites for formally-employed workers who earn less than Z$200 per month)—should never have been written into the loan in the first place.
13. For example, tuberculosis increased sharply in the early 1990s due to high-density suburb overcrowding, according to the Harare City Council (*FG*, 20/5/93).
14. The "Class C" accounts ("PUPS") paid, at the time, 9% to the depositor, which translated into a 23% effective rate for the top tax bracket. A quarter of the funds raised had to go towards low-income housing finance, a ratio easily met by the high level of effective demand. Although a substantial government subsidy was involved in the scheme, most loans went to self-help builders, a mainstay of Bank housing philosophy. The minimal collateral was some proof of income. Some 2,000 loans were made by building societies in the first four years of the Class C scheme, through 1990, worth Z$200 million.
15. Schlyter (1987:26,29) explains why US AID might have been ideologically pre-disposed to rejecting the building brigades:

    > I was told in Harare that the politicians responsible for housing made a world wide tour to study housing strategies. They were startled by the urban housing situation of many African countries. They did not like the views of the large squatter areas, nor were they impressed by the upgraded squatter areas. It was still a substandard they did not want to accept in Zimbabwe. They did get impressed, however, when visiting the suburbs of Havana and other places on Cuba. The Cubans could proudly claim success in building with brigades... The building brigades are presented as the socialist element in the Zimbabwean housing policy.

The Zimbabwean government attempted to impose one small collective component onto a system that had already become profoundly market-oriented, and given the added cost of labour that the (now formal sector) brigades represented in relation to informal builders, it was no wonder they failed to make an impact.

16. Some actions were taken in August, but interest rates in October increased from 13.25% to 13.75% for owner-occupied housing, while the rate for non-owner occupied housing rose from 13.75% to 18.25%, and the down-payment rose from 30% to 40%. Nevertheless, according to the chairperson of the of Association of Building Societies of Zimbabwe, there was little reaction in the market (*FG*, 12/10/90).
17. One company acquired 4,000 300 square meter sites for employees, each of which would cost Z$8,000 for servicing. According to the City of Harare's acting director of housing, "When the land is made available to the company for servicing for its employees, title will remain with the individual workers, which makes a substantial incentive for workers to remain with particular companies" (*FG*, 8/3/91). The implications for maintaining class power are rather obvious.
18. One of the most creative schemes was attempted by Old Mutual, which donated forty-seven hectares of land in Bulawayo to the local council for high-density housing, in order that nearby land it owned could be sold as an industrial park complete with neighboring labor supply.
19. It was not clear what the Bank considered "successful" in terms of women's access to housing finance, since many legal barriers in the transfer of property ownership to women remained even a decade after independence.
20. The first mention of such a secondary market was in the 1985 National Council of Savings Institutions' "Housing Finance in Zimbabwe" and later reported in the *Financial Gazette* (18/5/90). But it was only in January 1996 that a secondary mortgage market finally received support from Association of Building Societies (*FG*, 25/1/96).
21. The point may have been moot, for although by 1994 the Rent Board had accumulated a long backlog of applications to have rents increased under existing rent controls, landlord Moffit Saunders termed the Rent Board's determinations "more realistic" than previously (*FG*, 15/12/94).
22. To facilitate and amplify this approach, the Bank even set up a Harare training programme aimed at municipal authorities from the entire southern and eastern African region.
23. Thanks to advocacy by the NGO Housing People of Zimbabwe, cooperatives had finally made breakthroughs in government land policy and building society financing, and won allocation of 262 stands in 1994. There were 34 co-operatives at that stage, most of which were officially registered (a process that took 30-36 months). Three quarters of the cooperatives were based in Harare, and a dozen originated at their members' workplaces. More than 7,000 families were involved, with the vast majority earning below $500 per month. But the ideological foundation for this

social movement was extremely shaky, as witnessed by the discursive strategy chosen by Killian Munzwa of Housing People: "Let us underline our attempt to move away from the words 'provide,' 'provision,' and 'beneficiary' towards words that imply more people-based or market-driven solutions" (as if such solutions are intrinsically compatible) (*FG*, 8/7/93, 25/8/94, 19/1/95).

chapter ten

Farm Finance and Uneven Rural Development

Introduction

Zimbabwe's Independence was gained in part because peasant producers, starved for land, gave support to guerrillas of ZANU. Yet ZANU promises of land redistribution were never kept. Even the controversial 1993 Land Designation Act was "shelved," Lazarus Nzarayebani complained to parliament in late 1994, because "it is not in conformity with the World Bank and IMF" and instead served government only "to save its face" (*FG*, 9/2/95).[1] In contrast, a variety of market-related mechanisms, especially credit, were adopted in order to foster a "peasant miracle" which in reality never extended much beyond the top 10% of black farmers. Moreover, white commercial farmers were lured ever deeper into debt in the late 1980s as financial speculation in land became rife and export opportunities beckoned, leading to a reorientation of agricultural production.

The use of credit by different strata of Zimbabwean farmers represents, in essence, the capacity to extend over time the need to realize value from production to pay for present consumption, and in the process to extend their spatial reach. Financiers include the Agricultural Finance Corporation (AFC) and its partners in the World Bank and foreign foundations, and local commercial banks with long histories of serving white farmers. Agriculture is roughly stratified as follows: 4,800 Large Scale Commercial Farms (LSCFs) (controlled mainly by white farmers and farm corporations); 8,500 black Small Scale Commercial Farms (SSCFs) (formerly "African Purchase Area" farms); 57,000 Resettlement Area (RA) farms; and approximately a million Communal Area (CA) "peasant" households, of which 10% produce 90% of all CA maize output (World Bank 1995b, v.II: 83). (The latter three categories can be considered "small farmers.")

More than two thirds of Zimbabweans gain their livelihood from the land. The last difficult century through which they have struggled—the legacy of colonial land dispossession, establishment of labor reserves, and civil war—has been reviewed by a host of researchers and need not be revisited here (Phimister 1975; Palmer 1977; Lan 1985; Ranger 1985). For most farmers in the post-Independence era, work has remained primarily a form of subsistence activity, subject to various social and environmental pressures which sometimes leave even such a modest economic status untenable (Alexander 1995). Small farmers are not alone in suffering the vagaries of weather, erratic state programs, international commodity fluctuations, input price inflation and the like. LSCF farmers (and their quarter of a million farmworkers) also discover intractable problems associated with this most raw and contradiction-ridden of capitalist enterprise, including chronic overproduction (in average or above-average rainy seasons), the extremely competitive nature of the supply side (farming itself), and the tendency to extreme corporate concentration in inputs, financing, marketing, processing, distribution, and retailing. It is here that debt appears most attractive as a means of displacing contradictions across space and time. But, as in other rural Third World settings now coming under critical investigation, such an approach is also increasingly viewed as futile, misguided, and even damaging (Howell 1990; Ferguson, 1991; Adams and Fitchett 1992; Shipton 1992).

To understand how Zimbabwe's agricultural credit programs have expanded and in some cases contracted, in the process exacerbating uneven geographical development, also requires a brief look at the theory of rural "dualism," which is summarized in the next section. The dualist approach draws sustenance from the spatial skew of the circulation of money, most obviously in terms of the location of bank branches and the logistics of financial services. The limits of this approach are witnessed, however, through microeconomic studies of peasant savings and credit. The operations of "savings clubs" and the prospects for transforming these into credit-granting organizations are reviewed, followed by an appraisal of the rise and fall of formal lending to small farmers in historical and contemporary periods. A concluding section further probes dualistic approaches to the problem of uneven development and entertains the question of whether credit is actually necessary for small farmers under Zimbabwean conditions.

The dual market thesis

Methodologically, development agencies and some researchers utilize a dualistic developed/underdeveloped intellectual framework which in Zimbabwe at first blush appears inviting based upon surface-level distinctions and separateness between colonial-capitalist entrepreneurs and a peasantry supposedly unexposed to market forces.[2] Beyond descriptive historical analysis, dualism as a critique of the racial distribution of rural resources provides a basis for addressing underdevelopment through "extensive" (labor-intensive and spatially-expansive) agricultural policy. As a result, Zimbabwe's post-Independence epoch has been littered with uncritical arguments tying poverty to institutional constraints (e.g., apparent lack of market mechanisms), and wealth to strategic "choices," rather than capturing both within the same (unified) structural conceptual apparatus. Nowhere is the legacy of this work more visible, and its limitations so revealing, as in rural finance.

At the time of Independence, a three-volume report on peasant credit based on a dualist approach was issued by the Whitsun Foundation (1980), suggesting a massive expansion of credit into CAs, foreshadowing subsequent AFC policy. Shortly thereafter, Dan Ndlela (1981:149)—ordinarily a far more critical scholar—completed a policy-oriented study of *Dualism in the Rhodesian Colonial Economy* which, neglecting to consider the theory of "articulations of modes of production" (Wolpe 1980), contended that "dualistic conditions in the land market and direct discrimination in the allocation of credit are the main reasons for dualism in the credit market." In a similar vein, the US Agency for International Development (1982:10,11) argued that to address the "dual economy" in the rural areas required "refinements and resources" to extend existing markets to small farmers (and to this end US AID initiated a grain depot system which proved unsuccessful; for a critique see Breslin 1992; Thompson 1991:117-128). A German Development Institute team (Radke et al 1986:vi) performed an in-depth analysis of Zimbabwe's small farmer finances, beginning with the premise that Zimbabwe's "sophisticated financial system" reflects "the inherited dualism of the economy and society." Norman Reynolds' explicitly dualist framework led directly to a stirring condemnation of state intervention in rural credit markets: "Low or subsidized interest rates to small farmers are among the most emotionally endowed pieces of socialist tradition" (1987:26). And the World Bank (1991, v.II:3) argued that "Any analysis of agriculture in Zimbabwe is necessarily dominated by the pervasive dualism that characterizes the sector—the result of public policy during the colonial period."

It is not as if such studies fail to produce important research findings and useful data. Rather, the essential practical implication of the dualist approach is to throw money at the problem of underdevelopment: if not in populist style aimed at meeting basic needs, then instead in the forms of high-priced credit (as an externally-imposed resorce entailing very little scope for local control) and other extensions of the existing market system. The elaborate framework constructed to rationalize such credit systems is illustrated by Ndlela (1981:147), who identifies the demand for small farmer debt in terms of rational microeconomic calculation: "The farmer is only likely to start borrowing in larger amounts in the event that his capital requirements increase. This may come about if, say, he starts to clear more land, use more fertilizer or improved seed, and so on." Conversely, this argument might well continue, a lack of small farmer borrowing—or a rise in arrears on existing debt which in turn makes further borrowing difficult—reflects a rational decision-making process, i.e., a lack of desire to extend farming operations. Yet in the late 1960s and early 1970s a profoundly extensive development process of small-scale farming was indeed the rule and, as noted below, this was the pre-Independence period when default rates on credit increased most dramatically. Moreover, while the availability of credit in the 1980s coincided with increasingly intensive expansion of small farmer output, the value of credit to small farmers may be deemed questionable in view of the extremely high arrears rates they sustained. In other words, the capacity or desire of small farmers to make rational utility-maximizing calculations is by no means as obvious as dualist theory posits.

The debate over small farmer borrowing behavior is not limited to Zimbabwe. Dualism has also been used in Lesotho by the World Bank and other agencies in order to show that traditional small farmers have the capacity to modernize, in large part through credit. As James Ferguson (1991:137) reports, "Although there is a degree of 'separateness' between livestock and cash, this can in no way be expressed as a division between 'traditional' and 'modern' sectors. In place of the vague formulas of dualism, which posit 'two economies' or two 'autonomous sectors' one can say quite precisely that what is at issue is rather a socially created 'one-way barrier' between cash and livestock, and a prestige complex centring on the 'livestock' domain so defined." The dualist framework nevertheless insists that by increasing small farmer access to markets and all the features associated with them—inputs, marketing, credit, distribution, etc.—the two economies will gradually become one. While it is beyond the range of the present study to investigate what Ferguson terms the "prestige complex" of peasant relationships, the argument's bearing upon credit should be evident. Dan Nabudere (1989:21-22) addresses such linkage directly:

> A kind of "Chinese Wall" was erected between these two sectors conceptually, with a series of "dual economy" theories propounded to support the division... The low-wage was in fact in turn the basis of the *credit-system* because credit can only be advanced on the *expectation* that some valuable material goods or services will be produced tomorrow... Such credit could never enrich those who produce to keep it going except those at the top and the middle, who appropriate or pick up bits.

While those at the very top of Zimbabwe's small farmer hierarchy may have prospered, the fact that access to credit is firmly interrelated with a set of other processes of uneven development means that indebted small farmers may end up less, not more, capable of improving their standards of living. This is particularly true at times, as shown below, when financial capital is expanding its own power and reach. Before making this case, however, the spatial and logistical constraints and opportunities for financing rural development through the extension of the money economy and its existing institutions are considered.

The geographical circulation of money

Savings and credit facilities are not easily available to small farmers, especially peasants, in the way they are for urban dwellers and LSCFs, and part of the reason for this is limited geographic accessibility of bank branches. Yet it is not sufficient to argue merely that the location of bank and building society branches is severely biased towards urban areas and some small towns and rural areas which are vastly removed from the majority of Zimbabwe's population (as dualism would suggest). While this is certainly true, it does not capture fully the degree to which the entire financial system (commercial and government) played a role in exacerbating uneven development of the rural sector, in part through draining rural areas of whatever funds were mobilized in savings institutions, and in part through extending credit and financial services in an unsustainable manner. Both these aspects are addressed in subsequent sections, where it is argued that the geographical decentralization of borrowers (relative to the concentrated location of financiers in the towns) is but one part of the problem. The spatial location of bank branches and related logistical features—such as the hours during which branches were open (a serious constraint to those travelling long distances to do business) and the cost of basic financial services—were supplemented by a geographic ebb and flow of funds that served not to develop, but to underdevelop areas because they had little relation to the production process (itself suffering intensifying contradictions) and little relation to organic processes of social organization.

The World Bank actually disputed the argument that uneven institutional location affected the development of agriculture: "Zimbabwe's cities, small towns and rural administrative centers are relatively well served by financial institutions" (1991a, v.III:148). This statement, erroneous at face value, can only be defended by reference to the Post Office Savings Bank (POSB), which by the mid-1980s claimed 167 offices, of which two-thirds were in 27 towns of less than 2,500 population, and only 13% in the eight cities with official (1982) populations of more than 25,000. While offering appropriate savings facilities (including limited paperwork for account-holders, with literature available in local languages), the POSB did not, however, extend credit facilities to anyone other than government. Of 850,000 POSB savings accounts in the mid-1980s, 55% had less than Z$20 in them, representing just 1.7% of total POSB deposits (other, much larger depositors were attracted by POSB's tax-free status and relatively high interest rates).

In contrast, two-thirds of commercial bank offices and 72% of building society branches were located in these eight largest cities, with 9% of banks and just 1% of building societies in towns of 2,500 or less (Radke et al 1986:19,100). To their credit, banks introduced mobile agency services to some areas in 1985 concomitant with the increased monetization of the countryside thanks to increased agricultural marketing and extension services. But without nearby formal banking offices, rural Zimbabweans were extremely limited in their ability to manage personal finances. Lacking the safety and interest earnings of savings accounts, they were denied some of bank money's functions as a store of value, a shortcoming particularly important given the rising inflation rate and uneven access to credit. And there were also substantial limits to the use rural people made of money in its other fundamental roles: as a measure of value and means of payment. The country's main newspaper noted with disgust that the average rural Zimbabwean still "had to rely on local traders to cash crop-payment cheques, often paying a hefty commission for the privilege or being forced to take part payment in goods they did not necessarily need. Indeed, some traders have gone further snapping up crops at far below official prices from farmers desperate for cash" (*Herald*, 28/10/85).

Thus the torpid expansion of branch facilities in the 1980s was a source of constant complaint. For example, in Mutoko—an exceptionally successful "growth point" (i.e., small town targeted for government support) in the war-ravaged northeast—the first full bank branch was only established in late 1990. Likewise Shamva, "in dire need of banks," was "yet to see a single bank, permanent or mobile established" a decade after Independence, according to the head of the local rural council (*Herald*, 18/3/90). For the commercial banks, the basis for profitable small town banking reverted largely to business from local government, as some rural council budgets exceeded Z$20 million, and as rural teachers and civil servants were "encouraged" to bank their salaries (*Industrial Review*, July 1987). But beyond this government-related demand-side market, there were only weak efforts by policy-makers to change conditions on the supply-side. In 1985, the Reserve Bank requested banks to expand their operations into 54 official growth points, and the banks conferred to decide which institutions would service each growth point once or twice a week.

The spatial expansion of the money economy never met the high expectations of increasingly literate rural dwellers. Even two years after the expansion program began, a respected local businessperson attacked the banks' geographical prejudices:

> A level of intolerance is being reached for their arrogance, pomp and ceremony, splendor and grandeur in the urban areas and their indifference and obliviousness to the plight of our rural folk. Government's herculean efforts to provide the needed infrastructure into the rural areas at great cost in both human and financial resources, and to provide tax and investment allowances and incentives in declared growth points so that, through a decentralization policy, the majority of our people may share in the economic life of this country are perceived as not having had any impact upon such financial institutions. The view is that these efforts, goals and aspirations have invited little else but mockery and ridicule. Contemptuously, they hold steadfast in their beliefs that rural folk offer little or no security compatible with their financial services criteria, steeped as they are in their traditions of capital-intensive, high-technology and profit-maximizing orientation. (*Zimbabwe Quarterly*, 3 [3], 7)

Fourteen years after Independence, the commercial banking system's reverse flow of funds—from parched rural to liquid urban settings—had still not improved. In 1994 Ted Makoni, president of the Zimbabwe National

Chamber of Commerce (representing small, black-owned businesses) criticized banks for "overprovision of banks in Harare, while rural areas were starved of any banking services. This understandably tarnishes your image as you are seen as suckers, who only follow wealth and money and could not care less how that wealth is generated" (*FG*, 5/5/94). In the countryside, according to Rasmussen (1990:122), "The people's and enterprises' dominant relation to the commercial banks is as savers, receiving only low interest rates, while the money saved is transferred to the city and then lent to larger enterprises."

Official censure had little effect. Attorney General Patrick Chinamasa "condemned banking institutions for closing doors to peasant farmers. The Zimbabwe banking system is 'too rigid, too formal and too insensitive' to the majority of peasants who contribute substantial sums of money to banks in the form of deposits but are unable to borrow" (*Herald*, 12/5/90). Yet the "rigidity" of the banking system was probably not the ultimate barrier to its geographical expansion. Instead, as Reynolds (1988:75) explains, there was also the prospect of immediate overaccumulation of capital in rural markets: "The danger for all participants, including banks who finance small rural enterprises, is that local markets with small demand can be quickly saturated by a communality of available materials and skills."

Aside from such geographic constraints and the limited underlying economic base on which to expand banking services, other logistical problems in mobilising rural savings arose from the banks' economic exclusivity.[3] Questions therefore emerged about the degree to which the banks and building societies actually desired an infusion of low-balance consumer accounts, especially in light of increasingly strenuous complaints lodged in the press and parliament about extreme congestion in branches during the first days of each month. That problem was exacerbated by the expansion of direct bank deposits of workers' salary payments, which may have proved an added convenience and safety measure on the savings side for a select number of relatively privileged workers, but as a side-effect provided a disincentive (the congestion) for wealthier clients as well as those who had irregular banking business to conduct (especially women from the informal sector).[4]

Prevailing trends to more exclusive banking services—which indeed have occurred across the globe concomitant with banking deregulation—reflected Zimbabwe's worsening polarization of wealth and the limits of bank efforts to extend the money economy down the income scale. Radke et al. (1986:17) insightfully explained the "inactivity" of fundraising in low-income markets in terms of the banks' *excess* liquidity (also a global phenomenon in the 1980s): "The banks currently suffer from a lack of investment opportunities and would not therefore know how to invest any additional funds raised" and hence suffered a lack of incentive to attract deposits from new sources.

These, then, were some of the reasons for the ceiling on bank expansion into rural markets. Recognising such factors was easy, but it soon became obvious that overcoming the locational and logistical friction involved would require a relatively radical approach to the *institutional form* of finance, since the World Bank (1991a, v.III:149) soundly rejected the idea that the AFC might become a retail bank: "a price distortion will be created, sending out a signal that rural banking operations are cheaper than they actually are." (Five years were lost, but finally in 1996, the AFC was forced, by virtue of losing its 100% government funding, to turn to retail banking to raise funds.) The only other option was to upgrade organic forms of savings and credit institutions.

Savings clubs and credit cooperatives

Was there a way around these various constraints to wider geographical circulation of funds in Zimbabwe? If banking halls were designed for transactions beyond the sphere of small farmer finances—and if those halls were fitted-out with luxury comforts for a more affluent urban customer base thus making their reproduction in rural areas more difficult—then surely a new set of more appropriate (and better-located) institutional forms would solve these problems? This was the primary hypothesis of the state and international lending agencies. The vehicles ranged from new kinds of savings clubs to group credit schemes. In reality, all of these failed to achieve the desired linkage between the formal financial system and small farmers, and the reasons are worth reviewing in detail.

"The fact is that in Zimbabwe cash hardly circulates outside of the cities," according to Reynolds (1988:77). This is true in relative terms (only 7% of income in one area Reynolds studied remained in the countryside after five months), but should not obscure the vast number of transactions involving money as a commodity. Aside from widespread informal lending for a profit, there were some organic, and some non-organic approaches to money. Savings clubs, for example, are generally divided into two types: informal rotating schemes, and formal savings clubs. Rotating savings clubs ("societies," "rounds," or "kutenderera") are mainly women's groups which, during the 1980s, averaged per capita savings of Z$15 to Z$30 per month. The women contribute the agreed sum and then, at each meeting, one member is paid the entire amount saved by the group over that period. This represents the extension of credit of a very limited sort, and varies from the early recipients of the funds (who receive interest-free credit for the entire cycle) to those who receive the funds at the end of the cycle and therefore technically are pure creditors.[5] In the field of finance these are probably the only mutual aid networks emanating from rural Zimbabwean communities' own capacity to organize in geographically specific (and often kinship-based) ways, but sadly there are no studies available to suggest the extent of their development.

Other types of savings clubs, however, are much better documented and internationally understood (largely because they are externally initiated). These are formalized clubs which generally meet weekly and involve records in pass books and coded stamps (to help illiterate peasants understand the money transaction). In 1963, a Jesuit missionary founded the first recorded formal club of this sort near Salisbury, whose members initially consisted of teachers and mission employees. Catholic teaching held that "the State should not take over work or responsibility from smaller groups when the smaller groups are able to do what is necessary on their own. The reason for this is that if people look to the State for their advancement they fail to acquire the ability to look after their own affairs and interests." Hence the savings and credit clubs would contribute "to the building up of social and individual moral character" (Chishawasha Mission, 1967, 5).

Subsequently, clubs attempted to evolve from simple savings into credit unions in the 1960s and 1970s with support from church groups, university researchers, and commercial producers and retailers of agricultural inputs.[6] However, the savings clubs and credit unions soon faltered. The "Savings Club Movement"—headquartered in Salisbury with fifteen employees—wound down its operations in 1976. In addition to the emerging civil war, problems cited include the limited capacity of the savers to handle credit matters, erratic member participation and excessive absenteeism. By 1980 there were just 200 clubs serving 4,000 members, but the numbers began expanding again.

A Savings Development Movement was registered as a cooperative after Independence, and proceeded to jettison the credit side of the balance sheet. Government agencies were "the most important promoters of savings clubs" during the 1980s, according to one report—although at least one company (Windmill Pvt. Ltd) claimed the initiative for founding 2,000 of the 5,000 clubs operating in 1984—and in the search for economies of distribution even attempted to organize the groups on a regional basis (Radke et al 1986:50). By that time, 140,000 mainly rural people, mostly women, belonged to savings clubs.

Indeed in the post-Independence era savings clubs—especially of the informal variety—were of importance because of their fundamental role in rural African women's mutual aid, income-generation, and household finances. Dianne Elson (1991:23) criticizes most structuralist analysis for overlooking the gendered nature of rural money relations, and develops the concept of "male bias" to clarify "bias against women farmers by public and private sector suppliers of the services and inputs they need (information, seeds, fertilizers, credit and marketing); and bias against women farmers in the control of resources within households." Both forms of bias are operative in Zimbabwe, and women's mutual aid has evolved as a result. Kate Truscott's (1987:10) study of savings clubs estimated upwards of 90% of participants were women, stemming from the fact that "men's security derives from their 'savings' in the form of land and cattle. A savings account is one way in which women can claim categorically to have money in her own right, and control over its use." Women make up more than 40% of the heads of household in some provinces due to early male deaths, male migration to commercial farms and other migrant labor relations, and yet generally have little or no access to land, credit and extension services, or even to cards for the marketing boards. Women also accomplish 73% of farm labor, 62% of livestock care, 81% of fuel gathering and chopping, and 96% of routine domestic tasks (Zwart 1990: i, ii, 7). Collective savings can thus be crucial for economic survival, and women leaders of savings clubs also tend to be high in local hierarchies of the ZANU Women's League, Village Development Committees, Ward Development Committees, churches and schools.[7]

The savings do not always circulate efficiently, however, since clubs usually bank their funds with a formal institution. Nearly half of group savings accounts in one survey were held by the Central African Building Society, with the POSB and Beverley Building Society accounting for one-fifth each. The nearest bank location was 80 km away from the base of some of the savings clubs surveyed (bank offices closed at 2PM), which meant that for about 90% of the clubs, a bus trip to deposit funds could be justified only through collecting savings for more than a month (as much as Z$400) before banking them (Radke et al 1986:55). Annual withdrawals typically account for a third to a half of annual savings, and usually occur in January for school fees and in September for agricultural inputs. Although savings decrease during those months, and although savings increase in the early winter as crops are paid for, average savings do not otherwise vary much (Chimedza 1984).

There appears a certain order to this arrangement. But questions remain as to the sustainability of the savings clubs in view of their non-organic nature and their very limited material impact in relation to the time involved in organizing them and the capacities that are necessary to make them fully effective. Michael Drinkwater (1991:224) concluded that "the insertion of an organization, such as a ward cooperative or savings club, into a communal area society in which the normative structures required to sustain a modern institution are fragile and only partially developed, is a sensitive and difficult task. Such organizations are not part of people's experience and thus they will not emerge autonomously." Notwithstanding a World Bank (1982d:8) assessment of Zimbabwe's savings clubs as "certainly one of the best examples of self-help in Africa," three quarters of the savings clubs surveyed by Brand (1987) were founded through government programs (and the average savings balance of members was only Z$11.48). If not drained by the negative real interest rates in bank savings accounts, the funds were overwhelmingly used for increasingly expensive agricultural inputs and school-related fees. Thus the transition from savings club to formal credit-oriented institution is an immensely difficult one when temporal and spatial constraints are added to the general difficulties of mere survival in the Zimbabwean countryside.

The savings club movement is not incapable of upgrading into credit programs. In limited instances credit is already extended within the savings club—typically for the purpose of a funeral or coping with an illness—but this is mainly accomplished through additional savings levies which members must pay, and involves interest-free repayment. Church-based savings programs also strengthened and shaped the subsequent growth of credit unions. The philosophy of the Catholic missionary Silveira House, implemented from 1968, was that a two-year savings record among those with a common bond (e.g., coming from the same village or church) would create the conditions for successful small-scale credit provision. Loans would be limited for productive purposes, and would not exceed 10% of a borrower's accumulated savings. By banking accumulated savings at an interest rate of around 8% (during the 1980s), loans from the credit union could be charged at a 13% rate and still leave sufficient spread to cover overhead expenses (if not bad loans). Savings per member would have accumulated to at least Z$80 and in theory this would provide the basis, ultimately, for building a large debtor base as exists in the credit union sector of advanced capitalist countries (Radke et al 1986:55).

But this vision of an African rural credit union movement was never fully executed, in no small part because the concomitant imposition of market rationality was not feasible under the circumstances. The necessary mathematical and financial calculations that small farmers would have to make, combined with the difficulties in budgeting over extended (and highly uncertain) periods of time—and at the very point that structural changes buffeted the young nation's agricultural markets—could not adequately be accomplished by peasant credit union members in just two years of savings-discipline training. Book-keeping and credit assessment skills were in short supply. Transport, marketing, and other material constraints continued to hamper the productive operations needed to service loans regularly. While the Savings Development Movement ran a resource and training center in Harare, and a National Association of Savings and Credit Unions was established in the mid-1980s, massive expansion according to the visions of many savings clubs proponents was unrealistic (World Bank 1991a, v.I:186).

The informal credit that is available typically comes at a high cost (a 120% annual interest rate is typical) and generates extravagant allegations of small farmer capacity to afford high interest rates (but no firm studies to date). Some analysts (Reynolds 1987; Rasmussen 1990) advocate the rapid growth of community-based credit unions even under such usurious lending terms, which is consistent with a positive view of high interest rates in the international literature based on the notion that high rates force higher levels of productivity, mitigate against the tendency to "distort" financial markets through below-market rates, and enhance cost recovery (Fry 1980; Galvis 1982). One World Bank researcher's view (prior to ESAP) was that "real interest rates on agricultural lending of up to about 7% could be tolerated without major changes in the relativities of input and output prices" (Kydd 1990:27). There are, in contrast, market-oriented reasons for avoiding high interest rates: the relative pricing of financial assets becomes distorted to the disadvantage of productive lending, and household liquidity preference under conditions of uncertainty is also damaged (Beckerman 1988; Burkett and Dutt 1991; van Wijnbergen 1983). Moreover, Truscott (1987:10) reports, "Almost universally in Zimbabwe, interest is regarded with suspicion and akin to robbery."

The primary problem remained, however, not the cost of credit available to small farmers, but that in practice the monetization of the countryside through credit faced enormous practical barriers, even with the catalysing role of government. A disastrous lending record in the 1980s provides substantial evidence.

Small farm credit policies

After Independence, loan volumes to small farmers increased dramatically, but the Rhodesian system by and large remained intact (partly because of the important role of the Whitsun Foundation in promoting continuity in policy-making). In 1980 the CA program expanded by a factor of six over the previous year in terms of the number of loans, and by a factor of ten in dollar terms. Purchase Area farmers increased from 1,545 loans in 1979-80 to nearly 4,000 the next season. For those who could provide security, the AFC demanded "Notes of Hand," mortgage bonds, chattel mortgages and reservations of ownership on the crop inputs delivered by the suppliers. As the state paved a potential route into the rural financial market, others—including traders, tobacco auction floors, and chemical and pesticide manufacturers—became interested. But, noted the World Bank (1982d:7), "In almost all cases they suffered heavy losses, primarily due to lack of management and this led to severe curtailment of abandonment of credit facilities" by the various commercial suppliers.

The Bank and a host of other foreign financial agencies (KfW, IFAD, EEC, BADEA, DANIDA and the Japanese government) stepped in to support the expanding AFC programs. In 1982, a Bank-funded US$30.4-million AFC "small farm credit project" was developed for 27,000 CA farmers and 4,000 SSCFs. The Bank essentially endorsed the AFC's existing operations, and within a few years of Independence 60% of the AFC's "moderately conservative" and "generally competent" staff (in the Bank's words) engaged in small farmer credit activity. The Bank approved many existing AFC procedures (including the stop order repayment system), and in the 1982 loan negotiations won conditionality on the project which included: interest rates at or above the commercial prime lending rate (except for below-market seasonal lending to CAs for the initial two years); assurances on conditions of staffing; and that the Bank would be consulted prior to the appointment of computer consultants and acquisition of AFC computer equipment (World Bank 1982d:42,43).

One immediate result of the Bank program was an increase in AFC credit to CA and RA farmers from Z$15 million in 1983/84 to Z$35 million in 1984/85. Even before that point, however, it was clear that the AFC's small credit extension was in fact producing mixed results even on its own terms. On the one hand the misnomered "peasant miracle"—whereby maize production reached an unprecedented 900,000 tons in 1983/84 (a poor rainy season)—was attributed partly to market incentives that were brought to the attention of a select group of small farmers via the eight-fold increase in the availability of subsidized AFC credit (World Bank, 1995b, v.II:88). On the other hand, though, for those many farmers who were not able to compete effectively against LSCF economies of scale, default levels began rising to dangerous levels. Drinkwater (1991 89) suggests that the market incentive turned negative in that "the increase in credit use means farmers have to market more to stay solvent... At the national level the picture might look encouraging, but at the household level it is commonly debts not profits that are on the rise."

How did Zimbabwe's AFC program fare over time? Berger (1989: 1026) argues that internationally in such microloan programs, "While arrearage is higher than commercial banks could tolerate, only in problem programs does it exceed 5% to 10% of the value of the loans outstanding." In Zimbabwe's AFC program, arrears on long and medium term loans were already 16% in 1983. However, the more important short-term arrears rate was 33% in 1983 (short-term loans outnumber long-term loans by ten-to-one). Arrears were worst for SSCFs (33.5%), followed by RA farmers (24%) and CA farmers (22%). The African Development Bank (1985:62) appraised the AFC, discovered the high arrears rates, and concluded, "Credit at viable repayment levels is therefore suited mainly to the better areas." This too was a questionable conclusion because *within* each geographical area there were huge class, sectoral, and crop differentiations in credit repayment performance. The World Bank (1991a, v.II:178) acknowledged that "the AFC's lending is biased towards better-off communal land farmers" although the Bank argued that the bias was not any worse than in other countries.

The geographical differentiation of AFC loans is reflected in the fact that during the 1980s, three fifths of CA loans were directed to Mashonaland (with its generally better land), and only 4% to Matabeleland. In contrast, only half of the loans to RA farmers were in Mashonaland, with another quarter in Manicaland. Of AFC loans to SSCFs, 58% were in Mashonaland, with another 20% in the Midlands (Kydd 1990:104, 105). As a further complicating factor, one survey conducted during the 1987/88 season suggested that certain of the sites showed vast usage of credit in comparison with others. The AFC borrowing rate of small farmers surveyed in Kandeya in Mashonaland Central was 55%; in Chirau in Mashonaland West, 21%; in Chiweshe in Mashonaland Central, 49%; in Buhera in Manicaland, 3%; in Zvishavane in the Midlands, 7%; in Chirumanzu in the Midlands, 6%; in Nyajena in Masvingo, 2%; and in Mutoko in Mashonaland East, 7%. Geographical proximity to marketing board depots was strongly correlated to borrowing levels (World Bank 1991a, v.I:130-145).

Gender bias also contributed to unevenness in the AFC small farmer credit program. In 1990, Zwart (1990:iv) noted that "One of the most discernible features around credit is the lack of an educational package linked to the credit for small producers. Farmers are poorly informed about the nature of loans, the nature of interest and procedures relating to repayment. Moreover, all forms are in English." In this respect, the high levels of rural women's illiteracy must have been a relatively significant factor, and women may also have found it difficult to acquire the AFC marketing board card (a prerequisite for credit) and to comply with an AFC (1989:2) credit condition to the effect that the small farmer must be "full time and reside on and manage the farm." Although figures are not available from the AFC, women made up an estimated 30% of borrowers, a far lower percentage than the proportion of women farmers (Adams 1989; Zwart 1990). (Women's first chance to get widespread access to credit was in 1982, when the Age of Majority Act was passed. Later, the World Bank paid growing attention to women's finance, commissioning various papers in the Women-in-Development tradition and endorsing a Women's World Banking affiliate.)

Small farm debt crisis

The arrears rates of AFC programs did not improve over time, as Table 10.1 makes clear. The ambitious expansion program was simply not geared to the existing realities facing small farmers: unpredictable markets for small farmer products; barriers and bottlenecks in input provision, product marketing and distribution, transport and communications; drought; and all manner of other non-economic factors. The reach of the AFC programs was so ambitious, nevertheless, that at one stage nearly a fifth of the CA farmers were borrowers. But AFC lending continued at relatively high levels far beyond what would have been considered prudent, even to the point that arrears rates of over 50% were recorded in 1987.

After 1987, the credit began to ebb. The AFC lent to 18% of the CA farmers (a total of 94,000) during the 1987/88 season, and 13% (50,000) during 1988/89. By 1991, the CA borrowing rate was down to 5% (World Bank 1991a, v.II:187). (In comparison, most African countries achieved no more than a 5% penetration figure, whereas Asian and Latin American small farmers average 15% access to formal credit.)

The average size of AFC CA loans also declined by about half during the late 1980s. SSCFs followed similar trends, with the number of AFC loans falling from 3,649 in 1981/82 to less than a thousand by decade's end, and RA farmers witnessed a 75% decline from 1984 to 1989, as the numbers of loans dropped from 20,000 to 5,000. The World Bank (1991a, v.II:176) commented: "The sketchy data that are available suggest that between 1985 and 1989, fertilizer sales to small farmers fell by about 10%... From this it may be deduced that farmers have reacted to the decline in AFC lending over 1985 to 1989 mainly by substituting cash for credit in their purchases of fertilizer" (hence having less cash to meet other needs).

Small farmers were not alone in experiencing the contradictions of finance in the post-Independence period, as a brief diversion to explore LSCF debt and speculation makes clear. The AFC initially proved its traditional loyalty to white farmers by deferring Z$55 million in LSCF debt repayments and extending more credit during the 1983-84 drought. In fact, comments Stoneman (1988:50), "The AFC could have been obliged to foreclose, forcing a high proportion of land on to the market at the same time; but the AFC (and thereby the farmers) were bailed out by government." Nevertheless the AFC was viewed with increasing distaste by many white farmers, leading its chief executive to complain in 1992 about "a negative campaign going on about the AFC between several farming leaders and the press." By the end of the 1980s the real value of AFC lending to large farms was 70% lower than in 1980, and the number of borrowers declined to around 700 (from 2,526 at Independence). While the average AFC large farm loan size doubled in real terms during the 1980s (to Z$160,000), the arrears ratio for LSCFs also rose menacingly at moments when large amounts of debt were outstanding, whether from government or commercial banks (Table 10.2).

The growing LSCF debt burden was exacerbated by two other phenomena directly related to the rising financial circuit of capital in the late 1980s: dramatic increases in land prices, and trade and currency liberalization. At the time of Independence, according to the World Bank (1986a:41-43), "land prices plummeted and panic sales were common," a condition that lasted until 1981. Even in the mid-1980s, prices were 30%-45% below real 1975 prices, and (the Bank predicted) "the factors responsible are unlikely to change in the short term." But in the late 1980s nominal land value soared, as the general crisis of overaccumulation reached a climax in financial (stock market and property market) speculation. In 1990 alone, tobacco farms witnessed a 100%+ land price increase, ranches soared by 100% and other mixed farms rose 50%+, according to the country's main farm real estate agent (interview, January 1991). While this encouraged even more LSCF indebtedness, such price increases also made expansion difficult, and a leading tobacco farmer announced in mid-1990 that "the tobacco industry supports government's efforts to discourage speculating on land."

Relief from overvalued land finally came in the form of the generalized collapse of real estate prices. Yet by early 1995, LSCFs had again fallen massively into debt, with aggregate commercial farm loans at Z$3.2 billion, much of which was considered unrepayable (*FG*, 9/2/95). A year earlier, when the AFC was owed Z$146 million in unpaid loans by commercial farmers, the AFC's ability to sell the equipment it had seized as collateral was impossible because of poor LSCF liquidity (*FG*, 5/5/94, 9/2/95).

Unevenness in rural Zimbabwe was exacerbated in other respects during the 1990s. The key features of structural adjustment affecting rural land and credit markets were trade liberalization and currency devaluation. Although LSCFs understood they would experience higher costs on imported inputs associated with liberalization, their general standing as the primary foreign exchange generators in the economy (via tobacco exports) persuaded many that there was no way they could lose from ESAP (Moyo and Skalnes 1990). The consumer goods many had grown accustomed to—such as Mercedes cars and consumer electronics—would be in much more plentiful supply. With the transition to market-oriented agriculture clearly underway in 1990, *The Farmer* told its LSCF constituency of "the exciting things" ESAP had in store, reporting on farmers' success in retooling with ostrich ranching, roses, and exotic fruits and vegetables for European niche markets.[8]

Currency devaluation would have, the World Bank (1991a, v.II:15) agreed, "a skewed distribution of benefits, with the farmers in the commercial sector gaining more than subsistence farmers." Tobacco, for example, was well-irrigated during the 1991-92 drought and, thanks to currency devaluation, sustained itself as the primary foreign currency earner (until the price dropped effectively in half in 1993 due once again to global overproduction). Hundreds of LSCF farmers switched into tobacco, and most LSCFs grew maize only to supply their workers with subsistence foodstuff; the massive food shortages of 1992-93 can in large part be traced to the power of the Bank in setting agricultural priorities. The pre-drought sale of stockpiled grain (mandated by the Bank), the crash of land prices, the doubling of interest rates during 1991, a general credit crunch, and the continuing deterioration of international cash crop prices (already in 1992 at their lowest levels in recorded history) are just a few indications of the volatility of rural capitalist crisis and of the limits to its displacement in the sphere of finance.

As ESAP was progressively introduced, small farmers were meant to make up the difference in maize production, but an examination of the economics of lending to small farmers makes clear the limits of credit as a growth strategy. Crops for which a clear positive correlation between small farmer borrowing and yield exists are cotton, maize, and soybeans, largely because of the importance of fertilizer and chemicals bought on credit. Typically, financiers' costs of making credit available to small farmers are 15%-22% of the amount of the loan, including a 4% default rate. In Zimbabwe, the AFC cost runs at 24% due to very high administration costs (11%), with bad debt pegged at a low 4% as was the case in the mid-1980s (Reynolds 1988:6).

Yet to small farmers, even standard AFC loans of a few hundred dollars (depending on the crop package) represent enormous burdens when, according to one Agriculture Ministry survey in 1988/89, average net farm profit was just Z$735 (and non-farm income was Z$374). The average small farm had 3.28 hectares under crops, the net crop profit per hectare was Z$136, with the net crop profit per hour of labor Z$0.31. Maize was responsible for half (51%) of the cultivated area, followed by groundnuts (12%), pearl millet (11%), finger millet (8%), cotton (6%), and sunflower (5%). The average component of income represented by livestock appreciation and trading was Z$287 (40%) (World Bank 1991a, v.III:130-145). Truscott (1987:4) concludes that "the communal household economy rests on a narrow base and is fragile in that it is dependent on one or two crops or activities for a major source of income." Under such conditions, debt easily became a slippery slope to financial ruin. In the Midlands, Drinkwater (1991:217) found, "many farmers who have obtained loans through the cooperatives and do not have access to an outside wage income, have become horribly indebted. These are farmers who repaid their original [1985/86] loans. They have thus succumbed in just two seasons—1985/86 and 1986/87."

The World Bank, however, continued to focus on crop production based on credit, although its AFC scheme was capable of tapping into the small farmer's income stream only through the marketing boards' stop-order system. Stop-order repayment proved an insufficient incentive for small farmers, since it was relatively easy to evade either through the black market or through marketing produce via friends or relatives. Over time, such microeconomic financial constraints would destroy the basis for visionary credit schemes. The Bank, however, was simply not dissuaded by the soaring AFC arrears in the mid and late 1980s. As one Bank researcher (Kydd 1990:18) insisted,

> *It is known* that the financial requirements for production in communal land areas are substantial; that they have grown fast in the 1980s, due to production increases and technical changes in the direction of greater input use; that production of crops for the market and consequent requirements for seasonal inputs is strongly skewed towards the better-watered areas; that oxen, ploughs and yokes are basic items of equipment to which all households aspire as a "minimum kit."

The World Bank recognized the need to continue the small farmer credit program to meet the "substantial" financial needs of even peasants, but the difficulties associated with the arrears crisis became overwhelming. The watershed year for defaults was 1987, when the AFC's bad debts rose to more than 60% of total AFC costs, from 18% the year before. Thanks to government operating subsidies and government-guaranteed loans totalling Z$38 million a year by 1989 (by comparison with total agricultural subsidies of Z$170 million in 1989), the AFC continued to run a surplus (Z$8.4 million in 1989) (Kydd 1990:106). But the depth of the subsidies (Z$9.1 million for small farm credit alone in 1989), in the context of generalized fiscal crisis, brought the AFC under threat as ESAP was implemented.

From the perspective of the small farmer, it is more difficult to assess the perception of the AFC, or of credit more generally, given divergent experiences. Drinkwater (1987:3) studied the impact of the AFC small farmer scheme in Chiwundura (in the Midlands):

> In just three years of taking loans, their accumulating debts have already become a source of great worry to them. Women farmers with migrant worker husbands have been more fortunate in having an exit option available, by being able to obtain inputs through their husbands instead. Most others using credit, though, feel that for the foreseeable future they have little alternative but to continue to use loans for acquiring inputs. For these farmers therefore the struggle is to find strategies which will ameliorate the negative effects of credit.

Drinkwater found that small farmers responded to the negative effects of credit in both individual ways—typically by reducing their use of commercial fertilizer and attempting to acquire increased amounts of organic fertilizer (manure or compost)—as well as through group strategies: "In the farmers' terms, the access issue is not simply one of effecting the most efficient delivery systems of externally supplied and controlled resources. Rather it is one of expanding their own capacity to use effectively a combination of resources which they have more complete control over."

In RA areas, a somewhat different sense of the basis for AFC loan defaults—stemming from conflicts with the moral economy of land—was reported by a *Sunday Times* journalist (Mwale 1992:9):

> The resettled farmers felt that the Government was trying to run their lives for them and wanted to be left alone to pursue their former traditional life-styles in which they regarded the land as their rural homes where they would settle with their extended families, do as they liked with it, die, be buried on it and bequeath it to their children. This means they could go and look for employment in the urban areas, leaving behind some family members, even wives and children, occasionally sending them some money and paying them some visits. On retirement from their jobs, they would then go back and die and be buried there. If they happened to die in the urban areas, their bodies

> would be transported there for burial. Since such practices have amounted to under-utilization and degradation of land, the government sought to discourage them and emphasize the need to use the land to its maximum capacity for the sake of the nation. This led to a number of resettled farmers fleeing the resettlement areas with their AFC debts unpaid. They accused the AFC of "exploitation" through what they alleged to be its exorbitant interest charges and unreasonable conditions.

At the time the agricultural credit project was formally appraised in 1989, the World Bank "recommended" the AFC take action to reduce the arrears rate from 48% in 1988 to 35%, 25% and 15% in subsequent seasons. (AFC arrears, including commercial farm loans, had averaged just 19% until 1986.) The dramatic rise in arrears was due, according to the Bank (1989b:12,31), to droughts; an 18-month breakdown of AFC's computer system; the erosion of the stop order system; and the concentration of AFC officers in Harare instead of in the field. The Bank failed to note that to be found behind each reason (aside from the drought) was the Bank's own procedural approval and conditionality on the original 1982 loan. Moreover there was no mention of the fact that AFC infrastructure expenditure soared at precisely this point due to expanded staff and equipment spending, and was exacerbated later by a new Z$40-million headquarters in the fashionable Kopje district of Harare. (In 1991, in addition to a Z$25.4-million allocation for construction of provincial offices, staff housing, and the new head office, another Z$7.5-million was spent on other office equipment and automobiles.) Notwithstanding such precedent, the Bank approved another twenty-year US$36.3 million loan, and assumed that arrears rates would drop as mandated. The opposite happened: by 1990 arrears had reached 80% for CA farmers, 68% for SSCF farmers and 77% for RA farmers, and were also rising for LSCF farmers (Tables 10.1 and 10.2).

So it was that policy-makers and international development financiers discovered that deep-rooted contradictions in Zimbabwe's agricultural system—with regard to the uneven input supplies, chronic excess production, and unpredictable state-controlled marketing and distribution rules faced by small farm producers—are not easily resolved through the perceived "dualist" framework. In other words, recourse to credit does not overcome such contradictions, but rather displaces them temporarily. The AFC ultimately sunk tens of millions of dollars into small farm loans during the 1980s. Simultaneously, small farmers found new forms of resisting state financial domination—most obviously through outright default—and the underlying contradictions intensified. Indeed unless the lasting residues were cleared away (through the full-fledged devaluation of finance entailed in unconditional debt write-off) they would reappear again and again.[9]

Table 10.1

AFC ARREARS RATIOS AND LOSSES PER Z$ LOANED
COMMUNAL AREA, SMALL SCALE COMMERCIAL
AND RESETTLEMENT AREAS

YEAR	CA	SSCF	LOSSES PER Z$ LOANED	RA	LOSSES PER Z$ LOANED
1982/83	.21	.38	.11	.22	.17
1983/84	.37	.40	.19	.39	.12
1984/85	.36	.34	.19	.39	.10
1985/86	.35	.28	.07	.39	.19
1986/87	.42	.47	.10	.55	.59
1987/88	.66	.64	.08	.73	.14
1988/89	na	na	.16	na	.26
1989/90	.80	.68	.28	.77	.30

Source: Kydd 1990:101-104.

Table 10.2

AFC LARGE SCALE COMMERCIAL FARMER
ARREARS RATIOS AND PROFITS PER Z$ LOANED

YEAR	ARREARS RATIO	PROFITS PER Z$ LOANED
1983/84	na	.11
1984/85	.13	.06
1985/86	.22	.07
1986/87	.19	.08
1987/88	.28	.07
1988/89	.35	.07

Source: Kydd 1990:101-104.

In an effort to address the default problem, the Bank began applying more specific conditions to AFC small farmer loans in 1989. Initially a primary target was the agricultural services cooperative movement, which the Bank believed was receiving far too much government support (see Nyathi 1990 for a much more realistic assessment to the contrary). It was a relatively easy target, for by most accounts the 527 registered cooperatives were operating as a generally ineffectual means of employment creation for some 125,000 members (many of whom were ex-combatants), and there were few resources and little capacity to enter the formal agricultural markets. Genuinely collective cooperatives registered by government numbered 312 (with just 13,200 members), but less than 100 of these had actually been allocated land by 1989. Thus subsistence farming (far less competitive than sophisticated LSCFs) became difficult under the organizational conditions which the cooperatives faced. But the Bank's conditionality (1989a, ii) nailed the coffin shut for even those cooperatives that could have survived with government assistance:

> Government should formalize its recently adopted policy of gradually reducing its involvement in the affairs of cooperatives; the Government should not restrict competition among various input suppliers that has probably resulted in improved services and lower prices. The cooperatives need to adjust and rationalize their operations to meet any fair competition and agricultural service cooperatives should operate on commercial principles.

Aside from an ebbing of credit and a stranglehold on subsidized cooperative development, there were other policy shifts in the early 1990s necessitated by the AFC's increasingly disastrous financial position. In nominal terms, in 1991 AFC profits dropped 44% from the previous year (to Z$4.3 million) and although the value of loans granted in 1990/91 rose from Z$180.1 million to Z$229.8 million, loans to CA farmers declined from 44,000 worth Z$33.4 million to 33,000 worth Z$26.4 million; and AFC credit to SSCFs declined from 844 loans worth Z$4.5 million, to 761 worth Z$3.6 million.

And yet, even though it had failed to truly confront the growing arrears problem either practically or intellectually, the World Bank continued lending to the Zimbabwe government, but with the proviso that the AFC shift its resources back to commercial farmers. The AFC initially found little resistance from small farmers to such a policy shift—except in terms of rollover of existing debt once the drought became unbearable in 1992. Given the pariah status that its small farmer defaulters suffered, this was perhaps not surprising. Mandated to enforce the security clauses, the AFC and police increasingly relieved small farm borrowers of their meager farm utensils in the early 1990s, which were paraded before front-page newspaper photographers as a warning to others, but with no apparent effect. As AFC credit to small farmers declined, some companies—especially the ZFC fertilizer company—suffered and began to extend their own credits (Kydd 1990:42).

As drought became widespread in 1992, small farmer demands for rollover of existing debt grew. Some pyrrhic victories were won, for the AFC apparently approved loans in 1992 but these were soon canceled due to insufficient funds (*FG*, 24/6/93). In July 1992, a newly-formed Indigenous Commercial Farmers' Association requested Z$75 million in financing support, as well as changes in the rescheduling of loans so that "all farmers get assistance regardless of the type of crop and area." The Association welcomed the Z$400-million emergency injection by the Reserve Bank into financial institutions to ameliorate the effects of the drought, but "felt the terms and conditions... were grossly unfair and detrimental to indigenous commercial farmer recovery." A month later, the Zimbabwe Farmers' Union (ZFU) sought a Z$29-million debt write-off for its members, concessional lending rates for the 1992/93 season, a reduction in current interest rates, and grace periods. ZFU president Gary Magadzire complained that the ZFU had "on many occasions recommended to financial institutions a number of what it considered to be prerequisites to small-holder credit. These were a financial package that included finance, financial management training and a savings component" (*FG*, 24/6/93). None of the requirements were met.

Although the AFC retreated rapidly from small loans, it never shook the bad debt problem, which also extended to LSCFs. With the crash in tobacco prices in 1993, the AFC collected just 20% of loan repayments from 400 major tobacco farmers who had borrowed Z$386 million in seasonal and long-term loans. Moreover, fears of black market activity increased along with small farmer overindebtedness, according to AFC chief executive Taka Mutunhu, who assigned his officers "to milling companies to identify clients. Regular visits would also be made to AFC clients' homes to check whether they had sold their produce" (*FG*, 15/7/93, 8/7/93). In mid-1994, Mutunhu conceded that of a 1993 budget approaching Z$300 million, losses due to small farmer defaults would require Z$45 million in provisions, but even that was not adequate and by March 1994 the AFC was facing an additional Z$11.3 million deficit for small farm credit (*FG*, 4/8/94). It was only by halting the stop-order method of loan recovery in 1994 that the AFC managed to increase recoveries (*FG*, 24/11/94).

Notwithstanding the excess debt of the 1980s, the credit crunch a few years later, and a renewal of bad debt in the 1990s, the World Bank continued with agricultural lending. Its own interests in continuing to pump credit into the countryside were tied to the broader attempt to supply Zimbabwe with loans denominated in foreign currency, in terms of ESAP. Of course, to acquire hard currency loans for small farm credit during a period of currency devaluation made no economic sense in its own right. Government—and hence taxpayers—bore the responsibility for the foreign exchange risk in international loans. Government's subsidy to the AFC amounted to 50% of the interest rate spread due merely to the Zimbabwe dollar's late 1980s depreciation, which a Bank analyst conceded was a "substantial additional transfer" (Kydd 1990:3). And the massive 1990s devaluation of the Zimbabwe dollar required an even more substantial subsidy to cover repayment of the Bank's hard currency loans. Without a trace of irony, nevertheless, Bank economists Deininger and Binswanger (1995) drew the crucial lesson from Zimbabwe's rural finance disaster that "credit subsidies... must be eliminated in order to bring market prices more in line with the agricultural profit potential of the land."

A future in group credit?

The Bank's strategy then shifted perceptibly. The main Bank officer responsible for the AFC program continued to promote agricultural credit, but far less through the traditional AFC small farmer loan. Instead, two other routes were identified: group lending schemes, and pressure on commercial bankers to begin lending to the top 10% of CA farmers who produce some 90% of the maize crop (interview, June 1992).

There was no indication that the latter approach would succeed, however, because precisely at the time the Bank wanted to put emphasis on a more selective approach to credit provision, the commercial credit markets dried up entirely. No commercial bank loans to new farm clients were available in 1992, not only because of the debilitating drought, but because the Bank's macroeconomic structural adjustment team had in 1991 forced short-term interest rates up to abnormally high nominal levels (in excess of 40%), thus drawing funds into money markets and effectively destroying locally-oriented credit schemes, whether in the rural areas through the commercial banks, or for housing in urban areas through building societies, or for emergent small business.

As for group lending, the Bank's new emphasis on long-term development of this approach is important. Group lending—based on the principles that risk can be reduced through peer pressure and administrative costs of lending passed to the group of borrowers itself—has been proven effective in expanding the financial system under certain circumstances, with reported large-scale success in schemes found in Bangladesh (Grameen Bank), Indonesia (Bank Rakyat Indonesia-Unit Desa System) and Bolivia (PRODEM), among other places. In Zimbabwe, sporadic reports of success—including Z$400,000 lent by the European Union and a German foundation to 70 Matabeleland farmers with 98% repayment (*FG*,

12/5/94)—generated hopes for group lending. The Bank (1991d:135), after all, placed this financial innovation in rather grandiose historical context:

> The letter of credit, a contract that emerged in the Middle Ages in Italy, increased the scope of exchange and contributed to the expansion of international trade. By better defining creditors' rights in regard to a firm's assets, public liability companies—an innovation in late eighteenth-century England—allowed firms to take risks and attract resources to activities that otherwise could not have developed. Since the 1970s, leasing contracts have allowed enterprises to reduce the risks associated with large investments in equipment. In Bangladesh, the Grameen Bank found innovative ways to lend to low-income groups while keeping defaults low. This was achieved by establishing contracts that made the community, not only the borrower, responsible for payments.

But the terms of these arrangements—especially the issue of subsidies—remain highly contested. Even Jackelen and Rhyne (1991), two "market-oriented" proponents of group lending, concede that Grameen's highly publicized group lending philosophy relies upon subsidies of over US$5 million per year, since management "sees itself in the role of transferring benefits from donors to the most disadvantaged sectors of society." In Zimbabwe, Bratton (1985) argues that on classic efficiency grounds group lending is superior, but the precise form in which groups are constructed has a great deal to do with the validity of this argument. Bulk buying discounts had much to do with the group scheme's popularity. The partially-successful Silveira House worked on a "voluntary joint liability" basis, whereas early (and unsuccessful) AFC schemes required a form of "involuntary joint and several liability." Radke et al. (1986:xii, 91) suggested that "Joint and several liability leads to higher rates of loan repayment in very good seasons, while the voluntary approach produces better results in very poor seasons. In 'normal' seasons there is no significant difference between the two schemes." It was clear, they found, that AFC group lending was "not successful," with groups "in danger of collapsing." Yet like the AFC, the World Bank ultimately decided to base the expansion of group lending on mandatory joint liability, "which has potential for reducing operating costs and enhancing repayment performance." Aware of the danger, the Bank researcher also conceded that "it is clear that it is not a panacea" (Kydd 1990:5).

One reason is that joint liability credit is gender biased, since the groups are "composed of farmers who are generally considered the most knowledgeable. The people taking a strong position in these groups are men," as Zwart (1990:5) (a Bank researcher) found. There are, on the other hand, group schemes that are directly tied to production projects in which women have prospered. Truscott (1987:10) worked with such farmer groups (not necessarily having access to joint liability credit), and reported, "Women use farmer groups to overcome some of their own constraints particularly through gaining access to extra labor, technology (in the form of draught power and implements) and access to knowledge."

Nevertheless what stands out is the broader process by which groups form largely for the benefit of those—in the form of either state or capital—intent on further monetising the small farmers. This is easily recognized from a rational-choice perspective, from which Reynolds (1987:7) critiques the concept:

> Group loans are made on the basis of joint liability. This legal form gives apparent security to the bank, but works poorly in practice. Groups are usually formed just to obtain credit and do not have the discipline derived from other common pursuits. Hence when one farmer defaults, the others are left in a quandary; to repay their loan, thereby in part acknowledging their membership and their liability for unpaid loans, or to default themselves. Even if defaults are met, the group will have been broken. The difficulty is that group credit is, in its single purpose form, a device to benefit the bank, not the borrower.

Thus another problem with the group approach is that it can lead to farmers wasting their time and energy collecting debts from friends and family, not to mention heightened conflicts created in the process. Moreover, the "free rider problem"—in which peer pressure was not actually effective in assuring repayment—was demonstrated in one Midlands farm group where Drinkwater (1991:216) reports that "a full 40% of the money recovered by the AFC was actually profit owed to [a minority of] farmers marketing surpluses," following which many of the farmer leaders simply emigrated from the area rather than face the group's debts.

Finally, a potentially fatal contradiction in policy emerged: the AFC prohibited farmers from borrowing in group schemes if they were already in "serious arrears" on AFC debts. Since these included a good many leading small farmers (including village elders and ward councillors) who would otherwise be mainstays in the group operations, there was every likelihood the scheme would not get off the ground. Although the World Bank (1991a, v.III:146, 189) ultimately advocated joint-liability Grameen Bank style group credit, this was accompanied by the acknowledgment that

> In general, Zimbabwe's experience to date with group lending has not been favorable. The organization of groups is initially expensive and

> time-intensive, with residential training in group organization being provided for committee members and eventually, it is planned, for all members. Initial indications, after less than a season of operation, are that major problems have become apparent which will require time and determination to tackle.

In other words, the long-term solution (more credit for groups) for a problem (excessive credit flows to individuals that resulted in default) caused by the AFC and World Bank was prohibited by the very conditions imposed by the AFC and the Bank to address the problem in the short-term.

Conclusion: Do small farmers need credit?

At least one result of the self-defeating strategy of market-based, credit-oriented land reform was the embarrassed, near-complete absence of rural finance in the 36-page section ("Agricultural Sector Development") of the World Bank's 1995 Country Economic Memorandum entitled *Achieving Shared Growth*.[10] Indeed, "the development of a market-assisted land redistribution process will be a complex and challenging task," the Bank (1995c:36) went on to remark in 1995, as if only just discovering the task at hand (and as if, in citing the "complexity" of reform, preparing a justification for future failure).

Even if the profile of rural small-scale credit programs is necessarily much lower in Zimbabwe today, the approach, particularly as applied to women farmers, remains convenient—intellectually, politically, and financially—as a means for the Bank and like-minded agencies to deflect criticism that they are not reaching the poorest of the poor with their market-oriented development formulas. The Bank, for instance, announced a newish-sounding US$200-million global line of credit aimed at poor women in August 1995, just prior to the Beijing gender conference, leading critics to suggest this was merely a new "fashion statement." Replied Bank gender expert Minh Chau Nguyen, "Fashion comes and fashion goes but I don't think it is a fashionable area. Investing in women, particularly in credit for micro-enterprises, is a very effective way for reducing poverty" (*African Agenda,* October 1995).

But is credit the most useful input for African peasant women? The preceding pages have documented some of the more irrational, unsuccessful, and uneven of ventures aiming at the monetization of the masses of Zimbabwe in the context of a rural economic structure profoundly biased in favor of large-scale farming. In short, credit exacerbated the plight of small farmers and exposed their vulnerabilities to the vagaries of state interference (including pricing policies influenced by large capitalist interests and bureaucratic manoeuvers [Herbst 1990]), speculative financial markets, hostile weather, and external attempts to alter the chosen configuration of land, environment, cultural norms, material inputs, crop choices, etc. A top-down credit system such as promoted by the Rhodesian government, the Whitsun Foundation, the post-Independence AFC, the World Bank, and other such agencies is not, the evidence suggests, a product that is greatly appreciated by small farmers of any type. Perhaps, then, the most important conclusion, intellectually, is the need to transcend dualist theory in our conceptualization of small farm credit in rural Zimbabwe.

Certainly, the availability of credit assists in drawing small farmers into tightly structured capitalist markets, and therefore credit programs will invariably emerge from the state, development agencies, and capitalist interests (even if vast market distortions, high interest rates, and the like subsequently force out the least productive of these farmers). Thus if full-fledged monetization of small farmers is out of the question (for all the reasons reviewed above), then stratification is at least feasible. This, apparently, is the basis for the World Bank's (1991a, v.II:177,187) rather weak attempt to justify continued support for what was a manifestly unsuccessful rural credit scheme:

> Although it has been found that credit is not strongly linked to the adoption of what may be called high input farming characteristics, nevertheless, credit recipients are more successful (profitable) farmers. This may be regarded as providing some evidence that the AFC has had a degree of success in concentrating credit on those farmers which are able to make better-than-average use of resources, irrespective of the scale of their production... At the national level, there are strong links between use of credit and indicators of "market orientation" in farming and intensity of input use... For the AFC, this last conclusion is somewhat reassuring, suggesting that its campaign to cut back the number of borrowers is beginning to leave it with a core of good farmers distributed across the various economic strata in communal areas.

This sort of rationalization is aimed not only at restoring the status of the wretched AFC as a viable borrower, but also, implicitly, at restoring the dualist analytical approach. But the evident bankruptcy of both the credit program and the intellectual framework leads to another conclusion: simply, that it is rather telling that the following question is rarely asked: *Why do Zimbabwean small farmers (especially peasants) need credit?*

This is a particularly striking query in view of the implicit answer that most small farm borrowers provided during the late 1980s: we do not need credit so much that we will bend over backwards to repay AFC loans in order to preserve our credit rating. Drinkwater (1987:1,21) showed that "improving farmers' access to credit in Chiwundura has placed many of them in serious difficulties" which were compounded by "an overzealous launching of a group credit scheme" and the "doubtful viability of high cost fertilizer packages" inappropriate for the erratic Midlands climate. He criticizes the "incorporation" of peasants into agricultural markets through credit:

> Either it is taken for granted that it is in peasant farmers' interests to have improved access to these externally supplied and controlled resources, and thus to be thoroughly incorporated within a single, state-regulated national economy, or because incorporation is the main concern, it is an irrelevance whether or not such access is entirely beneficial to peasant producers... In Zimbabwe, few of those researchers who have even attempted to write from the perspective of peasant or communal area farmers' interest, have questioned whether incorporation may not be wholly desirable.

This is by no means a new issue, and the small farmers' response—widespread default on AFC loans—resembles rather closely the historical experience from colonial Rhodesia, as well as from other southern Africa countries where modernization approaches to development have been enforced. Ferguson (1991:58) studied a 1975 World Bank report on Lesotho, and commented on the ideas that guided the country's development strategy:

> In an LDC, where the cash economy is on such a precarious basis, there must be [according to the Bank] "a conspicuous lack of credit for the purchase of farm inputs," and it is obvious that "credit will play a critical role in all future major agricultural projects." It is never explained exactly why the need for credit is so critical. It is true that most Basotho invest very little in agriculture probably due to their intelligent appreciation of the low potential and high risks of capital intensive farming in Lesotho but this is usually not a matter of being unable to obtain the cash to make such an investment. Most families have access to wage-earnings or remittances, and this money most commonly comes in large lumps which could easily be used for agricultural inputs, but for the most part is not. Yet in the "development" picture, the need for credit is almost an axiom. Needing credit is part of what it means to be an LDC.

A similar degree of skepticism was also expressed by Sababathy Thillairajah, a World Bank economist whose critical study of the Bank's African small farmer credit programs was reported in the *Financial Gazette* in 1993:

> Those cooperative rural credit and banking operations in the villages

> with the least direct financial input from donor agencies did best... [My advice to colleagues is] leave the people alone. When someone comes and asks you for money, the best favor you can give them is to say "no"... We are all learning at the Bank. Earlier we thought that by bringing in money, financial infrastructure and institutions would be built up—which did not occur quickly. (*FG*, 20/5/93)

But, Thillairajah's colleagues would presumably reply, the main reason for the promotion of rural credit is to enable small farmers to gain better access to markets through increasing productivity, a function (so the argument goes) dependent mostly upon the availability of funds (and rarely on the cost of funds). Thus a primary goal of government and agribusiness is to help expand the scope of credit (Bratton 1986; Ndoro 1984). In particular, fertilizer companies operating in Zimbabwe have found that smallholder credit leads to greater use of inorganic fertilizers, and hence greater production (Blackie 1986:23). Nevertheless, Truscott (1987:7) reports that in one case study area (Wedza),

> farmers have generally improved their productivity *without* widespread access to loans. Certainly, the majority of members of farmer groups do not get loans. In fact they have largely funded their improvements in productivity from their own resources which are a) sales of produce; b) remittances and c) wages (mainly from casual labor)... Interestingly, the data show that savings *do not* supply any significant resource for production inputs.

If this line of reasoning has anything to recommend it, then Nabudere (1989:22) again provides an appropriate conclusion:

> The argument which then holds that the rural poor need agrarian reform in order to improve their own lot, but on the basis of credit which will enable them to improve their productivity and modernize production, has to be repudiated for what it is—A BIG LIE!... A correct policy must aim at *empowering* the people to use the land to produce food and other products for their *own needs* and those of the country. If such reform is to be tied to the *debt bondage* of foreign monopoly demands, even in the food sector, the land may be placed in the hands of the poor, but the benefits will accrue to the commodities markets, the banks and the petro-chemical industries which will maintain the credit channels to exploit the countryside.

All of this, finally, confirms the heterogeneity of rural households in their relations to finance, not only in class and gender terms, but more generally across space and (within households) over time (and through history). Clearly, this unevenness itself becomes a barrier to what may be an even more important function of finance in the rural areas: displacing the economy's—most particularly the financial system's—vast pool of overaccumulated capital in a manner that further expands and sustains the geographical and social character of Zimbabwean capitalism.

In contrast, a progressive alternative to this framework would incorporate several components: on the basis of collective organizational form, a financial system should be firmly integrated into a people-oriented development process—and in doing so accommodate all people (especially dominated groups such as women) in their quest to acquire socially essential (and socially-defined) goods in a manner that also enhances their struggles for control over their lives and over a fair share of society's resources. Sadly, however, the power to transcend official dualist policy and market-oriented credit programs in the context of a general crisis of overaccumulation is, at this stage, unreasonable to expect from unorganized small farmers in Zimbabwe; default will remain their natural response to the expansion of rural financial markets. And as desperate as conditions faced by so many indebted small farmers became during the 1980s, what lay ahead, under the economic and social changes wrought by structural adjustment, was still worse.

Notes

1. The permanent secretary responsible for land redistribution replied that in 1994-95, 17 farms encompassing 52,000 hectares had in fact been acquired (it was not clear whether this included a farm that Land Minister Witness Mangwende allocated for himself, or those of other senior politicians, in what became a minor scandal). The three high-publicity designation cases prior to 1997 involved farms owned by Ndabiningi Sithole (see Chapter Six), by former RF cabinet member Henry Elsworth (who had allegedly mistreated neighbouring workers trespassing on his property), and by Goromonzi mushroom farmer Garry Seaman, who, according to ZANU party officials, subjected his workers to sub-human treatment and called his dog Robert Mugabe out of disrespect for the president (in the latter two cases, the farmers denied the allegations and the designations remained mere threats). But there remain more than 4,000 large commercial farms on Zimbabwe's better agricultural lands which contain an estimated one million hectares of unutilised land that could be made suitable for redistribution (Wiener 1988).
2. In this respect see Sibanda's (1985) attack upon the dualist paradigm of Arrighi (1973:347), who once argued that "the extension of credit, which could possibly come only from European sources, to African farmers was hampered and therefore a constant lack of financing was bound to hold

back their development." In many respects, it is argued below, the overabundance of certain types of credit did just as much to hold back rural development.

3. In the mid 1980s, minimum opening deposit requirements ranged from Z$10 (Bank of Credit and Commerce) to Z$500 (Grindlays), and banks began limiting the number of free transactions permitted each month to less than five. Building societies, which had an even more obvious urban bias, required a minimum opening balance of Z$20 at that point, yet the three societies claimed 550,000 savings accounts, with two thirds of the largest society's accounts having less than Z$100. These smaller accounts were responsible for 79% of all building society transactions in the mid 1980s, but at an estimated transaction cost of Z$1.13 per transaction, so the usual retailing benefits of high volumes at the low end of the market were not necessarily realized in banking (Radke et al 1986:15,25).
4. Tellingly, one response of the Central African Building Society to this condition was not to expand the scope of services towards more efficient mass market retailing, but instead to move towards niche marketing of new "Gold Class" banking halls for the rich: "Set in luxurious, spacious surroundings, these banking halls offer a personal, free and speedy service to Gold Class clients exclusively" (*Financial Gazette*, 6/8/92). Similarly, Barclays and other banks raised the minimum balance on savings accounts to Z$100 in late 1991 thus shutting out further low-income savers.
5. Such schemes are similar in form to South African *stokvels*—whose roots are in 19th century Transkeian women's mutual aid groups that emerged at the time migrant male labour systems developed—and to other women's collective savings schemes that exist elsewhere in the Third World such as West Africa, Indonesia and Peru (Berger 1989).
6. By 1967 there were two dozen groups in the Catholic network with 2,300 members and £11,000 in savings, including four credit unions. In 1968, the National Council for Credit Unions was established with thirty savings clubs and eleven credit unions. In 1970, savings stamps, R$2 savings books and certificates were widely introduced in order to support the clubs, and interest rates were thereby calculated in a more systematic manner. By 1976, 500 savings clubs served 20,000 members, a ten-fold increase on the late 1960s (Smith 1984:7).
7. As reasons for saving through the clubs, most respondents cite the bulk ordering economies of scale achieved through interest-free collective financing (a fifth of the clubs were involved in gardening activities, with fertilizer the main item consumed); the possibility of saving small amounts (in comparison to minimum deposit requirements of the formal financial system); and savings discipline (fines are levied against non-savers, and competition exists through the "shouter system" whereby contributions are announced) (Brand, 1987). Most clubs engage in a variety of collective activities during the dry season: production of craft goods, soap, school uniforms and foodstuffs such as bread; gardening; contracting out of labour for weeding and harvesting; and raising of chicken and other live-

stock. Where the productive economy is healthy, savings clubs tend to proliferate. Drinkwater (1991:223) reports that "financial success [for savings clubs] depends on whether it can manage to establish a depot" for storing produce. In one province in Manicaland Province, 533 clubs existed in the most prosperous district, while two rather depressed districts claimed just 37 registered clubs each (Radke et al 1986:108).

8. Crocodile farming had represented a high hope, as international prices increased 200% in the late 1980s, but the booming industry massively overproduced at both the global and national scale, and Zimbabwean producers crashed in early 1991. Likewise, the ostrich market plummeted during the early 1990s, partly because of what the head of the Zimbabwe Ostrich Producers' Association called the "rather short-sighted" export of live birds, and partly because of additional local supply (an increase from 100 producers in 1989 to 250 in 1994) (*FG*, 1/12/94).

9. To illustrate, converting savings clubs and other collective small farmer organizations into vehicles for group credit, required solving this problem, since the arrears on AFC loans suffered by many of the more sophisticated savings clubs' members actively prevented the conversion of peasant groups into credit schemes. Formal group lending required both a track record in savings and a relatively arrears-free credit history.

10. The Bank (1995b, v.II:85) blamed the collapse of the various AFC small farmer credit systems upon "weak loan appraisal and monitoring systems, the inflexibility of the credit packages in terms of form and timing, many cases of excessive lending in relation to farmer debt servicing capacity, several years of drought, and a general perception among farmers that the AFC was not serious about recovering its 'development' loans." There was no acknowledgement that the Bank was in any way responsible for any of the first three of the five causes, however. As for the Bank report's (1995b, v.II:109) recommendations, there was merely one vague sentence: "The improved availability of credit, whether in cash or in the form of production inputs, has been shown to be an important factor in the commercialisation of smallholder production."

chapter eleven

Premonitions of Adjustment

Introduction

"International finance capital has, since the Lancaster House Agreement, been the major factor in the internal and external policies of the state in Zimbabwe." So pronounced Zimbabwe's leading political-economic analyst, Ibbo Mandaza (1986b:53), as early as the mid-1980s.

Most commentators, in contrast, cite the 1990 adoption of ESAP (the Economic Structural Adjustment Programme) as the point at which policy-makers—either through "homegrown" compulsion, or pressured by the World Bank, International Monetary Fund, US AID and other "donors" (an inappropriate term for what are in fact bilateral lenders with a neo-liberal agenda)—embarked upon a no-going-back switch from traditional import substitution industrialization to what was intended to be a manufacturing-based export-led orientation (i.e., an attempt to mimic Newly Industrialising Countries). The point is of potential political importance, for in contrast to those who harbor doubts about the "sustainability" or desirability of the local capital accumulation process dating to the mid-1970s, some "post-1990 critics" (especially Colin Stoneman 1990, 1992) have invested enormously in the contrary argument that post-Independence Zimbabwe harbored a coherent, successful economy until it was forced—or suicidally chose—to liberalize.

If one easily grows weary of Zimbabwe's "were they pushed or did they jump?" debate (see Dashwood 1996, for a summary and critique), questions of "structure" and "agency" in relation to international financial pressure are nevertheless explicitly taken up at the end of the next chapter. But to provide some initial context, John Week's (1996:116) summary seems reasonable, looking back on Zimbabwe and most Third World countries during the 1980s and early 1990s:

> The result of structural adjustment programs, implemented at the national level, is to deprive governments of country status. The effect of trade liberalization and eliminating capital controls is to render each government's fiscal and monetary policy increasingly derivative from the norm established across countries by structural adjustment prgrams themselves. If a government cannot run a fiscal deficit over (say) 5% of GDP for fear of capital flight, if the monetary authorities cannot set a prime rate below the London inter-bank rate for the same reason, if the state cannot tax mining companies in excess of the level prevailing in (say) Peru for fear they will relocate, then governments retain their country status in little more than form.

Regardless of the balance of local and international power, it is critical that we record the numerous premonitions of structural adjustment prior to Finance Minister Chidzero's July 1990 budget speech. For objectively, Mandaza is correct to prefigure ESAP in social and economic policies adopted just a few years after Independence (as previous chapters have also suggested). Moreover, with the Third World debt crisis unfolding throughout the post-Independence era, Zimbabwe's own experiences dabbling in international financial markets were indicative of increasingly universal power relations leading, in the main, towards accentuated uneven development throughout the world. The rapid intensification in the unevenness of "globalization," after all, coincides with the 1980s onset of structural adjustment policies, especially those central features aimed at manipulation of space and time, namely trade liberalization and financial deregulation.

There is a voluminous literature and confusing array of arguments regarding aspects of adjustment that bear relevance to Zimbabwe. Tackling this literature can be attempted, in this and the following chapter, by highlighting some of the most decisive aspects of Zimbabwe's international financial relations. For example, it was an early (1984) debt crisis that raised awareness (but no real contingency plans) about the dangerous path ahead. The growing role of foreign loan "conditionality" during the 1980s set the stage not only for specific sectoral policy interventions (documented here are energy, transport, health and education, construction, posts and telecommunications, and foreign consultancies more generally; earlier chapters covered rural and urban development).

In addition, the far more self-destructive loosening of financial and trade regulations was central to ESAP, although again precursors could be identified during the 1980s. Subsequently, as Chapter Twelve demonstrates, the failure of the first round of ESAP to bear fruit during the period 1990-95 can be understood as a logical consequence of dynamics operating at both local and global levels. The Zimbabwe case is particularly important because of its once-strong possibilities for resistance along the way, heightened by the country's symbolic role in the community of Third World nations.

The story begins, however, with a survey of the variety of alliances between international financiers—mainly in the World Bank—and Zimbabwean bureaucrats, financiers, and some national capitalists. These alliances help explain the surprisingly weak response of Zimbabwean leaders to historic opportunities in the mid and late 1980s in which there was a real possibility of catalyzing Third World resistance to international finance. They reflect both the difficult constraints imposed locally by economic stagnation, as well as the local class-forming process which was discussed at length in Chapter Seven. The result was an intensification of conditionality measures on loans to specific sectors of the economy, which then set the stage for financial deregulation, trade liberalization, and finally for ESAP itself.

Alliances and conflicts in Zimbabwe

The 1979 Lancaster House compromise and its various aborted predecessors reflected an understanding by geopoliticians like Henry Kissinger and (later) Margaret Thatcher, both that Zimbabwe's reintegration into the international economic system should be a priority, and that an infusion of a £750 million World Bank-managed "Zimbabwe Development Fund" (promised but never delivered) would be necessary to accomplish this by, in effect, bribing the liberation movement and the Rhodesian Front to maintain links to the West during a period when this was by no means certain. As Robert Mugabe commented at the time, "It seems to us as if its purpose is to bind Zimbabwe politically and economically and it would compromise our Independence" (Martin and Johnson 1981:255).

A revealing aspect of political transition concerned repayment of the existing Rhodesian foreign debt, which amounted to £102.3 million of pre-UDI London stock market securities and R315 million borrowed from South Africa during UDI. One pre-Reagan Era US Agency for International Development (1979:55-56) report to Congress suggested that Zimbabwe's debts at Independence would be substantial (deferred servicing costs were R$139 million in 1977 alone), with the danger that "financial resources are diverted away from development efforts and the provision of services which could benefit the poor." However, in what was one important early test of Mugabe's political will, the Rhodesian foreign debt was paid nearly in full. As the former chief economist in the Finance Ministry, Norman Reynolds, confided, "That was one of the crucial decisions. We had to have people talk to Mugabe to persuade him not to default on that debt" (interview July 1987).

A significant reason for placing stress on moderation was Zimbabwe's relevance to South Africa and the rest of the region. The Reagan-era US AID (1985:44) (as one example) displayed a strong geographic consciousness in the mid-1980s: "A successful multi-racial political model in Zimbabwe can set a positive example for peaceful change in South Africa. A successful mixed economy in Zimbabwe can have beneficial spillover effects within the region and can demonstrate an alternative to failed Marxist economies."

South African apartheid-era rulers were apparently opposed to any peaceful model (Hanlon 1986a, 1986b; Johnson and Martin 1989). Colin Stoneman (1985:10), moreover, noticed a short-term convergence of the programs of devaluation (International Monetary Fund) and destabilization (South Africa): "there can be no doubt that Zimbabwe's [1984] payments crisis was partly caused by South Africa, and that this was the means whereby the IMF gained a lever on Zimbabwean economic policy" (see also Maganya 1987). But the longer-term perspective prevailed, and once the ANC and other radical South African political parties were unbanned in 1990, they were bombarded by conventional wisdom to the effect that only an international infusion of funding under the direction of the IMF and World Bank, followed by an unequivocal export-orientation, would provide the breathing space that a new, highly unstable democratic government might need to ensure the continuity of capitalism (Bond 1994a).

Along with Weeks (1996), taking into consideration the global processes, we might conclude that the Zimbabwean economy's turn to foreign debt dependence during the 1980s was structural in nature, preordained to a certain degree by the necessary displacement of overaccumulated capital (in various settings across the world) into global financial circuits (Bond 1991b), enthusiastically facilitated through the bourgeoisification and compradorization of once-radical government leaders. This is not to say, of course, that the only important determinants of Zimbabwe's emerging geopolitical status were international financial relationships. In addition to South African destabilization Zimbabwe also committed a few diplomatic transgressions in the post-Independence period, which Herbst (1990:231) refers to as "high-profile statements with little actual costs." The Reagan administration cut aid to Zimbabwe on occasion based, for example, on a Foreign Ministry official's insult to former president Jimmy Carter on US Independence day (over the issue of Reagan's reluctance to impose sanctions on SA) and on Zimbabwe's 1983 Security Council opposition to Reagan's invasion of Grenada and failure to condemn the Soviet shooting of Korean Air Lines flight 007 (Anonymous 1985).

Moreover, the extent of Zimbabwe's debt dependency was continually mediated by alternating alliances and conflicts, especially involving the government bureaucracy. For example, although the World Bank's Whitsun Foundation proxy was looked upon with disdain by ZANU leader Mugabe during the late 1970s, a new round of alliances between local elites and the World Bank began forming in earnest six months after Independence when Zimbabwe formally became a member of the Bank and IMF. Another five months later the first major Bank loan had been signed. A year after Independence, six Bank and IMF officers appeared at the Zimbabwe Conference on Reconstruction and Development ("Zimcord"), organized by then-Minister of Planning and Economic Development Bernard Chidzero for the purpose of drawing in development funding from governments and international aid agencies.

Zimcord (1981:87,91) generated commitments of Z$900 million in loans and grants over the course of three days, and both Bretton Woods institutions heaped praise on government plans for the economy, including the extraordinary presumption that the economy would grow by 8% annually for the foreseeable future. The Bank staff were "in complete agreement with the diagnosis presented by [Chidzero] and in the documentation for this Conference" and the Bank promised US$120 million per year in new loans. The IMF representative was particularly pleased that "it is the government's objective to promote growth within a context of price and financial stability." As Stoneman (1988c:55) put it, "A perhaps cynical view might be taken that, in encouraging borrowing, the IMF recognized that it had as yet no means of exerting leverage on Zimbabwean economic policy."

By mid-1982, Chidzero was arranging an IMF loan but denying that "the IMF would impose any conditions as Zimbabwe was already restructuring its economy." Though it was "a sensitive issue not for public debate," he made statements to Parliament claiming "devaluation of the dollar is not imminent and is not being contemplated." But less than three months later Chidzero announced a 20% decline in the currency, conceding that it "had been under consideration for some months." Also in late 1982, interest rates were pushed up to 9.5%, a move Chidzero pointed out with pride to the World Bank in private correspondence (World Bank 1983a:Annex IX). Soon afterwards, an editorial by the government-owned *Herald* (26/3/83) complained that "Zimbabwe has a democratically elected people's government and therefore, the people, its supporters have the right to know what the IMF asked of this country."

The effective devaluation reached nearly 40% within eighteen months and was accompanied by cuts of US$200 million in development spending and a reduction of the maize subsidy. Other effects were quickly apparent to poor and working-class people: the price of the staple maize meal increased by 100% during 1982-83, bread 30%, and cooking oil 25%. The much-heralded public health program, which had seen state spending increases of 27.5% and 47% the first two years after Independence, suffered a 9% decline in spending in 1982-83, which reduced its share of the budget to pre-Independence levels (Davies and Sanders 1987:12-15). The main beneficiaries of the devaluation were agricultural and minerals exporters.

As austerity was experienced in many aspects of life, so too government's servicing of the foreign debt became increasingly difficult. In early 1983 Chidzero predicted Zimbabwe's ratio of debt payments to export earnings—which had soared from 4% at Independence to 16%—would "decline sharply until we estimate it will be about 4% within the next few years, depending on the world's economic position... Zimbabwean manufacturers would be in a position to capture the (export) market when the world economy reflated and recession receded" (*Herald*, 22/2/83). The World Bank (1982b:3) issued a report which concurred: "The debt service ratios should begin to decline after 1984 even with large amounts of additional external borrowing."

The bait was taken and large new foreign loans flowed into Zimbabwe. But in point of fact, even as the world economy began to pick up nicely, the predictions were found wanting. Zimbabwe's debt servicing ratio spiralled upwards to an untenable 37% of export earnings by 1987. Moreover, manufacturing exports (aside from ferrochrome and cotton lint) withered in relation to other exporters (Riddell 1990:345).

Indeed manufacturers found themselves in a somewhat contradictory situation under these conditions. Thanks to the inward-orientation and limited but powerful tools of financial regulation in the Rhodesian UDI economy, the residual power of national productive capitalists—particularly manufacturers—continued to fundamentally influence Zimbabwean political economy. Encompassing a quarter of national economic activity and represented by the powerful Confederation of Zimbabwe Industries (CZI), manufacturers were as fully able to enforce their interests as the export-oriented (mainly white) farming elite and the multinational mining giants. As Reginald Green (1987:264) reported, "The internal lineup is not stable—the Reserve Bank of Zimbabwe has for some years seen external debt service and external debt reduction as absolute priorities, while enterprises (who face reduced import allocations) back either rescheduling or replacement borrowing."

On the whole, productive enterprises did not do badly, notwithstanding continual complaints about the shortage of foreign exchange and the doubling of interest rates. Manufacturers had access to a World Bank Manufacturing Rehabilitation Loan (1981), a Bank Manufacturing Export Loan (1983), and the Export Incentive Scheme, as well as enjoying the very generous depreciation allowances introduced at the trough of the late 1970s crisis (thus keeping fixed capital costs extremely low). And they prevented implementation of a controversial 1983 World Bank deindustrialization initiative by arguing that, notwithstanding monopolies and high protection, much of Zimbabwean industry was indeed internationally efficient.

This latter conflict is a good example of how the material interests of Zimbabwean manufacturers inherently contradict Bank philosophy, and thus of how tenuous were the alliances between national capitalist class fractions and international finance in the early 1980s. In particular, the "Jansen Report," a study by Doris Jansen (1983:109) commissioned by the Bank, targeted iron, steel, and non-ferrous metals: "The country would save foreign exchange by closing them down instead of running down their fixed capital. The ensuing massive lay-offs of workers would be undesirable but a study of alternative product lines and more efficient use of existing plant and machinery should be undertaken."

The CZI's response was swift and sharp: chief economist Roger Riddell objected in the strongest terms to Jansen's methodological approach and conclusions. Where Jansen (1983:128) argued that "the ultimate goal should be to end price control and to let market forces set all prices," a tough rejoinder characteristic of (the often-sought, rarely-identified) "patriotic national bourgeoisie" was provided by Riddell (1983:21): "Both these statements are derived directly from a neo-classical perspective of efficient resource allocation in the context of perfect competition—a situation far removed from the workings of the present Zimbabwe economy."[1]

The rather fragile balance of forces at that stage mainly reflected the combination of endogenous overaccumulation crisis and exogenous pressures (mainly drought and increased defense spending arising from South African destabilization), which together pushed the Zimbabwean budget deep into deficit by 1984.

The first crisis

The IMF responded to the 1984 fiscal deficit by terminating a US$315 million line of credit (an action hushed up for six months, and then downplayed by Chidzero) (*Herald*, 23/8/84). Subsequently, reports Stoneman (1990:2), "the government took care to meet all debt obligations in full, without any rescheduling, and established a high (and rising) credit rating." Chidzero went on to organise what he termed "very constructive, friendly and frank" talks involving Mugabe and the IMF in late 1984, in which the Finance Minister denied differences in basic policy orientation, stressing mainly disputes over timing: "We had differences of views on the size of government expenditures on subsidies—not food subsidies as such, we have no problem with the IMF over that" (*Herald*, 18/4/85).

Mugabe's own recollections, interestingly, were different: "There is current pressure from the IMF to cut government spending on education and defence but the government has a way of overcoming this pressure" (*Herald*, 13/2/85). Yet within a few years the much-trumpeted education subsidies were indeed under threat as World Bank "cost-recovery" policies gained momentum. The budget cuts were hitting hard elsewhere as well; food subsidies, which had risen from 5.2% of total government spending at Independence to 7.7% a year later, subsequently fell to 5.3% by 1985/86 (Davies and Sanders 1987:9).

With intensified restrictions applied to profit repatriation (from 50% to 25%) during a forex crisis in 1984, a substantial current account surplus emerged in 1985. Indeed 1985 was a good economic year, and ZANU won the second national election handsomely. But renewed creditworthiness and Chidzero's continuing refusal to reschedule the foreign debt (against the wishes of many in industry) did not make foreign borrowing any cheaper.[2] When the debt payment/exports ratio rose to 32% in 1987, it was at a time when real global interest rates had reached levels of 6% (after an average of 0-1% during the 1970s). At this stage, Chidzero turned in desperation to Standard and Barclays for short-term loans, and attempted to improve relations with international commercial banks.

Surprisingly, however, Zimbabwe was rated only "C" quality by *Euromoney* debt evaluators in 1987, on the basis of the following criteria:

> Who holds the decision-making power in a country and what approach do these power figures take toward foreign creditors? Incorporated into this is the degree of nationalism and anti-Western sentiment displayed by key political actors and their attitude toward foreign investment and foreign business in general. This factor also encompasses the degree to which key actors display pragmatism in their actual dealings with foreign businesses and creditors. A specific issue is the politicization and visibility of the debt issue, in particular, the level of domestic hostility toward the IMF and how much this is reflected by leading power players. (Hughes 1987:1)

By such subjective measures, Zimbabwe earned "C+" on position of power structure, "B-" on political turmoil, "C-" on debt, "C-" on relations with the international financial community, "C+" on regime stability. Zimbabwe's sovereign risk rating was 47 (compared to South Africa with 38), largely based on the high debt service ratio and a debt/GDP ratio of 46%. Foreign debt at that point was US$2.2 billion, but *Euromoney* also noted that "Despite its rhetoric and a heavy debt service burden the debt issue does not appear to be politicized and no prominent actor advocates repudiation given the country's dependence on foreign aid inflows" (Hughes 1987:38, 39).

Nevertheless, intellectual critics multiplied quickly. "It seems the government was too anxious to establish its credentials with the financial world," Thandike Mkandawire (1984:40, 43) concluded. "Although the question of whether IMF staff or local economists devised the austerity program touches upon the very important issue of national sovereignty, it is probably no consolation to the victims of such programs that they are 'home-made'." Arnold Sibanda (1989:153) was more explicit: "Such packages reveal the ready formation of class alliances, and that a developing country that does not restructure its internal economy, and its relations with imperialism, will find itself forced to do so as a matter of course."

Even Chidzero seemed to confirm this: although Zimbabwe was "a blue-eyed boy" to the IMF until the 1984 budget deficit, the IMF soon created "if you like, a psychological-political situation which we can't ignore" (*Herald*, 23/8/84, 18/4/85). With such widespread sentiments, mixed with anger over the short-circuiting of the post-Independence socio-economic transformation, expectations were high that Zimbabwe would play an important international role in contesting Third World debt and structural adjustment during the crucial period of the mid and late 1980s.

The fiction of Third World solidarity

It is arguable that ZANU leadership won—and then squandered—far more significant opportunities to resist conditionality, both for Zimbabwe and for allies in the Non-Aligned Movement, which Mugabe chaired from 1986 to 1989. Zimbabwe's representatives also chaired the seventh session of the United Nations Conference on Trade and Development (1987), the IMF/World Bank Development Committee (1987-90), and the UN Security Council (1990-91). There were occasional outbursts at the IMF and Bank during this crucial period, even by Chidzero,[3] reflecting intrinsic conflicts between Zimbabwe and the multilateral agencies. But a brief survey of rhetoric and actions taken suggests that constraints Zimbabwe faced in challenging international finance were overwhelming.

The central issue was posed in the broadest possible terms in 1983:

> We must ask ourselves: How much pressure can these nations be expected to bear? How far can the poorest peoples be pushed into further reducing their meager standards of living? How resilient are the political systems and institutions in these countries in the face of steadily worsening conditions? I don't have the answers to these important questions. But if these countries are pushed too far, and too much is demanded of them without the provision of substantial assistance in their adjustment efforts, we must face the consequences. And those will surely exact a cost in terms of human suffering and political instability. A cost eventually to be paid by themselves and by the rest of the world, which may well prove far greater than the cost of helping them NOW... The economic distress of the poorest nations is a time bomb ticking away. We delay defusing it at our peril!

Thus the president of the World Bank, A.W. Clausen (1983:9, 15), addressed his board of directors, who proceeded to adopt a series of holding actions on the debt crisis. With no meaningful debt relief on the table, by the mid-1980s international financiers had reached mythical proportions in anti-imperialist discourse. Tanzanian president Julius Nyerere labelled the IMF "a neo-colonial institution which exploits the poor to make them poorer and serves the rich to become richer," and even Nigeria's military ruler complained of the "bad doctor who administers the same treatment to all patients, no matter what their ailments. Following IMF lending conditions leads to street riots here tomorrow" (*Herald*, 13/2/85).

Such complaints had little effect. Following appeals by Nyerere and

Fidel Castro in 1983 for a Third World debtor's cartel—considered far too radical by many leaders with substantial personal foreign bank accounts—IMF pressure on Latin nations was intensified in the mid-1980s in order to avoid a major case of debt repudiation, no matter what the social cost. At the 1985 World Bank/IMF meeting in Seoul, for example, the "Baker Plan" was introduced, and won Chidzero's praise, even though it would not apply to Zimbabwe due to insufficient foreign debt and relatively high average incomes (*Herald*, 6/11/85, 12/12/85).

Chidzero was subsequently offered the chair of the 22-member IMF-Bank Development Committee at the institutions' October 1986 annual meetings. The advanced capitalist countries were, at that point, searching far and wide for US$50 billion in fresh capital to bail out the World Bank (it later emerged that US$85 billion would be necessary). This entailed the appointment of a new Bank president, former US Republican Party congressman Barber Conable, who would be sophisticated enough to sell the Bank to hostile fractions of the US Congress and international political establishment. In taking the Development Committee post, Chidzero noted the obvious: "Developing countries are exporting capital back to the industrialized countries, almost subsidising them. We will have to do something dramatic about this" (*Herald*, 23/10/86).

In fact, nothing dramatic to halt reverse flows of capital was tried; instead the committee's executive secretary travelled to Harare in 1987 to bask in what he termed the "new era in cooperation between developing countries, donors and the IMF and World Bank" (*Herald*, 19/12/87). The only sour note, perhaps, was Chidzero's position against debt-for-nature swaps (which reflected widespread Third World nationalist sentiments, particularly in relation to proposals to turn the Amazon over to international sovereignty) (*Southern African Economist,* October/November 1989).[4]

Capitulating to nearly any initiative emanating from international financial centers, Chidzero accepted an inferior European Community debt relief proposal (later approved by the G-7 countries in Toronto) for the rest of Africa during his first Development Committee meeting in early 1987 (although he ruled out the possibility of debt relief for Zimbabwe) (*Herald*, 10/4/87). He advocated moderate reforms (such as the "menu approach" with its exit bond buy-backs, debt-equity swaps, interest caps, etc), and was clearly opposed to even raising the possibility of stronger relief or Third World solidarity (*Herald*, 28/1/88).

Tellingly, the 1989 IMF/Bank annual meeting was characterized by Chidzero in the following terms: "Curiously enough, debt was not the central issue. It was at the back of everyone's mind. But those who are primarily concerned with the debt issue have been saying: 'Look, the game is being played. Don't upset the apple-cart too much'" (*Southern African Economist*, November 1989). Meanwhile, however, the commercial bank loan tap had been turned off and even conditional aid to the Third World was slowing by the end of Chidzero's reign as Development Committee chair in 1990. Indeed, the transfer of net financial resources from South to North soared from nothing in 1987 to in excess of US$50 billion in 1989.[5]

This was also the period of Mugabe's portentous but ultimately overrated reign as leader of the Non-Aligned Movement (NAM). "Both [the NAM and the Development Committee posts] will enable Zimbabwe to provide an input into global discussions and negotiations on issues of trade and finance that reflected NAM and North-South preoccupations," claimed Chidzero (*Southern African Economist*, November 1989). Immediately following Mugabe in the hierarchy of the 1986-89 NAM was Peruvian president Alan Garcia, an enthusiastic though unsuccessful promoter of a unilateral debt repayment limitation of 10% of foreign currency earnings. The NAM 1986 conference in Harare produced strong rhetoric but no substantive collective action on the debt. As Zimbabwe Congress of Trade Unions general secretary Morgan Tsvangirai later complained, "At the time of Zimbabwe's leadership of the NAM, this was our worst period for debt servicing. We paid 35% of our forex earnings to the banks. But the government's priorities of that time were misplaced, so we missed the opportunity to lead the Third World" (*Southern Africa Report*, July 1991).

Another opportunity for action arose while Chidzero chaired the important seventh meeting of UN Conference on Trade and Development in mid-1987. He mulled over a proposal for converting debts to grants under terms of "co-responsibility" for the debt crisis, but ultimately remarked, "contrary to what some people expected, there was no confrontation between the developed and developing countries" at the UNCTAD meetings (*Herald*, 6/6/87, 24/7/87, 20/8/87).

There could well have been such a confrontation, as this was at precisely the moment that Zambian president Kenneth Kaunda publicly broke with the IMF, accusing it of "conducting a smear campaign" against Zambia. "It was our genuine desire to work with the IMF and World Bank," complained Kaunda, "and we did so honestly but reached a stage where the programs headed by the IMF became completely unbearable." The Zambian position was supported by Zimbabwe's *Herald* newspaper and by Zimbabwean Foreign Minister Nathan Shamuyarira, by public demonstrations of ordinary Zambian workers, and by the secretary-general of the Organization of African Unity. But without a concerted effort at

UNCTAD, Zambia ultimately succumbed to pressure and returned to the fold of international finance a few months later (*Sunday Mail*, 17/5/87; *Chronicle*, 8/5/87; *Herald*, 12/5/87; 7/5/87).

Shortly afterwards, at the September 1987 meetings of the Commonwealth group of nations, Britain's Nigel Lawson announced a plan to reduce the interest (not capital) burden of Third World debt, and the IMF's Michel Camdessus promised to search for more fresh loan money from central banks (*Herald*, 25/9/87). Chidzero overstated the gains from these inconsequential schemes: "Even though the new solutions were not always perfect, they generated a feeling of optimism among developing countries" (*Herald*, 5/11/87).[6] In reality, oft-made promises to debtors—new direct foreign investment, new flows of financial capital, better interest rates and borrowing terms, greater power and respect within international economic fora, a return to economic growth, etc, etc—in exchange for punctual repayments and endorsement of structural adjustment all generally failed to materialize during the 1980s.

Worse, evolving international trade relationships would make debt even harder to bear. Terms of trade fell dramatically from the early 1970s through the late 1980s. Then, according to even the World Bank and OECD, the December 1993 General Agreement on Tariffs and Trade (GATT) agreement would cost Africa a net value of US$2.6 billion in trading revenue annually by the year 2002, not including the social costs of associated unemployment and adjustment or the lost import tariff revenues. At the same time, Zimbabwe suffered the loss of the 1964-92 trade deal with South Africa (which privileged textiles), and in response (along with Zambia) raised tariffs on South African imports. Visions of regional trade harmony—either from the neo-liberal African Development Bank or the far more progressive African National Congress (as spelled out in its 1994 *Reconstruction and Development Programme*)—were likely to disintegrate as individual Southern African countries aspired to export-platform status or fell into submissive bilateral relations with either South Africa or their traditional colonial trading partners (Bond, 1997).

Thus, by the time Zimbabwe surrendered its leading positions in most of the international fora where debt could be raised, Third World external finances were in such tatters that what had seemed unreasonable and excessively cheeky in the mid-1980s—namely, stating the absolute impossibility of foreign debt repayment—was obvious. The United Nations "New Agenda for Development of Africa in the 1990s" even argued that the US$270 billion African debt should be canceled outright. The United States had, after all, found it feasible to cancel half of the Polish debt and US$7 billion in Egyptian military debt (the latter for Gulf War support).

In such cases, excessive external indebtedness served as the basis for positive incentives to support blunt American ideological and geopolitical interests. Of course, most Third World countries could not attract such incentives and instead were subject to the less-forgiving power of financial markets.

Then, in 1995, the unthinkable happened when World Bank staff let leak a paper promoting a "Multilateral Debt Facility" for Africa that would write off US$11 billion of multilateral debt (the catch, of course, was that recipients would include only those countries committed to orthodox structural adjustment) (*African Agenda,* October 1995). The reasons for the new proposal were simple. First, as the report conceded, "The fragmented approach followed thus far by the international financial community to address the debt problem of the poorest countries has reached its limit." Second, the Bank perhaps realised that it had created a bureaucratic monster in the form of 8,000 debt rescheduling negotiations in Africa alone between 1984 and 1992. With African finance ministry staff thus deployed, the Bank witnessed a corresponding decline in the number and quality of new loans negotiated, and with US$4 billion in new Bank loans earmarked for Africa annually it was embarrassing that by the early 1990s, US$14 billion in funds were still awaiting disbursement due to the limited absorptive capacity of many African countries' civil service (practically wrecked as they were in the early 1990s by wage, benefit, and morale cuts). (As noted below, such bottlenecks were also internal to the Bank, and Zimbabwe suffered enormously due to the Bank's failure to disburse 1990-91 loans until March 1992.)

No matter the merits of the case, the US$11-billion proposal still fell far short of Sub-Saharan Africa's total foreign debt (and was only a third of outstanding debt to multilateral lenders), although the document also expressed a vain hope that the Paris Club of donor countries and the London Club of commercial bankers might follow suit with debt relief.[7] Perhaps more importantly, upon mention of the proposal in the *Financial Times* in September 1995, the Bank's new president, James Wolfensohn, instantly clarified that this was merely a discussion document; he then failed to table the idea at the next month's IMF/World Bank meetings. Instead, under the guidance of leading US Treasury Department official Lawrence Summers (formerly Bank chief economist and author of the internal December 1991 memo arguing that "The economic logic of dumping a load of toxic waste on Africa is impeccable"), most of the donor country surplus funds which would have been contributed to such an African Multilateral Debt Facility were instead being pledged to a US$50-billion bailout fund. That fund, to be run by the IMF, was solely devoted to protecting international private sector investors who were sinking billions of pension and money market funds into the emerging financial markets. Such a fund was deemed necessary in the wake of the US$57-billion US-led bailout of the former structural adjustment poster-child, Mexico, earlier in 1995. Debate on African debt relief would simply be postponed again, until at least late 1996.

It was clear that Zimbabwe's role in the cruel international fora which devised and endorsed such redistributive, reverse-Robin Hood policies had apparently mattered very little to either the welfare of Third World peoples or to its own international balance sheet. Instead of being rewarded for adopting painful economic policies or for "letting the game be played" (as Chidzero had put it)—rewards perhaps in the form of debt cancellation in the early 1990s—Zimbabwe's ostensible honor was merely gaining access to additional, potentially crippling amounts of new foreign credit, tightly regulated by loan conditionality.

The omen of conditionality

The international financial agencies' desire for control of the direction of Zimbabwe's economy is so great, Reginald Green concluded (1987:255), that even when Zimbabwe declines to take on excessive short-term credit, "the Fund, Bank and several bilaterals oppose this apparently orthodox approach to the use of Fund credit presumably because it would limit macroeconomic conditionality leverage especially if Zimbabwe sought neither a SAP nor a Paris Club rescheduling." In the years prior to ESAP's introduction, microeconomic project loan conditionality was even more common, and was so widespread in most foreign-funded sectors of the economy as to provide a disturbing omen for the macroeconomic conditionality that was inevitably imposed in the early 1990s.

Zimbabwe was not unique, for as Joe Hanlon (1991:198) observes, "The IMF and World Bank have tried to muscle in and take a dominant role through 'conditionality'" in many places. In 1990 the Bank's chief economist, Stanley Fischer (who lived for many years in then-Rhodesia), explained two new ways to "maintain overall leverage" through conditionality: "slow disbursement loans" in which money is released only in response to agreed policy changes, and "hybrid loans" in which project loans are linked more directly to conditionality. In addition, "coordination" and "co-financing" are used to harmonize policy approaches and to leverage existing donor funds into World Bank projects.

To illustrate such ambitious conditionality goals, which reflect the agencies' aims of creating a free-market "enabling environment," recall from Chapter Nine that US AID found that its "achievements in project implementation have influenced the evolution of housing policy in Zimbabwe" (Abt Associates 1988:56). The World Bank (1995a:17) was ultimately to boast that although "During the 1980s, the policy dialogue between the Bank and the government was, at times, strained due to differences of view regarding the appropriate timing, sequencing and pace of macroeconomic and structural reform," the Bank's focus on sectoral lending gradually "fostered an awareness of the need for a broad-based economic policy reform" and "in conjunction with the informal work and advice provided by the Resident Mission, was instrumental" in shaping ESAP.

The World Bank—Zimbabwe's single largest project lender with more than US$700 million in credits during the 1980s—had initially provided loans "confined largely to sectors where there was some agreement on policy and where some success was possible in the prevailing distorted macroeconomic environment," as one report (World Bank 1995c:16) put it. These sectors included energy, railroads, agriculture, health and family planning, urban development, infrastructure and small business. The manufacturing sector was temporarily supported, as discussed below, by a US$75-million Export Revolving Fund.

But conditionality was imposed on many of the Bank loans which included: a 25% increase in interest rates for urban small businesses; an end to official support for agricultural cooperatives and tougher repayment conditions for peasant borrowers; and a veto of a proposed light commuter rail line for Harare's distant Soweto-style black township just as a crippling transport crisis threatened the township's future (Maliyami 1990a). Some key urban and rural aspects of loan conditionality were reviewed in Chapters Nine and Ten.

Although Mugabe occasionally protested—for example, during his first state visit to post-apartheid South Africa, he told parliament that the IMF and World Bank were becoming "less and less accountable" (*FG*, 18/8/94)—and his ministers often deeply resented the interference, his government did nothing to extricate itself from conditionality. As in the case of housing and rural credit, the same general lessons—the ability of the Bank to gain power through debt, and impose conditions ostensibly aimed at solving "dualistic" development problems through expansion of the market into undeveloped areas—are evident in sectoral lending such as energy, transport, health, education, construction, and posts and telecommunications, and in the requirement that foreign consultants be utilized. Each is considered in turn.

Energy

Energy was one of the primary sectors of Bank interest, responsible for more than US$150 million of loans during the 1980s. The Bank was active in energy lending during the colonial era, and at Independence immediately returned to the Hwange colliery for a huge expansion project that was essentially an extension of UDI-era plans.[8] A strategy for energy began to emerge shortly thereafter. The Bank (1982a:68, 71) and United Nations Development Programme conducted an energy sector assessment which stressed the extraordinary damage done to the environment through energy-related deforestation. The logical conclusion of this might have been to increase the retail supply of electricity to deprived urban and rural areas. To the contrary, however, the Bank and UNDP found that "income levels will not rise sufficiently to encourage fuel substitution by the African population" and that therefore "an extensive reforestation program is urgently needed." These conclusions were based on the assumption of "rational energy pricing policies" (to replace the subsidized rate structure then in operation), by which the Bank and UNDP revised the income elasticity demand for energy down from 1.5 to 1, which in turn justified a far smaller emphasis on providing retail electricity.

At Independence, only 14% of households—and virtually no households in rural areas—had access to electricity, due largely to the combination of Rhodesian racial discrimination and high connection fees. There was clearly room for growth in the energy sector through residential electrification—with resulting multiplier effects in electrical machinery and appliances as well as increased local entrepreneurial activities and benefits accruing from public health improvement, lessened deforestation, and women's time saving (in cooking and firewood collecting)—but this depended on a strong political commitment that would extend electricity provision beyond market determinations of affordability.

Instead, in 1982 the US$105-million Bank loan for the expansion of the Wankie power plant called for the Electricity Supply Commission (ESC) and Zimbabwe Electricity Supply Authority (ZESA) to raise retail prices by 60%. The Bank's (1982c:33, 40-41) objectives were to avoid debt-financing for investment until the point at which ZESA's debt/equity ratio fell below 60/40, and to keep short-term debt lower than 10% of total debt (both of which were provisions explicitly included in a nine-point conditionality menu).

The result was a flat energy consumption growth rate for 1981–84, by comparison with 9% annual growth for 1971–81. The Zimbabwe government, assisted by the Federal Republic of Germany, attempted to get a rural electrification scheme going in 1985, but two years later still only 20% of households were electrified. In 1987 the Bank granted a US$44.4-million loan for refurbishing the Kariba facilities conditional on "economic pricing for energy products" based on a study prepared by Coopers and Lybrand which anticipated an 18% economic rate of return (in contrast to an "estimated opportunity cost of capital in Zimbabwe of 5%" at the time).

At this point the Bank (1987b:14, 15, 19, 33, 39) expressed reservations over "institutional risks related to ZESA, which may have difficulty in properly and efficiently administering project execution," notwithstanding the fact that "the Bank has made a strong impact on strengthening the organization of the power subsector and its financial situation." It was subsequently revealed that Bank energy sector funds were being diverted by top ZESA personnel to London bank accounts (*FG*, 13/8/92). Moreover, from December 1992 through February 1993, ZESA defaulted on Bank loan repayments worth Z$150 million (*FG*, 18/2/93).

While ZESA certainly deserved blame for the breakdown of much of the electricity system in mid-1992—and for other occasional periods when rationing was imposed due to inadequate contingency measures—there was also substantive criticism levelled at the Bank. For example, Dan Ndlela (1984:73) found that local manufacturing linkages to the energy sector were virtually ignored in Bank energy sector lending:

> The metal product branch was perhaps the worst casualty of the foreign aid boom. Exceptionally large projects resulting from the external aid boom have definitely worked against the prospects of the metal branch, e.g. the acceptance of the World Bank funded project of the Hwange Thermal power complex on the World Bank rules of the best tender was taken without due consideration of the key role played by this branch in the economy. That these terms have been used to exclude local firms with a capability of constructing certain components of the Thermal Power Project does not augur well with building up national production.

The Bank's bias towards thermal power was revealed in the veto of a proposed expansion of the Kariba South hydroelectric plant in 1989. According to the *Financial Gazette* (19/5/89), "The World Bank is understood to be considering the withholding of all future loans for Zimbabwe's electric power projects because the Zimbabwe government, against expert advice, has decided to proceed with the Z$300 million Kariba South Extension scheme." Soon frustrated ZESA researchers complained publicly that the bias towards thermal power and other aspects of conditionality had resulted in an "apparent inability of the Bank to carry out timely reviews and decisions on ZESA's investment prgrams" (*Energy and Communications*, March 1991).

Furthermore, the Bank's external financing guideline represented "an extremely onerous condition as it imposes high tariffs on consumers, with negative consequences on the economy." In sum, the researchers continued, "*The World Bank's influence and policies in the electricity sector are therefore inconsistent with the Bank's supposed support for the country's economic structural adjustment program*" (original emphasis).

More importantly, though, retail consumers were the main victims of Bank conditionality on loans to an electricity system which at Independence had the potential to help lead a basic needs economic strategy, but which failed to expand to unserved areas and which failed on administrative and management terms where the Bank exercized considerable clout. ZESA was later "permitted to adjust consumer tariffs to cover specific cost categories agreed with the Bank" thanks to a conditionality on the second tranche of the Bank's (1995a:27) ESAP loan and, as a result, "large tariff increases [were] effected."

One result was that by early 1996, ZESA was only providing electricity to 21% of the population. Promises continued; within a decade electricity would reach half the population and within four decades all Zimbabweans would have power. This would depend in part upon a proposed 1600 megawatt dam and hydropower station planned for the Batoka Gorge, to be financed by the Bank (in the process destroying Africa's greatest whitewater river run, directly below Victoria Falls) (*FG*, 25/1/96).

Transport

Another example of the Bank's failure to properly carry through its own program was a US$43 million Bank loan to rehabilitate Zimbabwe's rail transport sector. Not only were there long delays and alterations, US$6.2 million of the credit was ultimately canceled. The loan, meant to raise the availability of locomotives in the National Railways of Zimbabwe (NRZ) fleet from 55% in 1981 to 75% in 1984, unveiled the flexible manner in which Bank project lending can swing in vain from objectives such as export-oriented infrastructural development (the original purpose) to what became the crucial subtext: ending government subsidies more generally.

"The key objective of the program loan was achieved but not through the means envisaged during preparation of the program," according to the Bank's own review (1989e:i, ii, 5, 6, 13, 25). "Since the problem of subsidies was pervasive in the economy and the effect of removals of subsidies on the rest of the economy was highly uncertain, government and the

Bank agreed that the best way to tackle the issue was to undertake a study of the problem in the railways and to implement its recommendations in a subsequent railways project." The Zimbabwe government agreed that subsidies (especially on transport of agricultural produce) should be phased out—from 17% in 1981 to 10% by 1982 and nothing by 1983—and apparently "complied with" all covenants in the loan agreement. Yet when the Bank looked more closely in 1989 it discovered that "NRZ's reliance on government subsidies increased throughout the program."[9] Also of note is the fact that, reminiscent of Ndlela's critique of the Wankie Colliery deal, Zimbabwe firms received only US$2.5 million in contracts relating to the project (7%, in contrast to India's 29%).

It was back to the drawing board for another round of restructuring in the early 1990s, and in its 1994 report, *Adjustment in Africa,* the Bank noted that the NRZ had now become a "model" for other African parastatals on the basis of having raised its revenue by 75% and cut its deficit in half after one year of adjustment (this was shortly after having refused to make payments to its pension fund of at least Z$40 million, or as the workers alleged, Z$196 million) (*FG*, 13/5/93). Meanwhile, tariffs had been increased by 50% over 18 months in 1993-94 and the work force cut by 3% (*FG*, 2/6/94). However, another early 1994 Bank report noted that the NRZ's financial situation was actually much worse than indicated in its financial statements (because the return on capital was based on book value, not market value, an accounting technique adopted because the Bank now insisted on an internal rate of return of 12%). Moreover, the NRZ's request for government subsidies—to serve as debt relief on Bank loans—would not help matters, according to the Bank itself (*FG*, 17/2/94). Indeed, the NRZ's loss of several million dollars in 1994 (at the time the Bank lauded NRZ as a model) was the result of "rampant unaccountability," according to Coopers and Lybrand in that year's audit (*FG*, 12/1/95). In February 1994, 48% of the NRZ's locomotives were out of service (Hawkins 1994:49).[10]

Health

With respect to ending state subsidies more generally, some of the most controversial aspects of Bank project loan conditionality affected areas where Zimbabwe was making progress in meeting basic needs, including health and education. The subsidy cuts that accompanied IMF macroeconomic conditionality were mentioned earlier, but microeconomic project loans also represented powerful levers on social programs, for while they did not reduce the scale of the programs, they often threatened to denude them of their ability to provide basic services at little or no cost to the very poor.

For example, a Bank (1990:iii) health-care financing program argued for an "increase in user charges" and the establishment of insurance prgrams as a means of reducing government involvement. The philosophy of cost recovery, initially adopted by the Ministry of Health in 1985, began to be applied with a vengeance from 1991. Official fee exemptions for the poor were erratic. In 1992, within a year of the implementation of user charges, the maternal mortality rate had doubled even in Harare due to fees imposed for ante-natal checkups and hospital care. In early 1993 fees at rural clinics were temporarily suspended as a drought-recovery measure, but by early 1994 the fees were reintroduced and increased (in some cases by more than 1,000%) (Bijlmakers, Bassett, and Sanders 1995–96).

By early 1994, Health Minister Timothy Stamps readily admitted that the (nominal) per capita spending on health had fallen by 37% since 1990 and medical services were now inaccessible to the majority of Zimbabweans (*FG*, 13/1/94). The government, Stamps said, was now "so miserly that we are killing ourselves because we want to save a few cents." Stamps called the Bank's 1993 report *Investing in Health* a "Catch 22" because it praised Zimbabwe as a model for health care at the same time other Bank ESAP policies were destroying the health system. Oxfam issued a 1994 report highly critical of the Bank on health policy, and as Minister of Mines Eddison Zvobgo observed in January 1994, Zimbabwe's post-Independence slogan "Health for All by the Year 2000" had become "Death for All by the Year 2000" (*EIU*, 3/94).

At this stage, a public squabble broke out between Stamps and the World Bank's Zimbabwe mission chief, Christiaan Poortman, regarding the health budget. When Stamps complained that the Bank considered health a social expenditure which "had to be cut" (*FG*, 13/1/94), Poortman took the rare step of denying the criticism: "Over the last several years, the Bank has consistently defended the need to maintain real expenditures in Zimbabwe's social sectors" (*FG*, 3/2/94). And by the time of the Bank's April 1995 *Country Economic Memorandum*, an entirely different tune was indeed being played. For poor households, the Bank scolded, health fees "have been high" and the fee exemption system "does not function effectively," with young mothers the most likely to be excluded by high user fees. Thus all maternal and child health fees "should be suspended and free basic health services, including immunizations, preventive care and [treatment of] infectious diseases, should be maintained." Citing a United Nations finding that 30% of Zimbabweans have no access to health services, and with infant and maternal mortality rates "unacceptably high" in rural areas and increasing in Harare, the Bank suggests reversing the trend in health spending (World Bank 1995b, v.II:56-61).

More generally, ESAP intensified Zimbabwe's (and indeed Africa's) health problems, for as Sanders and Sambo (1991:163) point out, "the current AIDS epidemic in Africa is inextricably linked to socioeconomic and political factors" attributable to structural adjustment such as

> urban drift, mainly as a result of increasing landlessness, and urban poverty as a result of contraction of cash incomes and inflation. Accompanying declines in formal sector employment in most of Africa have led to increased dependence on informal income, which for women has often meant resorting to prostitution.

Of Zimbabwe's eleven million citizens, approximately 10% were HIV-positive during the early 1990s, a situation that dramatically reduced income-generation and added new expenditures to the already overstretched budgets of affected households and kinship networks. The particular features of Zimbabwean political economy—such as the migrant labor system and the vulnerability to drought suffered by peasants with no access to irrigation—can be blamed for the high rate of infection, but there can be no doubt that ESAP exacerbated the susceptibility of poor Zimbabweans to disease.

Government's response to decaying health conditions and to adjustment-related poverty in general—aside from lower per capita spending, the November 1991 "Social Dimensions of Adjustment" program and the October 1993 "Poverty Alleviation Action Plan" (relaunched in January 1995)—was underwhelming, even the World Bank (1995c:10) conceded (at the same time it was judging ESAP "highly satisfactory"). As Bijlmakers, Bassett and Sanders (1996:70) remarked, "the proposed measures hardly involve any structural changes that may improve the plight of the poor."

Education

State-funded education was another important site of struggle over loan conditionality. Facing the first debt and conditionality crisis in 1984, Mugabe explained that "The argument put forward by the IMF is that the money should be used in the productive sector but we insist that education is equally productive since it produces men [sic] who serve in all sectors of the economy" (*Herald*, 13/2/85). There followed a sustained attack by international funders on various aspects of Zimbabwe education policy, ranging from teachers' salaries to school computers. Education Minister Fay Chung (1992:20) complained, "The Zimbabwe government insisted on maintaining its pay scales, although the World Bank equally adamantly insisted that too much education and overpaid teachers were the main causes of Zimbabwe's budget deficit... Today the World Bank is advising us to retain unqualified teachers, not because it is educationally better to do so, but because it is financially better to do so."

Chung, however, was by no means against the Bank's overall approach to education, including cost recovery.[11] It is noteworthy that in contrast, the CZI publicly rejected the introduction of school fees at primary level as "detrimental to ESAP in that the future employment of children dropping out of school for failure to pay school fees would be severely affected, thereby creating a shortage of badly needed trained manpower" (*FG*, 12/12/91).[12] But Chung's opposition to certain aspects of conditionality was well known. Political scientist Jonathan Moyo (*FG*, 9/7/92) noted that her removal from her ministerial position in mid-1992 "has fuelled theories that the demotion was because of her opposition to World Bank policies on education."

But in the 1995 *Country Economic Memorandum*, the Bank again appeared to get the message, acknowledging that "the quality of education has suffered in recent years due to budget cutbacks." Spending on primary schooling fell from 5% of GDP during the late 1980s to 3.6% in 1994, and should, the Bank suggested, be raised back to 4%-4.5%. Moreover, the new school and exam fees "are causing serious hardships for low-income households," and primary fees should thus be canceled in high-density suburbs (World Bank 1995b, v.II:50-56).[13] The Bank (1995c:29) also acknowledged that "The introduction of school fees has led to concerns that poorer parents may limit the number of children educated and further the existing gender bias, which favors the education of boys."

Construction

It would be a mistake, hence, to suppose that the Bank had a monolithic market-driven (gender-insensitive) approach to all aspects of the economy and society, particularly in view of the "kinder, gentler Bank" strategy unveiled in the 1995 *Country Economic Memorandum*.[14] On occasion the Bank applied conditionality of a rather different sort than that described above. For example, the Bank (1995a:33) had prohibited use of its ESAP financing for the import of tobacco processing machinery, due to the health effects of smoking. Another example is the Bank's support for what it termed "affirmative action" in the construction industry.

The 1991 Bank loan of the equivalent of Z$100 million to support the Zimbabwean construction industry carried with it conditionality to the effect that black contractors get preferential treatment on major tenders for all public sector works.[15] How did the affirmative action program fare?

The code was formally introduced in 1993, and required that all government construction projects below Z$10 million (later Z$3 million) be contracted to members of the Zimbabwe Building Contractors Association (ZBCA)[16] and that provisions be made on larger contracts to subcontract at least 7.5% to its members. More than 360 black contractors joined the ZBCA, but 300 of these failed to renew their membership a year later because only three companies received the bulk of the benefits. As Simbarashe Makunike (1994:4) observed, "A lot of the contractors have watched with resentment and frustration the creation of elite black contractors and the invasion of their market by some foreign contractors, mostly from the former Eastern European countries."

Major construction firms responded to the code by selling or offering shares to indigenous entrepreneurs. Emblematic of the process and outcome was the case of Leo Mugabe, the president's nephew, who bought a 51% stake in Wallen Construction (insisting, at the same time, that he would "never be a front for anybody"). In 1994, Leo Mugabe successfully intervened to force a reevaluation of construction bids for a new Harare International Airport, with support from most of the cabinet, and in 1995 his syndicate won formal approval for what would be a Z$1.2 billion project even though it finished behind three other tender offers in the ratings and was described by Ministry of Transport officials as architecturally "overscaled and ill-considered" and as entailing "one of the least desirable procurement methods" (*FG*, 16/12/93; 19/10/95).

Posts and telecommunications

It would also be a mistake to discount the role of resistance to the Bank offered by those in the bureaucracy who had both different visions (and in some cases material interests), and a sense of the long-term implications for their jobs.[17] For example, a 1990 Bank study (financed by Japan) on proposed Cotton Marketing Board adjustments was, a year later, "gathering dust at the Ministry of Agriculture," according to one report (*Herald*, 4/7/91). Moreover, the Bank did not get its way on proposals to restructure the National Parks and Wildlife Management in 1994, as opposition from hunting tour operator (and Vice President) Joshua Nkomo materialized (*FG*, 24/11/94). When in 1994 the Bank's International Finance Corporation prepared a privatization package for the government-owned Sabi Gold Mine, this was also rejected (*FG*, 15/12/94). And, conceded the Bank (1995c:31) ruefully, "due to government's reluctance, the Bank was not able to prepare or provide support for a comprehensive public expenditure review [during the first phase of ESAP], which was critically needed prior to major budgetary cuts."

Perhaps most revealing of intragovernmental power relations is that when the Bank over-reached on privatization—for example in its initial effort to split the Posts and Telecommunications Corporation (PTC) into a (profitable) phone company and a severely-rationalized postal service acting on cost recovery principles[18]—sufficiently strong resistance emerged from within the parastatal itself. Yet that particular suggestion was opposed by the PTC board not out of its desire to better serve the Zimbabwean public, but on grounds that "it is a strategic industry." The majority of Zimbabweans without personal telephone access who would logically have united with the board—for fear that Bank recommendations would forever preclude expanding services to the poor, as is the case internationally—were prevented from doing so because PTC acting chairman Edward Makoni initially lied when he denied a *Financial Gazette* report on the proposed privatization.[19]

Jonathan Moyo (1992:4) responded, "Just imagine the chaos that would result from this proposal!" In the spotlight, suddenly, was not merely the economic philosophy of privatization, but the broader question of the social distribution of the country's resources:

> Maybe the World Bank's rationale is that Zimbabweans will get their mail at workplaces. The trouble with that assumption is that it fails to recognise that, because of other World Bank policies, many have no workplaces because they are unemployed or are about to be retrenched. No sensible Zimbabwean politician would run for public office on the platform that if elected he would ensure that the PTC does not deliver mail to the homes of citizens as a cost-recovery measure. Only an unaccountable foreign institution such as the World Bank would insist on such measures and this goes to show that, contrary to its propaganda about structural adjustment with a human face, the World Bank is in point of fact an enemy of democracy.

Later, an opening emerged for private cell-phone systems (against government's wishes) when in 1995 the Supreme Court deemed the PTC's erratic phone service monopoly to be a violation of constitutional rights of expression. This would have much the same effect as privatization in intensifying the PTC's latent commercial instincts, and would further exacerbate unequal access to telecommunications between the small elite market and the vast majority of Zimbabweans. Fearful of private sector competition (in particular, an alliance between Strive Masiyiwa and two foreign companies) and probably desiring an option for state officials and friends to get in on the cell phone action, the government temporarily squashed the initiative, again anecdotally suggesting the occasional limits of international financial power against local bureaucratic and patronage-related sabotage.

Consultancies

Another aspect of conditionality that riled leading Zimbabweans was the Bank's habit of force-feeding consultants, usually foreign-based with good personal connections to Bank staff.[20] It was becoming obvious that "The donors and African governments together have, in effect, undermined capacity building in Africa. They are undermining it faster than they are building it, or at least as fast," acknowledged the Bank's Africa chief, Edward Jaycox, at a Washington, DC conference in 1993. Technical assistance "is not welcome, there is no demand for it really, except on the donor side," he conceded, while promising, "We are not going to write these [macroeconomic and sectoral] plans anymore. This is a wake up call on that. We are not going to do that anymore. Africa will have to find that domestic capacity" (*FG*, 27/5/93).

And yet in a 1994 review of its housing program, the Bank (1994:11) rigidly criticized the Zimbabwe government for rejecting its advice that the huge sum of US$7.5 million—a full 20% of the US$36.5 million Urban I loan—be spent on consultants to help implement the poorly-designed program.[21] To enhance government cost recovery on the agricultural services prgram, the Bank deployed the most controversial foreign consultant Zimbabwe had ever suffered, Doris Jansen (who wrote the 1983 report CZI feared would deindustrialise Zimbabwe), for the purpose of measuring—again using the discredited domestic resource cost methodology—where to seek a greater return on public investments in small farmer irrigation (World Bank 1995b, v.II:109). And by 1995 the *Financial Gazette* (9/11/95) expressed annoyance that the Bank and IMF

> have mooted another suspicious idea of recruiting retired banking "experts" to serve in needy countries... Obviously these jobless men and women, grouped under a new World Bank organization named the Senior Volunteer Advisory Service, will be transported, housed and salaried out of the donor funds granted to the recipient country by the World Bank itself. Thus it is being said that the new scheme is an attempt by the World Bank to create jobs in the Third World for the jobless aged from donor nations. What most developing countries need today is tightly focused funding aimed at greater self-sufficiency, not elderly advisors alien to the needs and conditions of recipient countries.

What is important in all of these examples of project and sectoral conditionality is not merely the specific issue at hand, but also the evidence of the Bank's ability to recommend and usually (though not always) enforce changes in government policy. It should be clear from the examples, as well, that the Bank sometimes went about its work in a seemingly haphazard manner. Yet there were at least two areas where conditionality was both consistent and unyielding: trade liberalization and financial deregulation. The early manifestations of pressure in these areas will be examined next, beginning with finance.

Financial regulation and monetary stability

Even though ESAP was crafted to suit the wishes of global-scale banks and corporations, their domination of time (through finance) and space (through trade) would not be an easy accomplishment in a country whose state financial controls and import-export system had together developed as one of the world's most rigorous regulatory regimes during the 1960s and 1970s. It is appropriate to consider the Zimbabwean government's finance and monetary policies in this recent historical context, for a full decade of pressure was required before international financiers fundamentally weakened the system inherited from Rhodesia. During the 1980s, a number of short-term financial management measures were gradually taken—of which steady interest rate increases and a few non-interest controls of financial ratios (when it was necessary to stave off crisis) were the most important—which led, ultimately, to the full-fledged deregulation of finance and establishment of high, positive real interest rates alongside trade liberalization and price decontrol during the 1990s era ESAP.

Upon taking power, Zimbabwe's state financial bureaucracy maintained the bulk of Rhodesian-era regulations over financial institutions and even added a few others. The additional controls stemmed from the Finance Ministry's realization, from early 1984, that growing imbalances in flows of financial funds would have to be dealt with in an interventionist manner. As noted in Chapter Eight, this was a result of increasingly speculative economic tendencies and growing inequality in access to financial assets. Zimbabwe was also faced with a foreign exchange crisis at that stage which required proactive measures to prevent outflows of corporate profits and foreign share investment funds.

In March 1984, for example, the Finance Ministry acquired Z$200 million in overseas stock market shares privately held by Zimbabweans, and also imposed a variety of other stringent "blocked funds" controls on foreign remittances (including the pension benefits of ex-Rhodesians). The occasional tightening of exchange control regulations generated some grumbling among elites, but all things considered the regulations were supported by domestic capital in view of chronic foreign exchange shortages (which in turn stemmed, in large part, from excessive post-Independence luxury consumption imports by the minority of wealth-holders; the trade-off was evident enough). For capital, a reassuring conclusion about those interventions was offered by accountants Deloitte Touche (1990:5): "A close analysis of post-Independence Zimbabwe reveals a pragmatic and indeed conservative government policy as far as monetary and financial strategies are concerned."

This attitude was also evident with respect to new institutions created by the Finance Ministry and Reserve Bank to support financial, trade and local commercial liberalization (e.g., the Zimbabwe Investment Centre in 1987, the Indigenous Business Development Centre in 1990, and Zimtrade and the Venture Capital Company of Zimbabwe in 1991). Some of the post-Independence financial institutions aimed at expanding financing to indigenous businesses were examined in Chapter Seven. In addition, it must be added that during the early years of ESAP, Zimtrade nearly closed down due to delays in the provision of anticipated government support, while the Zimbabwe Investment Centre was criticized for neither succeeding in reducing red tape nor for reversing the disinvestment trend (*FG*, 19/9/91, 4/6/92).

Regarding the "pragmatic and indeed conservative" monetary and financial regulation, there are several categories to consider, which broadly fit a chronological evolution of policy choices. On the one hand, the state maintained an unsure hand on the reins of financial capital, ensuring that its only routes for speculative investment were at least local ones (the stock exchange and real estate), as opposed to following international capital flight to offshore financial centers, as was underway across most of the Third World at the time. On the other hand, however, the strategic direction of the new policies was set at a bad time in the early 1980s, during a brief period of excessive monetary laxity. The tools utilized—mainly manipulation of interest rates and requirements relating to liquid assets and prescribed assets—did not address the underlying problems of productive sector overaccumulation and its displacement into financial circuits.

In 1980, the money supply (M1) rose by 34%, in part because of deficit-financing directly through the banks. In February 1981 the Reserve Bank imposed the first Bank Rate increases in two decades (from 4.5% to 6%) The next rate increase, from 6% to 9%, quickly followed in mid-1981 and had a dramatic impact on liquidity in the economy, as the money supply declined by 10%. In August 1982, further measures were adopted and M1 growth declined abruptly while M2 increased by just 1% from September 1982 to September 1983 (compared to a 19% increase over the previous twelve months).[22] The *Economist's* (21/8/84) comments on Zimbabwe's monetary slowdown are revealing: "To an outsider, that looks like overkill."

By late 1983 the deep recession forced a reversal of monetary strategy. Commercial banks' minimum liquid asset ratio was dropped from 35% to 30% (though it was increased again to 40% in the late 1980s). The banks lent much more aggressively during 1983, increasing their outstanding advances from Z$375 million to Z$450 million. The drought-ridden agricultural sector borrowed 50% more, as did the distribution sector (RAL *EGE*, December 1983, March 1984). Indeed, as shown in Chapter Eight, bank liquidity remained high throughout much of the decade, as reinvestment of profits into new plant and equipment was spurned by productive capital. As the government's budget deficit mounted in the mid-1980s, the Reserve Bank in 1987 forced banks to buy 91-day, non-interest bearing (and non-liquid) "special bills" to mop up liquidity and to finance government.

Such non-interest regulatory controls "caused banks the most headaches," according to bank economist Girdlestone (1990). But both interest rate changes and non-interest controls were ultimately ineffectual in addressing the tensions between rising financial and declining productive circuits of capital. In sum, the sorts of policies adopted in the early years of Independence were badly suited to addressing the underlying problem of emerging financial overaccumulation (which in turn largely reflected the limits to reinvestment of productive capital). The subsequent higher interest rates and monetary tightening had an unwanted effect on both growth (especially in the black housing market, as described in Chapter Nine) and, surprisingly, inflation.

Inflation quickly became a key monetary target, notwithstanding the fact that, according to Rob Davies (1983:7), "in Zimbabwe there does not appear to be even a statistical relationship" between money supply and inflation, much less a causal relationship. The deeper-rooted problems in the economy—such as corporate concentration and disproportionalities stemming from generalized overaccumulation—were not seriously addressed, and instead a temporal fix began to emerge through expanding financial markets. State policies could seemingly only adapt to such financial expansion—misdirecting it into speculative markets through the higher interest rate structure—rather than attempting to control it and channel it more effectively into the productive circuit of capital.

Thus even as rising inflation dragged real interest rates down to negative levels, the Finance Ministry and Reserve Bank reduced financial capital's earnings through higher liquidity requirements (which meant banks had to maintain more cash in their vaults) and prescribed asset requirements (by which institutional investors had to invest a larger share of their assets in government securities). Yet the banks apparently deemed this situation acceptable, for meanwhile, their rate spread (the difference between what banks charge borrowers and what they pay savers) increased substantially. Speculative investment markets had become extremely attractive, and banks prospered through increased loans for trading in real estate and share. Moreover, sufficient amounts of the banks' "substantial" profits continued to accrue to overseas headquarters (Government of Zimbabwe 1990). The financial system remained "nicely protected and profitable," the World Bank (1989d:23,56) confirmed, in part because "the depth of the country's capital market places Zimbabwe ahead of many countries, including Chile, Korea, India, Singapore and Greece."

Thus although the state intervened in the financial markets, it largely corroborated rather than challenged the markets' dynamics. Prescribed assets were an important example of the temporary equilibrium established between financial control and speculation in the context of the deeper crisis of overaccumulation. Notwithstanding prescribed asset rates for institutional investors of up to 60%, "It should be emphasized that there is little evidence of direct crowding out of the private business sector, owing to its weak demand for credit in this period [1980-87]," the World Bank (1989d:23) conceded.[23]

But even if regulations such as prescribed assets were relatively unimportant to the direction and tempo of funding flows in the Zimbabwean economy, financial institutions were nevertheless still viewed by black bureaucrats with a certain amount of hostility, largely on the basis that such a tiny percentage of loans were available to black borrowers. The World Bank (1989d:55) reported "considerable mistrust between the government and private financial sector—especially the foreign-owned part that accounts for the bulk of the monetary system—and a strong feeling that it could not be entrusted with implementing the government's priorities."

Thanks to the Bank's tutelage, however, those priorities would change dramatically during the 1990s, as is documented in Chapter Twelve. Not only did they entail profound changes in financial regulation that served to shorten the temporal horizons of investment capital, they also conclusively lengthened Zimbabwean capital's spatial reach, through promotion of more extensive trade relations. Again, though, the seeds of the new policies were sown during the first decade of Independence.

Trade promotion

The linkages between the two types of liberalization, finance and trade, are important. Chidzero spelled these out as early as 1982, in a self-imposed promise of conditionality (in a letter to the World Bank [1983a:Annex IX, 39]): "We are convinced that we could appreciably increase the volume of our exports through liberalization of credit facilities." But there was not much choice, for in subsequent years, according to Davies, Sanders and Shaw (1991:21), "Relations [between Zimbabwe and the World Bank] deteriorated somewhat when attempts to borrow further in order to increase the Export Revolving Fund were met by greater Bank conditionality, with an insistence on moves towards trade liberalization."

In a sense, trade liberalization began in late 1982, with the high-profile devaluation of the Zimbabwe dollar. The World Bank (1983a:3,13) soon heralded "important policy directions—including an outward-looking, export-oriented industrial strategy." Indeed, the list of conditionality on a 1983 Export Revolving Fund loan gave a sense of the priority that devaluation took:

> The government is discussing with the IMF a stabilization program which stipulates a number of measures including: an exchange rate adjustment (as a result of the dialogue, the government devalued the Zimbabwean dollar by 20% on December 9, 1982 in order to restore export competitiveness that had been eroded by large increases in labor costs and high domestic inflation); an adjustment in the basket of currencies on which the value of the Zim dollar is determined; a reduction in the budgetary deficit; limitations to wage and salary increases; and ceilings to short-term external debt and domestic credit. The negotiations are at an advanced stage and are expected to be successfully concluded shortly.

Devaluation was to be one of the most contested aspects of international financial conditionality, for it represents the fastest means of devaluing a country's labor power, and since the power of local manufacturing capital was often mobilized to oppose further devaluations. It was not merely progressive economists such as Ndlela (1986) or Davies (1983) who took public stands against devaluation. For UDC Ltd chairman (and former CZI president) Alan Paterson, devaluation was "an unacceptable alternative... Perhaps by liberalising external borrowing and improving the speed of decision making, government would encourage the private sector to take a greater role in this vital enterprise [foreign exchange generation]" (*Industrial Review*, July 1987).

As noted in Chapter Six, devaluation was not the only means of promoting trade liberalization. In 1984 the Export Incentive Scheme was introduced (allowing exporters to retain hard currency) and by late 1985, dubious comparisons between Zimbabwe and Asian Newly Industrialized Countries were ventured (*Herald*, 12/12/85). A joint World Bank and UN report on Zimbabwe noted possible "success stories" in manufacturing exports (*Sunday Mail*, 6/10/85), although no marketing studies were subsequently carried out indicating sure-fire "success stories" (indeed no marketing studies were released at all in the lead-up to the full-fledged trade liberalization of the 1990s). So whereas in late 1986 and thereafter, the Bank threatened to withdraw the Export Revolving Fund if Zimbabwe did not more decisively liberalise, there was no firm proof of even the *likely* effect this would have on industry (*Herald*, 23/10/86, 2/4/87, 29/5/87). Nevertheless, according to the Bank (1995c:16), the 1986 debate with government officials "intensified the Bank's policy dialogue, but it was not supported by the Bank's senior management, essentially on the grounds that it was too risky to proceed without a demonstrated commitment to trade liberalization."

More vague promises were still ahead. The following year, the Bank (1987c:70) report *A Strategy for Sustained Growth*—credited with winning over a critical mass of government bureaucrats—suggested that "it is highly difficult to predict which manufacturing subsectors will enjoy rapid growth, but there is sufficient evidence on the responsiveness of Zimbabwe's manufacturing sector to be optimistic on its export prospects... The European market is likely to be central to growth in manufactured exports."[24] Former CZI chief economist Riddell responded, "Strikingly, the Bank fails to provide evidence to support such a bland conclusion." Indeed, if the Bank's *Strategy for Sustained Growth* was adopted, Riddell (1990:382-383) predicted,

> there would be a major loss of control of major aspects of the economy, making planning for the future direction more difficult and increasing external vulnerability. Second, [new foreign borrowing to pay for imported capital goods] would have adverse implications for debt servicing just at the time when the country's dangerously high debt-servicing ratio would be falling. Third, the World Bank's own estimates suggest that their proposed 20% devaluation would induce a 6% fall in real wages while the price increases of the parastatals would be expected to add a further 2% to the cost of living of low-income groups... It therefore needs to be asked whether the marginal changes predicted would be worth the extremely high level of risk involved.

The risks included a major restructuring of Zimbabwe's manufacturing plant and equipment. By 1990, (pro-liberalization) CZI chief economist Mike Humphrey was compelled to warn, "In the early phase of the prgram an extensive process of rationalization will have to occur in many of the existing manufacturing companies. Companies will have to concentrate on a much-reduced product range, with greater production runs" (*Africa South,* May/June 1990). All of this fit the broad contours of what the Bank and other international financiers were promoting across the globe.

Humphrey's otherwise credulous (and very high-profile) promotion of ESAP was one way of differentiating the CZI of the late 1980s/early 1990s (especially following an April 1988 memo) from the CZI of a decade earlier (Skalnes:1993). By 1987, according to Peter Gibbon (1995:9), white CZI leaders "could distinguish themselves from the remnants of UDI-style politics" by working more closely with government on potential (but always theoretical) sanctions against apartheid South Africa, on the operation of the Beira Corridor Group (to permit an alternative export route than through Johannesburg), and on the design of industrial policy in roundtable discussions also involving the World Bank and United Nations. The Bank (1987a, 1987c) converted CZI to liberalization using the argument, oft-repeated by Humphrey, that *earlier rounds of (Rhodesian-era) import substitution were now essentially exhausted,* and that there was no alternative but for Zimbabwe to face outward (Stoneman and Cliffe 1989:137).

In addition to making amends with manufacturers, the Bank had much greater access to the Zimbabwe government during the late 1980s, and in 1991 claimed—as Lionel Cliffe (1991:28) put it—to be "'much more on the inside' than in earlier years. In late 1990, for example, there were, in the course of one month, thirty World Bank missions looking at some aspect or another of the economy."

Conclusion: Premonitions of economic collapse

The World Bank was accompanied by other international institutions in its imposition of conditionality on project, sectoral and macroeconomic loans, as has been shown in the past three chapters. Of greatest importance, perhaps, the IMF continued to monitor Zimbabwe even after cutting off its credit line in 1984. According to Riddell (1990:383) the IMF "sees the problems of public finance and of an 'overvalued' exchange rate as critical, while it advocates, more specifically, a simplification of investment procedures, an ending of all price controls as soon as possible and, for manufacturing specifically, a more outward orientation."

Zimbabwe accepted these macroeconomic recommendations (even before receiving a US$484 million IMF structural adjustment loan in

January 1992), and went even further. The 1991 "Framework for Economic Reform" promised that by the end of 1995 there would be a 25% cut in the civil service, and the demise of all labor restrictions, price controls, exchange controls, interest rate controls, investment regulations, import restrictions, and government subsidies. Privatization of parastatals was practically the only major ingredient in the typical structural adjustment recipe that Zimbabwe was able to forego (but even so, parastatal commercialization was pursued with vigor and by 1995 "rapid privatization of the key parastatals" providing telecommunications, electricity, water and transportation had become a central World Bank demand) (World Bank 1995c:35).[25]

Stoneman's (1990:5) prediction should be noted at this stage: "Historically, structural adjustment policies have no record of success, whereas Zimbabwe has been following proven policies of industrial protection... By 1995 the failure of World Bank policies will be indisputable." In fact, as the penultimate chapter shows, the date at which such a conclusion could have been reached was probably closer to late 1991.

Notes

1. Hanlon (1991:177) reports that "By 1986 the World Bank had abandoned the narrow deindustrialisation strategy it had tried to impose on Zimbabwe and other Third World states." Indeed, notwithstanding the Bank's miscalculation in circulating the controversial Jansen Report, there was always room for an alliance of some sort between national productive capital and international finance. CZI leaders like Alan Paterson (president in 1982) knew that the discipline of international finance—even enforced currency devaluation which would raise manufacturers' input costs—could serve his constituents' interests against a potentially "socialist" state: "If it brings in assistance from the IMF it's perhaps a good thing for the country" (*Herald*, 9/12/82). Paterson was subsequently head of UDC, Ltd—a finance house partly owned by the Bank's International Finance Corporation—and may not have exemplified the Zimbabwean industrialist. But by the late 1980s, the CZI had convinced the Bank to take a much more sympathetic view of local manufacturers as potential exporters.
2. The World Bank (1987c:20-22) noted that with regard to external private debt, Zimbabwe had adopted a "highly conservative policy." Of US$420 million per annum in new loans during the 1980s, an average of US$110 million came from commercial banks. The cost of both commercial bank and World Bank loans were high: "Multilateral borrowing is almost entirely on non-concessional terms to Zimbabwe—a reflection of her creditwor-

thiness—but has the major advantage of long maturities."

3. In late 1985, for example, Chidzero complained of "the IMF breathing down our necks" as balance of payments problems developed, and he remonstrated that in economies like Zimbabwe's, "market forces tended to mean market power, which was concentrated in the hands of dominant groups and monopolies... Naturally this line of thinking is not accepted by the IMF or the US, but this is the reality of developing countries" (*Herald,* 12/12/85).
4. Yet by early 1991, Chidzero was seriously considering a debt-for-nature swap on Zimbabwe's debt (*Sunday Mail,* 21/4/91). Strong critiques of such swaps can be found in Potter (1988) and Anonymous (1987).
5. The full name of the Development Committee, ironically, is the "Joint Ministerial Committee on the Transfer of Real Resources to Developing Countries." It is interesting to note, in the same spirit, that although a major Bank (1984, 38) statement on Africa, *Toward Sustained Development,* argued that "The starting point [for state investment] has to be a realistic assessment of expected resources," the Bank (1984:7) estimated a positive net capital inflow to Africa of US$5 billion in 1985-87, and soon thereafter (1986c:40) estimated a projected net annual inflow of US$8.5 billion from 1986-90.
6. "Optimism" could certainly not be attributed to ordinary citizens of Third World countries. For example, the late 1980s witnessed major trade union conferences on Latin American debt, and, according to *International Labor Reports,* "Most of the trade unions at all three meetings proposed one radical solution to the problem of their countries' debt problems: non-payment. After all, they argue, workers have already paid more than enough. Nothing has improved since Third World countries, especially in Latin America, got their first loans from Europe in the 1820s" (Farge 1990:17).
7. Instead, typical of financial market attitudes was the successful early 1990s gambit by British banks—including Barclays, Standard Chartered and Grindlays which had exposure in Zimbabwe—to draw US$350 million out of Third World governments in loans the banks had previously acknowledged to be unrepayable, and for which they had received tax credits for writing off as such (*FG,* 29/4/93).
8. Some of the energy sector's early foreign liabilities were simply unnecessary. International agency financing for the Hwange power plant came from the Bank's International Finance Corporation (a US$20 million loan, its largest in Africa) and the US Export Import Bank, and included a guarantee to Anglo American Corporation that its nearby coal mine would attain a 12.5% profit rate. As Makgetla (1983:IX, 24) remarked, "Serious questions arose about the project's impact on the government budget and the Zimbabwean economy as a whole," since it was easier to approve the

Rhodesian-era project than consider a variety of alternative energy sources.

9. The Bank's NRZ loan—mooted in 1980, begun in 1981, meant to conclude in 1984, and actually concluded in 1986—was only reviewed in September 1989. In 1986, the subsidies were still at least 7% of NRZ expenditures, and accounted for a quarter of all government parastatal subsidies.
10. The Bank blamed many of the problems (especially the long delays) on the "NRZ's slow preparation of tender documents... [and] NRZ's non-compliance with agreed procedures. In many respects, NRZ senior staff never fully accepted the rationale for Bank procedures and their relevance to NRZ's situation." Yet it is in just such administrative areas that the Bank typically excels, and—had it been involved in closer monitoring—could easily have intervened to ensure that simple tenders were issued. To illustrate, in the early 1990s, staff shortages became so severe that NRZ spent nearly Z$1 million between 1991 and 1993 on repairs, of which "more than half were sent to backyard garages, where NRZ employees received kick-backs," according to a report by an internal committee. "Owing to lack of panel-beaters and spray painters, every job to repair accident damages was sub-contracted," the committee reported (*FG*, 24/3/94).
11. On the Bank's 1988 *Education in Sub-Saharan Africa: Policy Adjustment, Revitalisation and Expansion*, Chung (1989:25) said that "On the whole I like it," and was then asked by an interviewer,

> A pervasive theme of the Report is the promotion of private schools and the increased privatization of finance. Zimbabwe has one of the largest private school sectors in Africa. In addition, much of the responsibility for school construction is currently passed on to local communities. Many families are hard pressed to meet the costs of school fees and uniforms. What are your reactions to the World Bank recommendation is this are?
> CHUNG: I feel that to some extent they are correct, because the responsibility for children must remain with the parents who decided to have them. I think it would be wrong for the government to take over all responsibility from the parents.

12. This was unusual, for typically, business concerns about the withdrawal of subsidies were immediately self-interested. In his effortless manner, Eric Bloch complained at length in a *Financial Gazette* column about the pain of cost recovery, mentioning in passing education and health but focusing mainly on National Parks entrance fees, the nonresident airport departure tax, and the 2,000% increase (from 10c to Z$2) in the fee he was charged to enter the bar at the Bulawayo airport (*FG*, 14/7/94).

13. As for university fees, however, the Bank argued that these should rise to 50% of actual costs.
14. For example, yet another surprising attack on cost recovery was found in the Bank's 1995 *Country Economic Memorandum* analysis of urban infrastructure. Moreover, in rural areas, the Bank argued, "the public sector could continue to assume capital costs for the construction of water points" while communities should pay maintenance costs. And the Grain Marketing Board—which suffered enormous annual deficits (Z$1.4 billion in 1994)—received unusual praise, for playing a "social/developmental role" in marginal areas. More generally, the Bank recommended "a social safety net which can ensure a socially acceptable minimum consumption level" and slated ESAP's Social Dimensions of Adjustment (SDA) programme for incompetent targeting, excessive administrative costs and its lengthy application forms. It also condemned the SDA fund for carrying "a social stigma, which ought to be avoided" (World Bank, 1995b, v.I:61-67). The most logical explanation for this string of reversals was the intensity of unending public attacks (by President Mugabe and his cabinet, the *Financial Gazette* and CZI, trade unions, and high-profile NGOs like Oxfam) on the Bank's role in denuding Zimbabwe of its best-recognized social investment programmes, while the economy remained at pre-ESAP levels of output.
15. More consistently, however, the Bank also argued that Zimbabwean construction firms should attempt to divert 20% of their business to export markets, while making virtually no linkage between the construction industry and the low-income housing crisis (*FG*, 7/9/90, 19/9/91).
16. The ZBCA as an institution left much to be desired; perhaps predictably, one leading white construction official concluded that it was "so weak that it amounts to nothing more than a paper administration office. As an organisation, they have very little credibility in the professional contracting industry. Their leaning towards politics and the current infighting do not auger well for their image and reputation" (*FG*, 16/6/94).
17. Resistance was not limited to conditionality by the Bank. In 1994, the PTC declined a Z$150 million loan from the Commonwealth Development Corporation due to what were described as "harsh" conditions (*FG*, 6/1/94).
18. The *FG* (9/7/92, 16/7/92) reported that the Bank "is understood to have recommended the abolition of the door-to-door delivery of letters and proposed that Post Office Savings Bank be converted into a commercial bank."
19. This was in order "to maintain healthy relations with government because the issue was 'very sensitive,'" according to the *Financial Gazette* (16/7/92). Makoni later explained to the newspaper, "We are 100% owned

by government and we have to be very careful in how we deal with them. We do not want to deal with government in the Press.:. I was not up to doing your paper any harm at all."

20. The author was offered (and rejected) one such consultancy by the Bank in mid 1992, in the course of an on-the-spot interview with its main agricultural officer; the consultancy would have entailed attempting to persuade Harare commercial banks to open their doors to the top fraction of small farmers. What with the Bank having recently acknowledged 80% default rates for peasant farmers in its AFC programme, and given Zimbabwean bank attitudes to such borrowers (see Chapter Ten), this appeared a classic case of programme design in H Street, Washington DC, with very little prospect of success in the field.
21. The main foreign consultants who did get jobs through Urban I were assigned to transport, road safety equipment, and motor vehicle administration, areas in which Zimbabwe had plenty of excess domestic capacity. The Bank's locally-based Urban I consultants were employed to carry out "aspects of civil engineering," and the Bank failed to document in its *Project Completion Report* (1994:12) why a foreign currency loan was required to pay for such services.
22. There were, however, few other changes in interest rates during the 1980s. At the end of 1989, commercial banks were required to reduce their minimum overdraft rate ("base lending rate") to 11.5% and were prohibited from charging interest rates in excess of 14% for productive investment purposes (as against 15.5% for consumption). The hire purchase lending base rate was reduced from 20% to 14%, with a maximum of 18%.
23. Interestingly, reflecting the Bank's (1991c:15) easy approach to data interpretation, a report on South Africa aimed at a rapprochement with the liberation movement draws a wholly different lesson about Zimbabwe's prescribed asset requirements: "the more important long-run effects was (*sic*) to allow an unsustainable accumulation of public debt and diverted (*sic*) resources from investment into public consumption." And of course ESAP, warmly endorsed by the Bank in early 1991, included a dramatic increase in public external debt.
24. Such optimistic projections continued during the 1990s, no matter the profusion of evidence to the contrary. A few months after Zimbabwe's volume of manufacturing output fell by 20% during early 1995, the Bank (1995c:35) intoned, "The potential for higher exports exists in several sectors—mining, agriculture, tourism and manufacturing," if only Zimbabwe would "provide a more market-friendly environment" and private firms would modernise and seek "foreign partners and external markets." Agricultural and mining products were specified (cotton, horticulture,

sugar, oilseeds, platinum) but notably, the Bank again provided no examples of potentially-successful manufacturing exports.

25. Privatisation had been justifiably delayed, as International Finance Corporation's Southern African representative Mwanghazi Mwachofi recorded, because its beneficiaries would be "perceived to be the rich and privileged" of Zimbabwe and because the existing political leadership preferred to use parastatals "to perpetuate existing jobs" (*FG*, 14/7/94). Later, Mugabe conceded to privatisation on grounds that the proceeds would go into a National Investment Trust to advance the economic interests of black Zimbabweans" (*FG*, 11/1/96).

chapter twelve

Eternal Suffering for the African People (ESAP)

Introduction

"Deep down," the novelist Chengerai Hove divulged (1994:71),

> I harbor fear, a persistent fear which, like an ominous shadow, refused to abandon me. There is the smell of the Structural Adjustment Programme in the wind, with its flags swamping those of political independence. "Sure Advice to Poverty" local pub humorists have nicknamed this World Bank-IMF economic beverage. It tastes sour from the beginning, a cartoonist once wrote as he watched friends and foes losing jobs in Harare's industries under the banner of "die today so as to live tomorrow."

ESAP was most often redubbed "Eternal Suffering for the African People" in colloquial discourse, but 1991–95 was also a period of eternal suffering for at least some badly-exposed fractions of overaccumulated capital, as devalorization finally began in earnest. What, one may ask in retrospect, was the point of it all?

Introduced by Finance Minister Chidzero in 1990, ESAP's formal programmatic shape and projected results were only revealed in the January 1991 *Framework for Economic Reform, 1991-95*. That supposedly "home-grown" document (tellingly, written in American English, as are all World Bank documents) offered the following predictions:

- Reaching 5% growth annually, the economy would have grown in excess of 4.3% for eight consecutive years (1988-95)—in spite of the fact that the longest stretch of positive growth since 1973 had been just three years.
- The overall budget deficit would shrink to 5% of GDP. And although Zimbabwe's foreign debt would initially increase from US$2.4 billion in early 1991 to a projected US$4 billion in 1995, repaying the debt would become easier. The debt service ratio (repayments as a percentage of export earnings)—which peaked at 35% in 1987 and fell to 24% in 1990—would drop further, to 18.5% by 1995, in spite of the addition of US$3.5 billion in new loans in the intervening years (US$1.9 billion of which would meanwhile be repaid).
- Private sector investment would rapidly overtake government investment, doubling from levels of the late 1980s, and total investment, which averaged less than 20% of GDP in 1985-90, would reach 25% by 1993 and remain there.
- Inflation, running at 20% in early 1991, would be down to 10% by 1994.
- Relative to the rest of the economy, exports would grow by about one third from late 1980s levels; specifically, mining exports would increase from less than US$400 million in 1990 to more than US$500 million in 1994, manufacturing exports would double from US$400 million in 1988 to US$800 million in 1995, and agricultural exports, which were in decline since 1988, would grow steadily through 1995.
- Except for 1991, Zimbabwe would have better terms of trade in its dealings with the world economy over the subsequent five years.
- New direct foreign investment would flood in (US$30 million a year in 1992-95) notwithstanding the fact that such investment flooded out during the 1980s.

Considering what actually transpired during the first half of the 1990s, a similarly-optimistic but farfetched prediction made by Chidzero precisely a decade earlier—8% annual economic growth through the 1980s—springs to mind, as does the resounding endorsement of Chidzero's planning by the World Bank and IMF at the 1981 Zimcord conference. From the late 1980s, the Bank promoted ESAP with as much temerity as did Chidzero, notwithstanding the fact that from 1989 rather mixed signals were emerging from a general equilibrium econometric model used to simulate Zimbabwe's economy. This is worth a moment's consideration, for in the scenario that most closely resembled ESAP, Bank modelers Elbadawi and Schmidt-Hebbel (1991:55,57) forecast the following:

> Reducing the consolidated public sector deficit over 1991-95 has major benefits for macroeconomic stability and long-term growth prospects in Zimbabwe. The domestic debt to GDP ratio starts to decline, allowing domestic real interest rates to fall, which reinforces the initial fiscal adjustment and spurs private investment... One final word on investment and growth is in order. Our simulations show ***a slight decline in GDP growth over the 1991-95 projection horizon, reflecting the contractionary effects of lower public consumption***. However, lower real interest rates spur private fixed capital investment, raising the share of total gross fixed capital investment in 1995 from 23.3% of GDP in 1988 to 24.8% under fiscal adjustment. (emphasis added)[1]

To translate the formal economic argument, in short, cutting government spending would limit growth, yes (though the Bank never revealed this finding to the Zimbabwean public), but private sector vitality would compensate soon enough.

In reality, growth only reached 5% during one year (1994), and averaged just 1.2% from 1991-94 (the last year full data are available; 1995 was flat while in 1996 generous rains generated hopes for a more substantial upturn). Inflation averaged 29% during 1991 to 1994, and never dropped anywhere near the 10% goal. The budget deficit was nearly 9% of GDP in 1991-94 (with no prospect of getting down to the targeted 5% from a drought-related high of 13% in 1994/95). Investment in 1993 was less than 19% of GDP, far short of the 25% target (*Zimbabwe Economic Review*, September 1995). But to get a more nuanced picture reflected in these disappointing numbers, it is worth looking more closely at the results of ESAP in the fields of trade, foreign debt, industrial output, investment and employment. Following this exercise, it will be helpful to reconsider the roles of time and space in reorganising the ESAP economy, and later to document the hopes and ambitions, actions and reactions of different social forces.

What we will conclude from examining trade, debt, output, investment and employment is that Zimbabwe suffered continuing overaccumulation of capital, intensified international competition, and yet profoundly uncompetitive production processes during the early 1990s. But while the ESAP experience was certainly bedeviled by these underlying dynamics of capitalist crisis, ESAP's defenders will reply that other forces external to the logic of reforms—the drought, durable fiscal deficits and severe losses by parastatals—all threw the model off track. True, yet the 1992-93 and 1993-94 rainy seasons were fine. Moreover, in the field of trade, enormous (unanticipated) devaluation of the currency should have boosted exports dramatically. Instead of growing, as discussed in more detail below, the real value of exports crashed and the visible balance of trade—which had been positive through 1988 (when the surplus was an impressive Z$923 million)—immediately went into deficit and plummeted to negative Z$1.9 billion in 1991 and negative Z$3.9 billion in 1992. The trade deficit remained deeply in the red in 1993 (negative Z$1.6 billion) and 1994 (negative Z$2.1 billion).

And this was accomplished by mortgaging the future at a rate unparalleled in the country's history. ESAP was to require US$3.5 billion in new foreign loans over five years (as against existing external debt of US$2.5 billion in the late 1980s). Initially, government had experienced severe liquidity problems because foreign donors delayed making ESAP-related loans or grants. These were ostensibly to become available in 1990-91 but did not, in fact, transpire until May 1992 (in the case of the Bank) and June 1992 (in the case of others), apparently because of both distrust that the program would truly be implemented, and the funders' need to maintain leverage over the Zimbabwe budget. As a result, government repeatedly turned to (inflationary) financing from the domestic banking sector—where real (after-inflation) rates of interest regularly reached unprecedented levels of 10%—as well as to an expensive US$155 million foreign commercial bank loan in mid 1991 (Gibbon 1995:13).

As a result, in the 1992/93 fiscal year, interest payments on both foreign and domestic debt soared 15% more than projected due to exorbitant interest rates and dramatic (downward) exchange rate movements (World Bank, 1995a, 35). The ratio of foreign debt repayments to export earnings, which Chidzero had promised would stay below 20% during the 1990s, climbed to more than 30% by 1992, with no prospect of coming back down to the "safety zone" around 25% before the 21st century. By April 1994, foreign debt was US$4.2 billion, with projections of reaching US$5.2 billion by April 1995 (*FG*, 20/10/94).[2]

One of the main causes of untenable foreign debt was that with financial liberalization, large domestic corporate borrowers (including banks) began seeking funding overseas, discovering in the process that the nominal cost of overseas funds was as low as 7%, compared to in excess of 35%

for domestic loans.[3] As noted in Chapter Six, the Zimbabwe Reserve Bank subsidized, on an immense scale, protection against currency devaluation on behalf of domestic banks' offshore borrowing (the subsidy essentially amounts to the difference between the seductively low "nominal" interest rate on foreign loans and the "real" rate at which the loans must be repaid, in hard currency, as the Zimdollar plunges in value). Reserve Bank losses in buying forward cover were Z$2 billion in 1991 alone, and were still estimated by the World Bank (1995b, v.II:21) at Z$600 million in 1994.

Meanwhile, overaccumulated manufacturing capital devalued dramatically in 1992 (the manufacturing growth rate was –9.5%) and again in 1993 (–12.5%). A slight recovery occurred in subsequent years (led by textiles, which were momentarily competitive after the massive currency devaluation). The 1992 depression (–6.3% overall GDP growth) was followed by a mediocre upturn in GDP in 1993 (recorded optimistically at 4.3%) and somewhat stronger growth (5%) in 1994 (following another 13% currency devaluation). But with 86% of manufacturing and mining firms below capacity in May 1993, World Bank Harare representative Kapil Kapoor begged for "a recovery in fixed investment, especially in the productive sector" (*FG*, 27/5/93, 15/7/93) on grounds, as a 1995 Bank report (1995b, v.I:6) alleged, that "The manufacturing sector uses capital very inefficiently and has a very high incremental capital to output ratio."

Yet as noted in Chapter Six, the Bank (1995b, v.II:129-130) also acknowledged that—based on its 1993 sample of manufacturers—Zimbabwean firms could increase their output by as much as 80% (an astonishingly high figure) before hitting technical barriers, by using existing equipment and modes of operation. In other words, notwithstanding the unprecedented industrial devaluation that occurred during the 1992-93 manufacturing depression, Zimbabwe's fixed capital stock had still not suffered sufficient destruction to meet the competitive demands of the lean, mean, global economy.

After a rise in manufacturing output during 1994, the devaluation of chronically overaccumulated industrial capital resumed in 1995. The manufacturing output index fell 20% from 1994 levels, at one point (January 1995) dropping to a level 5% lower than in 1980 (and during the first half of 1995 averaging just 7% higher than in 1980). Good rains in early 1996 would slow the deindustrialization process, but as noted below, several sectors still went to the wall.

The devaluation of labor was also proceeding apace. As the first five years of ESAP drew to a close, the Bank (1995b, v.II:3) boasted, "Labor intensive sectors, such as wood products and textiles, have benefitted from the sharp reduction in real wages, reinforcing the expansion of exports."

(Textiles, we shall see, may have benefitted, but not enough to offset the damage done by trade liberalization.) The major factors in lowering real wages were soaring inflation and rising unemployment. Inflation ravaged workers, with the Zimbabwe Congress of Trade Unions reporting in 1996 that their members found themselves on average 38% poorer than in 1980 and 40% poorer than in 1990. According to the ZCTU (1996:68), the biggest losers in direct standards of living (average annual earnings) as a percentage of 1980 levels were civil servants (–65%), domestic workers (–62%), construction workers (–56%), teachers (–50%), and farmworkers (–48%), with miners (–20%) and manufacturing employees (–19%) the "best off." Adding this to the falling "social wage"—thanks largely to new cost recovery policies for health, education and many other social services, as well as the unprecedented interest rates on consumer credit—workers and poor people faced an unprecedented financial crisis during the early 1990s.

But dramatically lower wages did not, as orthodox theory would suggest, translate into more jobs. Unemployment remained rampant, with a tiny fraction of the 200,000 annual school-leavers able to find formal sector employment. Based on data from the Bank and International Labor Organization, the ZCTU (1996:15) estimated a crash in non-agricultural sector employment from 939,800 in 1991 to 844,000 in 1992. According to Bank (1995b, v.II:14) estimates, of a total labor force of about 4.1 million, only 1.244 million were formally employed in 1991, and this dropped to 1.217 million in 1993. Indeed, notwithstanding a reported US$800 million in new investment during a 30 month period in 1992-1994, just 35,000 new jobs were created (Hawkins 1994:52).

These are only some of the preliminary indications of the impact of Eternal Suffering for the African People. Prior to examining how the process was understood by Zimbabweans themselves, this chapter reviews the two areas—finance and trade—in which time and space were most actively manipulated by international financial power to exacerbate Zimbabwe's uneven development. Then the pro-ESAP perspective of the World Bank and government is considered, followed by a catalogue of complaints about structural adjustment from business, labor and more eclectic popular perspectives. A concluding attempt is made to sort out the divergent discourses and attribute blame, so as to better move forward with alternative policies.

Financial deregulation and sado-monetarism

Arising from the legacy of growing speculative bubbles in certain financial markets (Chapter Eight) and strict controls in others (Chapter Eleven), the Finance Ministry's 1990 plan for the deregulation of finance would, in theory, be more sophisticated than simply an immediate decontrol of interest rates, exchange controls and exchange rates. The Zimbabwe program was aimed at correcting "a number of inherent weaknesses," according to the Finance Ministry (Government of Zimbabwe 1990:20-21): "A corset of controls... limited entry of newcomers... bias against small and aspiring entrepreneurs and the rural sector... The Stock Exchange has not been used as an active vehicle for the redistribution and broadening of the ownership of the productive base of the economy."

To address such problems, there would be additional forms of state intervention—particularly in establishing new institutional forms (such as the IBDC, Venture Capital Company, group credit schemes and the like)—but within the broader context of a market-oriented philosophy. Of course, most of the institutional reforms specified in the 1990 Finance Ministry plan seemed to have been drawn directly from the previous year's World Bank (1989d:xiii) report on the financial system, which advocated

> measures to encourage more, and more innovative, investment finance, especially by the capital market; this could include a gradual reduction in prescribed assets requirements, the encouragement of the use of the stock exchange and corporate debentures, and the encouragement of new and riskier lending activities through allowing new institutions (subject to appropriate prudential requirements), new instruments and greater interest rate flexibility.

In this spirit, the Finance Ministry's financial deregulation plan aimed to persuade banks to "display a national character in their allocation of credit without of course compromising prudence and sound banking practices... (Credit controls) will be relaxed enough to encourage productive borrowing while at the same time remaining strict enough to dampen any potential inflationary pressures." The Finance Ministry also requested that the "highly concentrated" banks establish a much larger, decentralized branch network (see Chapter Ten). International banks would be warmly invited to enter Zimbabwe, and yet notwithstanding periodic relaxation of currency controls—such that by 1995 Zimbabwe boasted a relatively convertible currency, with full repatriation of earnings and dividends to foreign investors—capital transfers still faced restrictions. And internal to the ZSE, government would initiate "deliberate policy measures" to increase "attractive script on the market," including the possibility of tax breaks for privately-owned companies to go public (Government of Zimbabwe 1990:21-22).

In short, with financial speculation such a powerful force in the economy at the time the plan was drafted, there would be no "free-for-all" market solution (*Financial Times*, 21/8/89). The Finance Ministry instead recognized the need for

> synchronization of the financial liberalization policy with the reductions in the fiscal deficit. Thus the financial liberalization, whether in regard to monetary policy instruments or the institutional structure of the financial system has to be gradual, increasing its speed when the fiscal deficit is drastically pared down. It is also necessary that the financial sector should be operating competitively eliminating opportunities for collusion amongst banks, so liberalized interest rates would be determined freely by market forces. (*Herald*, 28/2/91)

Zimbabwe's banks celebrated the proposed trade and financial liberalization (*FG*, 12/4/90, 10/8/90), even as the Finance Ministry (correctly) predicted that their non-performing loans would rise. (No one had any suspicion, however, that debt-related defaults would be threatened as early as mid 1992 at two of the country's largest export-oriented companies, Cone Textiles and Hunyani paper and packaging.)[4] The financial liberalization plan posited that the antidote for non-performing loans would be a strong "secondary market" in which such paper could be bought and sold (*Herald*, 28/2/91). At that very moment, interestingly, such secondary financial market activity (sometimes called securitization) was wreaking havoc in the US, and by the mid 1990s the secondary market—now taking the form of "derivatives" of other financial paper—would cripple major international investors ranging from Orange County, California to England's Barings Bank to Japan's Daiwa Bank (as noted in Chapter Ten, US AID was a recklessly enthusiastic sponsor of this aspect of financial liberalization). At least during the first phase of ESAP, the secondary market failed to get off the ground in Zimbabwe, fortunately.

Notwithstanding some efforts by the Finance Ministry and Reserve Bank to control the pace of financial deregulation, contradictions quickly emerged. Monetary policy again became a much more activist—and dangerous—tool in the liberalization process. There was initially, in late 1989, a rearrangement of controls over financial flows, as some interest rates increased but as finance houses experienced cuts in their base lending rates from 20-23% to 14% (supported by a 5% cut in liquidity rates to 15%), which would free Z$30 million for new lending. Financial institutions were then caught off guard in mid 1990 when deposit rates were allowed to rise by 2%. Lending rates for productive investment increased 0.5%, except for consumption lending, where the interest rate cap was removed.

The rationale, according to one account, was that "The higher deposit rates would encourage savings while the punitively high interest rates on consumption lending would make it more costly for people to buy luxury vehicles or boats." The Finance House Association welcomed the policy shift, although its "members would have preferred to see the cap also removed on productive expenditure so that rates could follow or equal the degree of risk" (*FG*, 16/8/90). Commercial bankers complained, however, about paying the new minimum requirement of 5% interest on current-account demand deposit accounts was too high (*African Business*, October 1990).

As never before, government policy, as expressed for example by Reserve Bank chair Kenneth Moyana, was caught between a rock and a hard place: "It is absolutely necessary that the Reserve Bank actively pursue a restrictive monetary policy, with a view to curbing money-supply growth and inflation without at the same time choking off the desirable real growth and structural transformation of the economy" (*African Business*, October 1990). But "transformation" would have to wait, since speculative markets continued bubbling. A final burst of speculation pulled the money supply up 35% from mid 1990 to mid 1991. With the abandonment of key price controls in early 1991, the inflation rate also rose above 30% for the first time in living memory. As even bank economists pointed out, price decontrol "did more to add to inflation and distortion of relative prices than it helped business viability. This approach also puts into question the credibility of the whole program in the eyes of the general public and market participants" (*Zimbank Review*, Third Quarter 1991).

This was the point that exceptionally harsh monetary tightening was deemed necessary by authorities with more power than Chidzero and Moyana. When the IMF and World Bank insisted on still tighter monetary policy in mid 1991, interest rates on certain government securities rose from 27.5% to 44% in a single day, rates on bankers acceptances soared, and the average rate paid on 90-day NCDs swelled from 32.5% to 40%. The reverberations shattered the stock market (as discussed in Chapter Eight) and led merchant banks to "sharply curtail lending to clients pending the stabilization of the money market" (*FG*, 31/10/91).

Anticipated international financial support was not immediately forthcoming (although as noted earlier, soon foreign debt would reach untenable levels). Donors assembled at the annual meetings of the IMF and World Bank in October 1991 to ostensibly provide Zimbabwe with Z$4 billion in foreign currency loans and aid. Even so, according to Elisha

Mushayakarara of the Finance Ministry, "To date [November 1991] only a few [donors] have translated their pledges into disbursable resources" (*FG*, 14/11/91), and it was only in the middle of 1992 that most promises were finally kept (Gibbon 1995:14).

Thus to lubricate an otherwise strait-jacketed economy, bank minimum liquidity rates had to be lowered dramatically at the end of 1991, from 40% to 10%. But with far higher interest rates in the money markets, the private sector remained paralysed, and government borrowing from domestic markets—largely a function of delays in disbursement of foreign-pledged loans and grants—was therefore important simply to mop up the available funds (*FG*, 5/12/91).

The issue for firms in the productive sector wasn't, therefore, the oft-cited but rarely-documented allegation that government "crowded out" the private sector credit markets,[5] but rather the high rates. As Zimbabwe Development Bank managing director Rindai Jaravaza explained, "The effect of these [monetary] measures will be to discourage capital investment for cost reasons but may also increase the risk of project failure given the potential for increased product market competition that the overall reform program entails" (*FG*, 12/12/91). Later, confirmed a ZCTU (1996:54) study, "Firm-level evidence now points to high interest rates as one of the major constraints to investment."

The policy of "sado-monetarism"—as it was termed in other lands—was so severe that even some financial institutions faced crisis. As noted in Chapter Nine, building societies suffered serious losses of deposits in the financial shake-out beginning in 1991, since the Post Office Savings Bank and money market offered savers substantially higher returns. "The monetary authorities do not appear to be willing to accord housing finance any degree of priority in the short-term, and the situation has become extremely serious," complained the outgoing president of the Association of Building Societies, Richard Parke (*FG*, 12/12/91). The general manager of Founders, Keith Evans, added, "We accept that with ESAP they are putting rates up to get real rates. But when you do that you can't leave one sector behind." Evans demanded building society access to the money market since "the over-the-counter retail market was proving inadequate." For obvious reasons, the turbulent monetary policy left Evans and his colleagues "apprehensive as to additional measures which can be expected during the remainder of the restructuring period" (*Herald*, 12/12/91).

One of the underlying arguments for raising interest rates—to stimulate savings—also came under attack (and this time correctly so) by *Financial Gazette* commentator Eric Bloch:

> By far the greater part of Zimbabwe's population exists at or below the

> Poverty Datum Line and, unavoidably, must therefore spend what funds as they may be able to obtain on meeting the costs of the absolute essentials of life. Therefore, no matter how much they may desire to do so, they are unable to save and invest, irrespective of the attractiveness of interest rates. (*FG*, 11/6/92)

Similarly, Joseph Muzulu's (1993) econometric study of the relationship between interest rates and savings in Zimbabwe found no statistically significant link. Rates of saving remained below 20% of GDP throughout ESAP. But bank spreads (the difference between the rates paid to deposit and charged to borrowers) rose when the commercial bank lending rate soared to a peak of 47.5% in November 1992; the rate remained above 30% over subsequent years even when inflation subsided 20%-24%.

One way in which high interest rates did affect savings, however, was in attracting a flood of "hot money" to Zimbabwe, which was described in detail in Chapter Eight. During 1994, the increase in funds in bank Foreign Currency Deposit Accounts following currency liberalization was responsible for raising the level of the broad money supply (M2) by a full 5%, which in real terms was three quarters of the money supply increase in the economy that year (ZCTU 1996, 86). And this required yet higher interest rates (to "sterilize" the hot money inflows) so as not to contribute further to inflation.

As *Financial Times* correspondent and University of Zimbabwe business professor Tony Hawkins conceded, "The irony of the Zimbabwe case is that although liberalization appears to be working in attracting capital inflows and the return of capital flight, it has been having a perverse effect on inflation and the exchange rate, leaving industrialists muttering gloomily about de-industrialization" (*FG*, 28/6/95). (This would not be considered "ironic," of course, from the standpoint of the theory and extensive historic evidence in this book, showing precisely such a role for finance in exacerbating uneven development.)

In sum, as a result of treating symptoms of the financial overaccumulation phenomenon with mild and uneven reformist medicine—and notwithstanding government's expressed attempts to moderate the potential ill-effects of financial liberalization—something close to a free-for-all did in fact result in the early stages of the program: capital flight and hot money in-flows, deindustrialization and extremely high interest rates, and the crash of financial speculation. As the government itself later admitted to the World Bank, there was "inadequate preparation of a financial sector reform strategy, to provide for the institutional reforms needed to complement the interest and exchange rate deregulations implemented early in the program" (World Bank 1995a:48).

These financial and monetary phenomena were all the more extreme because they were accompanied by trade liberalization, which added to the growing disaster two other distinct features: conspicuous luxury goods consumption; and the demise of basic industries (such as textiles) which could have been a backbone for a better-articulated combination of local production, employment and consumption.

The failure of trade liberalization

The World Bank (1995c:7) expressed delight in 1995 that "trade liberalization proceeded without delays... [and] the foreign exchange control system has been largely dismantled. All current account transactions have been freed from exchange controls and import licensing and the exchange rate is now market-determined" (although "anomalies remained in the tariff/tax structure"). Yet it should have been fairly obvious right at the outset of trade liberalization, in late 1989, that tampering with the complex system of protective tariffs, duties and quotas would have disastrous results. With the first serious reduction in import controls—instead of Z$500 as the minimum amount requiring an import license, the new figure was Z$5,000—the hedonistic tendencies of Zimbabwe's elites were given free reign. According to Stoneman (1990:5),

> there is evidence of a big increase in the importing of luxury consumer goods, especially computers, video recorders and color TVs, and a halving of the black market value of the Zimbabwe dollar as those with spare local funds try to mobilise the necessary foreign exchange. This may be only a small foretaste of the consequences of liberalization, should the phasing, monitoring, or consequent corrective action prove deficient. It may thus be one of history's ironies that the African country which best showed the viable alternative to World Bank structural adjustment policies, itself embraced them just before they became widely discredited.

Stoneman's predictions appear to be correct, particularly regarding conspicuous consumption in the midst of intensifying poverty.[6] Following the 1991 introduction of the Open Guaranteed Import License (OGIL) to allow yet more imports, one manufacturer complained (*FG*, 21/11/91), "This particular World Bank scheme is a recipe for disaster. That is, unless you would rather buy a bottle of scotch to drown your troubles than buy a spanner, a nut and bolt or spares for your car." He criticized the profusion of

> expensive motor cars, of which we seem to see more and more new BMWs and Mercedes on the road than ever before—more it seems

> even than in rich countries like Germany. Every such car I see makes me think of the twenty or more people I could employ if I were granted the forex for raw materials for my factory. The haphazard introduction of certain goods on OGIL, and the panic that followed are indicative of a total lack of foresight and planning. It was blatantly obvious that introducing certain items to the OGIL list whilst actually reducing real import licenses would create havoc. Was this a crazy World Bank scheme, or a crazy Reserve Bank scheme?

In the same spirit, asked a letter-writer (C.Frizell of Harare) to the *Financial Gazette* (18/2/93), "How can our professional beggars so abjectly and convincingly beg for international aid (because they have so mismanaged our country) when Australian beer, French brandy, SA wine, German luxury cares and many, many other trinket items are freely available? The mind boggles—one either needs aid, or has enough money for luxury goods." Added columnist Di Mitchell (*FG*, 15/12/94), "ESAP has yet to deliver. The supermarkets and boutiques; the luxury stores of the low-density suburbanites contrast glaringly with the hordes of young people toting their vegetables, fruit, flowers and trinkets around the streets in a desperate endeavor to stay alive. Beggars, street kids, vagrants, common sights in the major capitals of the world, are now here to stay in Zimbabwe."

Excessive imports of luxury goods were just the beginning of the miscalculations. Perhaps the most striking reflection of the coming trade crisis was the widespread abuse of the OGIL system to stockpile raw materials and machinery. Cement is a good example of the speculative purchasing problem associated with OGIL. The Zimbabwe Building Contractors Association quickly expressed its "deep concern" that "A lot of big contractors in the country have imported a lot of cement which is more than they can consume. What is eventually going to happen is that these contractors, on finding that the cement has lost its potency, will sell it to the small contractors who will be desperate for their commodity to complete their projects" (*FG*, 26/9/91).

Bloch complained that in assessing import priorities, government had not analysed production inputs effectively: "The OGIL imports are of no benefit to production and market shortages continue to prevail" (*FG*, 28/11/91). Later, according to the ZCTU (1996:3), "tariffs on imported inputs were raized so that by 1995, tariffs on inputs were generally higher than those on finished products."

The trade deficit exploded during the early 1990s, and not only because, as Gibbon (1995:13) reports, the "increase in imports was roughly double that anticipated." In addition, rather than demonstrating the potential for export-led growth, ESAP had ensured export-led decline, as exports dropped a crippling 17% in US dollar terms between 1990 (US$1.753 billion) and 1992 (US$1.531 billion), with projected 1993 (post-drought) figures barely improved from the year before (at a level just 9% higher than in 1981) (World Bank 1995b, v.I:163). This was not purely due to agricultural failure (or the temporary rise in demand for formerly-exported food products) in 1992, for manufactured exports fell 19% in US dollar terms in 1991 (from US$537 million to US$434 million), although they recovered somewhat (to nearly US$500 billion) in subsequent years (ZCTU 1996:52). The demise of some export incentives was often blamed, and government succumbed to pressure to provide export incentives in its 1995/96 budget.

Even the World Bank (1995a:29) began to recognise that the anticipated benefits of trade liberalization were not materializing as planned:

> Having now moved rapidly to establish an economy that is subject to international competition, sustained growth will depend on promoting exports to maintain an external equilibrium. At present, the underlying capacity to export is weak... In aggregate, these concerns appear to contribute to the more muted supply response than would have been desired at this time of the program's implementation.

The capacity to export was weak partly because the favorable 1964 trade agreement Zimbabwe had enjoyed with South Africa expired in 1992 and was not renewed until mid 1996. This was due to the fact that the textile industry had by then restructured such that its own local production inputs had dropped from nearly 100% of the finished product to less than 25%. On the grounds that Zimbabwe had become a thorough-fare for dumping, South African producers successfully lobbied their own government—including post-apartheid trade and industry ministries headed by nominally-progressive ANC leaders—to delay the extension or renegotiation of the 1964 agreement.

A related problem, as the ZCTU (1996:62) put it, was that Zimbabwe failed to qualify as a "least-developed country" except for the purposes of gaining additional World Bank loans (at a lower interest rate): "Countries in this category escape most obligations under the GATT/WTO, and even ordinary developing countries are allowed a wide range of concessions. Thus, although the international institutions in theory recognise the vulnerability of poorer countries to free trade, they continue to force Zimbabwe to take risks and deny itself concessions that it could benefit from."

In contrast, during the decade of the 1980s—when protective tariffs prevented many Zimbabwean exporters from access to cheap inputs—manufactured exports had risen by an average of 5% annually (led by non-traditional exports), and total exports rose by 9% annually for 1985-90. Based on this momentum, Colin Stoneman (writing for the ZCTU) aptly concluded of the subsequent 1990-94 results that, "This is a dismal record for a policy whose main *raison d'etre* was salvation through higher exports, and cannot simply be blamed on the 1992 drought, for exports fell by over 3% in 1991 before any impact of the drought could be felt, whereas in the comparable drought year of 1987 they had actually risen" (ZCTU 1996:61).

Likewise, in late 1995 Zimtrade's Mike Humphrey now acknowledged the need for "a much greater involvement of the state" in industrial policy, in view of the fact that

> export performance over the period of ESAP had not been impressive, even in terms of the limited targets set... In many of the regional markets we have lost market share to various other countries, not least of which has been South Africa. This has been due to a number of factors which have made or products increasingly uncompetitive, such as poor quality, poor delivery times, bad customer service and follow up, price and lack of competitive suppliers' credit. (*CZI Industrial Review,* November 1995)

All of this should have been easy to predict in advance. (While feverishly working to shift CZI's position from inward- to outward-looking, Humphrey had notably failed to generate marketing studies for Zimbabwe's exports.) As Stoneman (ZCTU 1996:49) concluded, trade liberalization "has tended to turn manufacturers into traders... (as) firms have tended to stop manufacturing products locally, preferring to import them directly and then sell them to local consumers."

Meanwhile, much other evidence began to accumulate on the efficacy of ESAP, not merely in terms of the enormous disruptions in financial and trade patterns just reviewed, but with respect to the vast gamut of official controls and private sector norms that ESAP was meant to revolutionise. Such evidence would be seen from rather divergent perspectives, however, and it is worth reviewing commentary and analysis by the government and World Bank, by business interests, and then by representatives of ordinary people.

The discourse of adjustment 1: The government and World Bank

In order, first, to understand the growing hegemony of neo-liberal discourse (the "Washington Consensus")—particularly the ubiquitous assertion that orthodox, market-led structural adjustment is the only route to economic prosperity—it is useful to briefly survey the World Bank's own evaluations of its first ESAP loan. The first evaluation included an 18-page contribution by the Zimbabwe Finance Ministry, possibly the government's most thoughtful and self-critical review of economic policy.[7]

Even a cursory survey helps situate the ongoing failures of Zimbabwean socio-economic policy-makers within a global context, for it was not merely direct World Bank or US AID loan conditionality on projects (or within financial and trade liberalization) that was responsible for the terribly unsuccessful and unjust outcomes. More importantly, it was the sense that Zimbabwe had joined the group of nations "undergoing economic reform"; that in spite of the 1992 drought there remained a "firm official commitment" to liberalization; and that Zimbabwe's elites were now responsible international citizens, promoting the noble causes of open markets and foreign investment.

Rewarding such widespread sentiment within what Mugabe (1989:358) had termed ZANU's "very powerful bourgeois group," the Bank's (1995a:23) *Project Completion Report* for ESAP gave the best possible final grade for the first stage of the utterly failed program: "highly satisfactory." How could this be? How, when even among Zimbabwe's business intelligentsia Bank advice came to be regarded as a bad joke (as we shall see below), did its staff continue to dispute the obvious?

The answer may partly have to do with vanity—or, more precisely, the need for loan officers to justify their and their colleagues' work—for the Bank (1995a:17) acknowledges playing "a key role in the dissemination of the program and in building support amongst the wider donor community." Hence Bank staff (1995a:24) also rated their own performance as "highly satisfactory" (again, top marks) for identification and appraisal, and "satisfactory" for preparation assistance and supervision.[8]

As for Zimbabwe government officials, the Bank (1995a:23-24) was just as generous, rating ESAP's preparation as "highly satisfactory" and its implementation and operation as "satisfactory." The Bank concluded that macro and sector policies and financial objectives were "substantially" achieved (again, the highest mark), and that institutional development, poverty reduction, public sector management and private sector development were "partially" accomplished. Project sustainability was deemed "likely."

Interestingly, government's own contribution to the ESAP *Project Completion Report*,[9] written in June 1994, was rather more defensive, for it complained that the "poorly articulated framework for dealing with the social dimensions of adjustment priorities for alleviating poverty... left the government vulnerable to—generally unfounded—accusations regarding its investments in human resources, and pressures to adopt ill-thought out programs." Hence from government's perspective, the framework was not wrong, merely "poorly articulated" and hence criticisms were "generally unfounded."

As for implementation problems, the government rationalized, they occurred because "the starting position [not a full-fledged crisis] muffled the sense of urgency needed to implement the wide ranging and complex elements of the program," in particular deficit shrinkage, privatization, and the Social Dimensions of Adjustment (SDA) fund. Over time, government continued, "the sense of urgency at the decision-making level began to accelerate. However, the analytical base for decision-making was not always in place, so policy reforms were delayed, or made on the basis of incomplete evaluation of options and implications" (World Bank 1995a:48-50).

And yet, the government insisted, had ESAP been implemented more forcefully and if "pursuit of program targets" had been more aggressive, this "might have placed the whole program in jeopardy" because

> an underlying risk associated with the program, that of perceptions of a skewing of benefits in favor of the white minority and black elites, was not adequately catered for in the early development of the program. This perception has arisen despite the fact that the privileged position of minorities was being sustained by the regulatory regime being dismantled under ESAP. As a result, some measures have had to be introduced to more explicitly cater for indigenous business interests. (World Bank 1995a:49)

The argument, implicitly, is that the skewed benefits in favor of white and black elites were merely a (presumably incorrect) *perception*, devoid of reality in light of the dismantling of previous regulatory privileges which hurt those very elites. (Government's only apparent concession to this "perception" was the rapid attempt to create a black petty bourgeoisie.)

If the government bureaucrats who contributed to the report truly believed that ESAP did not result in more uneven distributions of income and wealth, they did nothing to document this extraordinary, counter-intuitive belief. The Bank's own *Project Completion Report* assessment failed to conduct any income or racial (or gender) income distribution so as to determine whether or not the widespread "perception" of skewed benefits to elites was correct. As argued below (and in Chapters Seven and Eight), there was certainly a degree of suffering by a few unfortunate white and black elites, namely non-competitive manufacturers and those speculators whose financial bubbles burst. But such nuanced "class fraction" analysis would have no place in such an evaluation; instead, government favored outright denial that Zimbabwe's uneven development was intensifying due (even in part) to ESAP.

Observers may shake their heads in wonder at the myopia of a report which, after all, "has a restricted distribution and may be used by recipients only in the performance of their official duties. Its contents may not otherwise be disclosed without World Bank authorization."[10] This was government confessing to the World Bank, not to Zimbabwean society at large, for aside from some belated coverage in the *Financial Gazette* (22/6/95), the evaluation was indeed kept out of the hands of the millions of Zimbabweans adversely affected by ESAP.

A few months later, the Bank's June 1995 *Performance Audit Report* (conducted by a different set of staff) offered much the same line of analysis, alleging—without any supporting evidence—that "Most people agree that the reforms were relevant and necessary" and that "For most firms, there have been clear gains resulting from the trade and exchange rate liberalization..." (World Bank 1995c:8, 10). The report contains no polling data or firm cost-benefit analyses (contrasting the costs of high real interest rates and benefits of collapsing real wages, for example, with the skewed benefits of increased access to luxury goods and other imports).

On the one hand the *Performance Audit Report* confirms a key Bank (1995c:7) justification: "ESAP's implementation was complicated by a severe drought, which hit Zimbabwe in 1992. The drought contributed to a major fall in GDP that year, leaving the country in its worst recession since independence in 1980." The passive wording here—ESAP was "complicated by" drought, which "left" Zimbabwe in recession—is slippery but effective.

On the other hand, though, the report (World Bank 1995c:10-13) does acknowledge some severe problems. "In reviewing the considerable literature on ESAP and discussing its impact with various groups in the field, what emerges is a sense that ESAP has, to date, entailed considerable pain but little visible gain." Moreover, "it would appear that some basic questions were not explicitly addressed at the outset," namely job creation, income earning abilities of "informal sector participants" and prospects for residents of the communal areas. The Bank also considered ESAP an example of failure to accomplish "proper sequencing," specifically in reducing the fiscal deficit first; yet the same report advocated increased state spending on education, health and civil servant salaries (the wage bill of government had fallen from 16% of GDP in 1990 to 12% in 1995).[11]

Finally, the Bank concedes, "The failure to address these issues squarely means that ESAP (along with other ongoing government initiatives) may not be sufficient [*sic*] to better the lot of the majority of Zimbabweans and progressively eliminate the socio-economic dualism underlying present economic disparities and social tensions within a politically acceptable time frame." The semantic elision here implies that orthodox macroeconomic policies are "necessary but not sufficient" to reduce poverty; this is a seductive way to avoid the more appropriate conclusion that such policies *cause* poverty.[12]

To eliminate "dualism" and combat poverty, the *Performance Audit Report* recommends more power for the World Bank: "Although the Bank encouraged the government to incorporate an SDA program under ESAP, it was less effective in influencing its detailed design and monitoring its implementation through appropriate conditionality" (World Bank 1995c:10). In other words, the social wage would not have crashed quite so far had the Bank been more involved in confirming the need for social investments.

Is this credible? After all, the Bank's Manuel Hinds (1990:15) once candidly explained the objectives of both liberalization measures and "the overall model chosen to integrate the economy into the international markets... These measures should aim at avoiding the appropriation of rents by suppliers of nontradables and workers. That is, they should maintain the real wage low, so that excess profits accrue to capital." Such objectives were met, with the proviso that "excess profits" accrued not to productive capital necessarily but largely to financiers (domestic and especially international). With labor now harshly disciplined and overaccumulated capital suffering sharp devaluation, Zimbabwe's economy was now sufficiently open that, as the 1990s progressed, perhaps the World Bank could afford to become somewhat kindler and gentler.

But a neo-classical economic "human capital investment" approach underlay this rhetoric, with consequent limits for redistributive social policy. For when it came to deregulation of markets, the Bank barely budged from orthodoxy. In November 1995, Bank Poverty Mission consultant Tony Addison (1995:4-8) asserted, "When we assess the impact of adjustment policies on the poor, it is also important to keep in mind what would have happened to poverty in the absence of ESAP (the 'Counterfactual')." The answer, he argued, was to be found in the example of maize market deregulation (ironically, the Bank had earlier in 1995 suggested direct subsidization of yellow maize at 30%-40% below market prices).

Addison demonstrated to audiences of civil servants, NGOs and academics that following the early 1990s deregulation, "hammer-milled" maize (*mugayiwa*) became available to consumers at dozens of small local black-operated mills at a much lower price than state-subsidized roller meal. The latter originated from Grain Marketing Board maize (bought from commercial farmers), was milled by large-scale corporate millers, and was sold in ordinary shops. The price of roller meal soared in the early 1990s when the subsidy was removed (at the World Bank's insistence). Prior to that, in 1990, a 5 kg bag of roller meal cost Z$5.16 (in 1993 dollars), but as Addison put it, "Poor consumers therefore helped to pay for the monopoly profits of the large-scale millers." When the subsidy was lifted in June 1993, the price rose by 55%, to Z$8.83. By that time, newly-deregulated *mugayiwa* cost an average of Z$5.50 per 5 kg bag. Hence the *mugayiwa* appeared to be less expensive than roller meal (after the maize subsidy was cut), and because it was less refined had more nutritional value as well.

But in warmly praising the deregulation, Addison not only failed to take into account the fact that Bank-supported ESAP deregulation had caused the roller meal price to soar, he also ignored the cost of maize distribution and sales (typically included as a "mark-up" on roller meal sold to consumers in shops). For consumers of *mugayiwa*, additional costs now included the expense in transport and time that consumers faced trying to get hold of unmilled grain and bring it from the countryside (or alternatively buying it in urban areas); the time and expense of travelling to and from the hammer mill; and the cost of time spent queuing for the grain to be milled (at that time conservatively estimated by UNICEF at three quarters of an hour). Addison did not acknowledge these additional costs — or that they were mainly borne by women — and hence his claim that unsubsidized *mugayiwa* was "20%-47% cheaper than roller meal" was most questionable. Nor, on the production side, did he address what even the pro-liberalization *Financial Gazette* (10/6/93) conceded was the "widespread exploitation of communal farmers by businessmen being reported in many parts of the country" following the deregulation of maize.

Nevertheless, as discussed in Chapter Eleven, the Bank did recognise the rapid rise in poverty during ESAP and took some measures to adjust its own stingy image. But the combination of Bank and government excuses for ESAP's failure, and their mutual insistence upon continuing along the neo-liberal path, meant that a full-fledged economic strategy debate could not begin, no matter the quality of opposing arguments (which in the case of the ZCTU, as described below, was quite impressive).

In a far more thoughtful review of ESAP's implementation than the Bank or government mustered, Gibbon (1995:13-14) listed the three most important mistakes: donor failure "to punctually disburse the [ESAP] funding"; the Bank's "apparent second thoughts on the program's content"; and the Bank's foolish recommendation that the Grain Marketing Board sell off

600,000 tons of accumulated maize stocks (at a loss) just prior to the devastating 1992 drought.[13] Each mistake sharply exacerbated Zimbabwe's financing and balance of payments crises. But even if implementation had been less flawed, ESAP probably would have generated sharp criticism from its many victims—particularly poor and working people, but also (to a degree) business elites. In stark contrast to the Bank's narcissism, their evaluations were often quite bitter.

The discourse of adjustment 2: Victimized businesses

What had appeared to be relatively warm relations between business and government as ESAP began (see Chapter Six), broke down quickly. By the middle of 1992, the *Financial Gazette* (23/7/92) surmised that economic policy mistakes were bringing the entire economy to the edge of an abyss:

> The private sector has evidenced tremendous resilience over the past 27 years but we doubt that it will be able to sustain the latest blow [another interest rate hike], or if it does, how long it will go on like this and whether the sacrifice is necessary. The Reserve Bank's monetary policies have created a minefield out of the money market. Company liquidations have become the order of the day as heavily borrowed companies fail to meet the increased interest rates and send workers onto the streets to swell the ranks of the unemployed. The retrenchments, together with the increases in the prices of the public's daily necessities, have extensively eroded consumer demand. Many companies are sitting on stocks that nobody will buy. Still, they have to service the loans with which they purchased the stock. The Zimbabwe stock market, a barometer of the economy's health, has been in a downward spiral, indicating that the economy is in terminal stress. Some banks would have long since closed shop were it not that they have stopped competing against each other. They are leading a hand-to-mouth existence, occasionally throwing a lifebelt to those most threatened with extinction.

There is revealed in this excerpt a healthy dose of realism, yet nevertheless also a continuing failure by business analysts to recognise and reconcile the principal contradiction that had emerged with the displacement of overaccumulated capital into Zimbabwe's financial sector: the self-destructive tendencies embedded within the power of money.

Yet to have suggested, at the outset of ESAP, that such classically Zimbabwean "despondency" (as it is so often termed) would characterize the business community within two years, would have been to attract great scorn. Capital's initial confidence in ESAP was impressive, especially in the brief period from mid 1990 (when the brunt of the program was unveiled) to mid 1991 (just before the financial markets crashed). Although doubts about implementation capacity may have worried some, there were few critics. Speaking to the Confederation of Zimbabwe Industries in November 1990, even economist Rob Davies remarked, "Now is a good time to implement ESAP" (though he warned the industrialists to beware of potential "political unrest sparked off by a vocal middle class urban constituency") (*CZI Industrial Review*, December 1990).

The February 1991 interest rate increase passed almost unremarked, and when a Paris donor conference in April 1991 provided Chidzero with US$700 million in loan commitments, businesses prepared for a major foreign exchange spending spree (*Africa South*, May 1991). Imports picked up dramatically. Although the Central Statistical Office's regular poll of business confidence covering the period May-August 1991 recorded negative levels for transport equipment and foodstuffs industries, there was overall positive feedback and clear signs of business confidence for the chemical, petroleum, and paper, printing and publishing industries (*Herald*, 28/11/91). One indication of ESAP's success to that point, in the words of Eric Bloch, was that "goods in short supply—packaging materials, textile inputs—are now readily available" (*FG*, 26/9/91).[14]

However, confidence eroded extremely quickly when monetary variables—soaring inflation (in the wake of the lifting of price controls) and money supply aggregates—led the Reserve Bank of Zimbabwe to devalue the currency by more than 35% over a period of three months and to double short-term interest rates in September 1991, both apparently at the behest of the World Bank. By late 1991 a barrage of complaints surfaced.

Most importantly, perhaps, it quickly became clear to many inward-oriented businesses that effective demand was now slipping away. According to Peter Johnston, managing director of clothing producer Saybrook, the OGIL system had not helped his industry (even though clothing had been championed by the CZI to become a major exporter): "The unemployed will probably not buy much of our products, whilst the few breadwinners will find it difficult to buy clothing for their dependents" (*FG*, 28/11/91). Worse, the effective demand constraint generated a new market in second-hand clothing, an unintended consequence of foreign charitable donations (*FG*, 18/3/93). Clothing also suffered from high interest rates, the removal of some export incentives and the four-year termination of the South African trade agreement (exports actually fell from Z$400 million in 1993 to an estimated Z$290 million in 1994). From

1992 to 1994, more than 60 clothing firms shut down (*FG*, 24/11/94) and by 1995 the industry was operating at only 65% capacity (ZCTU 1996:48).

Businesses began to realize that, in the words of the *Financial Gazette* (21/11/91), "sufficient time and finance may not be available to allow them to re-tool and re-orientate before competing imports enter the local market." The only bright spot was that thanks to currency devaluation the tourist industry boomed (visitors rose from half a million in 1989 to 750,000 in 1992 and more than one million in 1994).

The consensus among corporate opinion-makers, increasingly, was that liberalization was good in principle but that the government was implementing ESAP with its usual ham-handedness. And there can be doubt that during the fragile period from mid-1991 through early 1992, some of the problems with ESAP were undoubtedly the government's fault. The *Southern African Economist* (December 1991/January 1992) cited

> piecemeal and uncoordinated and even panicky responses. Some economists blame such panicky responses on the fact that a government used to running a command economy finds it hard to allow market forces to operate. At the first sign that it is losing control, the government moves quickly to impose controls in different forms. This has been the case in the 5% penalty on second drawings for tobacco paper, the 50% deposit on OGIL imports, which was quickly dropped and the 10% surcharge duty on OGIL imports and an additional Z$0.70 per kilogramme duty on all imported cement and clinker.

In this erratic context, the government's perpetual tendency to raise expectations about ESAP and its vulgar marketing of the program were also objectionable to the more enlightened among Zimbabwe's corporate elite.[15] Meanwhile, the Finance Ministry's failure to control OGIL abuse—speculative purchasing and stockpiling of raw materials and luxury consumption goods by firms and wealthy individuals—severely prejudiced the anticipated capital goods investment drive.

Predictably, the World Bank (1995a:48) blamed the continued investment strike on the "lack of confidence in the government's commitment" to ESAP based on "a weak partnership between government and the private sector... [and] mutual suspicion, feeding on poor communications." But the *Financial Gazette* (26/9/91) conceded that in reality "There has been a large element of irresponsibility on the part of some concerns in the private sector, which will go a long way towards undermining the reform program."

In another camp altogether, indigenous business leaders and black corporate managers had become among the most acerbic critics of ESAP, for now their prized access to regulatory favors, foreign exchange and state patronage relationships were thrown into question. The *Financial Gazette* (28/10/93), in a controversial editorial, conceded that "There is a real danger of this peaceful country being plunged into ugly and destructive racial animosity" because "With ESAP, the black bosses have become a liability rather than being an asset." In the past, "Black executives were used to window-dress white companies. In this way they would be conduits to government when it came to negotiations on price control, labor disputes and foreign currency allocations."

In the same spirit, entrepreneur Sam Gozo turned this balance sheet on its head,

> ESAP is now more of a burden than an asset. I would say it should be scrapped and emphasis placed on self-reliance where Zimbabwe should put together available resources to good use and actually engage in a policy of regional economic integration and close cooperation with the new South Africa... There is no small black business which can survive under the present regulations. The money is scarce and if you get it, it would be so expensive that you cannot afford to pay it back. (*FG*, 3/2/94)

With growth and restored profitability nowhere on the horizon, it was not long before even large-scale capital began questioning the program.[16] Just two months after ESAP's official launch, Sam Moyo (1991:2) had reported "signs of division among the business groups... segments of the CZI not having been consulted are not in step with the general agreeability of the CZI to the program." By late 1993, the *Financial Gazette* (16/12/93) declared that the CZI was itself "one of the victims of the economic reform program" in the wake of membership criticism and desertion, financial mismanagement, and a crisis of staff morale, not to mention (white) ethnic leadership squabbles.

Even more strikingly, several Zimbabwean financiers rapidly deserted their hard-won (if uneasy) alliance with the state and international finance. Founders Building Society prepared for the worst by developing a "Job Loss Mortgage Protection Plan" to protect the newly-unemployed from default on their housing bonds (*FG*, 12/9/91). And a new complaint emerged: monetary policies had become so tight that they were "fuelling inflation and further depressing the economy," as conservative commentator Eric Bloch put it (*FG*, 11/6/92). Inflation was measured by the IMF at 43% in mid 1992, but when a group of bank chief executives pleaded to the Finance Ministry for lower interest rates, the response was "that the recommendations were in conflict with the proposals and targets set down by the International Monetary Fund." The bankers responded by informing IMF officials visiting Harare that "ESAP does not mean destroying the productive sector which is what is happening at the moment. What we are saying is that there is no point in achieving targets only to find that the productive sector is no more" (*FG*, 6/8/92).

As documented below, large-scale deindustrialization appeared a likely possibility as trade deficits soared, debt repayment levels reached unprecedented heights, and interest rates remained extraordinarily high (often more than 10% in real terms). Jonee Blanchfield, deputy president of the CZI confirmed:

> The single most troublesome feature for industry this year [1992] has been interest rates. Zimbabwean industry should now be investing heavily in new capacity, in new capability and in training, if we are to meet the challenge of a free market economy. Instead, most of us are working ourselves into the ground just to repay the banks... High interest rates threaten to derail ESAP and threaten to deindustrialise this country. (*FG*, 7/1/93)

Standard Bank economists continued to worry in early 1993 that "unless government abandons IMF-stipulated monetary targets, real money supply growth will continue to fall this year with a consequent decline in output" (*FG*, 18/3/93). The *Financial Gazette* (17/6/93) soon protested the secretive manner in which interest rates were determined: "Monetary policy is the domain of the general public as well and should be kept fully involved, through debate, in the formulation of such policy." Naturally the "public" was not involved in any manner, and as a result smaller retail and commercial businesses became increasingly angry about the high rates. As Zimbabwe National Chamber of Commerce president Ted Makoni complained in late 1994, "This situation does not enhance the country's capacity to retain the existing infrastructure as too many businesses are going to the wall" (*FG*, 22/12/94).

When an Oxfam report appeared in 1993 that was critical of the impact of structural adjustment policies on African economic growth, the *Financial Gazette* (13/5/93) joined the chorus of business critics concerned about the overall direction of policy: "Oxfam's forthright report should be used by African countries to draw the world's attention to the economic malaise that has been inflicted on Africa partly by the World Bank and IMF." At the end of 1993 the *Financial Gazette* (30/12/93) editorialized, "The IMF and World Bank continue to express faith in the reform process because they have no real alternative to putting their money where their mouth is. But throwing billions of dollars at Zimbabwe every year is simply enabling the government to avoid the hard choices it needs to make about spending."

Perhaps most bluntly, *Financial Times* correspondent and University of Zimbabwe business professor Tony Hawkins angrily traced government's ESAP boosterism to its source in Washington: "Every year, the World Bank officials dutifully prepare invariably over-optimistic assessments designed to show the worst is past and that the client state, whose economy is under the microscope, is on the brink of sustained recovery." Added UN Development Programme resident representative to Zimbabwe Carlos Lopez, "The World Bank figures are always exaggerated to give a rosy picture of whatever it is they are involved in" (*FG*, 27/1/94).

Hawkins went on to lambast the Bank for pretending—at a Paris Consultative Group donor meeting in March 1995—that ESAP was still, as ever, "on track." Eight weeks later the IMF suspended US$120 million in a credit line to Zimbabwe due to both budget overruns and—ironically, to be sure—excessive foreign borrowing. Commented Hawkins,

> Either the Bank knew in March that all was far from well, but refused to let on publicly for fear of undermining the donor meeting, or it hopelessly misread the situation. If it chose the first route of not letting on publicly, then its newfound commitment to transparency is not worth the paper it is written on. Either way, the World Bank's credibility has suffered an enormous setback, and the money spent on employing public relations experts to rebuild its image and credibility would be better spent on poverty alleviation. The World Bank's conduct in the Zimbabwean case raises a very serious issue. If the Bank had done its job properly, then Zimbabwe's budget and public sector crises need not have reached the dimensions that they have since. The debt burden would be less; the new taxes to be imposed would be less severe and the public spending cuts less drastic... the Bank has needlessly delivered 11 million Zimbabweans into the hands of harsher austerity than should have been necessary. (*Southern African Economist*, June/July 1995)

Reactions by international financiers to the emerging problems and criticisms were somewhat underwhelming, as the World Bank failed to make logical alliances with Zimbabwe's private sector elite. The Bank's Poortman, desperate for an African success story, appeared as little more than a propagandist when (in contrast to the CZI) he claimed in November 1991—with inflation and interest rates soaring and financial markets and production crashing—that Zimbabwe's economic reforms were "on course" (*FG*, 7/11/91). By 1993, this refrain had become unconvincing, *Financial Gazette* editorialist Iden Wetherell (1993:4) contended:

> Everybody repeats the official mythology that the recent drought has slightly derailed ESAP, while insisting (the wish being father to the thought) that economic reform is otherwise on course. The most notable representative of this starry-eyed approach is the World Bank's chief in Harare, Mr Christiaan Poortman. His emollient statements over the past 18 months reflect the devotion of a faith unmoved by facts.

Business confidence sagged further in 1994 due to the demise of export incentives and the continuation of extremely high interest rates (*EIU*, June 1994). Manufacturers complained about "the high cost of money, lack of export incentives, high duties on raw materials and the adverse impact of the delayed re-negotiation of a trade agreement with South Africa... [while] the overall situation of capacity utilization remained negative" (*FG*, 1/12/94).

Matters degenerated further still for industry in 1995, as First Merchant Bank announced that without "the reintroduction of subsidies or export bonus payments to give the [manufacturing] companies a fighting chance of survival" (i.e., without a reversal of ESAP in key areas), the result would be full-fledged deindustrialization: "After the businesses, jobs and export revenues have been impaired or destroyed, manufacturers point out, a far greater investment of funds will be needed than the amount needed now to prevent the current situation from getting to that crisis point" (*Quarterly Guide to the Economy*, June 1995).

There were signs that it may have been too late for at least two of the sectors for which ESAP proponents had generated great export hopes in 1990. Using an index which sets the 1980 volume of manufacturing output at 100, clothing output in early 1995 was 80 (compared to the 1991 peak of 190) while textiles fell to 75 (from 1991 production levels of 250). The *Financial Gazette* (22/6/95) now even called for new protective tariffs—"The threat of deindustrialization is real, as evidenced by the textile industry, and now the automotive sectors"—and listed a full set of criticisms of government's policies, which are worth citing at length:

> The government goes to Paris in March with its economic credibility in tatters. It has failed to meet all key targets it set itself at the commencement of the reform program... All pronouncements of uniformity of purpose between the government and the donors are now a mere facade... [as witnessed by] the rushed and uncoordinated introduction of consumptive taxes over the past two weeks. An income tax surcharge to raise desperately-needed revenue to balance the books has been brought in

> under the guise of a drought levy. Announcement of intentions to privatise or liquidate loss-making parastatals have been part of last-minute attempts to satisfy donor demands. The cancellation of the entire Public Sector Investment Programme in addition to these other rushed decisions so close to March cannot be mere coincidence. Contrary to World Bank assertions that these measures should yield growth in the medium to long-term, we see a reversal of the economic resurgence which commenced last year. (*FG*, 9/2/95)

By late 1995, CZI president Jonah Wakatama listed further complaints about the implementation of ESAP:

> implementation of policy decisions still slow, rampant inflation eroding real disposable incomes; resultant high interest rates inhibiting economic growth; unclear tariff regime threatening existing industries; flight of capital from productive sector to money markets; poor financial management in the public sector; and increased unemployment with a number of companies going under (*CZI Industrial Review*, November 1995).[17]

At the end of the day, however, Wakatama's deputy, Blanchfield (1994:11), was perhaps most honest: "We in the private sector accept all the goodies but carp *ad infinitum* about the inconveniences and the often necessary, unpopular decisions. We make press statements with zealous hyperbole. We overreact without understanding." Indeed, the occasional victims aside, leading members of the business community—particularly holders of financial assets—were after all the greatest beneficiaries of luxury goods imports, declining real wages, the new-found ability to move money out of the country, commercial deregulation and so many other aspects of liberalization.

But for whatever reason, we can safely conclude that in seeking "to maintain the real wage low, so that excess profits accrue to capital" both the World Bank and Zimbabwe government ignored perhaps the most important implementation advice tendered by the Bank's Manuel Hinds (1990:17), which was, simply, "In carrying out all these activities, a close alliance between government and private agents must be developed." The same failure to make "popular" alliances—notwithstanding yearnings from organized labor—is evident when considering bottom-up perspectives on ESAP.

The discourse of adjustment 3: Popular anguish and official reaction

A third of Zimbabweans are today unable to afford a basic food basket (60% of household expenditure), shelter (another 25%), minimal clothing, education, health care and transport. Price increases over the five years from 1990-94 amounted to 173% for all goods, but 237% for food and 316% for medical care (Bijlmakers, Bassett, and Sanders 1996:64). As even the World Bank (1995c:30-35) had to acknowledge, poverty increased sharply during the period of ESAP and "Programmes set up to help alleviate these transitional problems have not been as effective as planned."

Consumption remains extremely skewed, with the top 10% of Zimbabweans consuming 34% of all goods and services, and the bottom decile consuming just 3%. "This level of inequality is high," the Bank recognises, ranking Zimbabwe among the world's most unequal countries (Botswana, Brazil, Chile, Guatemala, Honduras, Kenya and South Africa).

Moreover, the trends generated by Zimbabwe's exemplary social policy during the first decade of independence—reducing infant mortality from 86 to 49 per 1,000 live births, raising the immunization rate from 25% to 80% and life expectancy from 56 to 62 years, doubling primary school enrollment, etc—witnessed ominous reversals. The problem, according to the Bank (1995c:9), was that "Budget cutting appears to have been an end in itself," leading to "the widely reported 'brain drain' of experienced teachers and health workers in the public sector, despite no official retrenchments in these areas." This was particularly true during the brief reign of Ariston Chambati, but the Bank's innocence is questionable, as previous chapters documented.

Crime statistics are also revealing. From 1989 to 1993 (the latest available data), the number of house or car break-ins soared from 43,274 to 65,392 (51%); incidents of stock theft rose doubled from 6,765 to 13,776 (105%); and robbery also doubled from 5,842 to 11,564 cases (98%).

But unemployment was the most glaring reflection of ESAP's failure. It was worsened not only by the shrinkage of the civil service, but by private sector retrenchments, which accounted for eight out of ten lost jobs during the first two years of ESAP (World Bank 1995b, v.II:14). The CZI experienced some confusion on how to handle the issue of widespread retrenchment, witnessed by the change from Humphrey's honesty in March 1990 about anticipated employment cutbacks to, in September 1991, a deceitful quote from the CZI's in-house magazine (*The Industrialist*,

September 1991): "Much harm has been done by the disaster rumor-mongers prophesying massive retrenchments as a result of ESAP."

More harm than the retrenchments themselves? Between January 1991 and July 1992, more than 4,000 private sector employees lost their jobs. Attempts to sort out the resulting problems through collective bargaining (rather than through traditional Ministry of Labor decree) were ineffectual in the new environment, because, according to then-Labor Minister John Nkomo, "Unfortunately our confidence has been betrayed. Our social partners have not conducted themselves in a responsible manner" (*FG*, 20/8/92).

One clear indication of the breakdown in the social accord between government and business was the tendency of companies to price-gouge after controls were lifted, and to stockpile to create artificial shortages. There were frequent allegations of such behavior by the Consumer Council of Zimbabwe—essentially a market-oriented middle-class group in the tradition of the Western-style consumer movement—and these were given a relatively high profile in the state-controlled media, although in a manner mainly designed to persuade consumers that their interests were being protected within the framework of ESAP.[18]

Other social forces increasingly voiced discontent. Students chimed in as expected: "ESAP has also severely affected the student," remarked a writer in the University of Zimbabwe student magazine. "Few, if any, will manage to buy textbooks this year... ESAP tends to mean Especially Students Are Prone to Suffering" (*Focus* v.1:1992). As noted, opposition also emerged from black entrepreneurs. Douglas Ruhukwa, vice president of the Indigenous Business Development Centre argued, "ESAP is an animal we don't know. All we know is it has been a failure in Africa and has recorded a few successes elsewhere. It is well known that IMF and World Bank recipes do not bring dramatic economic changes in countries they are prepared for, and it won't be different with Zimbabwe" (*FG*, 5/12/91).[19]

As for the middle classes (especially civil servants left unprotected), according to Sam Moyo (1991:11), "It remains to be seen how, in the absence of widespread consultation, the government will contain their pressures. Special subventions for the amelioration of the problems confronting this class may become necessary for the political stability that the program requires."

As ESAP generated economic fallout unprecedented in recent memory, substantial political instability emerged, worse than anything experienced since the mid 1980s ZANU-ZAPU conflict. As early as September 1991, the *Financial Gazette* (5/9/91) editorialized frankly about a possible scenario:

> The socio-economic hardships may force many Zimbabweans to go into the streets and show their disenchantment with the system. Many will remember the so-called IMF riots in places like Sudan and Zambia... While we do not advocate the oppression and suppression of the masses, it would be very unfortunate if the government were to be swayed by the popular view to abandon the program because of the difficulties that it would have necessitated.

Indeed two years later, bread riots broke out in high-density suburbs of Harare, skillfully deflected by ZANU into attacks on bread suppliers. But already, deep-rooted alienation and jokes about ESAP reflected the popular desire to simply abandon the reforms. Nearly nine out every ten trade unionists polled by Lloyd Sachikonye viewed ESAP negatively. But, noted Sachikonye (1995a:127-128), "much of the workers' understanding and critique of ESAP relates more to its effects rather than [to] its rationale and objectives," and hence when organized resistance did emerge (such as a banned May Day 1992 anti-ESAP demonstration that led to the prosecution of the "ZCTU Six"), its "amorphousness and porousness to state manipulation proved a weak basis for sustainability."

Notwithstanding a weak legacy of trade union organising and advocacy, worker confidence and unions' ambitions were by no means snuffed. In 1994 industrial action was revived by postal and telecommunications workers, Air Zimbabwe engineers (four days), bank employees (six days), construction workers (four days), and physicians (which led to the firing of all junior doctors). Strikes were down in 1995 (as they were, too, and quite dramatically, in South Africa, after a very active 1994). But rather than signalling the acquiescence of trade unionists to ESAP, this may have been more a reflection of an unusual and temporary conjuncture, in which the demotion of Nathan Shamuyarira from Foreign Minister to Labor Minister generated a need to rapidly reestablish a power base. The ZCTU had long been under attack—through powerful divide-and-rule tactics—from Shamuyarira's predecessor Nkomo, and its critique weakened steadily during the early 1990s until it finally won a begged-for corporatist-style pact with government. By mid 1995 its paper *The Worker* was proudly declaring the unions' new-found influence.[20]

But corporatist philosophy would not thrive under conditions of continuing structural crisis. Another major burst of unorganized social protest occurred in November 1995, along Samora Machel Avenue and other streets of Harare's financial district. Catalysed by police brutality but grounded in socio-economic desperation, a large protest march called by the ZimRights human rights group against careless police shootings of civilians was haplessly managed by Home Affairs Minister Damiso

Dabengwa. As *Horizon* (December 1995) reported, "frustration over the unemployment rate, soaring prices and poverty created by structural adjustment" were the basis for the destruction of property (especially government vehicles) that followed: "Jobless masses in the capital's burgeoning population were motivated by 'survival instincts' to loot shops in the city centre." According to ZimRights' Reginald Matchaba-Hove, "structural adjustment and the ethics of materialism had created 'a culture of violence' in society."

The only concession to the ugly mood was a realization of the need for consultations with non-governmental organizations and representatives of impoverished social forces, particularly in official poverty studies and, perhaps, even in the design of the next stage of ESAP. Necessary as it was, though, this slight opening would not be sufficient. With growth and profitability finally returning thanks largely to good rains in 1996, but with inflation still above 20% and public sector wage offers in the low single digits, unprecedented civil service militancy emerged, signalling the great gap between rulers and subjects. For nearly a fortnight in mid 1996, a strike of more than two thirds of the civil service paralysed government. Daily demonstrations in downtown Harare attracted the support of ZCTU leadership, who had grappled unsuccessfully for several years to incorporate the civil servants' organization into the trade union movement. ZCTU president Gibson Sibanda threatened a general strike in solidarity with the civil service, and public sector workers refused to compromise on wage demands and protection for strike leaders. Just back from a honeymoon after a lavish wedding, Mugabe revealed his lack of comprehension of civil service grievances. The government quickly folded to worker demands.

But the occasional victory from below did not sway political elites from the neo-liberal path. Aside from occasional populist posturing by Mugabe—whose oft-repeated land reform promises kept rural hopes high and whose May 1996 doubling of the minimum wage boosted spirits (until for most workers it was revoked, on grounds the announcement had been a press mistake)—Zimbabwean officials did not appear sympathetic. Emblematic of the elites' venal attitude were remarks by Tichaendepi Masaya, Minister of State for Finance, Economic Planning and Development, who when confronted with evidence of problems caused by ESAP in 1994 was adamant that the policies—especially intensified cost recovery efforts in urban areas—would not budge. According to the *Southern African Economist* (May 1994), Masaya openly bragged

> that some of these measures were introduced to encourage people to move out of towns and "go back to the rural areas" to make use of the infrastructure which the government has built over the years to uplift

> the living conditions of the rural folk... "To those able bodied people who choose to be idle in towns I would say, let them rot."

Amongst ZANU politicians, the exception proved the rule. Thus Sidney Malunga, a progressive MP until his suspicious 1994 death in a car accident, could be brutally honest because of his long isolation from power: "To the masses of Zimbabwe, the poor people of Zimbabwe, the sum total of ESAP can best be described as a loathsome economic monster which is ravaging and destroying decent lives by incapacitating the poor and further condemning them to abject poverty" (*FG*, 10/3/94). And things were not improving by the time ESAP 1 entered its final year, as preparations were made for ESAP 2 (a new five-year plan in the same spirit). In a late 1994 Gallup International poll, 62% of Zimbabweans anticipated increased hardship in the future, higher than any of the other 45 countries surveyed (*FG*, 5/1/95).

Hove's "persistent fear" appeared increasingly universal. According to a survey of 200 poor people by the Africa Community Publishing and Development Trust (1995:1),

> ESAP was listed as a cause of poverty even more often than drought and the shortage of land. The combination of retrenchment on a large scale, with a sharp increase in the price of basic goods and having to pay for health and education, has driven many families into poverty.

And the future? With ESAP 2 looming in 1995, Professor Hawkins spelled out the challenge:

> Its provisions will mean a great deal for those still at school, those seeking tertiary education, those desperately hunting for work, those needing land and water, homes and telephones. Who is fighting in their corner? Where is their voice in the debate? (*Southern African Economist*, June/July 1995)

Sadly, the answer was to be found neither in the traditional left intelligentsia nor in the unions. With a few exceptions—many in the University's Institute of Development Studies—the former largely suffered the classic "failure of analytic nerve." And reflecting its continuing corporatist orientation, the ZCTU commissioned a report in 1996, *Beyond ESAP*, that contained some powerful critiques of ESAP but yet that reflected a naive faith—reminiscent of modernization theory—in "the economy's" ability to reverse "enclavity," "dualism," and uneven development more generally:

> The evolution of a well articulated economy on the path towards economic development requires that the impetus for growth involve the incorporation and participation of the majority of the labor force in productive activities. It is this bottom-up approach to economic trans-

> formation that smooths out the discontinuities in the economy thereby leading to the evolution of an inter-linked and mutually reinforcing gradation of activities based on all scales of production. (ZCTU 1996:16)

Blinkered by the need to remain relevant to reforming ESAP, *Beyond ESAP* in fact codified many of neo-liberalism's worst conceptual errors and policy recommendations, such as avoiding "subsidization of nonproductive uses," means-testing "welfare and relief funds," "trimming the public sector," "repeal any regulations... that discriminate against non-formal sector activities or small-scale firms" (there is no mention of whether these include worker safety and health measures), "have the peasant captured by the market," "close government collaboration with private business" on industrial policy (with no mention of labor's involvement!), and the like (ZCTU 1996:20-21, 58).

The ZCTU's surrender was particularly disturbing in the field of finance, where notwithstanding sensible advice to avoid foreign borrowing, options to promote "financial resource mobilization" included "government selling off its assets using the proceeds to reduce the stock of debt" and "encourage people to save by providing incentives that would encourage them to invest in shares quoted on the Zimbabwe Stock Exchange." Regarding fiscal policy, "current debt needs to be reduced substantially" and there is a "need to redirect government funds away from recurrent towards capital expenditure"—but without considering the potential harm to social programs that would logically result.

Worst of all, the ZCTU (1996:61) effectively conceded that "There can be no return to pre-ESAP policies, partly because of the stranglehold that foreign creditors have on policy through the substantial debt that has accumulated, paradoxically, because of the failure of the policy." Instead, it was the ZCTU's own failure to give content to the popular anti-ESAP outrage that reflected not the "failure of the policy" but instead ESAP's success in reducing all analysis to modernization theory and all policy discourse to facilitating capital accumulation.

Reactions are sometimes as revealing as events themselves, for a society defines its prospects in large part through its understanding of its problems. And here, as much of this chapter has documented, most representatives of officialdom and corporate Zimbabwe—and even to an extent the ZCTU leaders and technocrats—were blind, in comparison to those suffering most.

Conclusion: Blame for ESAP?

In the wake of this review of ESAP's abject failure, the logical task of a conclusion is to show how the different discourses surrounding economic policy provide divergent intellectual grounds for attributing blame, and hence, thus, for crafting future policies. Assuming that conceptually, one can begin to control for the drought factor,[21] the challenge is to sort out the different ways in which failure was comprehended and in which a way forward was suggested. For aside from a natural disaster (drought) theory of economic crisis (to which Zimbabwe's state-owned press was prone), we have come to recognise three sets of questions that emerged during the 1990s to shed light on the economic and social crisis:

- Were structural barriers to capitalist growth responsible for the disappointing record of market liberalization?
- Or was ESAP's design "necessary but insufficient" for both growth and development?
- Or instead was the culprit ESAP's half-hearted implementation by government bureaucrats who had different agendas or insufficient capabilities?

This chapter has provided cross-cutting evidence of all three sentiments, emanating at different times from at least three different sectors of the Zimbabwe economy and society. To begin with the last, was ESAP's implementation sabotaged by lack of commitment? After all, warned Michel Camdessus of the IMF in 1990, "There is no 'third way' between central planning and a market economy. [It is] a mistake to take a piecemeal approach" (*Financial Times*, 20/4/90). In Zimbabwe, this reservation was widely expressed by business elites in the run-up to the introduction of ESAP. *Zimbabwe Quarterly* editorialist Mervyn Thompson, for example, had remarked in mid 1989,

> We are surely at an economic reform crossroads. The strong suspicion is that government does not wholeheartedly accept economic reform—because they do not believe in it. The current system works perfectly well for a small clique of politicians and bureaucrats who have no interest in change... There is still a suspicion that government will only undertake any form of liberalization as a stop-gap measure and revert to some form of state ownership/control of industry at a later date. (*Zimbabwe Quarterly*, v.3, #3)

Although tempered during first months of ESAP, this theme was repeated again and again in bourgeois argumentation as the contradictions embedded within the program became overwhelming. Even for perceptive observers such as Hawkins (1994:50-52), the impression left was of ESAP's "uneven implementation... Some of the policies are open to criticism, but for the most part it is implementation that is at fault":

> Where for instance is the promised tariff commission, and the threatened monopolies commission?... Where is the new banking act; where is the Securities and Exchange Commission? What has happened to the frequently promised export processing zones?... Where too is the government headed on privatization? What is the point in transforming a parastatal into a 100% state-owned private company?... Here again government is perpetuating uncertainty, sending signals that suggest that its commitment to reform is less than whole-hearted, with adverse ramifications for private sector investment.

But was Hawkins missing the wood for the trees? ***For ESAP was, in fact, largely implemented.*** The three exceptions usually cited are fiscal discipline, parastatal privatization (subsidies were meant to have fallen from Z$629 million in 1990/91 to Z$40 million in 1994/95, but instead increased over the period) and the Social Dimensions of Adjustment strategy (as if this were indeed a genuine goal of ESAP, which is most doubtful). These three defects aside, the government was able to claim, by mid 1994, the following accomplishments:

- 18,000 government jobs were abolished (with retrenchees numbering 7,000) and the civil service wage bill was reduced from 15.3% of GDP in 1990 to 11.3% in 1994 (World Bank 1995c:20);
- the foreign exchange control system was dismantled;
- tariffs were lowered (except for some "import-competing activities") to the 15-25% range (i.e., even below the GATT requirement of 30%, which was only meant to take effect by the year 2005),
- there was extensive liberalization of foreign investment regulations;
- price controls were eliminated;
- many local zoning and trading restrictions were abolished; and
- labor markets were largely deregulated (particularly regarding wage determination and employers' rights to hire and fire).

Yet as noted above, the devastation of both the real wage and social wage caused by such measures did not necessarily serve all capitals' interests. We have observed discourses of victimized businesses, which generally reflected dissatisfaction that the vision of manufacturing resurgence through liberalization proved ultimately no more than a mirage, and that instead, a shrinking domestic market and rising imports threatened dozens of established firms' very survival. But how to articulate this, particularly when the major voice of industry—the CZI—had shifted its position so emphatically in favor of ESAP (Skalnes 1993; Dashwood 1996)?

If there was such a creature, the "patriotic national bourgeoisie" could doubtlessly have improved profits by advocating economic restructuring to kick-start local industrial accumulation; financial reforms to blunt speculation and reduce interest rates to levels approximating the real growth rate; new tariff policies to enhance local production; spatial reorganization to reduce the colonial-era geographical inefficiencies; labor market reforms to enhance skills and productivity; substantive land reform to generate a stronger rural kulak class; and better targeting of housing subsidies and credit flows to provide a stronger and far more sustainable basis for accumulation in the construction sector, to name a few examples. These reforms were not terribly difficult to conceptualise (Robinson 1988), and were pursued in countries such as South Korea without apparent economic distress. But such a program would have threatened too many sectoral interests, particularly the increasingly powerful financial industry, and only the ZCTU (1996) began, in a very tentative manner, to develop an alternative along these lines.

Instead, and notwithstanding the barrage of grievances from producers facing extinction, a *laissez faire* brand of business ideology prevailed. For when not demanding further shrinkage of the state, the most powerful of Zimbabwe's capitalists—financial and commercial fractions—had every reason to celebrate. "The economy has evidenced some dramatic advances" under ESAP, asserted their leading spokesperson, Eric Bloch (*FG*, 5/1/95).

> The extent that inflation has declined, the significant reductions in direct taxation, the liberalization of trade and virtual elimination of import controls with a consequential elimination of most shortages, the immense relaxations of exchange controls, a somewhat more stable currency exchange rate environment, and the extent of new investment in the last two years are but a few indicators of the achievements of ESAP to date.

More sober observers—including even the World Bank at times—would have acknowledged the terrible social costs of such achievements. But clearly, the benefits of ESAP were real for a substantial section of the Zimbabwean capitalist class. For others, if benefits were not yet apparent and costs were mounting heavily, it would be easy to retreat to the hope that the market reforms were "necessary but insufficient," hence maintaining the possibility that if ESAP could be augmented with other measures not envisaged by the programe's architects, growth and development would finally emerge in a virtuous synthesis, as opposed to Zimbabwe's actual early 1990s record of economic decline and underdevelopment.

This second sentiment was the position adopted, at the end of the day, by the Zimbabwe Congress of Trade Unions. No matter that it may have been misleading to trade union constituents, and politically would exacerbate corporatist processes that tend to generate greater "insider-outsider" polarization. In the wake of more than a decade of debilitating paternalism and outright repression, including sophisticated attempts to tear the union federation apart through divide-and-rule strategies, it may be easier to understand—though not condone—the ZCTU's confusion.

In contrast, the third perspective was that ESAP was misguided from the start, serving bankers' needs above all others, destroying local productive capacity and setting real standards of living (and "human capital investment") back decades, and focusing on exporting to an increasingly hostile international economy which was mired in recession, at a time international competition was tougher than ever and commodity prices at their lowest in history. This perspective has informed the critique that has emerged throughout this book, regarding not only many components of ESAP but also finance-driven economic and social policies more generally.

Jameson Timba (1992:4), an employee of the Collective Self-Financing Scheme (a small NGO funder of agricultural cooperatives) expressed this view simply, but quite accurately:

> Zimbabwe's economic structural adjustment program came in part as a result of the lame economy that the new government inherited, and the inappropriate economic policies adopted at independence. From a financial perspective, the money market in Zimbabwe has been awash with liquidity, meaning that the economy has been able to mobilise savings, however no sizeable investments have been channelled back into the economy... This Economic Structural Adjustment Programme, dubbed "Economic Structural Acquired Poverty," is supposedly a home-grown set of economic measures designed to make the Zimbabwean economy more competitive. However its prescriptions are in no way different from the prescriptions of the IMF and the World Bank which have caused havoc and continued marginalization of the poor of most Third World countries. The only difference between the Zimbabwean prescription from that of the IMF is that the policy document on ESAP is published on Zimbabwean newsprint.[22]

And in a sense, Zimbabwe was "in no way different" from many other societies which permitted financial power—global and local—to reign at key moments. A reinterpretation of the universality of financial power, particularly under conditions of global and local overaccumulation, lies ahead in the concluding chapter.

Notes

1. The econometricians, it must be noted, proceeded to test their work by considering "a worsening external environment resulting from a prolongation and deepening of the current oil price shock" (which in reality, at the time of the Gulf War, was but a momentary blip).
2. This caused ongoing confusion. In 1994 Barings termed Zimbabwe's record as a debtor "virtually immaculate" (FG, 15/12/94), and the World Bank (1995b, v.II:9) confirmed that Zimbabwe "has remained current on all external debt obligations"—perhaps forgetting ZESA's failure to repay Z$50 million in Bank loans for several months during 1992-93 (*FG*, 18/2/93). Just as the Bank's Zimbabwe office gave a clean financial bill of health in 1995, its Johannesburg mission chief Isaac Sam lumped Zimbabwe with Nigeria and Tanzania as countries that are "not likely to obtain any more finance in the international capital markets as long as they are debt ridden and demanding that the debts should be written off" (*RSA Review*, March 1995).
3. Harare alderman John West was one of a very few government officials who recognised the problem: "When the government borrows from foreign sources there is a real problem. Every US dollar borrowed is a claim on Zimbabwe's goods and services and can only be repaid, with interest, out of this country's visible and invisible exports. This is the worst feature of ESAP" (*FG*, 17/2/94).
4. Cone eventually shut down in late 1994, unable to repay Z$266 million in debt—the local IFC representative considered that it "could never be competitive"—and with it, brought down 6,000 jobs and a good part of Chitungwiza's economy. Hunyani stumbled precariously but managed to convert Z$60 million in bank loans into a 37% dilution of the company's equity, with other major government shareholders—the Mass Media Trust and the IDC—bailing the company out at the request of Foreign Minister Nathan Shamuyarira (in 1994 a controlling share in Hunyani was purchased by the rapidly-growing tobacco-based conglomerate TSL Ltd) (*FG*, 26/1/95).

   The textile industry was perhaps an extreme case, given its role as the primary manufacturing victim of ESAP. The chair of David Whitehead Textiles Ltd complained in the company's 1994 annual report that return on capital of 11% was "well below money market rates" which in turn led to "continued deferral of necessary capital expenditure." Indeed David Whitehead's fixed assets actually declined from 1992-94 by Z$8.5 million (to Z$151 million). The poor 1994 results (which, however, were twice as good as those recorded in 1993) were blamed on declining consumer buying power and the fact that "The international market for textile products was generally stagnant" (*FG*, 8/12/94).

5. Even progressive analysts, such as ZCTU (1996:7) and Saunders (1996), adopted the crowding out thesis uncritically, notwithstanding all the evidence to the contrary.
6. Ironically, however, at roughly the same time, Stoneman was reported saying that ESAP "will be generally beneficial" if implemented correctly and if sensitive to the vulnerable (*Financial Gazette*, 7/9/90).
7. The January 1995 *Project Completion Report* (World Bank 1995a) (by the Bank's Southern Africa Department) covers the Bank's US$175 million 1992-94 (first tranche) structural adjustment loan, the linchpin of a multi-donor credit agreement in excess of US$500 million. The Zimbabwe government contributed a major statement on its accomplishments to the report. This was followed by a less-sanguine *Performance Audit Report* (World Bank 1995c) by the Operations Evaluation Department in June 1995, which termed the first tranche only "marginally successful" and which the Zimbabwe government decided not to formally respond to. The second report highlighted problems with government fiscal policy, parastatal reform, and the social dimensions programme. Inbetween, the Bank's Southern Africa Department issued a Country Economic Memorandum on Zimbabwe entitled *Achieving Shared Growth* (World Bank 1995b).

   There were other donor assessments of ESAP, including by the powerful United States Agency for International Development and the secretive International Monetary Fund. The Bank's view, is most important because of its proximity to government officials and its leadership among donors.
8. The only even mildly-negative self-appraisal was the Bank's (1995a:18, 30) admission of Danish funder DANIDA's criticisms (that Bank coordination of other donors was too slow, that donors lacked consistency in their approach "to major areas of economic policy," and that the Bank did not "accommodate their desire to provide grant [instead of loan] finance"; telling flaws, these, but apparently not deemed sufficiently fatal to omit from the first evaluation, or on the other hand to rebut).
9. This was apparently a highly-valued contribution, for the letter of transmittal from the Office of Director-General for Bank Operations Evaluation cites the government's "excellent assessment of the programme's performance and implementation lessons"; the Director-General's reading of the report was not terribly accurate in other places either, for it claimed, "Overall, the project outcome rates as satisfactory" when in fact the *Project Completion Report* had cited ESAP as "highly satisfactory" (World Bank 1995a, Memorandum to the Executive Directors and the President 22). The second evaluation also made this mistake.
10. Without a trace of irony, the Bank (1995c:13) concluded that among ESAP's lessons are "the importance of popular ownership and participa-

tion throughout the process of adjustment.. An open, transparent dialogue can help generate realistic expectations, reduce uncertainty, and contribute to a unified sense of national ownership for reforms." What an open, transparent dialogue should apparently *not* contribute to, however, is a decision that the reforms are too costly, and the benefits too skewed; hence specific information critical to such a cost-benefit analysis is studiously ignored.

11. The most obvious way to cut the government budget was a reduction in defense spending, particularly in light of the diminished regional threat (what with peace in Mozambique and a political settlement in South Africa). But notwithstanding growing pressure from the Bank and corporate media—"government has no qualms about allocating over Z$2 billion to defense," complained the *Financial Gazette* (21/9/95)—other powerful forces prevented this. After all, Chidzero had conceded in a rare unguarded moment, defense spending was necessary "to purchase the loyalty of generals and servicemen" (*FG*, 4/8/94).
12. There were many taken in by the middle-ground approach, in part because it combined apparently constructive criticism with an ongoing engagement with power. The once left-leaning cabinet minister Fay Chung (1993:1) argued that "The transition from a largely centrally-controlled economy to a market-based economy in Zimbabwe was a necessary step, but it was not without many painful teething problems." The generally pro-business commentator Tony Hawkins (1994:50), too, found that "Structural adjustment is a necessary—but not a sufficient—condition for self-sustaining economic growth." Similarly, the oppositional sensibility of ZCTU secretary general Morgan Tsvangirai had waned to the point, in 1996, that he conceded in his foreword to *Beyond ESAP*, "While acknowledging that SAPs are necessary, the study shows that they are insufficient in fostering development" (ZCTU 1996:i). And from an academic perspective, in their survey of Southern African structural adjustment programmes, Thomas Ohlson, Stephen John Stedman and Rob Davies (1994:252, 303) observe that Zimbabwe's structural adjustment programme "led to increased disease and food insecurity at a time of reduced state spending on health and medicine" but that, nevertheless, "The crisis of economic productivity is so vast and compelling that it is impossible to counsel against the structural adjustment programmes of the international financial institutions." Missing here is any sense that SAPs may have *intensified* the productivity crisis via deindustrialisation stemming from poorly phased tariff removals, extremely high interest rates, emasculation of state education and health programmes, and the general promotion of speculative, acquisitive tendencies which accompany the prosperity of tiny petty bourgeois and bourgeois enclaves, while workers and peasants surrender a third or more of their standards of living. The "necessary but insufficient" argument falls apart under closer scrutiny.
13. Although there is no mention of the maize fiasco in the Bank's input to the *Project Completion Report*, the lessons learned by the government (as told to the Bank [1995a:50]) are revealing: "Given the drought cycle in

Southern Africa, it was reasonable to suppose that a drought could occur during the life of the programme... Lack of a coherent contingency plan has led to a 'knee-jerk' reaction—in the form of excessive and underfinanced stock building—by the Grain Marketing Board, which threatened the fiscal foundations of the recovery from the drought." Diplomatically, nothing is mentioned of the Bank's prior role in depleting the GMB stocks.

14. Ironically, within the next months, Zimbabwe's largest packaging company (Hunyani) and textile firm (Cone) would effectively go bankrupt.
15. The *Financial Gazette* (21/11/91) was especially derogatory:

    The little that has been made public about the campaign indicates that this is going to be one of those propaganda exercises with government manifesting its usual but deplorable intolerance of views contrary to its own. The present campaign appears aimed at treating ESAP as some form of magic wand, some form of religion. Indeed the campaign aims at commercialising and trivialising a very important reform programme. The government seems keen to portray ESAP as a wholesome and faultless commodity, such as a detergent or toothpaste, which the public is being exhorted to get hooked on.
16. Partly this reflected the fact that "Zimbabwe's top managers face a decline of between 25% and 30% in real incomes" according to Green Line Salary Surveys in 1993 (even though "purchasing power" remained equivalent to Japanese executives). Other anecdotal evidence of corporate stress emerged from a huge downturn in the casino industry, "as a result of falling disposable incomes in the upper-middle income group which forms the bulk of its domestic clientele" (*FG*, 25/2/93, 20/5/93).
17. On the other hand, successes achieved to date included:

    reduction almost to a level of elimination of regulatory controls; broadening of business perspective to regional and international levels; competition promotion which induced improved management practice and improved customer care; and investment inflows even though they remained lower than expected.
18. As something of an alternative to the Consumer Council, the Finance Ministry also established a monthly "watchdog group... billed as the think-tank on ESAP" in May 1992, but it was delegated to the Zimbabwe Association of Business Organisations (also headed by Chidzero) which had no particular interest in representing the majority of Zimbabweans. Other members of the committee came from the Commercial Farmers' Union, the CZI, the Zimbabwe National Chamber of Commerce, the Chamber of Mines, and banks. In its first three months, the group—chaired by the deputy secretary in the Ministry of Finance—held just one meeting, and was subsequently rarely heard from (*FG*, 27/8/92).
19. Such sentiments show the limits to the CZI strategy of promoting small entrepreneurial finance—one of Humphrey's main contributions to the 1990 debate on ESAP, as noted in Chapter Seven—as a means of forging alliances with this ideologically-important sector of civil society.
20. Shamuyarira was named Minister of Industry and Commerce in 1996, and

for the first time brought organised labour into international trade negotiations, leading to a long-awaited rapprochement with South Africa. At the same time, the ZCTU (1996:8) requested "a truly national compromise" on economic policy with government, employers and other civic groups along the lines of South Africa's (ultimately extremely weak) National Economic Development and Labour Council.

21. To what degree was the early 1990s (especially 1992) drought responsible for ESAP's failure? Economically, the ratio of agricultural production to total production (at constant 1980 factor costs) fell from a post-Independence high of 16.1% in 1985 to 12.2% in 1991 to 9.9% in 1992, before rising to 14.4% again in 1993. Within the agriculture sector, multiplier effects are more important for non-tobacco crop production. (Indeed, commercial tobacco farmers drained most of the country's scarce irrigated water during the drought and hence increased production steadily from 135,000 tonnes in 1989/90 to 235,000 tonnes in 1993/94.) Maize fell from its record high of 1.8 million tonnes in 1985/86 to 900,000 in 1989/90, 780,000 in 1990/91, 605,000 in 1991/92 and just 12,615 in 1992/93, before recovering to 1.3 million in 1993/94. The three other major crops by weight—wheat, cotton and sunflower—followed a similar, but less extreme, pattern as maize. Yet as the World Bank (1995b, v.II:84) noted, "The average annual national rainfall has been only moderately lower since 1986 than during the early 1980s... [and] climatic factors cannot explain the broader contrast between the early 1980s agricultural growth and the virtual stagnation since then."

    Socially, it is difficult to assess the drought's destruction in comparison to the devastation caused by ESAP. But to cite just one control group indicator (the only one the author has encountered), health researchers discovered that during the early 1990s "almost a third of the households in Chitungwiza [Harare's main satellite township] said they had reduced the amount of sadza [the staple maize meal] they consume. In [rural] Murehwa district this was only 5%. It is argued that if reduced sadza consumption was to be attributed to the drought, the reverse would have been found, as most of the rural population relies on agriculture. One can only conclude that the harsh economic climate is responsible for the reduced food consumption" (Bijlmakers, Bassett and Sanders 1995:253).

    Historically, the previous period of sustained economic crisis—1974-78—was a time of extremely good rains, while the late 1960s and early 1970s period of booming growth witnessed years of severe drought.

22. On this latter matter it was apparently true that the January 1991 *Framework for Economic Reform* was actually typeset (if not printed, and even written) by the Bank, for it appears in American (not British) English.

Part Four

Lessons from Zimbabwe

chapter thirteen

Conclusion: Financial Power and Progressive Resistance

Introduction

This book has shown that the operations of financial markets have exacerbated the scope, degree, and socio-economic costs of uneven development in Zimbabwe. It is not our purpose, however, to expend more effort condemning the country's bankers and insurers, the speculators and rentiers, the financial bureaucrats and ever-gullible (or worse) politicians, the domestic and international capitalists, or the international mandarins and technocrats of the IMF, World Bank, and the like. Instead, with this final chapter, we reconsider the historical and contemporary evidence in Zimbabwe primarily in order to draw lessons of more general interest in at least three broad areas: finance and crisis theory; finance and uneven development; and the politics of financial power with respect to power blocs, ideology, and popular resistance.

What is the nature of that evidence? Briefly, over the course of Zimbabwe's colonial and post-colonial history, three dynamics (Gramsci's "organic movements") converged again and again at different scales: a) transformations in the sectoral direction of accumulation, generally in the context of overaccumulation crisis; b) geographical restructuring; and c) decisive interactions between productive and financial circuits of (both global and domestic) capitalism. There were several intervals of special significance:

- the 1890s, when overaccumulated London financial capital flowed through the British South African Company and London and Bulawayo Stock Exchanges into speculative land and mining shares, and on that basis ultimately propelled full colonial domination, hastened African proletarianization, and compelled a broader agro-mineral expansion which profoundly shaped development during the following decades;

- the 1930s, when—following a global (and, to a lesser degree, domestic) crisis of overaccumulation culminating in a financial-speculative spiral—gold again played its traditional role as international store of value of last resort, thereby ensuring a basis for post-Depression accumulation oriented to manufacturing, in the context of diminished international trade and investment;

- the 1950s, when international financial capital overheated—and then too rapidly cooled—the spatially-extensive economy of the Central African Federation, and when the displacement of domestic overaccumulation tendencies into spatial and temporal fixes proved unsustainable, leaving the economy skewed in crucial directions and requiring unprecedented state intervention in the financial markets;

- the 1970s, when overaccumulation in well-developed manufacturing industries reached dramatic levels, partly as a function of tight state controls over the financial circuit of capital required to prevent capital flight; leading directly to

- the late 1980s and early 1990s, as financial markets exploded with speculation (and then partially imploded) and as international financial interests gained dominance in the local economy, successfully removing trade and financial restrictions at the cost of sinking Zimbabwe into a profound economic depression.

During each of these periods, the impact of finance on temporal and spatial development was different. Comparisons are, therefore, made at risk. Yet each period was notable because the interactions of finance, space, and new paths of accumulation helped set the scene for important intercapitalist conflicts which in turn helped define a broader social experience. This impact is worth considering in more depth, with an eye to theoretical explanation.

In teasing out theoretical lessons, however, we would want to avoid disempowering—through the deployment of a monolithic explanation of the inexorable logic of capital—the variety of opponents of uneven development in Zimbabwe and elsewhere. We would be amiss, therefore, to leave the problems of resistance to the imagination.

Zimbabwe's experience

Uneven development in Zimbabwe was fraught with conflict, and even if much of the conflict this book describes was intercapitalist (involving a tiny minority of the country's people) rather than across class lines, understanding the competing interests nevertheless offers a good window on Zimbabwe's history and future. For we have seen that the relative positions of various circuits of capital (often mistakenly identified merely as class "fractions" or as their institutional surface forms) were often the best indicators of the nature of capital accumulation at a given point in time.

To illustrate, struggles over who would gain the profits and who would bear the burdens of uneven development pitted, at different stages, agricultural versus mining versus manufacturing capitals (throughout); financial versus agricultural capitals (especially during the 1920s); financial versus commercial and industrial capitals (1950s and 1990s); and domestic versus foreign capitals (until the 1960s, and again in the 1990s). Moreover, there were revealing power struggles between the state and capital as well (1930s and 1960s-90s).

The various confrontations took place on a geographical stage which, barring the Depression and War periods of relative delinking, expanded significantly until the late 1950s (and again following Independence in 1980). During much of the earlier period, the domestic financial system was itself relatively shallow, but ever-widening. From the beginning of the century, following the late 1890s crash of speculative financial investments in land and mining, the banks were usually accommodating with credit (within the parameters of colonial banking). Before encountering severe devaluation in the late 1920s, the financial system also facilitated an expansive geographical transmission of funds through branch banking, even if this ultimately generated a net drain of funds from rural areas to the two major cities (Chapter Two).

Unevenness in geographical flows of capital between London and Salisbury was far worse during and after World War II, this generated fierce controversies which ultimately led to an extension of state regulatory responsibilities in the late 1950s and early 1960s. At that point, as overaccumulation became a problem once again, ascendant financial power was itself incorporating new kinds of un- or under-regulated institutions and practices. A wide variety of financial forms appeared during the 1950s which corresponded to changing conditions of space (largely for the lubrication of trade) and time (for the financing of state, corporate, and personal expenditures), until the financial system became "top-heavy," in the words of the local business journal in the late 1950s.

In the early 1960s, a dramatic decline of financial power followed as an economic crisis borne of overinvestment and falling Federation revenues led to substantial emigration and bankrupted many debtors (especially homeowners). What was significant here was the degree to which international banks and multinational corporations turned on and then off investments aimed at *both* cash crop/raw material exports *and* luxury goods import substitution (Chapter Three). But the most important disproportionalities that emerged at this point were less within the productive circuit of capital than in the built environment, which received a far greater amount of investment than could be sustained (Chapter Four).

In sum, evidence from the first seventy-five years of the Rhodesian economy suggests that as capitalism matured, the conflicts over the direction and pace of flows of capital through the manufacturing, mining, and agricultural circuits of capital often stemmed from deeper tensions, indeed often directly from capitalist crisis tendencies. These were exacerbated by the periodic ascendance of domestic finance—and/or they diminished the capacity of the domestic economy to withstand the interventions of international finance—though not without running the risk of a (white, often right-wing) "populist" backlash, most impressively in the 1930s and 1960s.

Add to this sort of pattern the uneven restructuring of space by finance—at urban, rural, and regional scales—and the result is convincing evidence that the elusive search for a balance in processes of capital accumulation, and hence broader social reproduction, hinged largely on the manner in which space and time could be manipulated within the financial circuit. Indeed, the art of managing the economic benefits of space and time, largely through alternating fits of financial control and decontrol, would prove to be one of the colonial-capitalist state's most important and, at times (such as the mid-1960s), satisfying challenges. It was most difficult, however, at the peak of financial power, when tendencies to uneven development were exacerbated by financial capital's investment decisions.

One of the starkest examples of this convergence of rising finance and intensifying uneven development comes from the 1950s and early 1960s, when Salisbury and its close-in black township Harari both adopted the form they have tod y (now as Harare and Mbare) as a result of the role financial capital playe . in relation to other processes of spatial and economic development (Chapter Four). Here we find a striking example of the manner in which overaccumulated capital makes its way into financial circuits and undermines a potentially sustainable trajectory of accumulation. In the case of the uneven urban development of Salisbury, that trajectory would ostensibly have included a vast increase in commodified housing for blacks, while maintaining a balanced flow of finance into other facets of the built environment (industrial and commercial property, infrastructure, housing for whites, etc.).

Yet this did not happen; financiers and developers overbuilt speculative commercial offices in the Salisbury Central Business District, and made only half-hearted efforts to penetrate the townships, where effective demand was extremely limited in any case. As a result, industry failed to conclusively shed the costs of reproduction of its black workforce and instead a legacy of state-provided housing was established (one that required active undoing by international financial agencies at the time of Independence two decades later).

One lesson is that a balanced flow of finance into urban property investment may only be possible under conditions in which money is, in the words of the Southern Rhodesian war-time statistician, the "handmaid, and not the master" of capital-in-general during a stage of economic crisis. Otherwise, the displacement of overaccumulation through space and time fosters its own set of contradictions, which, in the context of the relationship between a distorted Southern Rhodesian economy and Salisbury's CBD and black townships, prevented the city's full transition from administrative-commercial-agricultural center into a site for more symmetrical and sustained accumulation.

There was, later, during the period of Unilateral Declaration of Independence, a much more impressive macroeconomic trajectory, which, as a result of a controlled reflation of the financial system, briefly balanced the capital goods and consumer goods departments of production.[1] But the rapid economic growth experienced from 1966 to 1974 was achieved via Rhodesia's enforced partial autarchy in relation to the world economy, especially so with respect to the repressed financial markets (Chapter Five).

Overaccumulation crisis subsequently followed, and fundamentally shaped development prospects accompanying Independence (hence the importance of an accurate theoretically-derived analysis of the 1970s downturn). Whereas many political economists are satisfied with blaming the

1974-78 depression on variables exogenous to the economy (civil war, drought, oil shocks, etc.), the argument advanced here instead is that, regardless of such factors, the huge investment spree of the mid-1970s—led by the base metals and transport capital goods industries and augmented by overinvestment in general consumer goods such as clothing, textiles, and furniture (and declining consumption in luxury goods ranging from cars to carpets to pharmaceuticals)—ensured that an overproduction problem would exist for many years to come.

The massive contraction of the building materials and construction industries (at a time low-income black housing was on the increase) testified to the manner in which the economy's "luxury goods" bias affected not only the primary productive circuit, but also the secondary circuit of capital, where overbuilding of (white) residential buildings had been prevalent. The subsequent building contraction also highlights the failure of a spatial fix to emerge in the late 1970s, for example, through decentralised regional development strategies. Similarly, the potential for a temporal fix was also limited by the immobilising effect of the major mid-1970s investments, by residual regulatory and policy constraints on the exercise of financial power, and by a diminishing lack of confidence in the RF project. The lack of a role for financiers in the transition to Zimbabwe was emblematic of the difficulties faced in displacing the crisis through either foreign- or local-sourced financial mechanisms.

The logical consequence of Zimbabwe's overaccumulation legacy and lack of immediate opportunities for extensive spatial and temporal development was a medium-term build-up of financial power, reflecting from the mid-1980s a decisive switch of funds out of productive investment and into various financial and speculative markets. The result, by the late 1980s, included such phenomena as the rise of a new financial elite within and around government bureaucracies; property and share speculation; partial and extremely uneven restructurings of the urban and rural built environment; an increasingly desperate search for external markets; and high levels of foreign debt followed by diminishing capacity to control the contours of the economy from the vantage point of the nation-state.

Thus overaccumulation crisis dating from the mid-1970s persisted through the late 1980s, and productive capital withered. The stagnation of output and decline in fixed investment had nothing to do with the government's "socialist" rhetoric, nor, in the case of manufacturing, much to do with the lack of foreign currency which is normally blamed for the investment strike. Nor was continuing racial bias in economic power relations responsible, in the main, for stagnation. Instead, the economy's productive sectors faced relatively universal barriers to growth, including lack of balance in output (and production processes) across firms and sectors; overinvestment and overproduction; limited domestic and global markets; and stagnation (Chapter Six).

As the class character of the state leadership—including personal accumulation strategies—became crystal clear in the mid-1980s, the rise of finance began in earnest. Occasional hostile rhetoric aside, Finance Minister Bernard Chidzero was extremely accommodating to bankers—through the mediation of international financial power—in the face of a racially-coded class bias in banking seemingly unaltered from pre-Independence days. New forms of corruption in both banking and the government's financial bureaucracy seemed to cement the power of domestic finance (Chapter Seven).

Thus capital flows through the financial system moved into higher gear from the mid-1980s, as financial markets hosted unprecedented speculation in shares and property through 1991 (Chapter Eight). The role of pension funds was particularly important in the centralization of capital that fuelled speculation, and this serves notice to the working-class and their representatives about at least one direction for resistance. The irony was that working-class pensioners financed some of the more extreme forms of property speculation, which in turn made finding even a rudimentary home impossible during unprecedented land price inflation (Chapter Nine).

Indeed, uneven flows of finance lowered the prospects of homeownership for all residents of urban low-density and high-density residential areas. This was partly a function of the contradictory role of such flows, in trying to both displace overaccumulated capital bottled in the liquid financial system, and expand the homeownership base of society into the black working class. Rural financial flows were just as uneven, with large commercial farmers maintaining their traditional access to an accommodating financial system (including debt write-offs during drought) while small farmers suffered an inappropriate expansion of credit as a *quid pro quo* for the lack of a serious state land reform policy. The small farmers' response—mass defaults on World Bank loans passed through the farm credit parastatal—provides microeconomic evidence of the inability of credit to successfully displace conditions of overaccumulation for long (Chapter Ten).

As financial power increasingly determined the social and spatial coordinates of the economy during the 1980s, so too orthodox means of addressing stagnation—structural adjustment, financial and trade liberalization, and full-fledged reintegration into the world system—emerged and became dominant. Yet within months of the initiation of the Economic Structural Adjustment Programme, a disaster had befallen the Zimbabwean economy, exacerbated by the drought, with 1992 production levels across manufacturing and agriculture between 10% and 40% lower than under conditions of normal stagnation.

Many of the economic problems could be traced to the Zimbabwe bureaucrats' lack of comprehension of the effective dynamics of the world economy, which had no use for the country's over-estimated manufacturing export capacity and which paid prices for raw materials lower than at any time in recorded history—yet which submerged the country in a new round of hard currency debt to ostensibly pay for the capital goods which would successfully restructure the economy. Net new capital investment not only did not occur at anything like the rates advertised. Deindustrialization was the rule, and the ranks of the permanently unemployed swelled to new heights (Chapters Eleven and Twelve).

It was (and remains) the period in Zimbabwe's history which most conclusively demonstrates how financial power translates into uneven development. But it was not unique, for (as discussed next) it fit a historical pattern of overaccumulation, financial market machinations, and political economic restructuring.

Zimbabwe's cycles of capital accumulation

Most of the features of uneven spatial, temporal and sectoral development in the post-Independence era, as described in Part Three, are consistent with both the historical patterns observed in Part Two and the theoretical arguments of Part One. They suggest that deep-rooted, repetitive dynamics of finance and uneven development can be identified as necessary (not contingent) processes, reflecting "incurable structural contradictions," as Gramsci might put it.

One way to assess the theory is by considering repetitive historical processes that appear as a "cycle" of capital accumulation. With a sweeping view of the recent history of accumulation in Zimbabwe, we might periodize such cycles into booms and busts that roughly correspond to fifteen-year waves. Due to the limited availability of comparable macroeconomic data, a synthetic argument about the role of finance in the accumulation cycle is only feasible from the mid-1950s through the early 1990s (notwithstanding the fact that the early 1930s and mid-1990s each bear witness to huge declines in production and to financial crisis which are consistent with the notion of a cycle of accumulation).

Although the data are limited, they do suggest the existence of a fifteen year "Kuznets cycle," during which changes in fixed capital investment (measured here as a ratio of GDP) are of greater significance and greater reliability in tracking macroeconomic vitality than changes in consumption

(Figure 13.1). (It is interesting to note here the dramatic fall in relative consumption expenditure in the early 1970s, which, coming at a stage in the cycle when economic growth was rising, helps dispel the inordinate focus on effective demand that often bedevils analysis of semiperipheral economies.) As a ratio of economic activity as a whole, investment levels rose to untenable levels during the late 1950s, the mid-1970s, again in the early 1990s.

More detail is gained by examining the rhythms of specifically *manufacturing* investment, output and inventory build-up (Figure 13.2). Here the dramatic swings in investment from year to year are impressive reminders of the "lumpiness" and corresponding volatility of capital flows. The sharp investment downturns of 1961-62, 1976-77, and 1982-84 seemed to respond to a 10-20% increase in inventory build-up, which signalled capitalists to refrain from new short-term investments.

As noted in Chapters Six, Eleven and Twelve, the most recent investment upturn is more difficult to interpret given that it involved a qualitative shift. Zimbabwean manufacturers shifted investment strategies from 1989 so as to gear up for international competition and changing domestic market conditions. In relation to manufacturing output, investments hit an historical peak in 1991, but inventories also began to accumulate at high levels as domestic demand slumped in 1992-93 (the latest data available) (Figure 13.3). Notwithstanding the financial crash that began during 1991 and dramatic rise in real interest rates that followed, the manufacturing sector's overaccumulation problem was not yet at an end, as the 1995 deindustrialisation proved.

In addition, other substantial fixed investments were made in the late 1980s (as well as the late 1950s and early 1970s) *in the built environment* (witnessed by official measures of building plans approved, as shown in Figure 13.4). By separating real estate into component parts (Figure 13.5), it appears that commercial property investment as a share of total property investment is a good indicator of overall developer confidence, and is the catalyst for a building boom. On the other hand, public investment (civil works, public buildings, etc.) has the capacity to play something of a countercyclical role, as is apparent from the rise in its relative importance in the early 1960s and early 1980s.

Having reviewed some of the patterns of uneven sectoral, spatial, and temporal development in Zimbabwe, we turn next to evaluate how these feed back into some of the corresponding theoretical concepts. There are several areas that can be reviewed in light of the Zimbabwe experience. First, revisiting the role of finance in overaccumulation crisis allows us to posit four theoretically-informed arguments that each have clear political implications. These are then reaffirmed when, in subsequent sections, we consider finance in the spheres of uneven sectoral development, of uneven spatial development, of uneven development of scale, and of shifting political power blocs. Following these theoretical inquiries, we will conclude with a concrete assessment of political prospects to be pursued at the various intersections of finance and uneven development in Zimbabwe, and internationally.

Finance, "finance capital" and overaccumulation crisis

Chapter One was devoted to constructing a Marxist framework of finance which would root money and credit initially in the deepest processes of capital accumulation, and then trace this through to the surface form of the financial system as the accumulation process unfolded. In working through the possible lines of argument, we came to rely heavily upon the idea that overaccumulation is a central and necessary tendency in capitalism and that it is only displaced—not resolved—by the financial system's capacity to generate debt and speculation and thus implement a temporal fix. The contradictions remain, to bubble up later, often somewhere else. In turn, the exercise of power vested in a rising financial system is affected by any number of contingencies (some of which are comprehensible not through structural formulae, but through a concrete class analysis of agency, as was attempted in Chapter Seven), and that power is subject to diminution by a host of financial vulnerabilities.

This was the starting point to considering how finance relates to overaccumulation crisis. Now, working through the lessons from Zimbabwe, we can address a variety of related theoretical problems in Marxist financial and development economics, in the process establishing future lines of inquiry. The first challenge concerns "finance capital," the concept that caused such a lengthy and politically-debilitating detour among scholars and leaders working from the tradition of *Capital*. For what, even in Zimbabwe, may appear on the surface as a monolithic "finance capital" configuration capable of managing crisis tendencies is revealed, after further inspection, as an unstable set of shifting finance-led alliances which are as prone to self-destruction as are the mountains of debt and speculation through which financial capital achieves temporary authority.

Recall that the periodic rise of finance during capitalist crisis is sometimes mistaken for the emergence of a new epoch of capitalist relations, since the exercise of financial power appears to impart a wholly new set of conditions for accumulation under the hegemony of "finance capital" which in turn seem to have the capacity to resolve the contradictions of capitalism. There were numerous rebuttals to Hilferding's thesis on theoretical grounds, most convincingly in the observation that the intimidating financial edifice is typically built upon the sand of chronic overaccumulation within productive capitalist circuits. "Breakdown" would inexorably result, argued Henryk Grossmann.

The evidence from Zimbabwe is revealing. In the late 1950s-early 1960s and late 1970s-1980s (the two periods which most easily lend themselves to consideration of empirical evidence), the collapse of fixed capital investment was the immediate response to a build-up of manufacturing inventories which signalled overaccumulation, and was followed by a massive flow of overaccumulated capital from productive circuits into financial circuits of capital (Chapters Three, Five, Six and Eight). Such rudimentary empirical observations do not "prove" the necessary tendencies towards overaccumulation and the rise of finance, and they certainly do not confirm an inherent tendency towards the breakdown of capitalism.

But they do provide striking evidence of endogenous limits to accumulation. And alongside the earlier (1930s-era) evidence of the decline of financial power during crisis, Zimbabwe's experience with rising (and then crashing) finance on the base of overaccumulated productive capital gives very little support to the idea of an increasingly more powerful and omniscient "finance capital" power bloc. (However, it must be conceded that, at the international scale, the continued predominance of financial capital in the 1990s, at the same time unprecedented vulnerabilities continue to emerge, does leave the question of financial control unresolved. We take this up again momentarily.)

The point, however, is that much contemporary political economic analysis implicitly assumes as immutable the power, the philosophy, and the agenda of "international finance capital," and hence makes fatal concessions to the concepts, language, and political agenda of neo-liberalism. The "post-Fordist" project and social contracts associated with the most popular international approach to radical political economic analysis today—Regulation Theory (especially in Western Europe and South Africa)—are an example of this danger (Clarke 1988, Bond 1991a). As was the case with "finance capital" theory seventy years ago, Regulation Theory focuses inordinately upon institutional arrangements which prevent full-fledged breakdown and instead accompany the switch from one "regime of accumulation" to another.

It is true, as noted in Chapter One, that within the corpus of Marxist theory the regulation approach has generated useful insights into the emergence of temporal and spatial fixes in the levelling of finance-production-reproduction disproportionalities.[2] Yet it was also pointed out that notwithstanding such new institutional forms, capitalism would have trouble sustaining what Aglietta termed its rising post-war "threshold of resistance" to crisis. And indeed in retrospect it is clear that global capitalism only temporarily witnessed "regulation" in both the specific sense (state control over money) and the larger sense (a coherent framework within which accumulation can proceed). Today there appears no sign of a universal new regime of accumulation at the global scale to replace the well-articulated (mass production/mass consumption) Fordist model, at least not until the financial overhang in the world economy and overaccumulation of fixed capital and inventories are all resolved through devaluation.[3]

In the process of the contemporary crisis, the very financial tools which stabilised effective demand and created investment pools were transformed into an Achilles Heel for capitalism at the global level (as well as in Zimbabwe). Consumer credit expanded far too quickly and wildly and the subsequent contraction denuded regulatory authorities of traditional tools of counter-cyclical stimulation (Chapter Twelve). Pension funds proved to be the reservoir that financed all manner of speculative and ultimately self-destructive investments (Chapter Eight). In one country, Zimbabwe—and quite possibly also at the scale of the world economy—the relationship between overaccumulation crisis and the rise of finance repeatedly ends where the theory suggests it should, in the economic catastrophe of financial crashes, not in the equilibrating harmony of "regulation."

As a second broad proposition, the concrete manner in which overaccumulation was experienced in Zimbabwe tends to reinforce concern about the detailed problems of "disproportionalities" and "disarticulation." The former is reflected in the perpetual lack of balance between production of Department One capital goods and Department Two consumer goods (following the course described by Hilferding), though Zimbabwe suggests no particular logic as to which Department leads the way into crisis. The latter expresses the differential weight between luxury and basic needs products within the consumer goods industries (consistent with the Latin American development theory developed by de Janvry).

We will return, in the next section, to an evaluation of uneven development across sectors of the economy. Across the historical and contemporary span of discussion, though, this point is important because it focuses attention on the class character of the social formation during accumulation crisis. It does so by showing how shifts in circuits—not simply fractions—of capital corresponding to differential exposure to overaccumulation were often the basis for the formation of political power blocs (more in the spirit of van der Pijl than of Poulantzas). Those blocs which managed the devaluation of overaccumulation and the subsequent restructuring were generally attuned to the need to even out disproportionalities (as in the 1930s recovery and the 1966-74 boom), if not to the moral justification for better articulating the production and consumption of luxury and basic needs goods.

While we can follow the traces of earlier debates in the Marxist tradition here, much of this represents relatively unfamiliar ground for Zimbabwean scholarship, particularly when extended by the consideration of uneven spatial development in urban (Chapters Four, Eight and Nine) and rural settings (Chapters Four and Ten). Here we observed that flows of funds through the productive circuits of capital were articulated, to some degree, with built environment formation in a manner which proved vital for surplus absorption and for the reproduction of labor. Ultimately though, this combination was to prove inherently contradictory; we return in a subsequent section to a consideration of uneven spatial development during accumulation crisis.

Why does this second proposition matter, politically? Mainly because from a progressive perspective, Zimbabwe's economic problems have usually been identified more with respect to "underconsumption" than to the economic structure's bias and hence its tendency to differential overaccumulation. This led, on the one hand, to Independence-era policy decisions based on the implicit faith that the Rhodesian economic crisis could be resolved through expanding state spending, and by leaving the productive sphere essentially untouched.[4] On the other hand, after ten ineffectual years of rising relative state spending, the attempt in 1990 to kick-start the disarticulated industrial economy by subjecting it to international competition for the first time in many decades was an unmitigated policy disaster. The possibility for taking advantage of potential domestic production-consumption linkages, especially those associated with a shift to mass provision of basic needs goods such as housing, went unexplored.

Third, we might consider more closely what Zimbabwe's experience has unveiled about the different roles of finance in the accumulation process, as well as in crisis formation and displacement. The "accommodating" function—i.e., lubricating the payment system and facilitating investment—which is so well-reported in orthodox texts, lost its centrality. Reflections of this failure to perform as was socially expected during a period of financial ascendance in the context of overaccumulation, were the inability of the credit system to penetrate black townships in late 1950s and early 1960s Salisbury (Chapter Four) and 1980s Harare (Chapter Nine), and of the payments system to adequately monetize small farmers in post-Independence

Zimbabwe (Chapter Ten). Instead, two other functions periodically emerged and dominated: control and speculation. Let us briefly consider each of these.

Throughout Zimbabwe's history, financial control (not by a "finance capital" bloc but by financial flows of capital) was most obviously manifested through the uneven development of the urban built environment (Chapters Four, Eight and Nine), as well as in terms of the sectoral unevenness of the economy. But perhaps more significantly, when financial control was periodically exerted at the global scale—through the City of London prior to UDI, and later through the World Bank and IMF—impressive flows of international resources into Southern Rhodesia and Zimbabwe were still incapable of sustaining the domestic financial fix to overaccumulation. This was the case in each of the periods of crisis: the late 1890s, late 1920s, and early 1930s; the late 1950s and early 1960s; and the 1990s (Chapters Two, Three, and Eleven). As a result, the rise of speculation (Chapters Two, Four and Eight) was followed in each case by domestic financial calamity. In other words, both domestic and international financial control and all that they implied, were no answer to organic problems whose financial "solutions" were exhausted.

Indeed, occasions of speculative ebb and flow reveal extremely significant linkages between finance and overaccumulation. As noted above, these took the form of shortish fifteen-year cycles in the built environment, but might also indicate even deeper patterns of accumulation over long-cycles of fifty to sixty years (the numerous contingencies within Zimbabwean and international capitalism make the Kondratieff cycle difficult to verify at this stage). The upshot of this approach is to highlight the inherent tendency in capitalism for periodic bouts of overaccumulation in productive sectors to filter into financial circuits.[5]

But even if displacement of overaccumulation crisis can occur through time (via credit and speculative market investments), there is a fourth broad argument concerning finance and overaccumulation crisis which undermines Grossmann's breakdown thesis, perhaps fatally: the role of space in displacing overaccumulation. This is the subject of a subsequent section, but to treat uneven spatial development fully requires also considering uneven sectoral development and the uneven development of scale and why these are intensified during periods when finance is ascendant.

Finance and uneven sectoral development

In Chapter One, uneven development was considered in terms, first, of sectoral unevenness between production, reproduction and finance, much of which had to do with changes in the nature of the accumulation process; second, of uneven geographical development; and third, of uneven development of scale in political economic processes. The central argument was that uneven development was exacerbated at times when finance was ascendant, i.e., when financial power had increased authority to restructure social, spatial and economic relations. This often occurred within the framework of a shift from an accommodating function to one more bound up in speculative and control functions.

Subsequently, stark evidence was presented concerning the relationships between finance, production and reproduction. In Zimbabwe there were several types of disproportionalities and disarticulations that arose in the course of the accumulation process:

- between the supposedly "dual" sectors of the society;
- within the consumer goods department of production (between luxury and consumer goods, and between outward-oriented and inward-oriented consumer goods);
- within production itself (Department One capital goods and Department Two consumer goods); and
- between different sectors of production (manufacturing, agriculture and mining, and outward vs. inward sectors).

The rise of finance during particular periods highlighted disproportionalities such as the excessive capital invested in the futile search for minerals in the 1890s and the crisis of agricultural overproduction in the late 1920s (Chapter Two). In addition there were problems of disproportional infrastructural development and manufacturing production in the late 1950s (Chapters Three and Four), as well as the rise of finance during a stage of long-term stagnation in the productive sectors in the mid-and late 1980s (Chapters Five through Ten).

Within the sphere of production, finance also generated significant distortions, for example, in corporate overindebtedness in the late 1980s. As share speculation boomed, the growing confidence of companies in taking on greater amounts of debt reached untenable levels, at a time when the international law of value began to operate more forcefully under the banner of ESAP. At that point, the World Bank and IMF exercised unprecedented financial power over Zimbabwe, forcing production in an export-oriented direction at the expense, even, of local food security (Chapters Eleven and Twelve).

Historically, state financing interventions in the sphere of production may have temporarily balanced some of the disproportionalities (though not the broader problem of disarticulated development). The state was occasionally able to direct credit into strategic industries, for example, during World War II and UDI, which private capitalists would not otherwise support (Chapters Three and Five). But this capacity came to an end in the 1980s, for several reasons. In part it was because the overwhelming character of petty-bourgeois state managers in the context of an unsure state monopoly capitalist framework was parasitical, not productive (Chapter Seven). In part state intervention failed because the financial institutions that were meant to serve as investment vehicles—whether BCCI, Zimbank, SEDCO, AFC, IDC, etc.—were inappropriate or thoroughly ineffectual (Chapter Seven). To illustrate, small farmers received excessive amounts of credit in relation to the material processes which would have supported the flood of finance, leading ultimately to mass defaults (Chapter Ten). Finally, the underlying logic of the overaccumulation crisis required not more state-led strategic investments in the existing structure of capitalist industry, but rather devaluation consistent with the economy's limited effective demand. Again, this was only accomplished with the introduction of ESAP. (An entirely different set of options, leading to increased state investment in basic needs industries, was ignored entirely.)

Disarticulated development, especially in the reproduction process, was just as convoluted, but not only in the 1980s. In the 1950s, the overaccumulation problem was traced to—and to some degree regulated through—the reproduction process where consumer credit and home mortgage bonds were increasingly important for the white population's emerging consumption norms (Chapter Three). Tellingly, the reproduction process did not include the black population, which was both left out of hire purchase schemes and whose expectations of getting access to home loans were dashed by the early 1960s (Chapter Four). Much the same sorts of barriers were witnessed in the post-Independence era, as high-density suburbs received a marginal amount of housing finance, while the state ended its own role in low-income housing construction (Chapter Nine). In contrast, reproduction processes were never endangered for those at higher income levels, even if they took extremely distorted forms. In sum, far from stabilising capitalism, as Aglietta argued was the case for advanced industrial countries, the interplay between finance and these reproduction processes ultimately exacerbated social tensions and maintained Zimbabwe's extreme form of disarticulated development.

Finance and uneven spatial development

Under such circumstances, the second area of uneven development to consider is geographical manifestation of unevenness. When faced with the limits of the temporal fix (provision of credit), financial power could sometimes organize a spatial fix, simply by moving devaluation around. The specter raised by the Chemical Bank president—"every creditor ransacks the globe attempting to locate his collateral" (Chapter One)—demonstrates the transition from finance as an accommodating agent in the development of the productive forces of capitalism, to finance as both a controlling power and a speculative vehicle gone awry. Hence uneven spatial development was to a large degree affected by the role of finance in determining important aspects of the social formation.

Recall the theoretical arguments concerning both uneven development of sectors and uneven development of space. In what are now known as the advanced capitalist societies, the development of credit systems was encouraged by the need to ameliorate disequilibria that had arisen from the evolution of capitalist production and reproduction. The accommodating aspects of finance permitted sufficient centralization of capital so as to funnel money to where the rate of surplus value extraction was highest. In turn, this would ensure that where such disequilibria did create shortages (and hence potential profits), there would be capital to finance the necessary investment.

The expansion of the accommodating role of finance occurred on a spatial stage which, though mediated by cost factors such as transport and communications, progressively widened out under conditions of steady accumulation. When operating in an accommodating mode, finance thus paved a more level sectoral and spatial expansion path for capital. However, as was observed in repeated occasions, when tensions in the underlying productive circuits could no longer be displaced into the financial circuit, finance took on more pernicious speculative and control functions.

In contrast to the advanced capitalist world, in many peripheral economies the imposition of well-developed financial institutions in the context of a poorly-organized system of surplus value extraction had a rather different—and far more powerful—effect. There was little initial evidence of any amelioration of differences or disproportionalities within the productive circuit of capital (Chapter Two). Indeed Phimister posited that it was the unevenness of global capitalism in the last half of the nineteenth century which was most responsible for the flood of City of London capital into late nineteenth century Africa. Thus in contrast to the incremental expansion of financial capital that should presumably have occurred in an unknown setting within a region afflicted by notorious geopolitical turmoil, Southern Rhodesia experienced an unsustainable flood of finance in the 1890s, and abruptly, a subsequent cessation.

Precisely this incident—the financial accentuation of an underlying boom-bust phenomenon—predetermined a most uneven socio-spatial structure for early twentieth century Southern Rhodesia. It profoundly affected the subsequent articulation of capitalist and pre-capitalist modes of production, generating the basis for disarticulated development. Neil Smith's argument that the logic of uneven development (at the global scale) is "prior to the problematic of articulation of modes of production" can be verified by the role of finance—especially in its speculative form—in the first decades of Southern Rhodesian settler capitalism.

From shortly after the Pioneer Column's arrival in 1890, speculative investors confirmed the power of finance over space. But there was an added dimension which reveals much more about the relations between circuits of capital. The system of surplus value had not even begun to mature when speculative capital arrived in the 1890s. As a result it was *only with the crash of finance* and the dwindling of new fictitious capital formation that the laws of motion of capitalist expansion could truly become operative, and the penetration of capitalist relations into pre-capitalist settings could occur. The motor force was still finance, but now because of the residual need to realise some minimal return from such huge financial investments in land and mining titles, shares, and the like. Those left holding devalued paper capital in the late 1890s suffered, while the physical capital itself (especially the assets of the British South Africa Company) required, for its valorization, the "superexploitation" of labor.

Thus extreme speculative activity by City financial capital was probably most responsible for the socio-spatial strategy of the BSAC and other settlers. That strategy was, simply, to construct a brutal system of surplus value extraction that would spare no pre-capitalist pocket from superexploitation, and would immerse a large agro-mineral space-economy in a profoundly distorted logic of capital-labor relations. It was, therefore, not at the peak of financial ascendance but only after the crash, that the colony's social relations of production and spatial structure were forged.

The necessary unevenness of this socio-spatial formation is also of interest in constructing a general theory of finance and uneven development. *A priori,* one might anticipate the advent of a technologically-advanced settler capitalism in Southern Rhodesia (in comparison, say, to the peasant-style settler agriculture of the nearby Transvaal Boers) to offer a much more rapid means of levelling differences between the settler and indigenous political economies (in part through a more systematic process of proletarianization funded by highly centralized financial capital). In reality, the opposite occurred in Southern Rhodesia. Capitalist expansion in the wake of the excessive financial investments left huge areas of space and population dependent upon formal wage-labor in mines, towns, and commercial farms, *but without being fully incorporated into a capitalist system of reproduction.*Proletarianization occurred, certainly, but not the balanced development of the circuits of capital (especially consumer durables) which was needed to sustain the proletariat in the somewhat better-articulated style of other economies.[6]

The next stage, from the 1910s through the 1920s, witnessed the establishment of more traditional relations between production and finance. But the inherited uneven spatial structure of colonial capitalism was, in the process, cemented. Partly this was a result of the accommodating role of a growing banking network in ensuring that the colony's belt of arable land was properly commodified to collateralize further loans. The geographical organization of the colony was geared from early on (the 1910s) to a process of labor recruitment and land alienation that made sense in rational-capitalist terms but also generated, as a byproduct, increasingly asymmetrical social and spatial development characterized by diverse capitalist-precapitalist relations. The Rhodesian achievement of an apartheid spatial container for the articulations of modes of production was no mean feat, and was not concluded until the 1960s, when the last of the major forced removals and social control mechanisms were implemented.

But the seeds of the most important facets of unevenness—large-small farm and urban-rural differentiation—were sewn under the influence of bursts of financial ascendance, first due to the need to gain some returns on the huge amount of capital invested in the mining boom, and later, following the crash of tobacco in the late 1920s, in restructuring agricultural markets to assure a return on loans to white farmers. In each case finance intensified geographical distinctions by heightening the returns (and the risks) that arose from maximum utilization (and hence overproduction) on both farming and mining land. The financing itself enhanced the concentration and centralization of capital and extended the geographical reach of the productive circuit of capital. Crashes of finance typically led productive capital to emerge even more strongly (even in the 1930s and mid-1960s), and with a greater capacity to exploit the spatial configuration that finance had only sketched out in visionary form—in fictitious capital—during the frenzy of speculation.

In addition to the spatially-accommodating features of finance during these periods (especially the expansion of the payments system) and to spatially-significant bouts of financial speculation (in mining and land acquisition during the 1890s, and farm debt in the 1920s), there also emerged the role of financial control. The basis for control was the persistent effort of the duopolistic Standard Chartered and Barclays banks to extract surpluses from the colony to their headquarters. This did not go uncontested, for in comparison to other areas of the British empire the system of financial profit repatriation and asset transfer was a negotiated, two-way process in Southern Rhodesia. This was a function of higher degrees of settler autonomy, particularly with respect to limited foreign indebtedness (Southern Rhodesia avoided an unreasonable repayment burden during the early 1930s when most extractive economies were hit by falling commodity prices and rising loan payments). Nevertheless, the ability of the imperial banks to control flows of funds through domestic and international circuits had a direct influence on the tempo and scope of accumulation across space, something observed not only in Southern Rhodesia but also in South Africa.

The control function of finance was also applied to the monetization of indigenous society, itself a formidable task which entailed all manner of extra-economic tactics. Indeed the exercise of financial control through the geographical expansion of capitalist relations, especially in the 1890s and 1920s, created significant "friction" against finance, ranging from indigenous uprisings, to struggles between different circuits of capital as Southern Rhodesian capitalism matured, to financial crashes, to the emergence in the 1920s of state interventions (beginning with the Land Bank and leading to increasingly important financial and monetary regulatory mechanisms). Some friction also took the form of the vast spatial distances between those who raised and those who used banking capital; the former were in Cape Town and the latter in the mining districts ranging from Bulawayo up the Midlands to Salisbury.

The point here is that none of these disequilibrating factors—the non-levelling effect of distorted proletarianization, the emergence of sustainable articulations of modes of production only after the first crash of finance, or the problem of friction in financial flows and power relation—fundamentally modify the general argument that finance exacerbates uneven development at particular moments in the accumulation process.

Likewise, during the 1930s global depression, finance lost some weight, signified by the fact that gold began to replace money as a store of value and that there were greater challenges (by the new Currency Board system) to even the accommodating (monetary) role of the London-headquartered banks. As finance declined, there was a rapid rise of mining and manufacturing, and a subsequent move in the early 1950s by productive capitalists, especially in outlying geographical areas, to gain even greater control of local financial capital.

But finance-driven unevenness inevitably returned, as the 1950s ended with excessive financial speculation, this time led by commercial office construction. Although Harvey suggests that speculation generates "chaotic ferment out of which new spatial configurations grow," the capacity of financial speculation in Salisbury to lay the ground for a new round of spatially-sustainable accumulation was rather limited. In Southern Rhodesia at that stage of the broader accumulation cycle, speculation tended to have a centralising, concentrating effect. Moreover, not only were fictitious paper shares and opulent real estate an outlet for overaccumulated capital, in the process the scene was also set for financial chaos in firms and in residential and industrial real estate markets. So rather than creating new spatial configurations appropriate to a reconstructed accumulation strategy, the speculative role of finance more often left efforts along these lines stunted.

We observed, for example, strong evidence of the difficulties financiers had in funding low-income black housing during periods of excessive liquidity—the late 1950s and late 1980s—as speculative Central Business District commercial buildings instead attracted built environment investment funds (Chapters Four, Eight and Nine). Something similar was underway in rural areas during both periods, also confirming the theory of uneven development through uneven flows of finance. Speculation in farmland was important, as were attempts to develop small farm borrowing. Neither proved sustainable (Chapter Ten).

But speculation was not the only financial cause of systematic unevenness between large and small commercial farmers. The control functions of credit had similar impact in the 1950s and 1980s, as seen, respectively, through the liberal-capitalist Native Land Husbandry Act, and the extension of markets and market-related technical services (led by credit). The World Bank backed both strategies, and both proved to be enormous failures on their own terms, and in terms of a better articulated development trajectory. The Land Husbandry Act was accompanied by a "Partnership" ideology which was firmly opposed by peasants; likewise, the modalities of 1980s rural credit included an attempt to control peasant production through the Grain Marketing Board's stop-order system, and again the resistance was fierce and took the form of black markets and mass debt default.

The common denominator in the restructuring of space by finance, however, was the *combination* of speculative and control functions. Historically, this was clearly the case with respect to speculative booms in land and real estate.[7] Spatial processes during the 1980s illustrate the combination of speculation and control rather well. The urban areas witnessed speculative waves of finance into real estate (only marginally directed to working-class homebuyers), followed by just as dramatic reversals of funding flows (Chapters Eight and Nine).

The rural areas, likewise, witnessed land speculation in commercial farmland and increasing levels of farm debt, as well as partial penetration of market relations to small farms largely through AFC credit supplied by the World Bank. With respect to growth points, control was exercised by banks (which resisted small town locations) and by the World Bank (which resisted non-market industrial policy) in limiting the scope for industrial decentralization (Chapters Nine and Ten). Again, what the evidence suggests is that the combination of overaccumulated financial capital in search of speculative capital, with increasing levels of financial power, has generalisable—if highly differentiated—effects on development. The outcome was always accentuated unevenness.

We have seen, therefore, that the uneven development of space in Zimbabwe has been fundamentally affected by the rise of finance in a manner that can be generalized across time. But can it be generalized across different scales?

Finance and uneven development of scale

The third sphere of unevenness—unevenness of the scale at which political economic determinations are made—is worthy of at least brief attention. There is an omnipresent dynamic of unevenness across scale in capitalist development, but the levers of financial power work more efficiently at different scales at some stages of the accumulation process than at other stages. Moreover, the control functions of finance at one scale—usually international financial control over the national economy—can have a debilitating effect on financial control at local levels, as changes in interest rates, currency values, state subsidies, and other variables distort local financial packages beyond recognition (and in the process, render ineffectual international aid agencies' own project lending).

Much depends on the spatial centralization of financial capital, and hence upon the degree of concentration and local control of financial institutions. The power of local (but foreign-controlled) banks in issuing currency—one of three scales de Brunhoff identifies as being of importance in monetary relations—peaked in the late 1930s, just as a Currency Board (highly constrained, though, by British colonial rules) took over printing money (Chapter Two). In the 1930s and 1940s, financial power diminished in absolute terms and in scale terms from empire-wide to local levels. Simultaneously, the centralization of money capital was proceeding, assisted by the emergence of many new institutional forms in the 1950s. Thus during the mid-1950s financial power was re-established conclusively at the national level with the introduction of a Central African Federation Reserve Bank (Chapter Three).

But there are also other scales to consider. The point was also made that the spatial centralization of financial capital in the built environment of the Salisbury Central Business District was a reflection of the operative power of finance at a scale that spanned the Central African Federation (Chapter Four). The exercise of national-level power over finance during the 1960s and 1970s was the most impressive indication that in the wake of a crash of finance, financial power could be controlled to serve the needs of productive capital. In contrast, the most obvious use of financial power at the global scale in contemporary times is the World Bank's and IMF's programme of restructuring national economies in harmony with the international law of value, something to which Zimbabwe succumbed following a period of harmless socialist rhetoric and strategic confusion (Chapters Eleven and Twelve).

Within this spectrum of different scales of financial power, the accumulation process must be given primary analytical attention. As overaccumulation sets in, the rise of finance is important to the power of the nation-state, in particular its capacity to regulate both labor and money in the manner de Brunhoff suggests. This capacity varied enormously, as we have seen, but the coincidence in the 1950s of expanded state activity in labor reproduction through township housing and policing (Chapter Four), and the emergence of a central bank (Chapter Three) testify to at least certain linkages in the exercise of power at the national scale, in both cases very much to do with the *truncated* nature of the rise of finance. And likewise the collapse of finance in the early 1960s was the basis for a state that was all the more powerful in the 1970s because of UDI Rhodesia's orientation to domestic accumulation (Chapter Five).

Yet notwithstanding such bouts of financial repression and state intervention, it was evident, particularly in the late 1980s, that when overaccumulation becomes acute, the speculative function of finance can coexist with the control function at a national level (Chapter Eight). But in turn control of the national economy easily shifts to the global sphere, where the World Bank and IMF remain hegemonic and where the ultimate arbitrator of value, the interest rate (positive in real terms), was determined. The fact that Zimbabwean bankers arose in futile protest against extremely high interest rates did not appear to intimidate the Bretton Woods institutions much (Chapter Twelve).

The geopolitical role of finance, thus, becomes centralized as overaccumulation and financial power are generalized. But the modalities of international financial control of countries remain subject to debate. According to Stephanie Griffith-Jones (1987:37), for instance, "the greater the geopolitical importance of the debtor county to the government(s) of the country where most of the creditor banks have headquarters, the larger leverage debtor governments have to extract favorable deals." This somewhat misleading line of argument fails to take into account the spreading influence of financial power in its own right, which coincided, in the late 1980s, with the demise of bipolarity in the world system. (After all, Zimbabwe, while geopolitically very important during the Cold War, never extracted especially "favorable" deals from creditors.)

Understanding power relations at the international scale requires deeper theoretical and historical inquiry, if we are to transcend orthodox interpretations of geopolitics. This is not the place for an exposition of how global overaccumulation played itself out from the 1970s, and how the transfer of overaccumulated capital to Third World borrowers coincided with their own crisis of (luxury goods) import substitution industrialization (Bond 1991b). Needless to say, though, excessive liquidity in global financial markets has been of such importance to a present-day imperialism that financiers have easily replaced colonial rulers, multinational corporations and the CIA as the power behind the thrones of so many Third World countries.

It is important, in sum, to amend our understanding of the role of finance in the temporal displacement of crisis to account for scale. Zimbabwe offers plenty of historical precedents in this respect, drawing from the 1890s, 1920s, 1950s, and 1980s. The limits of the national scale are most obvious when reviewing the lessons of ESAP, in the context of a transition from local financial power during the late 1980s—with its substantial profits and ability to circulate funds at will (Chapters Seven and Eight)—to international finance during the early 1990s.

The limits to growth that domestic capital faced in 1980s Zimbabwe (Chapter Six) could not be realistically addressed when effective demand remained low, when the state did little to spur new basic needs industries, and when the financial system failed to adequately funnel increasing levels of liquidity into productive investments. Nor could sustainable growth occur on the back of speculative temporal and spatial fixes (epitomized by the rise of markets in fictitious paper wealth like real estate titles and the ZSE). Indeed the very success of these investments—in terms of volume of magnitude and rates of return—foreshadowed their certain failure. It was not hard to see that the growth of the speculative markets far outpaced the extraction of surplus value which could be realized in the economy as a whole, and that it would be only a matter of time before the futility of the paper titles adequately representing the underlying values of land and companies would be exposed.

There were other options, including another sort of temporal fix—the increased rate of turnover of capital—which, from the beginnings of bills of exchange and other early forms of credit, has been implicit in the social power of money. Whereas banks traditionally achieved such improvements in shortening turnover time of financial capital at local and national scales, this became much more of a global process in the 1970s and 1980s. By the late 1980s the rest of the world had perfected the highly-profitable art of turning over financial capital in geographically uneven ways—such as the currency and interest rate swaps and derivatives which became all the rage during the global rise of finance—and this appeared so enticing to Zimbabwe that the Reserve Bank made international financial market trading functions a high technical-architectural priority in its new Z$130 million headquarters. Yet as quick and easy as international arbitrage operations might seem to a country with chronic foreign exchange constraints, it was likely that this sort of temporal displacement would not succeed, either, if not matched by a transformation in the economic base.

The increased rate of turnover of capital at a local scale should also have taken the form of speed-up at the point of production, usually measured as higher labor productivity. But this was in fact a negligible fix in a context in which a steady erosion of real wages and intensified absolute surplus value extraction had already reached their limits. Thus increased productivity would instead depend upon a shift into relative surplus value extraction: a new set of machines to do the nation's manufacturing, mining, agricultural, and even service work.

To get to this stage, a variety of ideological and material twists and turns would be necessary in the late 1980s and early 1990s. Given the residual strength of various forces which stood to lose from this transition, the impetus for the far-reaching changes would have to come in part from external forces—international financial agencies—no matter how much this would later be denied. But the flaws in the approach were in assuming first, growing (and easily-accessible) international markets; second, an easy switch out of outmoded machinery (which remained underutilised in the local markets); and third, the capacity to maintain macroeconomic balances such that currency devaluation, interest rates, inflation and the like would not destroy the capacity for long-term investment.

All such assumptions proved false by the early 1990s, yet although this was the most substantial practical and intellectual refutation of the programme of financial power, the power of money at the global level was not obviously affected by Zimbabwe's collapse. To reduce financial power would require more than the demise of domestic finance as a consequence of the necessary structural contradictions in the accumulation process; it would also require struggle. And it is here that both Hilferding's sense of the omnipotence of "finance capital" and Grossmann's conviction that finance is wrought with vulnerability come into clear focus. For the phenomenon of financial power in Zimbabwe's history—and elsewhere as well—was often met by various kinds of resistance, organised by both the state and forces within business and civil society, to which we turn next.

Financial power, vulnerability, and resistance in colonial Zimbabwe

The rise of financial power was documented in Southern Rhodesia during the 1890s, mid-1920s, and 1950s. In each case the period of financial ascendance lasted less than a decade, was accompanied by rising vulnerability, and resulted in substantial devaluation of financial assets. But each period had a crucial impact on the subsequent evolution of the economy and on uneven spatial arrangements.

The pattern may have changed, of course, in contemporary Zimbabwe. Although local speculative fevers and excessive domestic debt emerged in the mid-1980s and reached untenable levels in 1991, as the theory would suggest, residues of speculation continued in the stock market for a few subsequent years. In large part this was because the overarching power of international finance continued and indeed still appears capable of being sustained into the foreseeable future.[8] It is dangerous to make predictions about the ability of the global system to respond to renewed financial fragility in the coming uncertain period. But given the rich historical evidence of relationships between capital accumulation and political alliances and ideologies in colonial Zimbabwe, we can review historical cases of financial power and vulnerability so as to inform future resistance.

We observed that there were three extremely important shifts in the national political landscape: during the early 1900s, the early 1930s and early 1960s—in other words, in the wake of the collapse of financial power. (There is also an increasing degree of instability in 1990s Zimbabwe, whose economic and political implications remain unclear but which are addressed later.) First, recall that during the 1880s and 1890s, the ebb and flow of international financial power—in the form of the City of London—had an enormous impact on colonial development, and were responsible (according to Phimister) for the direction and momentum of the "Scramble for Africa." For newly-settled Rhodesia, the City provided sufficient support to take control of land, put up telegraph poles and establish a railroad. Although resistance in the form of the Ndebele and Shona uprisings of the or1890s was crushed (and in any event was not, to our knowledge, specifically directed against the financial backers of settler colonialism), financial vulnerability prevailed. The demise of the Bulawayo stock exchange and the drought of investment funds from London in the late 1890s forced a reversal of the minerals extraction strategy. Speculative mining capitalists (led by the British South Africa Company) began a campaign of proletarianization and promoted an agricultural industry staffed with expatriate working- and middle-class Britons. The collapse of financial power was thus a prerequisite for beginning a new and more sustainable process of colonial capital accumulation.

Secondly, a new round of national restructuring occurred following the rise and fall of financial power in the 1920s and 1930s. In particular, the crash of international financial markets during 1929-33 was fortunate for gold-producing Southern Rhodesia. In the colonies in the early 1930s, political economic conflict turned to some degree on debt-related problems (especially many African colonies' external debt, and in Southern Rhodesia, white farmers' debts to the state Land Bank). But it was the subsequent sea-change in the colony's political economy (emblematised by the Reform Party's 1933 electoral victory) that was most important. This resurgence was due mainly to the rise of gold—i.e., to the role of a metallic money as a store of value in the context of financial collapse—which undergirded an impressive economic upturn that lasted a full decade. The inward-oriented recovery permitted the state to adopt numerous new functions, including provision of social welfare to poor whites, more effective repression of the indigenous population, and new industrial policies and projects that the colony's capitalists could not or would not attempt.

In the third case, financial power again rose during the mid-1950s, notwithstanding intensifying state efforts to gain regulatory control of financial flows. There was striking evidence of financial ascendance to be found in the Salisbury skyline, in the form of towering bank headquarters and other speculative property investments. As in earlier periods, financial power had a profound impact on the built environment, as the huge amounts of money required for project financing could only come as a result either of international inflows or highly centralised local financial capital. Both were available, yet as underlying crisis tendencies emerged in the early 1960s, both were then withdrawn, exacerbating the demise of the built environment and cementing uneven development, as shown earlier.

The most vivid reflection of the inadequacy of financial power in supporting a more even form of expansion during the 1950s was the failure to commodify township housing, which effectively left industrial capital and the state responsible for collective consumption through the years of Rhodesian Front rule. At the same time, right-wing populism began to prosper in the white electorate in the late 1950s, gathering momentum in the early 1960s at precisely the moment financial power collapsed (witnessed by the extremely high default rates and closure of five out of eight building societies). One logical outcome was the election of the Rhodesian Front to government.

For black nationalists beginning to gain confidence during the same period, an important strategic error was made. With the encouragement of white liberals, the nationalist entrée to the circuit of financial capital—in the form of "friendly societies"—was an attempt to join rather than contest the rule of financial power. The crash of the friendly societies was an interesting parallel, for the black population, to the demise of financial power for whites. Because contracting financial markets were certainly not open to the black nationalist petty bourgeoisie, the turn to guerrillaism can be read, in one sense, as a political displacement of contradictions surfacing from the underlying economic crisis, into the sphere of race relations.[9]

Finally, it is interesting that the transition from Rhodesia to Zimbabwe in the late 1970s was notable for the lack of financial power exercised. This reflected both the domestic limits to solving such a severe case of overaccumulation through temporal and spatial fixes at a time of political instability, and the failure, at that stage, of the World Bank (and imperialism more generally) to directly impose a neo-liberal financial logic on the transition.

But indicators of both domestic and international financial power were increasingly obvious during the 1980s, in the form of a distinctly influential bureaucratic financial elite, rising values of financial assets, a return to property speculation, greater reliance on sources of domestic credit as the basis for urban and rural development policy, and a large (and growing) foreign debt. What with all the financial resources expended through the 1980s, growth continued sputtering along, until full-fledged devaluation was imposed beginning in 1991. But as a subsequent section shows, a measure of popular resistance to financial power and its contradictions also appeared during the late 1980s and early 1990s. To understand the nature of this resistance, however, requires developing a typology of the ideological orientations we have encountered in the various reactions to financial power.

A typology of financial power and resistance

In each instance of rising financial power—mid-late 1890s, mid-late 1920s, late 1950s-early 1960s, late 1980s-early 1990s—there were dichotomous impulses in the economy that led either towards financial power and liberalised finance, or to a form of financial repression often based on either official or what we might consider "popular" (or populist) resistance to finance. In fact, financial power and resistance both took rather divergent forms, depending upon the broader conditions of accumulation and the political balance of forces. Table 13.1 depicts the wide nature of ideologies bound up in the swings from financial power to resistance.

Table 13.1

TENDENCIES OF FINANCIAL POWER AND RESISTANCE

FINANCIAL POWER		RESISTANCE	
A	**B**	**C**	**D**
liberal	conservative	nationalist	socialist
internationalist	national-oriented	protectionist	internationalist
"democratic"	authoritarian	authoritarian	democratic

Consider some of the variants of financial power and resistance that have appeared in Zimbabwe's history according to this typology, which can be augmented by van der Pijl's (1984) typology of ruling global ideologies and interests.[10] First, *Tendency A* is the philosophy of liberal, internationalist financiers who are not unwilling, as in the case of the World Bank and aid agencies in the early 1990s, to espouse a content-less "democratic" ideology. This tendency is consistent with van der Pijl's notion of a "money capital concept." In Zimbabwe, to illustrate, there springs to mind the financial elite's support for "Partnership" in the 1950s, the cautious Rhobank "planned transition to majority rule" in the late 1970s, and in the early 1990s the vocal opposition of financiers, led by Chidzero, to Mugabe's ultimately empty threat to institute a one-party state.

Turning next to *Tendency C,* the money capital concept stood opposed to a "productive capital concept," which took on many more of the characteristics of nationalism, industrial protectionism, and authoritarian populism. The apex of this was certainly the Nazi project; locally there was no more committed advocate than Ian Smith (and John Handford's *Portrait of an Economy Under Sanctions, 1965-1975* is a key text in this tradition). Whereas money capital respects the rules of the market, the productive capital concept easily ignores them by invoking subsidies, tariffs, capital controls, directed credit, and even nationalization and other infringements of property rights, in the interests of industrial growth.

Van der Pijl argues convincingly that both such tendencies can and did co-exist in the conception of what he terms "finance capital" (a rather different usage than Hilferding's). This conception captures *laissez faire* internationalism (the money capital concept) and "state monopoly capitalism" (the productive capital concept) in a synthetic ideology of corporate liberalism. That ideology corresponds to what Regulationists consider the "progressive," intensive Fordist regime of accumulation, which was dominant in the global economy for the major part of the twentieth century. Given the room for terminological confusion, such short-hand, heuristic devices as these must be applied with extreme caution.[11] For whereas van der Pijl's typology seems to accurately capture the nature of the accumulation process and the accompanying ideology of corporate liberalism during the *high-growth period* of advanced capitalism (not, van der Pijl notes, the subsequent monetarist, neo-liberal phase that began in the late 1970s), the Zimbabwe case introduces important caveats particular to semi-peripheral (and in this case racially-biased) modes of accumulation.[12]

An important question is whether van der Pijl's "finance capital" can exist on the periphery of the world economy. Based on a case study of both repressed and liberalised financial regimes in Peru, Paul Burkett (1987:1) argues that neither the money capital concept nor the productive capital concept can claim dominance: "Historically, the uneven development of capital accumulation on a global scale has inhibited industrialization in the Third World, and this has not only stunted the financial development process... but has also eventually led to enaction of interest rate restrictions by the state." There is an uncomfortable tension between Third World production and finance in this description, as both are impeded as a result of global processes, and as finance accommodates a dependent form of non-industrialising economic activity. This, according to Burkett (1987:1), is the result of the peculiar *class relations* that arise from "the competitive dynamic of capital accumulation, including the concentration and centralization of capital and the uneven development inherent in the accumulation process." Burkett (1987:7) specifies the way in which closely controlled Third World economies can be controlled by small, tight-knit producer groups which have a considerable stake in, for example, interest rate policies:

> In short, the political forces favoring interest rate restrictions may not conflict with the economic forces of regressive rationing of subsidised credit, and this lack of conflict may be due to simultaneity of economic and political hegemony... (C)heap credit is dispensed to wealthy landowners and large firms in exchange for political support.

Just this sort of linkage, observed in Zimbabwe on more than one occasion, is crucial to assessing how changes in the productive circuit of capital affect the local financial circuit. In turn the example highlights the geographically-specific nature of the way in which capitalists operating in productive and financial circuits sometimes form alliances, and sometimes aim instead, in their search for individual profits, to undermine each other. In areas characterised by underdevelopment, it is not necessarily the case that productive and financial circuits are in conflict.

Indeed, there has apparently never been a durable "finance capital" synthesis in Zimbabwe's history, primarily because the economy has been far more unbalanced and superexploitative than any in the West. Yet at times, nevertheless, there was a degree of ideological coherence between leading fractions of capital. This was really only the case during those periods when domestic financiers exercised influence over the broad direction of accumulation in the productive circuits. There were, for example, indications of ideological fusion within the capitalist class during the expansive 1950s era, at the height of the Central African Federation (when international financiers were also very important) and in the domestic financiers' development of the Salisbury Central Business District with the support of rapidly-centralising mining and industrial capital. Perhaps Zimbabwe's most obvious manifestation of the "finance capital" concept at the national scale occurred in the late 1980s during the pre-implementation stage of ESAP. At this point there arose "a more or less general awareness that society is in a particular condition, and that it is in need of a 'bankers' solution,' because the situation elicits 'bankers' arguments,'" as van der Pijl (1984:33) describes the phenomenon. The bankers' arguments also appealed to certain industrialists who believed increasingly in internationalism—either in search of new markets and inputs (mainly spare parts for rotting machinery) or, more cynically, in search of means of acquiring hard currency for speculation or straightforward capital flight.[13]

However, reflecting semi-peripheral fragility, this latter-day "finance capital" consensus was not to last, at least not with any passion throughout the productive circuit of capital. Within eighteen months of ESAP's implementation, not only were huge, potentially export-oriented industrialists like Cone Textiles and Hunyani packaging facing extinction, Zimbabwe's bankers were even appealing desperately to international financial power—in the form of the IMF—to retract the single most decisive component of the "bankers' solution," punishingly high real interest rates.

The point here is that a lasting synthesis of the money capital concept and the productive capital concept was never realised in Zimbabwe. Either financial power was excessively destructive in relation to productive capital, or finance was subject to substantial repression. Rarely were the two in harmony ideologically, and when they were it was for a very short time. Given Zimbabwe's historical and contemporary particularities, therefore, it is appropriate to hypothesise other, different types of financial power and resistance from van der Pijl's money capital and productive capital concepts, more finely attuned both to the contradictions of accumulation faced by Zimbabwean capitalists and to the possibilities of popular resistance.

If there is an ideal-type, indigenous form of financial power in Zimbabwe, then, it is cast from a *conservative* die, as described in *Tendency B*. Financiers operating with such a world view always attempted to maintain some semblance of the status quo when under pressure, but yet were unable to express this conservatism as a coherent accumulation strategy. The banks lacked classically liberal instincts for full-fledged deregulation—recall (from Chapter Eleven) the "cozy" "corset of controls" that both the World Bank and Chidzero remarked upon in the late 1980s, and the banks' willingness to, as the *Financial Gazette* put it in mid-1992, "throw each other lifebelts" (Chapter Twelve). In this conservative, uncreative tendency can also be found the main ideological voice of capital-in-general, the *Financial Gazette*, which although a stalwart defender of human rights in principle, drifted towards authoritarianism in practice (especially when condemning soft-hearted politicians and potential IMF rioters, as in September 1991), at the same time its internationalist instincts were continually battered by the sad reality of Zimbabwe's impotence in exporting anything much more than tobacco and other primary commodities to the world market. At the level of state rhetoric, the populist developmentalism of a Bernard Chidzero was a consistent official companion of this tendency.

And while it would not yet qualify as a tendency of financial power, there are nevertheless germs of such a conservative and authoritarian ideology in the Indigenous Business Development Centre, the Affirmative Action Group and other aspirant petty-bourgeois forces. Self-consciously "indigenous" entrepreneurship may well continue to grow, even under the debilitating conditions currently being imposed upon Zimbabwe by the world economy, and could even become dominant within a few decades depending upon the nature of future intercapitalist power struggles. For while capable of bitterly attacking the currently hegemonic version of financial power—particularly when denied access to credit—the IBDC, AAG and various politicians appear to be cut from much the same cloth as the aspiring black nationalists of the early 1960s, in the sense they are readier to join rather than contest the basic rules of capitalism under financial power. They are very much encouraged in this by the traditional nationalists (led by Mugabe), to the discomfort of the small but important black financial bourgeoisie. Moreover, some of the same rhetoric of conservative populism can be found in several small political parties that have lined up to the right of ZANU.[14]

It is important not to overstate the case, however. An explicitly *domestic or national-oriented* version of financial power—such as existed in South Africa, briefly but most explicitly, following the imposition of sanctions and disinvestment by the major international banks[15]—is difficult to identify throughout Zimbabwe's history, primarily due to the foreign sources of bank headquarters. (The international linkages of Rhodesian-era banks were challenged, ineffectually, by a national-oriented bloc of white labor and merchants in the 1950s.)

There is in *Tendency D,* finally, the left-popular approach: a lively critique of financial power and, potentially, the reconstruction of the financial circuit of capital in which finance would be simultaneously "repressed" (with respect to the determination of resource-allocation) but also capable of empowering subordinate classes in democratic, community-based movements. What are the political prerequisites for such a tendency?

Conclusion: Progressive resistance to financial power in Zimbabwe

It is possible, though perilous, to trace nascent progressive resistance to financial power in contemporary Zimbabwe, and to make projections about the prospects for future resistance. It is difficult because the ruling party, after all, maintains centre-right political leanings while disguising its persistent authoritarian tendencies with leftist rhetoric. Although there are occasional rumors of ZANU's eventual split into left and right wings, this is likely to be wishful thinking. Moreover, the one left-leaning opposition party that arose from the ashes of ESAP (Austin Chakaodza's Movement for Popular Democracy) fell back quickly, having failed to draw aboard logical allies in civil society. The die-hard residues of socialist discourse in ZANU may well make formal left party-building a difficult if not impossible proposition in coming years, notwithstanding *Moto* magazine's urgent July 1995 call for the establishment of a workers' party.

Instead, Zimbabwe's explicitly left-popular currents are perhaps best represented by a small group of intellectuals, some ex-combatants (particularly in Matabeleland), university students, some elements within the Zimbabwe Congress of Trade Unions (ZCTU), and a few urban social movements that are beginning to emerge publicly. To illustrate the potential, one formidable intellectual, Arnold Sibanda (1987:19-20), has set out something of a call for

> new political and economic strategies for development, strategies which are popular-based and internally oriented. Such strategies mean the need for political structures that are popular and dynamic, that demand from multilateral financial institutions and transnational corporations benefits for national development and are strong enough to reject the demands of imperialism where these contradict those of the nation. Africa needs popular radical politics, it needs political regimes that place the people first, that realise the need to industrialise and develop national economies instead of leaving them as captive suppliers of the materials, markets and cheap labor for international monopoly capital. Africa needs to curb the outward flow of its much needed capital and other resources. If this does not happen, an ominous social crisis looms large over the continent.

Such concerns uppermost in his mind, ZCTU general secretary Morgan Tsvangirai made the following rather disturbing prognosis just prior to the 1991 financial crash:

> What we are looking for in Zimbabwe is a democratic space. Because what is going to be sacrificed in this programme [ESAP] is democracy. When people go to the streets, complaining about these things, the state will be forced to use power to quell these riots, and in fact one of the ironies is that we are arming our own people—the police and the army—to turn against our people... At the end of the day we become the marginalised group, because the government has put itself in a position so that it cannot take a stand against the IMF. The only way to defend against international capital marginalising further the indigenous businessman, the worker, the peasant, is to have all these groups together... There will not immediately be any flashpoints, you will have a lot of dropouts. The real flashpoint will be the combination of those social effects, and the declining standard of living, and unemployment. As everybody says, it is a timebomb. (*Southern Africa Report,* July 1991)

There were, in fact, the occasional flashpoints (the Zimbabwe versions of "IMF riots" in October 1993 and November 1995), and as a result Mugabe in late 1995 threatened to simply shut down any democratic space in which to protest. Moreover, Tsvangirai remained relatively "marginalised," as he put it, in formal Zimbabwean politics, reflected in the ZCTU's terribly unsuccessful initial attempt to organise anti-ESAP mass action (in mid-1992). In spite of the labor movement's growing coherence and material strength (Sachikonye 1995b), Tsvangirai's allies in civil society remained relatively weak (Raftopoulos 1991; Saunders 1995). Thus trade union rhetoric drifted aimlessly during the early 1990s, until entreaties for a corporatist deal were rewarded in 1995 when a new Labour Minister (Shamuyarira) finally provided ZCTU access to government's neo-liberal policy-making process. If the ZCTU was mistaken in taking this direction, however, Tsvangirai would be the leader workers would want to set matters right (or rather left) at the first promising opportunity. Hints of labor's potential were found in the successful mid-1996 public sector strike, which paralyzed the country's ruling machinery for more than a week.

In general, Zimbabwe's civil society discourse has thus far lacked either much content (in comparison to South Africa's) or any discernible consensus on the most important political issues. Some examples of commentary by leading intellectuals reveal, appropriately, an optimism of the will and (mainly but not entirely) a distinct pessimism of the intellect. Norbert Tengende (1992:5, 7, 22), for instance, calls for a return to the "values and goals of the liberation struggle," including the revival of "popular participatory structures created during the war that were suppressed after independence" and suggests that "the crisis presents significant openings for the advance of democratic claims by social groups." Yet ultimately he warns that "The informal sector organisations may reflect the same authoritarianism identified with the formal sector. It is evidenced in Zimbabwe where the discourse of domination of the ruling party is appropriated by the leaders of some such associations, thus recreating in microcosm the same strategies of domination as the national level."

Richard Saunders (1992) offers a more hopeful vision of the potential for eventual civil society challenges to the hegemony of ruling ideas:

> Concretely, the enduring crisis is more accurately described as an interlocking series of challenges from university students, trade unionists, unemployed youth, disgruntled ex-combatants, "democratic" white capitalists and other groups and class fractions, in response to various policies and public relations blunders by the ZANU leadership (and particularly the President). Here one can point to the gelling of a loosely articulated, generally leaderless "populist frontism" based on the disillusionment of diverse social fractions with ZANU's rhetoric and practice. This heterogeneous "opposition" has seized upon some of the more obvious failures of ZANU's own programme, prominently featuring such issues as the corruption of leadership, declining standard

> of living of the "povo", arrogance of the "chefs" and the suppression of freedom of expression and organisation.

Ibbo Mandaza (1991:28) correctly insists, "it is the *civil society*—of which the educated petty bourgeoisie is an important element—that can help temper this political instinct on the part of the African petty bourgeoisie once it has attained political power in this era of the dominance of international capital." In particular, "working-class civil society" (Mayekiso 1996) continued to be, for even advocates of a Marxist-Leninist vanguard party, a most critical element. According to Kempton Makamure (1991:118),

> We in Zimbabwe today stand in a situation where the working class is the vanguard for political liberty and for democratic institutions. The position is incontrovertible. The working class is spurring on all other democratic elements in our society. It is pushing the liberals towards the political radicals and the radicals towards a revolutionary socialist perspective for a new democracy in Zimbabwe. Without fully recognising and activating the political and economic potential of the working class in Zimbabwe all talk about democracy and pluralism is cheap political chatter for the amusement of the capitalist class.

One such radicalization process, uneven as ever (for political consciousness ebbed and flowed throughout the post-independence period), was to be found in acutely concentrated form amongst students. Under the leadership of Arthur Mutambara (1991:141), for instance, the University of Zimbabwe Student Union declared a

> maximum programme—to fight for the establishment of a truly egalitarian socialist Zimbabwe... [through] the establishment of a broad-based mass democratic movement consisting of progressive organisations of workers, consumers, peasants, lecturers, teachers, students, unemployed people, churches, political parties and the entirety of the democratic professional fraternity.

In a far more feasible vein, Lloyd Sachikonye (1995b) notes of the 1990s that "For the first time since its independence, a broad coalition of social forces have emerged to oppose the ESAP measures; the Mugabe government is currently encountering its most serious legitimacy crisis." But there was a long road from legitimacy crisis—always the turf on which rank populism and fragile "united front" politics grows fastest—to concrete changes in living conditions, in power relations, and in the strength of various democratic organisational forms.[16]

And that road still winds seductively through nationalist, instead of internationalist territory, in the process leaving many potential allies stranded in cul-de-sac detours. The target, of course, must still be international financial capital. "Popular demonstrations against officially constructed austerity plans are reported almost daily," remarked Arrighi, Hopkins and Wallerstein (1989:73-74) of the late 1980s:

> The more these popular struggles focus in each national setting on whatever regime is in office, and so become focused on who speaks in the name of that national people as a whole, the more will such struggles weaken the workings of the world-scale class-forming process and strengthen the interstate system. The more, on the other hand, the popular movements join forces across borders (and continents) to have their respective state officials abrogate those relations of the interstate system through which the pressure is conveyed, the less likely they are to weaken, and the more likely they are to strengthen, the pivotal class-forming process of the world-economy.

This probably remains true in the late 1990s and beyond. For even if no striking example of either abrogation of interstate relations[17] or of civil society internationalism has since come to pass,[18] there continue nevertheless a healthy variety of popular struggles against financial power, even if these are mainly reactive in nature (Walton and Seddon 1994). Indeed, although there may be important national and local particularities, the austerity plans are becoming ever similar throughout the interstate system, under the broad determination of financial power.

Finally then, what lessons from Zimbabwe, if any, for the rest of the world's progressive forces? I remain convinced, from the theoretical investigations that have preceded and followed the empirical evidence, that we must think globally about financial power and act locally but act nationally and internationally as well. Moreover, with the decline of industrial power relative to financial power, I find it revealing that trade unionism has waned at the international scale (or, perhaps worse, turned towards national-corporatism, as also appears the case in Zimbabwe). In the context of financial power over nation-states and of the degradation of nationalist movements (such as Zimbabwe's), this is not an opportune historical moment either to initiate corporatist relations with state and capital or to attempt to take formal state power. Thus it should not come as a surprise that traditional working-class movements have given way to broader, social-movement challenges to the uneven development of international capitalism (Bond and Mayekiso 1996).

Can social movements walk this tightrope, and react to financial power in an internationalist manner that ultimately addresses the causes—in industrial overaccumulation and decline—rather than merely the symptoms? After all, if (from Chapter One) Simon Clarke is correct that "The power of money is... the irreducible form, and the most abstract embodiment, of the social power of property," then to take up campaigns against financial power will continue to entail struggle that cuts to the very heart of international capitalism.

Notes

1. This, however, was accomplished by cementing even more extreme racial structures of production and consumption; hence the Rhodesian Front strategy generated untenable articulations and disarticulations of modes of production and social relations which led to guerrilla war.
2. These included the increasing roles of state debt and regulatory policy in managing monetary liquidity (Chapters Three, Five and Eleven); new "consumption norms" (and the development of consumer credit to match, including the hire purchase business that fostered financial development in 1950s Southern Rhodesia)(Chapter Five); and long-term contractual savings (especially pension funds)(Chapter Eight). These are impressive innovations, which had the affect of ameliorating crisis by displacing overaccumulation into growing financial markets which in turn supported effective demand and, to some degree, new fixed investment.
3. This is probably worth much greater reflection. The leading regulationist, Alain Lipietz (1985:126-127) may have raised expectations in arguing (initially in 1983) that such overaccumulation can continue to be ***partially devalued:***

   > The current rise in interest rates is therefore the concentrated expression, specific to credit money, of the devalorization of values-in-process. By the rise in the "actualization rate" that it implies, it depreciates the fictitious capital (shares and debentures) which measures the assets tied up in fixed capital.

   This stance proved to be incorrect by the time the English-language edition of *The Enchanted World* was published in 1985. Lipietz focused on the supposed transition from one near-extinct regime of accumulation characterised by heavy industry (Fordism) to a new "flexible" regime, and therefore missed the underlying importance of the rise of finance. The interest rate increase engineered by the US Federal Reserve in 1979 was not, in the first instance, geared to devalorisation (although it did this, to some extent), but on the contrary represented a ***symptom of the rise of finance*** instead. Thus it did not "depreciate" fictitious capital such as stock market shares, but on the contrary encouraged enormous shifts in capital from productive to financial circuits—and concomitant shifts in political power to financiers—such that a new regime of deregulation ultimately ***expanded*** the scope of such financial markets in the 1980s. Thus fictitious capital was less and less useful as a "measure" of assets tied up in fixed capital.

   Lipietz also argued in *The Enchanted World* that high real interest rates were responsible for the subsequent decline in new fixed capital expenditure. Yet the stagnation of fixed capital expenditure beginning in the mid 1970s reflected not only the high rate of interest, but more importantly, the general surplus of fixed capital in the world economy. Thus it is questionable how the "pseudo-validation" Lipietz refers to—in essence, the capacity of accumulation to proceed on the basis of financial expansion—is meant to stabilise the inherently unstable movement of capital through productive and financial circuits and to beckon the next regime of accumulation. Moreover, such a conception is as theoretically unfaithful to Marx (notwithstanding Lipietz's protestations in other works) as was Hilferding, and just as misleading politically. Brenner and Glick (1991:114-115) correctly critique Lipietz's "new class compromise that would secure, simultaneously, the socio-technical requirements for transcending the productivity crisis and the economic and political requirements for society-wide consent and stability... Because the regulationists' diagnosis of the current crisis is faulty, Lipietz's prescription will not work, and the proposed political bargain is therefore unviable."

4. Stoneman's otherwise insightful writing contributed to this belief, we saw, and his subsequent defence of the post-Independence decade of stagnation and the speculative rise of the Zimbabwe Stock Exchange as a reflection of economic policy success was equally as mistaken (*Southern African Review of Books,* September-October 1991).
5. Grossmann was quite correct when he observed that "The worst orgies of speculation are possible in a period when, with the transition from individual forms of property to its social form in share-capital, enormous fortunes accumulated over several decades are thrown on to the market and sacrificed on the exchange." In contemporary Zimbabwe, the "worst orgies" appeared in two forms: control by institutional investors of the pension funds of workers and civil servants, and their speculative employment in the Zimbabwe Stock Exchange and commercial property, which in turn led to overvaluation of fictitious capital and a crash (Chapter Eight).
6. Over the next few decades, settler capital did prove capable of valorising many of the speculative, spatially-extensive investments such as the telegraph, rail-road and land grabs. But full valorisation of labor power was not on the agenda (as was the case under the racially more liberal Partnership schemes of the late 1950s), simply because for economic reasons it did not have to be.
7. Smith (1990:125) argues that "the historical rhythm of investment in the built environment forges specific geographical patterns which in turn strongly influence the agenda of capital accumulation." This argument is not necessarily supported by Zimbabwe's historical evidence. Ironically, the Kuznets cycle, initially so appealing as a fifteen year temporal marker of overaccumulation and devaluation, does not adequately capture the nature of financial-speculative restructuring of space, especially urban real estate markets, in the 1950s and late 1980s. Speculation in the built environment during these two periods was more directly a function of the rise

of finance than it was (as Smith would have it) the basis for an expansion of productive sector fixed investment. While the collapse of finance in 1974 coincided with inordinate overinvestment in global real estate markets in relation to an emerging overaccumulation crisis, the productive sector rhythm in UDI Rhodesia actually peaked later (manufacturing investment was unprecedented, after all, from 1974-76).

8. Considered in terms of an overused historical metaphor, the 1928 Southern Rhodesian crash followed by the 1929-33 global financial crisis may not suffice as an accurate precursor for the coming period, given the much more flexible systems of crisis displacement. Nevertheless, as many observers (including captains of finance such as speculator George Soros and IMF Managing Director Michel Camdessus) have warned, an international financial crash is a distinct possibility in the wake of catalysts ranging from stock market corrections, violent currency fluctuations, speculative investments gone badly awry, property collapses and financial bankruptcies. Under such conditions the World Bank, IMF and other powerful international financial actors may also lose resources, status and their current power over Zimbabwe and the rest of the Third World. (On the other hand, the tenacity of the Bank, IMF and GATT/WTO, in the face of stiff resistance from various quarters during the 1980s and 1990s, also throws open the possibility of their transformation into a prototype for a form of world government.)
9. The armed struggles of ZANU and ZAPU later gained the support of China and the Soviet Union, respectively, which meant that there was a momentary engagement with "Marxism-Leninism." But this was, as noted in Chapter Six, ultimately a disguise for classically authoritarian nationalism, and it was at just at the point that such a left-popular (even socialist) ideological legacy would have been useful—when financial power dominated Zimbabwe's economy in the mid and late 1980s—that many ZANU leaders' politics turned to corruption and *compradorism*.
10. Van der Pijl's approach is used here because it is particularly capable of focusing attention on the circulation of capital, not merely its institutional appearance (or "fractional" form). As a result, this framework provides a more nuanced perspective of the expansion of capital through space and time, and through different (productive and financial) circuits—one more able to identify why imperialist proclivities were more likely at certain points in the accumulation process, and with particular tempos, than at others.
11. A different (and perhaps just as compelling) view is Eric Helleiner's (1995:164) observation not of a *synthesis* but instead of the *replacement* of the money capital concept by the productive capital concept in the post-war era:

> The endorsement of capital controls at Bretton Woods represented a dramatic departure from traditional liberal financial practices. This departure had its roots in a kind of socio-ideological structural break that took place across the industrial world in the wake of the economic and financial crises of the early 1930s. Largely discredited by the crises, the private and central bankers who had dominated financial

politics in the 1920s were increasingly replaced in positions of financial power by Keynesian-minded economists, industrialists and labor leaders. This new "bloc" of social forces rejected the bankers' laissez-faire ideology in the financial arena in favor of a more interventionist approach that would make the financial sector serve their broader economic and political objectives.

12. This is not to say that the same laws of motion of capital (which inform van der Pijl) failed to operate in a predictable manner in Southern Rhodesia, as witnessed (from the 1950s) by powerful tendencies to concentration, centralisation, extreme hierarchical structures of production, and the shift of control of significant sections of capital from family-owned firms to supervisory management and directors, funded substantially by the pension and insurance funds of a privileged portion of the working-class. The state monopoly capitalist element was also present from quite early on (the 1940s), and the liberal internationalism of financiers was not in doubt through the mid 1960s—until financial repression was imposed—and again in the 1980s. But unlike advanced capitalist settings, there was no easy unification of these diverse currents in a hegemonic corporate liberal ideology, in the manner of van der Pijl's "finance capital."
13. The difference between the CZI in the early and late 1980s was personified by the different degrees of respect which the then chief economists afforded World Bank export-oriented industrial policy advice: Roger Riddell not at all, Mike Humphrey fawningly.
14. The early 1990s witnessed a few parties—the Zimbabwe Unity Movement, the tiny ZUM-breakaway Democratic Party, and the even smaller National Progressive Alliance (NPA)—striking anti-ESAP positions. Yet they also support free enterprise with unlimited foreign remittances of profits and, in the case of the NPA, the scrapping of minimum wages. ZANU(Ndonga) showed some of the same tendencies. This confusion was embodied in the person of Enos Nkala, once a founding ZANU nationalist leader, convert to socialism, Minister of Finance, victim of the Willowvale corruption purge, employee of Lonrho, confidant of opposition leader Ndabiningi Sithole, and ultimately anti-ESAP critic of Mugabe and Chidzero from the populist right. In sum, Zimbabwe opposition politicians appeared a self-destructive lot, and present no challenge in the immediate future to ZANU.
15. This was articulated in the late 1980s writings of SA Reserve Bank Deputy Governor Jan Lombard, and the closely-related "inward industrialisation" strategy temporarily adopted by the Development Bank of Southern Africa.
16. Saunders (1995:24,25) correctly cautions, "In this context of weak internal organisation and pressures from the state and dominant party, any talk of civics' leading role—or indeed, the emergence of a national civics 'movement' as in South Africa—seems at very best premature.... Thus, while both ESAP and widespread dissatisfaction with the political *status quo* have provided plenty of raw material for mobilisation and for the

emergence of coalitions and joint agendas among a range of civics, little of this type of organising has taken place."

17. It may indeed be true that as in the 1930s, the only prospect for an entirely new direction of development that would give hope for the majority of people in the world in the 1990s is through hastening the fall of financial power, and that lies in widespread default on the Third World debt, increased South-South cooperation and semi-autarchic, inward-oriented accumulation. "The response to the challenge of our time imposes what I have suggested naming 'delinking'," Samir Amin argues (1990:xvi). "Delinking is not synonymous with autarchy, but rather with the subordination of external relations to the logic of internal development." Amin here recommends "refusing to submit to the demands of the globalized law of value, that is to the alleged 'rationality' of the system of world prices." There is not a single government, at this writing, which is anywhere near considering such a challenge to international financial power.
18. The Malaysia-based Third World Network, the "50 Years is Enough!" coalition calling for reform of the IMF and World Bank, various networks of international environmentalists, some of the Canada-US-Mexico popular alliances, and the Zapatista movement in Chiapas, Mexico all portend future progress in this regard. The international financial sanctions campaign against Pretoria was perhaps the best precursor.

Figures

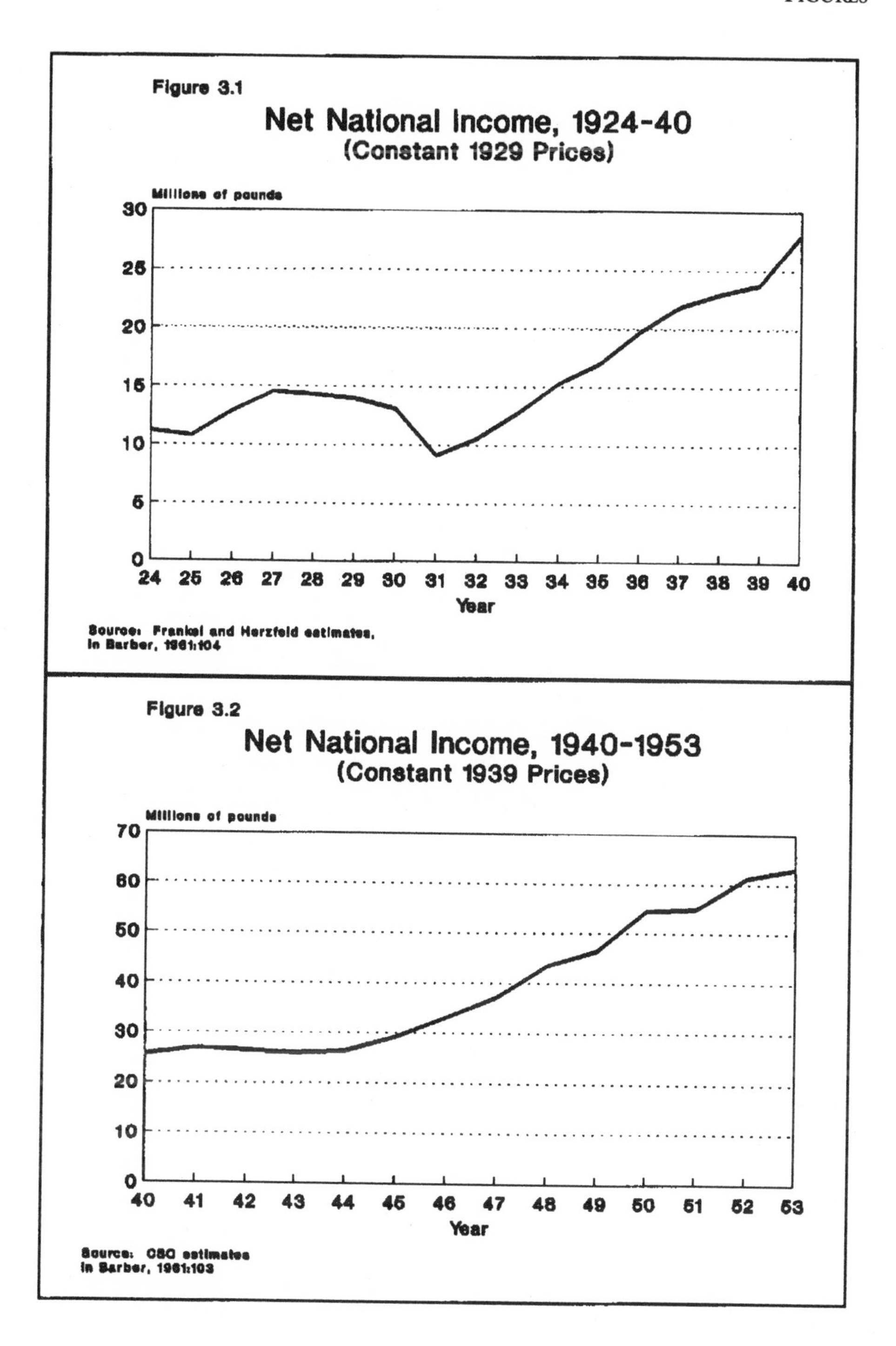
Figure 3.1
Net National Income, 1924-40
(Constant 1929 Prices)
Millions of pounds
30
25
20
15
10
5
0
24 25 26 27 28 29 30 31 32 33 34 35 36 37 38 39 40
Year
Source: Frankel and Herzfeld estimates,
in Barber, 1961:104
Figure 3.2
Net National Income, 1940-1953
(Constant 1939 Prices)
Millions of pounds
70
60
50
40
30
20
10
0
40 41 42 43 44 45 46 47 48 49 50 51 52 53
Year
Source: CSO estimates
in Barber, 1961:103

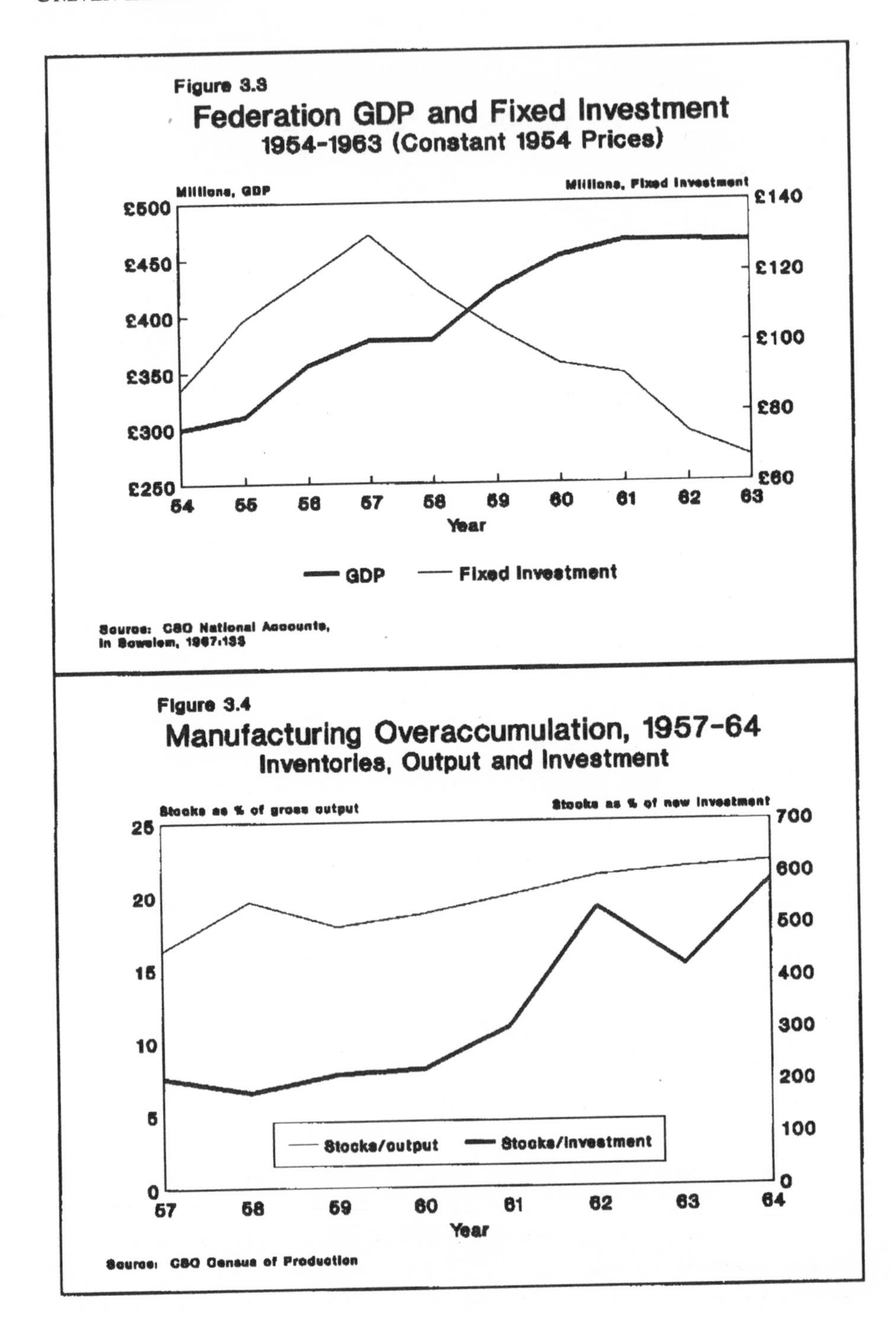
Figure 3.3
Federation GDP and Fixed Investment
1954-1963 (Constant 1954 Prices)
Millions, GDP
Millions, Fixed Investment
£500
£450
£400
£350
£300
£250
£140
£120
£100
£80
£60
54
55
56
57
58
59
60
61
62
63
Year
GDP
Fixed Investment
Source: CSO National Accounts,
in Bowslem, 1967:133
Figure 3.4
Manufacturing Overaccumulation, 1957-64
Inventories, Output and Investment
Stocks as % of gross output
Stocks as % of new investment
25
20
15
10
5
0
700
600
500
400
300
200
100
0
Stocks/output
Stocks/investment
57
58
59
60
61
62
63
64
Year
Source: CSO Census of Production

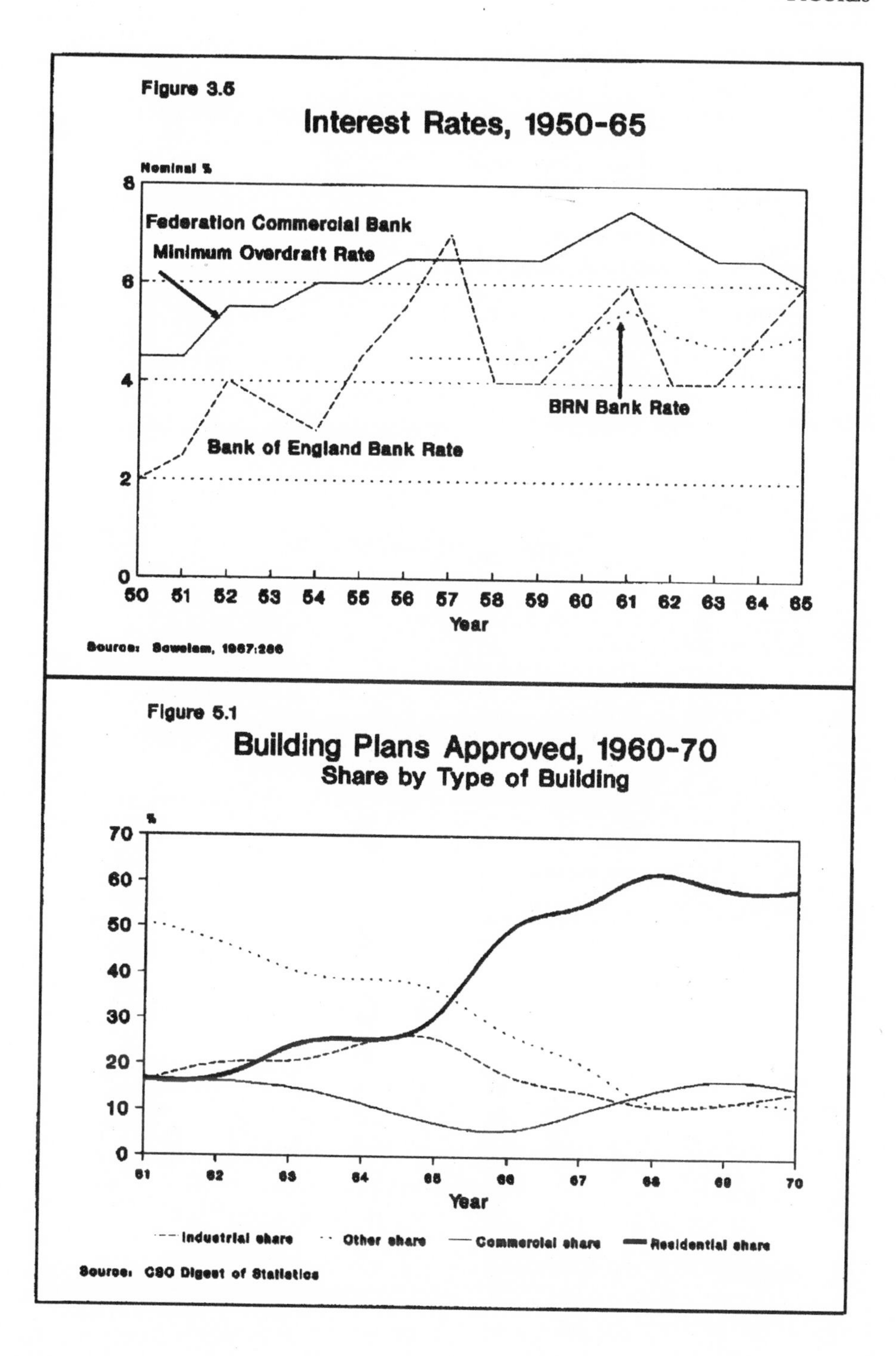
Figure 3.5
Interest Rates, 1950-65
Nominal %
8
6
4
2
0
Federation Commercial Bank
Minimum Overdraft Rate
BRN Bank Rate
Bank of England Bank Rate
50 51 52 53 54 55 56 57 58 59 60 61 62 63 64 65
Year
Source: Sowelem, 1967:286
Figure 5.1
Building Plans Approved, 1960-70
Share by Type of Building
%
70
60
50
40
30
20
10
0
61 62 63 64 65 66 67 68 69 70
Year
Industrial share
Other share
Commercial share
Residential share
Source: CSO Digest of Statistics

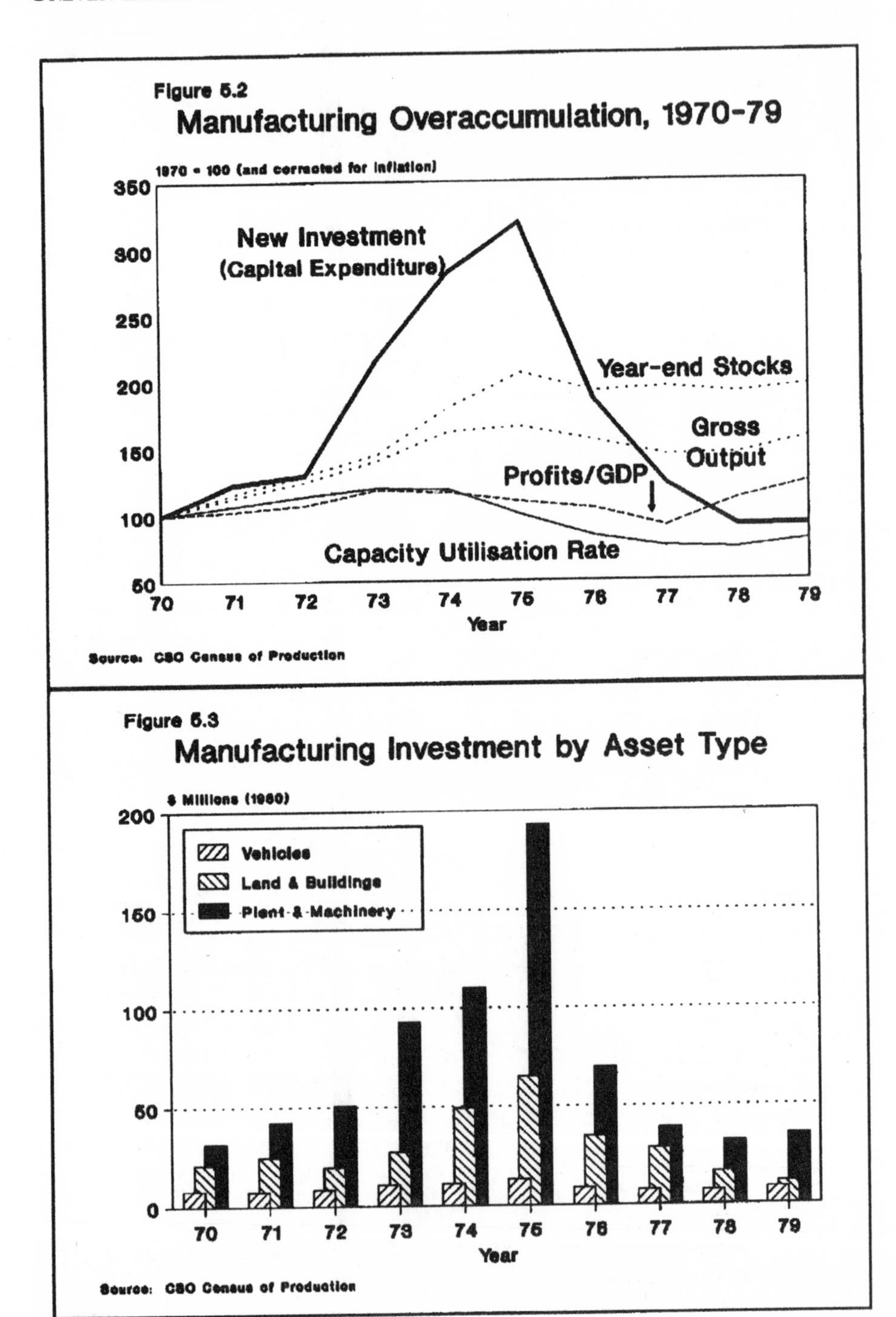
Figure 5.2
Manufacturing Overaccumulation, 1970-79
1970 = 100 (and corrected for inflation)
350
300
250
200
150
100
50
New Investment
(Capital Expenditure)
Year-end Stocks
Gross
Output
Profits/GDP
Capacity Utilisation Rate
70
71
72
73
74
75
76
77
78
79
Year
Source: CSO Census of Production
Figure 5.3
Manufacturing Investment by Asset Type
$ Millions (1980)
200
150
100
50
0
Vehicles
Land & Buildings
Plant & Machinery
70
71
72
73
74
75
76
77
78
79
Year
Source: CSO Census of Production

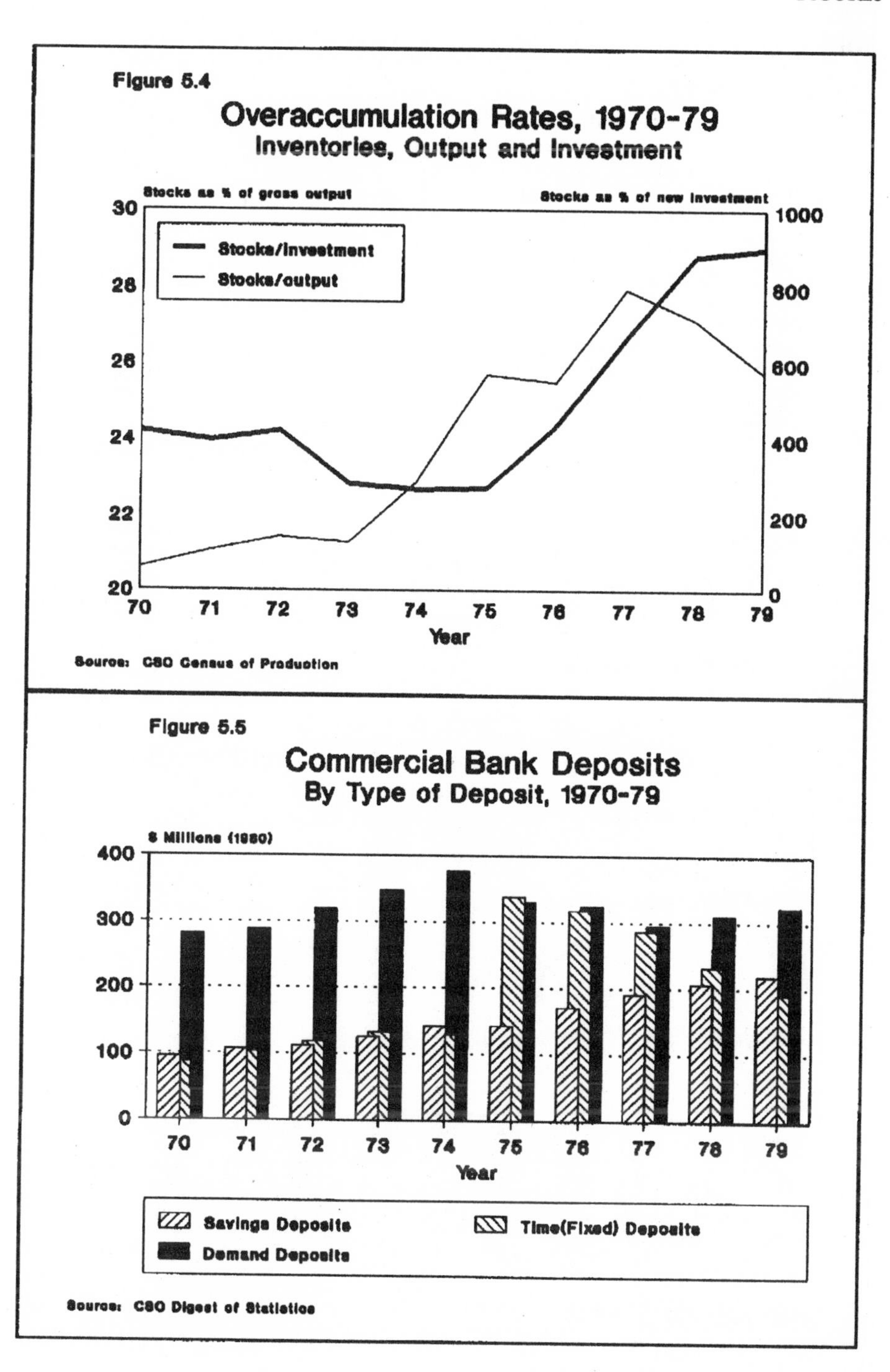
Figure 5.4
Overaccumulation Rates, 1970-79
Inventories, Output and Investment
Stocks as % of gross output
Stocks as % of new investment
Stocks/investment
Stocks/output
30
28
26
24
22
20
1000
800
600
400
200
0
70 71 72 73 74 75 76 77 78 79
Year
Source: CSO Census of Production
Figure 5.5
Commercial Bank Deposits
By Type of Deposit, 1970-79
$ Millions (1980)
400
300
200
100
0
70 71 72 73 74 75 76 77 78 79
Year
Savings Deposits
Time(Fixed) Deposits
Demand Deposits
Source: CSO Digest of Statistics

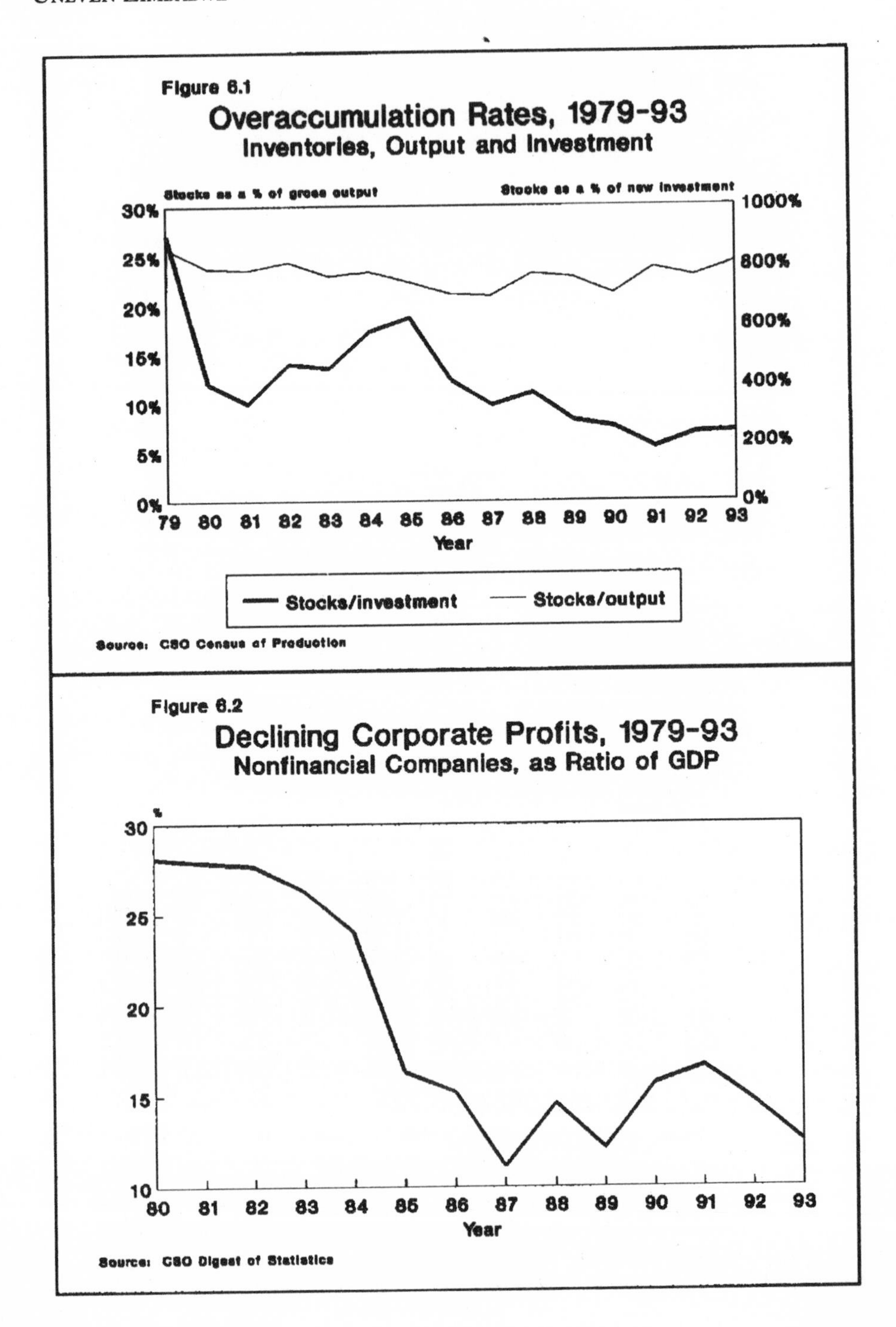
Figure 6.1
Overaccumulation Rates, 1979-93
Inventories, Output and Investment
Stocks as a % of gross output
Stocks as a % of new investment
30%
25%
20%
15%
10%
5%
0%
1000%
800%
600%
400%
200%
0%
79 80 81 82 83 84 85 86 87 88 89 90 91 92 93
Year
Stocks/investment
Stocks/output
Source: CSO Census of Production
Figure 6.2
Declining Corporate Profits, 1979-93
Nonfinancial Companies, as Ratio of GDP
%
30
25
20
15
10
80 81 82 83 84 85 86 87 88 89 90 91 92 93
Year
Source: CSO Digest of Statistics

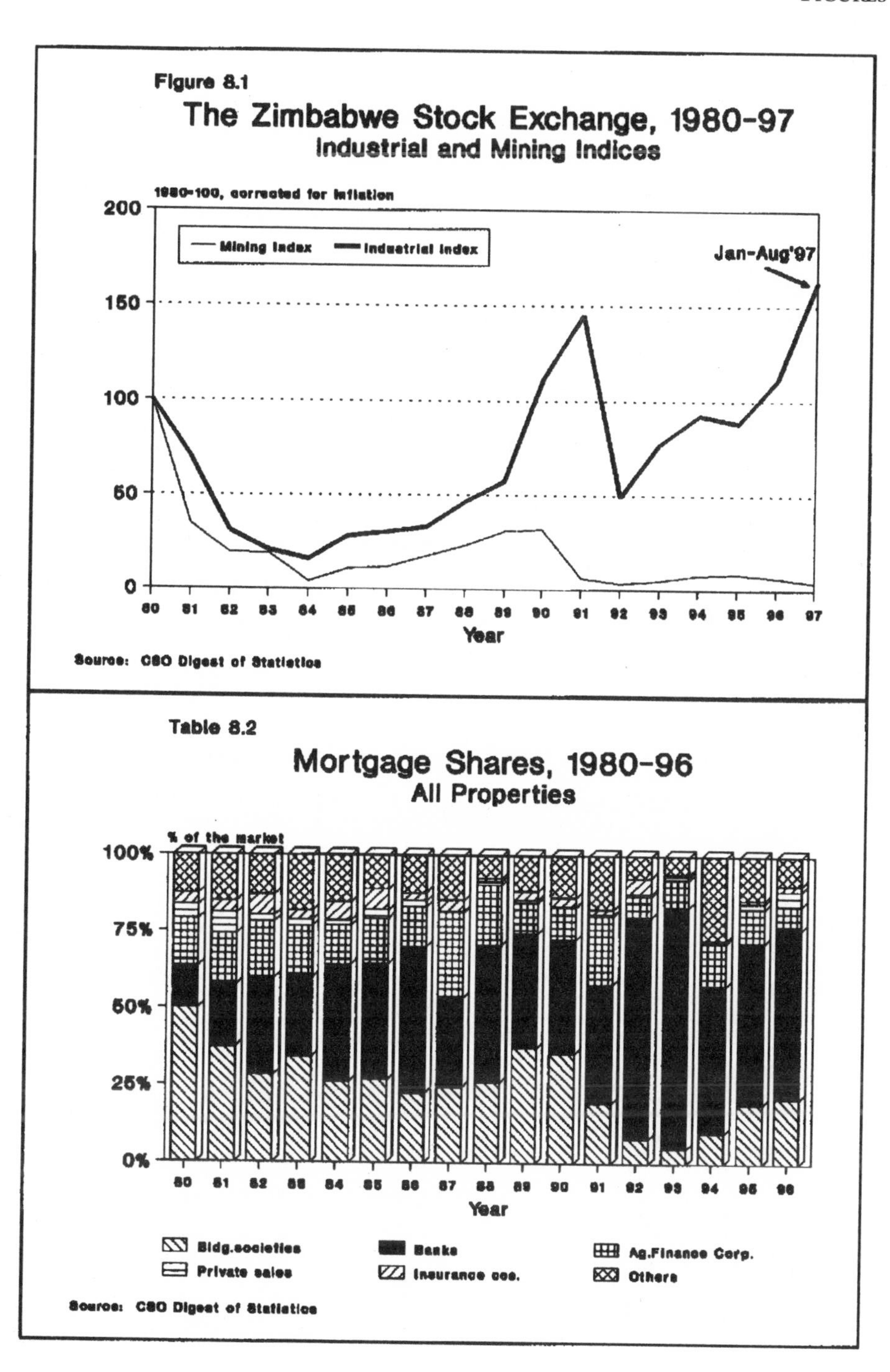
Figure 8.1
The Zimbabwe Stock Exchange, 1980-97
Industrial and Mining Indices
1980=100, corrected for inflation
Mining Index
Industrial Index
Jan-Aug'97
200
150
100
50
0
80 81 82 83 84 85 86 87 88 89 90 91 92 93 94 95 96 97
Year
Source: CSO Digest of Statistics
Table 8.2
Mortgage Shares, 1980-96
All Properties
% of the market
100%
75%
50%
25%
0%
80 81 82 83 84 85 86 87 88 89 90 91 92 93 94 95 96
Year
Bldg.societies
Banks
Ag.Finance Corp.
Private sales
Insurance cos.
Others
Source: CSO Digest of Statistics

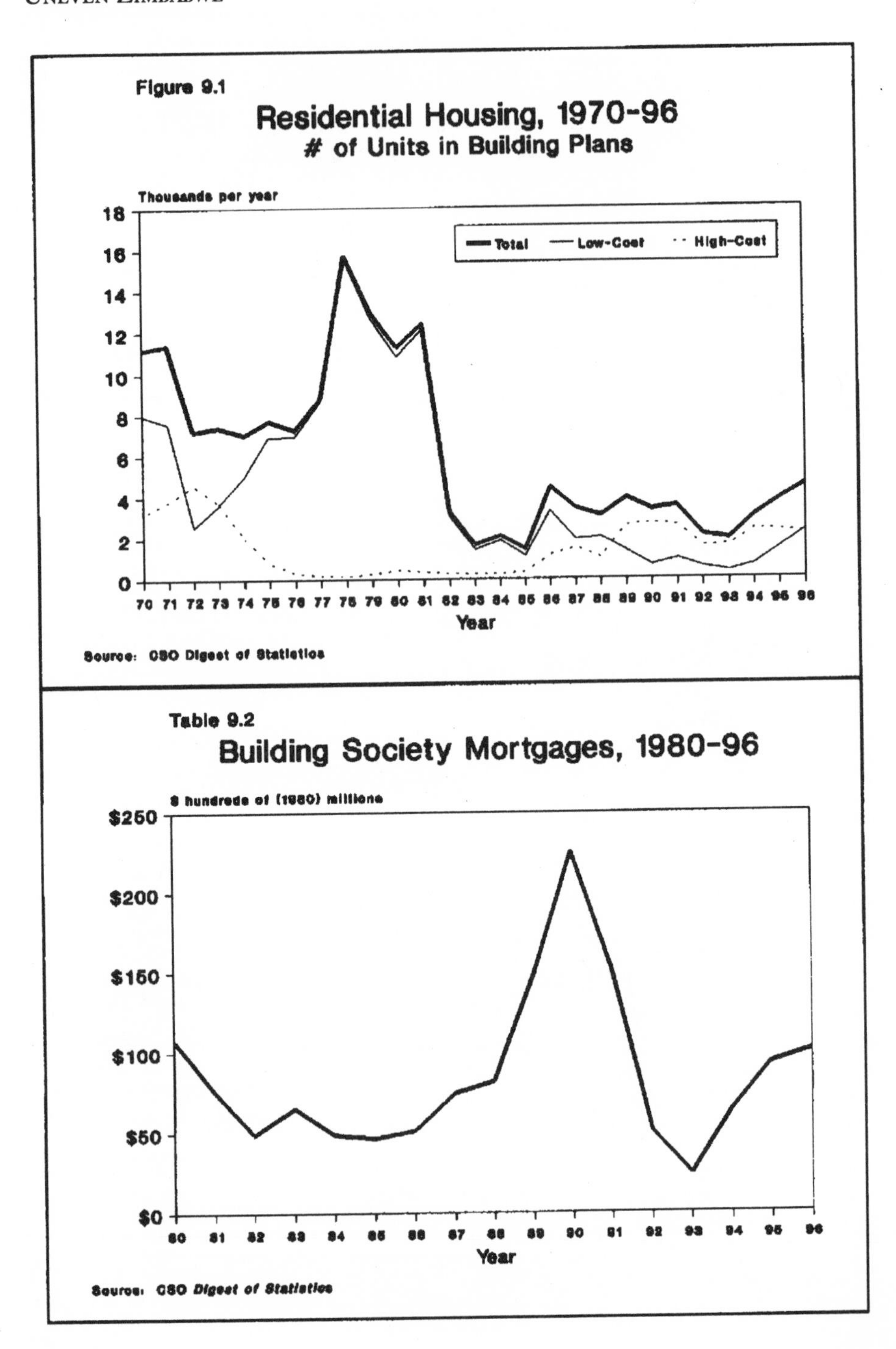
Figure 9.1
Residential Housing, 1970-96
# of Units in Building Plans
Thousands per year
18
16
14
12
10
8
6
4
2
0
Total
Low-Cost
High-Cost
70 71 72 73 74 75 76 77 78 79 80 81 82 83 84 85 86 87 88 89 90 91 92 93 94 95 96
Year
Source: CSO Digest of Statistics
Table 9.2
Building Society Mortgages, 1980-96
$ hundreds of (1980) millions
$250
$200
$150
$100
$50
$0
80 81 82 83 84 85 86 87 88 89 90 91 92 93 94 95 96
Year
Source: CSO Digest of Statistics

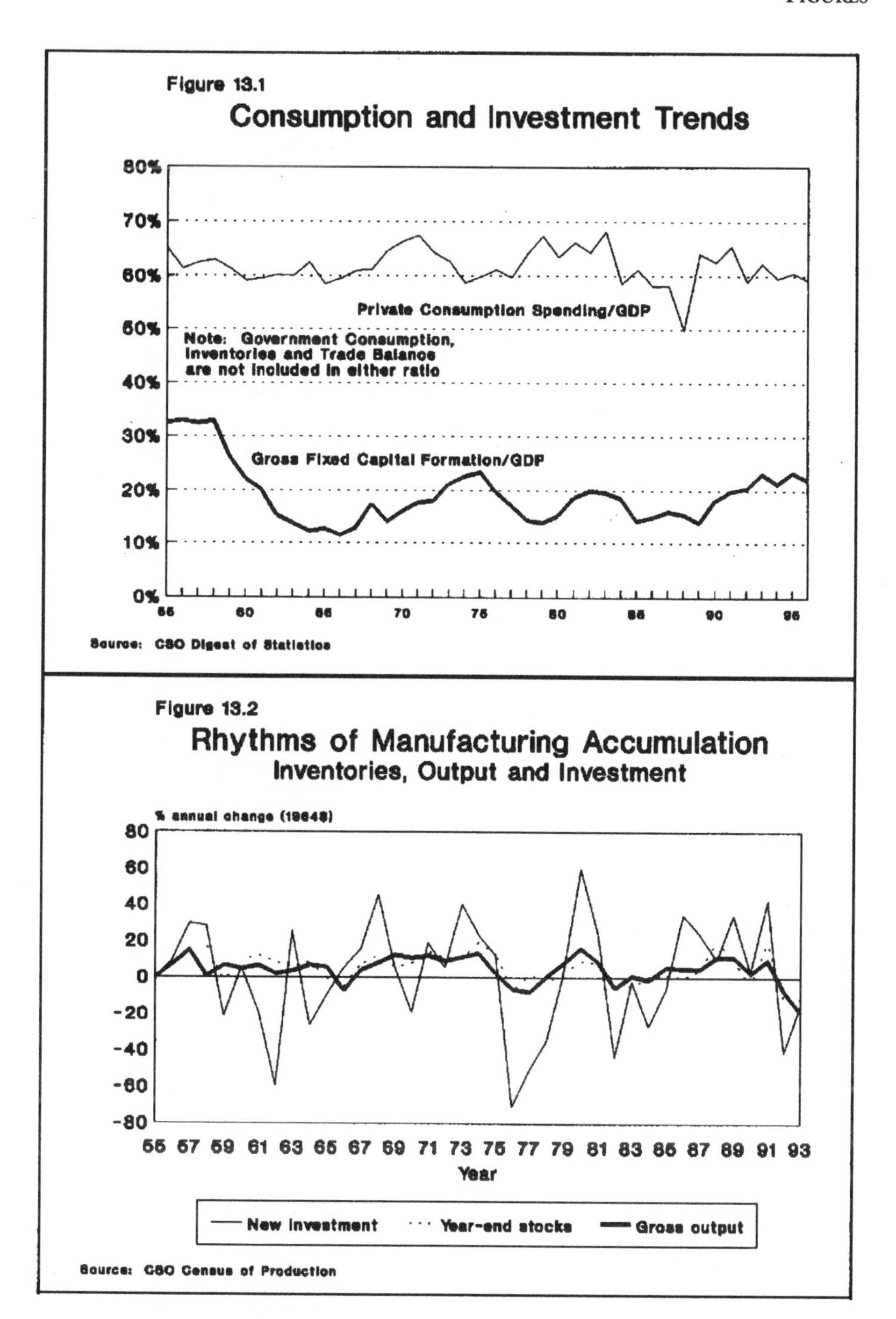
Figure 13.1
Consumption and Investment Trends
80%
70%
60%
50%
40%
30%
20%
10%
0%
55
60
65
70
75
80
85
90
95
Private Consumption Spending/GDP
Note: Government Consumption, Inventories and Trade Balance are not included in either ratio
Gross Fixed Capital Formation/GDP
Source: CSO Digest of Statistics
Figure 13.2
Rhythms of Manufacturing Accumulation
Inventories, Output and Investment
% annual change (1964$)
80
60
40
20
0
-20
-40
-60
-80
55 57 59 61 63 65 67 69 71 73 75 77 79 81 83 85 87 89 91 93
Year
New investment
Year-end stocks
Gross output
Source: CSO Census of Production

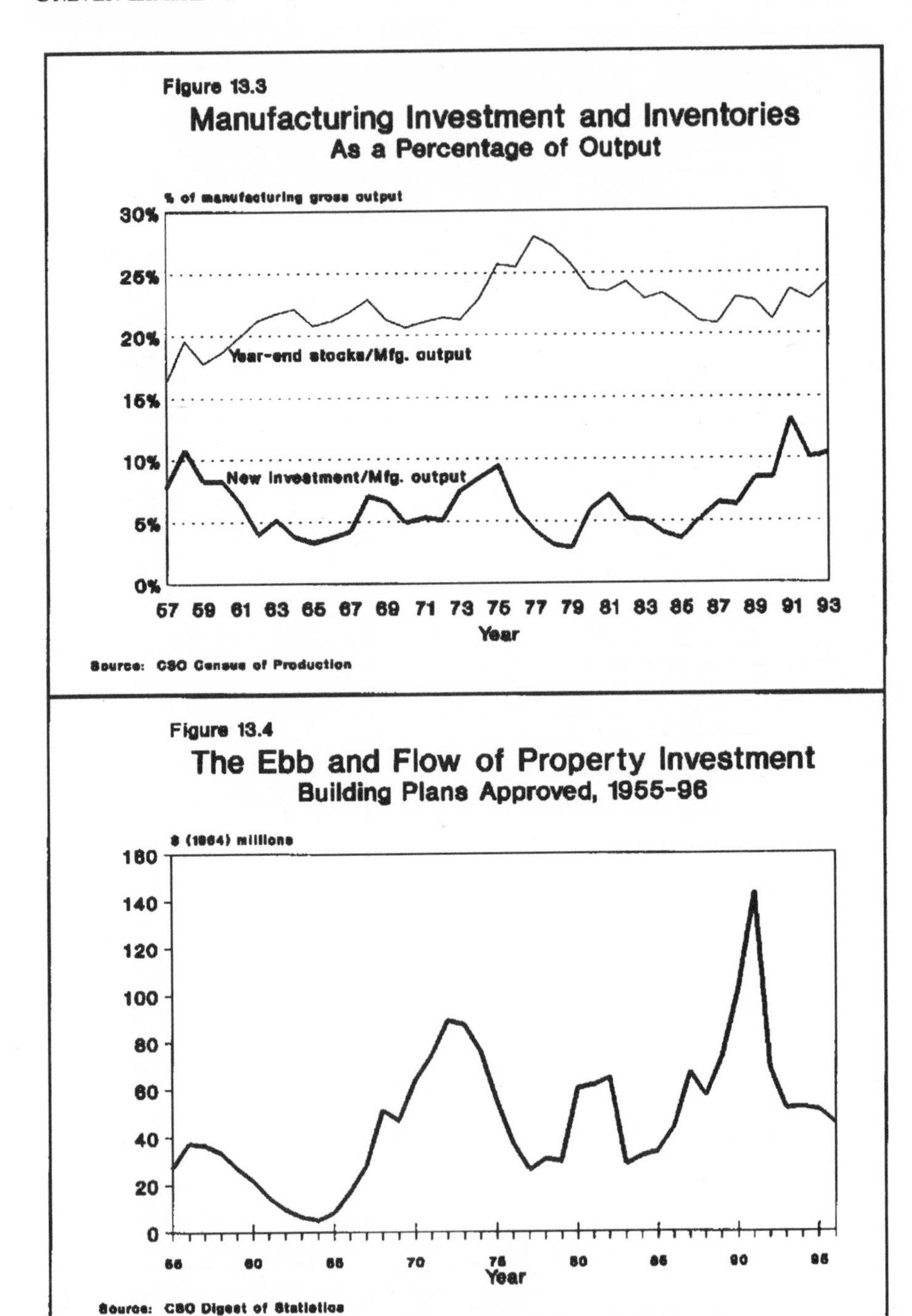

Figure 13.3
Manufacturing Investment and Inventories
As a Percentage of Output

Source: CSO Census of Production

Figure 13.4
The Ebb and Flow of Property Investment
Building Plans Approved, 1955–96

Source: CSO Digest of Statistics

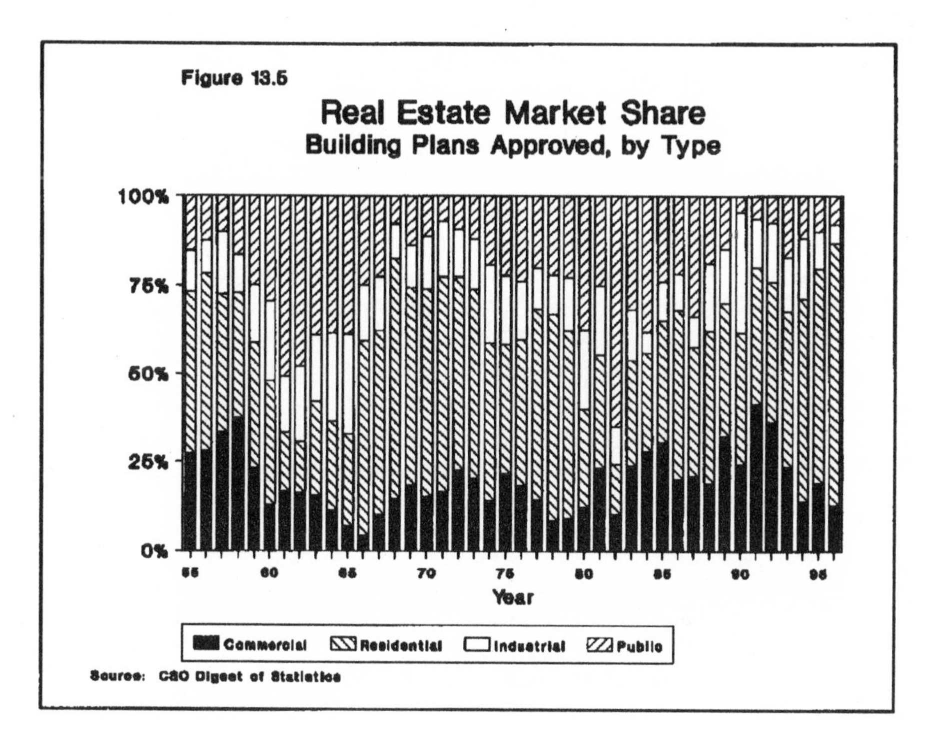
Figure 13.5
Real Estate Market Share
Building Plans Approved, by Type
100%
75%
50%
25%
0%
55
60
65
70
75
80
85
90
95
Year
Commercial
Residential
Industrial
Public
Source: CSO Digest of Statistics

Bibliography

NEWSPAPERS AND MAGAZINES

Africa South (Johannesburg)
African Agenda (Johannesburg)
African Business (London)
Chronicle (Bulawayo)
Commerce (Salisbury)
Dataworld Shareworld Crosstables (Harare)
Economic Review (Harare)
Economist Intelligence Unit (London)
Energy and Communications (Harare)
Executive Guide to the Economy (Harare)
The Farmer (Harare)
Financial Gazette (Harare)
Financial Times (London)
Focus (Harare)
Herald (Salisbury, Harare)
Horizon (Harare)
Industrial Review (Harare)
The Industrialist (Harare)
Liepziger Volkszeitung (Liepzig, Germany)
Moto (Gweru)
Newsletter of the National Property Association (Harare)
Northern News (Harare)
Northern News (Lusaka)
Parade (Harare)
Property and Finance (Salisbury)
Quarterly Guide to the Economy (Harare)
Read On (Harare)

Southern African Economist (Harare)
Southern Africa Report (Toronto)
Sunday Mail (Harare)
The Sunday Times (Harare)
The Sunday Times (London)
Weekend Gazette (Harare)
Zimbabwe Money and Capital Market Review (Harare)
Zimbabwe News (Harare)
Zimbabwe Quarterly (Harare)

GOVERNMENT DOCUMENTS

Advisory Committee (J. Phillips, J. Hammond, L.H. Samuels, and R.J.M. Swynnerton) (1962), *Report of the Advisory Committee: The Development of the Economic Resources of Southern Rhodesia with Particular Reference to the Role of African Agriculture*, Salisbury: Southern Rhodesia Ministry of Native Affairs.

Agricultural Finance Corporation (1989), "1989 Annual Report," Harare: Agricultural Finance Corporation.

Central African Federation (1959), "Notes on the Currency Media of Southern Rhodesia from the Time of the Charter and of Federation of Rhodesia and Nyasaland," Salisbury: Federal Information Department.

Central African Federation Information Department (1960), *Handbook to the Federation of Rhodesia and Nyasaland*, London: Cassell.

Central Statistical Office (various years), *Bulletin of Statistics.*

______ (various years), *Census of Production.*

______ (various years), *Digest of Statistics.*

______ (various years), *National Income and Expenditure Report.*

______ (1947), "The Banking System of Southern Rhodesia, 1936-46," Unpublished report, Salisbury.

______ (1948), "Central Bank for the Rhodesias and Nyasaland," Unpublished report, Salisbury.

______ (1965), "Report on the Urban African Budget Survey in Salisbury, 1963/64," Report S/32/350, Salisbury: Government Printer.

______ (1989), *Zimbabwe: Statistical Yearbook*, Harare: Government Printer.

City of Harare (1985), "Annual Report of the Director of Housing and Community Services for the Year Ended 30 June, 1985," Harare.

______ (1986), "Annual Report of the Director of Housing and Community Services for the Year Ended 30 June, 1986," Harare.

______ (1987), "Annual Report of the Director of Housing and Community Services for the Year Ended 30 June, 1987," Harare.

Government of Southern Rhodesia (Plewman Commission) (1958), "Report of the Urban African Affairs Commission," Government Printer, Salisbury.

Government of Zimbabwe (various issues), *Hansard*, Harare: Government Printer.

______ (1980), "Five Year Plan: Low Cost Housing Construction Programme 1980/85," Memorandum by the Ministry of Local Government and Housing, Salisbury.

______ (1981), "Records of Zimbabwe Conference on Reconstruction and Development Proceedings," Ministry of Planning and Economic Development, Salisbury, 23-27 March.

______ (1982), *Transitional National Development Plan*, Harare: Government Printer.

______ (1986a), *Second Five Year National Development Plan*, Harare: Government Printer.

______ (1986b), *Socio-Economic Review, 1980-85*, Harare: Government Printer.

______ (1987), "National Action and National Shelter Strategies up to the Year 2000," Submission to the Tenth Session of the UN Commission on Human Settlements, Nairobi.

______ (1990), "Economic Policy Statement: Macroeconomic Adjustment and Trade

Liberalisation," Republic of Zimbabwe, Ministry of Finance, Economic Planning and Development, Harare, 26 July.
______ (1991a), "Zimbabwe: A Field for Investment," Harare: Government Printer.
______ (1991b), "Zimbabwe: A Framework for Economic Reform, 1991-1995," Harare: Government Printer.
Government of Zimbabwe Department of Information (1987), "Standard Bank Dispute Settled," Press release 589/87/SK/GT/ME, Harare, November 10.
______ (1988), "Support Small Businessmen, Nkomo Tells Banks," Press release 91/88/SK/PR, 26 February.
Registrar of Banks and Financial Institutions and Registrar of Building Societies (1984), "Report for the Year Ended the 31st December 1983," Harare: Government Printer.
Registrar of Insurance (1982), "Report for the Year Ended the 31st December 1980," Harare: Government Printer.
Registrar of Pension and Provident Funds (1982), "Report for the Years Ended the 31st December 1979 and 31st December 1980," Harare: Government Printer.
Reserve Bank of Zimbabwe (various issues), ***Reserve Bank Quarterly Economic and Statistical Review***, Harare: Reserve Bank.
United States Agency for International Development (1979), "A Report to the Congress on Development Needs and Opportunities for Cooperation in Southern Africa," Annex A, Zimbabwe, Washington, DC: US AID.
______ (1980), "Zimbabwe: Zimbabwe Shelter Project," Project Paper 613-HG-001, Washington, DC: US AID.
______ (1982), "PAAD Authorization: Zimbabwe Agriculture Sector Assistance Program," Project Paper 613-0209, Washington, DC: US AID.
______ (1985), "Zimbabwe: Country Development Strategy Statement FY 1987," Washington, DC: US AID.
United States Senate Foreign Relations Committee (1992), *The BCCI Affair*, Subcommittee on Terrorism, Narcotics and International Operations, Washington, DC.
Zimcord (1981), "Records of Conference Proceedings," Ministry of Planning and Economic Development, Salisbury.

BOOKS AND ARTICLES

Abt Associates, Inc (1988), "AID Evaluation: Zimbabwe Low-Cost Shelter," Washington, DC: US Agency for International Development.
Adams, D.W. and D. Fitchett (1992), ***Informal Financing in Developing Countries***, Boulder: Westview.
Adams, J.M. (1989), "Female Wage Labour in Rural Zimbabwe," Unpublished paper, Faculty of Land Economics, Cambridge University, March.
Addison, T. (1995), "Poverty and Adjustment Policies: Findings to Date," Report of the World Bank Poverty Mission to Zimbabwe, 22 November.
Africa Community Publishing and Development Trust (1995), ***The Suffering are the Cornerstone in Building a Nation — Community Views on Poverty, Poverty Alleviation and Wealth Creation***, Harare, Africa Community Publishing and Development Trust.
African-American Institute/American Bar Association Conference (1982), "Investment in Zimbabwe," Conference Proceedings, New York, 26 March.
African Development Bank (1985), "Appraisal Report of the Agricultural Line of Credit to the Agricultural Finance Corporation, Zimbabwe," Report ADB/ZMB/ALC/85-01, Ibadjan: African Development Bank.
Aglietta, M. (1979)[1974], ***The Theory of Capitalist Regulation***, London: Verso.
Alexander, J. (1993), "The State, Agrarian Policy and Rural Politics in Zimbabwe: Case Studies of Insiza and Chimanimani Districts, 1940-1990," Doctoral dissertation, Oxford University, Oxford.

_____ (1995), "State, Peasantry and Land Resettlement in Zimbabwe," *Review Of African Political Economy*, 61.

Amin, S. (1990), *Delinking*, London: Zed Press.

Anderson, P. (1987), "The Figures of Descent," *New Left Review*, 161.

Angel, S. (1995), "The Future Lies in a Global System of Competitive Cities," *Countdown to Instanbul*, 1.

Anonymous (1985), "US Trying to Neutralize `Stubborn' Zimbabwe," *Moto*, 49.

Anonymous (1987), "Fire Sale on Debt: Will the Third World Lose in a `Win-Win' Situation?," *Dollars and Sense*, June.

Armstrong, K., A. Glyn and J. Harrison (1991), *Capitalism Since 1945*, Oxford: Basil Blackwell.

Arrighi, G. (1973a)[1967], "The Political Economy of Rhodesia," in G. Arrighi and J. Saul, *Essays on the Political Economy of Africa*, New York: Monthly Review.

_____ (1973b)[1969], "Labor Supplies in Historical Perspective: A Study of the Proletarianization of the African Peasantry in Rhodesia," in G. Arrighi and J. Saul, *Essays on the Political Economy of Africa*, New York: Monthly Review.

Arrighi, G. and J.S. Saul (1973)[1968], "Socialism and Economic Development in Tropical Africa," in G. Arrighi and J.S. Saul (Eds), *Essays in the Political Economy of Africa*, New York: Monthly Review.

Arrighi, G., T. Hopkins and I. Wallerstein (1989), *Antisystemic Movements*, London: Verso.

Askes, J. (1971), "The Changing Pattern of Banking in Rhodesia Since 1960", *Rhodesian Journal of Economics*, 4.

Astrow, A. (1983), *Zimbabwe: Revolution that Lost its Way?*, London: Zed Press.

Banana, C. (1987), *Towards a Socialist Ethos*, Harare: College Press

Barber, W.J. (1961), *The Economy of British Central Africa*, London: Oxford University Press.

_____ (1967), *Rhodesia: The Road to Rebellion*, London: Oxford University Press.

Barnes, T. (1992a), "The Fight for Control of African Women's Mobility in Colonial Zimbabwe, 1900-1939." *Signs*, 17.

_____ (1992b), "Ideologies and the Construction of Class Amongst African Women in Colonial Zimbabwe, 1930-1960," African Studies Institute Seminar Paper, University of the Witwatersrand, Johannesburg, 30 March.

Barnes, T. and E. Win (1992), *To Live a Better Life*, Harare: Baobab Books.

Batezat, E., M. Mwalo and K. Truscott (1988), "Women and Independence:The Heritage and the Struggle," in C. Stoneman (Ed), *Zimbabwe's Prospects*, London: Macmillan.

Beach, D.N. (1977), "The Shona Economy: Branches of Production," in R. Palmer and N. Parsons (Eds), *The Roots of Rural Poverty in Central and Southern Africa*, London: Heinemann.

_____ (1994), *The Shona and their Neighbours*, Oxford: Basil Blackwell.

Beak, G.H.M. (1967), "The Growth of Banking and Financial Institutions," *Rhodesian Journal of Economics*, 1.

Beckerman, P. (1988), "The Consequences of `Upward Financial Repression,'" *International Review of Applied Economics*, 2, 2

Bennell, P. (1991), "Market Power and Mark-Ups: Manufacturing Industry in Zimbabwe, 1970-86," Working Paper in Economics, Department of Economics, University of Zimbabwe, Harare.

Beresford, W.M.P. (1990), "Private Finance of Low Cost Shelter and Infrastructure: The Zimbabwe Case," in US AID (Ed), *Mobilizing Local Resources for Economic Development in an Urbanizing Africa*, Proceedings of a Regional Policy Workshop, US AID, Nairobi, 25-28 September.

_____ (1992), "Low Income Home Loan Lending: The Zimbabwean Experience," Paper presented to the Home Loan Guarantee Company "Strategic Think Tank," Johannesburg, 9-10 July.

Berger, M. (1989), "Giving Women Credit: The Strengths and Limitations of Credit as a Tool for Alleviating Poverty," *World Development*, 17, 7.

Bhebe, N. (1989), "The Nationalist Struggle, 1957-1962," in C. Banana (Ed), *Turmoil and*

Tenacity, Harare: College Press.
Bhila, H. (1982), *Trade and Politics in a Shona Kingdom, the Manyika and their Portuguese and African Neighbours, 1575-1902*, Harlow: Longman.
Bijlmakers, L., M. Bassett and D. Sanders (1995), "Health and Structural Adjustment in Rural and Urban Zimbabwe: Some Interim Findings," in P.Gibbon (ed), *Structural Adjustment and the Working Poor in Zimbabwe*, Uppsala: Nordiska Afrikainstitutet.
_____ (1996), *Health and Structural Adjustment in Rural Zimbabwe*, Uppsala: Nordiska Afrikainstitutet.
Blackie, M. (1986), "The Elusive Peasant: Zimbabwe's Elusive Agriculture Policy, 1965-1986," Unpublished paper, Harare: CIMMYT.
Bond, P. (1990), "The New US Class Struggle: Financial Industry Power vs. Grassroots Populism," *Capital and Class*, 40.
_____ (1991a), *Commanding Heights and Community Control: New Economics for a New South Africa*, Johannesburg: Ravan Press.
_____ (1991b), "Geopolitics, International Finance and Capital Accumulation: Zimbabwe in the 1980s and 1990s," *Tijdschrift voor Economische en Sociale Geografie*, 5.
_____ (1992a), "Finance and Uneven Urban Development in 1950s Salisbury: Contradictions in the Central Business District," *Geographical Journal of Zimbabwe*, 23.
_____ (1992b), "Re-Using the Spaces of Confinement: From Urban Apartheid to Post-Apartheid without Post-Modernism," *Urban Forum*, 3, 1.
_____ (1993a), "Economic Origins of Black Townships in Zimbabwe: Contradictions of Industrial and Financial Capital in the 1950s and 1960s," *Economic Geography*, 69, 1.
_____ (1993b), "Housing as an Investment: A Report on Zimbabwe's Housing Crisis and on Public-Private Reform of the Housing Finance System through Pension/Provident Fund Investments," Paper prepared for the Zimbabwe Congress of Trade Unions Department of Health and Social Welfare, Harare, August.
_____ (1994a), "From Apartheid to Neo-Liberalism in South Africa," in K.Danaher (ed), *50 Years is Enough: The Case Against the World Bank and the International Monetary Fund*, South End Press, Boston.
_____ (1994b), "Money Power and Social Movements: Finance and the Geopolitics of Uneven Development in Southern Africa," in S. Corbridge, R. Martin and N. Thrift (Eds), *Money, Power and Space*, Oxford: Basil Blackwell.
_____ (1997), "Regional Resource Flows: Integration or Disintegration for Southern Africa?," *Development Update*, 2.
Bond, P. and M. Mayekiso (1996), "Developing Resistance, Resisting `Development': Reflections from the South African Struggle," in L.Panitch (ed), *Are There Alternatives?*, London: Merlin Press.
Bottomore, T. (1981), "Introduction to the Translation," in R. Hilferding, *Finance Capital*, London: Routledge and Kegan Paul.
Brand, V. (1987), "Savings Clubs in Zimbabwe: A Survey Report," Unpublished paper, University of Zimbabwe School of Social Work, Harare.
Bratton, M. (1985), "Financing Smallholder Production: A Comparison of Individual and Group Credit Schemes in Zimbabwe," University of Zimbabwe Department of Land Management Working Paper 1/85, Harare.
_____ (1986), "Farmer Organisation and Food Production in Zimbabwe," World Development, 14, 3.
Braunderhjelm, P. and G. Fors (1994), "The Zimbabwean Manufacturing Sector: Current Status and Future Development Potentials," Report to the Confederation of Zimbabwe Industries, November.
Breckenridge, K. (1992), "The South African Gold Standard Crisis and the Dialectics of Value," Paper presented at the University of the Witwatersrand Graduate Seminar, Johannesburg, 5 August.
Brenner, R. and M. Glick (1991), "The Regulation Approach: Theory and History," *New Left*

Review, 188.
Breslin, N. (1992), "US AID and Food Insecurity in Rural Zimbabwe," Paper presented to the MA Seminar, University of the Witwatersrand, Johannesburg, 23 September.
Brewer, A. (1980), *Marxist Theories of Imperialism: A Critical Survey*, London: Routledge and Kegan Paul.
Broad, R. (1988), *Unequal Alliance*, Berkeley: University of California Press.
Bryan, D. (1995), *The Chase Across the Globe: International Accumulation and the Contradictions for Nation States*, Boulder, Westview Press.
Burdette, M. and R. Davies (1987), "The Zimbabwe Economy: Prognostications and Realities after Six Years," *Zambezia*, 14, 1.
Burgess, R. (1978), "Petty Commodity Housing or Dweller Control? A Critique of John Turner's Views on Housing Policy," *World Development*, 6, s9-10.
_____ (1985), "The Limits of State Self-Help Housing Programmes," *Development and Change*, 16.
Burkett, P. (1987), "Financial `Repression' and Financial `Liberalization' in the Third World: A Contribution to the Critique of Neoclassical Development Theory," *Review of Radical Political Economics*, 19, 1.
Burkett, P. and A.K. Dutt (1991), "Interest Rate Policy, Effective Demand, and Growth in LDCs," *International Review of Applied Economics*, 5, 2.
Butcher, C. (1986), "Low Income Housing in Zimbabwe: A Case Study of the Epworth Squatter Upgrading Programme," Department of Rural and Urban Planning Occasional Paper 6, University of Zimbabwe, Harare.
_____ (1992), "Standards and the Affordability Crisis Facing Low Cost Housing Delivery in Zimbabwe," Paper delivered to the Zimbabwe Institution of Engineers' Seminar on Low Cost Housing and Associated Technology, Harare, 29 May.
Cain, P.J. and A.G. Hopkins (1980), "The Political Economy of British Expansion Overseas," *Economic History Review*, 33, 4.
Centre of African Studies (1979), "Zimbabwe: Notes and Reflections on the Rhodesian Question," Mimeo, Maputo: Centre of African Studies, March.
Chang, E. and P. Montiel (1995), "A Measure of Stock Market Integration," Conference on Stock Markets, Corporate Finance and Economic Growth, World Bank, Washington, DC, February 16-17.
Chanakira, N. (1990), "Zimbabwe's Stock Market is Inefficient and Defies Textbook Theory," *Financial Gazette*, 18 May.
Chandavengerwa, M. (1994), "Banks have to be Market-Oriented," *Financial Gazette*, February 3.
Cheater, A. (1984), *Idioms of Accumulation*, Gweru: Mambo Press.
_____ (1986), *The Politics of Factory Organization*, Gweru: Mambo Press.
Chidzero, B. (1957), *Nzvengamutsvairo*, Salisbury.
_____ (1961), *The Influence of International Trusteeship on Tanganyika*, Oxford: Oxford University Press.
_____ (1979), *Education and the Challenges of Independence*, Geneva: International University Exchange Fund.
Chidzero, B. and K. Moyana (1979), "The Structure of the Zimbabwean Economy and Future Manpower Implications," in *Zimbabwe Manpower Survey*, Vol Two, Geneva: International University Exchange Fund.
Chimedza, R. (1884), "Savings Development Movement Evaluation," Unpublished paper, University of Zimbabwe Department of Land Management, Harare.
Chimombe, T. (1983), "The Role of Banks and Financial Institutions in the Accumulation and Reinvestment of Capital in Zimbabwe," Masters dissertation, Department of Economics, University of Zimbabwe, Harare.
Chinyoka, B. (1988), "The Role of Financial Institutions in the Development of Small-Scale Industries in Zimbabwe," in the Promotion of Small-Scale Entrepreneurs and National Development Symposium organised by Konrad Adenauer Stiftung, Parliament of

Zimbabwe, and Zimbabwe National Chamber of Commerce, 23-26 October.
Chishawasha Mission (1967), "An Approach to the Credit Union Movement in Rhodesia," Salisbury: Chishawasha Mission.
Christopher, A.J. (1977), "Early Settlement and the Cadastral Framework," in G. Kay and M.A.H. Smout (Eds), *Salisbury: A Geographical Survey of the Capital of Rhodesia*, London: Hodder and Stoughton.
Chung, F. (1989), "Policies of Primary and Secondary Education in Zimbabwe: Alternatives to the World Bank Perspective," Interview, *Zimbabwe Journal of Educational Research*, 1, 1.
______ (1992), "Zimbabwe Obeys the World Bank at its Peril," *Horizon*, July.
Civic Groups Housing Project (1995), Untitled, unpublished paper, Harare.
Clarke, D. (1980a), *Foreign Companies and International Investment in Zimbabwe*, Gwelo: Mambo Press
______ (1980b), "The Monetary, Banking and Financial System in Zimbabwe," in United Nations Conference on Trade and Development, *Zimbabwe: Towards a New Order: An Economic and Social Survey*, Working Papers, Geneva, Vol 1.
Clarke, S. (1988), *Keynesianism, Monetarism and the Crisis of the State*, Aldershot: Edward Elgar.
Clausen, A.W. (1983), "Address to the Board of Governors," Washington: World Bank, 27 September.
Cliffe, L. (1981), "Zimbabwe's Political Inheritance," in C. Stoneman (Ed), *Zimbabwe's Inheritance*, London: Macmillan.
______ (1991), "Were they Pushed or did they Jump: Zimbabwe and the World Bank?," *Southern Africa Report*, March.
Cobbing, J. (1976), "The Ndebele Under the Khumalos, 1820-1896," Doctoral dissertation, University of Lancaster.
Cole, R.L. (1973a), "The Building Societies and the Housing Market," *Rhodesian Journal of Economics*, 7, 1.
______ (1973b) "The Insurance Industry in Rhodesia," *Rhodesian Journal of Economics*, 7, 2.
______ (1973c), "The Finance Houses in Rhodesia," *Rhodesian Journal of Economics*, 7, 4.
______ (1974), "Commercial Banking in Rhodesia," *Rhodesian Journal of Economics*, 8.
Confederation of Zimbabwe Industries (1986), "Zimbabwe's Manufacturing Industry: The Key to National Development," Harare: Confederation of Zimbabwe Industries.
Crick, W.F. (Ed) (1965), *Commonwealth Banking Systems*, Oxford: Clarendon Press.
Crossley, J. and J. Blandford (1975), *The DCO Story*, London: Barclays Bank International Limited.
Dashwood, H. (1996), "The Relevance of Class to the Evolution of Zimbabwe's Development Strategy, 1980-1991," *Journal of Southern African Studies*, 22, 1.
Davies, D.H. (1981), "Towards an Urbanization Strategy for Zimbabwe," *GeoJournal*, 5, Supplementary Issue 2.
Davies, R. (1982), "Discussion Note on Chapter 13," in M. Fransman, *Industry and Accumulation in Africa*, London: Heinemann.
______ (1983), "Effects of Money Supply, Inflation and Interest Rates on Economic Growth," in Zimbabwe Current Economic Issues conference proceedings, Professional Conferences Zimbabwe Private Limited, 23-24 August.
______ (1986), "Trade, Trade Management and Development in Zimbabwe," Unpublished paper, Department of Economics, University of Zimbabwe, Harare.
Davies, R. and D. Sanders (1987), "Stabilisation Policies and the Effects on Child Health in Zimbabwe," *Review of African Political Economy*, 38.
Davies, R., D. Sanders and T. Shaw (1991), *Zimbabwe's Adjustment without the Fund*, Innocenti Occasional Papers 16, Florence: UNICEF.
Davies, R. and C. Stoneman (1981), "The Economy," in C. Stoneman (Ed), *Zimbabwe's Inheritance*, London: Macmillan.
Davies, R.J. and N. Dewar (1989), "Adaptive or Structural Transformation? The Case of the Harare, Zimbabwe Housing System," *Social Dynamics*, 15, 1.
Davis, M. (1985), "Urban Renaissance and the Spirit of Postmodernism," *New Left Review*, 151.

_____ (1991), *City of Quartz*, London: Verso.
de Brunhoff, S. (1976), *Marx on Money*, New York: Urizen Books.
_____ (1978), *The State, Capital and Economic Policy*, London: Pluto Press.
Deininger, K. and H. Binswanger (1995), "Rent-Seeking and the Development of Large-Scale Agriculture in Kenya, Zimbabwe and South Africa," *Economic Development and Cultural Change*, 43, 3.
Deloitte and Touche (1990), "Doing Business in Zimbabwe," Harare: Deloitte Haskins and Sells.
Demirguc-Kunt, A. and R. Levine (1995), "Stock Markets and Financial Intermediaries: Stylized Facts," Conference on Stock Markets, Corporate Finance and Economic Growth, World Bank, Washington, DC, February 16-17.
Demirguc-Kunt, A. and V. Maksimovic (1995), "Stock Market Development and Firm Financing Choices," Conference on Stock Markets, Corporate Finance and Economic Growth, World Bank, Washington, DC, February 16-17.
Dewar, N. (1987), "Salisbury to Harare: Citizen Participation in Public Decision-Making Under Changing Ideological Circumstances in Zimbabwe," *African Urban Quarterly*, 2, 1.
Drinkwater, M.J. (1987), "Loans and Manure: The Dilemma of Access," Mimeo, Department of Agricultural Technical and Extension Services and Department of Sociology, University of Zimbabwe, Harare, May.
_____ (1991), *The State and Agrarian Change in Zimbabwe*, London: Macmillan.
Duggan, W. (1980), "The Native Land Husbandry Act of 1951 and the Rural Middle Class of Southern Rhodesia," *African Affairs*, 79.
Elbadawi, I. and K. Schmidt-Hebbel (1991), "Macroeconomic Adjustment to Oil Shocks and Fiscal Reform," Policy, Research and External Affairs Working Papers WPS 772, World Bank, Washington, DC.
Elson, D. (1991), "Gender Analysis and Economics in the Context of Africa," Paper presented at the CODESRIA Workshop on Gender Analysis and African Social Science, Dakar, September.
Farge, J. (1990), "Trade Unions Say No," *International Labour Reports*, 40.
Ferguson, J. (1991), *The Anti-Politics Machine*, Cape Town: David Philip.
Fine, B. (1981), "Nationalism and Class Struggle in Zimbabwe," *Capital and Class*, 11.
Fine, B. and C. Stoneman (1996), "Introduction: The State and Development," *Journal of Southern African Studies*, 22, 1, March.
Frankel, S.H. (1938), *Capital Investment in Africa*, Oxford: Oxford University Press.
Frost, D.L. (1989), "Annual Report," Paper presented to the Annual General Meeting of the National Property Association, Harare, 31 October.
_____ (1991), "Future Development of the Construction Industry from the Developers' Point of View," Paper presented to Annual General Meeting of the Construction Industry Federation of Zimbabwe, July.
Fry, M. (1980), "Saving, Investment, Growth and the Cost of Financial Repression," *World Development*, 8, 3.
Galvis, V. (1982), "Analytical Aspects of Interest Rate Policies in Less-Developed Countries," *Savings and Development*, 6, 3.
Gann, L. and M. Gelfand (1964), *Huggins of Rhodesia*, London: Allen and Unwin.
George, S. (1988), *A Fate Worse than Debt*, Harmondsworth: Penguin.
Gibbon, P. (1995), "Introduction," in P.Gibbon (ed), *Structural Adjustment and the Working Poor in Zimbabwe*, Uppsala: Nordiska Afrikainstitutet.
Gilliomee, H. (1989), "Aspects of the Rise of Afrikaner Capital and Afrikaner Nationalism in the Western Cape, 1870-1915," in W. G. James and M. Simons (Eds), *The Angry Divide*, Cape Town: David Philip.
Girdlestone, J.A.C. (1983), "Industry's Role in Zimbabwe's Economic Recovery," Paper presented to Mashonaland Chamber of Industries Seminar, "Industry's Role in Zimbabwe's Economic Recovery," 23 November.
_____ (1990), "Independence Cause for Concern Within Financial Sector," *Financial Gazette*, 12

April.
Goldring, M. (1980), "Mr. Mugabe Counts His Friends," BBC Radio Four interview, London: British Broadcasting Corporation, 19 December.
Goldstein, J. (1988), *Long Cycles: Prosperity and War in the Modern Age*, New Haven: Yale University Press.
Gordon, D. (1978), "Capitalist Development and the History of American Cities," in W. Tabb and L. Sawyer (Eds), *Marxism and the Metropolis*, New York: Oxford University Press.
______ (1980), "Stages of Accumulation and Long Economic Cycles," in T. Hopkins and I. Wallerstein (Eds), *Processes of the World System*, Beverly Hills: Sage.
Grafftey-Smith, A.P. (1954), "Some Thoughts on the Future Federal Central Bank," Paper presented to the Rhodesian Economic Society, Salisbury, April.
Gramsci, A. (1978)[1920s], *Selections from the Prison Notebooks*, Q. Hoare and G.N. Smith (Eds), New York: International Publishers.
Grant-Suttie, R.I. (1965), "The Rhodesias and Nyasaland," in W.F. Crick (Ed), *Commonwealth Banking Systems*, Oxford: Clarendon Press.
Green, R. (1985), "IMF Stabilisation and Structural Adjustment in Sub-Saharan Africa: Are They Technically Compatible?," *IDS Bulletin*, 16, 3.
______ (1987), "Toward Sub-Saharan Debt Bargaining," in S. Griffith-Jones (Ed), *Managing World Debt*, New York: St. Martin's Press.
Griffith-Jones, S. (1987), "Debt Crisis Management: An Analytical Framework," in S. Griffith-Jones (Ed), *Managing World Debt*, New York: St. Martin's Press.
Grossmann, H. (1992)[1929], *The Law of Accumulation and Breakdown of the Capitalist System*, London: Pluto.
Hall, R. (1989), *My Life with Tiny*, London: Faber.
Handford, J. (1976), *Portrait of an Economy Under Sanctions, 1965-1975*, Salisbury: Mercury Press.
Handover, G. (1977), "Rhodesia's Place in the Economic World," in J. Dornan (Ed), *Rhodesia Alone*, Washington, DC: Council on American Affairs.
Hanlon, J. (1986a), *Beggar Your Neighbour: Apartheid Power in Southern Africa*, London: James Currey.
______ (1986b), *Apartheid's Second Front*, London: Penguin.
______ (1988), "Destabilisation and the Battle to Reduce Dependence," in C. Stoneman (Ed), *Zimbabwe's Prospects*, London: Macmillan.
______ (1991), *Mozambique: Who Calls the Shots?*, London: James Currey.
Harvey, D. (1982), *The Limits to Capital*, Oxford: Basil Blackwell.
______ (1985a), *The Urbanization of Capital*, Oxford: Basil Blackwell.
______ (1985b), "The Geopolitics of Capitalism," in D. Gregory and J. Urry (Eds), *Social Relations and Spatial Structures*, London: Macmillan.
______ (1989a), *The Urban Experience*, Oxford: Basil Blackwell.
______ (1989b), *The Condition of Postmodernity*, Oxford: Basil Blackwell.
______ (1992), Private correspondence, 7 July.
Hawkins, T. (1994), "Lessons of Adjustment from Zimbabwe," in K. Kapoor (Ed), *Africa's Experience with Structural Adjustment: Proceedings of the Harare Seminar*, Washington, DC: The World Bank.
Heath, HR.A. (1990)[1979], *Service Centres and Service Regions in Rhodesia*, Supplement to Zambezia, Harare: University of Zimbabwe Press.
Helleiner, E. (1995), "From Bretton Woods to Global Finance: A World Turned Upside Down," in R. Stubbs and G.R.D. Underhill (Eds.), *Political Economy and the Changing World Order*, New York: St. Martin's Press.
Herbst, J. (1990), *State Politics in Zimbabwe*, Harare: University of Zimbabwe Press.
Hilferding, R. (1981)[1910], *Finance Capital*, London: Routledge and Kegan Paul.
Hinds, M. (1990), "Outwards vs. Inwards Development Strategy: Implications for the Financial Sector," Washington, DC: World Bank.
Hove, C. (1994), *Shebeen Tales: Messages from Harare*, Harare: Baobab Books.

Howard, M.C. and J. King (1989), *A History of Marxian Economics*, Volume 1, Princeton: Princeton University Press.
Howell, J. (Ed)(1990), *Borrowers and Lenders*, London: Overseas Development Institute.
Hughes, J. (1987), *Sovereign Risk*, London: Euromoney Publications.
Humphrey, M. (1989), "An Ownership Profile of Zimbabwe's Manufacturing Sector," Position paper, Economics Department, Confederation of Zimbabwe Industries, Harare.
Iliffe, J. (1983), *The Emergence of African Capitalism*, London: Macmillan.
_____ (1990), *Famine in Zimbabwe*, Gweru: Mambo Press.
Innes, D. (1984) *Anglo American and the Rise of Modern South Africa*, New York: Monthly Review.
International Finance Corporation (1992), *Emerging Stock Markets Factbook*, Washington, DC: World Bank Group.
Irvine, A.G. (1957), "The Growth of Commercial Banking in the Federation," *Property and Finance*, September.
Jackelen, H. and E. Rhyne (1991), "Towards a more Market-Oriented Approach to Credit and Savings for the Poor," in United Nations Capital Development Fund, Tokyo Forum on Less Developed Countries, New York: United Nations.
Jansen, D.J. (1983), "Zimbabwe: Government Policy and the Manufacturing Sector: A Study Prepared for the Ministry of Industry and Energy Development," Unpublished paper sponsored by the World Bank, Washington, April.
Johnson, P. and D. Martin (1989), *Apartheid Terrorism*, London: James Currey.
Joyce, P. (1974), *Anatomy of a Rebel: Smith of Rhodesia*, Salisbury: Graham Publishing Company.
Jucker-Fleetwood, E.E. (1964), *Money and Finance in Africa*, London: George Allen and Unwin.
Kadhani, X. (1986), "The Economy: Issues, Problems, Prospects," in I. Mandaza (Ed), *Zimbabwe: The Political Economy of Transition, 1980-1986*, Dakar: CODESRIA.
Kazembe, J. (1986), "The Women Issue," in I. Mandaza (Ed), *Zimbabwe: The Political Economy of Transition, 1980-86*, Dakar: CODESRIA.
Keegan, T. (1986), *Rural Transformations in Industrializing South Africa*, Johannesburg: Ravan Press.
Kondratieff, N. (1979)[1926], "The Long Waves of Economic Life," *Review*, 2.
Kosmin, B. (1977), "The Inkoya Tobacco Industry of the Shangwe People," in R. Palmer and N. Parsons (Eds), *The Roots of Rural Poverty in Central and Southern Africa*, London: Heinemann.
Kriger, N. (1988), "The Zimbabwean War of Liberation: Struggles within the Struggle," *Journal of Southern African Studies*, v.14, 2.
Kuznets, S. (1930), *Secular Movements in Production and Prices*, New York: Houghton Mifflin.
Kydd, J.G. (1990), "Rural Financial Intermediation," Background document for Agriculture Division, Southern Africa Department, Washington, DC: World Bank.
Lan, D. (1985), *Guns and Rain: Guerrillas and Spirit Mediums in Zimbabwe*, London: James Currey.
Lawyers Committee for Human Rights (1986), *Zimbabwe: Wages of War, A Report on Human Rights*, New York.
Lelyveld, J. (1985), *Move Your Shadow: South Africa, Black and White*, London, Abacus.
Lenin, V. (1986)[1917], *Imperialism*, Moscow: Progress Publishers.
Lessing, D. (1994), *Under My Skin: Volume One of My Autobiography, to 1949*, London, Flamingo.
Leys, C. (1959), *European Politics in Southern Rhodesia*, Oxford: Oxford University Press.
Libby, R. (1987), *The Politics of Economic Power in Southern Africa*, Princeton: Princeton University Press.
Lipietz, A. (1985)[1983], *The Enchanted World: Inflation, Credit and the World Crisis*, London: Verso.
Loney, M. (1975), *Rhodesia: White Racism and Imperial Response*, Harmondsworth: Penguin.
Lowe-Morna, C. (1989), "Revolution Changes its Course," *South*, July.
Mabin, A. (1989), "Waiting for Something to Turn Up? The Cape Colony in the Eighteen Eighties," in A. Mabin (Ed), *Organisation and Economic Change*, Southern African Studies

Vol. 5, Johannesburg: Ravan.
Madanhire, N. (1994), "Inconsistencies, Contradictions," *Financial Gazette*, 22 December.
_____ (1995), "Truth Commission Needed to Probe Instant Millionaires," *Financial Gazette*, 2 November.
Mafico, C.J.C. (1987), "Urbanisation and Low Income Housing in Zimbabwe: An Historical Perspective," Department of Civic Design Working Paper 33, University of Liverpool, Liverpool.
_____ (1991), *Low-Income Housing in Zimbabwe*, Aldershot: Edward Elgar.
Maganya, E. (1987), "Economic Liberalisation versus the Liberation Process in Southern Africa: The IMF Agreement with Particular Reference to Zambia and Tanzania," Paper (18) presented at International Seminar Series: Southern African Responses to Imperialism, University of Zimbabwe, Departments of Economics, Law and Political and Administrative Studies, 22-24 April.
Magdoff, H. and P. Sweezy (1987), *Stagnation and the Financial Explosion*, New York: Monthly Review.
Makamure, K. (1991), "The Struggle for Democracy and Democratisation" in I.Mandaza and L.Sachikonye (eds), *The One Party State and Democracy: The Zimbabwe Debate*, Harare: SAPES.
Makgetla, N. (1980), "Transnational Corporations in Southern Rhodesia," *Journal of Southern African Studies*, 5, 1.
_____ (1983), "Transnational Banks and Unequal Development in the Third World: The Case of Southern Africa," Doctoral dissertation in economics, Karl Marx Universitaet, Berlin.
Makunike, S. (1994), "ZBCA Squabbles Threaten Affirmative Action Showcase," *Financial Gazette*, 16/6/94.
Maliyami, S. (1990a), "The World Bank Trap," *Moto*, 84.
_____ (1990b), "Old Boys Network," *Moto*, 85.
Mandaza, I. (1986a), "Introduction," in I. Mandaza (Ed), *Zimbabwe: The Political Economy of Transition, 1980-1986*, Dakar: CODESRIA.
_____ (1986b), "The Post-White Settler Colonial Situation," in I. Mandaza (Ed), *Zimbabwe: The Political Economy of Transition, 1980-86*, Dakar: CODESRIA.
_____ (1991), "The One-Party State and Democracy in Southern Africa: Towards a Conceptual Framework," in I.Mandaza and L.Sachikonye (eds), *The One Party State and Democracy: The Zimbabwe Debate*, Harare: SAPES.
_____ (1995), "RIP Bridge-maker," *Financial Gazette*, October 12.
Mandaza, I. and L. Sachikonye (Eds)(1991), *The One Party State and Democracy: The Zimbabwe Debate*, Harare: SAPES Books.
Mandel, E. (1968)[1962], *Marxist Economic Theory*, London: Merlin Press.
_____ (1980), *Long Waves of Capitalist Development*, Cambridge: Cambridge University Press.
_____ (1989), "Theories of Crisis: An Explanation of the 1974-82 Cycle," in M. Gottdiener and N. Komninos (Eds), *Capitalist Development and Crisis Theory: Accumulation, Regulation and Spatial Restructuring*, London: Macmillan.
Manson, D.M and H. Katsura (1985), "Housing Needs Assessment Study: Zimbabwe," Urban Institute Project 3471 commissioned by the United States Agency for International Development, Washington, DC: The Urban Institute.
Martin, D. and P. Johnson (1981), *The Struggle for Zimbabwe: The Chimurenga War*, London: Faber.
Marx, K. (1967)[1867], *Capital*, New York: International Publishers.
_____ (1973)[1858], *Grundrisse*, Harmondsworth: Penguin.
Masimba, T. (1994), "Black People Urged to Be Their Own Saviours," *Financial Gazette*, 22 December.
Mathema, N.C.G. (1988), "Let us Fight Neo-Colonialism in Zimbabwe," Harare: Memorial Cooperative Society.
Matika, A.T.K. (1987), "Low Cost Housing Finance in Zimbabwe," Unpublished paper, Central

African Building Society, Harare, 1 October.
Maya, R.S. and H. Tongoona (1989), "Ownership Structure of the Manufacturing Sector," Zimbabwe Institute of Development Studies, Consultancy Report 9.
Mayekiso, M. (1996), *Township Politics*, New York: Monthly Review.
Metrowich, F.R. (1969), *Rhodesia: Birth of a Nation*, Pretoria: Africa Institute of South Africa.
Mitchell, D. (1980), *Zimbabwean Nationalist Leaders Who's Who*, Salisbury: D. Mitchell.
Mkandawire, T. (1984), "'Home made' (?) Austerity Measures: The case of Zimbabwe," Paper presented at seminar on Austerity Policies in Africa: Under IMF Control, Dakar, Senegal, 19-21 June.
Moore, D. (1992), "The Ideological Formation of the Zimbabwean Ruling Class," *Journal of Southern African Studies*, 17, 3.
Moyo, J. (1992), "Who is Responsible for Government Policies in Zimbabwe?," *Financial Gazette*, 6 August.
Moyo, N. (1991), "1992 should see Liberation of Zimbabwe's Parliament," *Financial Gazette*, 19/12/91.
Moyo, S. (1991), "A Preliminary Review of Zimbabwe's Structural Adjustment Programme," ZERO Working Paper 14, Harare: ZERO.
Moyo, S. and T. Skalnes (1990), "Land Reform and Development Strategy in Zimbabwe: State Autonomy, Class and the Agrarian Economy," Paper presented to the Conference on Land Policy in Zimbabwe After Lancaster, Harare, 13-15 February.
Mtetwa, R.M.G. (1976), "The 'Political' and Economic History of the Duma People of South-Eastern Rhodesia from the Early Eighteenth Century to 1945," Doctoral dissertation, University of Rhodesia.
Mugabe, R.G. (1979), "Preface" to "Zimbabwe: Notes and Reflections on the Rhodesian Question," Mimeo, Maputo: Centre of African Studies, March.
______ (1989), "The Unity Accord: Its Promise for the Future," in C. Banana (Ed), *Turmoil and Tenacity: Zimbabwe 1890-1990*, Harare: College Press.
Mumbengegwi, C. (1986), "Continuity and Change in Agricultural Policy," in I. Mandaza (Ed), *Zimbabwe: The Political Economy of Transition, 1980-1986*, Dakar: CODESRIA.
Mupandiki, S.N.C. (1985), "Zimbabwe: An Analysis of the Socio-Economic Geographical Situation and Prospects," Doctoral dissertation, Department of Geography, University of Hamburg, Hamburg.
Murapa, R. (1977), "Geography, Race, Class and Power in Rhodesia," Working Paper, Council for the Development of Economic and Social Research in Africa, presented at the Conference on the Special Problems of Landlocked and Least Developed Countries in Africa, University of Zambia, Lusaka, 27-31 July.
Murray, D. (1970), *The Governmental System in Southern Rhodesia*, Oxford: Oxford University Press.
Mutambara, A. (1991), "The One-Party State, Socialism and Democratic Struggles in Zimbabwe: A Student Perspective," in I.Mandaza and L.Sachikonye (Eds), *The One-Party State and Democracy*, Harare: SAPES.
Muzulu, J. (1993), "Exchange Rate Depreciation and Structural Adjustment: The Case of the Manufacturing Sector in Zimbabwe, 1980-91," Doctoral dissertation, University of Sussex.
Mwale, M. (1992), "Resettlement Programme: An Economic Policy of a Political Gamble?," *Sunday Times*, 19 January.
Mynors, H.C.B. (1949), "Southern Rhodesia: Report on the question of a central bank," Unpublished report for the Government of Southern Rhodesia, Salisbury.
Nabudere, D. (1989), "Land Reform and Credit for Agricultural Development," *Southern African Political and Economic Monthly*, v.3, 1.
National Council of Savings Institutions (1985), "Housing Finance in Zimbabwe," Report prepared for the Office of Housing and Urban Programs, United States Agency for International Development Consultancy Report, Washington, DC.
Ncube, W. (1989), "The Post-Unity Period: Developments, Benefits and Problems," in C. Banana

(Ed), *Turmoil and Tenacity: Zimbabwe 1890-1990*, Harare: College Press.
Ncube, T. (1995), "In Search of a Minister," *Financial Gazette*, 19 October.
Ndlela, D. (1980), "The Rhodesian Economy in a Historical Perspective, Part I," in United Nations Conference on Trade and Development, *Zimbabwe: Towards a New Order: An Economic and Social Survey*, Working Papers, Geneva, Vol Two.
_____ (1981), *Dualism in the Rhodesian Colonial Economy*, Lund, Sweden: University of Lund.
_____ (1984), "Sectoral Analysis of Zimbabwe's Economic Development with Implications for Foreign Trade and Foreign Exchange," *Zimbabwe Journal of Economics*, 1, 1.
_____ (1986), "The Current Economic Trends in Zimbabwe and Prospects for the Future," Konrad Adenauer Symposium, Parliament of Zimbabwe, Zimbabwe National Chamber of Commerce: Economic Systems and Development, Victoria Falls, 22-24 October.
Ndlovu, D. (1994), "White Business Community's Fear of Indigenisation False," *Financial Gazette*, March 3.
Ndoro, H. (1984), "The Agrarian Question: Agricultural Credit in Zimbabwe," Harare: Zimbabwe Institute for Development Studies.
Newlyn, W.T. and D.C. Rowan (1954), *Money and Banking in British Colonial Africa*, Oxford: Clarendon Press.
Nixson, F. (1982), "Import-Substitution Industrialization," in M. Fransman (Ed), *Industry and Accumulation in Africa*, London: Heinemann.
Nowak, M. (1989), "The Role of Microenterprises in Rural Industrialisation in Africa," in J. Levitsky (Ed), *Microenterprises in Developing Countries: Papers and Proceedings of an International Conference*, London: IT Publications.
Nyagumbo, M. (1983), "Zimbabwe's Socialist Dream an Uphill Struggle," Interview, *Moto*, 18, November.
Nyathi, A. (1990), *Tomorrow is Built Today*, Harare: Anvil Press.
Nyathi-Mdluli, V. (1980), "The Manufacturing Industry in Zimbabwe," in United Nations Conference on Trade and Development, *Zimbabwe: Towards a New Order: An Economic and Social Survey*, Working Papers, Volume One, Geneva.
Oakeshott, R. (1987), "Employee Ownership and Profit Sharing Systems as a Development Strategy in Zimbabwe," Unpublished paper, Zimbabwe Promotion Council, Harare.
Ohlson, T., S. Stedman, and R. Davies (1994), *The New is Not Yet Born: Conflict Resolution in Southern Africa*, Washington, DC: Brookings Institution.
O'Meara, D. (1983), *Volkskapitalism*, Cambridge: Cambridge University Press.
Ostergaard, T. (1991), "Industrial Policy in Zimbabwe: The Role of the National Bourgeoisie," Unpublished paper, Zimbabwe Institute of Development Studies, Harare.
Palmer, R. (1977a), *Land and Racial Domination in Rhodesia*, London: Heinemann.
_____ (1977b), "The Agricultural History of Rhodesia" in R. Palmer and N. Parson (Eds), *Roots of Rural Poverty in Central and Southern Africa*, London: Heinemann.
Patel, D.H. (1984), "Housing the Urban Poor in the Socialist Transformation of Zimbabwe," in M.G. Schatzberg (Ed), *The Political Economy of Zimbabwe*, New York: Praeger.
Payer, C. (1974), *The Debt Trap*, New York: Monthly Review.
_____ (1982), *The World Bank*, New York: Monthly Review.
Pearson, D.S. and W.L. Taylor (1963), *Break-Up: Some Economic Consequences for the Rhodesias and Nyasaland*, Salisbury: The Phoenix Group.
Phimister, I. (1975), "Peasant Production and Underdevelopment in Southern Rhodesia," *African Affairs*, 13.
_____ (1986), "Discourse and the Discipline of Historical Context: Conservationism and Ideas about Development in Southern Rhodesia, 1930-1950," *Journal of Southern African Studies*, 12.
_____ (1988a), *An Economic and Social History of Zimbabwe, 1890-1948: Class Struggle and Capital Accumulation*, London: Longman.
_____ (1988b), "The Combined and Contradictory Inheritance of the Struggle Against Colonialism," in C. Stoneman (Ed), *Zimbabwe's Prospects*, London: Macmillan.

_____ (1991), "Reshaping the Reserves: State Intervention in Southern Rhodesia, 1946-1962," Unpublished paper, Department of History, University of Cape Town.

_____ (1992), "Unscrambling the Scramble: Africa's Partition Reconsidered," Paper presented to the African Studies Institute, University of the Witwatersrand, Johannesburg, 17 August.

_____ (1993), "Rethinking the Reserves: Southern Rhodesia's Land Husbandry Act Reviewed," *Journal of Southern African Studies*, 19, 2.

Pollin, R. (1986), "Alternative Perspectives on the Rise of Corporate Debt Dependency: The US Postwar Experience," *Review of Radical Political Economics*, 18, 1-2.

Potter, G. A. (1988), *Dialogue on Debt*, Washington, DC: Center of Concern.

Radke, D., H. von Blanckenburg, J. Gottschalk, J. Hake, S. Hartig, and K. Maurer (1986), "Mobilization of Personal Savings in Zimbabwe through Financial Development," Berlin: German Development Institute.

Raftopoulos, B. (1991), "Beyond the House of Hunger: The Struggle for Democratic Development in Zimbabwe," Zimbabwe Institute for Development Studies Working Paper 17, Harare.

_____ (1993), "Zimbabwe: Race and Nationalism in a Post-Colonial State," Unpublished paper, Institute of Development Studies, University of Zimbabwe, Harare.

_____ (1995), "Nationalism and Labour in Salisbury, 1953-1965," *Journal of Southern African Studies*, 21, 1.

Rakodi, C. (1993), "Land, Housing and Urban Development in Zimbabwe: Trends in the Residential Property Market in Harare and Gweru," Paper of the Department of Urban and Rural Planning, University of Zimbabwe, Harare

Rakodi, C. and N. D. Mutizwa-Mangiza (1989), "Housing Policy, Production and Consumption: A Case Study of Harare," Teaching Paper 3, Department of Rural and Urban Planning, University of Zimbabwe, Harare.

Ramsey, D. (1974), "Productivity and Capital in Rhodesian Manufacturing, 1955-72," *Rhodesian Journal of Economics*, 8, 2.

Ranger, T. (1967), *Revolt in Southern Rhodesia*, London: Heinemann.

_____ (1985), *Peasant Consciousness and Guerrilla War in Zimbabwe*, London: Heinemann.

Rasmussen, J. (1990), "Small Urban Centres and Local Enterprises in Zimbabwe," in J. Baker (Ed), *Small Town Africa: Studies in Rural-Urban Interaction*, Seminar Proceedings 23, Scandinavian Institute of African Studies, Uppsala.

_____ (1992), *The Local Entrepreneurial Milieu: Enterprise Networks in Small Zimbabwean Towns*, Copenhagen: Centre for Development Research.

Rennie, J.K. (1973), "Christianity , Colonialism and the Origins of Nationalism among the Ndau of Southern Rhodesia, 1890-1935," Doctoral dissertation, Northwestern University, Chicago.

Reynolds, N. (1987), "Community, Financial Flows, and the Provision of Credit to Small Farmers and Businessmen," Mimeo, Harare: Zimbabwe Promotion Council (version published as "Credit for Small Farmers and Businessmen," *Zimbabwe Quarterly*, 1, 1).

_____ (1988), "The Potential Role of Small-Scale Enterprises," in the Promotion of Small-Scale Entrepreneurs and National Development Symposium organised by Konrad-Adenauer-Stiftung, Parliament of Zimbabwe, and Zimbabwe National Chamber of Commerce, 23-26 October.

Richards, B.C.J. (1956), "The Operations of the Bank of Rhodesia and Nyasaland," *South African Bankers Journal*, 53.

Riddell, R. (1983), "A Critique of `Zimbabwe: Government Policy and the Manufacturing Sector: A Study Prepared for the Ministry of Industry and Energy Development, April 1983, Submitted by Dr. Doris J. Jansen'," Unpublished paper, Confederation of Zimbabwe Industries, Harare, July.

_____ (1990), "Zimbabwe," in R. Riddell (Ed), *Manufacturing Africa*, London: Overseas Development Institute.

Robinson, P. (1988), "Relaxing the Constraints," in C. Stoneman (Ed), *Zimbabwe's Prospects*, London: Macmillan.

Roder, W. (1964), "The Division of Land Resources in Southern Rhodesia," *Annals of the*

Association of American Geographers, 54, 1.
Sachikonye, L. (1986), "State, Capital and the Trade Unions," in I. Mandaza (Ed), *Zimbabwe: The Political Economy of Transition, 1980-1986*, Dakar: CODESRIA.
_____ (1995a), "Industrial Relations and Labour Relations under ESAP in Zimbabwe" in P.Gibbon (ed), *Structural Adjustment and the Working Poor in Zimbabwe*, Uppsala: Nordiska Afrikainstitutet.
_____ (1995b), "From `Equity' and `Participation' to Structural Adjustment: State and Social Forces in Zimbabwe," in D.Moore and G.Schmitz (eds), *Debating Development Discourses: Institutional and Popular Perspectives*, London: Macmillan and New York: St.Martin's Press.
Sagit Stockbrokers (various issues), *Statistical Information on Companies Listed on the ZSE*, Harare.
Sanders, D. and A. Sambo (1991), "AIDS in Africa: The Implications of Economic Recession and Structural Adjustment," *Health Policy and Planning*, 6, 2.
Saul, J. (1993), *Recolonization and Resistance in Southern Africa*, Trenton: Africa World Press.
Saunders, M. (1990), "Annual Report," Paper presented to the Annual General Meeting of the National Property Association, 27 November.
Saunders, R. (1992), "Information in the Interregnum: The Press, State and Civil Society in Struggles for Hegemony, Zimbabwe 1980-1990", Doctoral dissertation, Department of Political Science, Carleton University, Ottawa.
_____ (1995), "Civics in Zimbabwe: Are They Making a Difference?," *Southern Africa Report*, 11, 1.
_____ (1996), "ESAP's Fables," *Southern Africa Report*, 12, 1.
_____ (1997), "Striking Back: Worker Militancy in Zimbabwe," *Southern Africa Report*, 13, 1.
Saxby, J. (1989), "The Transition to Socialism?", *Transformation*, 8.
Schmidt, E. (1991), "Patriarchy, Capitalism, and the Colonial State in Zimbabwe," *Signs*, 16.
Schumann, C.G.W. (1938), *Structural Changes and Business Cycles in South Africa, 1806-1936*, London: P.S.King and Son, Ltd.
Seidman, A. (1986), *Money, Banking and Public Finance in Africa*, London: Zed Press.
Sender, J. and S. Smith (1986), *The Development of Capitalism in Africa*, London: Methuen.
Shamuyarira, N. (1960), "Revolt of the Intellectuals: Eggheads Join the NDP," *Central African Examiner*, 18 June.
_____ (1965), *Crisis in Rhodesia*, New York: Transatlantic Arts.
Shaul, J.R.H. (1946), "American Loan and Bretton Woods," Unpublished paper, Central Statistical Office, Salisbury.
Shipton, P. (1992), "Debts and Trespasses: Land, Mortgages and the Ancestors in Western Kenya," *Africa*, 62, 3.
Sibanda, A. (1985), "Theoretical Problems in the Development of Capitalism in Zimbabwe: Towards a Critique of Arrighi," *Zimbabwe Journal of Economics*, 1, 2.
_____ (1987), "Foreign Exchange Auctioning as a Measure of Economic Liberalisation for Adjustment in Zambia: Problems and Prospects for African Economies," ZIDS Working Paper 11.
_____ (1988), "The Political Situation," in C. Stoneman (Ed), *Zimbabwe's Prospects*, London: Macmillan.
_____ (1989), "IMF-World Bank Impact on Zimbabwe," in B. Onimode (Ed), *The IMF, the World Bank and the African Debt: Vol.1, The Economic Impact*, London: Zed.
_____ (1990), "The Lancaster House Agreement and the Post-Independence State in Zimbabwe," Discussion Paper Series 9, Harare: Zimbabwe Institute of Development Studies.
Sibanda, M. (1989), "Early Foundations of African Nationalism," in C. Banana (Ed), *Turmoil and Tenacity*, Harare: College Press.
Simmel, G. (1971), "The Metropolis and Mental life," in D. Levine (Ed), *On Individuality and Social Forms*, Chicago: University of Chicago Press.
Skalnes, T. (1993), "The State, Interest Groups and Structural Adjustment in Zimbabwe," *Journal of Development Studies*, April.
Schlyter, A. (1985), "Housing Strategies: The Case of Zimbabwe," *Trialog*, 6.

_____ (1987), "Women Householders in Harare," Paper presented at seminar on Women and Housing in Harare and cited in Schlyter, "Zimbabwe."

_____ (1990), "Zimbabwe," in K. Mathe (Ed), *Housing Policies in the Socialist Third World*, London: Mansell Publishing."

Smith, A. (1984), "Savings and Development of Rural Savings Institutions," Paper presented at the Commonwealth Training Workshop on Rural Credit, Harare.

Smith, N. (1979), "Toward a Theory of Gentrification: A Back to the City Movement by Capital not People," *Journal of the American Planning Association*, 45, 2.

_____ (1982), "Gentrification and Uneven Development," *Economic Geography*, 58, 2.

_____ (1990)[1984], *Uneven Development*, Oxford: Basil Blackwell.

Smout, M.A.H. (1971), "Service Centres in Greater Salisbury, Rhodesia," Doctoral Dissertation, Faculty of Science, University of London, London.

_____ (1977), "The Suburban Shopping Centres," in G. Kay and M.A.H. Smout (Eds), *Salisbury: A Geographical Survey of the Capital of Rhodesia*, London: Hodder and Stoughton.

Soja, E. (1989), *Postmodern Geographies*, London: Verso.

Sowelem, R.A. (1967), *Towards Financial Independence in a Developing Economy*, London: George Allen and Unwin.

Standard Bank (1967), *Three Quarters of a Century of Banking in Rhodesia*, Salisbury: The Standard Bank Limited.

Stone, M. (1993), *Shelter Poverty*, Philadelphia: Temple University Press.

Stoneman, C. (1978) "Foreign Capital and the Reconstruction of Zimbabwe," *Review of African Political Economy*, 11.

_____ (1981), "The Economy," in C. Stoneman (Ed), *Zimbabwe's Prospects*, London: Macmillan.

_____ (1982), "Industrialization and Self-Reliance in Zimbabwe," in M. Fransman (Ed), *Industry and Accumulation in Africa*, London: Heinemann.

_____ (1985), "Strategy or Ideology? The World Bank/IMF Approach to Development," Paper presented at Conference on Economic Policies and Planning Under Crisis Conditions, Harare, 2-5 September.

_____ (Ed) (1988a), *Zimbabwe's Prospects*, London: Macmillan.

_____ (1988b), "A Zimbabwean Model?," in C. Stoneman (Ed), *Zimbabwe's Prospects*, London: Macmillan.

_____ (1988c), "The Economy: Recognising the Reality," in C. Stoneman (Ed), *Zimbabwe's Prospects*, London: Macmillan.

_____ (1990), "The Impending Failure of Structural Adjustment: Lessons from Zimbabwe," Paper presented to the Canadian Association of African Studies, Dalhousie University, 11 May.

_____ (1991), "World Bank's Strategy Carries Risk of Bloody Nose for Economy," *Guardian*, 25 April.

_____ (1992), "Policy Reform or Industrialisation," in R.Adhikari *et al.* (Eds), *Industrial and Trade Reform in Developing Countries*, Manchester, Manchester University Press.

Stoneman, C. and L. Cliffe (1989), *Zimbabwe: Politics, Economics and Society*, London: Pinter Publishers.

Sutcliffe, R.B. (1971), "Stagnation and Inequality in Rhodesia, 1946-68," *Bulletin of the Oxford Institute of Economics and Statistics*, 33.

Suter, C. (1992), *Debt Cycles in the World Economy*, Boulder, CO: Westview Press.

Sweezy, P. (1968)[1942], *The Theory of Capitalist Development*, New York: Monthly Review.

_____ (1972), "The Resurgence of Finance Capital: Fact or Fancy?," *Socialist Revolution*, 1, 8.

Sylvester, C. (1990), "Simultaneous Revolutions: The Zimbabwean Case," *Journal of Southern African Studies*, 16, 3.

_____ (1991), *Zimbabwe: The Terrain of Contradictory Development*, Boulder: Westview Press.

Taylor, J.C.B. (1985), "Zimbabwe: One Local Authority's Response to the Challenge of Decent Shelter," in T.L. Blair (Ed), *Strengthening Urban Management: International Perspectives and Issues*, New York: Plenum Press.

Teedon, P. and D. Drakakis-Smith (1986), "Urbanisation and Socialism in Zimbabwe: The Case of

Low-Cost Urban Housing," *Geoforum*, 17, 2.

Tengende, N. (1992), "State-Society Relations and the Potentials for the Struggles for Democracy in the Context of Adjustment: Zimbabwe as a Case Study," Unpublished paper, Roskilde University Centre, Denmark.

Thomas, B. (1972), *Migration and Urban Development: A Reappraisal of British and American Long Cycles*, London: Methuen.

Thomas, C. (1989), "Restructuring of the World Economy and its Implications for the Third World," in A. MacEwan and W.K. Tabb (Eds), *Instability and Change in the World Economy*, New York: Monthly Review.

Thompson, C. (1991), *Harvests Under Fire: Regional Co-Operation for Food Security in Southern Africa*, London: Zed Press.

Thompson, C.H. and H.W. Woodruff (1954), *Economic Development in Rhodesia and Nyasaland*, London: Dennis Dobson Ltd.

Ticktin, H. (1986), "The Transitional Epoch, Finance Capital and Britain: The Political Economy of Declining Capitalism," *Critique*, 16.

Timba, J. (1992), "The Impact of the Economic Structural Adjustment Programme on People Centred Development with Particular Reference to the Zimbabwe Collective/Worker Co-operative Movement in general and the work of the Collective Self Finance Scheme in Particular," Paper presented to the Third Working Commonwealth Conference on "Structural Adjustment and People Centred Development," Kuala Trengganu, Malaysia.

Tomlinson, R. and M. Addleson (Eds)(1987), *Regional Restructuring Under Apartheid*, Johannesburg: Ravan Press.

Truscott, K. (1987), "The Role and Function of Informal Farmer Groups," Paper presented to the Workshop "The Role of Informal Groups in the Rural Financial System," Harare.

Tsumba, L. (1980), "Money, Credit and Financial Flows in Zimbabwe," in *Zimbabwe: Towards a New Order: An Economic and Social Survey*, Working Papers Vol 1, Geneva: United Nations Conference on Trade and Development.

Tsvangirai, M. (1992), "Pension Funds: The Employees' and Union Viewpoints," Paper presented to the Zimbabwe Association of Pension Funds Annual Congress, 28 July.

United Nations (1975), "Special Report Concerning the Question of Southern Rhodesia on External participation in the Expansion of the Rhodesian Iron and Steel Commission," United Nations Security Council, New York, Special Supplement v3, 39141.

United Nations Conference on Trade and Development (UNCTAD) (1980), *Zimbabwe: Towards a New Order: An Economic and Social Survey*, Geneva, United Nations Conference on Trade and Development.

University of Zimbabwe (1981), "Business Opinion Survey," Harare: University of Zimbabwe Department of Business Administration.

Urban Institute (1990), *Urban Economies and National Development*, Report prepared for US Agency for International Development, Washington, DC.

van der Pijl, K. (1984), *The Making of an Atlantic Ruling Class*, London: Verso.

van Duijn, J.J. (1983), *The Long Wave in Economic Life*, London: George Allen and Unwin.

van Onselen, C. (1976), *Chibarro*, London: Pluto Press.

van Wijnbergen, S. (1983), "Interest Rate Management in LDCs," *Journal of Monetary Economics*, 12, 3.

Verrier, A. (1986), *The Road to Zimbabwe, 1890-1980*, London: Jonathan Cape.

Wainwright, H. (1994), *Arguments for a New Left*, Oxford: Basil Blackwell.

Wallerstein, I. (1979), *The Capitalist World Economy*, Cambridge: Cambridge University Press.

Walton, J. and D. Seddon (1994), *Free Markets and Food Riots*, Oxford: Basil Blackwell.

Weeks, J. (1996), "Regional Cooperation and Southern African Development," *Journal of Southern African Studies*, 22, 1.

Weinrich, A.K.H. (1975), *African Farmers in Rhodesia*, London: Oxford University Press.

Welensky, R. (1964), *Welensky's 4000 Days: The Life and Death of the Federation of Rhodesia and Nyasaland*, London: Collins.

West, M. (1990), "African Middle-Class Formation in Colonial Zimbabwe, 1890-1965," Doctoral dissertation, Department of History, Harvard University, Cambridge, MA.

_____ (1993), "Pan Africanism, Capitalism and Racial Uplift: The Rhetoric of African Business Formation in Colonial Zimbabwe," *African Affairs*, 92.

Wetherell, H.I. (1975), "N.H. Wilson: Populism in Southern Rhodesia," *Rhodesian History*, 6.

_____ (1993), "Good Governance: Separating the Reality and the Rhetoric," *Financial Gazette*, 9 June.

Whitsun Foundation (1979), "Finance for Low Income Housing," Project 4.02, Salisbury: Whitsun Foundation.

_____ (1980), "Peasant Sector Credit Plan for Zimbabwe," Project 3.04(2), Salisbury: Whitsun Foundation.

_____ (1981), "A Credit System for Financing Low-Income Housing in Zimbabwe," Project 4.06, Harare: Whitsun Foundation.

_____ (1983), "Money and Finance in Zimbabwe," Project 1.09, Harare: Whitsun Foundation.

Wield, D. (1980), "Technology and Zimbabwean Industry," in United Nations Conference on Trade and Development, *Zimbabwe: Towards a New Order: An Economic and Social Survey*, Working Papers, Geneva, Vol One.

Wild, V. (1997), *Profit for Profit's Sake*, Harare: Baobab

Wilson, D.C.K. (1980), "The Development of a Residential Neighborhood: American Principles Applied in Mabelreign, Salisbury," *Zimbabwe Science News*, 14, 9.

Wolpe, H. (Ed) (1980), *The Articulations of Modes of Production*, London: Routledge and Kegan Paul.

Woods, B. (1988), "Trade Union Organisation and the Working Class," in C. Stoneman (Ed), *Zimbabwe's Prospects*, London: Macmillan.

World Bank (1982a), "Zimbabwe: Issues and Options in the Energy Sector," Report of the Joint UNDP/World Bank Energy Sector Assessment Program.

_____ (1982b), "Report and Recommendation of the President of the IDA to the Executive Directors on a Proposed Credit in an amount equivalent to US$1.2 million to the Government of Zimbabwe for a Petroleum Fuels Supply Technical Assistance Project," Energy Division, Eastern Africa Regional Office.

_____ (1982c), "Zimbabwe: Power Project," Energy Division, Eastern Africa Regional Office.

_____ (1982d), "Zimbabwe: Small Farm Credit Project," Staff Appraisal Report, Southern Agriculture Division, Eastern Africa Projects Department.

_____ (1983a), "Report and Recommendation of the President of the International Bank for Reconstruction and Development to the Executive Directors on a Proposed Loan in an Amount Equivalent to US$70.6 million to the Republic of Zimbabwe for a Proposed Manufacturing Export Promotion Project," Eastern Africa Projects Department.

_____ (1983b), "Zimbabwe: Urban Sector Review," Water Supply and Urban Development Division, Eastern Africa Projects Department.

_____ (1984), *Toward Sustained Development in Sub-Saharan Africa: A Joint Program of Action.*

_____ (1985), "Zimbabwe: Urban Sector Review," Southern Africa Department.

_____ (1986a), "Zimbabwe: Land Subsector Study," Southern Agriculture Division, Eastern and Southern Africa Projects Department.

_____ (1986b), "Zimbabwe Staff Appraisal Report: Small Scale Enterprise Project," Regional Projects Department, Eastern and Southern Africa Regional Office.

_____ (1986c), *Financing Adjustment with Growth in Sub-Saharan Africa, 1986-90.*

_____ (1987a), "Zimbabwe: An Industrial Sector Memorandum," Southern Africa Department.

_____ (1987b), "Zimbabwe: Power II Project," Industry and Energy Operations, Southern Africa Department.

_____ (1987c), "Zimbabwe: A Strategy for Sustained Growth," Southern Africa Department, Africa Region.

_____ (1988), *Education in Sub-Saharan Africa—Policies for Adjustment, Revitalisation and Expansion.*

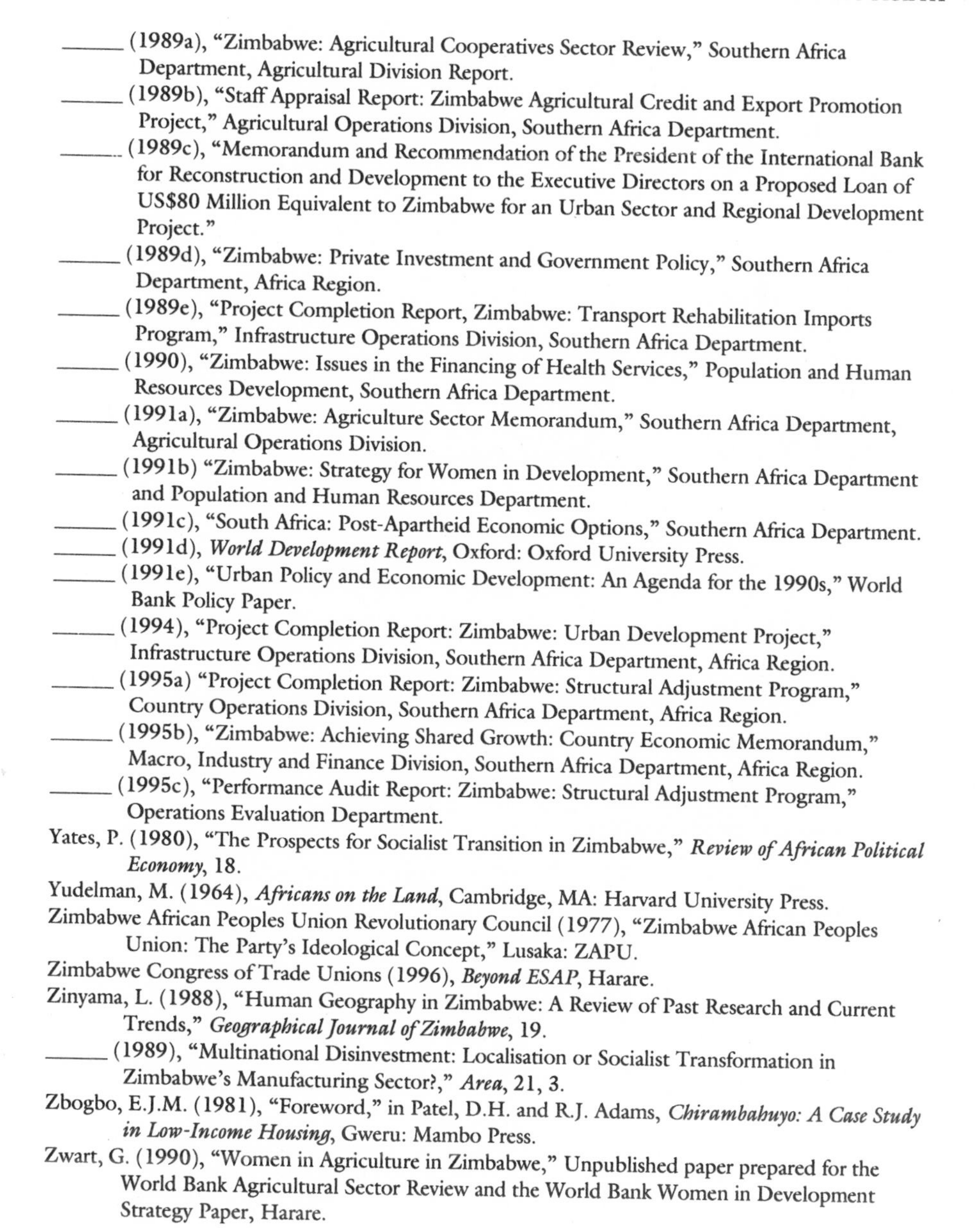

_____ (1989a), "Zimbabwe: Agricultural Cooperatives Sector Review," Southern Africa Department, Agricultural Division Report.

_____ (1989b), "Staff Appraisal Report: Zimbabwe Agricultural Credit and Export Promotion Project," Agricultural Operations Division, Southern Africa Department.

_____ (1989c), "Memorandum and Recommendation of the President of the International Bank for Reconstruction and Development to the Executive Directors on a Proposed Loan of US$80 Million Equivalent to Zimbabwe for an Urban Sector and Regional Development Project."

_____ (1989d), "Zimbabwe: Private Investment and Government Policy," Southern Africa Department, Africa Region.

_____ (1989e), "Project Completion Report, Zimbabwe: Transport Rehabilitation Imports Program," Infrastructure Operations Division, Southern Africa Department.

_____ (1990), "Zimbabwe: Issues in the Financing of Health Services," Population and Human Resources Development, Southern Africa Department.

_____ (1991a), "Zimbabwe: Agriculture Sector Memorandum," Southern Africa Department, Agricultural Operations Division.

_____ (1991b) "Zimbabwe: Strategy for Women in Development," Southern Africa Department and Population and Human Resources Department.

_____ (1991c), "South Africa: Post-Apartheid Economic Options," Southern Africa Department.

_____ (1991d), *World Development Report*, Oxford: Oxford University Press.

_____ (1991e), "Urban Policy and Economic Development: An Agenda for the 1990s," World Bank Policy Paper.

_____ (1994), "Project Completion Report: Zimbabwe: Urban Development Project," Infrastructure Operations Division, Southern Africa Department, Africa Region.

_____ (1995a) "Project Completion Report: Zimbabwe: Structural Adjustment Program," Country Operations Division, Southern Africa Department, Africa Region.

_____ (1995b), "Zimbabwe: Achieving Shared Growth: Country Economic Memorandum," Macro, Industry and Finance Division, Southern Africa Department, Africa Region.

_____ (1995c), "Performance Audit Report: Zimbabwe: Structural Adjustment Program," Operations Evaluation Department.

Yates, P. (1980), "The Prospects for Socialist Transition in Zimbabwe," *Review of African Political Economy*, 18.

Yudelman, M. (1964), *Africans on the Land*, Cambridge, MA: Harvard University Press.

Zimbabwe African Peoples Union Revolutionary Council (1977), "Zimbabwe African Peoples Union: The Party's Ideological Concept," Lusaka: ZAPU.

Zimbabwe Congress of Trade Unions (1996), *Beyond ESAP*, Harare.

Zinyama, L. (1988), "Human Geography in Zimbabwe: A Review of Past Research and Current Trends," *Geographical Journal of Zimbabwe*, 19.

_____ (1989), "Multinational Disinvestment: Localisation or Socialist Transformation in Zimbabwe's Manufacturing Sector?," *Area*, 21, 3.

Zbogbo, E.J.M. (1981), "Foreword," in Patel, D.H. and R.J. Adams, *Chirambahuyo: A Case Study in Low-Income Housing*, Gweru: Mambo Press.

Zwart, G. (1990), "Women in Agriculture in Zimbabwe," Unpublished paper prepared for the World Bank Agricultural Sector Review and the World Bank Women in Development Strategy Paper, Harare.

INDEX